D1739377

Subject Guide to Women of the World

Katharine Joan Phenix

The Scarecrow Press, Inc.
Lanham, Md., & London

SCARECROW PRESS, INC.

Published in the United States of America
by Scarecrow Press, Inc.
4720 Boston Way
Lanham, Maryland 20706

4 Pleydell Gardens, Folkestone
Kent CT20 2DN, England

British Cataloguing-in-Publication Information Available

Library of Congress Cataloging-in-Publication Data

Phenix, Katharine, 1952–
Subject guide to women of the world / Katharine Joan Phenix.
p.   cm.
To be used in conjunction with Index to women of the world from
ancient to modern times (1970) and Index to women of the world from
ancient to modern times : a supplement (1988), both compiled by
Norma Olin Ireland.
Includes bibliographical references.
1. Ireland, Norma Olin, 1907–   Index to women of the world from
ancient to modern times—Indexes.   2.   Women—Biography—Indexes.
I. Title.
Z7963.B6P45   1996   [HQ1123]   96-14228   016.92072—dc20   CIP

ISBN 0-8108-3190-2

Contents

Acknowledgments

Many thanks to Jorg Jemelka, spouse and superior technical assistant. Thanks also to women's studies librarians all over the country, and to the H.W. Wilson Company which supplied me with copies of their *Biography Index* for use as a subject guide.

Introduction

The *Subject Guide to Women of the World* is a subject index intended for a research audience requiring additional access points to published biographies of women. Material for this work is derived exclusively from two volumes previously compiled by Norma Olin Ireland. They are *Index to Women of the World from Ancient to Modern Times: Biographies and Portraits* (Westwood, MA: F.W. Faxon, 1970; dist. by Scarecrow Press) and *Index to Women of the World from Ancient to Modern Times: A Supplement* (Metuchen, NJ: Scarecrow Press, 1988). Together these books guide their users to approximately 24,096 women mentioned in 1,385 collected biographies and special magazine supplements. Entries are listed alphabetically by last name, followed by author, short title information, and page number of the original biographical source. Ireland's indexes are useful to those who require biographical information about women whose names are known. Used with the *Women of the World* and *Supplement*, this guide will identify women by occupation or subject area and lead the user to the woman's name and appropriate Ireland index.

We all know that many women who have lived extraordinary lives have been left out of or nearly forgotten in recorded history. A paragraph here and footnotes there are all we have to make us aware of their existence. A look at the body of this subject guide is enough to excite feminist pride and anger over the fact that women have done so much and received so little notice for it. Even those working from the premise that women have always been equal partners in any historical endeavor will be pleasantly surprised to see how basic female participation has been in all fields, eras and enterprises. As pioneers and criminals, queens and witches, founders and patrons, women have put themselves into every aspect of human existence and endeavor. The panorama of this information is not immediately available in the alphabetical listing of the names of women who appear in an assortment of collective biographies. The accomplishments of these women are richly displayed subject order. From Madame Moustache and Poker Alice, the gamblers, to Handy Betsy the blacksmith, to "Miss Bess" Farmer and "Blossom Dearie" we experience unusual careers, and then come full circle to women known as Moms, Ma, Mother, or Granny Dollar Callahan to find the full range of female activity throughout history.

Ireland has done a great service to scholars who are seeking out information about women identified in collected biographies. The names of women included in Joan and Kenneth Macksey's *The Book of Women's Achievements*, Clarke Newlon's *Famous Mexican-Americans*, or Elaine Showalder's *These Modern Women: Autobiographical Essays from the 20s* are not listed individually in any library card catalog or database. Their names, plus several sources of information about them are readily available in Ireland's books.

The missing link in the research process is that of subject access to particular women. Unless previous work has uncovered a complete guide to "women rice planters" or "female insurance agents I have known," each researcher is adrift among diverse biographical sources to find a proper name within an obscure profession or historical period. For the quick reference work of finding a famous woman from Oklahoma, the names of two female astronauts, or the first name of Henry VII's mother, a single subject source for all women recorded in reference books is essential.

The *Subject Guide to Women of the World* solves the problem. It turns the Ireland indexes inside out. *Women of the World* and the *Supplement* list women in alphabetical order by last name. This volume reverses the order by listing the women first by subject, then last name and dates. A researcher interested in a general subject area such as Civil War nurses, stunt pilots, or circus performers will find names here, then use the Ireland indexes to retrieve the citation for the biographical data. Here in the *Subject Guide*, numbers after the women's names and dates refer to the original index, 1 for *Women of the World* and 2 for the *Supplement*. There are 10,017 names in the first volume, 10,247 in the second, and 3,826 names which were listed in both.

Contents

It is a peculiarity of an index of women that some women are most famous for what happened to them than for what they did in their stated occupations: Mary Jo Kopechne is not known as a famous secretary, although that is the subject heading used for her here. We know her name because of Ted Kennedy's July 19, 1969 incident on the bridge at Chappaquiddick. Equally telling is that in this index Karen Gay Silkwood (1946–1974) is listed under "atomic power industry." Her life and death might have been considered unremarkable if it had not been for *Ms.* Magazine's expose on her deadly struggle with the industry over employee safety risks. This is also true for Betsy Ross, who obviously did not make a living as a flag maker, or Jean Harris, an educator, and also a murderer. This index also contains women who are famous not for their accomplishments but for particular incidents. Include in that group the murder, rape and Nazi victims, a freezing accident victim, and the "Indian captives."

We know other women as satellites of men. Alexander the Great, Sam Houston, Ben Franklin, etc. drew clusters around them. Mothers, spouses, daughters, sisters, friends, secretaries, models, and inspirations are just a few of the support roles under which women are listed. Looking at the lives and activities of these women is of interest to historians, biographers of men, and women's history scholars. In this subject guide, women are listed under the names of the men they influenced, and again as "Mothers of prominent men/women" or "Presidents' wives," etc.

Is it a happenstance of research propensity that some men and women are immortalized in history books while others live and die unrecorded? Far from being comprehensive, these indexes represent not history as it happened, but, sadly, only history as it has been written thus far. There are seafarers and whaling voyagers, covenanters, octogenarians and award winners in this index simply because a previous author or editor has already assembled the specific subject matter. We cannot use these materials, and by extension, this subject index as a complete body of information about the shape of the contributions and experiences of women in the past. For example, through published works, we can find the names of 42 women who were "Indian captives." Native American women who were similarly captured are still lost daughters of time.

Subject Headings

Subject headings can be misleading, and never more so than in this list of women we want to know about. Frequently their activities fall into headings we generally reserve for the exploits of men. These are the actors, authors, pilots, dentists, and business executives. Beyond standard lists, this index represents materials that trace the activities of women whose exploits reach beyond occupation and accomplishment.

Thanks to Ireland's infinitesimal analysis of such works as *The American Women's Gazetteer* by Lynn Sherr (NY: Bantam, 1976), which is a state by state guide to places associated with women, the subject term "Avenger" retrieves the story of Josefa. A gang of men followed her home and taunted her. She had threatened to slit the throat of the next man who called her a whore. When she made good her threat, they hanged her in the town square. Ireland's heading for her was "avenger," and under that term is where she is found in this index. Sherr's *Gazetteer* also provides us with "Noted well water donors" Lydia and Elizabeth Winchester, who provided the whole town with water during a time of extreme drought; "Highway beautifier" Jessie M. Honeyman, the "Sunshine lady" and "Noted mausoleum" of Leila Davidson Hansell, and the "Noted perfect wife" Sarah Davis, whose husband built a series of statues of them together to commemorate her after her death. The "Mexican Indian freak" term comes from the *People's Almanac*. Left untouched from the Ireland material, it refers to Julia Pastrana, the "ugliest woman alive." Her husband displayed her as a circus sideshow. She is listed under "Circus performer", and also under the pejorative term to reflect the attitudes that allowed this degrading behavior to happen. The term "Radio osteopath" comes from *Felton & Fowler's Famous Americans You Never Knew Existed* (NY: Stein & Day, 1979), describing Ruth Drown, a woman who claimed to heal with radio beams. *Incredible People*, by Kevin McFarland, includes a "One-eyed woman" and a "Silent woman." These headings and more illustrate the many ways we can find women making their lives known and not forgotten.

Nature of the Index

Name Authority

The *Subject Guide to Women of the World* uses the exact form(s) of the names found in the alphabetical indexes compiled by Ireland. This is because the user must know how Ireland listed them in her indexes. *Women of the World* and the *Supplement* each attempted to enforce name authority control. This is especially necessary in any work that attempts to record women's names, which change with marriage. Both used extensive "see" references from other forms of names. As with any work handling thousands of entries and dissimilar sources, however, there are mistakes and inconsistencies within and between the two titles.

The advantage of computerizing a large database is that long lists can be manipulated to juxtapose similar data fields. The mistakes in the first two books are evident when women are listed in order by birth and death dates. In this way, women with identical or nearly exact birth and death dates seen to hold similar name elements can be examined more closely. Often they are in fact the same woman with a different form of name.

A woman listed under the same occupation with two or more forms of may also turn out to be the same person. "Alice in Wonderland" brings together Hargreaves, Alice Liddell and Liddell, Alice. Horace Tabor's spouse, known locally as "Baby Doe" may be found under "Tabor, Horace—Spouse" as Tabor, Elizabeth Bonduel "Baby Doe." This is the way she is listed in the *Index to Women* and the *Supplement*. She is also found under McCourt, Baby Doe in the *Supplement*. By either name, she's identified here as a "Recluse" and Horace Tabor's spouse. By any name, she died frozen, poor and alone, in Leadville, Colorado. Jacqueline Lee Bouvier Kennedy Onassis is found under Kennedy in *Index* and Onassis in the *Supplement*. This index lists her under both names as "Kennedy, John F.—Spouse" and under "President's wives." Locate Robert Browning's mother under Browning, Robert— Mother as Wiedemann, Sara Anna and Browning, Sara Anna Wiedemann, or Tom Thumb's wife as Warren, Lavinia and Stratton, (Mercy) Lavinia Warren Bumpus.

Double or triple listings due to different forms or misspellings are numerous. There is Robbins, Margaret Drier and Robins, Margaret Drier, who was a sociologist and labor reformer. Barrington, Emily Dunning and Barringer, Emily Dunning are the same person listed twice under "Physicians and surgeons." Mills, Susan Lincoln Tolman and Miller, Susan Lincoln Tolman is the same person listed as a missionary, educator, and native Californian. Other misspellings are Elizabeth De Kooning, who is also listed as De Mooning, Sophie Tauber-Arp also spelled Taeber-Arp and Phyllis Chesler, found under Chester as well as under Chesler.

Rosemary Ruether, the contemporary feminist theologist is listed twice, once correctly and once under Reuther, Rosemary. Annette Funicello is found under Annette (Funicello) and under Funicello, Annette.

Even when the last name is the same, different arrangements or forms of first names become evident when listed by subject. Astronomer Wilhelmina Fleming is surely the same as Mina Fleming the astronomer, both listed in the *Supplement*, as are Marion G. "Pat" Robertson the flight attendant born in 1930 and Pat Marion Gordon Robertson the TV network analyst also born in 1930.

Clearly, a third authority control in this subject guide would hinder the use of the other indexes because of these inconsistencies and mistakes. Take, for example, Valerie Percy, the murdered daughter of Illinois state senator Charles Percy. She is listed in Ireland under the name Case, Valerie Percy because the story of her murder in the primary reference work is called "The Case of Valerie Percy." By any name, she is still a murder victim. By using that subject heading in the subject index, the researcher, using the name "Case, Valerie Percy" will find her in Ireland. The name index will lead to the original reference source. The user can correct the mistake then.

Our assumption is that the user of this book is looking for women identified with a particular subject area. This researcher will come upon all forms of names for the same woman by pulling out all names associated with a subject. Using all forms of names listed by Ireland guarantees the reader access to all the primary sources. It does not directly collect all the names used for one woman in the two indexes.

Subject Authority

The subject headings come directly from the Ireland material. Minimal subject authority control was exercised for the sake of consistency, using H.W. Wilson's *Biography Index* as a model. Some flavors were lost in the melting pot of standard terms. Wendy Campbell Purdie, who singlehandedly planted 200 acres of Sahara desert is found under "Horticulturist." Sadie Orchard was a stagecoach driver in New Mexico. She handled a six-horse hitch. She also ran a bawdy house with "fierce tongue and gutsy manner." Her subject headings are "Hotel owner and manager" "Restauranteur" and "Stagecoach driver." "See also" references will lead the user to "Bar owner" and "Saloonkeeper" for other characters cataloged here. The one apothecary is found under "Pharmacologists." "Belles" "Southern belles," and "Beauty", however, remain as described, as do "Salonists," "Hostesses," "Club leaders," etc. The subject headings reflect the social roles women have played.

Call it revenge. In this index the tavern maids are upgraded to tavern keepers, library workers to librarians and businesswomen to business executives. Accused witches and criminals are given credit as "Witches" and "Criminals."

Alphabetizing

The subject headings and the names of the women under the subject headings are in alphabetical order provided by the personal computer. The modern method is strictly by numerical, ASCII value. Acronyms are found at the start of each letter of the alphabet since capital letters are given lower value than small letters. In addition, Mac and Mc, Van der and Vander, Saint and St., O'D and Od etc., are not interfiled, as in older filing schemes and earlier indexes. For this reason, names in the *Subject Guide* will not be in the same order as listed in the Ireland material. Indeed, they may be pages away from each other.

Geographic Index

The geographic index is a secondary appendix to the subject content and left generally as listed in Ireland's books. For reasons of space, it excludes women from the US. The 15,188 American women account for 63% of the database. American women with state affiliation are listed under the name of the state in the general subject index. Not all women were originally listed with nationality. In all but in 61 cases, the country was found and included. Women from the Bible are listed without country, but given the subject term "Biblical." Women listed as "Jewish printers," (with no country) are not listed in the Country index but found as "Jewish leaders" in the subject fields. Some women had several countries, for example, England/US or Austria/Hungary. For the most part all countries for each woman are listed, so that Asian Americans are under Japan/US or China/US.

Some countries are updated. Germany replaces East and West

Germany. India replaces East India. No work was done to use current terms for countries within the USSR and Yugoslavia, and the continent of Africa. Rome, as in Roman empress, is listed as a country.

Some occupations are broken out by country, following the format of H.W. Wilson's *Biography Index*. This include Poets, Authors, Composers, Artists, Sculptors, etc. In the cases where no country was listed for the women in these occupations, the author of the reference source is used in its stead. This is also true of women who needed at least one subject heading to appear in this guide.

Database

The names of all women, with separate, searchable fields for first, last, dates, country, and up to five subject headings are in machine-readable form and available for a fee from the author (2419 Keystone Ct., Boulder, CO, 80304–1935).

Alphabetical Index by Subject

Coffin, Catherine, 1827–1947, 2
Craft, Ellen, 1826–1897, 1,2
Crandall, Prudence, 1803–1890, 1,2
Douglass, Sarah Mapps Douglas,
    1806–1882, 2
Foster, Abigail Kelley, 1810–1887,
    1,2
Gage, Frances Dana Barker, 1808–
    1884, 1,2
Greenwood, Grace, pseud., 1823–
    1904, 1,2
Grew, Mary, 1813–1896, 1,2
Grimke, Angelina Emily, 1880–1958,
    1,2
Grimke, Charlotte L. Forten, 1838–
    1915, 1,2
Grimke, Sarah Moore, 1792–1873, 1,2
Haviland, Laura Smith, 1808–1898, 2
Hickock, Hannah Hadassah, fl.
    1840s, 2
Holley, Sallie, 1818–1893, 1,2
Mott, Lucretia Coffin, 1793–1880,
    1,2
Murray, Ellen, fl. 1860s, 2
Pugh, Sarah, 1800–1884, 2
Remond, Sarah Parker, 1826–1887, 2
Robbins, Elizabeth Murray, d. 1853,
    2
Stone, Lucy, 1818–1893, 1,2
Swisshelm, Jane Grey Cannon, 1815–
    1884, 1,2
Tappan, Julia, 2
Tappan, Susan, 2
Truth, Sojourner, 1797–1883, 1,2
Tubman, Harriet Ross, 1820–1913,
    1,2
Van Lew, Elizabeth L. (Mrs. John),
    1818–1900, 1,2
Van Lew, Mrs. John, fl. 1860s, 1
Whitney, Anne, 1821–1915, 1,2
Wollman, Betty Kohn, 1836–, 2
Wright, Frances, 1795–1852, 1,2
Abortion reform
Chevalier, Marie-Claire, fl. 1970s, 2
Chevalier, Michele, 1934–, 2
Lohman, Ann Trow, 1812–1878, 2
Absalom—Daughter
Tamar, 1
Absalom—Daughter or Granddaughter
Maachah, 1
Accordianists
Farmer, Bess "Miss Bess", 1919–, 2
Accountants
    See also
    Bookkeepers

Boyd, Elizabeth, 1
Burge, Marianne, fl. 1970s, 2
Dickey, Francine, fl. 1970s, 2
Fairclough, Ellen, 1905–, 1
Hale, Larzette Golden, 1920–, 2
Ryan, Mary P. Van Buren, fl. 1930s, 1
Achilles—Slave
    Briseis, 2
Ackland, Major—Spouse
    Ackland, Harriet Christina Henrietta,
        Lady, 1750–1818, 1,2
Acrobats
    Charmon "the perfect woman", fl.
        1910s, 1
Action for Children
    Ambrosino, Lillian, 2
Activists
    See also
    Affirmative action
    AIM
    Alliance Movement workers
    Animal rights workers
    Antisuffragists
    Antivivisectionists
    Apartheid fighters
    Birth control advocates
    Black Panthers
    Civil rights leaders
    Equal Rights Amendment
    Euthanasia activist
    Feminists
    Grey Panthers
    Martha movement
    Political activists
    Prohibitionists
    Radicals
    Social activists
    Underground leaders
    Welfare rights activists
Abiertas, Josefa, d. 1922, 2
Agadjanova-Shutko, Nina, 1889–, 2
Alexander, Lucie, fl. 1970s, 2
Baez, Joan, 1941–, 1,2
Bernstein, Janice, 1931–, 2
Bolden, Dorothy, 1920–, 2
Booth, Heather, 2
Brown, Elaine, fl. 1960s, 2
Caldicott, Helen, 1938–, 2
Chambers, Marjorie Bell, 1923–, 2
Christy, Mary Rose, 2
Cleaver, Kathleen, 1945–, 2
Clusen, Ruth C., fl. 1970s, 2
Collins, Ella Mae, fl. 1950s, 2
Comden, Betty, 1915–, 1,2

Andre, Lona, 1915–, 2
Andreini, Isabella, 1562–1604, 1,2
Andress, Ursula, 1936–, 2
Andrews, Julie, 1935–, 1,2
Angel, Heather, 1909–, 1,2
Angeli, Pier, 1932–, 1,2
Angelou, Maya, 1928–, 2
Angelus, Muriel, 1909–, 1
Anglin, Margaret Mary, 1876–1958, 1,2
Ann-Margaret, 1941–, 1,2
Annabella, 1909–, 1,2
Annette (Funicello), 1942–, 1
Anspach, Susan, 1944–, 2
Arden, Eve, 1912–, 1,2
Arletty, (Leonie Bathiat), 1898–, 1,2
Armani, Vincenza, fl. 1560s, 1
Armond, Isabel d', fl. 1910, 1
Arnaud, Yvonne (Germaine), 1892–1958, 1,2
Arnaz, Lucie, 1951–, 2
Arnoul, Francoise, 1932–, 1
Arnould-Plessy, Jeanne Sylvania, 1819–1897, 1
Arthur, Beatrice, 1923–, 2
Arthur, Jean, 1905–, 1,2
Arthur, Julia (Ida Lewis), 1869–1950, 1,2
Arundale, Sybil, 1897–, 1
Arville, Camille d', 1863–, 1
Ashcroft, Peggy, Dame, 1906–, 1,2
Ashley, Elizabeth, 1939–, 2
Ashwell, Lena Simson, Lady, 1872–1957, 2
Astor, Mary, 1906–1987, 1,2
Ault, Marie, 1870–, 1
Avedon, Doe, 1
Avery, Phyllis, 1924–, 1
Ayres, Agnes, 1898–1940, 1
Bacall, Lauren, 1924–, 1,2
Bach, Catherine, 1954–, 2
Baclanova, Olga, 1899–1974, 2
Baddeley, Angela, 1904–, 1
Baddeley, Hermione, 1906–, 1,2
Baddeley, Sophia Snow, 1745–1786, 1
Bailey, Pearl Mae, 1918–, 1,2
Bain, Barbara, 1932–, 2
Bainbridge, Beryl, 1934–, 2
Bainter, Fay Okell, 1894–1968, 1,2
Baird, Dorothea, 1873–1933, 1
Bajor, Gizi, 1894–1951, 2
Baker, Alexina Fisher, fl. 1850s, 1
Baker, Ann, 1
Baker, Belle, 1898–1957, 1

Baker, Carroll, 1931–, 1,2
Baker, Frances, fl. 1670s, 1
Baker, Katherine, fl. 1670s, 1
Balfour, Betty, 1903–, 1
Balin, Ina, 1937–, 1
Ball, Lucille, 1911–1989, 1,2
Ballard, Kaye, 1926–, 1,2
Bancroft, Anne, 1931–, 1,2
Bancroft, Marie Effie Wilton, Lady, 1839–1921, 1,2
Bankhead, Tallulah Brockman, 1903–1968, 1,2
Banky, Vilma, 1898–, 1,2
Bannerman, Margaret, 1896–, 1
Bara, Theda, 1890–1955, 1,2
Barbour, Joyce, 1901–, 1
Bardot, Brigitte, 1934–, 1,2
Bari, Lynn, 1913–, 2
Bariatinski, Lydia Yavorska, Princess, 1874–1921, 1
Barker, Widow, fl. 1830s, 1
Barnard, Sophye, fl. 1910s, 1
Barnes, Binnie (Gertrude Maude), 1905–, 2
Barnes, Gertrude, fl. 1910s, 1
Barnes, Hattie Delaro, fl. 1910s, 1
Barnes, Mrs. John, 1816–, 1
Barrett, Ann Henry, m. 1825, 1
Barrie, Wendy, 1912–1978, 1,2
Barry, Ann Street, 1734–1801, 1
Barry, Elizabeth, 1658–1713, 1,2
Barry, Joan, 1901–, 1,2
Barry, Katie, fl. 1910s, 1
Barrymore, Diana, 1921–, 1
Barrymore, Ethyl Blythe, 1879–1959, 1,2
Barrymore, Georgiana Emma Drew, 1854–1893, 1,2
Bartet, Jeanne Julia Regnault, 1854–1941, 1
Bartok, Eva, 1929–, 1
Basquette, Lina, 1907–, 2
Bateman, Ellen, 2
Bateman, Isabel Mary, 1855–1934, 1
Bateman, Kate Josephine, 1842–1917, 2
Bates, Blanche Lyon, 1873–1941, 1,2
Bauer, Charita, d. 1985, 2
Bauer, Karoline Philippine A., 1807–1878, 1
Baupre, Mille., fl. 1600s, 1
Baxter, Anne, 1923–1985, 1,2
Baxter-Birney, Meredith, fl. 1970s, 2
Bayes, Nora, 1880–1928, 1,2

Bayne, Beverly, 1895–, 2
Beauchateau, Mlle., fl. 1600s, 1
Beauval, Mme., 1648–1720, 2
Beavers, Louise, 1902–1962, 2
Becker, Maria, 1920–, 2
Bedelia, Bonnie, 1948–, 2
Bee, Molly, 1939–, 1,2
Beecher, Janet, 1884–1955, 2
Bejart, Armande Gresinde Claire
Elizabeth, 1642–1700, 1,2
Bejart, Madeleine, 1618–1672, 1,2
Bel Geddes, Barbara, 1922–, 2
Bell, Marie, 1900–, 2
Bellamy, George Anne, 1731–1788, 1
Bellamy, Madge, 1900–, 1,2
Beller, Mary Linn, 1
Belmont, Eleanor Elise Robson,
1879–1979, 1,2
Belmore, Alice, 1870–1943, 1
Bennett, Constance, 1904–1965, 1,2
Bennett, Joan, 1910–, 1,2
Bennett, Laura, fl. 1870s, 1
Bennett, Leila, fl. 1920s, 2
Bentley, Irene, 1870–1940, 1
Berenson, Marisa, 1946–, 2
Berg, Gertrude, 1899–1966, 1,2
Bergen, Candice, 1946–, 2
Bergen, Polly, 1930–, 1,2
Bergere, Ouida, d. 1974, 2
Bergman, Ingrid, 1915–1982, 1,2
Bergner, Elisabeth, 1898–, 1,2
Bernard-Beere, Fanny Mary, 1856–
1915, 1
Bernhardt, Rachel, 1821–, 1
Bernhardt, Sarah, 1844–1923, 1,2
Berridge, Rachel, Countess of Clon-
well, m. 1901, 1
Bertinelli, Valerie, 1960–, 2
Berwin, Bernice, fl. 1930s, 1
Besserer, Eugenie, fl. 1920s, 2
Best, Edna, 1900–1974, 1,2
Betterton, Mary Saunderson, 1637–
1712, 1,2
Biancolelli, Caterina, 1665–1716, 2
Bicknell, Mrs., fl. 1700s, 1
Biddulph, Jessie Catherine Vokes,
1851–1884, 1
Billingsley, Barbara, 2
Bilton, Belle, Countess of Clancarty,
1868–1906, 1
Bingham, Amelia, 1869–1927, 2
Birch-Pfeiffer, Charlotte Karoline,
1793–1868, 1
Bisset, Jacqueline, 1944–, 2

Black, Karen Blanche Ziegler, 1942–,
2
Black, Shirley Temple, 1928–, 2
Blaha, Louise, 1850–1926, 1
Blaine, Vivian, 1924–, 1
Blair, Janet, 1921–, 1,2
Blair, Linda, 1959–, 2
Blake, Amanda, 1931–, 1,2
Blake, Marie, fl. 1920s, 2
Blakley, Ronee, 1946–, 2
Bland, Joyce, 1906–, 1
Blandick, Clara, 1880–, 2
Blane, Sally, 1910–, 2
Blaney, Norah, 1896–, 1
Blondell, Joan, 1909–1979, 1,2
Bloom, Claire, 1931–, 1,2
Blyth, Ann(e), 1928–, 1,2
Blythe, Betty, 1903–1972, 2
Boardman, Eleanor, 1898–, 2
Boland, Mary, 1880–1965, 1,2
Bolton, Mary Katherine, 1790–1830,
1
Bonavita, Rose (Rosina), 1921–, 2
Bond, Lilian, 1910–, 2
Bondi, Beulah, 1892–1981, 2
Bonehill, Bessie, fl. 1800s, 1
Bonstelle, Jessie, 1871–1932, 2
Boote, Rose, 1878–1958, 1
Booth, Agnes, 1841–1910, 1,2
Booth, Mary Devlin, 1840–1863, 1
Booth, Mary F. McVicker, 1849–
1881, 1
Booth, Shirley, 1907–, 1,2
Borboni, Paola, 1900–, 2
Borden, Olive, 1906–1947, 1,2
Bordoni, Irene, 1893–1953, 1
Borg, Veda Ann, 1915–1973, 2
Bosson, Barbara, 2
Boswell, Martha, 1909–1958, 1
Boswell, Vet, fl. 1930s, 1
Bouchier, Dorothy, 1910–, 1
Boucicault, Agnes Robertson, 1833–
1916, 1,2
Boudevska-Gantcheva, Adriana,
1878–, 1
Boutell, Elizabeth, fl. 1663, 1
Bow, Clara Gordon, 1905–1965, 1,2
Bowden, Dorris, 1915–, 2
Bowers, Elizabeth, 1830–1895, 1
Boyd, Belle, 1844–1900, 1,2
Bracegirdle, Anne, 1663–1748, 1,2
Bradley, Grace, fl. 1940s, 2
Bradna, Olympe, 1920–, 2
Brady, Alice, 1892–1939, 1,2

Devi, Indira, 2
Dewhurst, Colleen, 1926–, 2
Dey, Manju, 2
Dickinson, Angie, 1931–, 2
Dickinson, Anna Elizabeth, 1842–
  1932, 1,2
Dickson, Dorothy, 1896–, 1
Dickson, Gloria, 1916–1945, 2
Dietrich, Marlene, 1901–, 1,2
Diller, Phyllis Driver, 1917–, 1,2
Dixon, Adele, 1908–, 1
Dixon, Jean, 1896–1981, 2
Doble, Frances, 1902–, 1
Dodd, Claire, 1908–1973, 2
Dolly, Roszcika, fl. 1910s, 1
Domerque, Faith, 1925–, 2
Donahue, Elinor, 1937–, 1
Donnelly, Dorothy, 1880–1928, 1,2
Donnelly, Ruth, 1896–, 2
Doran, Mary, 1907–, 2
Doro, Marie, 1882–1956, 1
Dors, Diana Lee, 1928–, 1,2
Dorsch, Kathe, 1890–1957, 2
Dorval, Marie-Thomas, 1798–1849,
  1,2
Doucet, Catharine, 1875–1958, 2
Douglas, Donna, 1
Douglas, Helen Mary Gahagan,
  1909–1980, 1,2
Douglas, Loretta Mooney, m. 1895, 1
Douglass, Sarah Hallam, d. 1774, 1,2
Dove, Billie, 1900–, 1,2
Drake, Frances, 1908–, 2
Drake, Frances Ann Denny, 1797–
  1875, 2
Draper, Ruth, 1884–1956, 1,2
Dresser, Louise Kerlin, 1882–1965,
  1,2
Dressler, Marie, 1867–1934, 1,2
Drew, Ellen, 1915–, 2
Drew, Louisa Lane, 1820–1897, 1,2
Du Parc, Therese de Gloria, Mar-
  quise, 1633–1668, 2
Duff, Mary Ann Dyke, 1794–1857,
  1,2
Duke, Patty (Anna Marie), 1946–, 1,2
Duke, Robin, 1954–, 2
Dumesnil, Marie-Francoise, 1711–
  1803, 1,2
Dumont, Margaret, 1889–1965, 2
Duna, Steffi, fl. 1930s, 2
Dunaway, (Dorothy) Faye, 1941–, 1,2
Dunbar, Dixie, 1918–, 2
Duncan, Mary, 1903–, 2

Duncan, Sandy, 1946–, 2
Duncan, Vivian, 1902–, 1,2
Duncan sisters, Vivian and Rosetta, 2
Dunn, Josephine, 1906–, 2
Dunne, Irene Marie, 1898–, 1,2
Dunnock, Mildred, 1900–, 1,2
Dupree, Minnie, 1875–1947, 2
Durbin, Deanna, 1921–, 1,2
Durieux, Tilla, 1880–1971, 2
Duse, Eleanora, 1858–1924, 1,2
Dussault, Nancy, 1936–, 2
Duvall, Shelley, 1950–, 2
Dvorak, Ann, 1912–1979, 2
Dyas, Ada, 1843–1908, 1
Dybwad, Johanne, 1867–1950, 2
Eagels, Jeanne, 1890–1929, 1,2
Ebigwei, Patricia, fl. 1960s, 2
Eburne, Maude, 1875–1960, 2
Eddy, Helen Jerome, 1897–, 2
Eden, Barbara, 1924–, 2
Edwardes, Paula, fl. 1890s, 1
Eggar, Samantha, 1929–, 2
Eggerth, Martha, 1916–, 1
Eilers, Sally (Dorothea Sallye),
  1908–, 1,2
Eis, Alice, fl. 1910s, 1
Ekberg, Anita, 1931–, 1
Eklund, Britt, 1942–, 2
Eldridge, Florence, 1901–, 2
Ellers, Sally, 1908–1978, 2
Elliott, Maxine, 1868–1940, 1,2
Elliott, May Gertrude, 1874–1950, 2
Ellis, Mary, 1899–, 2
Ellis, Patricia, 1916–1970, 2
Ellsler, Effie, 1854–1942, 2
Elsie, Lily, 1886–1962, 1
Emerson, Faye, 1917–1983, 1,2
Emery, Isabel Winifred Maud, 1862–
  1924, 1
Entwistle, Sarah, m. 1781, 1
Erwin, June Collyer, 1
Espert, Nuria, 1938–, 2
Eucharis, 2
Eudocia (Eudoxia) (Anthenais), 401–
  460, 1,2
Evans, Edith Mary Booth, Dame,
  1888–1976, 1,2
Evans, Joan, 1934–, 2
Evans, Linda, 1943–, 2
Evans, Madge, 1909–, 2
Evelyn, Judith, 1913–1967, 1
Eytinge, Rose, 1835–1911, 1,2
Fabray, Nanette, 1920–, 1,2
Fairbrother, Louisa, 1816–1890, 1

Fairbrother, Sydney, 1872–, 1
Fairet, Marie, fl. 1540s, 1
Falana, Lola, 1947–, 2
Falk, Rossella, 1926–, 2
Falkenburg, Jinx, 1919–, 1
Farley, Elizabeth, fl. 1660s, 1
Farmer, Frances, 1913–1970, 2
Farr, Florence, d. 1917, 1
Farrell, Glenda, 1904–1971, 2
Farren, Elizabeth, 1759–1829, 1
Farren, Ellen, 1848–1904, 1
Farren, Maria Ann Russell, fl. 1830s, 1
Farrow, Mia Villiers, 1946–, 2
Faucit, Helen(a) Saville, 1817–1898, 1,2
Favart, Justine, d. 1772, 1
Fawcett, Farrah, 1947–, 2
Faye, Alice, 1915–, 1,2
Fazenda, Louise, 1895–1962, 2
Fealy, Maude, 1886–, 1,2
Fears, Peggy, 1906–, 2
Feigenblatt, Ann, fl. 1930s, 1
Feldon, Barbara, 1941–, 2
Fellows, Edith, 1923–, 2
Felton, Verna, 1890–1966, 1
Fenton, Lavinia Duchess of Bolton, 1708–1769, 1,2
Ferguson, Elsie, 1883–1961, 1
Feron, Madame, 1797–, 1
Ferrens, Norah, m. 1923, 1
Feuillere, Edwige, 1,2
Ffrangcon-Davies, Gwen, 1896–, 1
Fickett, Mary, 1
Field, Betty, 1918–1973, 1,2
Field, Kate, 1838–1896, 1,2
Field, Sally Margaret, 1946–, 2
Field, Virginia (Margaret Cynthia), 1917–, 2
Finch, Flora, 1869–1940, 1
Fischer, Lynn Conner, fl. 1970s, 2
Fisher, Carrie Frances, 1956–, 2
Fisher, Clara, 1811–1898, 1,2
Fiske, Mary Augusta Davey, 1865–, 1
Fiske, Minnie Maddern, 1865–1932, 1,2
Fitzgerald, Cissy, 1873–1941, 1
Fitzgerald, Geraldine, 1914–, 1,2
Fitzwilliam, Fanny Elizabeth Copeland, 1801–1854, 1
Flaminia, fl. 1565, 1
Fleming, Rhonda, 1923–, 1,2
Fletcher, Louise, 1936–, 2
Flickenschildt, Elisabeth, 1905–, 2

Flood, Ann, 2
Florence, Malvina Pray, 1830–1906, 1,2
Foch, Nina, 1924–, 1,2
Fonda, Jane, 1937–, 1,2
Fontaine, Joan, 1917–, 1,2
Fontanne, Lynn, 1887–1983, 1,2
Fontenelle, Miss, fl. 1790s, 1
Foote, Maria, 1797–1867, 1
Forbes-Robertson, Gertrude Elliott, Lady, 1874–1950, 1,2
Forbes-Robertson, Jean, d. 1962, 2
Ford, Constance, 1
Ford, Ruth, 1
Fortescue, Julia, m. 1862, 1
Fortescue, May, 1862–1950, 1
Foster, Gloria, 1936–, 2
Foster, Jodie, 1962–, 2
Foster, Susanna, 1924–, 2
Fox, Della May, 1870–1913, 1,2
Fox, Sidney, 1910–1942, 2
Francis, Arlene, 1908–, 1,2
Francis, Genie Ann, 1962–, 2
Francis, Kay, 1903–1968, 1,2
Francis, Noel, 2
Franklin, Bonnie Gail, 1944–, 2
Franklin, Irene, 1876–1941, 1
Frederick, Pauline, 1883–1938, 1,2
Freeman, Mona (Monica Elizabeth), 1926–, 2
Frier, Peg, fl. 1669s, 1
Friganza, Trixie, 1870–1955, 2
Fuller, Frances, 1907–, 2
Fuller, Loie, 1862–1928, 1,2
Fulton, Eileen, 2
Fulton, Maud, 1881–1950, 1
Funicello, Annette, 1942–, 1,2
Fyodorova, Victoria, 1945–, 2
Fyodorova, Zoya, 1911–, 2
Gaal, Franciska, 1904–, 2
Gabor, Eva, 1921–, 1,2
Gabor, Magda, 1918–, 1
Gabor, Zsa Zsa (Sari), 1919–, 1,2
Gallagher, Helen, 1926–, 2
Gallian, Ketti, 1913–1972, 2
Gam, Rita, 1928–, 1
Gannon, Margaret, 1829–1868, 1
Garbo, Greta Louisa Gustafson, 1905–, 1,2
Gardner, Ava, 1922–, 1,2
Gardner, Helen, fl. 1910s, 1
Garland, Judy, 1922–1969, 1,2
Garr, Teri, 1952–, 2
Garrett, Betty, 1919–, 2

Garson, Greer, 1908–, 1,2
Gateson, Marjorie, 1891–, 2
Gay, Maisie, 1883–, 1
Gaynor, Janet, 1906–1984, 1,2
Gaynor, Mitzi, 1931–, 1,2
Geddes, Barbara Bel, 1922–, 1
Geistinger, Marie, 1836–1904, 1
George, Gladys, 1904–1954, 2
George, Grace, 1878–1961, 1
George, Mademoiselle, 1787–1867, 2
Georges, Marguerite Josephine, 1787–
   1867, 1
Gerrard, Miss, fl. 1800s, 1
Gersten, Berta, 1896–1972, 2
Ghostley, Alice, 1926–, 2
Giatsintova, Sofiya, 2
Gibbs, Ann, fl. 1660s, 1,2
Gibbs, Marla, 1946–, 2
Gibbs, Mrs., fl. 1670s, 1
Gibson, Virginia, 1
Gibson, Wynne, 1907–, 2
Giehse, Therese, 1898–1975, 2
Gilbert, Anne Jane Hartley, 1821–
   1904, 1,2
Gilbert, Melissa, 1964–, 2
Gilbert, Mrs. G. H. "Grandma",
   1822–1904, 1
Gilchrist, Constance, 1865–1946, 1
Gilfert, Mrs. Charles, fl. 1810s, 1
Gillespie, Jean, 1
Gillespie, Marian, 1889–1946, 1
Gilman, Mabelle, fl. 1890s, 1
Gingold, Hermione Ferdinanda,
   1897–1987, 1,2
Gish, Dorothy, 1898–1968, 1,2
Gish, Lillian Diana, 1893–, 1,2
Glaser, Lulu, 1874–, 1
Glover, Julia, 1779–1850, 1
Glynne, Mary, 1898–, 1
Goddard, Paulette, 1911–, 1,2
Godowski, Dagmar, 1897–, 1
Goldberg, Whoopi, pseud., 1950–, 2
Gombell, Minna, 1893–1973, 2
Goodman, Dody, 1
Goodner, Carol, fl. 1920s, 1
Goodrich, Frances, 1891–1984, 1,2
Gordon, Julia Swayne, fl. 1900s, 1
Gordon, Mary Gilmour, 1882–1963,
   2
Gordon, Ruth, 1896–1985, 1,2
Gosnell, Winifred, fl. 1660s, 1
Grable, Betty, 1916–1973, 1,2
Graham, Gloria, 1925–, 2
Grahame, Margot, 1911–, 2

Gramatica, Irma, 1870–1962, 2
Granier, Jeanne, fl. 1900s, 1
Grant, Kathryn, 1933–, 1
Grant, Lee, 1929–, 2
Granville, Bonita, 1923–, 2
Gray, Coleen, 1922–, 1
Gray, Dolores, 1930–, 1
Gray, Gilda, 1901–1959, 1,2
Gray, Linda, 1940–, 2
Gray, Mary Alice Smith, 2
Grayson, Kathryn, 1923–, 1,2
Green, Ethel, fl. 1910s, 1
Greenwood, Charlotte, 1893–1978,
   1,2
Greenwood, Joan, 1921–, 1,2
Greer, Jane, 1924–, 2
Grenfell, Joyce Irene, 1910–1979, 1,2
Grey, Nan, 1918–, 2
Grey, Virginia, 1917–, 2
Grier, Pam, 1949–, 2
Griffies, Ethel, 1878–1975, 1,2
Griffith, Corinne, 1896–, 1,2
Grimes, Tammy Lee, 1934–, 1,2
Gross, Mary, 1953–, 2
Guilbert, Yvette, 1867–1944, 1,2
Guinan, Mary Louise Cecilia, 1884–
   1933, 1,2
Gurie, Sigrid, 1911–1969, 2
Guzik, Anna, 2
Gwynn, Nell (Eleanor), 1650–1687,
   1,2
Gwynne, Anne, 1918–, 2
Gwynne, Rose, 1650–, 1
Hackett, Joan, 1933–1983, 2
Hading, Jane, 1859–1941, 1
Hagen, Jean, 1924–, 2
Hagen, Uta, 1919–, 1,2
Hale, Louise Closser, 1872–1933, 1,2
Hall, Deidre, fl. 1970s, 2
Hall, Elizabeth, fl. 1660s, 1
Hall, Josephine, fl. 1890s, 1
Hall, Juanita, 1913–1968, 1
Hall, Pauline, fl. 1870s, 1
Hallam, Mrs. Lewis, m. 1793, 1
Hallam, Nancy, 1750–1775, 1,2
Hallam, Sarah, fl. 1760s, 1
Halop, Florence, 1
Hamel, Veronica, 1947–, 2
Hamilton, Cicely, 1872–1952, 1
Hamilton, Margaret, 1902–1985, 2
Hamlin, Sonya, 2
Hampshire, Susan, 1941–, 2
Hampton, Louise, 1877–1954, 1
Harding, Ann, 1901–1982, 1,2

Harlow, Jean, 1911–1937, 1,2
Harman, Catharine Maria, d. 1775, 1
Harned, Virginia, 1868–1946, 1
Harper, Valerie, 1940–, 2
Harris, Barbara, 1935–, 1,2
Harris, Julie, 1925–, 1,2
Harris, Rosemary, 1930–, 1
Harrison, Kathleen, 1898–, 2
Harry, Debbie, 1944–, 2
Hart, Dorothy, 1923–, 1
Hart, Kitty Carlisle, 1914–, 2
Hartley, Elda, fl. 1970s, 2
Harvey, Lilian, 1906–1968, 2
Haver, June, 1926–, 2
Haver, Phyllis, 1926–, 1
Havoc, June, 1916–, 1,2
Hawkes, Sylvia, fl. 1920s, 1
Hawn, Goldie Jeanne, 1945–, 2
Haydon, Julie, 1910–, 2
Hayes, Helen, 1900–, 1,2
Hayes, Susan Seaforth, 1943–, 2
Hays, Kathryn, 2
Hayward, Susan, 1918–1975, 1,2
Hayworth, Rita, 1918–1987, 1,2
Healy, Mary, 1918–, 1
Heckart, Eileen, 1919–, 1,2
Heiberg, Johanne Louise Patges, 1812–1890, 1
Heinkel, Susan, 1944–, 1
Held, Anna, 1873–1918, 1
Held, Anna, 1865–1918, 2
Hemingway, Margaux (Margot), 1955–, 2
Henderson, Florence, 1934–, 1,2
Henderson, Marcia, 1930–, 1
Hendrix, Wanda, 1928–1981, 2
Henley, Beth, 1952–, 2
Henner, Marilu, 1952–, 2
Henry, Charlotte, 1914–, 1,2
Hepburn, Audrey, 1929–1993, 1,2
Hepburn, Katharine, 1907–, 1,2
Herford, Beatrice, 1868–1952, 1
Herlie, Eileen, 1920–, 2
Herne, Chrystal Katharine, 1882–1950, 2
Herne, Katherine Corcoran, m. 1878, 1
Heron, Matilda Agnes, 1830–1877, 1,2
Hervey, Irene, 1910–, 2
Hibbard, Edna, 1895–1942, 1
Hilder, Vera Gertude, fl. 1930s, 1
Hill, Jenny, 1850–1896, 1
Hiller, Wendy, 1912–, 1,2

Hobart, Rose, 1906–, 2
Hobson, Valerie, 1917–, 2
Hodgkinson, Mrs. John, 1770–1803, 1,2
Hoey, Iris, 1885–, 1
Hoflich, Lucie, 1883–1956, 2
Hogquist, Emilie, 1812–1846, 1
Holden, Fay, 1895–1973, 2
Holliday, Judy, 1922–1965, 1,2
Holliday, Polly Dean, 1937–, 2
Holm, Celeste, 1919–, 1,2
Holman, Libby, 1905–1971, 1,2
Hopkins, Miriam, 1902–1972, 1,2
Hopper, Edna Wallace, 1864–, 1
Hopper, Hedda, 1885–1966, 1,2
Horne, Lena, 1917–, 1,2
Howard, Cordelia, 1848–1941, 2
Howard, Lisa, 1930–1965, 2
Howes, Sally Ann, 1930–, 1
Howland, Beth, 1947–, 2
Howland, Jobyna, 1880–1936, 2
Hudson, Rochelle, 1914–1972, 1,2
Hughes, Annie, 1869–1931, 1
Hughes, Jean Peters, 1926–, 2
Hughes, Margaret, d. 1719, 1
Hull, Josephine Sherwood, 1884–1957, 1,2
Hume, Benita, 1906–1967, 2
Hunnicut, Gayle, 1943–, 2
Hunt, Marsha (Marcia Virginia), 1917–, 2
Hunter, Kim, 1922–, 1,2
Huppert, Isabelle, 1955–, 2
Hussey, Ruth, 1914–, 2
Hutchinson, Josephine, 1904–, 2
Hutton, Betty, 1921–, 1,2
Hutton, Lauren, 1943–, 2
Hyams, Leila, 1905–1977, 2
Illington, Margaret, 1881–1934, 1
Inchbald, Elizabeth Simpson, 1753–1821, 1,2
Inescort, Frieda, 1901–, 2
Irving, Isabel, 1871–1944, 1
Irwin, Agnes, 1862–1938, 2
Irwin, Flora, fl. 1870s, 1
Irwin, May, 1862–1938, 1,2
Isaacs, Adah, 1835–1868, 1
Jackson, Anne, 1926–, 1,2
Jackson, Glenda, 1936–, 2
Jackson, Kate, 1948–, 2
James, Elizabeth, fl. 1660s, 1
Janauschek, Francesco (Fanny) Romana Magdalena, 1829–1904, 1,2
Janis, Elsie, 1889–1956, 1

Jean, Gloria, 1927–, 2
Jeanmaire, Renee Marcelle (Zizi), 1924–, 1,2
Jeans, Isabel, 1891–, 1
Jeans, Ursula, 1906–, 1
Jecks, Clara, fl. 1800s, 1
Jefferson, Cornelia Burke, fl. 1830s, 1
Jefferson, Mary Anne, fl. 1820s, 1
Jeffreys, Anne, 1923–, 1,2
Jeffreys, Ellis, 1868–1943, 1
Jergens, Adele, 1917–, 2
Jerome, Maude Nugent, 1873–1958, 1,2
Jewell, Isabel, 1909–1972, 2
Johann, Zita, 1904–, 2
Johns, Glynnis, 1923–, 2
Johnson, Celia, 1908–1982, 2
Johnson, Kay, 1904–, 2
Johnson, Mrs., fl. 1660s, 1
Johnson, Mrs. John, fl. 1790s, 1
Johnson, Rita, 1912–1965, 2
Jones, Avonia, 1839–1867, 1
Jones, Carolyn, 1933–1983, 1,2
Jones, Gail (Gayl), 1949–, 1,2
Jones, Grace, 1951–, 2
Jones, Jennifer, 1919–, 1,2
Jones, Marcia Mae, 1924–, 2
Jones, Marsha Mae [Marcia Mae], 1924–, 2
Jones, Shirley, 1934–, 1,2
Jordan, Dorothea Bland, 1762–1816, 1
Jordan, Dorothy, 1908–, 2
Jordan, Miriam, 1908–, 2
Jorgensen, Christine, 1926–, 1,2
Joy, Leatrice, 1896–1985, 1,2
Joyce, Alice, 1890–1955, 1
Joyce, Brenda, 1916–, 2
Joyce, Peggy Hopkins, 1893–1957, 1
Judge, Arline, 1912–1974, 2
June (June Howard Tripp), 1901–, 1
Kahn, Madeline Gail, 1942–, 2
Kalich, Bertha, 1874–1939, 2
Kamala, fl. 1900s, 2
Kaminska, Ida, 1899–1980, 2
Kane, Helen, 1910–1966, 2
Kate, Elinor, fl. 1910s, 1
Kean, Ellen Tree, 1805–1880, 1,2
Keane, Doris, 1885–1945, 1
Keaton, Diane, 1949–, 2
Keeler, Ruby (Ethel), 1909–, 1,2
Keeley, Mary Anne, 1806–1899, 1
Keene, Laura, 1820–1873, 1,2
Kellerman, Annette, 1888–1975, 1,2

Kellerman, Sally, 1937–, 2
Kelly, Grace Patricia, 1929–1983, 1,2
Kelly, Nancy, 1921–, 1,2
Kelly, Patsy, 1910–1981, 1,2
Kelton, Pert, 1906–, 2
Kemble, Elizabeth, 1761–1836, 1
Kemble, Fanny (Frances Anne), 1809–1893, 1,2
Kendal, Margaret (Madge) Robertson, Dame, 1848–1935, 2
Kendal, Margaret Robertson, 1849–1917, 1
Kendall, Kay, 1927–1959, 2
Kendall, Nancy, fl. 1970s, 2
Kent, Barbara, 1906–, 2
Kent, Dorothea, 1917–, 2
Kenyon, Doris, 1897–, 2
Kerr, Deborah Jane, 1921–, 1,2
Kerr, Joyce, m. 1924, 1
Keyes, Evelyn, 1917–, 2
Kholodnaya, Vera, 2
Kibbee, Lois, 2
Kidder, Kathryn, 1868–1939, 1
Kidder, Margot, 1948–, 2
Kimball, Corinne, 1873–, 1
Kimball, Grace, 1887–, 1
Kimball, Jennie, 1951–, 1
Kimbrell, Marketa, 1928–, 2
King, Morgana, 1930–, 2
Kingston, Gertrude, fl. 1900s, 1
Kinski, Nastassja, 1961–, 2
Kirk, Phyllis, 1930–, 1
Kitt, Eartha Mae, 1928–, 1,2
Knapp, Evelyn, 1908–, 2
Knepp, Mary, d. 1677, 1,2
Knight, Frances Maria, fl. 1676, 1
Knipper-Checkhova, Olga, 1870–1959, 2
Knowlden, Marilyn, 1925–, 2
Komisarjevskava, Vera, 1864–1910, 1
Korjus, Miliza, 1900–1980, 2
Kruger, Alma, 1871–1960, 2
Kurishima, Sumiko, fl. 1900s, 2
Kurtz, Swoosie, 1944–, 2
Kvapilova, Jana Kubesova, 1860–1907, 1,2
Kwan, Nancy, 1939–, 1
La Marr, Hedy, 1913–, 1,2
La Planche, Rosemary, fl. 1940s, 1
La Plante, Laura, fl. 1920s, 1
La Villiers (Devilliers), Mlle, fl. 1620s, 1
LaBlanc, Leonide, fl. 1860s, 1
LaPlante, Laura, 1904–, 2

Lacy, Harriette Deborah Lacy, 1807–1874, 1
Ladd, Cheryl Stoppelmoor, 1950–, 2
Ladynina, Marina, fl. 1930s, 2
Lake, Veronica, 1919–1973, 1,2
Lamour, Dorothy, 1914–, 1,2
Lanchester, Ella, 1902–, 1
Lanchester, Elsa (or Ella), 1902–1986, 1,2
Lander, Jean Margaret Davenport, 1829–1903, 1
Landi, Elissa, 1904–1948, 1,2
Lane, Abbe, 1932–, 1,2
Lane, Lola Mullican, 1909–, 2
Lane, Louisa, 1820–1897, 1
Lane, Priscilla, 1917–, 2
Lane, Rosemary, 1914–, 2
Lane, Sara, fl. 1890s, 1
Lang, June, 1915–, 2
Lange, Hope, 1933–, 1,2
Lange, Jessica, 1948–, 2
Langtry, Lillie Emilie Charlotte le Breton, 1853–1929, 1,2
Lansbury, Angela Brigid, 1925–, 1,2
Laporte, Marie Vernier, fl. 1610s, 1
Larrimore, Francine, 1898–, 1
Lasser, Louise, 1940–, 2
Laurie, Piper, 1932–, 1
Lavalliere, Eve, 1866–1929, 1
Lavin, Linda, 1937–, 2
Lawrence, Carol, 1934–, 1,2
Lawrence, Florence, 1886–1938, 1,2
Lawrence, Gertrude, 1898–1952, 1,2
Lawrence, Lillian, fl. 1890s, 1
Lawrence, Vicki, 1949–, 2
Lawson, Mary, 1910–1941, 1
Laye, Evelyn, 1900–, 1,2
Le Gallienne, Eva, 1899–, 1,2
LeBlanc, Georgette, 1875–1941, 1
LeMoyne, Sarah Cowell, fl. 1890s, 1
Leachman, Cloris, 1925–, 2
Leatherbee, Mary Lee Logan, 2
Leblanc, Leonide, fl. 1860s, 1
Lecourvreur, Adrienne, 1692–1730, 1,2
Lee, Auriol, 1880–1941, 1
Lee, Dorothy, 1911–, 2
Lee, Gwen, 1904–, 2
Lee, Gypsy Rose, 1914–1970, 1,2
Lee, Lila, 1901–1973, 1,2
Lee, Michele, 1942–, 2
Lee, Peggy, 1920–, 1,2
Leeds, Andrea, 1914–, 2
Leeds, Lila, 1928–, 2

Leigh, Elinor, fl. 1670s, 1
Leigh, Janet, 1927–, 1,2
Leigh, Vivien, 1913–1967, 1,2
Leighton, Margaret, 1922–1976, 1,2
Lenihan, Winifred, 1898–, 1
Lennox, Mary Anne Paton, d. 1864, 1
Lenya, Lotte, 1898–1981, 1,2
Leontovich, Eugenie, 1894–, 2
Leslie, Joan, 1925–, 1,2
Leslie, Miriam Florence Folline Squier, 1836–1914, 1,2
Leslie, Nan, 1926–, 1
Levey, Ethel, 1881–1955, 1
Lewis, Monica, 1925–, 2
Lightner, Winnie, 1899–1961, 2
Lillie, Beatrice, Lady Peel, 1894–, 1,2
Lincoln, Abbey, 1930–, 2
Lindfors, Elsa Viveca Torstendotter, 1920–, 1,2
Lindsay, Margaret, 1910–, 2
Lipman, Clara, 1869–, 1
Lipton, Peggy, 1947–, 2
Litton, Marie, d. 1884, 1
Livingston, Margaret, 1900–, 1
Lloyd, Alice, 1873–1949, 1
Lloyd, Doris, 1900–1968, 2
Lloyd, Marie, 1870–1922, 1,2
Lockhart, June, 1925–, 1,2
Lockwood, Margaret, 1916–, 1,2
Loftus, Marie Cecilia, 1876–1943, 1,2
Logan, Ella, 1913–, 1
Logan, Jacqueline, 1901–, 1,2
Logan, Olive, 1839–1909, 1,2
Lohr, Marie, 1890–, 1
Lollobrigida, Gina, 1927–, 1,2
Lombard, Carole, 1908–1942, 1,2
London, Julie, 1926–, 1,2
Long, Jane, fl. 1660s, 1
Long, Loretta, 2
Long, Shelley, 2
Longet, Claudine Georgette, 1941–, 2
Lopkova, Lydia, 1891–, 1
Lord, Marjorie, 1
Lord, Pauline, 1890–1950, 1,2
Loren, Sophia, 1934–, 1,2
Loring, Gloria Jean, 1946–, 2
Loring, Joan, 1
Lorne, Marion, 1888–1968, 1,2
Loudon, Dorothy, 1933–, 2
Louise, Anita, 1915–1970, 2
Louise, Tina, 1934–, 1
Love, Bessie, 1898–1931, 2
Lowrie, Mrs., fl. 1880s, 1
Loy, Myrna, 1905–, 1,2

Lucci, Susan, 2
Luce, Clare Booth, 1903–1987, 1,2
Lupino, Ida, 1918–, 1,2
Lyman, Dorothy, 2
Lynley, Carol, 1942–, 1,2
Lynn, Diana, 1926–1971, 1,2
Lynn, Sharon, 1907–1963, 2
Lyon, Sue, 1946–, 1
MacDonald, Christie, 1875–1962, 1
MacDonald, Cordelia, 1848–1941, 1
MacDonald, Jeannette, 1907–1965, 1,2
MacGrath, Leueen, 1914–, 1
MacGraw, Ali, 1939–, 2
MacKenzie, Giselle, 1827–, 1,2
MacLaine, Shirley, 1934–, 1,2
MacMahon, Aline, 1899–, 1,2
MacRae, Meredith, 1945–, 2
Mack, Helen, 1913–, 2
Mack, Nila, 1891–1953, 1,2
Mackaill, Dorothy, 1903–, 2
Macklin, Miss, fl. 1700s, 1
Macpherson, Jeanie, d. 1946, 2
Madison, Cleo, d. 1964, 2
Magnani, Anna, 1908–1973, 1,2
Main, Marjorie, 1890–1975, 1,2
Malina, Judith, 1926–, 2
Malkhazounie, Irma de, m. 1933, 1
Malloch, Elizabeth, fl. 1930s, 1
Mallory, Boots, 1913–, 2
Malone, Dorothy, 1925–, 2
Mana (Manna)-Zucca, Madame, pseud., 1894–, 1
Manchester, Helena Zimmerman, fl. 1930s, 1
Mann, Erika, 1905–1969, 1,2
Mannering, Mary, 1876–1953, 1
Manners, Diana, Lady, 1892–, 1,2
Mansfield, Jayne, 1933–1967, 1,2
Mantell, Lynda, m. 1925, 1
Mara, Adela, 1927–, 2
Mardyn, Mrs., 1789–, 1
Maretskaya, Vera, 2
Margo, 1918–1985, 2
Margolin, Janet, 1943–, 2
Maritza, Sari, 1910–, 2
Markham, Daisy, 1886–, 1
Marlowe, Julia, 1866–1950, 1,2
Mars, Anne Francoise Hippolyte Boutet, 1779–1847, 1,2
Marsh, Jean Lyndsey Tarren, 1934–, 2
Marsh, Joan, 1913–, 2
Marsh, Mae, 1895–1968, 2
Marsh, Marian, 1913–, 2

Marshall, Ann, 1661–1682, 1
Marshall, Penny, 1945–, 2
Marshall, Rebecca, 1663–1677, 1
Martin, Mary, 1913–, 1,2
Martinelli, Angelica, fl. 1579, 1
Masina, Giulietta, 1921–, 1,2
Mason, Marsha, 1942–, 2
Massey, Ilona, 1912–1974, 1,2
Mather, Margaret, 1862–, 1
Mathews, Joyce (Jane), fl. 1940s, 2
Matthews, Jessie, 1907–, 1,2
Matthews, Joyce, fl. 1940s, 2
Matthison, Edith Wynne, 1861–1898, 1
Mattocks, Isabella, 1746–1826, 1
Maxwell, Marilyn, 1922–, 1
May, Edna, 1878–1948, 1
May, Elaine, 1932–, 1,2
Mayne, Clarice, fl. 1910s, 1
Mayo, Virginia, 1920–, 2
McArdle, Andrea, 1963–, 2
McAvoy, May, 1901–1984, 1,2
McCalla, Irish, 1929–, 2
McCambridge, Mercedes, 1918–, 1,2
McClendon, Rose, 1884–1936, 2
McCracken, Joan, 1922–1961, 1
McCree, Junie, 1865–1918, 2
McDaniel, Hattie, 1895–1952, 1,2
McDonald, Marie Frye, 1920–, 1
McGuire, Dorothy, 1918–, 1,2
McKenna, Siobhan, 1922–, 1,2
McKenna, Virginia, 1931–, 1
McLaughlin, Emily, 1928–, 2
McLaurin, Kate, 1
McMillan, Lida, fl. 1800s, 1
McNair, Barbara, 1939–, 2
McNamara, Maggie, 1931–, 2
McNeil, Claudia, 1
McNichol, Kristy, 1962–, 2
McQueen, Butterfly (Thelma), 1911–, 2
McVey, Lucille, 1890–1925, 2
Meade, Julia, 1930–, 1
Meadows, Audrey, 1922–, 1,2
Meadows, Jayne Cotter, 1925–, 1,2
Melanie, 1948–, 2
Meller, Raquel, 1888–1962, 1
Mellon, Harriot, 1777–1837, 1
Melmoth, Charlotte, 1749–1823, 1,2
Mendl, Lady, 1865–1960, 1
Menken, Adah Isaacs, 1835–1868, 1,2
Menken, Helen, 1901–, 1
Menken, La Belle, fl. 1860s, 1
Mercer, Beryl, 1882–1939, 1,2

Mercouri, Melina (Maria Amalia), 1923–, 1,2
Meriwether, Lee, 1935–, 2
Merkel, Una, 1903–1986, 2
Merman, Ethel Agnes Zimmerman, 1908–1984, 1,2
Merrill, Dina, 1925–, 1,2
Merry, Anne Brunton, 1769–1808, 1,2
Methot, Mayo, 1904–1941, 2
Michael, Gertrude, 1910–1965, 2
Midler, Bette, 1944–, 2
Miles, Sarah, 1943–, 2
Miles, Vera, 1930–, 2
Millar, Gertie, 1879–1952, 1
Millar, Marjie, 1930–, 1
Millard, Evelyn, 1873–, 1
Miller, Ann, 1919–, 1,2
Miller, Marilyn, 1898–1936, 1,2
Miller, Patsy Ruth, 1905–, 1,2
Mills, Donna, 2
Mills, Hayley, 1946–, 1,2
Mills, Juliet, 1941–, 1
Mimieux, Yvette Carmen M., 1941–, 1,2
Minnelli, Liza, 1946–, 2
Minter, Mary Miles, 1902–1984, 1,2
Miranda, Carmen, 1909–1955, 1,2
Mirren, Helen, 1946–, 2
Mistinguett, 1873–1956, 2
Mitchell, Abbie, 1884–1960, 1,2
Mitchell, Maggie (Margaret Julia), 1832–1918, 2
Mitchell, Margaret Julia, 1832–1918, 1
Mitzie, 1891–, 2
Modjeska, Helena, 1840–1909, 1,2
Modotti, Tina, 1886–, 2
Monroe, Marilyn, 1926–1962, 1,2
Montansier, Marguerite Brunet, La, 1730–, 1
Montez, Maria, 1920–1951, 2
Montgomery, Elizabeth, 1933–, 1,2
Montgomery, Peggy "Baby Peggy", 1919–, 1
Moore, Colleen, 1902–, 1,2
Moore, Constance, 1922–, 2
Moore, Eva, 1870–1955, 1
Moore, Grace, 1898–1947, 1,2
Moore, Mary, 1861–1931, 1
Moore, Mary Tyler, 1937–, 1,2
Moore, Melba, 1945–, 2
Moore, Terry, 1929–, 1
Moorehead, Agnes, 1906–1974, 1,2
Moorehead, Natalie, 1901–, 2

Moran, Lois, 1907–, 1,2
Morant, Fanny, fl. 1870s, 1
Moreau, Jeanne, 1928–, 1,2
Morelli, Rina, 1908–1976, 2
Moreno, Rita, 1931–, 1,2
Morgan, Helen, 1900–1941, 2
Morgan, Michele, 1920–, 1,2
Morison, Patricia, 1914–, 1,2
Morley, Karen, 1905–, 2
Morris, Anita, 2
Morris, Clara, 1847–1925, 1,2
Morris, Elizabeth, 1753–1826, 1,2
Morris, Mrs., d. 1767, 1
Morris, Mrs. Owen, d. 1825, 1
Morrison, Adrienne, 1889–1940, 1
Moten, Etta, fl. 1930s, 1
Mowatt, Anna Cora Ogden, 1819–1870, 1,2
Mrinalini, fl. 1910s, 2
Muir, Jean, 1911–, 2
Munson, Ona, 1906–1955, 2
Murray, Alma, 1855–, 1
Murray, Kathryn, 1906–, 1,2
Murray, Mae, 1889–1965, 1,2
Musidora, d. 1957, 2
Mutchie, Marjorie Ann, 2
Myers, Carmel, 1899–1980, 2
Nash, Mary, 1855–, 1
Natwick, Mildred, 1908–, 1,2
Nazimova, Alla, 1879–1945, 1,2
Neagle, Anna, Dame, 1904–, 1,2
Neal, Patricia, 1926–, 1,2
Nedeva, Zlatina, 1877–1941, 1,2
Neff, Hildegarde, 1925–, 2
Negri, Pola, 1894–1987, 1,2
Neill, Noel, 2
Neilson, Julia, 1869–1957, 1
Neilson, (Lilian) Adelaide, 1846–1880, 1
Nelligan, Kate, 1951–, 2
Nelson, Harriet Hilliard, 1911–, 1,2
Nesbit, Evelyn, 1884–1967, 1,2
Nesbitt, Cathleen (Mary), 1888–1982, 1,2
Nethersole, Olga Isabel, 1870–1951, 1
Neuber, Frederike(a) Caroline Weissenborn, 1697–1760, 1,2
Newman, Phyllis, 1935–, 1,2
Nilsson, Anna Q., 1888–1974, 2
Nisbett, Louise Cranston, 1812–1858, 1
Nissen, Greta, 1906–, 1,2
Nixon, Marion, 1904–, 2
Nolan, Doris, 1916–, 2

Nolan, Kathy (Kathleen), 1933–, 2
Normand, Mabel Ethelreid, 1893–1930, 1,2
Norris, Mrs., 1661–1683, 1
North, Sheree, 1932–, 1
Norton, Mrs., fl. 1660s, 1
Norton-Taylor, Judy, 1958–, 2
Novak, Eva, 1898–, 2
Novak, Jane, 1896–, 2
Novak, Kim (Marilyn Pauline), 1933–, 1,2
Nurmi, Maila, 1921–, 2
Nuyen, France, 1939–, 1
O'Brien-Moore, Erin, 1908–, 2
O'Connor, Una, 1880–1959, 2
O'Dea, Anne Caldwell, 1867–1936, 1,2
O'Hara, Maureen, 1920–, 1,2
O'Neal, Tatum, 1963–, 2
O'Neil, Barbara, 1910–, 2
O'Neil, Nance, 1874–1965, 1,2
O'Neil, Sally, 1908–, 2
O'Neill, Eliza, 1791–1872, 1
O'Niel, Constance Mary, 1895–, 1
O'Sullivan, Maureen, 1911–, 1,2
Oakes, Betty, 1
Oberon, Merle, 1911–1979, 1,2
Oldfield, Anne "Nance", 1683–1730, 1,2
Oldmixon, Lady John, fl. 1740s, 1
Oldmixon, Mrs. George, d. 1836, 1
Oliver, Edna May, 1883–1942, 1,2
Orger, Mary Ann, 1788–1849, 1
Osata, Sono, 1919–, 1
Osborn, Margaret, fl. 1670s, 1
Osborne, Vivienne, 1896–1961, 2
Ottiano, Rafaela, 1894–1942, 2
Ouspenskaya, Maria, 1876–1949, 1,2
Owen, Catherine Dale, 1925–1965, 2
Page, Anita, 1910–, 2
Page, Gale, 1913–, 2
Page, Geraldine, 1924–1987, 1,2
Paget, Debra, 1933–, 1
Paige, Janis, 1923–, 1
Palmer, Betsy, 1926–, 1
Palmer, Lilli, 1914–, 1,2
Papas, Irene, 1926–, 2
Papathanossiou, Aspasia, fl. 1940s, 2
Parker, Cecilia, 1905–, 2
Parker, Eleanor, 1922–, 2
Parker, Jean, 1912–, 2
Parrish, Helen, 1922–1959, 2
Parsons, Estelle, 1927–, 2
Parton, Dolly Rebecca, 1946–, 2

Paterson, Pat, 1911–, 2
Patrick, Gail, 1911–, 2
Patrick, Lee Salome, 1912–1982, 2
Patterson, Elizabeth, 1875–1966, 2
Patterson, Nan, 1882–, 1
Paul, Mrs. Howard, fl. 1890s, 1
Pavan, Marisa, 1932–, 2
Paxinou, Katina, 1900–1973, 1,2
Pearce, Alice, 1
Pearson, Beatrice, 1920–, 1
Peel, Emma, 2
Peers, Joan, 1911–, 2
Pennington, Ann, 1893–1971, 2
Pepper, Barbara, 1912–1969, 2
Percy, Eileen, 1899–, 2
Perkins, Millie, 1938–, 2
Peron, Maria Eva (Evita) Duarte de, 1919–1952, 1,2
Perrine, Valerie, 1943–, 2
Perry, Antoinette, 1888–1946, 1,2
Peters, Bernadette, 1948–, 2
Peterson, Dorothy, 1930–1940, 2
Petty, Mrs., fl. 1670s, 1
Philbin, Mary, fl. 1920s, 1
Phillipps, Adelaide, 1833–1882, 1,2
Phillips, Margaret, 1925–, 1
Pickford, Mary Smith, 1893–1979, 1,2
Picon, Molly, 1898–, 1,2
Pierpont, Laura, fl. 1910s, 1
Piisimi, Vittoria, fl. 1570s, 1
Pilbeam, Nova, 1919–, 2
Pinto, Apolonia, 1854–, 1
Pitts, Zasu, 1900–1963, 1,2
Platt, Louise, 1915–, 2
Pleshette, Suzanne, 1937–, 1,2
Plisetskaya, Maya Mikhailovna, 1925–, 1,2
Plowright, Joan Anne, 1929–, 1,2
Poe, Elizabeth (Arnold) Hopkins, 1787–1811, 1,2
Pond, Nellie Brown, 1858–, 1
Ponisi, Elizabeth, 1818–1899, 1
Pope, Jane, 1742–1818, 1
Porter, Mary Ann, 1681–1765, 1
Potter, Mrs. Brown, fl. 1890s, 1
Powell, Eleanor, 1913–1982, 1,2
Powell, Jane, 1929–, 1,2
Power, Edith Crane, 1869–, 1
Powers, Stefanie, 1942–, 2
Prentiss, Paula, 1939–, 1,2
Previn, Dory Langan, 1929–, 2
Prevost, Marie, 1898–1937, 1,2
Price, Mrs., fl. 1670s, 1

Principal, Victoria, 1950–, 2
Pringle, Aileen, 1895–, 2
Printemps, Yvonne, fl. 1910s, 1
Pritchard, Hannah Vaughan, 1711–
1768, 1,2
Provine, Dorothy, 1937–, 1,2
Quinault, Mademoiselle, fl. 1700s, 1
Raabe (Niemann-Raabe), Hedwig,
1844–1905, 1
Rachel, (Elizabeth Rachel Felix),
1821–1858, 1,2
Radner, Gilda, 1946–1989, 2
Rae, Charlotte, 1926–, 2
Rae, Melba, 1
Rafferty, Frances, 1922–, 1
Rainer, Luise, 1910–, 1,2
Raines, Ella, 1921–, 1
Ralph, Jessie, 1864–1944, 2
Ralston, Esther, 1902–, 1,2
Rambeau, Marjorie, 1889–1970, 1,2
Randolph, Joyce, 1925–, 2
Rayburn, Kitty, fl. 1900s, 1
Raymond, Maud, fl. 1890s, 1
Reagan, Nancy, 1921–, 2
Redgrave, Lynn, 1943–, 1,2
Redgrave, Vanessa, 1937–, 1,2
Reed, Donna, 1921–1986, 1,2
Reed, Florence, 1883–, 1
Reeve, Ada, 1874–, 1
Reeves, Anne, fl. 1670s, 1
Rehan, Ada, 1857–1916, 1,2
Reid, Frances, 1
Reid, Kate, 1930–, 2
Reignolds, Catherine (Kate) Mary,
1836–1911, 2
Rejane, Gabrielle Charlotte, 1856–
1920, 1,2
Remick, Lee, 1935–, 1,2
Renaud, Madeleine, 1900–, 1,2
Revere, Anne, 1903–, 1
Revier, Dorothy, 1904–, 2
Reynolds, Debbie Marie Frances,
1932–, 1,2
Riccardo, Corona, fl. 1890s, 1
Rice, Florence M., 1907–1974, 2
Rich, Irene, 1891–, 1,2
Richards, Irene, m. 1917, 1
Richardson, Abby Sage, 1837–1900, 1
Riddle, Elizabeth, 1
Riefenstahl, Leni (Berta Helene
Amalia), 1902–, 2
Rigg, Diana, 1938–, 2
Ring, Blanche, 1872–1961, 2
Risdon, Elizabeth, 1887–1958, 2

Ristori, Adelaide, 1822–1906, 1,2
Ritchie, Anna Cora O. Mowatt,
1819–1870, 1
Ritter, Thelma, 1905–1969, 1,2
Rivera, Chita, 1933–, 1,2
Rivers, Joan, 1935–, 2
Roberti, Lyda, 1906–1938, 2
Roberts, Beverly, 1914–, 2
Roberts, Florence, 1861–1940, 1
Robertson, Mary Imogene, 1906–
1948, 1,2
Robins, Elizabeth, 1862–1952, 1,2
Robinson, Ann, fl. 1790s, 2
Robinson, Anna, m. 1905, 1
Robinson, Margaret A., fl. 1900s, 1
Robinson, Mary Darby "Perdita",
1758–1800, 1,2
Robson, Eleanor Elsie, 1880–, 1
Robson, Flora, Dame, 1902–1984, 1,2
Robson, May Mary Jeannette, 1858–
1942, 1,2
Rogers, Ginger, 1911–, 1,2
Rogers, Jean, 1916–, 2
Rolle, Esther, 2
Romanescu, Aristizza, 1854–1918, 2
Rorke, Kate, 1866–, 1
Rosay, Francoise, 1891–, 1
Rose Marie, fl. 1930s, 2
Rosedale, Roxanne, 1
Rosehill, Margaret Cheer, fl. 1700s, 1
Ross, Diana, 1944–, 2
Ross, Katharine, 1942–, 2
Ross, Marion, 1928–, 2
Ross, Oriel, 1907–, 1
Ross, Shirley, 1914–, 2
Roth, Lillian, 1910–, 1,2
Rousby, Clara Marion Jesse Dowse,
1852–1879, 1
Rouverol, Aurania, 1885–1955, 1
Rowlands, Gena (Virginia Cathryn),
1936–, 2
Rowson, Susanna Haswell, 1762–
1824, 1,2
Rudie, Yvonne, 1892–, 2
Rule, Janice, 1931–, 1,2
Rush, Barbara, 1930–, 2
Russell, Annie, 1864–1936, 1,2
Russell, Gail, 1924–1861, 2
Russell, Jane (Ernestine Jane Geral-
dine), 1921–, 1,2
Russell, Lillian, 1861–1922, 1,2
Russell, Rosalind, 1907–1976, 1,2
Rutherford, Ann, 1920–, 2
Rutherford, Margaret, 1892–1972, 1,2

Rutter, Margaret, fl. 1660s, 1
Ryan, Irene, 1903–1973, 2
Saint, Eva Marie, 1924–, 1,2
Saint Huberty, Cecile Clavel, 1756–
1812, 1
Sale, Virginia, 1
Sanda, Dominique, 1951–, 2
Sanderson, Julia, 1887–, 1
Sands, Diana Patricia, 1934–1973, 2
Sanford, Isabel Gwendolyn, 1917–, 2
Santlow, Hester, fl. 1720s, 1
Sarandon, Susan, 1946–, 2
Sarnoff, Dorothy, 1,2
Saunders, Margaret, fl. 1700s, 1
Savina, Marie G., 1854–1915, 1
Scheff, Fritzi, 1879–1954, 1,2
Schell, Maria Margarethe Anna,
1926–, 1,2
Schlamme, Martha, 1930–, 1
Schneider, Romy, 1938–1982, 1,2
Schroder, Sophie Burger, 1781–1868,
1
Schygulla, Hanna, 1943–, 2
Scott, Lizabeth, 1922–, 2
Scott, Martha, 1914–, 1,2
Scott-Maxwell, Florida, 1893–, 2
Seacombe, Mrs. Charles M., fl.
1930s, 1
Seal, Elizabeth, fl. 1720s, 1
Sebastian, Dorothy, 1903–1957, 2
Seberg, Jean, 1938–1979, 1,2
Seebach, Marie, 1830–1897, 1
Segal, Vivienne, 1897–, 2
Semmes, Myra Eulalie Knox, fl.
1860s, 1,2
Seyler, Athene, 1889–, 1
Seyrig, Delphine, 1932–, 2
Shannon, Effie, 1867–1941, 1
Shannon, Peggy, 1907–1941, 1,2
Shaw, Lilian, fl. 1910s, 1
Shaw, Mary G., 1860–1929, 1,2
Shaw, Wini, 1910–, 2
Shay, Dorothy, 1921–1978, 1,2
Shearer, (Edith) Norma, 1900–1983,
1,2
Shearer, Moira, 1926–, 1,2
Sheedy, Alexandra, 1962–, 2
Shelley, Gladys, 1918–, 1,2
Shepherd, Cybill, 1950–, 2
Sheridan, Ann (Clara Lou), 1915–
1967, 1,2
Shields, Brooke, 1965–, 2
Shields, Ella, 1879–1952, 1
Shipman, Nell, 1892–, 2

Shipp, Mary, 1
Shire, Talia, 1946–, 2
Shirley, Anne, 1918–, 2
Shoemaker, Ann, 1891–, 2
Shutta, Ethel, 1896–1976, 2
Siddons, Sara "Sally" Kemble, 1755–
1831, 1,2
Sidney, Sylvia, 1910–, 1,2
Signoret, Simone, 1921–1985, 1,2
Simmons, Jean, 1929–, 1,2
Simms, Hilda, 1920–, 1
Simon, Simone, 1914–1985, 2
Simpson, Sloan, 1917–, 2
Sinclair, Catherine Norton Forrest,
1817–1891, 1,2
Sinclair, Mary, 1922–, 1
Sitgreaves, Beverley, 1867–1943, 1
Skinner, Cornelia Otis, 1901–1979,
1,2
Skipworth, Alison, 1863–1952, 2
Skujeniece-Dambelkalne, Biruta,
1888–1931, 1
Slade, Elizabeth, fl. 1660s, 1
Slingsby, Mary Aldridge, 1
Smith, Alexis, 1921–, 2
Smith, Ethel, 1910–, 2
Smith, Jaclyn, 1947–, 2
Smith, Maggie, 1934–, 2
Smith, Mary Alice, fl. 1800s, 2
Smithson, Harriet Constance, 1800–
1854, 1
Smock, Rose Melville, 1873–, 1
Snezhina, Elena, 1881–1944, 1,2
Snodgrass, Carrie, 1946–, 2
Soldene, Emily, 1845–1912, 1
Solntseva, Julia (Yulia), fl. 1960s, 2
Somers, Suzanne, 1945–, 2
Sommer, Elke, 1941–, 2
Sondergaard, Gale, 1899–1985, 2
Sondergand, Gale, fl. 1920s, 1
Soray, Turkan, fl. 1970s, 2
Sorma, Agnes, 1865–1927, 2
Sothern, Ann, 1909–, 1,2
Spacek, "Sissy" (Mary Elizabeth),
1949–, 2
Spencer, Caroline Elizabeth, Lady,
1763–1812, 2
Spencer, Danielle, 1965–, 2
Spinelly, Andree "Spi", 1920–1930, 2
St. Clair, Catherine N., fl. 1850s, 1
St. James, Susan, 1946–, 2
St. John, Jill, 1940–, 1,2
Stagg, Mary, 1710–1730, 1,2
Stahl, Rose, 1870–, 1

Twilford, Mrs., fl. 1600s, 1
Twyford, Mrs., fl. 1670s, 1
Tyler, Odette, fl. 1880s, 1
Tyler, Priscilla Cooper, 1816–1889, 2
Tyson, Cicely, 1939–, 2
Uggams, Leslie, 1943–, 1,2
Ullman, Liv Johanne, 1939–, 2
Ulmar, Geraldine, 1862–1932, 1
Ulric, Lenore, 1892–, 1,2
Umeki, Miyoshi, 1929–, 1,2
Uphill, Susana, fl. 1660s, 1
Vaccaro, Brenda, 1939–, 2
Valli, Alida, 1921–, 2
Van Brugh, Irene, Dame, 1872–1949,
  1,2
Van Cleve, Edith, fl. 1930s, 1
Van Devere, Trish, 1943–, 2
Van Doren, Mamie, 1933–, 1,2
Van Fleet, Jo, 1922–, 1,2
Van Vooren, Monique, 1933–, 1
Vanbrugh, Violet, 1867–1942, 1
Vance, Vivian, 1912–1979, 1,2
Vanderbilt, Gertrude, 1889–1960, 1,2
Vanderbilt, Gloria Morgan, 1924–
  1965, 1,2
Varsi, Diane, 1937–, 1,2
Vaughan, Kate, 1852–1903, 1
Velez, Lupe, 1908–1944, 1,2
Venable, Evelyn, 1913–, 2
Venier, Marie, 1590–1619, 2
Vera-Ellen, (Vera-Ellen Rohe), 1926–
  1981, 1,2
Verbruggen, Susanna Percival, 1667–
  1703, 1
Verdugo, Elena, 1
Verrill, Virginia, fl. 1930s, 1
Vestris, Francoise-Rose, Madame,
  1743–1804, 2
Vestris, Lucia Elizabetta, Madame,
  1797–1856, 1,2
Victoria, Vesta, 1873–1951, 1
Vincent, Mary Ann Farlow, 1818–
  1887, 1,2
Vining, Matilda Charlotte, 1831–
  1915, 1
Vinson, Helen, 1907–, 2
Vitti, Monica, 2
Vokes, Rosina, 1858–1894, 1
Vokes, Victoria, 1853–1894, 1
Von Furstenberg, Betsy "Madcap
  Betsy", 1932–, 1,2
Vos, Elizabeth, fl. 1830s, 1
Wagner, Lindsay, 1949–, 2
Waldo, Janet, 2

Walker, Nancy, 1921–, 1,2
Walker, Nella, fl. 1920s, 2
Wall, Susannah, fl. 1790s, 2
Wallace, Grace, fl. 1910s, 1
Wallace, Nellie, 1870–1948, 1,2
Walsh, Blanche, 1873–1915, 1
Ward, Dorothy, 1890–, 1
Ward, Fannie, 1872–1952, 1
Ward, Genevieve, Dame, 1837–1922,
  1,2
Ware, Helen, fl. 1910s, 1
Warrenton, Lule, d. 1932, 2
Warrick, Ruth, 1915–, 2
Washinton, Fredi, 1903–, 2
Waters, Ethel, 1900–1977, 1,2
Watson, Lucile, 1879–1962, 1,2
Weaver, Affie, 1855–1940, 1
Weaver, Elizabeth, fl. 1660s, 1
Weaver, Marjorie, 1913–, 2
Weber, Lois, 1881–1939, 2
Webster, Harriet, m. 1862, 1
Webster, Margaret, 1905–1972, 1,2
Weigel, Helene, 1900–1971, 2
Welch, Raquel, 1940–, 2
Weld, Tuesday (Susan Ker), 1943–, 1,2
Wells, Becky Davies, 1781–1812, 1
Wentworth, Bessie, d. 1900, 1
West, Mae, 1892–1980, 1,2
Westley, Helen, 1875–1942, 1,2
Westman, Nydia, 1907–1970, 2
Westray, Elizabeth, fl. 1810s, 1
Wheatley, Mrs. Ross, fl. 1800s, 1
Whelan, Arleen, 1916–, 2
Whiffen, Blanche Galton, 1854–
  1936, 1,2
White, Alice, 1907–, 1,2
White, Betty, 1917–, 1,2
White, Pearl, 1889–1938, 1,2
White, Ruth, 1914–1969, 2
Whiting, Barbara, 1
Whitney, Eleanore, 1914–, 2
Whitty, May, 1865–1948, 1,2
Wicker, Ireene, 1905–, 1,2
Wieck, Dorothea, 1907–, 1,2
Williams, Cecilia, fl. 1800s, 1
Williams, Cindy, 1948–, 2
Williams, Esther, 1913–, 1,2
Williams, Kathlyn, fl. 1910s, 2
Williams, Maria Pray Mestayer, m.
  1850, 1
Wilson, Dorothy, 1909–, 2
Wilson, Elsie Jane, d. 1965, 2
Wilson, Lois, 1894–, 1,2
Wilson, Marie Katherine Elizabeth,
  1916–1972, 1,2

Brent, Anne, fl. 1600s, 2
Brent, Margaret, 1600–1671, 1,2
Brent, Mary, fl. 1638, 1,2
Brett, Catherina, d. 1764, 1,2
Brown, Kathryn, 2
Burlend, Rebecca, fl. 1900s, 2
Burt, Beryl, fl. 1970s, 2
Byrd, Mary Willing, fl. 1700s, 1,2
Caldwell, Margaret Hood, fl. 1940s, 2
Carter, Frances Ann Tasker, 1737–
   1797, 1
Chandler, Naomi, 2
Christian, Angela, 2
Colbry, Vera, fl. 1970s, 2
Columella, fl. 99BC, 2
Cooke, Katie, fl. 1970s, 2
Dubre, Hannah, fl. 1750s, 1
Eid, Aida, fl. 1950s, 2
Everett, Beverly, 2
Fanconi, Linda, fl. 1970s, 2
Forbes, Carol, 1913–, 2
Fuller, Electra, fl. 1870s, 1
Fuller, Laura, fl. 1870s, 1
Galland, Nancy, fl. 1970s, 2
Grieg, Connie, fl. 1970s, 2
Griffin, Hilda S., fl. 1970s, 2
Guyer, Cynthia, fl. 1970s, 2
Hanson, Jeanne, 2
Hardner, Luetta, fl. 1970s, 2
Haughland, Brynhild, 1905–, 1
Heard, Cuba, fl. 1970s, 2
Heuser, Laura, fl. 1970s, 2
Hind, (Ella) Cora, 1861–1942, 1,2
Huddleston, Barbara, 1939–, 2
Irene de Borbon de Parma, 2
Jacobson, Dorothy H., fl. 1960s, 2
King, Debbie, fl. 1970s, 2
Kinneberg, Sally, fl. 1970s, 2
Kongas, Lembi, fl. 1970s, 2
Leckband, Susanne M., 2
Lerza, Catherine, 2
Lewis, Tillie (Myrtle) Erlich, 1901–
   1977, 2
Machan, Cathy, fl. 1970s, 2
Mancini, Maria Pia, 1941–, 2
McArthur, Henrietta Duncan, 1945–,
   2
McKinnon, Jane Price, fl. 1970s, 2
Meagher, Mary, 1855–, 1
Meredith, Virginia, 1848–1936, 2
Moftakhari, Khorsid, 2
Molony, Winifred D., fl. 1940s, 2
Mowat, Vivia A., fl. 1910s, 1
O'Connell, Joan, fl. 1970s, 2

Paasnuori, Tynne, 1907–, 2
Pahlevi, Farah, 1918–, 2
Pinckney, Eliza Lucas, 1723–1793,
   1,2
Plank, Rosine, fl. 1970s, 2
Platt, Christina, fl. 1970s, 2
Ritchie, Jean, 1913–, 2
Rose, Ellen Alida, 1843–, 1
Rose, Flora, fl. 1910s, 2
Royal, Doris, fl. 1970s, 2
Russell, Lilla, 1885–1977, 2
Sanborn, Katherine Abbot, 1939–
   1917, 1
Sayre, Ruth Buxton, 1896–, 2
Sechler, Susan, fl. 1970s, 2
Sellers, Marie, fl. 1930s, 1
Sherman, Minna E., fl. 1910s, 1
Smith, Karen, 2
Stanley, Louise, 1883–1954, 2
Steffens, Sharon, fl. 1970s, 2
Strong, Harriet Williams Russell,
   1844–1929, 2
Thomas, M. Louise, fl. 1870s, 1
Valdez, Adelia Rivera de, 1874–, 2
Watkins, Elaine, 2
Wilson, Mary, fl. 1870s, 1
Wiser, Vivian, fl. 1950s, 2
Yegorova, Irina, 1901–, 2
Agrippa, Marcus Vipsanius—Spouse
   Marcella Claudia, the younger, m. 28
   BC, 1
Agrippina the Younger—Mother
   Agrippina I, The Elder, 13BC–
   33AD, 1,2
Agronomists
   Coming, Affra Harleston, d. 1699, 1
   Manigault, Judith Giton Royer, d.
   1711, 1,2
Ahab of Israel—Spouse
   Jezebel, 875–852BC, 1,2
Air Force nurses, American
   Hoefly, E. Ann, fl. 1940s, 2
Air Force officers, American
   Abbott, Mary N., fl. 1970s, 2
   Bakarich, Alexandra C., fl. 1960s, 2
   Beale, Jo A., fl. 1970s, 2
   Carl, Mary, fl. 1970s, 2
   Forbes, Katherine Frefusis, fl. 1940s,
   1
   Garrecht, Claire, 2
   Gibson, Joann, fl. 1970s, 2
   Harness, Arminta J., fl. 1970s, 2
   Johnson, Deborah G., fl. 1960s, 2
   Johnson, Lorna, 2

Mann, Chris C., fl. 1950s, 2
May, Geraldine Pratt, 1895–, 1,2
Orndoff, Carla, fl. 1960s, 2
Potter, Lorraine, fl. 1970s, 2
Smith, Allison, fl. 1970s, 2
Van Horn, June, 2
Watkins, Altheria, fl. 1970s, 2
Air Force officers, Austrian
  Bohannon, Grete M., 2
Air Force officers, Canadian
  Davey, Jean, fl. 1940s, 2
Air Force officers, English
  Hanbury, Felicity, fl. 1940s, 1
  McKinlay, Katherine, fl. 1940s, 1
  Pearson, Joan D. M., fl. 1940s, 1
  Salmon, Nancy Marion, fl. 1950s, 1
  Stephens, Anne, fl. 1930s, 1
Air Force officers, French
  Dumont, Laryse, 2
Air Force physicians and surgeons
  Nell, Patricia A., fl. 1960s, 2
Air Force pilots, American
  Ancar, Murlene B., 2
  Aune, Regina C., 2
  Baker, Betty L., 2
  Holley, Leslie, fl. 1970s, 2
  Holm, Jeanne M., fl. 1940s, 2
  Ryan, Patty, 2
  Shelly, Mary Josephine, 1902–1976,
    1,2
Air Force pilots, English
  Barnett, Henrietta, fl. 1950s, 1
Air stunts
  Leatherbee, Mary Lee Logan, 2
Air traffic controllers
  Beales, Iris, 1
  Harper, Katy, fl. 1970s, 2
Air travelers
  See also
  First air travelers
  Shuler, Marjorie, fl. 1920s, 1
  Whitney, Mrs. L. A., fl. 1910s, 1
Aircraft industry
  Carter, Amy, 1
  De Long, Sally, 1
  Hargis, Cheryl L., 2
  Kelly, Patsy, fl. 1930s, 1
  Miles, Mary Forbes-Robertson,
    1900–, 1
  O'Malley, Patricia, fl. 1930s, 1
  Page, Celeste Walker, fl. 1930s, 1
  Palmer, Bernice, fl. 1940s, 1
  Schwartz, Melainie, d. 1897, 2
  Smith, Quincy, fl. 1940s, 1

Soulsby, Elsie MacGill, gr. 1927, 1
Stewart, Sylvia, fl. 1940s, 1
Sullivan, Marie, fl. 1930s, 1
Wilson, Elva, 1
Wilson, Mabel K., fl. 1930s, 1
Airlines
  Gilbert, Edwinna, 1931–, 2
  Johnston, Marjane, 1
  Mark, Joyce, 1
  Perry, Margaret, fl. 1920s, 1
  Rich, Jean, pseud., 1923–1975, 2
  Stein, Camille L., 1894–, 1
  Thompson, Myrtle Grey, fl. 1950s, 1
  Winters, Midge, 1
Aisse, Mlle.—Friend
  Calandrini, Madame, fl. 1700s, 1
Akeley, Carl—Spouse
  Akeley, Delia Denning, 1865–1970,
    1,2
Akhnaton, King—Spouse
  Nefertiti, 1390– BC, 1,2
Akiba—Spouse
  Rachel, 1
Aknaton—Mother
  Tiy, 1400 BC, 1
Alabama
  Flowers, Emma Payne, 1892–, 2
  Graham, Annie Elsie Zimmerman,
    1904–, 2
  Jacobs, Pattie Ruffner, 1875–1935, 2
  Maples, Doris Elliott, 1918–, 2
  McCartney, Louise Smitt, fl. 1950s, 2
  Owen, Marie Bankhead, 1869–, 2
  Ruffner, Pattie Ruffner, 1875–1935, 2
  Stone, Mary Katherine, fl. 1960s, 2
  Waite, Mary George Jordon, 1918–, 2
  Wallace, Lurleen Burns, 1926–1968,
    1,2
  Wright, Carrie Newton, 1893–, 2
Alaska
  Allman, Ruth Wickersham, 2
  Anderson, Alyce E., 2
  Anderson, Junita, 1890–, 2
  Argetsinger, Louise H., 1904–, 2
  Arthur, Dolly, 1919–1975, 2
  Austin, Belinda, fl. 1879, 2
  Baranof, Anna, Princess, fl. 1790s, 2
  Berry, Ethel Bush, fl. 1890s, 2
  Brady, Elizabeth Patton, fl. 1880s, 2
  Brotherson, Shirley, fl. 1900s, 2
  Brower, Toctoo, fl. 1960s, 2
  Bullock, Edith R. "Tugboat queen", 2
  Carmack, Katie, fl. 1890s, 2
  Coleman, Ann, 1872–, 2

Dimond, Dorothea, fl. 1930s, 2
Drake, Marie, fl. 1910s, 2
Dusenbury, Elinor, fl. 1830s, 2
Egan, Neva McKittrick, fl. 1950s, 2
Etolin, Margaret, fl. 1840s, 2
Fischer, Helen, fl. 1950s, 2
Fitzgerald, Emily McCorkle, 2
Frost, Helen, 2
Gilman, Isabel Ambler, fl. 1900s, 2
Gruening, Dorothy, fl. 1930s, 2
Hakkinen, Elizabeth Sheldon, 1914–, 2
Hatcher, Cornelia, 2
Hering, Agnes Potts, 1874–, 2
Hermann, Mildred R., 1891–, 2
Ivanof, Vera, fl. 1890s, 2
Jenne, Crystal Snow, 2
Jones, Wendy, fl. 1940s, 2
Kellogg, Fanny, fl. 1870s, 2
Klondike Kate, 1881–1957, 2
Maksoutoff, Mariia, fl. 1860s, 2
McFarland, Amanda, 1837–1898, 1,2
McLane, Enid Stryker, 1896–, 2
Neakok, Sadie Brower, fl. 1880s, 2
Nelson, Klondy Esmerelda, 1897–, 1
Ost, Ruth Elin, 1886–1953, 2
Painter, Charlotte, fl. 1970s, 2
Paul, Tillie, fl. 1950s, 2
Peterson, Jetret Stryker, 1895–, 2
Pullen, Harriet Smith, 1859–1947, 2
Romuald, Mary, 1895–, 2
Shelikof, Natalya, fl. 1780s, 2
Simpson, Belle Goldstein, 1900–1930, 2
Snow, Anna Rablen, 1861–, 1,2
Sparks, Mildred Hotch, 1901–, 2
Stepovich, Matilda, fl. 1950s, 2
Troy, Dorothy, fl. 1930s, 2
Troy, Helen, fl. 1930s, 2
Von Wrangell, Baroness, fl. 1830s, 2
Walsh, Louise Forsyth, 1886–1971, 2
Walsh, Mollie, d. 1902, 2
Watson, Lillian Smith, d. 1967, 2
Wester, Zula Swanson, 1892–1973, 2
White, Josephine, 1873–1956, 2
Willard, Carrie McCoy White, 1853–, 2
Wright, Laura Beltz, fl. 1950s, 2
Yanaovskii, Irina Baranof, fl. 1810s, 2
Albert I—Spouse
Marie Victoire, 1850–1922, 1
Alcibiades—Spouse
Hipparette, 2
Alcott, Louisa May—Mother
Alcott, Abigail (Abba) May, 1800–1877, 1,2

Alexander I—Mistress
Naryshkin, Madame, fl. 1800s, 1
Alexander I—Spouse
Elizabeth, Alexeievna, 1779–1826, 1
Alexander II—Spouse
Dolgorukky, Katherine, 1846–1922, 1
Alexander Severus—Mother
Julia Mamaea, d. 235, 1
Alexander VI, Pope—Mistress
Farnese, Giulia, fl. 1400s, 2
Alexander the Great—Mistress
Thais, fl. 300BC, 1
Alexander the Great—Mother
Olympias, 360–410, 1,2
Alexander the Great—Spouse
Roxana, d. 309 BC, 1
Alexis—Mother
Dalassena, Anna, d. 1105, 1
Alfonso IX of Leon—Spouse
Berengaria, Queen, fl. 1200s, 1,2
Alfred of Northumbria—Spouse
Cuthburge, fl. 800s, 1
Alfred the Great—Daughter
Elfled, d. 918, 1,2
Ali, Mohammed—Mother
Clay, Odetta Lee Grady, 2
Ali, Mohammed—Spouse
Ali, Veronica, 1955–, 2
Alice in Wonderland
Hargreaves, Alice Liddell, 1852–1934, 2
Liddell, Alice, 2
Allen, Ethan—Spouse
Allen, Frances Buchanan, m. 1784, 1
Allen, Mary Brownson, 1733–, 1
Allen, Fred—Spouse
Hoffa, Portland, 1910–, 1
Allen, Steve—Spouse
Meadows, Jayne Cotter, 1925–, 1,2
Alliance for Displaced Women
Sommers, Tish, 2
Alliance movement workers
Gay, Bettie, 2
McDonald-Valesh, Eva, fl. 1890s, 2
Altamish—Daughter
Rezia, Sultana, fl. 1220s, 1
Amana Society—Founder
Heinemann, Barbara, 1795–1883, 2
Amazons
Sutherland, Jane, Countess of, 1545–1929, 1
Ambassadors
See
Diplomats

Ambulance drivers
McKinlay, Katherine, fl. 1940s, 1
Stewart, Gwenda, fl. 1900s, 2
American Association of University
Women
See
AAUW
American Civil Liberties Union
See
ACLU
American Crafts Council
Webb, Aileen Osborn, 1892–1979,
1,2
American Indian Movement
See
AIM
American Library Association
Lowrie, Jean Elizabeth, 1918–, 2
Martin, Allie Beth, 1914–1976, 2
American Paper Institute
Pace, Norma, 1923–, 2
American Red Cross
See
Red Cross
American Revolution
Adams, Anne, fl. 1770s, 1
Allen, Maria, fl. 1770s, 1
Almy, Mary Gould, 1735–1808, 2
Anderson, Nancy, 2
Arnett, Hannah White, 1733–1824,
1,2
Arnold, Margaret Shippen, 1760–
1804, 1,2
Bache, Sarah, d. 1798, 1
Bache, Sarah Franklin, 1743–1808,
1,2
Baddeley, Mary O'Callaghan, fl.
1760s, 2
Bailey, Ann "Mad Ann", 1742–1825,
1,2
Bailey, Anna Warner "Mother Bai-
ley", 1758–1851, 1
Baldwin, Alice, fl. 1770s, 1
Barker, Penelope Pagett, fl. 1770s, 2
Barlow, Rebecca Sanford, fl. 1770s, 1
Barnett, Susannah, fl. 1770s, 2
Barrett, Meliscent, fl. 1770s, 1,2
Bates, Ann, fl. 1770s, 2
Beckham, Mrs., fl. 1770s, 1
Beekman, Cornelia Van Cortlandt,
1752–1847, 1,2
Belcher, Elizabeth, fl. 1770s, 2
Benjamin, Sarah Matthews, 1744–
1861, 1

Berry, Mrs. Sidney, fl. 1770s, 1
Bevier, Mrs. J., fl. 1770s, 1
Biddle, Rebecca, fl. 1770s, 1,2
Bidlack, Mrs. Gore, fl. 1770s, 1
Bishop, Mrs. Samuel, fl. 1770s, 2
Blair, Hannah Millikan, 2
Bland, Martha Dangerfield, fl. 1770s,
2
Bolling, Susanna, 2
Borden, Mrs., fl. 1770s, 1,2
Bowen, Mary, fl. 1770s, 1
Brady, Mary Quigley, 2
Bratton, Martha, d. 1816, 1,2
Brevard, Mrs., fl. 1770s, 1
Brewton, Mrs. Robert, fl. 1770s, 1
Brown, Hannah, fl. 1770s, 1,2
Brown, Mary Buckman, 1740–1824,
1
Bull, Mary, fl. 1770s, 2
Bulloch, Mary Deveaux, m. 1760, 1
Burr, Eunice Dennie, 1729–1805, 1,2
Butler, Behethland, 1764–, 1
Butler, Rehethland Foote, 1764–, 1
Cadillac, Marie Therese Guyon, m.
1687, 1
Caldwell, Hannah Ogden, 1737–
1780, 2
Caldwell, Rachel, 1739–1825, 1,2
Campbell, Jane Cannon, 1743–1836,
1,2
"Captain Molly", 1751–1800, 1
Carter, Hannah Benedict, 1733–
1780, 1
Caswell, Mary McIlweane, m. 1750, 1
Champe, Elizabeth, 1780–, 2
Champion, Deborah, 1753–, 1,2
Channing, Mrs., fl. 1770s, 1
Chase, Deborah, 1760–, 1
Chittenden, Elizabeth Meigs, m.
1750, 1
Cilley, Elsie, 2
Clarke, Hannah, 1737–1827, 1
Clay, Ann, fl. 1770s, 2
Clay, Elizabeth, 1750–1827, 1
Clifford, Anna Rawle, 1757–1858, 2
Clinton, Cornelia Tappen, m. 1770, 1
Clyde, Mrs., fl. 1770s, 1,2
Clymer, Elizabeth Meredith, m.
1765, 1
Cobb, Lydia, fl. 1770s, 1
Coffin, Keziah Folger, m. 1740, 1
Coffin, Mrs. Peter, fl. 1770s, 1,2
Conyngham, Anne, fl. 1770s, 1
Cook, Elizabeth, fl. 1740s, 1

Cooke, Hannah Sabin, 1722–, 1
Cooper, Polly, fl. 1770s, 2
Corbin, Margaret Cochran "Captain Molly", 1751–1800, 1,2
Cranch, Mary, d. 1811, 1
Cranch, Mrs. Richard, fl. 1770s, 1
Crough, Mary, 1740–1818, 2
Cruger, Anne de Lancey, fl. 1770s, 2
Curwen, Abigail Russell, fl. 1770s, 2
Daggett, Polly, fl. 1770s, 1
Dana, Mrs., fl. 1770s, 1
Danielson, Sarah Williams, 1737–, 1
Darragh (Darrah), Lydia Barrington, 1728–1789, 1,2
Daviess, Mrs., fl. 1770s, 1
Dickinson, Sarah, fl. 1770s, 1
Dillard, Mrs., fl. 1770s, 1
Dissoway, Mrs., fl. 1770s, 1
Dowdy, Betsy, 2
Draper, Mary Aldis, 1718–1810, 2
Drinker, Elizabeth Sandwith, 1734–1807, 1,2
Easson, Mary, fl. 1770s, 2
Eastman, Mary Butler, d. 1837, 2
Edgar, Rachel, fl. 1770s, 1
Eliott, Sabrina, fl. 1770s, 1
Elliott, Ann, 1762–1848, 1
Elliott, Susannah Smith, fl. 1750s, 1,2
Ellsworth, Abigail Wolcott, 1756–1818, 1,2
Elmendorf, Mary, fl. 1770s, 2
Emmons, Lucretia, fl. 1770s, 2
Espy, Jean, d. 1781, 1
Fanning, Anne Brewster, 1753–1813, 1
Farrand, Rhoda Smith, fl. 1760s, 1,2
Ferguson, Elizabeth Graeme, 1737–1801, 1,2
Ferguson, Jane Young, fl. 1770s, 2
Fitzhugh, Anne, 1727–1793, 1,2
Floyd, Joanna Strong, fl. 1770s, 1
Forbes, Dorothy (Dolly) Murray, fl. 1740s, 2
Franklin, Agnes, Lady, fl. 1740s, 2
Franks, Rebecca, 1760–1823, 1,2
Fraser, Mrs. Alexander, fl. 1890s, 1
Frazier, Mary, fl. 1760s, 2
Fulton, Sarah Bradlee, 1740–1835, 1,2
Gaston, Esther, fl. 1770s, 1,2
Gaston, Margaret, 1755–, 1
Gaylord, Katherine Cole, 1745–1840, 1
Gaylord, Mrs., 2
Geiger, Emily, fl. 1760s, 1,2

Gibbes, Mrs. and Mary Ann, fl. 1770s, 1,2
Gibbes, Sara Reeve, 1746–1825, 1,2
Gorman, Mary, fl. 1770s, 2
Graydon, Rachel, fl. 1770s, 1,2
Green, Alice Kollock, d. 1832, 1
Griffith, Maria Thong Patterson, fl. 1770s, 2
Griffiths, Dorcas Pringle, fl. 1770s, 2
Griswold, Ursula Wolcott, fl. 1770s, 1
Hagidorn, Mary, fl. 1770s, 1,2
Hall, Mrs. Daniel, fl. 1770s, 1,2
Hamilton, Anne Kennedy, 1760–1836, 1
Hamilton, Elizabeth Schuyler, 1757–1854, 1,2
Hancock, Dorothy Quincy, 1750–1828, 1,2
Harrison, Jemima Condick, 1755–1779, 2
Hart, Nancy Morgan, 1735–1840, 1,2
Hart, Ruth Cole, 1742–1844, 1
Harvey, Mrs., fl. 1770s, 1
Hendee, Hannah Hunter, fl. 1770s, 2
Hewes, Deborah, fl. 1770s, 2
Heyward, Elizabeth Mathews, fl. 1760s, 1,2
Hill, Margaret Francis, fl. 1770s, 2
Honeyman, Mary Henry, fl. 1770s, 1
Hooper, Ann(e) Clark, fl. 1760s, 1,2
Hopton, Sarah, fl. 1770s, 1
Howell, Mary, fl. 1770s, 2
Hull, Elizabeth Clarke, 1732–1826, 1
Hull, Sarah, 1755–1826, 1
Hulton, Ann, fl. 1760s, 1,2
Humaston, Abi, 1759–1847, 1
Humphreys, Sarah Riggs, 1711–1787, 1
Huntington, Martha Devotion, d. 1794, 1
Hutchinson, Elizabeth, fl. 1750s, 1
Inman, Elizabeth Murray Campbell Smith, 1726–1785, 2
Israel, Hanna Erwin, 1743–1821, 1,2
Ives, Lucy, fl. 1770s, 1
Izard, Alice, 1745–1832, 1
Jackson, Elizabeth Hutchinson, fl. 1770s, 1,2
Jackson, Mrs., fl. 1770s, 1
Jemison, Mary Dehewamis, 1740–1831, 1,2
Johnson, Anne Jennings, m. 1766, 1
Johnson, Jemima Suggett, 1753–1814, 1,2

Jones, Mrs. Willie, d. 1828, 1
Keith, Mary Isham, 1737–, 1
Knight, Kitty, 2
Knight, Mary Worrell, 1759–1849,
1,2
Knox, Lucy Flucker, 1756–1824, 1,2
Lane, Anna Maria, fl. 1770s, 2
Latham, Eunice Forsythe, fl. 1770s,
1,2
Lawrence, Elizabeth, fl. 1770s, 2
Ledyard, Mary, fl. 1770s, 1
Lee, Agnes Dickinson, fl. 1770s, 2
Lee, Rebecca Tayloe, d. 1787, 1
Lewis, Elizabeth Annesley, fl. 1740s,
1,2
Lewis, Elizabeth Washington, d.
1797, 1
Lightfoot, Susannah, fl. 1770s, 2
Livingston, Christina Ten Broek, fl.
1770s, 1
Livingston, Margaret Beekman, fl.
1740s, 1,2
Livingston, Susan, fl. 1770s, 1,2
Livingston, Susannah French, d.
1789, 1
Long, Mary M'Kinney, fl. 1770s, 1
Ludington, Sybil, 1761–1839, 1,2
Ludlow, Sarah, d. 1773, 1
MacAulay, Catharine Sawbridge,
1731–1791, 1,2
MacDonald, Mary, fl. 1770s, 2
Malessy, Madame, fl. 1700s, 1
Malone, Wyannie, fl. 1780s, 2
Mammy Kate, fl. 1770s, 1,2
Manter, Parnel, fl. 1770s, 1
Marshall, Mrs. Christopher, fl.
1770s, 1
Martin, Elizabeth Marshall, fl. 1770s,
1,2
Martin, Grace, fl. 1770s, 1
Martin, Rachel, fl. 1770s, 1
Martin family, fl. 1770s, 2
Mattoon, Mary Dickinson, 1758–
1835, 1
McCalla, Mrs., fl. 1770s, 1
McCalla, Sarah, fl. 1770s, 2
McClure, Mary, fl. 1770s, 1,2
McCrea, Jane, 1752–1777, 1,2
McIntosh, Sarah Swinton, fl. 1770s, 1
McKeehan, Mary, 1751–, 2
Mecom, Jane Franklin, 1712–1794, 2
Merrill, Mrs. John, fl. 1770s, 1
Mersereau, Charity, fl. 1770s, 1
Mills, Mary Gills, fl. 1770s, 1

Moffat, Olive, fl. 1770s, 2
Mooney, Hannah Gaunt, fl. 1770s, 1
Moore, Margaret Catherine Barry,
1760–1770, 2
Morris, Anne Elliott, d. 1948, 1
Morris, Margaret Hill, 1737–1816, 1,2
Morris, Mary Walton, 2
Morris, Mrs. Robert, 1824, 2
Moseley, Laura Wolcott, 1761–1814,
2
Motte, Rebecca Brewton, 1738–1815,
1,2
Munro, Mrs., fl. 1770s, 1
Murray, Mary Lindley, 1720–1782,
1,2
Myers, Mrs., fl. 1770s, 1
Nelson, Lucy Grymes, m. 1762, 1
Nixon, Mary, fl. 1770s, 2
Nonhelma, fl. 1770s, 2
Otterson, Mrs., fl. 1770s, 1
Paca, Mary Chew, m. 1763, 1
Page, Mrs. Jeremiah, fl. 1770s, 2
Parker, Ruth, fl. 1770s, 1
Patton, Mary, fl. 1770s, 2
Peabody, Elizabeth Smith Shaw,
1750–1813, 1
Percival, Mary Fuller, 1737–, 1
Perkins, Elizabeth Peck, 1735–1807,
1,2
Peters, Fannie Ledyard, 1754–1816,
1,2
Philipse, Mary, 1730–1825, 1,2
Pickens, Rebecca Calhoun, 1746–
1815, 1,2
Pitcher, Molly, 1754–1832, 1,2
Potter, Mrs., fl. 1770s, 1
Pratt, Elizabeth "Handy Betsy",
1750–, 1,2
Putnam, Deborah Lothrop, 1719–
1777, 1,2
Putnam, Susannah French, fl. 1770s, 1
Putney, Susannah, fl. 1770s, 2
Redmond (Redman), Mary, fl. 1770s,
1,2
Reed, Esther DeBerdt, 1746–1780,
1,2
Reid, Molly, fl. 1770s, 1
Reynolds, Phebe, fl. 1770s, 2
Richardson, Dorcas Nelson, 1740–
1834, 1,2
Riedesel, Frederica Louisa Charlotte
Massow, Baroness von 1746–1808,
1,2
Rinker, "Old Mom", 2

Ripley, Dorothy Brintnall, 1737–1831, 1
Rush, Julia Stockton, 1759–1848, 1,2
Russell, Mrs. Joseph, fl. 1770s, 1
Rutledge, Elizabeth Grimke, d. 1792, 1,2
Rutledge, Henrietta Middleton, 1750–, 1
Sampson, Deborah, 1760–1827, 1,2
Schlatter, Rachel, fl. 1770s, 2
Schuyler, Catherine van Rensselaer, 1733–1803, 1,2
Seavey, Helen, fl. 1770s, 2
Sevier, Catherine Sherrill "Bonny Kate", 1754–1836, 1,2
Sharpe, Jemima Alexander, m. 1748, 1
Shattuck, Mrs. Job, fl. 1770s, 1
Shattuck, Sarah Hartwell, fl. 1770s, 2
Shaw, Elizabeth, 1750–1816, 1
Shaw, Lucretia, 1737–1781, 1
Shell, Elizabeth Petrie, fl. 1770s, 1,2
Sherman, Rebecca Prescott, m. 1763, 1
Shubrick, Mrs. Richard, fl. 1770s, 1
Silliman, Mary Fish, 1736–1804, 1,2
Simms, Sarah Dickinson, fl. 1770s, 1
Sims, Isabella, fl. 1770s, 1
Skinner, Esther, 1731–1831, 1
Slocum(b), Mary Hooks (Polly), 1760–1836, 1,2
Smith, Elizabeth Quincy, 1722–1775, 1
Smith, Sarah, fl. 1770s, 2
Spalding, Mrs., fl. 1770s, 1
Springfield, Laodicea "Dicey" Langston, 1760–, 1,2
Stanley, Esther, 1697–1776, 1
Stark, Elizabeth Page (Molly), 1736–1814, 1,2
Stedman, Mrs., 2
Steel, Katherine Fisher, 1724–1785, 1,2
Steele, Elizabeth Maxwell, fl. 1770s, 1,2
Stephens, Martha Stewart Elliot, fl. 1770s, 1
Stirling, Kitty, 2
Stockton, Annis Boudinot, 1736–1801, 1,2
Story, Ann, 1742–1817, 1,2
Stow, Freelove Baldwin, 1728–, 1,2
Symmes, Susannah, fl. 1770s, 1
Tallmadge, Mary Floyd, 1764–1805, 1
Taylor, Nancy Savage, m. 1739, 1

Thomas, Jane Black, 1720–, 1,2
Threritz, Emily Geiger, 1760–, 1
Townsend, Sally, 1760–1842, 1,2
Trumbull, Faith Robinson, 1718–1780, 1,2
Van Alstyne, Nancy, 1733–, 1,2
Varnum, Molly, fl. 1770s, 1
Vassall, Elizabeth, fl. 1790s, 2
Vernooy, Catharine, fl. 1770s, 1
Vrooman, Angelica, fl. 1770s, 1
Waglum, Jinnie, fl. 1790s, 2
Walker, Martha I'Ans, fl. 1770s, 2
Walker, Mrs. John, fl. 1770s, 2
Walker, Mrs. John, fl. 1770s, 1,2
Walton, Dorothy Camber, fl. 1770s, 1,2
Ward, Nancy, 1738–1822, 2
Warne, Margaret Vliet "Aunt Peggy", 1751–1840, 1,2
Warner, Jemima, fl. 1770s, 1,2
Warren, Mercy Otis, 1728–1814, 1,2
Washington, Elizabeth Foote, d. 1812, 2
Washington, Jane Elliott, d. 1830, 1
Watts, Mary Stirling, fl. 1770s, 1
Webster, Abigail Eastman, 1737–1816, 1
Weston, Hannah Watts, 1758–1855, 1,2
Wharton, Susannah Lloyd, d. 1772, 1
Wheelock, Deborah Thayer, 1742–1815, 1
Whetten, Harriet Douglas, fl. 1860s, 1
Whetton, Margaret Todd, d. 1809, 1,2
Whipple, Katharine Moffat, fl. 1770s, 1
Whitley, Mrs., fl. 1770s, 1
Wick, Tempe, fl. 1770s, 2
Wilkinson, Eliza Yonge, fl. 1770s, 1,2
Williams, Anne Newton, fl. 1770s, 1
Williams, Mary Trumbull, m. 1771, 1
Wilson, Martha, 1758–, 1
Wilson, Mrs. Robert, fl. 1720s, 1
Wilson, Rachael Bird, m. 1771, 1
Winthrop, Hannah, 1726–1790, 1,2
Wister, Sarah, 1761–1804, 1,2
Witherspoon, Elizabeth Montgomery, d. 1789, 1
Wolcott, Laura Collins, m. 1789, 1
Woodhull, Ruth Floyd, m. 1761, 1
Woodruff, Hannah, 1730–1815, 1
Woods, Mrs., fl. 1770s, 1
Wooster, Mary Clag (Clapp), 1729–1807, 1,2

Wright, Mrs. David, fl. 1770s, 1
Wright, Prudence Cumings, 1739–1823, 1
Wyllys, Ruth Beldon, 1747–1807, 1
Wythe, Anne Lewis, 1726–, 1
Yonge, Mrs., fl. 1770s, 2
Young, Elizabeth Bennett, fl. 1770s, 2
Young, Mrs. Poyner, fl. 1770s, 1
Zane, Betty, 1766–1831, 1,2
American Stock Exchange
Roebling, Mary Grindhart, 1905–, 1,2
American Symphony Orchestra League
Thompson, Helen Mulford, 1908–1974, 2
Anarchists
Braut, Bessy, fl. 1910s, 2
Goldman, Emma, 1869–1940, 1,2
Anatomists
Arconville, Genevieve Charlotte d', 1720–1805, 2
Biheron, 1730–, 2
Ferreti, Zaffira, fl. 1800s, 2
Giliani, Alessandra, 1307–1326, 2
Manzolini, Anne Morandi, 1716–1774, 1,2
Morandi, Anna, 1716–1774, 2
Nachmias, Vivianne T., fl. 1960s, 2
Sabin, Florence Rena, 1871–1953, 1,2
Scharrer, Berta Vogel, fl. 1960s, 2
Staal (Stahl, Stael), Marguerite Jeanne Cordier D., 1693–1750, 1,2
Andersen, Hans Christian—Mother
Andersen, Anne Marie, 1767–1834, 1,2
Anderson, John—Mother
Anderson, Mabel, 1886–, 2
Anesthesiologists
Apgar, Virginia, 1909–1974, 2
Animal breeders
Fox, Gertrude Elizabeth Wilbur, 1878–1947, 1
Animal rights workers
See also
Bird protection
Johnston, Velma B., fl. 1950s, 1
Ross, Rita, fl. 1910s, 1
Animal trainers
See also
Dog trainers
Horse trainers
Martin, Helen Frances Theresa, 1912–, 1
Rasputin, Maria, 1898–, 2

Rogers, Anne Hone, 1929–, 1
Stark, Mabel, 1892–, 1,2
Woodhouse, Barbara, 1910–, 2
Animators
Keating, Anna-Lena, 2
Anne of Brittany—Daughter
Renee of France, 1,2
Anne, Queen—Friend
Masham, Abigail Hill, Lady, d. 1734, 1,2
Anne, Queen—Maid
Argyll, Jane Warbuton, fl. 1710, 1
Antarctica
Bernasconi, Irene, fl. 1960s, 2
Cahoon, Mary Odile, fl. 1970s, 2
Caria, Maria Adela, fl. 1960s, 2
Colin, Jane, fl. 1970s, 2
Cooney, Marion, fl. 1970s, 2
De Vries, Yuan Lin, fl. 1970s, 2
Denys, Charlene, fl. 1970s, 2
Dreschhoff, Gisela, fl. 1970s, 2
Fontes, Elena M., fl. 1960s, 2
Friedmann, Roseli Ocampo, 2
Harrower, Karen, fl. 1970s, 2
Haschemeyer, Audrey, 1936–, 2
Jones, Lois Marilyn, 1934–, 2
Kane, Martha, 2
Lindsay, Kay, fl. 1960s, 2
Marvin, Ursula B., 1921–, 2
Mathews, Rita, fl. 1970s, 2
McSaveney, Eileen, fl. 1970s, 2
McWhinnie, Mary Alice, 1922–1980, 2
Mikkelsen, Caroline, fl. 1970s, 2
Muchmore, Donna, fl. 1970s, 2
Muller-Schwarze, Christine, fl. 1960s, 2
Oliver, Donna, fl. 1970s, 2
Pearson, Jean, fl. 1960s, 2
Pujals, Carmen, fl. 1960s, 2
Ronne, Edith, fl. 1940s, 2
Samson, Julie Ann, fl. 1980s, 2
Scott, E. Nan, fl. 1970s, 2
Thomas, Jeanette, fl. 1970s, 2
Tickhill, Terry Lee, fl. 1960s, 2
Vickers, Julia, fl. 1970s, 2
Young, Pam, fl. 1970s, 2
Anthologists
Hemenway, Abby Maria, 1828–1890, 2
Sitwell, Edith, Dame, 1887–1964, 1,2
Wells, Carolyn, 1862–1942, 1,2
Anthropologists
Aberle, Sophia D., fl. 1920s, 2
Almy, Susan, 2

Benedict, Ruth Fulton, 1887–1947,
1,2
Blackman, Winifred, d. 1950, 2
Brown, Ina Corinne, fl. 1950s, 1
Bunzel, Ruth, fl. 1930s, 1
Colson, Elizabeth Florence, fl.
1970s, 2
Cone, Cynthia, 2
De Laguna, Fredica Annis, fl. 1940s,
2
Deloria, Ella Cara, 1888–1971, 2
Dunham, Katherine, 1910–, 1,2
Friedlander, Judith, 2
Geertz, Hildred, 2
Hurston, Zora Neale, 1901–1960, 1,2
Kongas, Lembi, fl. 1970s, 2
Mead, Margaret, 1901–1978, 1,2
Meggers, Betty Jane, 1921–, 1
Parsons, Elsie Worthington Clews,
1875–1941, 1,2
Patai, Raphael, fl. 1960s, 2
Powdermaker, Hortense, 1900–1970,
1,2
Reichard, Gladys Amanda, 1893–
1955, 2
Robeson, Eslanda Cardoza Goode,
1896–1965, 2
Robesson, Eslanda Cardoza Goode,
1896–1965, 1
Schuchat, Molly G., fl. 1970s, 2
Steedman, Elsie V., fl. 1930s, 1
Stevenson, Matilda Coxe Evans,
1849–1915, 1,2
Toshchakova, Dr., fl. 1950s, 2
Underhill, Ruth Murray, 1884–1984,
1,2
Van Lawick-Goodall, Jane, Baroness,
1934–, 1,2
Antiochus II—Spouse
Laodice, 2
Antiquarians
Castaing, Madeleine, 2
Earle, Alice Morse, 1851–1911, 1,2
Evans, Joan, gr. 1916, 1
Newman, Henriette, fl. 1930s, 1
Plongeon, Alice D. le, 1851–, 1
Radcliffe, Ann Ward, 1764–1823, 1,2
Antisuffragists
Bissell, Emily Perkins, 1861–1948, 2
Dodge, Josephine Marshall Jewell,
1855–1928, 2
Antivivisectionists
Cobbe, Frances Power, 1822–1904,
1,2

Kingsford, Anne Bonus, 1846–1888,
2
Stevens, Christine, 1918–, 1
Antoinette, Marie—Daughter
Angouleme, Marie Therese Charlotte,
1778–1851, 2
Antoinette, Marie—Friend
Polignac, Yolande Martine Gabrielle
de Polastron, 1749–1793, 1
Antoinette, Marie—Mother
Maria Theresa, 1717–1780, 1,2
Antonius "Critius", Marcus—Mother
Julia, fl. 63 BC, 1
Antony, Mark—Daughter
Antonia Major, fl. 900s, 1
Cleopatra Selene, 40 BC, 1
Antony, Mark—Spouse
Fulvia, fl. 40 BC, 1,2
Octavia, 69–11
BC, 1,2
Apartheid fighter
Myburgh, Helmine, 2
Apothecaries
See
Pharmacologists
Appalachia
Morgan, Hannah, fl. 1970s, 2
Archduchesses
Maria Theresa, 1717–1780, 1,2
Maria Theresa, 1855–1944, 1
Archeologists
Bell, Gertrude Margaret Lowthian,
1868–1926, 1,2
Bonaparte, Maria Annunciata, 1782–
1839, 1
Caetani-Bovatelli, Donna Ersilia, fl.
1870s, 1
Dieulafoy, Jeanne Paule Henriette Ra-
chel Magre, 1851–1916, 1
Dohan, Edith Hayward Hall, 1877–
1943, 2
Este, Isabella d' Marchioness of Man-
tua, 1474–1539, 1,2
Gibson, Margaret Dunlop, 1843–
1920, 1
Goldman, Hetty, 1881–1972, 2
Harrison, Jane Ellen, 1850–1928, 1
Hawes, Harriet Ann Boyd, 1871–
1945, 1,2
Hodgkin, Dorothy Mary Crowfoot,
1910–, 1,2
Horsford, Cornelia, 1861–, 1
Jameson, Anna Brownell Murphy,
1794–1860, 1,2

Garrard, Mary D., fl. 1970s, 2
Gray, Nicolette Mary Binyon, gr.
  1932, 1
Harris, Ann Sutherland, fl. 1970s, 2
Hattis, Phyllis, fl. 1970s, 2
Hauser, Alice, fl. 1970s, 2
Hollander, Anne, fl. 1970s, 2
Iskin, Ruth, fl. 1970s, 2
Jameson, Anna Brownell Murphy,
  1794–1860, 1,2
Love, Iris Cornelia, 1933–, 2
Metzger, Frances, fl. 1970s, 2
Waters, Clara Erskine Clement, 1834–
  1916, 1,2
Art researchers
  Ackerman, Margaret, fl. 1970s, 2
  Coerr, S. DeRenne, fl. 1970s, 2
  Dominquez, Rita, fl. 1970s, 2
  Kalmbach, Ann E., fl. 1970s, 2
  Rice, Frances, fl. 1970s, 2
Art teachers
  Bartlett, Jennifer, 1941–, 2
  Brown, Alice van Vechten, 1862–
    1949, 2
  Cassell, Rosalie, fl. 1970s, 2
  Daneshvar, Julia Prokofyena, 1912–,
    2
  Dodd, Lois, 1927–, 2
  Hall, Adelaide S., 1857–, 1
  Kingsbury, Martha, 2
  Knowlton, Helen Mary, 1832–1918, 2
  McAlister, Elizabeth, 1940–, 2
  Prang, Mary Amelia Dana Hicks,
    1836–1927, 1,2
  Purcell, Elinor, fl. 1750s, 1
  Sartain, Emily, 1841–1927, 1,2
  Sullivan, Mary Josephine Quinn,
    1877–1939, 2
Arthur, Chester Alan—Mother
  Arthur, Malvina Stone, 1802–1869,
    1,2
Arthur, Chester Alan—Sister
  McElroy, Mary Arthur, fl. 1880s, 1
Arthur, Chester Alan—Spouse
  Arthur, Ellen Lewis Herndon, 1837–
    1880, 1,2
Artists' models
  Anderson, Emily, 1805–, 2
  Bowdoin, Augusta (Lady Temple), 2
  Camden, Francis, 1760–1829, 2
  Catteano, Simonetta, 1456–1476, 2
  Cayetana, Duchess of Alba, d. 1802, 2
  Fourment, Helena, 1614–, 1,2
  Gioconda, Lisa Gherardini, 1474–,
    1,2

Grenfell, Mrs. William, 1769–1851, 2
  Kiki of Montparnasse (Prin, Marie), 2
  Mears, Mrs. John, d. 1765, 2
  O'Murphy, Louise, 1737–1814, 2
  Stoffels, Hendrickje, d. 1667, 2
Artists
  See also
    Architects
    Calligraphers
    Cartoonists
    Ceramic painters
    Construction artist
    Designers
    Enamellers
    Etchers
    Faience art
    Fiber artists
    Folk artists
    Gesso decorator
    Gesso worker
    Glass decorators
    Glass painters and stainers
    Graphic artists
    Illuminators
    Illustrators
    Interior designers
    Lithographers
    Murals
    Painters
    Plastic art
    Potters
    Rug art
    Sand painters
    Scenic designers
    Silk art
    Tapestry designers
    Tattoo artists
    Weavers
    Wood engravers
Artists, American
  Achey, Mary Elizabeth, 1832–1885, 2
  Alcott, May (Madame Neriker),
    1840–1879, 1
  Alexander, Francesca, 1837–1917, 1,2
  Allen, Margaret Newton, 1894–, 1
  Allen, Marion, 1862–1941, 1
  Apfelbeck, Marie Louise Bailey,
    1876–, 1
  Asher, Elise, fl. 1970s, 2
  Axley, Martha Frances, fl. 1930s, 1
  Aycock, Alice, 1946–, 2
  Bach, Florence Julia, 1887–, 1
  Bachrach, Elise Wald, 1899–1940, 1
  Badger, Mrs., fl. 1859, 1

Baily, Caroline A.B., fl. 1900s, 1
Ballou, Addie L., fl. 1860s, 1
Bank, Mirra, fl. 1970s, 2
Barnard, Elinor M., 1872–1942, 1
Barry, Iris Sylvia Crump, 1895–1969, 2
Bartlett, Jennie E., fl. 1880s, 1
Bascom, Ruth Henshaw, 1772–1841, 1
Baskin, Lisa Unger, 2
Bernstein, Theresa, 1
Beveridge, Hortense, fl. 1950s, 2
Birge, Priscilla, 2
Bishop, Isabel, 1902–, 2
Bohner, Blyth, 2
Bradley, Ora Lewis, fl. 1930s, 1
Brannan, Sophie Marston, fl. 1930s, 1
Brettesville, Sheila, fl. 1960s, 2
Briggs, Berta N., fl. 1930s, 1
Brinkley, Nell, 1888–1944, 1
Brown, Charlotte, fl. 1970s, 2
Brown, Vivian, fl. 1970s, 2
Brownscombe, Jennie Augusta, 1850–1936, 1,2
Burr, Frances, fl. 1930s, 1
Burroughs, Margaret, 1917–, 2
Byard, Carole, fl. 1970s, 2
Byard, Dorothy Randolph, fl. 1930s, 1
Carl, Katharine Augusta, fl. 1890s, 1
Carson, Karen, fl. 1970s, 2
Chase-Riboud, Barbara, 1939–, 2
Church, Angelica Schuyler, 1877–1954, 1,2
Clark, Kate Freeman, d. 1957, 2
Clubb, Laura A., 2
Cochran, Dewees, 1902–, 1
Cole, Olivia H. H., 1942–, 2
Cowles, Florence Call, 1861–1950, 2
Davis, Gladys Rockmore, 1901–, 1
Denes, Agnes, fl. 1970s, 2
Derby, Mary, fl. 1810s, 1
Dickinson, Eleanor Creekmore, 1931–, 2
Diemer, Emma Lou, 1927–, 2
Dix, Eulabee, 1878–1961, 1
Donaldson, Alice Willits, 1885–1961, 1
Donner, Vyvyan, fl. 1930s, 1
Donneson, Seena, fl. 1970s, 2
Dunkleman, Loretta, fl. 1970s, 2
Dwight, Mary Elizabeth, fl. 1930s, 1
Eakins, Susan MacDowell, 1851–1938, 2

Edelheit, Martha, fl. 1970s, 2
Eliasoph, Paula, fl. 1930s, 1
Emmet, Lydia Field, 1866–1952, 1
Fecit, Henrietta Johnston, fl. 1700s, 2
Fetherstone, Edith Hedges, fl. 1930s, 1
Floyd, Phyllis, fl. 1970s, 2
Ford, Irene De Pendall, fl. 1930s, 1
Foster, Barbara, fl. 1970s, 2
Francis, Miriam Ḇ., 1930–, 2
Freilicher, Jane, 1924–, 2
Fuller, Sarah E., 1829–1901, 1
Ginsburg, Estelle, fl. 1970s, 2
Goodbar, Octavia Walton, fl. 1930s, 1
Goodridge, Sarah, 1788–1853, 2
Gordon, Juliette, fl. 1970s, 2
Gorelick, Shirley, fl. 1970s, 2
Grant, Blanche C., fl. 1920s, 1
Gray, Sophie de Butts, fl. 1890s, 1
Green, Emma Edwards, 1890–1942, 2
Greenstein, Ilise, fl. 1970s, 2
Greenwood, Marion, 1909–, 1
Gross, Sandi, fl. 1970s, 2
Hale, Lilian Westcott, 1881–, 1
Hale, Susan, 1833–1910, 1,2
Hall, Horathel, fl. 1970s, 2
Hall, Vicki, fl. 1970s, 2
Hardy, Kay, 1902–, 1
Harmon, Lily, 1913–, 1
Harris, Joan Sutherland, fl. 1970s, 2
Harrison, Margaritta Willetts, fl. 1870s, 1
Hazleton, Mary Brewster, fl. 1890s, 1
Hekking, Avis, fl. 1900s, 1
Hering, Elsie Ward, 1871–1923, 1
Hill, Susan, 1940–, 2
Hiller, Susan, 1940–, 2
Holley, Bertha Delbert, fl. 1930s, 1
Honeywell, Annette, 1904–, 1
Honeywell, Martha Ann, 1787–, 1
Horne, Mrs. William Henry, fl. 1900s, 1
Huber, Alice, fl. 1890s, 1
Hughes, Toni (Martha Groomas), 1
James, Alice Archer Sewall, 1870–, 1
Jeffries, Rosalind, fl. 1970s, 2
Johanson, Patricia, 1940–, 2
Johnson, Buffie, fl. 1970s, 2
Joy, Josephine, 1869–, 1
Keith, Dora Wheeler, 1857–1940, 1
Kelly, Mary, 2
Kimmel, Marcia, fl. 1970s, 2
Klavun, Betty, 1916–, 2
Knapp, Hazel, 1908–, 1

Koedt, Anne, fl. 1960s, 2
Koehler, Florence, 1861–1944, 2
Kooning, Elaine de, 1920–, 2
Kramer, Louise, fl. 1970s, 2
Kramer, Marjorie, fl. 1970s, 2
Kuehn, Frances, 1943–, 2
Lakey, Emily Jane, 1837–1896, 1
Lea, Anna M., fl. 1880s, 1
Leach, Susan, fl. 1970s, 2
Legare, Mary Swinton, fl. 1840s, 1
Leslie, Ann, fl. 1880s, 1
Lijn, Liliane, 1939–, 2
Loeb, Clare Sparke, fl. 1970s, 2
Logan, Charlotte, fl. 1930s, 1
Lumain-Dain, Alexandra, fl. 1970s, 2
Lundeberg, Helen, 1908–, 2
MacNeil, Carol Brooks, 1871–, 1
Macomber, Mary Lizzie, 1861–1916, 2
Mann, Katinka, fl. 1970s, 2
Marcus, Marcia, fl. 1970s, 2
Marie of Wurtemberg, 1813–1839, 1
Marohn, Irma Elaine, fl. 1930s, 1
Martin, Maria, 1796–1863, 1,2
Mason, Alice Trumbull, 1904–1971, 2
Mason, Clara, fl. 1930s, 1
Mason, Maud M., 1867–1956, 1
Maxwell, Martha A., 2
McCannon, Dinga, fl. 1970s, 2
McCullough, Esther Morgan, fl. 1930s, 1
McLaughlin, Mary Louise M., 1847–1939, 1,2
Mellen, Mary B., fl. 1880s, 1
Mendelsohn, Celia, fl. 1930s, 1
Merriman, Helen Biglow, 1844–, 1
Metcalf, Augusta J. C., 1871–, 2
Meyerowitz, Helen, fl. 1970s, 2
Miss, Mary, 1944–, 2
Miyakawa, Kikuko, fl. 1930s, 1
Moore, Sarah, fl. 1910s, 1
Morell, Imogene Robinson, d. 1908, 1
Morgan, Barbara, 1900–, 2
Morgan, Samantha Jane Atkesan, 1843–1926, 2
Morris, Jenny, 2
Morse, Alice Cordelia, 1862–, 1
Nedwill, Rose, fl. 1930s, 1
Newby, Ruby Warren, fl. 1930s, 1
Newman, Eve, fl. 1960s, 2
Newman, Isadora, fl. 1930s, 1
Normandie, Elizabeth K. de, fl. 1870s, 1
Norton, Clara, fl. 1920s, 1

O'Day, Caroline Goodwin Love, 1875–1943, 1,2
O'Reilly, Gertrude, fl. 1900s, 1
Obey, Trudel Mimms, fl. 1970s, 2
Oehler, Bernice Olivia, fl. 1930s, 1
Okubo, Mine, fl. 1970s, 2
Orvis, Mrs., fl. 1870s, 1
Ostertag, Blanche, fl. 1890s, 1
Paddock, Josephine, fl. 1930s, 1
Page, Marie Danforth, 1870–1940, 1
Pattee, Elsie Dodge, 1876–, 1
Paxton, Ethel, fl. 1930s, 1
Peabody, Sophia, m. 1842, 1
Peixotto, Mary Hutchinson, m. 1897, 1
Pepper, Beverly, 1924–, 2
Post, Cornelia S., fl. 1860s, 1
Pre, Julia du, fl. 1880s, 1
Predmore, Jessie, 1896–, 1
Ransom, Sarah, fl. 1870s, 1
Reynal, Jeanne, 1902–, 2
Richardson, Ellen A., 1845–1911, 1
Robertson, Lucille, fl. 1930s, 1
Rosenthal, Doris, 1
Ruellan, Andree, 1905–, 1
Santoro, Suzanne, 1946–, 2
Sartian, Harriet, d. 1957, 1
Sawyer, A. R., fl. 1870s, 1
Sawyer, Helen Alton, 1
Schoor, Esther Brann, fl. 1930s, 1
Shankland, Eugenia, fl. 1910s, 1
Shapiro, Dee, fl. 1970s, 2
Shoff, Carrie M., 1849–, 1
Smallwood, Hannah T., fl. 1870s, 1
Smith, Garland, 2
Southworth, Ella, 1872–, 1
Startz, Jane, fl. 1970s, 2
Stewart, Margot, fl. 1970s, 2
Stuart, Jane, 1812–1888, 1,2
Stuart, Michelle, 2
Tait, Agnes, 1897–, 2
Tee-van, Helen Damrosch, fl. 1910s, 1
Thorward, Clara Schafer, fl. 1930s, 1
Toro, Petronella, fl. 1900s, 1
Tyler, Alice Kellogg, fl. 1890s, 1
Vanderbilt, Gloria Morgan, 1924–1965, 1,2
Varian, Dorothy, 1895–, 1
Walcott, Mary Morris Vaux, 1860–1940, 2
Walsh, Alida, fl. 1970s, 2
Walworth, Ellen Hardin (the younger), 1858–, 1
Wamsley, Lillian Barlow, fl. 1930s, 1

Ward, Miss E., fl. 1900s, 1
Weatherford, Dorothy, fl. 1970s, 2
Weisberg, Suzanne, fl. 1970s, 2
Weston, Mary Pillsbury, fl. 1870s, 1
Wilde, Jennie, fl. 1910s, 1
Willet, Anna Lee, 1867–1943, 1
Wolfe, Mildred Nungester, 1912–, 2
Wood, Beatrice, 1
Wormly, Mrs., fl. 1870s, 1
Zehr, Connie, 1938–, 2
Artists, Australian
 Cassab, Judy, fl. 1960s, 2
Artists, Austrian
 Dombrowski zu Papros und Krus.,
  Kathe Schonberger von (K.O.S.
  pseud), 1
 Kayne, Hilde, 1903–, 1
 Laucota, Hermine, 2
 Weil, Lisl, 1910–, 1
Artists, Belgian
 Kindt, Adele, 1805–, 1
 Peeters, Clara, 1594–1657, 2
Artists, Bohemian
 Esch, Mathilde, 1820–, 1
Artists, Brazilian Bonomi, Maria,
  1935–, 1
Artists, Canadian
 Farncomb, Caroline, fl. 1900s, 1
 Murray, Marjorie, fl. 1960s, 2
 Scott, Jeannette, 1864–, 1
 Stone, Sylvia, 1928–, 2
 Winsor, Jacqueline, 1941–, 2
Artists, Chinese
 Hsueh T'ao, fl. 760s, 2
 Wei Shuo, 2
Artists, Dutch
 Bodenheim, Nelly, 2
 Heer, Margaretha de, fl. 1650s, 2
 Knibbergen, Catherina van, fl. 1850s,
  2
 Oosterwisck, Maria van, 1630–1693,
  1,2
 Scheffer, Caroline, d. 1839, 1
Artists, English
 Allingham, Helen Paterson, 1848–,
  1,2
 Allingham, Margery, 1904–1966, 2
 Alma-Tadema, Laura Therese, Lady,
  fl. 1870s, 1,2
 Ayres, Gillian, 1930–, 2
 Barlow, Phyllida, 1944–, 2
 Base, Irene, 2
 Blackadder, Elizabeth, 1931–, 2
 Blow, Sandra, 1926–, 2

Bodichon, Barbara Leigh-Smith,
  1827–1891, 1,2
Cameron, Shirley, 1944–, 2
Carlile, Joan, 1600–1679, 2
Ciobotaru, Gillian Wise, 1936–, 2
Clough, Prunella, 1919–, 2
Cooke, Jean, 1927–, 2
Corbeaux, Fanny, 1812–1883, 1
Donagh, Rita, 1939–, 2
Donlevy, Alice Heighes, 1846–1929,
  1
Durrant, Jennifer, 1942–, 2
Evans, Leslie, 1946–, 2
Fell, Sheila, 1931–, 2
Frink, Elisabeth, 1930–, 2
Gili, Katherine, 1948–, 2
Granby, Marchioness of, fl. 1900s, 1
Grant, Sybil, 1879–, 1
Grey, Edith F., fl. 1890s, 1
Hambling, Maggi, 1945–, 2
Hayllar, Edith, 1860–1948, 2
Jaray, Tess, 1937–, 2
Lander, Hilda Cowham, 1
Leapman, Edwina, 1934–, 2
Loy, Mina, 1882–1966, 2
MacKenzie, Lucy, 1952–, 2
Moss, Marlow, 1890–1958, 2
Osborn, Emily Mary, 1814–1865, 2
Potter, Mary, 1900–, 2
Rosse, Susan Penelope, 1652–1700, 2
Rossetti, Lucy Maddox Brown, fl.
  1870s, 2
Rowe, Louise Jopling, 1831–1884, 1
Spencer, Jean, 2
Stillman, Marie Spartali, fl. 1860s, 1
Swynnerton, Annie Louisa, 1844–
  1933, 1
Taylor, Wendy, 1945–, 2
Tweedie, Ethel Brilliana, d. 1940, 1
Wakely, Shelagh, 1932–, 2
Wright, Emma Scholfield, 1845–, 1
Yhap, Laetitia, 1941–, 2
Artists, Finnish
 Ilvessalo, Kirsti, 1920–, 2
 Schjerfbeck, Helene, fl. 1860s, 2
 Soldan-Brofeldt, Venny, 1860–, 2
 Wiik, Maria, 1853–, 2
Artists, Flemish
 Eyck, Margaretha von, 1370–1430,
  1,2
Artists, French
 Antigna, Marie-Benezit Helene,
  1861–1880, 1
 Auzou, Pauline, 1775–1835, 1,2

Ride, Sally Kristen, 1951–, 2
Roman, Nancy Grace, 1925–, 1,2
Sitterly, Charlotte Moore, 1898–, 1
Aswapati—Daughter
Savitri, 1
Athapascan Indians
Fate, Mary Jane, 2
Atheists
O'Hair, Madalyn Murray, 1919–, 2
Athletes
See also
Specific sports
Brooks, Erica May, fl. 1920s, 1
Clanton, Reita, fl. 1970s, 2
Goss, Margaret, fl. 1920s, 1
Hawley, Gertrude, fl. 1920s, 1
Hsueh, Wu (Hsuen Su-Su), 1564–
1637, 2
Jackson, Jill, fl. 1940s, 2
Lester, Margaret, 1938–, 2
Marvingt, Marie, 1875–1963, 1,2
Pound, Louise, 1872–1958, 2
Rosenbaum, Ruth Broemmer, 1945–,
2
Stead, Karen, 2
Athletic directors
See
Physical directors
Atmospheric researchers
Kane, Martha, 2
Atomic power industry
Kankus, Roberta A., 1953–, 2
Savolainen, Ann W., fl. 1940s, 2
Silkwood, Karen Gay, 1946–1974, 2
Attalus—Daughter
Pipara, fl. 250s, 1
Aucassin—Friend
Nicolette, fl. 1100s, 1
Audubon, John James—Friend
Martin, Maria, 1796–1863, 1,2
Augustine, Saint—Mother
Monica (Monnica), Saint, 333–387,
1,2
Augustus, Duke of Sussex—Spouse
Murray, Augusta, d. 1830, 1
Augustus—Daughter
Julia, 39BC–14AD, 1,2
Augustus—Granddaughter
Julia, d. 28, 1
Augustus—Sister
Octavia, 69–11
BC, 1,2
Augustus—Spouse
Livia Drusilla, d. 29, 1,2
Scribonia, fl. 39 BC, 1

Aurangzeb—Daughter
Roopnager, Princess of, fl. 1860s, 1
Aurelian—Spouse
Severina, Ulpia, fl. 270s, 1
Aurelius, Marcus—Spouse
Faustina, Annia, the younger, 125–
175, 1,2
Austen, Jane—Governess
Sharpe, Miss, fl. 1780s, 1
Austen, Jane—Mother
Austen, Cassandra, 1729–1827, 2
Australia
Jones, Mary "Molly", 1762–1833, 1
MacArthur, Elizabeth Veale, 1786–
1850, 1
Authors
See also
Anthologists
Biographers
Child authors
Columnists
Correspondents
Critics
Cookbook authors
Diarists
Dramatists
Editors
Encyclopedists
Essayists
Health food authors
Humorists
Literary agents
Literary critics
Motion picture authors
Museum catalog author
Publicists
Radio authors
Religious authors
Reviewers
Scribes
Sportswriters
Television authors
Translators
Writers
Authors, American
Acosta, Mercedes de, 1
Adams, Juliette Aurelia Graves,
1858–, 1
Addington, Sarah, 1891–1940, 1
Akers, Susan Grey, 1889–, 1
Alden, Isabella MacDonald "Pansy",
1841–1930, 1,2
Alexander, Francesca, 1837–1917, 1,2
Alle, Marjorie Hill, 1890–1945, 1

Ames, Mary E. Clemmer, 1831–
  1884, 1,2
Anderson, Barbara Tunnell, 1894–, 1
Angelou, Maya, 1928–, 2
Anthony, Katharine Susan, 1877–
  1965, 1,2
Archer, Alma, fl. 1930s, 1
Arlen, Jeanne Burns, 1917–, 1
Armer, Laura Adams, 1874–1963, 1,2
Armstrong, Charlotte, 1905–1969,
  1,2
Armstrong, Margaret Neilson, 1867–
  1944, 1
Ashmun, Margaret Eliza, d. 1940, 1
Atkenson, Mary Meek, 1884–, 2
Atkinson, Oriana Torrey, 1894–, 1
Avary, Myrta Lockett, fl. 1910s, 1,2
Aylward, Ida, fl. 1930s, 1
Babson, Naomi Lane, 1895–, 1
Bacon, Alice Mabel, 1858–1918, 2
Bacon, Elizabeth, 1842–1933, 2
Badger, Mrs., fl. 1859, 1
Bailey, Carolyn Sherwin, 1875–, 1
Baker, Etta Iva Anthony, fl. 1930s, 1
Baker, Harriette Newell Woods, 1
Baker, Katharine Lee, 1859–1929, 2
Baker, Louise Maxwell, 1909–, 1
Baker, Nina Brown, 1888–1957, 1
Baldwin, Alice, fl. 1770s, 1
Ballaseyus, Virginia, 1893–, 1
Ballou, Addie L., fl. 1860s, 1
Banks, Elizabeth L., 1870–1938, 1,2
Bannon, Laura, d. 1963, 1
Barber, Edith Michael, 1892–1963, 1
Barber, Elsie Marion Oakes, 1914–, 1
Bard, Mary Ten Eyck, 1904–, 1
Barker, Ellen Blackmar, fl. 1880s, 1
Barker, Tommie Dora, 1888–, 1
Barnes, Margaret Ayer, 1886–1967,
  1,2
Barnes, Margaret Campbell, 1891–, 1
Barratt, Louise Bascom, fl. 1930s, 1
Barrow, Frances Elizabeth "Aunt
  Fanny", 1822–1894, 1
Bartlett, Anna Warner, 1827–1915, 2
Barton, Betsey, 1918–1962, 1
Bassett, Sara Ware, 1872–, 1
Bates, Sylvia Chatfield, 1
Bauer, Florence Ann Marvyne, 1
Baumer, Marie, 1906–, 1
Bayliss, Marguerite Farleigh, 1895–, 1
Beach, Cora M., 1878–, 1
Beam, Lura, 1887–, 1
Beard, Mary Ritter, 1876–1958, 1,2

Beatty, Bessie, 1886–1947, 1
Beck, Joan, fl. 1960s, 2
Becker, May Lamberton, 1873–1958,
  1
Beecher, Catherine Esther, 1800–
  1878, 1,2
Beek, Alice D. Engley, 1876–, 1,2
Bell, Ann, fl. 1930s, 1
Bell, Lilian, 1867–1929, 1
Bell, Margaret Elizabeth, 1898–, 1
Belle, Barbara, 1922–, 1
Benedict, Ruth Fulton, 1887–1947,
  1,2
Bennett, Dorothy Graham, 1893–
  1959, 1
Bennett, Helen Christine, 1881–, 1
Bergengren, Anna Farquhar, 1865–, 1
Berlin, Ellin Mackay, 1904–, 1
Bernstein, Aline Frankau, 1880–
  1955, 1,2
Best, Allena Champlin, 1892–, 1
Best, Molly, fl. 1920s, 1
Bevier, Isabel, 1860–1942, 1,2
Bialk, Elisa, 1912–, 1
Biddle, Ellen McGowan, fl. 1900s, 2
Bilbro, (Anne) Mathilde, fl. 1910s, 1
Bingham, Millicent Todd, 1880–1968,
  1,2
Bishop, Mary Axtell, 1859–, 1
Bitters, Jean Ray Laury, 1928–, 2
Blackwell, Alice Stone, 1857–1950,
  1,2
Blaisdell, Mary Frances, 1874–, 1
Blake, Lillie Devereaux, 1833–1913,
  1,2
Bloom, Vera, 1898–1959, 1
Bombeck, Erma, 1927–, 2
Bond, Carrie Jacobs, 1862–1946, 1,2
Bonelli, Mona Modini, 1903–, 1
Bonner, Mary Graham, 1895–, 1
Bonney, (Mabel) Therese, 1894–
  1978, 1,2
Booker, Edna Lee, 1
Booth, Alice, fl. 1930s, 1
Borgese, Elisabeth Mann, 1918–, 2
Bork, Florence L. Holmes, 1869–, 1
Bothwell, Jean, 1
Botta, Anne Charlotte Lynch, 1815–
  1891, 1,2
Bottome, Margaret McDonald, 1827–
  1906, 2
Bower, Bertha Muzzy, pseud., 1871–
  1940, 1
Bowles, Heloise, 1919–1977, 2

Boyd, Mrs. Orsemus Bronson, fl. 1860s, 2
Bradley, Ora Lewis, fl. 1930s, 1
Brandt, Mary Elizabeth, fl. 1930s, 1
Breck, Carrie Ellis, 1855–1934, 1,2
Breen, May Singhi, 1949–, 1
Brewster, Cora Belle, 1859–, 1
Bridges, Dorothy, fl. 1970s, 2
Brin, Ruth, 2
Bristol, Margaret, 1
Bro, Marguerite Harmon, 1894–, 1
Broadhurst, Jean, 1873–1954, 1
Brock, Emma Lillian, 1886–, 1
Bromley, Dorothy Dunbar, 1896–, 1
Brotherton, Alice Williams, d. 1930, 1
Brower, Harriette, 1869–1928, 1
Brown, Alice, 1856–1948, 1,2
Brown, Barnetta, 1859–1938, 1
Brown, Helen Dawes, 1857–1941, 1
Brown, Helen Gurley, 1922–, 1,2
Brown, Kate Louise, 1857–1921, 1
Brown, Marcia, 1918–, 2
Brown, Marion, 1908–, 1
Brownmiller, Susan, 1935–, 2
Bruce, Elizabeth M., fl. 1880s, 1
Bruff, Nancy, 1
Brush, Katherine Ingham, 1902–1952, 1
Bryan, Mary Edwards, 1838–1913, 1,2
Bryner, Edna, fl. 1930s, 1
Buchanan, Annabel Morris, 1888–, 1,2
Buckmaster, Henrietta, 1909–1983, 1,2
Buell, Sarah, fl. 1820s, 1
Burgwyn, Mebane Holoman, 1914–, 1
Burks, Frances, fl. 1930s, 1
Burnett, Hallie Southgate, 1908–, 1
Burton, Emma, 1844–1927, 1
Burton, Virginia Lee, 1909–1968, 1,2
Busbey, Katharine Graves, 1872–1959, 1
Bushnell, Adelyn, 1894–, 1
Bussenius, Luellen T., fl. 1930s, 1
Byers, Margaretta, 1901–, 1
Cabot, Ella Lyman, gr. 1904, 1
Calhoun, Eleanor, 1864–1957, 1
Calkins, Mary Whiton, 1863–1930, 1,2
Call, Annie Payson, 1863–, 1
Cameron, Anne, 1

Campbell, Helen Stuart, 1839–1918, 2
Campbell, Patricia Platt, 1901–, 1
Campbell, Valeria, fl. 1860s, 1
Cannon, Ida Maud, 1877–1916, 2
Carey, Emma Forbes, 1833–, 1
Carey, Ernestine Moller Gilbreth, 1908–, 1,2
Carey, Helen A., fl. 1930s, 1
Carlisle, Helen Grace, 1898–, 1,2
Carnegie, Dorothy Reeder Price, 1912–, 1
Carraway, Gertrude Sprague, 1896–, 1
Carrick, Jean Warren, fl. 1940s, 1
Carroll, Consolata, pseud., 1892–, 1
Carroll, Ruth, fl. 1930s, 1
Carroll, Ruth Robinson, 1899–, 1
Carson, Rachel Louise, 1907–1964, 1,2
Carter, Mary Gilmore, 1867–, 1
Cary, Elisabeth Luther, 1867–1936, 2
Cary sisters, 2
Castle, Marian Johnston, 1898–, 1
Caudill, Rebecca, 1899–, 1
Cavanah, Frances Elizabeth, 1899–, 1
Chaffee, Allen, fl. 1900s, 1
Chamberlin, Georgia Louise, 1862–1943, 1
Chandler, Elizabeth Margaret, 1807–1834, 1,2
Chanler, Beatrice Ashley, 1875–1946, 1
Charles, Bula Ward, 1887–1974, 2
Chase, Ilka, 1903–1978, 1,2
Chastain, Madye Lee, 1908–, 1
Cheney, Frances Neel, 1906–, 1
Cheney, Harriet V., fl. 1870s, 1
Chenoweth, Caroline Van Dusen, 1846–, 1
Chesler, Phyllis, 2
Chester (Chesler), Phyllis, 2
Chevalier, Elizabeth Pickett, 1896–, 1
Chidester, Ann, 1919–, 1
Child, Lydia Maria Frances, 1802–1880, 1,2
Chute, Beatrice Joy, 1913–, 1
Chute, Marchette Gaylord, 1909–, 1
Clappe (Clapp), Louise Amelia Knapp Smith, 1819–1906, 1,2
Clapper, Olive Ewing, 1896–1968, 2
Clark, Dorothy Park, 1899–, 1
Coates, Gloria, 1938–, 2
Coburn, Eleanor Habawell Abbot, 1872–, 1

Coit, Margaret Louise, 1919–, 1
Coker, Elizabeth Boatwright, 1909–, 1
Cole, Miriam M., fl. 1870s, 1
Colman, Jane, fl. 1770s, 1
Colt, Miriam Davis, fl. 1850s, 1,2
Colver, Alice Mary Ross, 1892–, 1
Comden, Betty, 1915–, 1,2
Conant, Helen C., fl. 1870s, 1
Conant, Helen S., 1839–1899, 1
Conde, Bertha, 1
Cone, Mary, fl. 1870s, 1
Conklin, Jennie M. Drinkwater, 1841–1900, 1
Converse, Harriet Maxwell, d. 1903, 2
Cook, Fannie Bruce, 1893–1949, 1
Cooke, Grace McGowan, 1863–, 1
Cooley, Anna Maria, 1874–1955, 1
Cooley, Winnifred Harper, fl. 1930s, 1
Cooper, Sarah Brown Ingersoll, 1835–1896, 2
Cooper, Susan Augusta Fenimore, 1813–1894, 1,2
Corbin, Caroline Elizabeth, 1835–, 1
Cornell, Sophia S., 1875–, 1
Corr, Mary Bernadine, 1858–, 1
Corson, Juliet, 1841–1897, 1,2
Cousins, (Sue) Margaret, 1905–, 1
Cowles, Fleur Fenton, 1910–, 2
Cowles, Florence Call, 1861–1950, 2
Cowles, Virginia Spencer, 1912–1983, 1,2
Coxe, Margaret, fl. 1870s, 1
Crawford, Phyllis, 1899–, 1
Crocker, Hannah Mather, 1752–1829, 1,2
Crockett, Lucy Herndon, 1914–, 1
Crownfield, Gertrude, 1877–1945, 1
Crowninshield, Mary Bradford, d. 1913, 1
Curtis, Georgina Pell, 1859–1922, 1
Cutler, Bessie Ingersoll, fl. 1910s, 1
Cutting, Mary Stewart, 1851–1924, 1
Dahlgren, Madeleine Vinton, 1835–, 1
Dalgliesh, Alice, 1893–, 1
Dall, Caroline Wells Healey, 1822–1912, 1,2
Dallam, Helen, fl. 1940s, 1
Dana, Mrs. William Starr, 1862–1952, 1
Daringer, Helen Fern, 1892–, 1
Darling, Flora Adams, 1840–1910, 1,2

Davidson, Hannah Amelia, 1852–, 1
Davis, Adelle, 1904–1974, 2
Davis, Katherine K., 1892–, 1
Davis, Minnie S., fl. 1880s, 1
Davis, Mollie Evelyn Moore, 1844–1909, 2
Davis, Rebecca Blaine Harding, 1831–1910, 1,2
Day, Martha, 1813–1833, 1
De Kroyft, Susan Helen Aldrich, 1818–1915, 1
De Lima, Sigrid, 1921–, 1
De Long, Emma J. Wotton, 1851–1940, 1
De la Torre(-Bueno), Lillian, 1902–, 1
Deasy, Mary Margaret, 1914–, 1
Dee, Sylvia, 1914–1967, 1
Delaney, Adelaide Margaret, 1875–, 1
Deming, Dorothy, 1893–, 1
Denni, Gwynne, 1882–1949, 1
Denning, Ann Eliza Webb Young, 1844–1908, 2
Dewey, Mary Elizabeth, 1821–, 1
Diamant, Gertrude, 1901–, 1
Diaz, Abby Morton, 1821–1904, 2
Dick, Dorothy, 1900–, 1
Dickinson, Anna Elizabeth, 1842–1932, 1,2
Dickinson, Mary Lowe, 1839–1914, 1
Dickson, Marguerite Stockman, 1873–1953, 1
Diehl, Anna Randall, fl. 1880s, 1
Dillard, Annie, 1945–, 2
Diller, Angela (Mary Angelica), 1877–1968, 1,2
Disney, Doris Miles, 1907–1976, 1,2
Dock, Lavinia Lloyd, 1858–1956, 1,2
Dodd, Martha Eccles, 1908–, 1
Dodge, Mary Abigail, 1833–1896, 1,2
Donaldson, Elizabeth W., fl. 1930s, 1
Doner, Mary Frances, 1893–, 1
Donez, Ian, 1891–, 1
Donnelly, Dorothy, 1880–1928, 1,2
Donnelly, Dorothy, Sister, 2
Dorsey, Ella Loraine, 1853–, 1
Dorsey, Sarah Anne Ellis, 1829–1879, 1,2
Douglas, Alice May, 1865–, 1
Douglas, Marjory Stoneman, 1890–, 1
Downes, Anne Miller, d. 1964, 1
Downing, Eleanor, fl. 1930s, 1
Downs, Mrs. George Seldon, 1843–, 1
Doyle, Agnes Catherine, fl. 1900s, 1

Doyle, Martha Claire MacGowan, 1869–, 1

Drake, Debra Bella (Debbie), 1932–, 1

Drew, Elizabeth Brenner, 1935–, 2

Drinkwater, Jennie Maria, 1841–1900, 2

Drouet, Bessie Clarke, 1879–1940, 1

Dubois, Mary Constance, 1879–1959, 1

Duckett, Elizabeth Waring, fl. 1860s, 1

Duncan, Rena Buchanan Shore, fl. 1930s, 1

Durant, Ariel K., 1898–1981, 2

Dye, Eva Emery, 1885–, 1,2

Dyhrenfurth, Hettie, fl. 1930s, 1

Dykeman, Wilma, fl. 1950s, 1

Eames, Jane, 1816–1894, 1

Earle, Alice Morse, 1851–1911, 1,2

Eastman, Elaine Goodale, 1863–1953, 1

Eastman, Mary Henderson, 1818–1887, 2

Eastman, Mary Huse, 1879–1963, 1

Eberle, Irmengarde, 1898–, 1

Edwards, Clara, 1925–, 1

Edwards, Joan, 1919–1981, 1,2

Eliot, Charlotte Champe Stearns, 1843–1929, 2

Ellet, Elizabeth Fries Lummis, 1812–1877, 1,2

Elliot, Kathleen Morrow, 1897–1940, 1

Elliott, Grace Loucks, fl. 1930s, 1

Ellis, Anna M. B., 1860–1911, 1

Ely, Helena Rutherford, 1858–1920, 1

Embury, Emma Catherine, 1806–1863, 1,2

Emery, Anne Eleanor McGuigan, 1907–, 1

Emrick, Jeanette Wallace, 1878–, 1

Enright, Elizabeth, 1909–, 1

Ephron, Nora, 1911–, 2

Erdman, Loula Grace, 1

Eron, Carol, fl. 1970s, 2

Eustis, Helen White, 1916–, 1

Evatt, Hariet Torrey, 1895–, 1

Eve, Sarah, fl. 1770s, 1

Ewing, Mary Emilie, 1872–, 1

Eyre, Katherine Wigmore, 1901–, 1

Fair, Ethel Marion, 1884–, 1

Fairbank, Janet Ayer, 1878–1951, 1

Fancher, Mollie, 1848–1916, 2

Farmer, Lydia Hoyt, 1842–1903, 1

Farnham, Eliza Wood Burhans, 1815–1864, 1,2

Farnham, Marynia L. Foot, 1899–1979, 2

Farrar, Eliza Ware Rotch, 1791–1870, 1,2

Faulkner, Nancy, 1906–, 1

Faulkner, Virginia L., fl. 1930s, 1

Fenner, Beatrice, 1904–, 1

Fenollosa, Mary McNeill, 1865–1954, 1

Fernald, M. E., 1839–1919, 1

Fieser, Mary, fl. 1970s, 2

Fine, Sylvia, 1893–, 1

Finley, Lorraine Noel, 1899–, 1

Finley, Martha Farquaharson, 1828–1909, 1,2

Finney, Emily Jex, d. 1952, 1

Finney, Gertrude Elva Bridgeman, 1892–, 1

Finney, Ruth Ebright, 1884–1955, 1,2

Firestone, Isabella Smith, 1874–1955, 1

Fisher, Anne Benson, 1898–, 1

Fisher, Harriet White, m. 1898, 1

Fisher, Mary Frances Kennedy, 1908–, 1,2

Fitzgerald, Sally Ridgefield, fl. 1970s, 2

Fitzgerald, Zelda Sayre, 1900–1948, 2

Flack, Marjorie, 1897–1958, 1

Flanner, Janet, 1892–1978, 1,2

Fleming, Elizabeth, fl. 1750s, 1

Flintham, Lydia Stirling, fl. 1780s, 1

Foley, Martha, 1897–1977, 1,2

Follen, Eliza Lee Cabot, 1787–1860, 1,2

Foote, Mary Anna Hallock, 1847–1938, 1,2

Ford, Eileen Otte, 1922–, 2

Forsee, Aylesa, fl. 1950s, 1

Fort, Eleanor H., 1914–, 1

Foster, Edna Abigail, d. 1945, 1

Fowler, Marie Louise, fl. 1930s, 1

Fowler-Billings, Katharine, 1902–, 1

Fox, Genevieve May, 1888–, 1

Franken, Rose, 1898–, 1

Franklin, Blanch Ortha, 1895–, 1

Fraser, Mary Crawford, 1851–, 1

Freedman, (Lois) Nancy Mars, 1920–, 1

Freeman, Jo, 1946–, 2

Freeman, Marilla Waite, 1

Friedan, Betty, 1921–, 2
Frings, Ketti Hartley, 1915–, 1
Frost, Elizabeth Hollister, 1886–
1958, 1
Frost, Jannett Blakeslee, fl. 1870s, 2
Fryberger, Agnes Moore, 1868–, 1
Fyan, Loleta Dawson, 1894–, 1
Gadsby, Mrs. James Eakin, fl. 1900s,
1
Gage, Matilda Joslyn, 1826–1898, 1,2
Gaines, Ruth, fl. 1910s, 1
Gaither, Frances, 1889–1955, 1
Gardener, Helen Hamilton, 1853–
1925, 1,2
Gardiner, Abigail, 2
Gardner, Mary Sewall, 1871–1961,
1,2
Garner, Elvira Carter, 1895–, 1
Garst, Shannon, 1899–, 1
Gates, Eleanor, 1875–1951, 2
Gay, Zhenya, 1906–, 1
Gerrish-Jones, Abbie, 1863–1929, 1
Gerson, Virginia, 1864–1951, 1
Geyer, Georgie Anne, 1935–, 2
Gibson, Anna L., fl. 1940s, 1
Gilchrist, Anne, 1828–1885, 1
Gilder, Jeannette Leonard, 1849–
1916, 1,2
Gilder, Rosamond, 1,2
Giles, Janice Holt, 1909–, 1
Gillespie, Marian, 1889–1946, 1
Gillespie, Marian, fl. 1930s, 1
Gilliam, Dorothy, fl. 1950s, 2
Gilman, Mary Rebecca Foster,
1859–, 1
Gilman, Mildred, 1898–, 1,2
Gilmore, Elizabeth McCabe, 1874–, 1
Gilmore, Florence MacGruder,
1881–, 1
Glenn, Mabelle, fl. 1940s, 1
Goertz, Arthemise, 1905–, 1
Goetschius, Marjorie, 1915–, 1
Goetz, Delia, 1898–, 1
Golden, Sylvia, 1900–, 1
Goldsmith, Margaret, 1897–, 1
Gonzales, Sylvia Alicia, fl. 1943s, 2
Goodman, Lillian Rosedale, 1888–, 1
Goodnow, Minnie, d. 1952, 1
Goodsell, Willystine, 1870–, 1
Gould, Elizabeth Lincoln, d. 1914, 1
Govan, Christine Noble, 1898–, 1
Graham, Elinor Mish, 1906–, 1
Graham, Rose, gr. 1898, 1
Grant, Blanche C., fl. 1920s, 1

Granville-Barker, Helen Gates, d.
1950, 1
Gray, Caroline E., d. 1938, 1
Green, Charlotte Hilton, 1889–, 1
Greene, Marie Louise, gr. 1891, 1
Greene, Sarah Pratt McLean, 1856–
1935, 1,2
Griffith, Corinne, 1896–, 1,2
Grimke, Charlotte L. Forten, 1838–
1915, 1,2
Groves, May Showler, 1888–, 1
Gruenberg, Sidonie Matsner, 1881–
1974, 1,2
Hager, Alice Rogers, 1894–, 1
Hahn, Emily, 1905–, 1,2
Haines, Helen Colby, fl. 1900s, 1
Haines, Helen Elizabeth, 1872–1961,
1,2
Hale, Louise Closser, 1872–1933, 1,2
Hale, Lucretia Peabody, 1820–1920,
1,2
Hale, Nancy, 1908–, 1
Hale, Susan, 1833–1910, 1,2
Hall, Addye Yeargain, fl. 1940s, 1
Hall, Adelaide S., 1857–, 1
Hall, Marjory, 1908–, 1
Halse, Margaret Frances, 1910–, 1
Hamilton, Nancy, 1908–, 1
Hapgood, Isabel Florence, 1850–
1928, 2
Hargreaves, Sheba, 1882–, 1
Harris, Bernice Kelly, 1894–, 1
Harris, Eliza, fl. 1860s, 1
Harris, Julia, 1875–, 2
Harrison, Edith Ogden, 1
Harrison, Marguerite, 1879–1960, 2
Hartman, Mrs. Gustave, 1900–, 1
Hartt, Mary Bronson, 1873–, 1
Haskell, Helen Eggleston, m. 1903, 1
Hathaway, Ann, fl. 1940s, 1
Hathaway, Katherine Butler, 1890–
1942, 1
Hauck, Louise Platt, 1883–1943, 1
Haven, (Alice) Emily Bradley Neal, 2
Hawes, Elizabeth, 1903–1971, 1,2
Hayes, Ellen, 1851–, 1
Haynes, Elizabeth A. Ross, 1883–
1953, 1,2
Hazard, Caroline, 1856–1945, 1,2
Hebard, Grace Raymond, 1861–
1936, 1,2
Hedden, Worth Tuttle, 1896–, 1
Hemingway, Clara Edwards, fl.
1940s, 1

Hemingway, Mary Welsh, 1908–, 1,2
Hemsley, Josephine, 1880–, 1
Herrick, Christine Terhune, 1859–
1944, 1,2
Hickock, Lorena A., 1893–1908, 1,2
Hill, Amelia Leavitt, fl. 1930s, 1
Hill, Carol, fl. 1930s, 1
Hill, Dedette Lee, 1900–1950, 1
Hill, Helen, d. 1942, 1
Hill, Margaret Ohler, 2
Hiller, Margaret, fl. 1930s, 1
Hillis, Marjorie, fl. 1930s, 1
Hobart, Alice Tisdale Nourse, 1882–
1967, 1
Hobson, Laura Kean Zametkin, 1
Hoerle, Helen, fl. 1930s, 1
Holberg, Ruth Langland, 1891–, 1
Hollingsworth, Thekla, fl. 1930s, 1
Holstein, Anna, 1824–1890, 1
Holt, Isabella, 1892–1962, 1
Holt, Rackham, 1899–, 1
Holton, Susan May, 1875–1951, 1
Hood, Marguerite Vivian, fl. 1940s, 1
Hormel, Olive Deane, fl. 1930s, 1
Hosford, Jessie Wiegand, 1882–, 2
Howar, Barbara, 1914–, 2
Howard, Alice Sturtevant, 1878–
1945, 1
Howard, Blanch Willis, fl. 1830s, 2
Howard, Elizabeth, 1907–, 1
Howard, Florence Ruth, 1902–, 1
Howe, Florence, 1919–, 2
Howe, Helen (Allen), 1905–1875, 1,2
Howland, Eliza W., fl. 1860s, 1
Hubbard, Margaret Ann, 1909–, 1
Hudson, Octavia, fl. 1940s, 1
Hueston, Ethel Powelson, 1887–, 1
Hughan, Jessie Wallace, 1875–1955,
1,2
Humphrey, Grace, 1882–, 1
Hunt, Mabel Leigh, 1892–, 1
Huntley, Florence, d. 1912, 1
Hurll, Estelle May, 1863–, 1
Hutten, Bettina, m. 1897, 1
Huxtable, Ada Louise Landman,
1921–, 2
Hyde, Madeline, 1907–, 1
Hyman, Libbie Henrietta, 1888–
1969, 1,2
Innis, Mary Quayle, 1
Ireland, Norma Olin, 1907–, 1,2
Irwin, Laetitia McDonald, fl. 1930s, 1
Isaacs, Adah, 1835–1868, 1
Jackson, Sherry, 1

Jasmyn, Joan, 1898–, 1
Jean, Elsie, 1907–, 1
Jebb, Caroline Lane Reynolds Slem-
mer, 1840–1930, 1
Jenkins, Sara, 1904–, 1
Jerome, Maude Nugent, 1873–1958,
1,2
Jessye, Eva, 1895–, 1,2
Johnson, Helen Louise Kendrick,
1844–1917, 2
Johnson, Osa Helen Leighty, 1894–
1953, 1,2
Johnston, Maria I., 1835–, 1
Johnston, Patricia, 1922–, 1
Johnstone, Margaret Blair, 1913–, 1
Jones, Amanda Theodosia, 1835–
1914, 2
Jones, Mary M., fl. 1930s, 1
Jones, Wendy, fl. 1940s, 2
Jordan, Elizabeth Garver, 1865–
1947, 1,2
Jordan, Grace Edington, 2
Jordan, Mildred, 1901–, 1
Judson, Clara Ingram, 1879–, 1
Kael, Pauline, 1919–, 2
Kahmann, (Mable) Chesley, 1901–, 1
Kahn, Ruth Ward, 1870–, 1
Kander, Lizzie Black, 1858–1940, 1,2
Kantor, Rosabeth Moss, 2
Kaup, Elizabeth Bartol Dewing,
1885–, 1
Kearney, Martha Eleanor, 1842–
1930, 1
Keen, Dora, 1871–, 1,2
Keller, Helen Adams, 1880–1968, 1,2
Kelly, Eleanor Mercein, 1880–, 1
Kelly, Florence Finch, 1858–1939, 1,2
Kelly, Myra, 1875–1910, 1,2
Kelly, Regina Zimmerman, 1898–, 1
Kennelly, Ardyth, 1912–, 1
Kerby-Miller, Wilma A., fl. 1960s, 2
Kerr, Sophie, 1880–1965, 1,2
Kimbrough, Emily, 1899–, 1,2
King, Frances, 1863–1948, 1
King, Grace Elizabeth, 1852–1932, 2
Kinkead, Elizabeth Shelby, fl. 1900s,
1
Kirk, Ellen Warner Olney, 1842–, 1
Kirkland, Caroline Matilda Stans-
bury, 1801–1864, 1,2
Kirkland, Winifred Margaretta, 1872–
1943, 1
Kirkus, Virginia, 1893–1980, 1,2
Kleeman, Rita Halle, 1887–, 1

Kluegel, Anne Jennings, 1880–, 1
Knight, Ruth Adams Yingling, 1898–, 1
Knox, Adeline Grafton, 1845–, 1
Knox, Helen Boardman, 1870–1947, 1
Kohut, Rebekah Bettelheim, 1864–1951, 1,2
Krantz, Judith, 1928–, 2
Krementz, Jill, 1940–, 2
Krey, Laura, 1890–, 2
Krout, Mary Hannah, 1857–1927, 1
La Motte, Ellen Newbold, 1873–1961, 1
Lacy, Mary Goodwin, 1875–1962, 1
Laidlaw, Harriet Burton, 1873–1949, 1,2
Lamb, Martha Joanna Reade Nash, 1826–1893, 1,2
Lambert, Janet Snyder, 1894–, 1
Landau, Genevieve Millet, fl. 1970s, 2
Landers, Olive Richards, fl. 1930s, 1
Landon, Margaret Dorthea Mortenson, 1903–, 1
Langer, Susanne Katherina Knauth, 1895–1985, 1,2
Langley, Adria Locke, 1
Lanza, Clara, 1859–, 1
Latham, Jean Lee, 1902–, 1
Lathrop, Dorothy Pulis, 1891–, 1
Lathrop, Rose Hawthorne, 1851–1926, 1,2
Lauferty, Lilian, 1887–1958, 1
Laughlin, Clara Elizabeth, 1873–1941, 1
Lawless, Margaret H. Wynne, 1847–, 1
Lawrence, Hilda, 1
Lawrence, Jeanette, fl. 1930s, 1
Lawrence, Mildred, 1907–, 1
Lay, Julia, fl. 1880s, 1
Lay, Margaret Rebecca, 1905–, 1
Le Favre, Carrica, fl. 1890s, 2
Le Vert, Octavia Celeste Walton, 1810–1877, 1,2
Lee, Gypsy Rose, 1914–1970, 1,2
Lee, Hannah Farnham Sawyer, 1780–1865, 1
Lee, Jennette Barbour Perry, 1860–1951, 1
Lee, Mary E., d. 1849, 1
Leech, Lida Shivers, 1873–, 1
Leech, Margaret Kernochan, 1893–1974, 1,2

Leighton, Margaret Carver, 1896–, 1
Leonard, Anita, 1922–, 1
Leonard, Florence, fl. 1940s, 1
Leslie, Eliza (Elizabeth), 1787–1858, 1,2
Lilly, Doris, 1926–, 1
Lincoln, Jennie Gould, fl. 1910s, 1
Lincoln, Mary Johnson Bailey, 1844–1921, 1,2
Lindbergh, Anne Spencer Morrow, 1906–, 1,2
Lindheim, Irma, 1886–, 1
Lippmann, Julie Mathilde, d. 1952, 1
Litchfield, Mary Elizabeth, 1854–, 1
Littledale, Clara Savage, 1891–1956, 1,2
Livingstone, Mabel, 1926–, 1
Lockwood, Mary Smith, 1831–, 1,2
Lofas, Jeanette, fl. 1970s, 2
Loftin, Tee, 1921–, 2
Logan, Celia, 1840–1904, 1
Logan, Mrs. John A., fl. 1890s, 1
Logan, Virginia Knight, 1850–1940, 1
Logasa, Hannah, 1879–, 1
Lombard, Helen Carusi, 1905–, 1
Long, Elsie, 1880–1946, 1
Lopata, Helena, 1925–, 2
Lothrop, Harriett Mulford Stone, 1844–1924, 1,2
Loud, Patricia Russell, 1926–, 2
Loveman, Amy, 1881–1955, 1,2
Lowe, Corinne Martin, 1882–1952, 1
Lowe, Martha Perry, 1829–1902, 1
Lower, Dorothy M., 1914–, 2
Lowitz, Sadyebeth Heath, fl. 1930s, 1
Lownsbery, Eloise, 1888–, 1
Luce, Clare Booth, 1903–1987, 1,2
Luhan, Mabel Ganson Dodge, 1879–1962, 1,2
Lummis, Dorothea, 1860–, 1
Lummis, Eliza O'Brien, fl. 1910s, 1
Lumpkin, Grace, 1
Lupton, Mary Josephine, fl. 1910s, 1
Lussi, Marie, 1892–, 1
Lutes, Della Thompson, d. 1942, 1
Lynch, Maude Dutton, fl. 1930s, 1
Lynch, Peg, 1
Lynd, Helen Merrell, 1896–1982, 2
M'Cleary, Dorothy, 1894–, 1
MacDougall, Priscilla Ruth, 2
MacGregor, Ellen, 1906–, 1
MacKaye, Julia Josphine Gunther, fl. 1890s, 1
MacLaine, Shirley, 1934–, 1,2

Macaulay, Fannie Caldwell, 1863–1941, 1

Mackenzie, Jean Kenyon, 1874–1936, 2

Mackie, Pauline Bradford, 1873–, 1

Mackin, Sarah Maria Spottiswood, 1850–, 1

Mannes, Marya, 1904–, 1,2

Mannix, Mary Ellen Walsh, 1846–1938, 1

Marble, Annie Russell, 1864–, 1

Marble, Callie Bonney, fl. 1910s, 1

Marlett, Melba Balmat Grimes, 1909–, 1

Marshall, Marguerite Moers, 1887–1964, 1

Marshall, Rosamond Van de Zee, 1900–1957, 1

Martin, Elizabeth Gilbert, 1837–, 1

Martin, George Madden, 1866–1946, 2

Marzolf, Marion, 2

Mason, Amelia Gere, d. 1923, 1

Mather, Sarah Ann, 1820–, 1

Mathews, Blance Dingley, d. 1932, 1

Mayer, Jane Rothschild, 1

McCabe, Lida Rose, 1895–1938, 1

McCall, Dorothy Lawson, 1888–, 2

McClintock, Katharine Morrison, 1899–, 1

McClurg, Virginia Donaghe, fl. 1920s, 1

McCrackin, Josephine Woempner Clifford, 1838–1920, 2

McCullough, Esther Morgan, fl. 1930s, 1

McDonald, Betty, 1908–1958, 1,2

McDonald, Lucile Saunders, 1898–, 1

McElroy, Colleen, 1935–, 2

McGauley, Minna Hoppe, fl. 1920s, 1

McGowan, Alice, 1858–, 1

McGraw, Eloise Jarvis, 1915–, 1

McIntosh, Maria Jane, 1803–1878, 1,2

McKenney, Eileen, d. 1940, 1

McKenny, Ruth, 1911–1972, 1,2

McKown, Robin, fl. 1960s, 1

McMeekin, Isabel McLenan, 1895–, 1

McSwigan, Marie, 1907–1962, 1

Mead, Margaret, 1901–1978, 1,2

Mears, Helen, 1900–, 1

Melville, Velma, 1858–, 1

Mercedes, Mary Antonio Gallagher, fl. 1910s, 1

Merriman, Helen Biglow, 1844–, 1

Metzelthin, Pearl Violetta, 1894–1947, 1

Millay, Edna St. Vincent, 1892–1950, 1,2

Miller, Alice Duer, 1874–1942, 1,2

Miller, Anna Jenness, 1884–, 1

Miller, Dora Richards, m. 1862, 1

Miller, Marion M., 1864–, 1

Millett, Kate, 1934–, 2

Mills, Nellie Ireton, 1880–1967, 2

Misch, Mrs. Ceasar, fl. 1910s, 1

Modell, Merriam, 1908–, 1

Molloy, Mary Aloysius, 1880–, 1

Montgomery, Elizabeth Rider, 1902–, 1

Moore, Anne Carroll, 1871–1961, 1,2

Moore, Annie Aubertine Woodward, 1841–1929, 1,2

Moore, Clara Sophia Jessup, 1824–1899, 1,2

Moore, Elizabeth Evelyn, 1891–, 1

Moore, Idora McClellan Plowman, 1843–1929, 1,2

Moore, Ruth, 1903–, 1

Moore, Vandi, 1912–, 2

Mordecai, Ellen, 1820–, 1

Mordecai, Rose, 1839–, 1

Morgan, Anne Eugenia Felicia, 1845–1952, 1

Morgan, Charlotte E., fl. 1930s, 1

Morgan, Marabel, 1938–, 2

Morgan, Maud, 1864–1941, 1

Morgan, Robin, fl. 1970s, 2

Morley, Margaret Warner, 1858–1923, 2

Morris, Constance Lily, d. 1954, 1

Morrison, Toni, 1931–, 2

Morrow, Elizabeth Cutter, 1873–1955, 1

Morton, Eliza Happy, 1852–1916, 1

Moser, Edwa Robert, 1899–, 1

Moses, Clara Lowenburg, 1865–1951, 1

Mosher, Edith R., fl. 1900s, 1

Moulton, Ellen Louise Chandler, 1835–1908, 2

Mudd, Emily Hatshore, 1898–, 1

Murray, Pauli, 1910–, 2

Mydans, Shelley Smith, 1915–, 1

Myers, Carlene Brien, fl. 1930s, 1

Nash, Eleanor Arnett, 1892–, 1

Nathan, Adele Gutman, fl. 1930s, 1

Neal, Alice B., m. 1946, 1

Nearing, Helen Knothe, 1904–, 2

Neilson, Frances Fullerton Jones, 1912–, 1
Newman, Isadora, fl. 1930s, 1
Nichols, Mary Sargeant Neal Gove, 1810–1884, 1,2
Nicholson, Margaret, 1904–, 1
Niehaus, Regina Armstrong, 1869–, 1
Niles, Blair Rice, 1887–1959, 1
O'Hair, Madalyn Murray, 1919–, 2
O'Hara, Mary, 1
O'Malley, Patricia, fl. 1930s, 1
O'Malley, Sallie Margaret, 1862–, 1
O'Neill, Rose Cecil, 1874–1944, 1,2
O'Reilly, Mary Boyle, 1873–, 1
Oberdorfer, Anne Faulkner, fl. 1940s, 1
Oemler, Marie Conway, 1879–1932, 1
Ogilvie, Elisabeth May, 1917–, 1
Okumura, Katsu, d. 1942, 2
Olds, Helen Diehl, fl. 1930s, 1
Oliver, Grace Atkinson, 1844–1899, 1
Olnhausen, Mary Phinney von, 1818–1902, 1
Ormsby, Mary Frost, 1852–, 1
Orton, Helen Fuller, 1872–1955, 1
Osborne, Letitia Osborne Preston, 1894–, 1
Osser, Edna, 1919–, 1
Overstreet, Bonaro Wilkinson, fl. 1930s, 1
Owen, Ruth Bryan, 1895–1954, 1,2
Ozick, Cynthia, 1928–, 2
Page, Celeste Walker, fl. 1930s, 1
Paine, Harriet Eliza, 1845–1910, 1
Paley, Grace, 1922–, 2
Palmer, Fannie Purdy, 1839–1923, 1
Palmer, Phoebe Worrall, 1807–1874, 1,2
Parker, Cornelia Stratton, 1885–, 1
Parker, Eleanor R., 1874–, 1
Parker, Lottie Blair, d. 1937, 1
Parker, Marjorie Holloman, fl. 1940s, 1,2
Parloa, Maria, 1843–1909, 1,2
Parmenter, Christine Whiting, 1877–1953, 1
Paterson, Anne, pseud., 1
Pattee, Alida Francis, d. 1942, 1
Paxton, Ethel, fl. 1930s, 1
Paxton, Jean Gregory, fl. 1930s, 1
Peare, Catherine Owens, 1911–, 1
Pearl, Lee, 1907–, 1
Peck, Anne Merriman, 1884–, 1

Peebles, Mary Louise, 1834–1915, 1
Peltz, Mary Ellen (Opdycke), 1896–1981, 1,2
Pennell, Elizabeth Robins, 1855–1936, 1,2
Perfield, Effa Ellis, fl. 1940s, 1
Perry, Eleanor Bayer, 1914–1981, 2
Perry, Nora, 1831–1896, 1,2
Peter, Frances, 2
Peterkin, Julia Mood, 1880–1961, 1
Peterson, Betty, 1918–, 1
Peterson, Virgilia, 1904–1966, 1
Petkere, Bernice, 1906–, 1
Peyser, Ethel R., fl. 1910s, 1
Phelps, Anna Elizabeth, fl. 1930s, 1
Phillips, Josephine, fl. 1860s, 1
Phillips, Marie Tello, 1874–1962, 1
Picken, Mary Brooks, 1886–, 1,2
Pierson, Louise John Randall, 1890–, 1
Pike, Mary Hayden Green, 1824–1908, 2
Pinkard, Edna Belle, 1892–, 1
Pinkerson, Kathrene Sutherand, 1887–1967, 1
Plassmann, Martha Edgerton, 1850–, 1
Plummer, Mary Wright, 1856–1916, 1,2
Poll, Ruth, 1899–, 1
Pollard, Josephine, 1840–1892, 1
Porter, Anne Porter, 1894–, 2
Portuondo, Josephine B. Thomas, 1868–, 1
Post, Emily Price, 1873–1960, 1,2
Pottker, Janice, 2
Poulssn, Ann Emile, 1853–1939, 1
Prang, Mary Amelia Dana Hicks, 1836–1927, 1,2
Pringle, Elizabeth Waties Allston, 1845–1921, 2
Putnam, Emily James Smith, 1865–1944, 1,2
Putnam, Mary T. S. L., 1810–1898, 1
Pyle, Katherine, d. 1938, 1
Rabb, Kate Milner, 1866–1937, 2
Ramsey, Grace Fisher, fl. 1930s, 1
Ratchford, Fannie Elizabeth, 1887–, 1
Rathbone (Rathbun), Mary Jane, 1860–, 1
Redfield, Ethel, 1877–, 1
Reed, Caroline Keating, fl. 1910s, 1
Rembaugh, Bertha, 1876–1950, 1
Reno, Itti Kinney, 1862–, 1

Rensselaer, Mariana Griswold, 1851–1914, 1
Reynolds, Belle, 1840–, 1
Reynolds, Helen Wilkinson, 1877–1943, 1
Rhoades, Cornelia Harsen, 1863–1940, 1
Rich, Louise Dickinson, 1903–, 1
Rich-McCoy, Lois, 1941–, 2
Richardson, Ellen A., 1845–1911, 1
Richardson, Harriet, gr. 1896, 1
Richardson, Hester Dorsey, m. 1891, 1
Rickert, Edith, 1871–1938, 2
Ripley, Elizabeth Blake, 1906–, 1
Ritner, Ann Gilliland, 1906–, 1
Rives, Hallie Erminie, 1
Robbins, Elizabeth Murray, d. 1853, 2
Robertson, Constance Noyes, 1897–, 1
Robertson, Mary Imogene, 1906–1948, 1,2
Robesson, Eslanda Cardoza Goode, 1896–1965, 1
Robins, Julia Gorham, fl. 1910s, 1
Robinson, Agnes Mary, 1857–, 1
Robinson, Evangeline, fl. 1930s, 1
Robinson, Mabel Louise, d. 1962, 1
Robyn, Louise, 1878–1949, 1
Roma, Caro, 1866–1937, 1
Rombauer, Irma von Starkloff, 1877–1962, 1,2
Rood, Helen Martin, 1889–1943, 1
Rose, Mary Davies Swartz, 1874–1941, 1,2
Ross, Nancy Wilson, 1907–, 1
Ross, Pat, 2
Rothery, Agnes Edwards, 1888–1954, 1
Rothrock, Mary Utopia, 1890–, 1
Roulet, Mary F. Nixon, fl. 1910s, 1
Ruffin, Margaret Ellen Henry, 1857–, 1
Runbeck, Margaret Lee, 1910–1956, 1
Sabin, Florence Rena, 1871–1953, 1,2
Sach, Emanie N., m. 1917, 1
Samuels, Margaret, fl. 1930s, 1
Schaeffer, Mary, 1
Schlafly, Phyllis Stewart, 1924–, 2
Schlauch, Margaret, 1898–, 1
Schlein, Miriam, 1926–, 1
Schmitt, Gladys Leonore, 1909–1972, 1,2

Schoff, Hannah Kent, 1853–1940, 1,2
Schoor, Esther Brann, fl. 1930s, 1
Scidmore, Eliza Ruhamah, 1856–1928, 1,2
Scott, Mary Augusta, 1851–1916, 1
Scott, Mary Sophie, 1838–, 1
Scudder, Vida Dutton, 1861–1954, 1,2
Seaman, Barbara, 2
Searing, Annie Eliza Pidgeon, 1857–1942, 1
Searing, Laura Catherine Redden, 1840–, 1
Sears, Cynthia Lovelace, 1937–, 2
Seaver, Blanche Ebert, 1891–, 1
Seed, Suzanne, fl. 1970s, 2
Senn, Margaret Lynch, 1882–, 1
Sergeant, Elizabeth Shepley, 1881–, 1
Settle, Mary Lee, 1918–, 1
Seymour, Flora Warren, 1888–, 1
Seymour, Harriet Ayer, 1876–1944, 1
Shaw, Ellen Eddy, fl. 1930s, 1
Shay, Edith Foley, 1894–, 1
Sheehy, Gail Henion, 1937–, 2
Shelton, Louise, 1867–1934, 1
Shephard, Esther, fl. 1920s, 1
Sherman, Minna E., fl. 1910s, 1
Sherwood, Emily Lee, 1929–, 1
Sherwood, Margaret Pollock, 1864–1955, 1
Sherwood, Mary Elizabeth Wilson, 1826–1903, 1,2
Shiber, Etta, 1878–1948, 1
Shindler, Mary B., 1810–1833, 1
Shinn, Milicent Washburn, 1858–1940, 1,2
Shippen, Katherine Binney, 1892–, 1
Showalter, Elaine, 2
Simms, Alice D., 1917–, 1
Simon, Charlie May, 1897–, 1
Sims, Marian McCamy, 1899–, 1
Skelsey, Alice F., fl. 1970s, 2
Skinner, Cornelia Otis, 1901–1979, 1,2
Slaughter, Linda, 1843–, 2
Smiley, Sarah Frances, 1830–, 1
Smith, Anita, 1922–, 1
Smith, Emily Adella, fl. 1880s, 1
Smith, Fanny I. Burge, fl. 1870s, 1
Smith, Hannah, d. 1939, 1
Smith, Julia, 1911–, 1,2
Smith, Julia Holmes, 1839–, 1
Smith, Lillian Eugenia, 1897–1966, 1,2

Smith, Mabell Shippie Clarke, 1864–1942, 1
Smith, Margaret Bayard Harrison, 1778–1844, 1,2
Smith, Mary Agnes Easby, 1855–, 1
Smith, Mary Stuart, 1834–, 1
Smith, Mrs. J. Henry, fl. 1860s, 1
Smith, Ruth Lyman, 1872–1926, 1
Snyder, Alice Dorothea, 1887–1943, 1,2
Snyder, Grace McCance, 1783–, 1
Sochen, June, fl. 1970s, 2
Sorensen, Virginia, 1912–, 1
Sosenko, Anna, 1910–, 1
Souder, Emily Bliss, fl. 1860s, 1
Soule, Caroline Augusta White, 1824–1903, 1,2
Spafford, Belle Smith, 1895–1982, 2
Speare, Dorothy, 1
Speare, Elizabeth George, 1908–, 1
Spencer, Cornelia Phillips, 1825–1908, 2
Spencer, Fleta Jan Brown, 1883–1938, 1
Spencer, Lilian White, 1873–1953, 1
Spiegel, Clara Gatzert, 1
Springer, Rebecca Ruter, 1832–1904, 1
St. John, Cynthia Morgan, 1852–1919, 1
Steele, Ann, fl. 1840s, 1
Stehling, Wendy, 2
Stellman, Jeanne M., fl. 1970s, 2
Stephens, Kate, 1853–1938, 2
Stephenson, Geneva, 1
Stern, Elizabeth Gertrude Levin, 1890–1954, 1,2
Stevens, Alice J., 1860–, 1
Stevens, Augusta de Grasse, 1865–1894, 1
Stevenson, Elisabeth, 1919–, 1
Stevenson, Sarah Ann Hackett, 1841–1909, 1,2
Stewart, Anna Bird, 1
Stockton, Louise, 1839–1914, 1
Stone, Grace Zaring, 1896–, 1
Stowell, Louise M. R., 1850–, 1
Strahan, Kay Cleaver, 1888–, 1
Strange, Micheal, 1890–1950, 1,2
Strange, Ruth May, 1895–1971, 1,2
Strasberg, Susan Elizabeth, 1938–, 1,2
Strawbridge, Anne West, 1883–1941, 1
Strickland, Lily Teresa, 1887–1958, 1,2

Stuart, Ruth McEnery, 1849–1917, 1,2
Suesse, Dana Nadine, 1911–, 1,2
Summerhayes, Martha, fl. 1870s, 1,2
Sumner, Bertha Cid Ricketts, 1890–, 1
Swados, Elizabeth, 1951–, 2
Sweet, Sophia Miriam, 1855–1912, 1
Swidler, Arlene Anderson, 2
Swiger, Elinor Porter, fl. 1970s, 2
Tafolla, Carmen, 1951–, 2
Talbot, Ellen Bliss, 1867–, 1
Taney, Mary Florence, 1861–, 1
Tarr, Florence, d. 1951, 1
Taylor, Rosemary Drachman, 1899–, 1,2
Tempski, Armine von, 1899–1943, 1
Tharp, Louise Marshall Hall, 1898–, 1
Thomas, Dorothy, fl. 1930s, 1
Thompson, Caroline Wadsworth, 1856–, 1
Thompson, Helen, 2
Thompson, Kay, 1911–, 1,2
Thompson, Mary Wolfe, 1886–, 1
Thorpe, Cleta, 1
Thurston, Ida Treadwell, d. 1918, 1
Tibbles, Suzette "Bright Eyes" La Flesche, 1854–1903, 2
Tomasi, Mari, 1
Tomkins, Juliet Wilbor, 1871–1956, 1
Toomer, Jean, 1894–1967, 2
Tovar, Ines Hernandez, 1947–, 2
Townsend, Virginia Francis, 1830–1914, 1
Tracey, Cateau Stegeman, fl. 1940s, 1
Trask, Kate Nichols, 1853–1922, 2
Tremaine, Marie, 1902–, 1
Trilling, Diana Rubin, 1905–, 2
Trout, Grace Wilbur, d. 1955, 1
Truman, Mary Margaret, 1924–, 1,2
Tuchman, Barbara Mayer Wertheim, 1912–, 1,2
Tufty, Barbara, fl. 1940s, 2
Turner, Eliza L. Sproat Randolf, 1826–1903, 2
Turner, Lida Larrimore, 1897–, 1
Turner, Nancy Byrd, 1880–, 1
Turpin, Edna Henry Lee, 1867–1952, 1
Tuthill, Cornelia, 1820–1870, 1
Tuthill, Louisa Caroline Huggins, 1798–1879, 1,2
Tuttle, Florence Onertin, 1869–, 1
Twomey, Kathleen, 1914–, 1

Ulmer, Edith Ann, fl. 1930s, 1
Underwood, Edna Worthley, 1873–, 1
Vail, Stella Boothe, fl. 1910s, 1
Van Rennsselaer, Mariana Alley Griswold, 1851–1934, 2
Van Sciver, Esther, 1907–, 1
Van Vorst, Marie Louise, 1867–1936, 1,2
Vanamee, Grace Davis, 1876–1946, 1
Vance, Marguerite, 1889–1965, 1
Vaupel, Ouise, fl. 1930s, 1
Venable, Mary Elizabeth, d. 1926, 1
Victor, Metta Victoria Fuller, 1831–1886, 1,2
Vining, Elizabeth Janet Gray, 1902–, 1
Von Hesse, Elizabeth F., fl. 1930s, 1
Von Klenner, Katherine E., fl. 1930s, 1
Von Tempski, Armina, 1899–1943, 2
Walden, Amelia Elizabeth, 1909–, 1
Walker, Mildred, 1905–, 1
Wallace, Mary Ella, 1855–1938, 1
Wallace, Mildred White, 1839–, 1
Wallace, Susan Arnold, 1830–1907, 1
Wallis, Mary D., fl. 1870s, 1
Waln, Nora, 1895–, 1
Walsh, Honor, fl. 1910s, 1
Wambuagh, Sarah, 1882–1955, 1,2
Warner, Anne Richmond, 1869–1913, 1
Washington, Margaret Murray, 1865–1925, 1
Watkins, Shirley, 1897–, 1
Watson, Virginia Cruse, fl. 1930s, 1
Waugh, Dorothy, fl. 1930s, 1
Wayman, Agnes R., fl. 1930s, 1
Webster, Alice Jean, 1876–1916, 1
Webster, Jean, 1876–1916, 2
Webster, Mary C., fl. 1870s, 1
Weeks-Shaw, Clara, fl. 1800s, 1
Weiman, Rita, 1889–1954, 1
Wells, Bernice Young Mitchell, 1
Werner, Kay, 1918–, 1
Werner, Sue, 1918–, 1
West, Maria A., fl. 1870s, 1
Wharton, Anne Hollingsworth, 1845–1928, 1
Wheaton, Elizabeth Lee, 1902–, 1
Wheelock, Julia Susan, fl. 1860s, 1
Whipple, Maurine, 1906–, 1
White, Barbara Erlich, fl. 1970s, 2
White, Helen Constance, 1896–, 1

White, Nelia Gardner, 1894–1957, 1
White, Olive Bernardine, 1899–, 1
Whiting, (Emily) Lilian, 1847–1942, 1,2
Whitney, Joan, 1914–, 1
Whitson, Beth Slater, 1879–1930, 1,2
Wiggin, Kate Douglas Smith, 1856–1923, 1,2
Williams, Blanche Colton, 1879–1944, 1
Williams, Colleen, 1
Williams, Mary Ann Barnes, 1
Williams, Sherley, fl. 1970s, 2
Willis, Pauline, 1870–, 1
Wilson, Dorothy Clarke, 1904–, 1
Winchester, Alice, 1907–, 1
Winn, Edith L., d. 1933, 1
Winnemucca, Sarah, 1844–1891, 2
Winslow, Anne Goodwin, 1875–, 1
Winslow, Helen Maria, 1851–1938, 1
Winslow, Ola Elizabeth, 1855–1977, 2
Winslow, Thyra Samter, 1893–1961, 1,2
Winter, Alice Vivian Ames, 1865–1944, 2
Wise, Jessie Moore, 1883–1949, 1
Wolff, Maritta M., 1918–, 1
Wollstein, Rose R., fl. 1940s, 1
Wood, Ethel Pope, fl. 1930s, 1
Wood, Frances Gilchrist, 1859–, 1
Woodrow, Nancy Mann Waddel, 1866–1935, 2
Woods, Bertha Gerneaux Davis, 1873–1952, 1
Woods, Kate Tannatt, d. 1910, 1
Woods, Katharine Pearson, 1853–1923, 2
Woolsey, Abby Howland, 1828–1893, 1,2
Woolsey, Caroline Caisson, fl. 1860s, 1
Woolsey, Harriet Roosevelt, fl. 1860s, 1
Woolsey, Jane Stuart, fl. 1860s, 1
Woolsey, Maryhale, 1899–, 1
Woolson, Abba Louisa Goold, 1838–1921, 1,2
Wooster, Lizzie E., 1870–, 1
Worden, Helen, 1896–, 1
Workman, Fanny Bullock, 1859–1925, 1,2
Wright, Anna Maria Louisa Perrott Rose, 1890–, 1

Wright, Helen, 1914–, 1
Wyatt, Edith Franklin, 1873–, 1
Wynne, Madeline Yale, 1847–, 1
Young, Ann Eliza Webb, 1844–1908,
    1,2
Young, Rose Emmet, 1869–1941, 1
Yu, Connie Young, 1941–, 2
Authors, Argentine
Mitre, Delfina Vedia de, 1821–1882, 1
Authors, Australian
Cato, Nancy, 1917–, 1
Chisholm, Caroline Jones, 1810–
    1877, 1
Cottrell, Ida Dorothy Wilkinson,
    1902–1957, 1
Drake-Brockman, Henrietta, 1901–, 1
Durack, Mary, 1913–, 1
Ercole, Velia, fl. 1930s, 1
Franklin, Jane Griffin, 1792–1875, 1
Glanville-Hicks, Peggy, 1912–, 2
Harrower, Elizabeth, 1928–, 1
Hill, Ernestine Hemmings, fl. 1930s,
    1
James, Winifred Lewellin, 1876–
    1941, 1
Mitchell, Mary, 1892–, 1
Morris, Myra, fl. 1930s, 1
Stewart, Dorothy M., 1891–1954, 1
Tennant, Kylie, 1912–, 1
Authors, Austrian
Dombrowski zu Papros und Krus.,
    Kathe Schonberger
    von(K.O.S.,pseud, 1
Gluck, Barbara Elisabeth, 1812–
    1894, 1
Kulka, Leopoldine, 1872–1920, 1
Selinko, Annemarie, 1914–, 1
Studer, Carmen, fl. 1940s, 1
Tonaillon, Christiane, 1878–1928, 1
Unschuld, Marie von, fl. 1900s, 1
Weil, Lisl, 1910–, 1
Authors, Bohemian
Goldsmith, Sophia, 1847–, 1
Authors, Brazilian
Nizia Floresta, 1810–1855, 1
Authors, Byzantine
Anna Comnena, 1083–1148, 1,2
Authors, Canadian
Andrews, Fannie Fern Phillips, 1867–
    1950, 2
Beaton, Maude Hill, fl. 1940s, 1
Beattie, Jessie Louise, 1896–, 1
Branscombe, Gena, 1881–1977, 1,2
Burton, Jean, 1

Chalmers, Audrey, 1893–1915, 1
Clark, Amy Ashmore, 1924–, 1
Conan, Laure, 1845–1924, 1
Cotes, Sarah Jeannette, 1862–, 1
Davies, Blodwen, 1897–, 1
De Sherbinin, Betty, 1917–, 1
Dumbrille, Dorothy, 1898–, 1
Dunham, (Bertha) Mabel, 1881–, 1
Eastwood, Alice, 1859–1953, 1,2
Ellis, Mina A., fl. 1900s, 1
Firestone, Shulamita, fl. 1970s, 2
Fleming, May Agnes, 1840–1880, 1
Foley, Pearl, 1
Fraser, Anne Ermatinger, d. 1930, 1
Grayson, Ethel Vaughan Kirk, 1
Greene, Eleanore D., fl. 1930s, 1
Hamm, Margherita Arlina, 1867–
    1907, 2
Howard, Kathleen, fl. 1900s, 1
James, Belle Robinson, 1868–1935, 1
Jamieson, Nina Moore, 1885–1832, 1
Kelly, Judith, 1908–1957, 1
Kimber, Diana Clifford, d. 1928, 1
King, Violet, fl. 1940s, 1
Laut, Agnes Christina, 1871–1936, 1
Livesay, Florence Hamilton Randal,
    m. 1908, 1
Lowe, Ruth, 1914–, 1
Macbeth, Madge Hamilton Lyons,
    1878–1965, 1
Mallette, Gertrude Ethel, 1887–, 1
McClung, Nellie Mooney, 1874–
    1951, 1
McWilliams, Margaret, 1875–1952, 1
Monk, Maria, 1816–1849, 1,2
Mowat, Angus, 1892–, 1
Murphy, Emily, 1868–1933, 1,2
Pearce, Theodocia, 1894–1926, 1
Pickthall, Marjorie Lowry Christie,
    1883–1922, 1
Reeve, Winnifred Eaton Babcock,
    1879–, 1
Salverson, Laura Goodman, 1890–, 1
Saunders, Margaret Marshall, 1861–
    1947, 1
Saunders, Marshall, 1861–1947, 1
Sheard, Virginia Stanton, d. 1943, 1
Sime, Jesse Georgina, 1880–, 1
Strickland, Susanna, 1802–1899, 1
Williams, Flos Jewell, 1892–, 1
Authors, Chilean
Iris, 1920–, 2
Authors, Chinese
Sung, Betty Lee, fl. 1940s, 2

Authors, Colombian
    Francisco Josefa de la Concep., 1671–
        1742, 1
    Gomez, Josefa Acevedole, 1803–
        1861, 1
    Santa Maria, Manuela Sanz de,
        1770–, 1
Authors, Cuban
    Avellaneda y Arteaga, Gertrudis
        Gomez, 1814–1873, 1
    Gonzalez, Luisa, fl. 1960s, 2
Authors, Czechoslovakian
    Saxl, Eva R., 1921–, 1
    Soltesova, Elena Marothy, 1855–, 1
    Svetla, Karolina Rottova, 1830–1899,
        1
    Svobodova, Ruzena Capova, fl.
        1910s, 1
    Varsova, Terezia, 1857–1942, 1
Authors, Danish
    Dinesen, Isak, pseud., 1885–1962, 1,2
    Fibiger, Mathilde, 1830–1871, 1
    Heiberg, Johanne Louise Patges,
        1812–1890, 1
    Ulfeld, Lenora Christine, 1631–1698,
        1
Authors, Dutch
    Bekker, Elizabeth (Betje), 1738–
        1804, 1
    De Jong, Dola, 1911–, 1
    Hollander, Xaviera, 1943–, 2
    Questier, Catherine, fl. 1650s, 1
    Reiss, Johana de Leeuw, 1932–, 2
    Toussaint, Anna Luisa Geertruida,
        1812–1886, 1
Authors, Egyptian
    Al-Taymuriyya, Ayesha, 1840–1902,
        1
    Nasif, Melek Hifni, 1886–1918, 1
Authors, English
    Acton, Eliza, 1799–1859, 1
    Adams, Bertha Leigh Grundy, d.
        1912, 1
    Alleine, Theodosia, fl. 1662, 1
    Arnold, Polly, 1906–, 1
    Ashton, Elizabeth, fl. 1700s, 1
    Astell, Mary, 1666–1731, 1,2
    Aubin, Penelope, fl. 1720s, 1
    Austin, Sarah, 1793–1867, 1
    Baird, Irene, fl. 1919, 1
    Baker, Mary, 1897–, 1
    Barrington, Emilie Isabel, 1842–
        1933, 1
    Beeton, Isabella Mary Mayson, 1836–
        1865, 1,2

Bell, Florence Evelyn Eleanor, Dame,
    1851–1930, 1
Bell, Gertrude Margaret Lowthian,
    1868–1926, 1,2
Berners, Dame Juliana, 1388–, 1
Berry, Mary, 1763–1852, 1,2
Bethan-Edwards, Matilda Barbara,
    1836–1919, 1
Bloomfield, Georgiana, Lady, 1822–
    1905, 1
Bonhote, Elizabeth, 1744–1818, 1
Bonner, Hypatia Bradlaugh, 1858–, 1
Borden, Mary, 1886–, 1
Brooke, Frances Moore, 1724–1789,
    1,2
Broster, Dorothy Kathleen, 1877–
    1950, 1
Buckrose, J. E., d. 1931, 1
Burton, Isabel Arundel, Lady, 1831–
    1896, 1
Cadell, (Violet) Elizabeth, 1903–, 1
Callcott, Maria, Lady, 1
Cameron, Mrs. Lovett, fl. 1890s, 1
Campbell, Margaret, fl. 1930s, 1
Cartwright, Julia, d. 1924, 1
Cary, Mary Rande, fl. 1650s, 1
Champion de Crespigny, Rose, m.
    1878, 1
Charques, Dorothy Taylor, 1899–, 1
Chetwynd, Mrs. Henry, 1858–, 1
Clifford, Anne, Countess of Dorset,
    1590–1676, 1,2
Cockburn, Catharine Trotter, 1679–
    1749, 1
Coghill, Mrs. Henry, fl. 1800s, 1
Cornwallis, Caroline Frances, 1786–
    1858, 1
Cotton, Anne, 2
Courtney, Janet Hogarth, fl. 1880s, 1
Crommelin, May, fl. 1890s, 1
Darby, Abiah Maude Sinclair, fl.
    1740s, 1
Darby, Deborah, fl. 1790s, 1
Davies, Eleanor Audley, 1603–1652, 1
De La Pasture, Elizabeth Lydia Rosa-
    belle Bonham, 1866–, 1
Dickens, Mary, fl. 1890s, 1
Duff-Gordon, Lucie, 1821–1869, 1
Duke, Winifred, fl. 1920s, 1
Edginton, May, 1
Elstob, Elizabeth, 1683–1765, 1,2
Erskine, Mrs. Steuart, fl. 1920s, 1
Eugenia, fl. 1699, 1
Everett-Green, Evelyn, 1856–1932, 1

Fanshawe, Anne Harrison, 1625–1680, 1

Forbes, (Joan) Rosita, 1893–, 1

Franklin, Eleanor Ann Porden, 1795–1825, 1

Gatty, Margaret Scott "Aunt Judy", 1807–1873, 2

Gaunt, Mary, fl. 1930s, 1

Giberne, Agnes, 1845–, 1

Graham, Maria, 1785–1843, 2

Graham, Winifred, 1873–1950, 1

Grant, Sybil, 1879–, 1

Gray, Nicolette Mary Binyon, gr. 1932, 1

Green, Evelyn Everett, 1856–1932, 2

Grier, Mary Lynda Dorothy, fl. 1940s, 1

Hall, Dawn Langley, 1929–, 2

Hamilton, Cicely, 1872–1952, 1

Hamilton, Mary Agnes Adamson, 1883–, 1

Hardy, Duffus, fl. 1870s, 1

Hardy, Isa Duffus, fl. 1890s, 1

Herbert, Elizabeth A'Court, 1822–1911, 1

Hill, Octavia, 1836–1912, 1,2

Houstoun, Mrs., fl. 1890s, 1

Howitt, Mary Botham, 1799–1888, 1,2

Hull, Eleanor H., 1860–, 1

Hutchinson, Lucy Apsley, 1620–1675, 1,2

Iremonger, Lucille Parks, gr. 1937, 1

Jenkins, Elizabeth, 1907–, 1

Jones, Emily Beatrix Coursolles, 1893–, 1

Jones, Mary, fl. 1700s, 1

Jourdaine, Clare Melicent, 1875–1925, 1

Kemble, Adelaide, 1814–1879, 1

Kempe, Margery, 1373–1440, 1,2

Kenealy, Arabella, fl. 1890s, 1

Kennard, Mrs. Edward, fl. 1890s, 1

Kernahan, Mrs. Coulson, 1858–1943, 1

Kingsley, Mary Henrietta, 1862–1900, 1,2

Kingston, Gertrude, fl. 1900s, 1

Lane, Margaret, 1907–, 1

Latimer, Mary Elizabeth Wormeley, 1822–1904, 1,2

Lawrence, Margery, 1880–, 1

Le Blonde, Elizabeth Frances, d. 1934, 1

Le Gallienne, Eva, 1899–, 1,2

Levett, Ada Elizabeth, gr. 1910, 1

Lind-af-Haageby, Emelie Augusta Louise, 1878–, 1

Little, Mrs. Archibald, fl. 1800s, 1

Loudon, Jane Webb, 1807–1858, 1

Lyster, Annette, fl. 1800s, 1

MacQuoid, Katharine Sarah, 1824–1917, 1

Magnus, Lady, fl. 1800s, 1

Makin, Bathsua, 1608–1675, 1,2

Mander, Rosalie Glynn Grylls, gr. 1927, 1

Mangnall, Richmal, 1769–1820, 1

Markham, Elizabeth, 1780–1837, 1

Mary, Lady, fl. 1720s, 1

Masham, Damaris Cudworth, 1658–1708, 1

Mathers, Helen, fl. 1890s, 1

McMinnies, Mary Jackson, 1920–, 1

Middlemass, Jean, 1850–, 1

Milinaire, Caterine, fl. 1970s, 2

Mill, Harriet Hardy Taylor, 1807–1858, 1

Mitton, Geraldine Edith, fl. 1900s, 1

Moir, Phyllis, fl. 1930s, 1

Montague, Elizabeth Robinson, 1720–1800, 1,2

Mordaunt, Elinor, 1877–1942, 1

Muilman, Teresia Constantia, fl. 1750s, 1

Muir, Florence Roma, 1891–1930, 1

Murray, Rosalind, 1890–, 1

Nepean, Edith, fl. 1910s, 1

Nevill, Dorothy, 1826–1913, 1

Norton, Frances Freke, Lady, 1640–1731, 1

Nugent, Maria, Lady, 1771–1834, 1

Olivia, Edith, 1879–1948, 1

Oman, Carola Mary Anima, 1897–, 1

Oxford and Asquith, Margo Tennant, 1864–1945, 1

Pakenham, Antonia, gr. 1950, 1

Pakington, Dorothy Coventry, d. 1679, 1

Pardo, Julia, 1806–1862, 1

Porter, Joyce, 1924–, 2

Raverst, Gwen Darwin, 1885–1957, 1,2

Remsen, Alice, 1896–, 1

Robinson, Mary Darby "Perdita", 1758–1800, 1,2

Rockley, Alicia-Margaret Amherst, 1941–, 1

Roydne, Agnes Maude, 1876–1956, 1
Russell, Rachel Wriothesley, Lady, 1636–1728, 1,2
Savery, Constance Winnifred, 1897–, 1
Savi, Ethel Winifred, 1865–, 1
Scott, Catherine Amy Dawson, 1863–1934, 1
Sewell, Anna, 1820–1878, 1
Sewell, Mary, 1797–1884, 1
Sharp, Evelyn, 1869–1955, 1
Sheridan, Clare Consuelo Frewen, 1885–, 1
Sherwood, Mary Martha, 1775–1851, 1
Smedley, Constance, 1881–1941, 1
Spry, Constance, 1886–1960, 1,2
Stanhope, Hester Lucy, Lady, 1776–1839, 1,2
Steen, Marguerite, 1894–1975, 1,2
Stirling, Anna Marie Wilhelmina Pickering, fl. 1800s, 1
Stockes, Mary D., fl. 1910s, 1
Stopes, Charlotte Carmichael, 1841–1929, 1
Struther, Jan, pseud., 1901–1953, 1
Swan, Annie S., fl. 1880s, 1
Trimmer, Sarah Kirby, 1741–1810, 1
Trotter, Catherine, 1679–1749, 1,2
Tweedie, Ethel Brilliana, d. 1940, 1
Waddell, Helen, 1889–, 1
Wakefield, Priscilla, 1751–1832, 1
Weston, Christine Goutiere, 1904–, 1
Whale, Winifred Stephens, fl. 1910s, 1
Williams, (Helen) Maria, 1762–1827, 1
Wilson, Harriette, 1789–1846, 1,2
Wright, Elizabeth M., 1863–, 1
Zimmern, Helen, 1846–1934, 1
Authors, Finnish
Canth, Minna Ilrika Wilhelmina Johansson, 1844–1897, 1
Gripenberg, Alexandra, 1856–1911, 1
Runeberg, Fredrika, 1807–1879, 1
Authors, French
Arman de Caillavet, Leontine Charlotte Lippman, 1844–1910, 1
Arvede, Barine, pseud., 1840–1908, 1
Audougard, Olympe, 1830–1890, 1
Aulnoy, Marie Catherine Jumelle de Berneville, Countess D', 1650–1705, 1
Broglie, Albertine Ida Gustavine de Stael, 1797–1838, 1

Costa (Coste), Blanche Marie de, fl. 1566, 2
Crequy, Renee Caroline, 1714–1803, 1
Curie, Eve, 1904–, 1,2
David-Neal, Alexandra, 1868–1969, 2
Delaru-Mardrus, Lucie, 1880–1945, 2
Epinay, Louise Florence Petronille de la Live d, 1726–1783, 1
Gay, Marie Francoise Sophie, 1776–1852, 1
Gournay, Marie le Jars de, 1565–1645, 1,2
Grammont, Elizabeth, 1641–1708, 1
Guerin, Eugenie de, 1805–1848, 1
Guyon, Jean Marie de la Motte-Guyon Bouvier, 1648–1717, 1
Gyp, 1850–1932, 1
Lambert, Marquise de, 1647–1733, 1
Lespinasse, Julie Jeanne Eleonore de, 1732–1776, 1
Montesson, Charlotte Jeane Beraud de la Haye de Riou, Marchioness of, 1737–1805, 1
Montpensier, Anne Marie Louise d'Orleans, Duchesse de, 1627–1693, 1,2
Motteville, Dame Langlois de Francoise Bertaut, 1615–1689, 1
Remusat, Claire Elisabeth, 1780–1821, 1
Simone, Benda, Madame, 1877–1967, 2
Tencin, Claudine Alexandrine Guerin de, 1685–1749, 1
Weil, Simone, 1909–1943, 1,2
Authors, German
Anneke, Mathilde Franziska Giesler, 1817–1884, 2
Dransfield, Hedwig, 1871–1925, 1
Francois, Luise von, 1817–1893, 1
Hahn-Hahn, Ida, 1805–1830, 1
Hamilton, Edith, 1867–1963, 1,2
Hildeck, Leo, pseud., fl. 1800s, 1
Hoechstetter, Sophie, fl. 1800s, 1
Huch, Ricarda, 1864–1947, 1,2
John, Eugenie (E. Marlett), 1
Kahlenberg, Hans von, pseud., fl. 1800s, 1
Kurz, Isolde, 1853–, 1
Lipsius, Marie, 1
Lita (Litte) of Regensburg, fl. 1544, 2
Mann, Erika, 1905–1969, 1,2
Marriot, Emil, pseud., fl. 1900s, 1

Authors, Roman
  D'Aragona, Tullia, 1510–1556, 1,2
Authors, Romanian
  Bibesco, Marie, 2
  D'Istria, Dora, pseud., 1829–1888, 1
  Hasdew, Julia, 1869–1888, 1
Authors, Russian
  Alliluyeva, Svetlana Stalina, 1926–, 1
  Antin, Mary, 1881–1949, 1,2
  Dashkova (Dashkoff), Ekaterina Ro-
    manova, 1743–1810, 1,2
  Hakimova, Professor, fl. 1970s, 2
  Kovalevski, Sonya, 1850–1891, 1,2
  Luban, Francia, 1914–, 1
  Novikoff, Olga Kireev (O.K. pseud.),
    1840–1925, 1
  Papashvily, Helen Waite, 1906–, 1
  Radziwill, Catherine, 1
  Scott, Miriam Finn, 1882–1944, 1
  Seifullina, Lidiia V., 1889–1954, 1
  White, Rose Rubin, fl. 1930s, 1
Authors, Scottish
  Bannerman, Helen, 1863–1946, 1,2
  Curry, Peggy Simson, 1912–, 1
  Graham, Clementina Stirling, 1782–
    1877, 1
  Grant, Anne McVickar, 1755–1838,
    1,2
  Haldane, Elizabeth Sanderson, 1862–
    1937, 1
  Halkett, Anne Murray, Lady, 1622–
    1699, 1,2
  Hamilton, Elizabeth, 1758–1816, 1
  Jay, Harriet, 1863–1932, 1
  Lorimer, Norma Octavia, fl. 1900s, 1
  MacKenzie, Agnes Mure, 1891–, 1
  Stuart, Louisa, 1757–1851, 1
  Walker, Susan Hunter, m. 1904, 1
Authors, South African
  Faulkner, Mary, 1903–1973, 2
  Joseph, Helen, 1906–, 2
Authors, Spanish
  Caballaro, Fernan Bohl von Faber,
    pseud., 1796–1877, 1
  Medina-Sidonia, Duchess of, 1936–, 2
  Palencia, Isabel de, 1881–, 1
  Pineda, Mariana, 1804–1831, 1
  Sabuco, Oliva Barrera, 1562–, 2
Authors, Swedish
  Beskow, Elsa Maartman, 1874–, 1
  Key, Ellen Karoline Sofia, 1849–
    1926, 1
  Kock, Karin, 1891–, 1
  Morris, Edita, 1902–, 1

Authors, Swiss
  Marcet, Jane, 1769–1858, 1,2
  Moos, Hortensia Gugelberg von,
    1659–1715, 1
  Spyri, Johanna Heusser, 1827–1901,
    1,2
  Syrkin, Marie, 1900–, 1
Authors, Tasmanian
  Meredith, Louisa Anne Twamly,
    1812–1895, 1
Authors, Turkish
  Adivar, Halide Edib, 1883–1964, 2
Authors, Welsh
  Piozzi, Hester Lynch Thrale Salus-
    bury, 1741–1821, 1,2
Authors—Children's books
  Abbott, Eleanor Hallowell, 1872–
    1958, 1,2
  Adams, Harriet, 1893–1982, 2
  Alcott, Louisa May, 1832–1888, 1,2
  Andrews, Jane, 1833–1887, 1,2
  Anglund, Joan Walsh, 1926–, 2
  Applegarth, Margaret Tyson, 1886–,
    1
  Aulaire, Ingri D'Mortenson, 1904–,
    1,2
  Barto, Agnia, 1906–1981, 2
  Bawden, Nina, 1925–, 2
  Beskow, Elsa Maartman, 1874–, 1
  Bianco, Margery Williams, 1881–
    1944, 2
  Blume, Judy Sussman, 1938–, 2
  Blyton, Enid Mary, 1897–1968, 2
  Brazil, Angela, 1868–1947, 2
  Brink, Carol Ryrie, 1895–1981, 1,2
  Brown, Abbie Farwell, 1871–1927, 2
  Brown, Frances, 1816–1879, 2
  Brown, Margaret Wise, 1910–1952, 2
  Brown, Margery, 1920–, 2
  Burnett, Frances Eliza Hodgson,
    1849–1924, 1,2
  Byars, Betsy, 1928–, 2
  Carlson, Natalie Savage, 1906–, 2
  Charlesworth, Maria Louisa, 1819–
    1880, 1,2
  Clarke, Rebecca Sophia "Sophie
    May", 1833–1906, 1
  Coatesworth, Elizabeth Jane, 1893–,
    1,2
  Conkling, Hilda, 1910–, 1,2
  Corbett, Elizabeth Francis, 1887–
    1981, 1,2
  De Trevino, Elizabeth Borton,
    1904–, 2

DeAngeli, Marguerite, 1889–, 1,2
Dodge, Mary Elizabeth Mapes, 1831–1905, 1,2
Doudney, Sarah, 1843–, 2
Douglas, Amanda Minnie, 1831–1916, 1,2
Estes, Eleanor Ruth Rosenfeld, 1906–, 1,2
Ets, Marie Hall, 1895–, 1,2
Ewing, Juliana Horatio Orr Gatty, 1841–1885, 1,2
Farjeon, Eleanor, 1881–1965, 1,2
Ferris, Helen Josephine, 1890–1909, 1,2
Field, Rachel Lyman, 1894–1942, 1,2
Fox, Paula, fl. 1970s, 2
France, Georgina Cave, 1868–1934, 2
Gag, Wanda Hazel, 1893–1946, 1,2
Giovanni, Nikki, 1943–, 2
Gordon, Dorothy Lerner, 1889–1970, 1
Gray, Elizabeth Janet, 1902–, 1,2
Greenaway, Kate (Catherine), 1846–1901, 1,2
Hamilton, Cicely Viets Dakin, 1837–1909, 2
Henry, Marguerite, 1902–, 1,2
Ishimova, Alexandra, fl. 1820s, 2
Johnston, Annie Fellows, 1863–1931, 2
Keary, Annie, 1825–1879, 1,2
Kumin, Maxine Winokur, 1925–, 2
Kunhardt, Dorothy, 1901–1979, 2
Lane, Rose Wilder, 1867–1957, 1
Lenski, Lois, 1893–1974, 1,2
Lively, Penelope, 1933–, 2
Lobel, Anita Kempler, 1934–, 2
Luling, Elizabeth, 1930–, 2
Martineau, Harriet, 1802–1876, 1,2
May, Sophie, pseud., 1833–1906, 2
Meadowcraft, Enid LaMonte, 1898–1966, 1,2
Meigs, Cornelia, 1884–1973, 2
Miller, Harriet Mann, 1831–1918, 1,2
Molesworth, Mary Louise Stewart, 1839–1921, 1,2
Mozley, Harriett, 1803–1852, 2
Nesbit, Edith, 1858–1924, 1,2
Opie, Iona, 2
Perkins, Lucy Fitch, 1865–1937, 2
Porter, Eleanor Hodgman, 1868–1920, 1,2
Potter, Helen Beatrix, 1866–1943, 1,2
Rice, Alice Caldwell Hegan, 1870–1942, 1,2

Richards, Laura Elizabeth Howe Ward, 1850–1943, 1,2
Sawyer, Ruth, 1880–1970, 2
Segal, Lore, 2
Segur, Sophie Rostopchine, Comtesse de, 1799–1874, 2
Seredy, Kate, 1896–1975, 1,2
Singmaster, Elsie, 1879–1958, 1,2
Sneve, Virginia Driving Hawk, 1933–, 2
Spyri, Johanna Heusser, 1827–1901, 1,2
Stolz, Mary, 1920–, 1,2
Stretton, Hesba, pseud., 1832–1911, 1,2
Sutcliffe, Rosemary, 1920–, 2
Tappan, Eva March, 1854–1950, 2
Tastu, Amable, Madame, 1798–1885, 2
Thorpe, Rose Almora Hartwick, 1850–1939, 1,2
Viorst, Judith, 2
Warner, Susan Bogert, 1819–1885, 1,2
Wells, Carolyn, 1862–1942, 1,2
White, Eliza Orne, 1856–1947, 2
Wilder, Laura Ingalls, 1867–1957, 1,2
Wojciechowska, Maia Teresa, 1927–, 2
Woolsey, Sarah Chauncey, 1835–1905, 1,2
Yates, Elizabeth, 1905–, 1,2
Yonge, Charlotte Mary, 1823–1901, 1,2

Authors—Fairy tales
Deharme, Lise, 1902–, 1,2
Authors—Short stories
Adler, Renata, 1938–, 2
Andrews, Jane, 1833–1887, 1,2
Andrews, Mary Raymond Shipman, 1860–1936, 1,2
Atwood, Margaret Eleanor Killian, 1939–, 2
Banning, Margaret Culkin, 1891–1982, 1,2
Barker, A. L., 1918–, 2
Benson, Sally Smith, 1900–1972, 1,2
Birstein, Ann, fl. 1970s, 2
Bowles, Jane Sydney, 1917–1973, 2
Boyle, Kay, 1902–, 1,2
Cather, Willa Sibert, 1873–1947, 1,2
Chapone, Hester Mulso, 1727–1801, 1,2
Chopin, Kate O'Flaherty, 1851–1904, 2
Cooke, Rose Terry, 1827–1892, 1,2

Cullinan, Elizabeth, fl. 1950s, 2
D'Arcy, Ella, 1851–1939, 2
Deledda, Grazia, 1875–1936, 1,2
Du Jardin, Rosamond Neal, 1902–
1963, 1,2
Elsner, Gisela, 1937–, 2
Engel, Marian, fl. 1970s, 2
Ferber, Edna, 1887–1968, 1,2
Fleisser, Marieleuse, 1901–1974, 2
Forbes, Kathryn, pseud., 1909–1966,
1,2
Frankau, Pamela, 1907–1967, 1,2
Freeman, Mary Eleanor Wilkins,
1852–1930, 1,2
Gale, Zona, 1874–1938, 1,2
Genlis, Stephanie Felicite de Crest de
Saint-Aubin, Comtesse de, 1746–
1830, 1,2
Gerould, Katherine Elizabeth Fuller-
ton, 1879–1944, 1,2
Gibbons, Stella Dorothea, 1902–, 2
Gilliatt, Penelope Ann Douglas,
1924–, 2
Godden, Rumer, pseud., 1907–, 1,2
Goquiiolay-Arellano, Remidios,
1911–, 2
Gordimer, Nadine, 1923–, 1,2
Gordon, Caroline, 1895–1981, 1,2
Goudge, Elizabeth, 1900–1984, 1,2
Grau, Shirley Ann, 1929–, 1,2
Hall, Sharlot Mabridth, 1870–1943,
1,2
Hawker, Mary Elizabeth, 1848–
1908, 2
Hazzard, Shirley, 1931–, 2
Highsmith, Patricia, 1921–, 2
Hill, Susan, 1942–, 2
Hunt, Violet, 1866–1942, 1,2
Jewett, Sarah Orne, 1849–1909, 1,2
Jhabvala, Ruth Prawer, 1927–, 2
Kaschnitz, Marie Luise, 1901–1974, 2
Kavan, Anna (Helen Edmonds),
1901–1968, 2
Konig, Barbara, 1925–, 2
Konopnicka, Maria Wasilowska,
1842–1910, 1,2
Lagerlof, Selma Ottiniana Louisa,
1858–1940, 1,2
Lavin, Mary, 1912–, 2
Lessing, Doris May, 1919–, 1,2
Manley, Mary de la Riviere, 1663–
1724, 1,2
Mannin, Ethel Edith, 1900–1978, 1,2
Mansfield, Katherine, pseud., 1888–
1923, 1,2

Matsubara, Hisako, fl. 1970s, 2
McCullers, (Lula) Carson Smith,
1917–1967, 1,2
Meigs, Cornelia, 1884–1973, 2
Meylan, Elisabeth, 1937–, 2
Michaelis, Karin, 1872–1950, 1,2
Millin, Sarah Gertrude Liebson,
1889–1968, 1,2
Mowatt, Anna Cora Ogden, 1819–
1870, 1,2
Murfee, Mary Noailles, 1850–1922, 1
Murfree, Mary Noailles, 1850–1922, 2
O'Brien, Edna, 1930–, 2
O'Connor, Mary Flannery, 1925–
1964, 1,2
Oates, Joyce Carol, 1938–, 2
Olsen, Tillie, 1913–, 2
Parker, Dorothy Rothschild, 1893–
1967, 1,2
Parsons, Alice Beal, 1886–1962, 1,2
Patton, Frances Gray, 1906–, 1,2
Porter, Katherine Anne, 1890–1980,
1,2
Potts, Jean, 1910–, 2
Rhys, Jean, 1894–1979, 2
Richards, Laura Elizabeth Howe
Ward, 1850–1943, 1,2
Ritchie, Anna Cora O. Mowatt,
1819–1870, 1
Roberts, Kate, 1891–, 2
Ross, Lillian, 1926–, 2
Seghers, Anna, pseud., 1900–1983,
1,2
Shelley, Mary Wollstonecraft God-
win, 1797–1851, 1,2
Sinclair, Jo, pseud., 1913–, 1,2
Singmaster, Elsie, 1879–1958, 1,2
Slesinger, Tess, 1905–1945, 1,2
Spencer, Elizabeth, 1921–, 1,2
Stafford, Jean, 1915–1979, 1,2
Taylor, Elizabeth Coles, 1912–1975,
1,2
Terry, Rose, 1827–1892, 1
Triolet, Elsa, 1896–1970, 1,2
Warner, Sylvia Townsend, 1893–
1978, 1,2
Welty, Eudora, 1909–, 1,2
West, Dorothy, 1910–, 2
Wharton, Edith Newbold Jones,
1862–1937, 1,2
Wilson, Ethel Davis, 1888–1980, 2
Wohmann, Gabrielle, 1932–, 2
Woolson, Constance Fenimore, 1840–
1894, 1,2

Autograph dealers
  Benjamin, Mary A., 1
Autoharpists
  Carter, June, 1929–, 2
  Carter, Maybelle Addington, 1909–
    1978, 2
  Faye, Rita, 1944–, 2
  MacArthur, Margaret Crowl, 1928–,
    2
Automobile industry
  Pullinger, Dorothee, 2
  Stearns, Mary Beth, d. 1973, 2
Automobile racers
  Fillipis, Maria Theresa de, 2
  Guthrie, Janet, 1937–, 2
  Jennkey, Madame, 2
  Laumaille, Madame, fl. 1890s, 2
  Levitt, Dorothy, fl. 1900s, 2
  Locke-King, Mrs., fl. 1900s, 2
  Lorentz, Baroness de, 2
  Moss, Pat, fl. 1960s, 2
  Mudge, Genevra Delphine, fl. 1890s,
    2
  Muldowney, Shirley "Cha Cha",
    1940–, 2
  Murphy, Paula Mulhauser, fl. 1970s, 2
  O'Neil, Kitty, 1948–, 2
  Petrie, Kay, fl. 1930s, 2
  Ramsay, Alice Huyler, fl. 1900s, 2
  Stewart, Gwenda, fl. 1900s, 2
  Thomas, Mrs. E., fl. 1920s, 2
  Trautmann, Claudine, fl. 1970s, 2
  Wisdom, Ann, fl. 1960s, 2
Avenger
  Josefa, 2
Aviation experts
  Hager, Alice Rogers, 1894–, 1
Aviation instructors
  Hall, Elizabeth, 1
Aviation patrons
  Guest, Amy Phipps, fl. 1920s, 2
  Rex, Peggy, fl. 1920s, 1
  Tusch, Mary E. Hall, 1875–1960, 1
  Wright, Katherine, 1874–1929, 1
Aviators
  See
  Pilots
Avon
  Albee, P.F.E., fl. 1880s, 2
Award winners
  See
  4–H scholarship winners
  Carnegie Medal winners
  Ceres Medal winners

Federal Women's Award winners
Mothers of the year

B

B'Nai B'rith
  Alpert, Miriam, d. 1976, 2
  Perlman, Anita, fl. 1970s, 2
Bach, Johan Sebastien—Mother
  Bach, Elisabeth Laemmerhirt, 1644–
    1694, 2
Bach, Johan Sebastien—Spouse
  Bach, Anna Magdalena Wulken,
    1700–1760, 1
  Bach, Maria Barbara, d. 1720, 1
Bachofen, Johann Jakob—Mother
  Merian, Valeria Bachofen, 1796–
    1856, 1
Backgammon players
  Jacoby, Mary, fl. 1930s, 2
Bacon, Nathaniel—Spouse
  Bacon, Elizabeth Duke, fl. 1650s, 2
Bacteriochemists
  Yermol'yeva, Ziraida Vissarionovna,
    1898–, 1
Bacteriologists
  Bliss, Eleanor Albert, 1899–, 1
  Broadhurst, Jean, 1873–1954, 1
  Dick, Gladys Rowena Henry, 1881–
    1963, 1,2
  Downs, Cora, fl. 1930s, 2
  Evans, Alice Catherine, 1881–1975,
    1,2
  Fleming, Amalia, Lady, 1909–, 2
  Gage, Nina Diadamia, 1883–1948, 1
  Hamilton, Alice, 1869–1970, 1,2
  Hart, Fanchon, fl. 1930s, 1
  Hill, Justina Hamilton, 1893–, 1
  Lancefield, Rebecca Craighill, 1895–
    1981, 2
  McCoy, Elizabeth, 1920–1970, 2
  Metchinkoff, Elie, 1845–1916, 2
  Meyer, Margaret, 1923–, 2
  Pennington, Mary Engle, 1897–1952,
    1,2
  Prigosen, Rosa Elizabeth, fl. 1930s, 1
  Rabinowitch-Kempner, Lydia, 1871–
    1935, 2
  Stone, Hannah Mayer, 1894–1941,
    1,2
  Tunnicliff, Ruth, 1876–1946, 1
  Williams, Anna Wessels, 1863–1954, 2

Badminton players
Devlin, Judy, fl. 1950s, 2
Hashman, Judy Devlin, 1935–, 2
Haubrich, Karen, fl. 1970s, 2
Takagi, Noriko, fl. 1960s, 2
Bagpipe players
Turnbull, Edith, 2
Bainton, Frederick—Spouse
Hardenberg, Anna, 2
Baker, Sir Samuel—Spouse
Baker, Lady Samuel, fl. 1830s, 1
Bakers
Bercovitz, Helen, 2
Dwyer, Karen, fl. 1970s, 2
Haughery, Margaret Gaffney, 1813–
1882, 1,2
Korman, Nadine, fl. 1970s, 2
Rudkin, Margaret Fogarty, 1897–
1967, 1,2
Ballet dancers
Adams, Diana, 1926–, 1
Adelaide, La Petite, fl. 1910s, 1
Allard, Marie, 1742–1802, 1,2
Alonso, Alicia, 1921–, 1,2
Anderson, Ib, 1954–, 2
Andreianova, Elena, 1821–1855, 2
Aroldingen, Karin von, 1941–, 2
Ashley, Merrill, 1950–, 2
Baldine-Kosloff, Alexandra, 2
Baronova, Irina, 1919–, 1
Basquette, Lina, 1907–, 2
Bausch, Pina, 1940–, 2
Beretta, Caterina, 2
Beriosova, Svetlana, 1932–, 1,2
Bettis, Valerie Elizabeth, 1919–1982,
1,2
Bigottini, Emilie, 1784–1858, 2
Bonfanti, Marie, 1847–1921, 1,2
Boris, Ruthanna, 1918–, 1
Bozzacchi, Guiseppina, fl. 1870s, 2
Brae, June, 1918–, 1
Brianza, Carlotta, 1867–, 2
Callaghan, Domini, 1923–, 1
Camargo, Marie Anne de Cupis de,
1710–1770, 1,2
Campanini, Barbara, 1721–1799, 2
Carlson, Carolyn, 2
Caron, Leslie, 1931–, 1,2
Cerito, Fanny, 1821–1899, 1
Cerrito, Fanny, 1817–1909, 1,2
Charrat, Janine, 1924–, 1
Chase, Lucia, 1907–, 1,2
Chauvire, Yvette, 1917–, 1
Chouteau, Yvonne, 1929–, 1

Clayden, Pauline, 1922–, 1
Collins, Janet, 1923–, 2
Crespe, Marie-Madeleine, 1760–
1796, 2
Dale, Margaret, 1922–, 1
Danilova, Alexandra Alicia, 1906–,
1,2
Danilova, Maria, 1793–, 2
De Valois, Ninette, 1898–, 1,2
Duvernay, Pauline, 2
Emarot, Celestine (Marguerite Ade-
laide), 2
Ewing, Lucia Chase, fl. 1930s, 1
Farrell, Suzanne, 1945–, 1,2
Farron, Julia, 1922–, 1
Fedorovitch, Sophie, d. 1953, 1
Ferraris, Amalia, fl. 1850s, 2
Field, Laura, fl. 1930s, 1
Fifield, Elaine, 1931–, 1
Fontaine, Mademoiselle de la, 1655–
1738, 2
Fonteyn, Margot, Dame, 1919–, 1,2
Fracci, Carla, 1936–, 2
Franca, Celia, 1921–, 1,2
Fraser, Moyra, fl. 1930s, 1
Genee, Adeline, 1878–, 1
Gilmour, Sally, 1921–, 1
Gollner, Nana, 1920–, 1
Grahn, Lucile, 1819–1907, 1,2
Gregory, Cynthia, 1946–, 2
Grey, Beryl, 1927–, 1
Grisi, Carlotta, 1819–1899, 1,2
Guimard, Marie-Madeleine, 1743–
1816, 1,2
Haydee, Marcia, 1937–, 2
Hayden, Melissa, 1923–, 1,2
Heinel, Anne (Anna), 1752–1808, 2
Hernandez, Amalia, fl. 1950s, 2
Hightower, Rosella, 1920–, 1
Howard, Andree, 1910–, 1
Inglesby, Mona, 1918–, 1
Istomina, Avdotia, 1789–1848, 2
Jackson, Suzanne, 1944–, 2
Jaffe, Susan, 2
Jamison, Judith, 2
Jeanmaire, Renee Marcelle (Zizi),
1924–, 1,2
Kain, Karen Alexandria, 1951–, 2
Kariyeva, Bernara, 2
Karsavina, Tamara, 1885–1978, 1,2
Kaye, Nora, 1920–1987, 1,2
Kchessinska, Mathilde, 1872–, 1
Kent, Allegra, 1938–, 2
Kholodnaya, Vera, 2

Kirkland, Gelsey, 1952–, 2
Kschessinska, Marhilde, 1871–, 2
Kyasht, Lydia, 1886–, 1
Lafontaine, Mlle, 1665–1738, 1
Le Clercq, Tanaquil, 1929–, 1,2
Lee, Mary Ann, 1823–1899, 1,2
Legnani, Pierina, 1863–1923, 1,2
Linn, Bambi, 1926–, 1
Livry, Emma, d. 1863, 2
Lopkova, Lydia, 1891–, 1
Makarova, Natalia Romanova,
  1940–, 2
Marchand, Colette, 1925–, 1
Mariemma, fl. 1940s, 1
Mariquita, 183?–1922, 1
Markova, Alicia, Dame, 1910–, 1,2
May, Pamela, 1917–, 1
Maywood, Augusta, 1825–1876, 1,2
Mazzo, Kay, 1947–, 2
McBride, Patricia, 1942–, 1,2
Medina, Maria, 2
Mouravieva, Martha, 1837–1879, 2
Moylan, Mary Ellen, 1926–, 1
Nerina, Nadia, 1927–, 1
Nijinska, Bronislava, 1891–1972, 1,2
Nikova, Rina, 2
Novak, Nina, fl. 1940s, 1
Novitskaya, Anastasia, 1819–, 2
Pagava, Ethery, 1932–, 1
Page, Ruth, 1900–, 1,2
Park, Merle, 1937–, 2
Petipa, Marie Sourovschikova, fl.
  1860s, 2
Plisetskaya, Maya Mikhailovna,
  1925–, 1,2
Preobrazhenskaya, Olga, 1871–, 1,2
Prevost, Francoise, 1680–1741, 1,2
Reed, Janet, fl. 1940s, 1
Rees, Rosemary, fl. 1940s, 1,2
Riabouchinska, Tatiana, 1918–, 1
Romanova, Maria, 2
Sabirova, Malkia, 1943–, 2
Salle, Marie, 1707–1756, 1,2
Schanne, Margrethe, fl. 1950s, 1
Schoop, Trudi, 1904–, 1,2
Senger-Bettaque, Katharine, 1862–, 1
Seymour, Lynn, 1939–, 2
Shatner, Marcy, 1947–, 2
Shearer, Moira, 1926–, 1,2
Sibley, Antoinette, 1939–, 2
Skolow, Anna, 1915–, 2
Skorik, Irene, fl. 1940s, 1
Slavenska, Mia, 1917–, 1
Smirnova, Tatiana, 2

Subligny, Marie-Therese Perdou de,
  1666–1736, 1,2
Taglioni, Amalia, 1801–1881, 2
Taglioni, Maria, 1804–1884, 1,2
Tallchief, Maria, 1925–, 1,2
Tallchief, Marjorie, 1927–, 1,2
Tamiris, Helen, 1902–1966, 1,2
Tester, Dorothy Julia, m. 1884, 1
Tharp, Twyla, 1941–, 2
Toumanova, Tamara, 1917–, 1
Turnbull, Julia Anna, 1822–1887, 2
Ulanova, Galina Sergeyevna, 1908–,
  1,2
Vaganova, Agrippina, 1879–1951, 1
Valois, Ninette de, 1898–, 1
Verdy, Violette, 1933–, 2
Vestris, Therese, 1726–1808, 2
Vollmar, Jocelyn, 1925–, 1
Vyroubova, Nina, 1921–, 1
Watts, Heather, 1953–, 2
Wilde, Patricia, 1928–, 1
Zorina, Vera, 1917–, 1,2
Zucchi, Virginia, d. 1930, 1,2
Ballet managers
  Crosnier, Madame, 2
  Rambert, Marie, Dame, 1888–1982,
    1,2
Balloonists
  Blanchard, Sophie, Madame, d. 1819,
    1,2
  Bradley, Lucretia, fl. 1850s, 1
  Brewer, Mrs. Griffith, fl. 1900s, 1
  Drever, Miss, fl. 1900s, 1
  Durof, Madame, fl. 1879s, 1
  Gamerin, Madam, 2
  Garnerin, Elisa, fl. 1790s, 1
  Graham, Margaret, fl. 1850s, 1
  Harbord, Mrs. Assheton, fl. 1900s, 1
  Montalembert, Marchioness de, fl.
    1780s, 2
  Mudie, Rosemary, fl. 1950s, 1
  Piccard, Jeannette R., 1895–1981, 1,2
  Sage, Letitia Ann, fl. 1780s, 1,2
  Thible, Madam, fl. 1780s, 1,2
  Tible, Marie, fl. 1780s, 1
  Wise, Louisa, fl. 1800s, 1
  Wolf, Constance, 1905–, 1
Balzac, Honore de—Spouse
  Hanska, Evelina von, 1804–1882, 1
Band leaders
  Benson, Ivy, 2
  Hutton, Ina Ray (Odessa Cowan),
    1916–1984, 2
Bandit queen
  Starr, Belle Shirley, 1848–1889, 1,2

Beecher, Henry Ward—Spouse
  Beecher, Mrs. Henry Ward, fl.
    1800s, 1
Beekman, Gerardus—Spouse
  Beeckman, Magdelen, d. 1730, 2
Bees
  Tupper, Ellen S., 1822–, 1
Beethoven, Ludwig von—Mother
  Beethoven, Maria Magdelena van,
    1746–1787, 2
Beggars
  Broadway Rose, fl. 1940s, 1
Behavioral scientists
  Wedel, Cynthia Clark, 1908–, 2
Bell, Alexander Graham—Daughter
  Grosvenor, Elsie May Bell, 1878–, 2
Bell, Alexander Graham—Mother
  Bell, Eliza Grace Symonds, 1809–
    1897, 2
Bell, Alexander Graham—Spouse
  Bell, Mabel Gardner Hubbard,
    1857–, 1,2
  Hubbard, Mabel Gardiner, m. 1877, 1
Belles
  See also
  Southern belles
  Adair, Ellen, fl. 1800s, 1
  Adams, Abigail (Mrs. William Ste-
    phens Smith), 1765–, 1
  Byrd, Evelyn, 1709–, 1,2
  Carmichael, Anne, d. 1840, 1
  Caton sisters, fl. 1780s, 2
  Chase, Kate, 1840–1899, 1,2
  Chevalier, Sally, 2
  Chew, Peggy, 1759–, 1
  Custis, Eliza Parke, c. 1794, 1
  DeLancey, Alice, m. 1767, 1
  Dudley, Lady, fl. 1870s, 1
  Franks, Rebecca, 1760–1823, 1,2
  Hamilton, Elizabeth Schuyler, 1757–
    1854, 1,2
  Hazeltine, Nellie, fl. 1880s, 2
  Ibbotson, Mrs., fl. 1800s, 1
  Knight, Mary Worrell, 1759–1849,
    1,2
  Langtry, Lady de Bathe, m. 1899, 1
  Livingston, Cora, 1806–1873, 2
  Mitchell, Mattie (Duchess de Roche-
    foucauld), 2
  Robinson, Hannah, fl. 1700s, 1
  Schaumberj, Emilie, fl. 1860s, 1,2
  Seymour, Mary Julia, 1769–1808, 1
  Smith, Rebecca, 1772–1837, 1
  Taylor, Fanny, d. 1857, 2

  Wentworth, Frances Deering, Lady,
    d. 1813, 1,2
  Willing, Elizabeth, fl. 1780s, 1
Belshazzar—Mother
  Belshazzar's mother, 1
Bennett, Tony—Spouse
  Bennett, Sandy, 1940–, 2
Benny, Jack—Spouse
  Livingstone, Mary, 1908–1983, 1,2
Beorhtric—Spouse
  Eadburga, fl. 800s, 1
Berle, Milton—Spouse
  Berle, Ruth, fl. 1980s, 2
Berlin, Irving—Mother
  Baline, Leah, 2
Berzelius, Jon Jacob—Spouse
  Berzelius, Betty Poppius, Baroness,
    1811–1884, 1
Bhima, King—Daughter
  Damayanti, Princess, 1
Bhimsi—Spouse
  Padmini of Chitore, fl. 1300s, 1
Biblical
  Basmath, 1
Bibliographers
  Colcord, Mabel, 1872–, 1
  Greene, Belle da Costa, 1883–1950, 2
  Mudge, Isador(e) Gilbert, 1875–
    1957, 2
  Sellers, Kathryn, 1870–1939, 1
Bibliophiles
  Adele of Assisi, fl. 1200s, 2
Bicyclists
  See
  Cyclists
Big Brothers, Inc.
  Black, Joyce M., fl. 1940s, 2
Bigamists
  Vaughn, Theresa, 1898–, 2
Billionaires
  Hill, Margaret Hunt, 1815–, 2
  Schoellkipf, Caroline Hunt, 1923–, 2
Billy the Kid—Friend
  Deluvina, 1848–, 2
Bingham, Ann Willing—Sister
  Willing, Elizabeth, fl. 1780s, 1
Biochemists
  Brown, Rachel Fuller, 1898–, 1
  Cori, Gerty Theresa Radnitz, 1896–
    1957, 1,2
  De Vries, Yuan Lin, fl. 1970s, 2
  Emerson, Gladys Anderson, 1903–,
    1,2
  Farr, Wanda Kirkbride, 1895–, 1

Fuchs, Elaine, 1950–, 2
Fulford, Millie Wylie, 2
Hodgkin, Dorothy Mary Crowfoot, 1910–, 1,2
Horning, Marjorie G., 2
Krasnow, Frances, fl. 1930s, 1
Lucid, Shannon W., fl. 1970s, 2
Mary Alma, fl. 1960s, 1
McClintock, Barbara, 1902–, 2
Neufeld, Elizabeth Fondal, fl. 1970s, 2
Ratner, Sarah, fl. 1960s, 2
Russell, Jane Anne, 1911–1967, 2
Schweber, Miriam, fl. 1970s, 2
Seifert, Florence Barbara, 1897–, 1
Stoll, Alice, fl. 1960s, 2
Vennesland, Birgit, fl. 1960s, 2
Wrinch, Dorothy M., 1894–, 1
Biographers
Andreas-Salome, Lou, 1861–1937, 1,2
Anthony, Katharine Susan, 1877–1965, 1,2
Atherton, Gertrude Franklin Horn, 1857–1948, 1,2
Bedford, Sybille, 1911–, 2
Berteaut, Simone, 1923–, 2
Bowen, Catherine (Shober) Drinker, 1897–1903, 1,2
Cavendish, Margaret, Duchess of Newcastle, 1624–1674, 1
Forster, Margaret, 1938–, 2
Fraser, Antonia Pakenham, Lady, 1932–, 2
Haslip, Joan, fl. 1970s, 2
Howe, Julia Ward, 1819–1910, 1,2
Meigs, Cornelia, 1884–1973, 2
Mitford, Nancy Freman, 1907–1973, 1,2
Newcastle, Margaret Cavendish, Duchess of, 1624–1694, 1,2
O'Casey, Eileen, 1924–, 2
Philby, Eleanor, fl. 1970s, 2
Randall, Ruth Elaine Painter, 1892–1908, 1,2
Ross, Ishbel, 1897–1975, 1,2
Ross, Lillian, 1926–, 2
Sackville-West, Victoria Mary, 1892–1962, 1,2
Sandoz, Mari, 1896–1966, 1,2
Sitwell, Edith, Dame, 1887–1964, 1,2
Tappan, Eva March, 1854–1950, 2
Winwar, Frances, 1900–, 2
Woodham-Smith, Cecil Blanche Fitzgerald, 1896–1977, 1,2

Biologists
See also
Bacteriologists
Botanists
Geneticists
Molecular biologists
Neurobiologists
Physiologists
Radio biologists
Zoologists
Brooks, Matilda Moldenhauer, 1,2
Bruce, Mary, Lady, 2
Cahoon, Mary Odile, fl. 1970s, 2
Clark, Eloise E., 1931–, 2
Denys, Charlene, fl. 1970s, 2
Driessche, Therese Vande, fl. 1960s, 2
Eddy, Bernice, fl. 1950s, 2
Gantt, Elizabeth, 2
Howland, Ruth B., fl. 1930s, 1
Hubbard, Ruth, fl. 1950s, 2
Lepeshinskaya, Ol'ga Borisovna, 1871–1963, 1
Mathews, Rita, fl. 1970s, 2
McWhinnie, Mary Alice, 1922–1980, 2
Mosher, Edna, fl. 1930s, 1
Murray, Margaret Ransone, fl. 1930s, 1
Pastori, Giuseppina, 1891–, 2
Patrick, Ruth, 1907–, 2
Pereyaslawzewa, Sophia, fl. 1890s, 1
Rabinowitch-Kempner, Lydia, 1871–1935, 2
Richardson, Harriet, gr. 1896, 1
Sedlak, Bonnie, fl. 1970s, 2
Stevens, Nettie Maria, 1861–1912, 2
Stickel, Lucille Farrier, fl. 1950s, 2
Walker, Norma Ford, 1893–1968, 1
Williams, Hannah English, 1692–1722, 1,2
Young, Pam, fl. 1970s, 2
Biophysicists
Franklin, Rosalind Elsie, 1920–1958, 2
Guttman, Rita, fl. 1930s, 2
Khalafalla, Aida, fl. 1970s, 2
McClintock, Martha, 1947–, 2
Quimby, Edith Hinckley, 1891–, 1,2
Bird protection
Wright, Mabel Osgood, 1859–1934, 1,2
Birth control advocates
Sanger, Margaret Higgins, 1883–1966, 1,2

Botev, Khristo—Mother
  Botyo, Ivanka Petrova, 1830–1910, 2
Bottling industry
  Ocloo, Esther, fl. 1940s, 2
Boudinot, Elias—Spouse
  Boudinot, Mrs. Elias, 2
Bourbon, Duc de—Mistress
  Prie, Jeanne Agnes Berthelot de Pleneuf, 1698–1727, 1
Bourbon, Duke of—Mistress
  Dawes, Sophia, 1790–1840, 1
Bourbon, Francois de—Spouse
  St. Pol, Marie de, Countess of Pembroke, d. 1592, 1
Bowdoin, James II—Spouse
  Bowdoin, Elizabeth Erving, 1731–1803, 2
Bowdoin, James III—Spouse
  Bowdoin, Sarah, 1761–1826, 2
Bowery Queen
  Hull, Millie, 2
Bowlers
  Anderton, Carol, 2
  Benton, Bonnie, 2
  Cook, Judy, 2
  Cordes, Georgene, 2
  Costello, Patty, 1946–, 2
  Fothergill, Dorothy, fl. 1970s, 2
  Garms, Shirley Rudolph, 1924–, 1
  Giovinco, Lucy, fl. 1970s, 2
  Haefker, Annedore, fl. 1970s, 2
  Harris, Maureen, fl. 1970s, 2
  Hoffman, Martha, fl. 1960s, 2
  Jacobson, D. D., fl. 1970s, 2
  Knechtges, Doris, fl. 1950s, 2
  Koester, A. J., fl. 1910s, 2
  Ladewig, Marion, 2
  Matthews, Merle, 2
  McCutcheon, Floretta Doty, 1888–1967, 1,2
  Merrick, Marge, fl. 1960s, 2
  Miller, Dorothy, 1920–1940, 2
  Miller, Elizabeth, fl. 1960s, 2
  Morris, Betty, 2
  Nichols, Lorrie, fl. 1970s, 2
  Oartner, Beverly (Beva), fl. 1960s, 2
  Ortner, Beverley, fl. 1960s, 2
  Simon, Gloria, 2
  Small, Tess, fl. 1940s, 2
  Soutar, Judy Cook, 1944–, 2
  Sperber, Paula, 1951–, 2
  Taylor, Joan, fl. 1970s, 2
  Wood, Frieda, fl. 1970s, 2
Boxers
  Bermudez, Marion, 2
  Donahue, Hessie, fl. 1880s, 2

Poillon, Charlotte, fl. 1900s, 2
Poillon, Katherine, fl. 1900s, 2
Saunders, Nell, 2
Shain, Eva, fl. 1970s, 2
Stokes, Mrs., 2
Trimiar, Marian "Tyger", 1953–, 2
Boxing judges
  Polls, Carol, fl. 1970s, 2
Braillists
  Mueller, Magdalene, fl. 1960s, 2
Brann, Governor—Spouse
  Brann, Martha Cobb, 1882–1961, 2
Brendan the Voyager—Mother
  Cara, fl. 400s, 1
Bridge builders
  Joyce, Margaret, fl. 1500s, 1
Bridges, Lloyd—Spouse
  Bridges, Dorothy, fl. 1970s, 2
Bright, Bill—Mother
  Bright, Mary Lee, 2
Brigittine Order
  Persson, Birgitta, 1303–1373, 2
British Drama League
  Fogerty, Elsie, 1866–1945, 2
Broadcasters
  Gillott, Jacky, 1939–, 2
  Laski, Marghanita, 1915–, 1,2
  Rayner, Claire, 1931–, 2
Brokers
    See also
    Investment brokers
  Bollmann, Mary O'R, fl. 1930s, 1
  Claflin, Tennessee, 1846–1923, 1,2
  Elgenmann, Ingrid, fl. 1970s, 2
  Howe, Patricia M., fl. 1950s, 2
  Hughes, Paula, 2
  Hume, Jo Ann, 1955–, 2
  Jarcho, Alice, fl. 1960s, 2
  Karmel, Roberta S., 1937–, 2
  O'Bryan, Mollie, 2
  Oboussier, Helene, fl. 1920s, 2
  Ovitz, Carol, fl. 1970s, 2
  Roebling, Mary Grindhart, 1905–, 1,2
  Shaw, Susan, 2
  Taylor, Kathleen DeVere, fl. 1930s, 1
  Woodhull, Victoria Claflin, 1838–1927, 1,2
  Wuhsha, fl. 1098, 2
Bronte sisters—Mother
  Bronte, Maria Branwell, 1783–1821, 2
Brook Farm
  Barlow, Almira, 2
  Bruce, Georgiana, 2

Dwight, Marianne, 2
Ripley, Sophia Willard Dana, 1803–
1861, 2
Brower, Charles D.—Daughter
Neakok, Sadie Brower, fl. 1880s, 2
Brower, Charles D.—Spouse
Brower, Toctoo, fl. 1960s, 2
Brown, John—Friend
Pleasant, Mary Ellen "Mammy",
1814–1904, 1,2
Brown, John—Spouse
Brown, Dianthe, d.c. 1832, 1
Brown, Mary Anne Day, 1816–1844,
1
Browne, William—Spouse
Browne, Mary Burnet, fl. 1700s, 2
Browning, Robert—Mother
Browning, Sarah Anna Wiedemann,
d. 1849, 1
Wiedemann, Sarah Anna, fl. 1810s, 1
Browning, Robert—Sister
Browning, Sarianna, d. 1903, 1
Brutus, Decimus Junius—Spouse
Sempronia, fl. 70sBC, 1
Brutus, Marcus Junius—Mother
Servilia, fl. 80sBC, 1
Bryan, William Jennings—Spouse
Bryan, Mary Elizabeth Baird, 1861–
1930, 2
Bryant, William Cullen—Mother
Bryant, Sarah Snell, fl. 1780s, 1
Snell, Sarah, fl. 1780s, 1
Bryologists
Britton, Elizabeth Gertrude Knight,
1858–1934, 2
Buchanan, James—Mother
Buchanan, Elizabeth Speer, 1767–
1833, 1,2
Buchanan, James—Niece
Johnston, Harriet Lane, 1833–1903, 1
Lane, Harriet, 1830–1903, 1,2
Buchwald, Art—Spouse
Buchwald, Ann, 1921–, 2
Buck, Pearl—Mother
Sydenstricker, Caroline Stulting,
1892–, 2
Buckland, Frank—Spouse
Buckland, Mrs. Frank, fl. 1800s, 1
Building industry
Boustany, Myrna, 2
Carter, Betty, 2
Clapp, Hannah, fl. 1860s, 2
Gjurich, Gilda B., fl. 1950s, 2
Phillips, Sarah Bowman, fl. 1850s, 2

Pontalba, Micaela Almonester, Bar-
oness, 1795–1874, 2
Uhl, Alice, fl. 1890s, 2
Bullfighters
Angeles, Maria de Los, 2
Atienzar, Maribel, 1959–, 2
Cintron, Conchita, 1922–, 2
Gaucin, Dona Maria de, 2
Los Angeles, Maria de, fl. 1970s, 2
Torera, La Nina, fl. 1970s, 2
Bunche, Ralph—Grandmother
Johnson, Lucy Ann Taylor, 1855–, 1
Bunche, Ralph—Mother
Bunche, Olive Agnes Johnson, 1885–
1917, 1
Bunyan, John—Spouse
Bunyan, Elizabeth, d. 1691, 1
Burgoyne, John—Spouse
Burgoyne, Charlotte Stanley, fl.
1770s, 2
Burlesque
Britton, Sherry (Edith), 2
Lee, Gypsy Rose, 1914–1970, 1,2
Rowland, Betty Jane, fl. 1930s, 2
Sothern, Georgia, 1917–, 2
St. Cyr, Lili, 1917–, 1,2
Burns, Robert—Inspiration
Campbell, Mary, d. 1786, 2
Burns, Robert—Mother
Burns, Agnes Broun, 1732–1820, 2
Burns, Robert—Spouse
Armour, Jean, 2
Burns, Jean, 1767–1834, 1
Burr, Aaron—Daughter
Burr, Theodosia Alston, 1783–1813,
1,2
Burr, Aaron—Friend
Hassel, Miss, fl. 1800s, 1
Moncrieffe, Margaret, fl. 1780s, 1,2
Burr, Aaron—Spouse
Burr, Theodosia Prevost, d. 1794, 1
Jumel, Elizabeth (Eliza) Bowen,
1769–1865, 1,2
Burton, Richard—Spouse
Arundell, Isabel, 1831–, 2
Burton, Sybil, 2
Taylor, Elizabeth, 1932–, 1,2
Business consultants
Gilbreth, Lillian Moller, 1878–1972,
1,2
Hicks, Beatrice Alice, 1919–, 1,2
Wertz, Jeanne, 2
Business educators
Gibbs, Katharine, 1865–1934, 2
Kozlova, Olypiada, fl. 1910s, 2

Lelash, Ethelyn L., fl. 1930s, 1
Rattley, Jessie Menifield, fl. 1950s, 2

Business executives

Abbott, Sarah, fl. 1970s, 2
Abel, Hazel Hempel, 1888–1966, 1,2
Abrabanel, Benvenida, d. 1560, 2
Alexander, Mary (Polly) Pratt Provoost, 1693–1760, 1,2
Amen, Marion Cleveland, fl. 1930s, 1
Anderson, Gertrude E. Fisher, 1894–, 1
Anthony, Sarah Porter Williams, fl. 1830s, 1
Arbus, Loreen, 2
Archibald, Anne, fl. 1930s, 1
Arden, Elizabeth, 1884–1966, 1,2
Askwith, Margaret Long, fl. 1930s, 1
Auerbach, Beatrice Fox, 1887–1968, 2
Ayer, Harriet Hubbard, 1849–1903, 2
Beales, Hannah, fl. 1760s, 1
Berliner, Constance Hope, fl. 1930s, 1
Beshar, Christine, 2
Binger, Delphine, fl. 1930s, 1
Binner, Madame, fl. 1930s, 1
Bissell, Anna, d. 1934, 2
Blakeway, Sarah, fl. 1741, 1
Bleicher, Blanche O., fl. 1930s, 1
Blondin, Catharine F., fl. 1930s, 1
Bloodworth, Bess, fl. 1930s, 1
Bloom, Helene C., fl. 1970s, 2
Boehm, Mildred Witt, fl. 1930s, 1
Bogardus, Annetje Jane, 1638–1663, 1,2
Bollmann, Mary O'R, fl. 1930s, 1
Bonfield, Lida, fl. 1930s, 1
Boylston, Sarah, fl. 1760s, 1
Brasher, Judith, fl. 1737, 1
Brogliatti, Barbara Spencer, 1946–, 2
Brosnan, Mary, fl. 1930s, 1
Brown, Eleanor McMillen Stackstrom, fl. 1920s, 1,2
Brown, J. Margarethe, fl. 1970s, 2
Brown, Sarah, fl. 1750s, 1
Brupbacher, Alice, fl. 1930s, 1
Bullock, Edith R. "Tugboat queen", 2
Burt, Alene, fl. 1930s, 1
Campbell, Amelia M., fl. 1930s, 1
Cannan, Mary, fl. 1763, 1
Cella, Phyllis A., 2
Charlick, Edith, fl. 1920s, 1
Charren, Peggy, 1928–, 2
Clark, Catherine T., 1906–, 2
Clark, Katherine, 1602–1671, 1,2

Clewer, Lisa, fl. 1970s, 2
Cochran, Jacqueline, 1910–1980, 1,2
Coffin, Dionis Stevens, fl. 1640s, 1
Coffin (Coffyn), Dionis Stevens, fl. 1640s, 2
Cohen, Barbara, 1901–, 1
Connor, Catherine, 2
Converse, Thelma, Lady Furness, fl. 1930s, 1
Cookman, Helen Cramp, fl. 1930s, 1
Cowley, Mary, fl. 1741, 1
Crabb, Mary, fl. 1730s, 1
Crimmins, Mary Bety, fl. 1960s, 2
Crowley, Mary M., fl. 1930s, 1
Cumming, Rose Stuart, fl. 1930s, 1
Cunningham, Mary Elizabeth, 1951–, 2
Cupps, Anita, 1948–, 2
Custin, Mildred, 1906–, 1
Daniels, Angela B., fl. 1930s, 1
Davenport, Elizabeth Wooley, fl. 1650s, 1,2
Davis, Arlene Palsgraff, d. 1964, 1
Davis, Frances, fl. 1970s, 2
Davis, Hannah, d. 1863, 1,2
Davis, Tobe Collier, 1893–, 1
De Mott, Margorie Mahon, fl. 1930s, 1
Deimer, Catherine, d. 1761, 1
Dillon, Mary Elizabeth, 1885–, 1
Ducray, Anne, fl. 1760s, 1
East, Henrietta Maria, fl. 1760s, 1
Edgerly, Anne R., fl. 1930s, 1
Ehmann, Freda, d. 1932, 2
Erb, Letitia H., 1895–, 1
Esty, Janet Marie Dearholt, 1944–, 2
Eumachia, 2
Farley, Rosalie La Flesche, 1861–1900, 2
Farmer, Mary, d. 1687, 2
Faulds, Mrs. David, m. 1885, 1
Fendi, Adele, 2
Fippinger, Grace, 1948–, 2
Fisher, Harriet White, m. 1898, 1
Ford, Gertrude H., fl. 1930s, 1
Frederick, Christine McGaffey, 1883–1970, 1,2
Gabor, Jolie, 1896–, 1
Gates, Hazel Rhoads, Sr., 1891–1973, 2
Gill, Elizabeth Mary, fl. 1870s, 1
Gillett sisters, fl. 1860s, 1
Gilmore, Gladys Chase, fl. 1930s, 1
Gleason, Kate, 1865–1933, 2

Goodrich, Frances Louisa, 1856–1944, 1,2
Goodwin, Sarah, 1745–1756, 1,2
Goon, Toy Len Chin, 1,2
Gordon, Edith Frances, fl. 1930s, 1
Graham, Bette Clair Nesmith, d. 1980, 2
Green, Blanche, fl. 1940s, 2
Greene, Amy, 2
Gregg, Dorothy, 2
Grieg, Connie, fl. 1970s, 2
Hall, Marjory, 1908–, 1
Hanssen, Hertha I., fl. 1930s, 1
Harriman, Mary Williamson Averill, 1851–1932, 1,2
Hart, Daisy, 2
Haughery, Margaret Gaffney, 1813–1882, 1,2
Haynes, Elizabeth A. Ross, 1883–1953, 1,2
Hennessey, Alice E., fl. 1970s, 2
Herrick, Elinore Morehouse, 1895–1964, 1,2
Hershey, Lenore, 1920–, 2
Hershman, Aleene, fl. 1950s, 1
Hewitt, Ann, 2
Heywood, Anne, 1913–1961, 1
Hilder, Vera Gertude, fl. 1930s, 1
Hines, Eleanor Culton, fl. 1930s, 1
Hoederlin, Lillina Ottilie, fl. 1930s, 1
Holton, Susan May, 1875–1951, 1
Horn, Berta, fl. 1930s, 1
Hough, Marti, 2
Hughes, Michelle, 2
Hume, Jo Ann, 1955–, 2
Husted, Marjorie Child, 1892–, 1,2
Hyde, Helen Smith, fl. 1930s, 1
James, Margaret Hodges, 1880–, 2
Jardim, Anne, fl. 1970s, 2
Jarvis, Lucy Howard, 1919–, 2
Johnson, Sonya Bortin, fl. 1930s, 1
Jones, Candy, 1925–, 1
Jones, Maude Hall, 1872–1954, 2
Jordan, Alice Boyer, fl. 1930s, 1
Joseph, Nannine, fl. 1930s, 1
Kalep, Elvy, 1
Kayshus, Effie, fl. 1930s, 1
Kellogg, Marion, fl. 1970s, 2
Kimball, Josephine, fl. 1930s, 1
Koernig, Anna Mabel, fl. 1930s, 1
Kohl, Marguerite C., 2
Kroc, Joan Beverly, 2
Lamson, Lucy Stedman, 1857–, 1
Lane, Columbia, fl. 1880s, 1

Lang, Natalie, 2
Lasky, Royle Glaser, 1930–, 2
Leach, Ruth Marian, 1916–, 1
Lee, Peggy, 1920–, 1,2
Lee, Rosamund, fl. 1930s, 1
Leigh, Dorian, 1919–, 1,2
Lenart, Marian F., fl. 1930s, 1
Leopold, Alice Koller, 1909–, 1,2
Lewis, Mary Carlile, fl. 1930s, 1
Licoricia of Winchester, 2
Lippincott, C. H., 1860–, 1
Lyman, Laura Elizabeth, fl. 1930s, 1
MacDougall, Alice Foote, 1867–1945, 1
Macklewain, Margaret, fl. 1730s, 1
Malsin, Lane Bryant, 1879–1951, 1,2
Maneck, Margaret Brown, fl. 1930s, 1
Matarazzo, Maria Pia Esmerelda, fl. 1970s, 2
McCabe, Rita, fl. 1960s, 2
McConner, Dorothy, fl. 1960s, 2
McCormick, Nettie Fowler, 1835–1923, 1,2
McCrea, Vera T., fl. 1930s, 1
McFadden, Dorothy L., fl. 1930s, 1
McKaig, Dianne, fl. 1970s, 2
Mendelsohn, Celia, fl. 1930s, 1
Mercereau, Ethel F., fl. 1930s, 1
Merzon, Ruth, fl. 1930s, 1
Mibtahiah, 400, 2
Minijima, Mrs. Kiyo, 1833–1919, 1
Mistrot, Ethel Reed, fl. 1930s, 1
Monmouth, Mrs. L. N., fl. 1880s, 1
Morgan, Rose Meta, 1
Morse, Fanny, fl. 1930s, 1
Mowat, Vivia A., fl. 1910s, 1
Muller, Gertrude Agnes, 1887–1954, 2
Munro, Beatrice Lounsbery, fl. 1930s, 1
Myers, Ella Burns, fl. 1930s, 1
Nadeau, Claudette, fl. 1970s, 2
Neighbors, Patricia, 2
Newman, Henriette, fl. 1930s, 1
Newton, Charlotte L., fl. 1870s, 1
Norton, Katherine Byrd Rodgers, fl. 1930s, 1
Nosworthy, Meta, fl. 1930s, 1
Novello, Mary, 1818–1908, 2
Noyes, Dorothy, fl. 1930s, 1
Nuthead, Dinah, 1695, 1,2
Ogilvie, Elizabeth, fl. 1930s, 1
Ogilvie, Gladys, fl. 1930s, 1
Ogilvie, Jessica, fl. 1930s, 1

Olivier, Frances, fl. 1930s, 1
Owens, Charlene B., fl. 1950s, 2
Paige, Mrs. Richard E., fl. 1930s, 1
Parnis, Mollie, 1905–, 1,2
Patterson, Lillian D., fl. 1930s, 1
Peasley, Mrs., fl. 1880s, 1
Peden, Katherine Graham, 1926–, 1
Peirce, Isabel, fl. 1930s, 1
Perkins, Elizabeth Peck, 1735–1807, 1,2
Pettit, Polly, fl. 1930s, 1
Phillips, Elizabeth, fl. 1770s, 1
Post, Marjorie Merriweather, 1887–1973, 2
Remington, Mrs. Mather, fl. 1870s, 1
Richards, Henrietta King, fl. 1930s, 1
Riis, Mary Phillips, fl. 1930s, 1
Riley, Ranny, 2
Roman, Mae, fl. 1930s, 1
Roney, Marianne, 1929–, 1
Rose, Ellen Alida, 1843–, 1
Rosenthal, Beatrice, 1930–1940, 2
Ruggles, Emily, 1827–, 1
Santi, Tina, 2
Saruya, Julia Salinger, fl. 1930s, 1
Saunders, Mary A., 1849–, 1
Schoeman, Johanna, 2
Scott, Dru, 2
Scovil, Cora, fl. 1930s, 1
Selby, Cecily Cannon, fl. 1970s, 2
Shaver, Dorothy, 1897–1959, 1,2
Shelton, Louise, 1867–1934, 1
Shepherd, Theodosia Burr Hall, 1845–1906, 1
Shorter, Susie I. L., 1859–1912, 1
Sidbury, Charlotte M., d. 1904, 2
Simon, Dorothy M., fl. 1960s, 2
Singer, Betty, fl. 1930s, 1
Slocum, Caroline Edna, fl. 1930s, 1
Slocum, Lillie, fl. 1870s, 1
Smith, Ida B. Wise, 1871–, 1
Smith, Thelma J., fl. 1970s, 2
Spain, Jayne, 1941–, 2
Spain, Jayne Baker, 1927–, 2
Speakman, Margorie Willoughby, 1890–, 2
St. George, Katharine, 1896–1983, 1,2
Stanford, Sally (Mabel Marcia Busby Goodan Fanster Bayham Spagnoli Rapp Gump), 1903–1982, 2
Stover, Clara Mae Lewis, 1882–1975, 2
Styers, Aleta, fl. 1960s, 2

Summers, Quinneth C., fl. 1930s, 1
Swallow, Frances, fl. 1700s, 1
Switlik, Lottie, 1
Thal, Augusta, fl. 1930s, 1
Totino, Rose, fl. 1950s, 2
Tresidder, Mary Curry, 1
Tuttle, Marguerite, fl. 1930s, 1
Van Vries, Margaret Hardenbroek, fl. 1660s, 2
Vanderlip, Candace Alig, fl. 1930s, 1
Washburn, Florinda, fl. 1850s, 1,2
Watson, Louise, fl. 1930s, 1
Weaver, Anna K., fl. 1870s, 1
White, Eartha Mary Magdalene, 1876–1974, 2
Whitman, Lucilla Mara de Vescovi, 1893–, 1
Wiedhopf, Louise Bartling, fl. 1920s, 1
Williams, Esther, 1913–, 1,2
Worman, Donna, fl. 1950s, 1
Wright, Laura Beltz, fl. 1950s, 2
Wuhsha, fl. 1098, 2
Zwick, Florence, 1894–, 2
Business managers
   Smith, Martha Turnstall, fl. 1860s, 1
Business researchers
   Goldmark, Pauline Dorothea, fl. 1890s, 1
Butler, Benjamin—Spouse
   Butler, Sarah Hildreth, 1816–1870, 1
Butler, Richard Austen—Spouse
   Butler, Sydney Elizabeth Courtauld, d. 1954, 1
Buttons, Red—Spouse
   Buttons, Alicia, fl. 1970s, 2
Buyers
   Dingman, Margaret Christian, fl. 1930s, 1
   Koch, Marion, fl. 1930s, 1
   Vigon, Ann, fl. 1930s, 1
Byrd, William—Daughter
   Byrd, Evelyn, 1709–, 1,2
Byrd, William—Spouse
   Byrd, Elizabeth (Betty) Carter, 1732–1760, 2
Byron, George Gordon—Friend
   Clairmont, Claire, 1798–1879, 1,2
Byron, Lord—Friend
   Guiccioli, Teresa Gamba, 1801–1873, 1

C

Cabaret owners
   Bricktop (Ada Smith), 1895–, 1

Cabinet members, Australian
Rankin, Anabelle, Dame, fl. 1970s, 2
Cabinet members, Belgian
Reimacker-Legot, Marguerite de, fl.
1960s, 2
Cabinet members, Canadian
Begin, Monique, fl. 1930s, 2
Cabinet members, Danish
Bang, Nina Henriette Wendeline,
1866–1928, 1,2
Cabinet members, English
Bondfield, Margaret Grace, 1873–
1953, 1,2
Smith, Mary Ellen, 1862–1933, 2
Cabinet members, Finnish
Sillanpaa, Mina, 1866–1952, 2
Cabinet members, Italian
Anselmi, Tina, 2
Cabinet members, Mauritanian
Kane, Toure Aissata, fl. 1960s, 2
Cabinet members, New Zealand
Howard, Mabel, 1893–1972, 2
Cabinet members, Norwegian
Hansteen, Kirsten, fl. 1940s, 2
Cabinet members, Polish
Kosmowska, Irena, 1879–1945, 2
Cabinet members, Russian
Kollontay, Alexandra Mikhailovna,
1872–1952, 1,2
Stasova, Helena, 1873–1966, 2
Cabinet members, Swedish
Sigurdsen, Gertrude, 1923–, 2
Thorsson, Inga, 1915–, 2
Cabinet members, Venezuelan
Casanova, Aura Celina, fl. 1960s, 2
Cadwalader, John—Daughter
Cadwalader, Frances, Lady Erskine,
1781–1843, 2
Caesar, Caius—Spouse
Livia Orestilla, fl. 12–41, 1
Caesar, Julius—Daughter
Julia, 83–54 BC, 1
Caesar, Julius—Mistress
Servilia, fl. 80sBC, 1
Caesar, Julius—Mother
Aurela, d. 54 BC, 1
Caesar, Julius—Spouse
Calpurnia, 59 BC, 1
Pompeia, fl. 61
BC, 1
Cagliostro, Alessandro di—Friend
"Seraphina", fl. 1780s, 1
Cain—Spouse
Cain's wife, 1

Caleb—Concubine
Maachah, 1
Caleb—Spouse
Azubah, 1
Calhoun, John—Spouse
Calhoun, Floride Calhoun, 1792–
1866, 1,2
California
Bailey, Pearl Mae, 1918–, 1,2
Black, Shirley Temple, 1928–, 2
Brown, Charlotte Amanda Blake,
1846–1910, 1,2
Covilland, Mary Murphy, 2
Hearst, Phoebe Apperson, 1842–
1919, 1,2
Higuera, Prudencia, fl. 1840s, 2
Hoover, Lou Henry, 1874–1944, 1,2
Martinez, Vilma S., 1943–, 2
Miller, Marion, 1862–, 2
Miller, Susan Lincoln Tolman, 1825–
1912, 2
Mills, Susan Lincoln Tolman, 1821–
1912, 1,2
Montanadon, Pat, 2
Murphy, Mary, d. 1979, 2
Pettit, Laura Mildred Tanner, 1895–,
2
Pico, Maria Antonia, fl. 1810s, 2
Priest, Inez Baber, d. 1973, 2
Priest, Ivy Maud Baker, 1905–1975,
1,2
Randall, Harriet Bulpitt, 1904–1975,
2
St. Johns, Adela Rogers, 1894–, 1,2
Caligula—Sister
Julia Livilla, fl. 39, 1
Caligula—Spouse
Lollia, Paulina, d. 49, 1,2
Call, Joe—Sister
Call, Miss, fl. 1900s, 2
Calligraphers
Bayes, Jessie, 1890–1934, 2
Chu Ching-Chien, 265–420, 2
Hsing Tz'u Ching, fl. 1570s, 2
Kello, Hester English, 1571–1624, 1,2
Kuan Tao-Sheng, 1262–1319, 2
Li Fu-Jen, Lady Li, 907–960, 2
Shinoda, Toko, fl. 1970s, 2
Traquair, Phoebe Anna Moss, 1852–
1936, 2
Ts'Ao Miao-Ch'ing, fl. 1300s, 2
Wei Fu-Jen, 272–350, 1
Yang Mei-Tzu, 2
Calvin, John—Spouse
Bure, Idelette de, fl. 1530s, 2

Cory, Fanny Young, fl. 1870s, 1
Hokinson, Helen Elna, 1893–1949, 1,2
Messick, Dale, 1906–, 1,2
Parker, Gladys, fl. 1930s, 1
Whitcher, Frances Miriam Berry, 1811–1852, 1,2
Carus—Spouse
Magnia Urbica, fl. 230s, 1
Casimir the Great—Sister
Elizabeth, 2
Castro, Fidel—Mother
Castro, Argez Lina Gonzales, d. 1963, 2
Catalyst, Inc.
Schwartz, Felice N., fl. 1960s, 2
Caterers
Moorland (Morland), Jane, fl. 1760s, 1
Catholic Church
Avery, Mary Ellen, 1927–, 2
Ayres, Anne, 1816–1896, 2
Bayer, Adele Parmentier, 1814–1893, 2
Bennett, Joyce, fl. 1970s, 2
Bohn, Carole, 2
Borgia, Francis, 2
Catholic Institution For Poor Girls
Maintenon, Francoise D'Aubigne, Marquise de, 1635–1719, 1,2
Catholic converts
Tekakwitha, Kateri, 1656–1680, 1,2
Catholic emancipator
Petre, Juliana, Lady, 1769–1833, 2
Catholic workers
Avery, Martha Gallison Moore, 1851–1929, 2
Chouteau, Bernice Menard, 1801–1888, 2
Day, Dorothy, 1897–1980, 1,2
Filhiol, Florence Miller, 1878–, 2
Catiline conspirator
Sempronia, 2
Cato, Uticensis—Daughter
Porcia, d. 42 BC, 1
Cato, Uticensis—Spouse
Marcia, fl.40s BC, 1,2
Cattle queens
Collins, Libby Smith, 1844–1921, 1
De Balli, Dona Rosa Maria Hinopsa, 1755–, 2
Cattle rustlers
Richey, Annie, 2
Cavalry officers
Durova, Nadezhada, 1783–1866, 2

Cell biologists
Harvey, Ethel Browne, 1885–1965, 2
Cellists
See also
Violincellists
Du Pre, Jacqueline, 1945–, 2
Garbousova, Raya, 1909–, 1
Harrison, Beatrice, 1892–, 1
Hilger, Elsa, fl. 1940s, 1
Kraeuter, Phyllis Marie, fl. 1930s, 1
Moorman, Charlotte, fl. 1960s, 2
Neveu, Ginette, 1919–1949, 2
Nevu, Ginette, 1919–1949, 2
Park-Lewis, Dorothea, fl. 1930s, 1
Ruegger, Elsa, 1881–1924, 2
Wellerson, Mila, 1910–, 1
Cenci, Francesco—Daughter
Cenci, Beatrice, 1577–1599, 1,2
Centenarians
Chapman, Maude, 1869–, 2
Christian, Annie, 1871–, 2
Davidson, Sophia, 1868–, 2
Davies (Davis), Mary, 1635–1752, 2
Fairbank, Lorena King, 1874–, 2
Farley, Carrie, 1869–, 2
Hank, Helen, 1870–, 2
Harper, Mary, 1866–, 2
Hartshorn, Emily, 1870–, 2
Howard, Estelle, 1871–, 2
Hull, Elizabeth, 1862–, 2
Kean, Jennie Whitlock, fl. 1870s, 2
Letch, Ida, 1867–, 2
Losh, Nancy, 1867–, 2
Malsbary, Sarah Mahon, 1868–, 2
Martin, Anna, 1869–, 2
McAndrew, Anna, 1868–, 2
McCrary, Elizabeth, 1869–, 2
Nave, Rufina, 1867–, 2
Otto, Alice, 1870–, 2
Pollatschek, Estelle, 1876–, 2
Racey, Linda, 1869–, 2
Roy, Mrs. Clarinda, 1863–, 2
Taylor, Ella, 1868–, 2
Watson, Anna, 1871–, 2
Ceramic painters
Hokinson, Helen Elna, 1893–1949, 1,2
Ceres Medal winners
Myrdal, Alva Reimer, 1902–, 1,2
Chair caners
Goodwin, Sarah, 1745–1756, 1,2
Chamberlain, Joseph—Spouse
Chamberlain, Mary Endicott, 1864–, 1

Chandler, Winthrop—Spouse
    Chandler, Anna Paine, 1738–1811, 2
Chanilly, Marquis de—Friend
    Mariana, Sister, fl. 1660s, 1
Channel Islands
    Hathaway, Sibyl Mary Collings, fl.
    1920s, 1
Chantrey, Sir Francis—Mother
    Chantrey, Mrs., d. 1826, 1
Chaplains
    Parvey, Connie, fl. 1970s, 2
Chaplin, Charles—Mother
    Chaplin, Mrs. Charles Hill, d. c1920,
    2
Chaplin, Charles—Spouse
    Chaplin, Lita Grey, 1908–, 2
Charity workers
    Chantal, Jeanne Francois Fremiot,
    1574–1641, 1,2
    Devney, Verona Stubbs, 1916–, 2
    Fisher, Dorothea, 1894–1974, 2
    Fouquet, Marie, Vicomtesse de Vaux,
    fl. 1600s, 2
    Hubbard, Gertrude McCurdy, 1829–
    1909, 2
    Julia Domna, 157–217, 1,2
    Montefiore, Judith Cohen, Lady, fl.
    1820s, 1,2
    Nilsson, Anna Q., 1888–1974, 2
    Prior, Margaret Barret Allen, 1773–
    1842, 1,2
    Sheffield, Mary E., fl. 1860s, 2
    Smith, Virginia Thrall, 1836–1903, 2
    Wise, Louise Waterman, 1874–1947, 2
    Wolf, Frument, fl. 1700s, 2
Charles, Duke—Spouse
    Krasinska, Francoise, 1742–1795, 1
Charles I—Daughter
    Mary of Orange, 1631–1660, 1
    Orleans, Henriette-Anne, Duchess
    d', 1644–1670, 1
Charles I—Spouse
    Henrietta Maria, 1609–1669, 1,2
Charles II—Mistress
    Gwynn, Nell (Eleanor), 1650–1687,
    1,2
    Keroualle, Louise Renee de, Duchess
    of Portsmouth and Aubigny, 1649–
    1734, 1,2
    Richmond and Lennox, Frances Te-
    resa, 1648–1702, 1
    Villiers, Barbara, 1640–1709, 1,2
    Walter, Lucy (Mrs. Barlow), 1630–
    1658, 1,2

Charles IX—Mistress
    Touchet, Marie, 1549–1638, 1
Charles IX—Spouse
    Elizabeth of Austria, 1554–1592, 1
Charles V—Spouse
    Jeanne de Bourbon, m. 1350, 1
Charles VII—Mistress
    Sorel, Agnes, 1409–1450, 1,2
Charles the Bald—Daughter
    Judith, the Merry Heart, fl. 860s, 1
Charles the Bold—Daughter
    Mary of Burgundy, 1457–1482, 1,2
Charles the Fat—Spouse
    Richardis (Richilda), d. 896, 1
Charles, Prince of Wales—Spouse
    Diana, Princess of Wales, 1961–, 2
Charlotte—Preceptriss
    Knight, Ellis Cornelia, 1758–1838, 1
Chase-Smith, Margaret—Mother
    Chase, Carrie Matilda Murray,
    1876–, 2
Checkers
    Huntley, Gertrude, fl. 1930s, 2
Cheese makers
    Smith, Joan Barton, 1942–, 2
Chemical engineers
    See also
        Metallurgists
    Hutchinson, Margaret H., fl. 1950s, 2
    Julliard, Jacqueline, fl. 1970s, 2
    Levanova, Svetlana, 2
    Quiggle, Dorothy, 1903–, 1
Chemists
    See also
        Bacteriochemists
        Biochemists
        Geochemists
        Organic chemists
        Pharmacologists
        Physical chemists
        Physio-chemists
    Apgar, B. Jean, 1936–, 2
    Arconville, Genevieve Charlotte d',
    1720–1805, 2
    Benerito, Ruth R., 2
    Bengston, Hertha, 1917–, 2
    Benson, Margaret, fl. 1970s, 2
    Berkowitz, Joan B., 2
    Bishop, Hazel Gladys, 1906–, 1,2
    Blodgett, Katharine Burr, 1898–
    1979, 1,2
    Blunt, Katharine, 1876–1954, 1,2
    Bodley, Rachel Littler, fl. 1870s, 2
    Bogert, L. Jean, fl. 1930s, 1

Brooks, Harriet, 1876–1933, 1
Caldwell, Mary Letitia, 1890–1972, 2
Carr, Emma Perry, 1880–1972, 1,2
Carter, Mary E., fl. 1970s, 2
Caserio, Marjorie C., fl. 1970s, 2
Chang, Marguerite Shue-Wen, fl. 1970s, 2
Cohn, Mildred, fl. 1960s, 2
Curie, Marie Sklodowska, 1867–1934, 1,2
Dehmer, Patricia, 1945–, 2
Dyer, Helen M., 2
Elion, Gertrude B., fl. 1960s, 2
Fieser, Mary, fl. 1970s, 2
Fischer, Charlotte F., 2
Good, Mary L., fl. 1970s, 2
Green, Arda A., d. 1958, 2
Harrison, Anna J., fl. 1970s, 2
Hayes, Dora, fl. 1970s, 2
Hiller, Alma Elizabeth, 1892–1953, 1
Jeanes, Allene R., fl. 1960s, 2
Johnson, Kristen, 2
Joliot-Curie, Irene, 1897–1956, 1,2
Karle, Isabella L., fl. 1970s, 2
Kaufman, Joyce, 2
Mack, Pauline Beery, 1891–, 1
Marcet, Jane, 1769–1858, 1,2
Martos, Flora, 1897–1938, 2
Moran, Juliette M., fl. 1960s, 2
Morgan, Agnes Fay, 1884–1968, 1,2
Murray, Rosemary, fl. 1970s, 2
Nobel, Anne C., fl. 1970s, 2
Noddack, Ida Eva Tacke, 1896–, 1,2
Orcutt, Ruby R. M., fl. 1930s, 1
Pennington, Mary Engle, 1897–1952, 1,2
Perlmann, Gertrude E., 1912–1974, 2
Petermann, Mary L., d. 1976, 2
Phelps, Almira Hart Lincoln, 1793–1884, 1,2
Pickett, Lucy W., fl. 1950s, 1,2
Richards, Ellen Henrietta Swallow, 1842–1911, 1,2
Sandberg, Marta Ehrlich, fl. 1930s, 1
Shotwell, Odette, fl. 1960s, 2
Siebert, Florence, 1897–, 2
Simon, Dorothy M., fl. 1960s, 2
Smith, Jean Wheeler, 1942–, 2
Snell, Cornelia Tyler, fl. 1930s, 1
Stellman, Jeanne M., fl. 1970s, 2
Sullivan, Elizabeth, fl. 1940s, 2
Swallow, Ellen, 1842–1911, 1
Telkes, Mari(a) de, 1900–, 1,2
Tesoro, Giuliana, fl. 1970s, 2

Tickhill, Terry Lee, fl. 1960s, 2
Van Straaten, Florence Wilhelmina, 1913–, 1,2
Wall, Florence Emeline, fl. 1920s, 1
Watson, Patricia, 1949–, 2
Webster, Eleanor, fl. 1930s, 2
Weiner, Ruth, fl. 1960s, 2
Young, Hoylande D., 2
Cherokee folklore
Green, Rayna Diane, fl. 1970s, 2
Cherokee Indians
Akyoka, fl. 1820s, 2
Brown, Catherine, d. 1823, 2
Callahan, Nancy "Granny Dollar", 1826–1931, 2
Ward, Nancy, 1738–1822, 2
Watie, Sarah Caroline Bell, 1820–, 2
Wilson, Florence, fl. 1840s, 2
Cherokee Indians—Friend
Lovely, Persis, fl. 1810s, 2
Chess players
Gaprindashvili, Nona, fl. 1960s, 2
Hastings, Lady Thomas, 2
Menchik-Stevenson, Vera, 1906–1944, 2
Chicana leaders
Cardenas, Teresa Torres, fl. 1970s, 2
Espinosa-Larsen, Anita, 2
Fallis, Guadalupe Valdes, 1941–, 2
Gonzales, Sylvia Alicia, fl. 1943s, 2
Hoyos, Angela de, fl. 1970s, 2
Lucero, Judy, fl. 1970s, 2
Lucero-Trujillo, Marcela Christine, fl. 1970s, 2
Moreno, Victoria, 1957–, 2
Perez, Soledad, 2
Rodriguez, Rosalinda, 1948–, 2
Sotomayer, Marta, fl. 1970s, 2
Tafolla, Carmen, 1951–, 2
Toscano, Carmen, 2
Tovar, Ines Hernandez, 1947–, 2
Trambley, Estela Portillo, 1936–, 2
Xelina, 1954–, 2
Chicano Welfare Rights Group
Escalante, Alicia, fl. 1960s, 2
Child actors
Baby Sandy, 1938–, 2
Chapin, Lauren, 1945–, 1,2
Collins, Cora Sue, 1927–, 2
Cummings, Quinn, 1967–, 2
Darling, Jean, 1929–1935, 2
Garner, Peggy Ann, 1931–1984, 2
Gloria Jean, 1926–, 2
Green, Mitzi, 1920–1969, 2

Hood, Darla, 1931–1979, 2
Jason, Sybil, 1929–, 2
King, Cammie, 2
Kornman, Mary, 2
McCormack, Patty, 1945–, 2
Morgan, Robin, fl. 1970s, 2
O'Brien, Margaret (Angela Maxine), 1937–, 1,2
Perreau, Gigi (Chislaine), 1941–, 2
Quigley, Juanita, 1931–, 2
Rudie, Evelyn, fl. 1950s, 1,2
Weidler, Virginia, 1927–1968, 2
Withers, Jane, 1926–, 1,2
Child authors
Ashford, Daisy, 1881–1972, 2
Crane, Nathalia Clara Ruth, 1913–, 1,2
Grosvenor, Kali Diana, 1960–, 2
Hudson, Virginia Cary, 1894–, 2
Straight, Dorothy, 1958–, 2
Child baseball players
Dickinson, Amy, 2
Child bride
Aurelia Philematium, 2
Child care
Creque, Bobbie Little, fl. 1970s, 2
Dodge, Josephine Marshall Jewell, 1855–1928, 2
Hughes, Dorothy Pitman, 1938–, 2
Child celebrities
Agresta, Kirsten, 2
Brown, Linda, 2
Gampbel, Lilit, 2
O'Hanlon, Virginia, 2
O'Neal, Tatum, 1963–, 2
Stead, Karen, 2
Child circus performers
Jones, Annie, 1865–1902, 2
Child development
Frank, Mary Hughes, 1919–, 1
Gans, Bird Stein, fl. 1930s, 1
Ovens, Florence Jane, fl. 1930s, 1
Wandling, Arlita R., fl. 1930s, 1
White, Edna Noble, 1879–1954, 2
Child gymnasts
Willim, Stephanie, fl. 1970s, 2
Child heroes
Miner, Hazel, 1914–1920, 2
Child of discrimination
Etienne, Gail, 1966–, 2
Child patent holders
Thompson, Mary, fl. 1960s, 2
Thompson, Teresa, 1952–, 2
Child pianists
Mozart, Maria Anna (Nannerl), 1751–1829, 1,2

Child pilots
Coupe, Betty Lou, fl. 1900s, 2
Smith, Elinor, 1911–, 1,2
Child poets
Davidson, Lucretia Maria, 1808–1825, 1,2
Davidson, Margaret Miller, 1823–1838, 1,2
Drouet, Minou, 1947–, 2
Child printers
Ella of Dessau, fl. 1690s, 2
Child psychologists
Blanchard, Phyllis, 1895–, 2
Roland, Jeanne Manon Philipon, 1754–1793, 1,2
Shinn, Milicent Washburn, 1858–1940, 1,2
Child radio personalities
Rose Marie, Baby, fl. 1930s, 1
Child singers
Jean, Gloria, 1927–, 2
Child spy
Marie, fl. 1910s, 1
Child tennis players
Foster, Joy, fl. 1920s, 2
Child welfare workers
Bertola, Mariana, fl. 1920s, 1
Birney, Alice McLellan, 1858–1907, 2
Reeves, Margaret, 1893–, 1
Schoff, Hannah Kent, 1853–1940, 1,2
Smith, Ruth Lyman, 1872–1926, 1
Child winner soap box derby
Cross, Laura, 1962–, 2
Childbirth experts
De Lyser, Femmy, 2
Childhood educators
Darden, Margaret Singleton, 1942–, 2
Dobbs, Ella Victoria, 1866–1952, 2
Gage, Lucy, 1876–1945, 2
Genlis, Stephanie Felicite de Crest de Saint-Aubin, Comtesse de, 1746–1830, 1,2
MacMillan, Margaret, 1860–1931, 1,2
Children's Defense Fund
Edelman, Marian Wright, 1939–, 2
Children's Foundation
Bode, Barbara, 2
Children's World Educational Center
Dias, Marie T., fl. 1970s, 2
Children's counselors
Wallerstein, Judith, fl. 1970s, 2
Children's librarians
Moore, Anne Carroll, 1871–1961, 1,2
Children's literature
Arbuthnot, May Hill, 1884–1969, 2
Massee, May, 1881–1966, 2

Miller, Bertha Everett Mahony, 1882–1969, 2
Chilperic I—Consort
Fredegund (Fredegonde), d. 597, 1,2
China
Bridgman, Eliza Jane Gillet, 1805–1871, 2
Fearn, Anne Walter, 1865–1939, 2
China painters
Coleman, Helen Cordelia, 2
Coleman, Rebecca, d. 1884, 2
Dodd, Jane Porter Hart, 1824–1911, 2
Faulkner, Lucy, fl. 1860s, 2
Hagen, Alice Mary Egan, 1872–1972, 2
Newton, Clara Chipman, 1848–1936, 2
Nourse, Mary Madeline, 1870–1959, 2
Powell, Louise Lessore, 1910–1930, 2
Sherwood, Rosina Emmett, 1854–, 1,2
Sparkes, Catherine, fl. 1870s, 2
Chippewa Indians
Maulson, Hannah, fl. 1970s, 2
Petersen, Andrea, fl. 1950s, 2
Chiropractors
Arnold, Alma Cusian, 1871–, 1
Choate, Rufus—Daughter
Bell, Helen Olcott Choate, 1830–1918, 1
Choctaw Indians
McCurtain, Jane, 2
Popkes, Opal Lee, 1920–, 2
Victor, Wilma L., fl. 1970s, 2
Choir directors
See
Choral conductors
Choral conductors
Bampton, Ruth, 1902–, 1
Davies, Clara Novello Davies, 1861–1943, 1
Deneke, Margaret, fl. 1930s, 1
Foster, Bertha M., fl. 1940s, 1
Garron, Etta R. Small, 1887–, 2
Gulesian, Grace Warner, 1884–, 1
Kentworthy, Ruth DeWolfe, 1889–1971, 2
Choreographers
Benesh, Joan Dorothy, 1920–, 1
Bettis, Valerie Elizabeth, 1919–1982, 1,2
Charrat, Janine, 1924–, 1
Childs, Lucinda, 1940–, 2

Cullberg, Birgit, 1908–, 2
Danilova, Alexandra Alicia, 1906–, 1,2
De Valois, Ninette, 1898–, 1,2
DeMille, Agnes George, 1905–, 1,2
Dunham, Katherine, 1910–, 1,2
Erdman, Jean, 1917–, 2
Franca, Celia, 1921–, 1,2
Graham, Martha, 1893–, 1,2
Greenfield, Amy, fl. 1970s, 2
Haney, Carol, 1924–1964, 1,2
Harriton, Maria, fl. 1960s, 2
Hernandez, Amalia, fl. 1950s, 2
Hightower, Rosella, 1920–, 1
Holm, Hanya Eckert, 1893–, 1,2
Humphrey, Doris, 1895–1958, 1,2
Inglesby, Mona, 1918–, 1
Koner, Pauline, 1912–, 1
Lang, Pearl Lack, 1922–, 2
Levi-Tanai, Sara, fl. 1940s, 1,2
Lopez, Pilar, fl. 1950s, 1
Losch, Tilly, Countess of Carmarvon, 1907–1975, 1,2
Monk, Meredith, 1942–, 2
Nijinska, Bronislava, 1891–1972, 1,2
Page, Ruth, 1900–, 1,2
Skolow, Anna, 1915–, 2
St. Denis, Ruth, 1877–1968, 1,2
Tamiris, Helen, 1902–1966, 1,2
Tharp, Twyla, 1941–, 2
Valois, Ninette de, 1898–, 1
Wigman, Mary, 1886–1973, 1,2
Wilde, Patricia, 1928–, 1
Chou Hsin—Concubine
T'a Chi, 1
Christian IV—Mother
Sophia of Mechlenburg, 2
Christian Scientists
Eddy, Mary Baker, 1821–1910, 1,2
Morgan, Mary Kimball, 1861–1848, 2
Stetson, Augusta Emma Simmons, 1842–1928, 2
Christian VII—Stepmother
Juliane Marie, 1729–1796, 2
Christian converts
Journeycake, Sally, fl. 1830s, 2
Christian—Daughter
Wales, Alexandra, m. 1863, 1
Christians
Acarie, Madame Barbe, 1566–1618, 1
Adela of Blois, 1062–1137, 1
Bullinger, Anna, 1504–1564, 1
Bunyan, Elizabeth, d. 1691, 1
Godolphin, Margaret Blagge, 1652–1678, 1

City planners
  McLain, Elizabeth, fl. 1970s, 2
  Ramati, Raquel, fl. 1970s, 2
  Smith, Chloetheil W., 1910–, 2
Civic leaders
  Black, Nellie Peters, 1851–1919, 2
  Douglas, Edna Mae, 1
  Evans, Anne, 1869–1941, 1
  Hogg, Ima, 1882–1975, 2
  Lea, Sally Wildy, d. 1884, 2
  Mier, Isabel Alonso de, 1886–, 2
  Montgomery, Catherine Lewis, fl.
    1960s, 2
  Mumford, Mary Eno Bassett, 1842–
    1935, 2
  Munford, Mary-Cooke Branch,
    1865–1938, 1,2
  Murray, Florence Kerins, 1916–, 2
  Sherwin, Belle, 1868–1955, 2
  Wells, Marguerite Milton, 1872–
    1959, 2
Civic reformers
  Landes, Bertha Ethel Knight, 1868–
    1943, 1,2
  Ueland, Clara Hampson, 1860–1927,
    2
Civic workers
  Berry, Harriet Morehead, 1877–
    1940, 2
  Biesele, Anna Emma John, 1888–, 2
  Congdon, Mary Glasgow Peek (Prin-
    cess Redwing), 1898–, 2
  Eisenhower, Barbara Jean, 1926–, 1
  Hayes, Anna Hansen, 1886–, 1,2
  Holmes, Kate Stone, 1841–1907, 2
  Kirksey, Lucile Hicks, 1904–, 2
  McCannel, Louise Walker, 1916–, 2
  Mendez, Ana G., 1908–, 2
  Miller, Elva Ruby Connes, 1908–, 2
  Miller, Myrtis Hawthorne, 1906–, 2
  Mills, Nellie Ireton, 1880–1967, 2
  Montgomery, Helen Barrett, 1861–
    1934, 1,2
  Morrison, Ann, d. 1957, 2
  Murat, Catherine (Katrina), 1824–
    1910, 2
  Pittinger, Alice Butterworth, fl.
    1910s, 2
  Romeu, Marta Robert de, 1890–, 2
  Sanders, Estelle Schulze, 1905–, 2
Civil Defense organizer
  Isaacs, Stella Charnaud (Baronness
    Swansborough), 1894–1971, 2
Civil engineers
  Barney, Nora Stanton Blatch, 1883–
    1971, 2

Carlin, Dorothy A., fl. 1930s, 1
Eaves, Elsie, 1898–, 1,2
McNally, Margaret, fl. 1930s, 1
Morgan, Julia, 1872–1957, 2
Richards, Lydia, 1863–1935, 2
Civil rights leaders
  Barnett, Ida B. Wells, 1862–1931, 1
  Bates, Daisy Lee Gatson, 1919–, 1,2
  Cox, Dinah, 1804–1909, 1
  Davis, Nancy L., fl. 1960s, 2
  Delaney, Catherine A., 1822–1894, 1
  Devlin, Bernadette Josephine, 1947–,
    2
  Gaines, Irene McCoy, 1892–1964, 2
  Hamer, Fannie Lou Townsend,
    1917–, 2
  Harris, La Donna Crawford, 1931–, 2
  Hill, Caroline Sherman Andrews,
    1829–1914, 1
  King, Coretta Scott, 1927–, 2
  Martin, George Madden, 1866–1946,
    2
  Moody, Anne, 1940–, 2
  Norton, Eleanor Holmes, 1937–, 2
  Ovington, Mary White, 1865–1951, 2
  Parks, Rosa Lee, 1913–, 2
  Pleasant, Mary Ellen "Mammy",
    1814–1904, 1,2
  Robeson, Eslanda Cardoza Goode,
    1896–1965, 2
  Robesson, Eslanda Cardoza Goode,
    1896–1965, 2
  Robinson, Ruby Doris Smith, 1942–
    1967, 2
  Sanders, Elizabeth Elkins, 1762–
    1851, 2
  Seidenberg, Faith, 2
  Takayama, Shigeri, 1899–1977, 2
  Terrell, Mary Eliza Church, 1863–
    1954, 1,2
Civil War
  A.M.B., Miss, fl. 1860s, 1
  Adams, Helen Balfour, 1848–1948, 1
  Agnes, fl. 1820s, 1
  Alden, Esther, c. 1847, 1
  Andrews, Eliza Frances, 1840–1932,
    1,2
  Andrews, Emma, fl. 1860s, 1
  Arnold, Mary Ellen, fl. 1860s, 1
  Babcock, Martha Cross, 1814–1873, 2
  Baker, Delphine P., 1828–, 1
  Baker, Mrs. E. H., fl. 1860s, 1
  Barrows, Ellen B., fl. 1860s, 1
  Baum, Mrs. A., d. 1910, 1

Beach, Elizabeth Jane, fl. 1860s, 2
Beck, Mrs., fl. 1860s, 1
Bickerdyke, Mary Ann Ball
  "Mother", 1817–1901, 1,2
Bigelow, Mrs. R. M., fl. 1860s, 1
Blalock, Mrs. L. M., fl. 1860s, 1
Bondurant, Mrs., 2
Booth, Mrs., fl. 1860s, 1
Boozer, Mary, fl. 1860s, 1
Boteler, Helen, fl. 1860s, 1
Botume, Elizabeth Hyde, fl. 1860s, 1
Boyd, Belle, 1844–1900, 1,2
Boyer, Margaret, fl. 1860s, 1
Bradford, Charlotte, fl. 1860s, 1
Bradford, Mary, fl. 1860s, 1
Bradford, Susan, 1846–, 1,2
Bradley, Amy Morris, 1823–1904, 1,2
Brady, Mary A., 1821–1864, 1
Bragg, Mrs. Braxton, fl. 1860s, 2
Brayton, Mary Clark, fl. 1860s, 1
Brooks, Mary Frances, fl. 1860s, 1
Brownell, Kady, 1842–, 1
Buckel, Cloe Annette, 1833–1912, 2
Buie, Mary Ann, fl. 1860s, 1
Burge, Dolly Sumner Lunt, 1817–, 1
Byson, Mary, fl. 1860s, 1
Cahal, Mary, fl. 1860s, 1
Campbell, Valeria, fl. 1860s, 1
Carroll, Anna Ella, 1815–1893, 1,2
Cary, Constance, fl. 1860s, 1
Chapin, Mrs. Herman, fl. 1860s, 1
Chapman, G. D., fl. 1860s, 1
Chase, Mary Wood, 1868–, 1
Chase, Nelly M., fl. 1860s, 2
Chesnut, Mary Boykin Miller, 1823–
  1886, 1,2
Clapp, Anna L., fl. 1860s, 1
Clarke, Amy, 1,2
Clay, Susanna Withers, m. 1815, 1
Cobb, Mary Ann, 2
Cohen, Octavia, 1718–, 1
Collins, Ellen, 1828–1913, 1,2
Colt, Henrietta L. Peckham, 1812–, 1
Coste, Marie Revenel de la, fl. 1860s,
  1
Cox, Lucy Ann, fl. 1860s, 1
Crouse, Nancy, fl. 1860s, 2
Cushman, Pauline, 1833–1835, 1,2
D'Oremieulx, Mrs. T., fl. 1860s, 1
Davis, Varina Anne Banks Howell,
  1826–1906, 1,2
Dawson, Sarah Morgan, 1841–, 1
Dorsey, Sarah Anne Ellis, 1829–
  1879, 1,2

Duckett, Elizabeth Waring, fl. 1860s,
  1
Duffee, Mary Gordon, 2
Dulaney, Evalina, fl. 1860s, 1
Dulany, Ida, fl. 1860s, 1
Duvall, Betty, fl. 1860s, 1
Edmondson, Belle, fl. 1860s, 1
Edmonston, Catherine Ann, fl.
  1860s, 1,2
Edson, Sarah P., fl. 1860s, 1
Ellis, Lizzie Rutherford, fl. 1860s, 2
Evans, Augusta Jane, 1835–1909, 1,2
Fales, Almirah L., d. 1868, 1
Farnham, Amanda C., fl. 1860s, 1
Felch, Amanda Farnham, 183—, 1
Fenn, Mrs. Curtis T., fl. 1860s, 1
Ford, Antonia, fl. 1860s, 1,2
Frietschie, Barbara, 1766–1862, 1,2
Gage, Frances Dana Barker, 1808–
  1884, 1,2
Gardner, Adaline, fl. 1860s, 1
Gardner, Bertha, fl. 1860s, 1
Gay, Mary Ann Harris, 1829–, 1,2
Gilmer, Louisa Fredericka, fl. 1860s,
  1
Gilmer, Loulie, fl. 1860s, 1
Gist, Malvina Black, 1842–, 1,2
Goodridge, Ellen, fl. 1860s, 1
Greble, Susan Virginia, fl. 1860s, 1
Greenhow, Rose O'Neal, 1815–1864,
  1,2
Grier, Maria C., fl. 1860s, 1
Griffin, Josephine R., fl. 1860s, 1
Griffin, Mrs. William Preston, fl.
  1860s, 1
Hadley, Piety Lucretia, fl. 1860s, 1
Hague, Parthenia Antoinette, fl.
  1860s, 2
Hall, Mrs. Dorian, fl. 1860s, 1
Hallowell, Mrs. M. M., fl. 1860s, 1
Harding, Elizabeth McGavock,
  1818–, 1
Harlan, Mrs. James, m. 1845/6, 1
Harmon, Amelia, fl. 1860s, 1
Harper, Ella, fl. 1860s, 2
Harris, Eliza, fl. 1860s, 1
Harvey, Cordelia Adelaide Perrine,
  1824–1895, 1,2
Hitz, Ann, fl. 1860s, 1
Hoge, Mrs. A. H., 1811–1890, 1
Holmes, Emma E., fl. 1860s, 1
Hosmer, Mrs. O. E., fl. 1860s, 1
Houston, Margaret Moffett Lea,
  1819–1867, 1,2

Hurd, Mrs. P. B., m. 1857, 1
Jackson, Eleanor Noyes, fl. 1860s, 1
Jackson, Mary Anna, m. 1857, 1
Johns, Annie E., fl. 1860s, 1
Johnston, Mrs. John T., fl. 1860s, 1
Johnston, Sarah R., fl. 1860s, 1
Johnstone, Mary H., fl. 1860s, 1
Jones, Calista Robinson, fl. 1860s, 1
Jones, Flora MacDonald, fl. 1860s, 1
Kelly, Amie, fl. 1860s, 1
Kirby, Mrs. William, fl. 1860s, 1
Kollock, Augusta J., fl. 1860s, 1
Lamb, Mrs. William, fl. 1800s, 1
Lawton, Sarah Alexander, fl. 1860s, 1
Lay, Julia, fl. 1880s, 1
Le Conte, Emma Florence, 1,2
Le Grand, Julia, fl. 1860s, 1
Lee, Henrietta Bedinger, fl. 1860s, 1
Lee, Mary Randolph Custis, 1806–
    1873, 1
Lee, Mrs. Joseph, 2
Loughborough, Mary Ann Webster,
    1863–1887, 1,2
Love, Mary, fl. 1860s, 1
Lowe, Lucy, fl. 1860s, 1
Lowell, Anna, fl. 1860s, 1
Mackall, Lillie, fl. 1860s, 1
Mann, Maria R., fl. 1860s, 1
Marsh, Mrs. M. M., fl. 1860s, 1
Maury, Betty Herndon, fl. 1860s, 1
May, Abigail Williams, 1829–1888,
    1,2
McCalla, Margaret, fl. 1860s, 2
McEwan, Hetty (Hettie) M., fl.
    1860s, 1,2
McGuire, Judith Brockenbrough,
    1813–, 1
McLure, Margaret A. E., fl. 1860s, 1
McMichael, Margaret T., fl. 1860s, 1
McSherry, Virginia Faulkner, fl.
    1860s, 1
McSweeney, Mattie, fl. 1860s, 1
Moon, Charlotte, 1829–1912, 1
Moon, Virginia, 1845–1926, 1
Moore, Clara Sophia Jessup, 1824–
    1899, 1,2
Moore, Eliza, 2
Moore, Jane Boswell, fl. 1860s, 1
Moran, Mrs. Harry Harrison, 1857–,
    2
Morgan, Henrietta Hunt, 1805–1891,
    1
Morgan, Martha Ready, fl. 1860s, 1
Morgan, Sarah, 1841–, 1,2

Morrison, Mary Anna, fl. 1860s, 1
Morton, Matt, fl. 1860s, 2
Muirson, Georgeanna, 1833–1906, 2
Murdock, Ellen E., fl. 1860s, 1
Murphree sisters, fl. 1860s, 2
Orman, Sarah, 2
Painter, Hettie K., fl. 1860s, 1
Palmer, Mary E., d. 1865, 1
Parrish, Lydia G., fl. 1860s, 1
Peake, Mary S., 1823–1862, 1
Pearsall, Rachel, fl. 1860s, 1
Perkins, Anne, fl. 1860s, 1
Phelps, Mrs. John S., fl. 1860s, 1
Phillips, Bettie Taylor, fl. 1860s, 1
Phillips, Eugenia Levy, fl. 1860s, 1,2
Phillips, Josephine, fl. 1860s, 1
Pickens, Lucy Petway Holcombe,
    1832–1899, 1,2
Pickett, LaSalle Corbell, 1843–, 1
Pierce, Tillie, fl. 1860s, 1,2
Piggott, Emeline, fl. 1860s, 1,2
Polk, Antoinette, 2
Pollock, Roberta, fl. 1860s, 1
Pomery, Lucy Gaylord, d. 1863, 1
Poppenheim, Mrs. C. C., fl. 1860s, 1
Powers, Lucy Gaylord, fl. 1860s, 1
Preston, Margaret Junkin, 1820–
    1897, 1,2
Pryor, Sara Agnes Rice, 1830–1912,
    1,2
Pugh, Mary Williams, fl. 1860s, 1
Ravenel, Charlotte St. Julien, fl.
    1860s, 1
Rawson, Mary, fl. 1860s, 1
Ready, Alice, fl. 1860s, 1
Revenel, Charlotte St. Julien, fl.
    1860s, 1
Ridley, Rebeccah C., fl. 1860s, 1
Roebling, Emily Warren, 1843–1903,
    1
Rogers, Loula Kendall, fl. 1860s, 1
Rouse, Mrs. Benjamin, 1800–, 1
Ruffin, Josephine St. Pierre, 1843–
    1924, 1,2
Russell, Lenie, fl. 1860s, 1
Russell, Tillie, fl. 1860s, 1
Salomon, Eliza, fl. 1860s, 1
Sansom, Emma, d. 1990, 1,2
Scales, Cordelia Lewis, fl. 1860s, 1
Schuyler, Louise Lee, 1837–1926, 1,2
Scott, Mrs. Taylor, fl. 1860s, 1
Seymour, Mrs. Horatio, fl. 1860s, 1
Sheads, Carrie, fl. 1860s, 1
Sheffield, Mary E., fl. 1860s, 2

Shelton, Mary E., fl. 1860s, 1
Shover, Felicia Lee Carey Thornton, fl. 1860s, 1
Simpson, Annie, d. 1905, 1
Simpson, Lucy Faucett, fl. 1860s, 1
Sims, Leora, fl. 1860s, 1
Smith, Cassie Selden, m. 1861, 1
Smith, Lucy, fl. 1860s, 1
Smith, Mrs. J. Henry, fl. 1860s, 1
Smith, Mrs. S. E. D., fl. 1860s, 1
Souder, Emily Bliss, fl. 1860s, 1
Springer, Mrs. C. R., fl. 1860s, 1
Stearns, Sarah Burger, 1836–, 1
Stinson, Virginia McCollum, fl. 1860s, 1
Stokes, Missouri, fl. 1860s, 1
Stone, Cornelia Branch, 1840–, 1
Stone, Kate, 1841–1907, 2
Stranahan, Marianne F., fl. 1860s, 1
Streeter, Elizabeth M., fl. 1860s, 1
Stuart, Flora Cooke, fl. 1860s, 1
Stuart, Jane, 1830–1891, 2
Sullivan, Betsy "Mother", fl. 1860s, 1
Sullivan, Mary Mildred Hammond, m. 1856, 1
Sutherlin, Mrs. W. T., fl. 1860s, 1
Taylor, Alice, fl. 1860s, 1
Taylor, Susie King, 1848–1912, 2
Terry, Ellen F., fl. 1860s, 1
Thompson, Sarah, d. 1909, 1
Titlow, Effie, fl. 1860s, 1
Toombs, Mrs. Robert, fl. 1860s, 2
Turchin, Nadine, 1826–1904, 1
Tynes, Mary Elizabeth, fl. 1860s, 1,2
Van Lew, Elizabeth L. (Mrs. John), 1818–1900, 1,2
Van Lew, Mrs. John, fl. 1860s, 1
Velazquez, Loretta Janeta, 1838–1897, 1,2
Wade, Jennie, fl. 1860s, 1,2
Wade, Mary B., fl. 1860s, 1
Wadley, Sarah L., fl. 1860s, 1
Walker, Mary Edwards, 1832–1919, 1,2
Waring, Mary D., fl. 1860s, 1
Waterbury, Kate E., fl. 1860s, 1
Watie, Sarah Caroline Bell, 1820–, 2
Wells, Mrs. Shepard, fl. 1860s, 1
White, Armenia, fl. 1860s, 1
Wilcox, Mrs. G. Griffin, fl. 1860s, 1
Winborne, Rebecca M., d. 1918, 2
Windsor, Mary Catherine, 1830–1914, 1
Wittenmyer, Annie Turner, 1827–1900, 1,2

Woerishoffer, Anna, 2
Woods, Mehitable Ellis, 2
Wormeley, Katharine Prescott, 1830–1908, 1,2
Wright, Mrs. Crafts J., fl. 1860s, 1
Wright, Rebecca, m. 1871, 1

Civil War lecturers
Dickinson, Anna Elizabeth, 1842–1932, 1,2

Civil War nurses
Adams, Martha, fl. 1860s, 1
Aiken, Lizzie, fl. 1860s, 1
Alder, Emily, fl. 1860s, 1
Allen, Phebe, fl. 1860s, 1
Alter, Belle Thompson, fl. 1860s, 1
Aston, Mary A., fl. 1860s, 1
Baker, Anna H., fl. 1860s, 1
Baldridge, Elizabeth Lee, fl. 1860s, 1
Ballou, Addie L., fl. 1860s, 1
Barker, Mrs. Stephen, fl. 1860s, 1
Barlow, Arabella Griffith, fl. 1860s, 1
Barry, Susan E. Hill, fl. 1860s, 1
Bell, Mary E., fl. 1860s, 1
Bengless, Catherine H. Griffith, fl. 1860s, 1
Billing, Rose M., d. 1865, 1
Bissell, Lucy J., fl. 1860s, 1
Blackmar, Miss, fl. 1860s, 1
Boyington, Mary K., fl. 1860s, 1
Breckinridge, Margaret Elizabeth, fl. 1860s, 1
Briggs, Mrs. M. M., fl. 1860s, 1
Brown, Nancy M. Nelson, fl. 1860s, 1
Brown, Susan L. McLaughlin, fl. 1986s, 1
Buckley, Lettie E. Covell, fl. 1860s, 1
Bucklin, Sophronia, fl. 1860s, 1
Budwin, Florena, 2
Bullard, Jennie Matthewson, fl. 1860s, 1
Bunnell, Mrs. Henrietta S. T., fl. 1860s, 1
Burnell, Helen M., fl. 1860s, 1
Canfield, Martha, fl. 1860s, 1
Cartwright, Emily J. Avery, fl. 1860s, 1
Chapman, Elizabeth, fl. 1860s, 1
Clark, Bell Vorse, fl. 1860s, 1
Cochran, Nannie M., fl. 1860s, 1
Cole, Helen Brainard, fl. 1860s, 1
Colfax, Harriet R., fl. 1860s, 1
Counts, Belle, fl. 1860s, 1
Cross, Sarah B., fl. 1860s, 1

Crossan, Clarissa Watters, fl. 1860s, 1
Cumming, Kate, 1835–1909, 1,2
Curry, Sadie, fl. 1860s, 1
Cutter, Carrie, d. 1862, 2
Dada, Hatte A., fl. 1860s, 1
Dana, Emily W., fl. 1860s, 1
Danforth, Ruth, fl. 1860s, 1
Daniels, Frances D, fl. 1860s, 1
Davis, Clara, fl. 1860s, 1
Davis, Mrs. G. T. M., fl. 1860s, 1
Day, Juliana, fl. 1860s, 1
Dieffenbacker, Frances A., fl. 1860s, 1
Divers, Bridget, fl. 1860s, 1
Dix, Dorothea Lynde, 1802–1887, 1,2
Dudzik, Josephine, 2
Dumas, Sarah J. Steady, fl. 1860s, 1
Dupee, Mary A., fl. 1860s, 1
Dye, Clarissa F., fl. 1860s, 1
Eccleston, Sarah Chamberlain, fl. 1860s, 1
Edmonds, (Sarah) Emma E., 1841–1898, 1,2
Eldred, Maria Olmstead, fl. 1860s, 1
Elliott, Melcinia, fl. 1860s, 1
Elmer, Emily Rowell, fl. 1860s, 1
Erving, Anne Princess, fl. 1860s, 1
Ewing, Elizabeth Wendell, fl. 1860s, 1
Fay, Delia A. B., fl. 1860s, 1
Fogg, Isabella, fl. 1860s, 1
Fowle, Elida Barker Rumsey, 1842–1919, 1,2
Fox, Mary Jane, fl. 1860s, 1
Frick, Rebecca E., fl. 1860s, 1
Fritcher, Elizabeth L., fl. 1860s, 1
Gardner, Mary Fryer, fl. 1860s, 1
George, Mrs. E. E., fl. 1860s, 1
Gibbons, Abigail Hopper, 1801–1893, 1,2
Gibson, Mrs. E. O., fl. 1860s, 1
Gilson, Helen Louise, 1835–1868, 1,2
Gordon, Sallie Chapman, 1805–1894, 1
Grass, Elizabeth, fl. 1860s, 1
Gridley, Ann Eliza, d. 1909, 1
Hagar, Sarah J., d. 1864, 1
Hahn, Anna, fl. 1860s, 1
Hall, Maria M. C., fl. 1860s, 1
Hall, Susan E., fl. 1860s, 1
Hamilton, Margaret, 1840–, 1
Hancock, Cornelia, 1839–1927, 1,2
Harrington, Cornelia, fl. 1860s, 1
Harris, Miss W. F., fl. 1860s, 1
Harris, Mrs. John, fl. 1860s, 1

Hawley, Harriet Foote, fl. 1860s, 1
Hayden, Mary F. Strahan, fl. 1860s, 1
Hayes, Margaret Meserolle, fl. 1860s, 1
Hazen, Fanny Titus, 1840–, 1
Hibbard, Julia A., fl. 1860s, 1
Hickey, Katherine Maloney, fl. 1860s, 2
Hill, Nancy M., fl. 1860s, 1
Hoisington, Lauretta H. Cutler, fl. 1860s, 1
Holstein, Anna, 1824–1890, 1
Home, Jessie, fl. 1860s, 1
Howe, Abbie J., fl. 1860s, 1
Howland, Eliza W., fl. 1860s, 1
Howland, Mary Woolsey, d. 1864, 1
Hunt, Elizabeth Pickard, fl. 1860s, 1
Husband, Mary Morris, fl. 1860s, 1
Jackson, Fannie Oslin, fl. 1860s, 1
Jobes, Mary Adelaide Daugherty, fl. 1860s, 1
Johnson, Ada, fl. 1860s, 1
Johnson, Lydia S., fl. 1860s, 1
Jones, Hetty A., fl. 1860s, 1
Kaiser, Lucy L. Campbell, fl. 1860s, 1
King, E. M., fl. 1880s, 1
Kingsbury, Emiline D., fl. 1860s, 1
Kripps, Susanna, fl. 1860s, 1
Lacey, Mary Roby, fl. 1860s, 1
Lane, Adeline A., fl. 1860s, 1
Law, Sallie Chapman Gordon, 1805–1894, 1,2
Leavitt, Adelia, fl. 1860s, 1
Lee, Mary W., fl. 1860s, 1
Lemmon, Sarah A. Plummer, fl. 1860s, 1
Loomis, Mary A., fl. 1860s, 1
Lowell, Susan R., fl. 1860s, 1
Lowry, Ellen J., fl. 1860s, 1
Maertz, Louisa, fl. 1860s, 1
Maish, Jennie Gauslin, fl. 1860s, 1
Mannon, Mary L., 1843–, 1
Marsh, Susan Ellen, fl. 1860s, 1
Maxfield, Mary B., fl. 1860s, 1
Maxon, Hannah W., d. 1910, 1
McKay, Charlotte E., fl. 1860s, 1
McMeens, Anna C., fl. 1860s, 1
McPeek, Allie, fl. 1860s, 1
Melton, Joanna, fl. 1860s, 1
Mendenhall, Elizabeth S., fl. 1860s, 1
Miller, Adaline, fl. 1860s, 1
Miller, Maria, fl. 1860s, 1
Mills, Susan Carrie, fl. 1860s, 1

Mitchell, Ellen E., fl. 1860s, 1
Morris, Matilda E., fl. 1860s, 1
Morton, Jane M., fl. 1860s, 1
Mott, Mollie C., fl. 1860s, 1
Munsell, Jane R., fl. 1860s, 1
Newman, Laura A. Mount, fl. 1860s, 1
Newsom, Ella King, fl. 1860s, 1
Nichols, Elizabeth B., fl. 1860s, 1
Oleson, Rebecca Lemmon, fl. 1860s, 1
Olnhausen, Mary Phinney von, 1818–1902, 1
Otis, Rebecca, fl. 1860s, 1
Palmer, Hannah L., fl. 1860s, 1
Parsons, Emily Elizabeth, 1824–1880, 1,2
Patterson, Sarepta C. McNall, fl. 1860s, 1
Pember, Phoebe Yates Levy, 1823–1913, 1,2
Pettes, Mary Dwight, fl. 1860s, 1
Phillips, Emaline, fl. 1860s, 1
Pollard, Carrie Wilkins, fl. 1860s, 1
Pollock, Mary B., fl. 1860s, 1
Porter, Eliza Emily Chappell, 1807–1888, 1,2
Pratt, Malinda A. Miller, fl. 1860s, 1
Price, Rebecca L., fl. 1860s, 1
Pringle, Mary, 1833–, 1
Rathnell, Maria L. Moore, fl. 1860s, 1
Reading, Sarah M., fl. 1860s, 1
Reynolds, Belle, 1840–, 1
Richards, Maria M. C. Hall, fl. 1860s, 1
Richardson, Mary A. Ransorn, fl. 1860s, 1
Risley, Alice Carey Farmer, fl. 1860s, 1
Ross, Anna Maria, fl. 1860s, 1
Russell, Mrs. E. J., fl. 1860s, 1
Sackett, Emma A. French, fl. 1860s, 1
Safford, Mary Jane (Joanna), 1834–1891, 1,2
Schram, Ann Maria B., fl. 1860s, 1
Scott, Harriet M., fl. 1860s, 1
Scott, Kate M., d. 1911, 1
Seelye, Sara Emma Edwards, 1841–1901, 2
Sharpless, Harrie R., fl. 1860s, 1
Shelton, A., fl. 1860s, 1
Simonds, Emma E., d. 1893, 1
Small, Jerusha R., fl. 1860s, 1
Smith, Adelaide W., 1831–, 1

Smith, Mary E. Webber, fl. 1860s, 1
Smith, Rebecca S., fl. 1860s, 1
Smythe, Amanda B., fl. 1860s, 1
Spaulding, Jennie Tileston, fl. 1860s, 1
Spencer, Emily P., fl. 1860s, 1
Spencer, Mrs. R. H., fl. 1860s, 1
Sprague, Sarah J. Milliken, fl. 1860s, 1
Sprague, Susannah, fl. 1860s, 1
Squire, Mary E., fl. 1860s, 1
Stanley, Cornelia M. Tomkins, fl. 1860s, 1
Starbird, Hannah Judkins, fl. 1860s, 1
Starr, Lucy E., fl. 1860s, 1
Stevens, Mary O. Townsend, fl. 1860s, 1
Stevenson, Sophie, fl. 1860s, 1
Stewart, Mary E. Pearce, fl. 1860s, 1
Stewart, Salome M., fl. 1860s, 1
Stubbs, Annie Bell, fl. 1860s, 1
Sturgis, "Mother", fl. 1860s, 1
Swartz, Vesta M., fl. 1860s, 1
Tannehill, Arabella, fl. 1860s, 1
Taylor, Catherine L., fl. 1860s, 1
Taylor, Nellie Maria, fl. 1860s, 1
Thomas, Mrs. E., fl. 1860s, 1
Thompson, Charlotte Marson, fl. 1860s, 1
Titcomb, Louise, fl. 1860s, 1
Tomkins, Cornelia M., fl. 1860s, 1
Tompkins, Sally Louisa, 1833–1916, 1,2
Townsend, Eliza L., fl. 1860s, 1
Trader, Ella King Newsom, 1838–1919, 1,2
Tyler, Adeline Blanchard, Sister, 1805–1875, 1,2
Tyson, Laura R. Cotton, fl. 1860s, 1
Usher, Rebecca R., fl. 1860s, 1
Vance, Mary, fl. 1860s, 1
Walker, Adeline, d. 1865, 1
Warnock, Susan Mercer, fl. 1860s, 1
Wheelock, Julia Susan, fl. 1860s, 1
White, Cynthia Elbin, fl. 1860s, 1
Whiteman, Lydia L., fl. 1860s, 1
Willard, Electra, fl. 1860s, 1
Willets, Georgiana, fl. 1860s, 1
Willson, Mary Eleanor, fl. 1860s, 1
Wiswall, Hattie, fl. 1860s, 1
Witherell, Mrs. E. C., fl. 1860s, 1
Woodley, Emily E. Wilson, fl. 1860s, 1
Woodworth, Mary A. E. K., fl. 1860s, 1

Woolsey, Abby Howland, 1828–
1893, 1,2
Woolsey, Caroline Caisson, fl. 1860s,
1
Woolsey, Georgiana M., fl. 1860s, 1
Woolsey, Harriet Roosevelt, fl.
1860s, 1
Woolsey, Jane Newton, fl. 1860s, 1
Woolsey, Jane Stuart, fl. 1860s, 1
Woolsey sisters, fl. 1860s, 1
Wright, Leonore Smith, fl. 1860s, 1
Young, Lucy A. Newton, fl. 1860s, 1
Young, M. A. B., d. 1865, 1
Civil War workers
Eaton, Mrs. J. S., fl. 1860s, 1
Fowle, Elida Barker Rumsey, 1842–
1919, 1,2
Hoge, Jane Currie Blaikie, 1811–
1890, 1,2
Livermore, Mary Ashton Rice, 1820–
1905, 1,2
Minor, Virginia Louisa, 1824–1894, 2
Simril, Harriet, fl. 1870s, 2
Whittenmyer, Annie Turner, 1827–
1858, 2
Claflin, Victoria—Mother
Claflin, Roxanna (Roxie), fl. 1850s,
1,2
Clare, Robert—Spouse
Clere, Elizabeth, fl. 1450s, 1
Clarinetists
Scheerer, Jeannette, 1900–1950, 2
Clark, Dick—Spouse
Clark, Kari, 1943–, 2
Clark, James Freeman—Mother
Clark, Martha Hull, fl. 1790s, 1
Classicists
Hamilton, Edith, 1867–1963, 1,2
Kober, Alice Elizabeth, 1906–1950, 2
Pomeroy, Sarah B., fl. 1970s, 2
Rao, Shanta, 1930–, 1
Swindler, Mary Hamilton, 1884–
1967, 2
Taylor, Lily Ross, 1886–1969, 2
Yourcenar, Marguerite, 1903–1987,
1,2
Claudius Appius—Spouse
Claudia, fl. 143BC, 1
Claudius I—Daughter
Antonia, Claudia, d. 66, 1
Octavia, 42–62, 1
Claudius I—Niece
Julia Agrippina, fl. 50 BC, 2
Claudius I—Spouse
Agrippina, The Younger, 15–59, 1,2
Messalina, Valeria, 24–49, 1,2

Plautia Urgulanilla, 84–, 1
Valeria Nessalina, fl. 40s, 1
Claudius Pulcher Appius—Slave
Verginia (2), fl.300sBC, 1,2
Clavecinists
Couperin, Marguerite-Louise, 1676–
1728, 2
Clay, Clement C.—Spouse
Clay, Susanna Withers, m. 1815, 1
Clay, Henry—Mother
Clay, Elizabeth, 1750–1827, 1
Clay, Henry—Spouse
Clay, Lucretia Hart, fl. 1800s, 1
Cleaver, Eldridge—Spouse
Cleaver, Kathleen, 1945–, 2
Clement, Rufus—Mother
Clement, Emma Clarissa Williams,
1874–1952, 1,2
Cleobulus—Daughter
Cleobuline, fl. 570BC, 1,2
Cleopas—Spouse
Cleopas, wife of, 1
Cleopatra—Daughter
Cleopatra Selene, 40 BC, 1
Cleophas—Mother
Mary, 1
Clergy
See also
Chaplains
Missionaries
Priests
Rabbis
Theologians
Anderson, Carol, 1946–, 2
Andrews, Mary Garard, 1852–, 1
Ashbridge, Elizabeth, fl. 1700s, 1
Babcock, Clara Maria, fl. 1880s, 1
Barnard, Hannah Jenkins, 1764–
1825, 1,2
Bartlett, Ella Elizabeth, fl. 1870s, 1
Bennedsen, Dorte, fl. 1950s, 2
Blackwell, Antoinette Brown, 1825–
1921, 1,2
Booth, Catherine Mumford, 1829–
1890, 1,2
Bowles, Ada C., 1836–, 1
Brooks, Nona L., fl. 1930s, 1
Brown, Olympia, 1835–1926, 1,2
Bruce, Elizabeth M., fl. 1880s, 1
Burleigh, Celia, fl. 1880s, 1
Campagnola, Iona, fl. 1970s, 2
Chapin, Augusta Jane, 1836–1905, 1,2
Cheek, Alison M., 1928–, 2
Coltman, Constance M., gr. 1911, 1

Comstock, Elizabeth Leslie Rous, 1815–1891, 1,2
Cook, Maria, fl. 1820s, 1
Cram, Nancy Gore, fl. 1810s, 1
Crane, Caroline Julia Bartlett, 1858–1935, 1,2
Damon, Ruth Augusta, fl. 1860s, 1
Danforth, Abbie Ellsworth, 1836–, 1
Danforth, Clarissa H., m. 1822, 1
Eastman, Annis Bertha Ford, 1852–1910, 2
Evans, Abigail, fl. 1950s, 2
Folsom, Mariana Thompson, fl. 1870s, 1
Fordham, Druecillar, fl. 1970s, 2
Frerichs, Margaret, fl. 1970s, 2
Gertmenian, Susan, fl. 1970s, 2
Gillett, Fidelia Woolley, fl. 1780s, 1
Gonzalez, Luisa, fl. 1960s, 2
Graves, Mary H., fl. 1870s, 1
Green, Patricia, 2
Gustin, Ellen G., fl. 1870s, 1
Hambly, Loveday Billing, 1604–1682, 1
Hanaford, Phebe Ann (Coffin), 1829–1921, 1,2
Harter, Lydia, fl. 1970s, 2
Hawkes, Daphne, 2
Haynes, Lorenza, 1820–, 1
Henderlite, Rachel, fl. 1940s, 2
Henrichsen, Margaret, fl. 1950s, 2
Hewett, Mary, d. 1853, 1
Heylyn, Mrs. Peter, fl. 1600s, 1
Heyward, Carter, fl. 1970s, 2
Hobart, Ella F., fl. 1860s, 2
Hoehler, Judy, fl. 1970s, 2
Hoskins, Jane, 1694–, 1,2
Hume, Sophia Wigington, 1702–1774, 1,2
Janes, Martha Waldron, 1832–, 1
Jenkins, Lydia A., fl. 1850s, 1
Johnstone, Margaret Blair, 1913–, 1
Jones, Mary C., 1842–, 1
Jones, Rebecca, 1739–1818, 1,2
Jones-Goldstein, Bonnie, fl. 1970s, 2
Koch, Bodil, fl. 1950s, 2
Laughland, Polly, fl. 1970s, 2
Leggett, Mary Lydia, 1852–, 1
Levis, Elizabeth, fl. 1750s, 1
Livermore, Harriet, 1788–1868, 1,2
Lobo, Maria Teresa, fl. 1970s, 2
Lowrie, Mrs., fl. 1880s, 1
Martin, Joan, 2
McGee, Pamela Jo Lee, 1947–, 2

Meadows-Rogers, Arabella, fl. 1970s, 2
Moore, Grace, fl. 1970s, 2
Murdock, Marian, 1849–, 1
Newman, E. E., fl. 1870s, 1
O'Daniels, A. M., 1828–, 1
Oliver, Anna, d. 1893, 1,2
Olson, Carol, fl. 1970s, 2
Patterson, Jane C., fl. 1870s, 1
Perkins, Sarah M. C., 1824–, 1
Pierce, Diane, fl. 1970s, 2
Potter, Lorraine, fl. 1970s, 2
Powell, Elizabeth M., fl. 1870s, 1
Roberts, Abigail Hoag, d. 1841, 1
Roberts, Fannie, fl. 1870s, 1
Rowand, Mary Louise Morris, 1918–, 2
Roydne, Agnes Maude, 1876–1956, 1
Russell, Letty Mandeville, fl. 1970s, 2
Rust, Norma, fl. 1970s, 2
Savage, Mary, fl. 1790s, 1
Shaw, Anna Howard, 1847–1919, 1,2
Smiley, Sarah Frances, 1830–, 1
Smith, Sarah, 1804–1877, 1
Soule, Caroline Augusta White, 1824–1903, 1,2
Spencer, Anna Carpenter Garlin, 1851–1931, 2
Stephenson, Sarah, 1738–1802, 1
Tan Sri, Fatimah, fl. 1970s, 2
Thompson, Ruth, fl. 1970s, 2
Truth, Sojourner, 1797–1883, 1,2
Uemura, Tamaki, fl. 1940s, 2
Van Cott, Margaret Ann Newton, 1830–1914, 1,2
Vrana, Ethel, 2
Warren, Elizabeth Hooton, 1598–1672, 1
Way, Amanda M., 1828–1914, 1,2
Webster, Mary C., fl. 1870s, 1
Whitcomb, Joanne, fl. 1970s, 2
Wilkes, Eliza Tupper, 1844–, 1
Willing, Jennie Fowler, 1834–1916, 1,2
Willis, Olympia Brown, 1835–1926, 1
Wilson, Rachel, fl. 1760s, 1

Clerical workers
Shattuck, Harriette Lucy Robinson, 1850–, 1
Cleveland, Grover—Mother
Cleveland, Ann(e) Neal, 1806–1882, 1,2
Cleveland, Grover—Sister
Cleveland, Rose Elizabeth, 1846–1918, 1

Cleveland, Grover—Spouse
 Cleveland, Frances Folsom, 1864–
  1947, 2
 Preston, Frances Folsom Cleveland,
  1864–1947, 1
Clisthenes—Daughter
 Agariste of Sicyon, 600–570BC, 2
Clodius Pulcher, Publius—Spouse
 Fulvia, fl. 40 BC, 1,2
Clothaire—Spouse
 Radegonde, 518–587, 1,2
Clothing industry
 See also
  Fashion critics
  Fashion designers
  Fur industry
  Milliners
  Seamstresses
  Textile industry
  Textile designers
 Nikiforova, Tatiana, 2
 Wagle, Premila, 1920–, 2
Clovis II—Spouse
 Berthildis, Abbess, d. 680, 2
Clowns
 See also
  Comedians
 Fratellini, Annie, fl. 1970s, 2
 Williams, Peggy Lenore, 1948–, 2
Club leaders
 Adams, Agnes Jones, 1858–1923, 1
 Ames, Minerva Ross, m. 1875, 1
 Argetsinger, Louise H., 1904–, 2
 Arnold, Margaret, 1912–, 1
 Ashley, Grace Bosley, 1874–, 1
 Avery, Nina Horton, 1840–1930, 1
 Baird, Irene, fl. 1919, 1
 Baker, Grace Green, fl. 1930s, 1
 Bancroft, Jane M., fl. 1880s, 1
 Barker, Eliza Harris Lawton, fl.
  1870s, 1
 Barnard, Anne Hawkins, fl. 1930s, 1
 Barnum, Charlotte P. Acer, 1865–, 1
 Batcheller, Mrs. Tryophosa Bates,
  1878–, 1
 Baxter, Alice, fl. 1900s, 1
 Bearden, Bessye J., 1891–1943, 1
 Berry, Martia L. Davis, 1844–, 1
 Blankenburg, Lucretia M. Long-
  shore, 1845–1937, 1,2
 Block, Anna Scott, fl. 1900s, 1
 Blum, Florence A., 1872–1959, 1
 Boone, Maggie Augusta, 1867–, 2
 Boyer, Sophie Ames, fl. 1930s, 1

Brenner, Dora, fl. 1930s, 1
Bridge, Edith McKenney, fl. 1930s, 1
Broomhall, Mrs. Addison F., fl.
 1900s, 1
Brown, Annie Florence, fl. 1920s, 1
Brown, Charlotte Emerson, 1838–
 1895, 2
Brown, Elizabeth Carolyn Seymour,
 fl. 1890s, 1
Brown, Emma Crane, fl. 1930s, 1
Brown, Laura A., 1874–1924, 1
Bryan, Mary Edwards, 1838–1913,
 1,2
Buchanan, Annie R., fl. 1930s, 1
Buchanan, Mrs. Robert, fl. 1890s, 1
Buchwalter, Mrs. Edward L., fl.
 1890s, 1
Burdett, Clara Bradley, m. 1878, 1
Burroughs, Nannie Helen, 1878–
 1961, 1,2
Burrows, Frances L. Peck, fl. 1880s, 1
Caraway, Glenrose Bell, fl. 1930s, 1
Carpenter, Mrs. Philip, fl. 1900s, 1
Carter, Cora C. C., fl. 1930s, 1
Chase, Kate Fowler, 1871–1951, 1
Chase, Lucetta, fl. 1930s, 1
Clark, Lois Pinney, fl. 1930s, 1
Clarke, Grace Giddings Julian, 1865–
 1938, 2
Cleaver, Ethelyn Hardesty, fl. 1930s,
 1
Clement, Emma Clarissa Williams,
 1874–1952, 1,2
Colt, Miriam Davis, fl. 1850s, 1,2
Conger, Mrs. Al, fl. 1900s, 1
Conklin, Jennie M. Drinkwater,
 1841–1900, 1
Cooper, Martha Kinney, 1874–, 2
Cotten, Sallie Sims Southall, 1846–
 1929, 2
Cramsie, Mary Isabel, 1844–, 1
Croly, Jane Cunningham, 1829–
 1901, 1,2
Cropper, Anna McLane, 1859–, 1
Cunningham, Ann Pamela, 1816–
 1875, 1,2
Danser, Fanny Root, fl. 1930s, 1
Davenport, Louise M., fl. 1930s, 1
Davis, Mrs. M. E., fl. 1890s, 1
Dawes, Helen B. Palmer, m. 1890, 1
Decker, Sarah Sophia Chase Platt,
 1852–1912, 2
Deere, Mary Little Dickinson, m.
 1862, 1

Maxfield, Winifred Hill, fl. 1930s, 1
Maxwell, Mrs. Lawrence, fl. 1910s, 1
McCartney, Katharine Searle, fl.
  1910s, 1
McCartney, Louise Smitt, fl. 1950s, 2
McClellan, Aurora Pryor, fl. 1910s, 1
McCrackin, Josphine, 1846–, 1
McDougall, Irene G., fl. 1930s, 1
McHenry, Mary Sears, fl. 1910s, 1
McHugh, Mrs. Bernard, 1894–, 1
McKee, Ruth Karr, 1874–1951, 1
Mendes, Grace P., fl. 1890s, 1
Meyer, Annie Nathan, 1867–1951, 1,2
Miller, Flo Jamison, fl. 1910s, 1
Miller, Marion, 1862–, 2
Mink, Sarah C., d. 1896, 1
Minot, Fannie E., m. 1874, 1
Moore, Eva Perry, fl. 1900s, 1
Morgan, Jessie Borrer, 1907–, 2
Morgan, Sarah Berrien Casey, fl.
  1910s, 1
Morris, Alice V. Shepard, fl. 1920s, 1
Morris, Constance Lily, d. 1954, 1
Moskowitz, Belle Lindner Iraels,
  1877–1933, 1,2
Mumford, Mary Eno Bassett, 1842–
  1935, 2
Nash, Mary McKinlay, 1835–, 1
Noble, Esther Frothingham, fl.
  1910s, 1
Nobles, Catherine, fl. 1890s, 1
Norman, Julie Bowie, 1889–, 2
Noyes, Ida E. Smith, m. 1879, 1
O'Mahoney, Katherine A., fl. 1910s,
  1
Ottman, Josephine Whitney, fl.
  1930s, 1
Page, Lucy Gaston, fl. 1910s, 1
Parson, Lillian Bendeka, 1896–, 2
Patterson, Mrs. Lindsay, fl. 1910s, 1
Pennybacker, Mrs. Percy V., 1861–, 1
Peterson, Jetret Stryker, 1895–, 2
Phelps, Anna Elizabeth, fl. 1930s, 1
Pierce, Elizabeth F., fl. 1910s, 1
Pitkin, Louisa Rochester, fl. 1900s, 1
Pittinger, Alice Butterworth, fl.
  1910s, 2
Plimpton, Hannah R. Cope, 1841–, 1
Pope, Sarah Lloyd Moore Ewing, fl.
  1890s, 1
Pouch, Helena R., fl. 1890s, 1
Prentiss, Harriet Doan, fl. 1930s, 1
Proctor, Nina Gregory, fl. 1930s, 1
Putnam, Mary Steiner, fl. 1910s, 1

Quinton, Amelia Stone, 1833–1926,
  1,2
Ramsey, Grace Fisher, fl. 1930s, 1
Ransford, Nettie, 1838–, 1
Rauh, Bertha, 1865–, 1
Read, Carrie R., fl. 1910s, 1
Reavis, Babs H., fl. 1930s, 1
Richardson, Ellen A., 1845–1911, 1
Riker, Ina Ambrose, fl. 1930s, 1
Ritchie, Mrs. John, fl. 1890s, 1
Robinson, Martha Gilmore, fl.
  1950s, 1
Roebling, Emily Warren, 1843–1903,
  1
Rohrer, Gertrude Martin, fl. 1940s, 1
Rose, Laura Martin, 1862–, 1
Rosenbery, Mollie R. M., fl. 1910s, 1
Ross, Letitia Roano Dowdell, d.
  1952, 1
Ross, Margaret Wheeler, d. 1953, 1
Ruffin, Josephine St. Pierre, 1843–
  1924, 1,2
Runcie, Constance Faunt le Roy,
  1836–1911, 1,2
Sanders, Sue A. Pike, fl. 1910s, 1
Scott, Mrs. Matthew T., fl. 1910s, 1
Senie, Claire M., fl. 1930s, 1
Severance, Carolina Maria Seymour,
  1820–1914, 1,2
Sewall, May Eliza Wright, 1844–
  1920, 1,2
Shera, Florence B., fl. 1950s, 1
Sherman, Mary Belle King, 1802–
  1935, 2
Sherman, Minna E., fl. 1910s, 1
Shippen, Mrs. William Watson, fl.
  1890s, 1
Shyler, Nettie Rogers, 1862–1939, 2
Slocum, Caroline Edna, fl. 1930s, 1
Smallwood, Delia Graeme, fl. 1910s,
  1
Smith, Beulah Morgan, fl. 1930s, 2
Smith, Emily L. Goodrich, 1830–, 1
Smith, Fannie Morris, fl. 1900s, 2
Smith, Mrs. J. Morgan, fl. 1910s, 1
Soper, Luella Hartt, fl. 1930s, 1
Sparks, Mildred Hotch, 1901–, 2
Spilman, Mrs. Baldwin Day, fl.
  1910s, 1
Stone, Cornelia Branch, 1840–, 1
Stovall, Kate Bradley, m. 1904, 1
Stovall, Thelma, 1919–, 2
Straus, Flora B. S., fl. 1930s, 1
Strauss, Anna Lord, 1899–1979, 1,2

Swanger, Ludmilla E., fl. 1930s, 1
Swormstedt, Mabel Godfrey, gr. 1890, 1
Talbert, Mary Burnett, 1862–1923, 1
Tench, Mrs. Frank Murray, fl. 1930s, 1
Thurman, Lucy Smith, 1849–4948, 1
Trout, Grace Wilbur, d. 1955, 1
Turner, Eliza L. Sproat Randolf, 1826–1903, 2
Turner, Lizabeth A., d. 1907, 1
Turner, Rose, fl. 1940s, 1
Van Meter, Pattie Field, fl. 1890s, 1
Vanamee, Grace Davis, 1876–1946, 1
Vivian, Mrs. Thomas J., fl. 1930s, 1
Waite, Mary George Jordan, 1918–, 2
Walker, Alice Brenard Ewing, fl. 1900s, 1
Wallace, Emma R., d. 1911, 1
Walworth, Ellen Hardin, 1832–1915, 1,2
Ward, Mary Alden, 1853–, 1
White, Doris Pike, fl. 1950s, 1
Wickins, Margaret Ray, fl. 1910s, 1
Wilbour, Charlotte B., fl. 1870s, 1
Wilcox, Mary R., fl. 1910s, 1
Williams, Fannie Barrier, 1855–1944, 2
Williams, Mary Ann Barnes, 1
Williams, Mattie, fl. 1920s, 1
Wilson, Anne Maynard K., fl. 1930s, 1
Winans, Sarah D., fl. 1910s, 1
Winter, Alice Vivian Ames, 1865–1944, 2
Woods, Kate Tannatt, d. 1910, 1
Wright, Mrs. S.J., m. 1883, 1
Zimand, Gertrude Folks, fl. 1930s, 1
Zuver, D. DeCourcy, fl. 1930s, 1
Coaches, Athletic
   See also specific sports
Hawley, Gertrude, fl. 1920s, 1
Coale, Anne Hopkinson—Daughter
   Coale, Mary Abby Willing, 1789–, 2
Coale, Francis—Sister
   Coale, Anne Hopkinson, fl. 1770s, 2
Coast Guard
Burton, Terry, 2
Lambine, Janna, fl. 1970s, 2
Snelson, Debra G., fl. 1970s, 2
Cogswell, Mason F.—Daughter
   Cogswell, Alice, fl. 1800s, 1
Coke, Sir Edward—Spouse
   Hatton, Elizabeth, Lady, fl. 1617, 1

Cole, Nat King—Daughter
   Cole, Natalie, 1950–, 2
Coleman, Ronald—Spouse
   Hume, Benita, 1906–1967, 2
Coleridge, Samuel—Spouse
   Coleridge, Sara(h) Henry, 1802–1852, 1,2
Colette, Sidonie Gabrielle—Mother
   Colette, Adele-Eugenie-Sidonie, d. 1912, 2
Collectors
   See also
   Art collectors
   Autograph collectors
   Food collectors
   Native American collectors
Barry, Eleanor, 2
Folger, Emily Clara Jordan, 1858–1936, 2
Garrison, Lucy McKim, 1842–1877, 2
St. John, Cynthia Morgan, 1852–1919, 1
College administrators
   See also
   College deans
   College presidents
Birjandi, Parvin, fl. 1950s, 2
Blanding, Sarah Gibson, 1898–1985, 1,2
Blank, Blanche, 2
Blunt, Katharine, 1876–1954, 1,2
Bohen, Halcyone H., 2
Bunting, Mary Ingraham, 1910–, 1,2
Daigler, Jeremy, 2
Dunnewald, Helen Bishop, 1891–, 2
Durant, Pauline, fl. 1870s, 2
Garsoian, Nina G., 2
Gildersleeve, Virginia Crocheron, 1887–1965, 1,2
Girgus, Joan, fl. 1970s, 2
Jubin, Brenda, fl. 1970s, 2
Kerby-Miller, Wilma A., fl. 1960s, 2
King, Lida Shaw, 1868–1932, 2
Madeleva, Mary, Sister, 1887–1964, 1,2
Meredith, Virginia, 1848–1936, 2
Mitchell, Lucy Sprague, 1878–1967, 2
Murray, Rosemary, fl. 1970s, 2
Muse, Martha Tritchel, fl. 1970s, 2
Ramos, Elaine Abraham, fl. 1970s, 2
Ritner, Susan, fl. 1970s, 2
Sette, Alice, fl. 1970s, 2
Slowe, Lucy Diggs, 1885–1937, 2
Talbot, Marion, 1858–1948, 2
Towle, Katherine Amelia, 1898–, 1,2

College deans
Cronkhite, Bernice Brown, 2
Douglass, Mabel Smith, 1877–1933, 2
Irwin, Agnes, 1841–1914, 2
Manoppo, Ani, fl. 1940s, 2
Marcus, Ann Lee, fl. 1970s, 2
Marshall, Clara, 1847–1931, 1,2
McIntosh, (Margaret) Millicent,
   1898–, 1
Mentschikoff, Soia, 1915–, 2
Pickel, Margaret Barnard, 1898–
   1955, 2
Preston, Ann, 1813–1872, 1,2
Putnam, Emily James Smith, 1865–
   1944, 1,2
Rabb, Harriet, fl. 1960s, 2
Rees, Mina S., 1902–, 1,2
Slowe, Lucy Diggs, 1885–1937, 2
College presidents
Ahrweiller, Helene, 1916–, 2
Claydon, Margaret, fl. 1950s, 2
Comstock, Ada Louise, 1873–1973, 2
Conway, Jill Ker, fl. 1970s, 2
Cross, Patricia, fl. 1960s, 2
Emerson, Alice Frey, fl. 1970s, 2
Farenthold, Frances (Sissy), 1926–, 2
Futter, Ellen Victoria, 1949–, 2
Gambrell, Mary L., 1898–1974, 2
Gannon, Ann Ida, Sister, fl. 1950s, 2
Glass, Meta, 1881–1896, 2
Gray, Hanna Holborn, 1930–, 2
Gulliver, Julia Henrietta, 1856–1940,
   2
Hazard, Caroline, 1856–1945, 1,2
Horner, Matina Souretis, 1939–, 2
Horton, Mildred Helen McAfee,
   1900–, 1
Jewett, Paulina, fl. 1970s, 2
Lyon, Mary Mason, 1797–1849, 1,2
Mattfield, Jacqueline Phillips, 1925–,
   2
McAfee, Mildred Helen, 1900–, 1,2
McBride, Katharine Elizabeth, 1904–
   1976, 1,2
McFee, Mildred H., 2
Mead, Elizabeth Storrs Billings, 1832–
   1917, 2
Miller, Susan Lincoln Tolman, 1825–
   1912, 2
Mills, Susan Lincoln Tolman, 1821–
   1912, 1,2
Palmer, Alice Elvira Freeman, 1855–
   1902, 1,2
Park, Rosemary, 1907–, 1,2

Pate, Martha B. Lucas, 1912–1983, 2
Patrick, Mary Mills, 1850–1940, 1,2
Pendleton, Ellen Fitz, 1864–1936, 1,2
Peterson, Martha Elizabeth, 1916–, 2
Reinhardt, Aurelia Isabel Henry,
   1877–1948, 1,2
Sabin, Ellen Clara, 1850–1949, 2
Scully, Jane, Sister, fl. 1970s, 2
Simmons, Adele, fl. 1970s, 2
Smith, Virginia Beatrice, 1924–, 2
Thomas, Martha Carey, 1857–1935,
   1,2
Thompkins, Pauline, 2
Thomson, Mary Moore Dabney,
   1887–, 2
Wexler, Jacqueline Grennan, 1926–, 2
Woolley, Mary Emma, 1863–1947,
   1,2
College professors and instructors
Arbuzova, Alla, 2
Armstrong, Barbara, 1934–1969, 2
Atwood, Margaret Eleanor Killian,
   1939–, 2
Babcock, Maud, fl. 1890s, 2
Baxter, Annette K., 2
Benson, Margaret, fl. 1970s, 2
Bernard, Jessie, 1903–, 2
Bervoets, Marguerite, 1914–1944, 2
Boyle, Kay, 1902–, 1,2
Burch, Linda, 2
Cade, Ruth Ann, 1917–, 2
Colton, Elizabeth Avery, 1872–1924,
   2
Comini, Alessandra, fl. 1970s, 2
Cotton, Elizabeth Avery, 1872–, 2
Couzin, Sharon, fl. 1970s, 2
Crist, Judith Klein, 1922–, 2
Dana, Mary Stanley Bunce Palmer,
   1810–1883, 2
Diemer, Emma Lou, 1927–, 2
Dixon, Marlene, 2
Donne, Maria Delle, 1776–1842, 1,2
Donnelly, Dorothy, Sister, 2
Downey, June, 2
Downs, Cora, fl. 1930s, 2
Egbert, Ercell Jan, 1895–, 2
Epstein, Cynthia Fuchs, fl. 1970s, 2
Evans, Mari, 1923–, 2
Ferebee, Dorothy, fl. 1920s, 2
Galindo, Beatrix, 1473–1535, 2
Greene, Maxine, 2
Hewitt, Mary Jane, fl. 1970s, 2
Hostetter, Helen, fl. 1910s, 2
Isom, Sarah McGehee, fl. 1880s, 2

Jones, Gail (Gayl), 1949–, 1,2
Jones, Lois Mailou, 1905–, 1,2
Kay, Herma Hill, 1934–, 2
Knowles, Marjorie Fine, fl. 1960s, 2
Law, Sylvia, fl. 1970s, 2
Leach, Abby, 1855–1918, 2
Lefkowitz, Mary L., fl. 1970s, 2
Lorde, Audre, 2
Mansfield, Arabella Babb "Belle",
    1846–1911, 1,2
Mengel, Nanette Vonnegut, 1913–, 2
Nicolson, Marjorie Hope, 1894–
    1981, 1,2
O'Neill, Catherine, fl. 1970s, 2
Owens, Elisabeth, fl. 1940s, 2
Patterson, Helen, d. 1974, 2
Pennell, Rebecca, fl. 1850s, 2
Picker, Jane Moody, 1930–1970, 2
Quitsland, Sonia, fl. 1970s, 2
Richter, Elise, 1864–1943, 2
Rose, Willie Lee, fl. 1970s, 2
Rossiter, Margaret, fl. 1970s, 2
Rothschild, Emma, 1948–, 2
Sanford, Maria Louise, 1836–1920, 2
Shalvi, Alice, 1926–, 2
Taub, Nadine, fl. 1970s, 2
Van Straaten, Florence Wilhelmina,
    1913–, 1,2
Wilson, Margaret D., fl. 1960s, 2
Young, Marilyn, 1927–, 2
Colman, Ronald—Spouse
Colman, Benita Hume, 1906–1967, 1
Colonial America
Alexander, Mary (Polly) Pratt Pro-
    voost, 1693–1760, 1,2
Axtell, Rebecca, Lady, fl. 1700s, 1,2
Bass, Mary, fl. 1770s, 1,2
Berkeley, Frances, fl.1630s, 2
Bett, Mum, fl. 1810s, 2
Blai(c)kley, Catherine, 1695–1771, 2
Bleecker, Ann(a) Eliza, 1752–1783,
    1,2
Bosomworth, Mary Musgrove Mat-
    thews, 1700–1760, 1,2
Boylston, Sarah, fl. 1760s, 1
Bradford, Cornelia Smith, d. 1772,
    1,2
Bradnox, Mary, fl. 1648, 1
Bradstreet, Anne Dudley, 1612–
    1672, 1,2
Brasher, Judith, fl. 1737, 1
Breintnall, Hannah, fl. 1750s, 1
Brent, Mary, fl. 1638, 1,2
Brewster, Lucretia, d. 1679, 2

Brittano, Susannah, d. 1764, 1
Broadwell, Mary, 1630–1730, 2
Brown, Sarah, fl. 1750s, 1
Browne, Charlotte, fl. 1750s, 1
Brownlow, Kate, fl. 1745, 1
Bunnell, Goodwife, fl. 1650s, 2
Burrows, Anne, 2
Byrd, Evelyn, 1709–, 1,2
Byrd, Mary Willing, fl. 1700s, 1,2
Cahill, Mary, fl. 1740s, 1
Cannan, Mary, fl. 1763, 1
Chandler, Anna Paine, 1738–1811, 2
Cheer, Margaret, fl. 1760s, 1,2
Clark, Katherine, 1602–1671, 1,2
Coffin, Anna, fl. 1700s, 2
Coffin, Dionis Stevens, fl. 1640s, 1
Coffin (Coffyn), Dionis Stevens, fl.
    1640s, 2
Colden, Jane, 1724–1766, 1,2
Coleman, Ann, fl. 1660s, 1
Coming, Affra Harleston, d. 1699, 1
Copley, Mary Singleton, 1710–1789,
    1,2
Corbin, Hannah Lee, 1728–, 2
Cowell, Hannah, d. 1713, 1
Cowley, Mary, fl. 1741, 1
Crabb, Mary, fl. 1730s, 1
Crathorne, Mary, fl. 1760s, 1
Crosse, Mary Fisher Bayley, 1624–
    1690, 1
Crouch, Mary, fl. 1780s, 1
Davenport, Elizabeth Wooley, fl.
    1650s, 1,2
Deimer, Catherine, d. 1761, 1
Digges, Elizabeth, d. 1699, 1,2
Dillingham, Mrs., d. 1636, 2
Dircken, Lysbert, fl. 1630s, 1,2
Dommet, Mrs. John, fl. 1730s, 1
Dotey, Faith, d. 1675, 2
Douglass, Sarah Hallam, d. 1774, 1,2
Downing, Lucy Winthrop, fl. 1630s,
    2
Draper, Margaret Green, 1727–1807,
    1,2
Drummond, Sarah Prescott, fl.
    1670s, 1,2
Dudley, Dorothy, d. 1643, 2
Dudley, Mary Winthrop, fl. 1630s, 2
Eliot, Ann(e) Mountfort, d. 1687, 2
Ellis, Mehetable, fl. 1760s, 1
Emerson, Mary, fl. 1760s, 1
Estaugh, Elizabeth Haddon, 1680–
    1762, 1,2
Eustis, Jane, fl. 1755, 1

Eve, Sarah, fl. 1770s, 1
Fages, Eulelia de Callis y, fl. 1780s, 1
Farmer, Mary, d. 1687, 2
Ferree, Mary Warenbuer, d. 1716, 1,2
Flanagan, Elizabeth, fl. 1770s, 2
Fleming, Elizabeth, fl. 1750s, 1
Flowerden, Temperance, fl. 1600s, 2
Forrest, Mistress, fl. 1600s, 2
Frankland, Agnes Surriage, Lady,
1726–1783, 2
Franklin, Ann Smith, 1696–1763, 1,2
Franklin, Elizabeth, fl. 1750s, 1
Galloway, Anne, fl. 1700s, 1
Gazley, Martha, fl. 1730s, 1
Glover, Elizabeth, fl. 1630s, 1,2
Goddard, Mary Katherine, 1738–
1816, 1,2
Goodwin, Sarah, 1745–1756, 1,2
Grant, Mrs. Sueton, fl. 1740s, 1
Green, Ann(e) Catherine Hoof,
1720–1775, 1,2
Green, Mary, fl. 1750s, 1
Hallam, Nancy, 1750–1775, 1,2
Harman, Catharine Maria, d. 1775, 1
Harnet, Mary, d. 1792, 1
Hazard, Mary, 1639–1739, 1
Heard, Elizabeth, fl. 1600s, 2
Hebden, Katharine, fl. 1640s, 1,2
Hendee, Mrs., 2
Henry, Ann(e) Wood, 1732–1799, 1,2
Hicks, Margaret, fl. 1600s, 1
Hill, "Nurse", fl. 1680s, 1
Hiller (Hillyer), Mrs., fl. 1740s, 1
Hoskins, Jane, 1694–, 1,2
Hubertse, Aulkey, 2
Hunt, Elizabeth, fl. 1770s, 2
Jackson, Mary, fl. 1740s, 1,2
Johnson, Mrs. Jacob, fl. 1770s, 2
Jones, Anne Scotton, fl. 1750s, 1
Jones, Margaret, d. 1648, 1,2
King, Elizabeth, d. 1780, 2
Kitchin, Hannah Chapman, m. 1751,
1
Knight, Sarah Kemble, 1666–1727,
1,2
Lancaster, Sarah, fl. 1730s, 1
Levis, Elizabeth, fl. 1750s, 1
Logan, Deborah Norris, 1761–1839,
1,2
Ludwell, Frances Culpeper Stephens
Berkeley, fl. 1600s, 1
Manigault, Judith Giton Royer, d.
1711, 1,2
Mankin, "Widow", fl. 1730s, 1,2

Marriott, Elizabeth, d. 1755, 1
Masters, Sybilla, d. 1720, 1,2
Merry, Anne Brunton, 1769–1808,
1,2
Montour, Catherine, Madame, 1684–
1752, 1,2
Moody, Deborah, Lady, 1600–1659,
1,2
Moorland (Morland), Jane, fl. 1760s,
1
Morris, Mrs., d. 1767, 1
Neale, Mary Peasley, fl. 1750s, 1
Netmaker, Benedicta, fl. 1740s, 1
Norris, Deborah, 1761–1839, 1
Nuthead, Dinah, 1695, 1,2
Nutt, Anna Rutter Savage, 1686–
1760, 1
Orne, Rebecca Taylor, 1727–, 2
Paisley, Mary Neale, fl. 1750s, 1
Parrish, Anne, 1760–1800, 1,2
Perry, Joanna, d. 1725, 1,2
Peyton, Catherine, fl. 1750s, 1
Philipse, Catharine Duval Van Cort-
land, fl. 1690s, 1
Philipse, Margaret Hardenbrook De-
Vries, 1650–1690, 1,2
Phillips, Catherine Payton, 1727–
1794, 1
Phillips, Elizabeth, 1685–1761, 2
Pratt, Margaret, fl. 1740s, 1
Prentice, Mrs. John, d. 1691, 1
Prince, Mary, fl. 1650s, 1,2
Pritchard, Mrs. Francis, fl. 1660s, 2
Purcell, Elinor, fl. 1750s, 1
Purcell, Mary, fl. 1750s, 1
Quick, Alice, fl. 1750s, 1
Raunall, Sarah, fl. 1760s, 1
Rensselaer, Maria van, fl. 1670s, 2
Rhodes, Mrs., fl. 1720s, 1
Ridgely, Sarah, fl. 1760s, 1
Rind, Clementina, 1740–1774, 1,2
Robbins, Caria, 1794–, 2
Robbins, Elizabeth Le Baron, 1745–
1829, 2
Roberts, Widow, fl. 1740s, 1
Robinson, Ann, fl. 1790s, 2
Robinson, Hannah, fl. 1700s, 1
Rosehill, Margaret Cheer, fl. 1700s, 1
Russel, Mrs. Ezekiel, fl. 1700s, 1
Salmon, Mary, fl. 1750s, 1,2
Scharibrook, Elizabeth, fl. 1760s, 1
Schuyler, Catherine van Rensslaer,
1733–1803, 1,2
Schuyler, Cornelia, fl. 1700s, 1

Schuyler, Margaretta, fl. 1930s, 1
Scott, Sarah, m. 1726, 1
Simmes, Sarah, fl. 1600s, 2
Skinner, Dorothy Wendell, 1733–1822, 2
Smith, Joanna, 1614–1687, 2
Smith, Margaret, fl. 1660s, 1
Smith, Martha Turnstall, fl. 1860s, 1
Stagg, Mary, 1710–1730, 1,2
Stamper, Mrs., fl. 1770s, 1
Stone, Verlinda Cotton Burdette Boughton, fl. 1650s, 1
Stoothoff, Saartze Kierstede von Borsum, d. 1693, 1
Swallow, Frances, fl. 1700s, 1
Tilton, Mary, fl. 1650s, 1
Timothy, Ann Donovan, 1727–1792, 1,2
Timothy, Elizabeth, 1700–1757, 1,2
Todd, Sarah, fl. 1750s, 1
Todd, Sarah, fl. 1730s, 1
Townley, Elizabeth Smith Carteret, fl. 1710s, 1
Tranchepain de Saint Augustin., Marie de, Sister, d. 1733, 1
Treby, Bridget, fl. 1760s, 1
Tucker, Ann, fl. 1760s, 1
Turell, Jane Colman, 1708–1735, 2
Turrell, Jane Colman, 1708–1735, 1
Van Alstyne, Nancy, 1733–, 1,2
Van Es, Elizabeth, fl. 1680s, 1
Van Rennselaer, Mari van Cortlandt, 1645–1689, 1,2
Voyer, Jane, fl. 1740s, 1
Walker, Mrs. Robert, d. 1695, 1
Walker, "Widow", fl. 1680s, 1
Wall, Susannah, fl. 1790s, 2
Watteville, Benigna Zinzendorf, 1725–1789, 1

Wells, Rebecca, fl. 1750s, 1,2
Wheatley, Phillis, 1753–1784, 1,2
Whitmore, Mrs., fl. 1760s, 1
Williams, Hannah English, 1692–1722, 1,2
Winslow, Anna Green, fl. 1770s, 1,2
Winslow, Penelope, fl. 1650s, 2
Winthrop, Margaret, 1591–1647, 1,2
Wright, Lucy, fl. 1780s, 1
Wright, Susanna, 1697–1784, 1,2
Wyatt, Margaret, fl. 1620s, 2
Wyatt, Mary, 1611–1705, 1
Yardley, Temperance Flowerdew Yardley West, Lady, 1593–1636, 1

Zellers, Christine, fl. 1740s, 1
Zenger, (Anna) Catharine Maulin, 1704–1750, 1,2
Zinzendorff, Anna Caritas Nitschmann, 1715–1760, 1
Colonna—Spouse
Mancini, Maria, 1639–1715, 1
Colony co-sponsor
Penalosa, Dona Eufemia, fl. 1590s, 1
Colorado
Blue, Virginia Neal, 1910–, 2
Brown, Clara "Aunt", fl. 1850s, 2
Chipeta, 1842–1880, 1,2
Decker, Sarah Sophia Chase Platt, 1852–1912, 2
Flowers, Ruth, 2
Gates, Hazel Rhoads, Sr., 1891–1973, 2
Greenberg, Ida, fl. 1940s, 2
Greenwood, Marie Chandler, 1901–, 2
Jacobs, Frances, 1843–1892, 2
Lubchenco, Portia, 1887–, 2
McCourt, Baby Doe, 1854–1935, 2
Petteys, Anna G., d. 1970, 2
Tabor, Elizabeth Honduel McCourt, 1854–1935, 1,2
Valdez, Adelia Rivera de, 1874–, 2
Coluberson, Eli—Spouse
Culbertson, Josephine Murphy, 1899–1956, 2
Columnists
Beale, Betty, 1912–, 1,2
Beckley, Zoe, fl. 1910s, 1,2
Blue, Miriam, 2
Bombeck, Erma, 1927–, 2
Bowles, Heloise, 1919–1977, 2
Brothers, Joyce, 1927–, 1,2
Brown, June, fl. 1970s, 2
Cheshire, Maxine, 1930–, 2
Dahl, Arlene, 1927–, 1,2
Fern, Fanny, pseud., 1811–1846, 1,2
Goodman, Ellen, fl. 1950s, 2
Graham, Sheilah, 1908–, 1,2
Greenfield, Meg, 1930–, 2
Hopper, Hedda, 1885–1966, 1,2
Ivins, Molly, fl. 1970s, 2
Kilgallen, Dorothy, 1913–1965, 1,2
Kuhn, Irene Corbally, 1900–, 1,2
Lague, Louise, 1947–, 2
Lambert, Eleanor, 1910–, 2
Landers, Ann, pseud., 1918–, 1,2
Lewis, Flora, 1920–, 2
Malloy, (Marie) Louise, d. 1947, 1

Maxwell, Elsa, 1883–1963, 1,2
McGrory, Mary, 1918–, 2
McLellan, Diane, 1937–, 2
Mehle, Aileen, 1,2
Myerson, Bess, 1924–, 1,2
Paddleford, Clementine Haskin, 1900–1967, 1,2
Parsons, Louella Oettinger, 1881–1972, 1,2
Paterson, Isabel Bowler, 1886–1961, 1
Percy, Eileen, 1899–, 2
Post, Emily Price, 1873–1960, 1,2
Quinn, Jane Bryant, 1939–, 2
Robb, Inez Callaway, 1901–1979, 1,2
Robinson, Elsie, 1883–1956, 1
Rodgers, Dorothy, 1909–, 2
Ryan, Joan, 2
Smith, Liz (Mary Elizabeth), 1923–, 2
Thompson, Dorothy, 1893–1961, 1,2
Van Buren, Abigail, pseud., 1918–, 1,2
Vanderbilt, Amy, 1908–1974, 1,2
Viorst, Judith, 2
Walker, Alice, 1944–, 2
Colville Indians
  Wilson, Ramona C., 1945–, 2
Comanche Indians
  Cox, Marie, fl. 1970s, 2
  Harris, La Donna Crawford, 1931–, 2
  Volborth, Judith Ivaloo, 1950–, 2
Comedians
  Allen, Grace (Gracie) Ethel Cecile Rosalie, 1905–1964, 1,2
  Arden, Eve, 1912–, 1,2
  Ball, Lucille, 1911–1989, 1,2
  Ballard, Kaye, 1926–, 1,2
  Bicknell, Mrs., fl. 1700s, 1
  Brice, Fanny Borach, 1891–1951, 1,2
  Brooke, Hillary, 1914–, 2
  Burnett, Carol, 1933–, 1,2
  Buzzi, Ruth, 1936–, 2
  Canova, Judy, 1916–, 1,2
  Carroll, Vinnette, 1922–, 2
  Clive, Catherine (Kitty) R., 1711–1785, 1,2
  Coca, Imogene, 1908–, 1,2
  Courtneidge, Cicely, 1893–1980, 1,2
  Daley, Cass, 1915–, 2
  Daniels, Bebe (Phyllis Virginia), 1901–1971, 1,2
  Davis, Joan, 1907–1961, 1,2
  Diller, Phyllis Driver, 1917–, 1,2
  Donnelly, Ruth, 1896–, 2
  Fields, Gracie, Dame, 1898–1979, 1,2

  Fields, Totie, 1931–1979, 2
  Florence, Malvina Pray, 1830–1906, 1,2
  Ghostley, Alice, 1926–, 2
  Grenfell, Joyce Irene, 1910–1979, 1,2
  Gwynn, Nell (Eleanor), 1650–1687, 1,2
  Hartman, Grace, 1907–1955, 1
  Held, Anna, 1873–1918, 1
  Hibbard, Edna, 1895–1942, 1
  Hill, Jenny, 1850–1896, 1
  Hutton, Betty, 1921–, 1,2
  Kelly, Patsy, 1910–1981, 1,2
  Kitchell, Iva, 1912–, 1
  Lanchester, Elsa (or Ella), 1902–1986, 1,2
  Lillie, Beatrice, Lady Peel, 1894–, 1,2
  Livingstone, Mary, 1908–1983, 1,2
  Lloyd, Marie, 1870–1922, 1,2
  Lorne, Marion, 1888–1968, 1,2
  Mabley, Jackie "Moms", 1894–1975, 2
  Marryat, Florence, 1838–1899, 1,2
  Mars, Anne Francoise Hippolyte Boutet, 1779–1847, 1,2
  Marshall, Penny, 1945–, 2
  May, Elaine, 1932–, 1,2
  Meara, Anne, 1924–, 2
  Normand, Mabel Ethelreid, 1893–1930, 1,2
  O'Brien, Virginia, 1921–, 2
  Oliver, Edna May, 1883–1942, 1,2
  Paige, Janis, 1923–, 1
  Pearce, Alice, 1
  Pearl, Minnie, 1912–, 2
  Pious, Minerva, 1909–, 2
  Pitts, Zasu, 1900–1963, 1,2
  Radner, Gilda, 1946–1989, 2
  Raye, Martha, 1916–, 1,2
  Rejane, Gabrielle Charlotte, 1856–1920, 1,2
  Reynolds, Debbie Marie Frances, 1932–, 1,2
  Rivera, Chita, 1933–, 1,2
  Rothman, Stephanie, 1925–, 2
  Rutherford, Margaret, 1892–1972, 1,2
  Ryan, Peggy, 1924–, 2
  Smith, Keely, 1932–, 1,2
  Talbot, Nita, 1930–, 1,2
  Talmadge, Constance, 1900–1973, 1,2
  Tomlin, Lily (Mary Jean), 1937–, 2
  Wallace, Nellie, 1870–1948, 1,2
  Winwood, Estelle, 1883–, 1,2
Comghall, Saint—Mother
  Briga, fl. 490s, 1

Commenus, Manuel—Spouse
  Irene, d. 1160, 1
Commodus, Lucius A. Aurelius—
  Concubine
  Marcia, fl. 180s, 1
Commodus, Lucius A. Aurelius—
  Spouse
  Bruttia Crispina, fl. 180, 1
  Crispina, fl. 180s, 1
Communications industries
  See also
  Telephone companies
  Brodsky, Linda G., 2
  Dawson, Mimi Weyforth, 1944–, 2
Communist leaders, American
  Stokes, Rose Harriet Pastor, 1879–
  1923, 2
  Whitney, Charlotte Anita, 1867–
  1955, 2
  Wiley, Olive Fucier Thomas, 1902–, 2
Communist leaders, Chinese
  Li Chen, 2
Communist leaders, Cuban
  Bunke Bider, Haydee Tamara, 1937–
  1967, 2
Communist leaders, Finnish
  Kuusinen, Hertta (Elina), 1904–1974,
  1,2
Communist leaders, Romanian
  Pauker, Ana Rabinsohn, 1894–1960,
  1,2
Communist leaders, Spanish
  Ibarruri, Dolores, 1895–, 2
  Mercader, Caridad, 2
Community leaders
  Cunningham, Minnie Fisher, 1882–
  1964, 2
  Gaines, Irene McCoy, 1892–1964, 2
  Gaston, Rosetta, 1885–, 2
  Hershey, Lenore, 1920–, 2
  MacLeish, Martha Hillard, 1856–
  1947, 2
  White, Eartha Mary Magdalene,
  1876–1974, 2
  Wright, Muriel Hazel, 1889–1975, 2
Community workers
  Blanks, Lily Faulkner, 1856–1942, 2
  Boggs, Lettie Vaughn, 1885–1971, 2
  Bowers, Mary, 2
  Boyd, Mamie Alexander, 1876–1973,
  2
  Brindley, Arabella Owens, 1892–, 2
  Browne, Rose Butler, 2
  Bryant, Ruth Flowers, 1917–, 2

Buck, Bertha Ann Stanley, 1913–, 2
Butler, Selena Sloan, 1872–1964, 2
Carter, Eunice Hunton, 1899–1970, 2
Charles, Bula Ward, 1887–1974, 2
Cline, Minerva Jane Mayo, 1847–, 2
Creque, Bobbie Little, fl. 1970s, 2
Dozier, Beverly Fisher, 1933–, 2
Duncan, Evelyne Weeks, 1906–, 2
Edwards, Elaine Schwartzenburg,
  1929–, 2
Ehinger, Aline N., 1891–, 2
Fairbank, Lorena King, 1874–, 2
Foster, Eleanor Long, d. 1910, 2
Frear, Esther Schaner, 1909–, 2
Fulbright, Roberta Waugh, 1875–
  1953, 2
Garnet, Sarah J. Smith Thompson,
  1831–1911, 1,2
Hall, Ruby Hibler, 1912–, 2
Hammett, Eliza Groves, 1860–1927,
  2
Hervin, Carrie B., fl. 1940s, 2
Hillis, Cora Bussey, 1858–1924, 2
Hosford, Jessie Wiegand, 1882–, 2
Houghton, Dorothy Deemer, 1890–
  1972, 1,2
Huntington, Hallie, 1898–, 2
Jasper, Teresa (Tessie), 1893–, 2
Jordan, Grace Edington, 2
Judd, Dorothy Leonard, 1898–, 2
Lewis, Mary Caulk, 1880–, 2
Marlar, Fannie Morteu, 1863–1948, 2
Mayer, Bessie Bruce, 1890–, 2
Mitchell, Lucy Miller, fl. 1900s, 2
Neff, Francine Irving, 1925–, 2
Osborn, Ethelinda Murray, 1918–, 2
Perkins, Zina Kartchner, 1883–, 2
Ridgely, Mabel LLoyd, 1872–1957, 2
Ritter, Nellie Miller, 1882–, 2
Romney, Lenore Lafount, 2
Scully, Violet Simpson, 1902–, 2
Simpson, Margaret Burnett, 1874–
  1974, 2
Smith, Beulah Morgan, fl. 1930s, 2
Stevens, Alice Hardie, 1900–, 2
Turpin, Ella Wheeler, 1876–, 2
Walsh, Louise Forsyth, 1886–1971, 2
Composers
  See also
  Hymnists
  Librettists
  Music arrangers
  Songwriters
Composers, American
  Aborn, Lora, 1
  Adair, Mildred, d. 1943, 1

Adams, Carrie B., 1859–1940, 1
Adams, Juliette Aurelia Graves, 1858–, 1
Ahbez, Eden, 1908–, 2
Alter, Martha, 1904–, 1
Anderson, Laurie, 1947–, 2
Appleton, Adeline Carola, 1886–, 1
Arlen, Jeanne Burns, 1917–, 1
Armstrong, Lil Hardin, 1898–1971, 2
Ashford, Emma Louise, 1850–1930, 1
Bailey, Marie Louis, 1876–, 2
Ballaseyus, Virginia, 1893–, 1
Bampton, Ruth, 1902–, 1
Barbour, Florence Newell, 1866–1946, 1
Barnett, Alice, 1896–, 1,2
Bartlett, Floy Little, m. 1908, 1
Bassett, Karolyn Wells, 1892–1931, 1,2
Bauer, Marion Eugenie, 1887–1955, 1,2
Beach, Amy Marcy Cheney, 1867–1944, 1,2
Beaton, Isabella, 1870–, 1
Becker, Angela, 1
Behrend, Jeanne, 1911–, 1
Belle, Barbara, 1922–, 1
Berckman, Evelyn, 1900–, 1,2
Bilbro, (Anne) Mathilde, fl. 1910s, 1
Bixby, Allene K., d. 1947, 1
Black, Jennie Prince, 1868–1945, 1
Black, Ruby Aurora, 1868–1945, 1
Blair, Kathleen, 2
Blake, Dorothy Gaynor, fl. 1940s, 1
Bley, Carla Borg, 1938–, 2
Bond, Carrie Jacobs, 1862–1946, 1,2
Bond, Victoria, 1949–, 2
Bonds, Margaret, 1913–1972, 2
Breen, May Singhi, 1949–, 1
Bridges, Ethel, 1897–, 1
Briggs, Cora S., 1
Briggs, Dorothy Bell, 1
Bristol, Margaret, 1
Britain, Radie, 1903–, 1,2
Brock, Blanche Kerr, 1888–, 1
Brown, Barnetta, 1859–1938, 1
Brown, Kate Louise, 1857–1921, 1
Brown, Mary Helen, d. 1937, 1
Buchanan, Annabel Morris, 1888–, 1,2
Buckley, Helen Dallam, 1899–, 2
Bugbee, L. A., d. 1917, 1
Burns, Annelu, 1889–1942, 1
Bush, Grace, 1

Calloway, Blanche, 1902–1978, 1,2
Capers, Valerie, fl. 1970s, 2
Carlisle, Una Mae, 1918–1956, 2
Carreau, Margaret, 1899–, 1
Carter, Betty, 1929–, 2
Castagnetta, Grace, 1912–, 1
Cheatham, Catharine "Kitty" Smiley Bugg, 1864–1946, 1,2
Clark, Mary Gail, 1914–, 1
Clarke, Helen J., fl. 1890s, 2
Clarke, Rebecca, 1886–, 1
Cleary, Ruth, 1942–, 1
Coates, Gloria, 1938–, 2
Cole, Ulric, 1905–, 1
Coleman, Satis Narrona, 1878–, 1
Collins, Judy Marjorie, 1939–, 2
Comfort, Annabel, fl. 1940s, 1
Coolidge, Peggy Stuart, 1913–1981, 2
Copeland, Bernice Rose, fl. 1940s, 1
Cornett, Alice, 1911–, 1
Cotton-Marshall, Grace, fl. 1940s, 1
Cowles, Cecil, 1901–, 1
Cramm, Helen L., d. 1939, 1
Crawford-Seeger, Ruth Porter, 1901–1953, 1,2
Crosby, Marie, fl. 1940s, 1
Crowe, Bonita, fl. 1940s, 1
Curran, Pearl Gildersleeve, 1875–1941, 1
Curtis, Natalie, 1875–1921, 1,2
Cushing, Catherine Chisholm, 1874–1952, 1,2
Da Costa, Noel, 1930–, 2
Dallam, Helen, fl. 1940s, 1
Daniels, Mabel Wheeler, 1878–1971, 1,2
Davis, Fay Simmons, d. 1942, 1
Davis, Genevieve, 1889–1950, 1
Davis, Katherine K., 1892–, 1
De Cevee, Alice, 1904–, 1
Diemer, Emma Lou, 1927–, 2
Dillon, Fannie Charles, 1881–1947, 1,2
Dlugoszewski, Lucia, 1931–, 2
Dodge, Cynthia Dodge, fl. 1940s, 1
Dodge, Mary Hewes, fl. 1940s, 1
Donez, Ian, 1891–, 1
Downey, Mary E., fl. 1940s, 1
Drake, Marie, fl. 1930s, 2
Duncan, Vivian, 1902–, 1,2
Dungan, Olive, 1903–, 1
Dusenbury, Elinor, fl. 1830s, 2
Dutton, Theodora, fl. 1940s, 1
Eakin, Vero O., 1900–, 1

Eberhart, Nelle Richmond, 1871–1944, 1,2
Edwards, Clara, 1925–, 1
Edwards, Joan, 1919–1981, 1,2
Ellis, Cecil Osik, 1884–, 1
Engberg, Mary Davenport, 1830–, 1
Erb, Mae-Aileen Gerhart, fl. 1940s, 1
Estabrook, Lizzie S (Touriee), 1858–1913, 2
Fauchald, Nora, 1803–1874, 2
Fenner, Beatrice, 1904–, 1
Fenstock, Belle, 1914–, 1
Fergus, Phyllis, fl. 1940s, 1
Fine, Sylvia, 1893–, 1
Fine, Vivian, 1913–, 1,2
Finley, Lorraine Noel, 1899–, 1
Fisher, Doris, 1915–, 1
Forman, Mrs. R. R., 1855–1947, 1
Fort, Eleanor H., 1914–, 1
Foster, Fay, 1886–1960, 1,2
Franklin, Blanch Ortha, 1895–, 1
Freer, Eleanor Everest, 1864–1942, 1,2
Gainsborg, Lolita Cabrera, fl. 1910s, 1
Galajikian, Florence Grandland, 1900–, 1,2
Gaynor, Jessie Lovel Smith, 1863–1921, 2
Genet, Marianne, fl. 1900s, 1
George, Anna E., fl. 1920s, 1
Gere, Florence Parr, fl. 1940s, 1
Gerrish-Jones, Abbie, 1863–1929, 1
Gest, Elizabeth, fl. 1940s, 1
Gideon, Miriam, 1906–, 1,2
Gillespie, Marian, 1889–1946, 1
Gober, Belle Biard, fl. 1940s, 1
Goetschius, Marjorie, 1915–, 1
Golson, Florence, fl. 1940s, 1
Goodman, Lillian Rosedale, 1888–, 1
Goodrich, Florence, fl. 1940s, 1
Graham, Shirley, 1907–1977, 1,2
Grant, Micki, fl. 1970s, 2
Griswold, Henrietta Dippman, fl. 1940s, 1
Gulesian, Grace Warner, 1884–, 1
Hammond, Fanny Reed, fl. 1940s, 1
Hanaford, Phebe Ann (Coffin), 1829–1921, 1,2
Harkness, Rebekah West, 1915–1982, 2
Harris, Letitia Radcliffe, fl. 1940s, 1
Harris, Margaret, 1943–, 2
Hatch, Edith, 1884–, 1

Heckscher, Celeste de Longpre, 1860–1928, 1
Hemingway, Clara Edwards, fl. 1940s, 1
Heyman, Katherine Ruth Willougby, 1877–1944, 1,2
Hier, Ethel Glenn, 1889–, 2
Higginbotham, Irene, 1918–, 1
Hill, Mabel Wood, 1870–1954, 1,2
Hokanson, Margrethe, 1893–, 1
Holden, Anne Stratton, 1887–, 1
Hollingsworth, Thekla, fl. 1930s, 1
Holst, Marie Seuel, fl. 1940s, 1
Hood, Helen, 1863–, 1
Housman, Rosalie Louise, 1888–1949, 1
Howe, Mary, 1882–1964, 1,2
Hudson, Octavia, fl. 1940s, 1
Hyde, Madeline, 1907–, 1
Irvine, Jessie S., 1836–1887, 2
Ivey, Jean Eichelberger, 1923–, 2
Jackson, Wanda, 1937–, 2
James, Dorothy, 1901–, 1,2
James, Inez Eleanor,
Jasmyn, Joan, 1898–, 1
Jean, Elsie, 1907–, 1
Jenkins, Cora W., 1870–1947, 1
Jerome, Maude Nugent, 1873–1958, 1,2
Jewell, Lucina, 1874, 2
Jewitt, Jessie Mae, fl. 1940s, 1
Jolas, Betsy, 1926–, 2
Jones, Abbie Gerrish, fl. 1930s, 1
Kahn, Grace LeBoy, 1891–, 1
Kerr, Anita, 1927–, 2
Kinscella, Hazel Gertrude, fl. 1940s, 1
Knouss, Isabelle G., fl. 1940s, 1
Knowlton, Fanny Snow, 1859–1926, 1
Kolb, Barbara Anne, 1939–, 2
Krogman, Mrs. C. W., d. 1943, 1
Kummer, Clare Rodman Beecher, 1888–, 1
Lang, Margaret Ruthven, 1867–1972, 1,2
Laufer, Beatrice, 1922–, 1,2
Lawnhurst, Vee, 1905–, 1
Lee, Julia, 1902–1958, 2
Lee, Norah, 1898–1941, 1
Lee, Peggy, 1920–, 1,2
Leech, Lida Shivers, 1873–, 1
Lehman, Evangeline, fl. 1940s, 1
Leonard, Anita, 1922–, 1

Lewis, Louise Hills, 1887–1948, 1
Liebling, Estelle, 1880–1970, 1,2
Lilioukalani, Lydia Kamekeha, 1838–1917, 1,2
Liston, Melba Doretta, 1925–, 2
Liszniewska, Marguerite Melville, fl. 1940s, 1
Logan, Virginia Knight, 1850–1940, 1
Long, Elsie, 1880–1946, 1
Lorenz, Ellen Jane, 1907–, 1
Lorenzo, Ange, 1894–1971, 2
Lynn, Cheryl, fl. 1970s, 2
MacKown, Marjorie T., 1896–, 1
Maley, Florence Turner, 1927–, 1
Mana (Manna)-Zucca, Madame, pseud., 1894–, 1
Manning, Kathleen Lockhart, 1890–1951, 1
Marschal-Loepke, Grace, fl. 1940s, 1
Marsh, Lucille Crews, 1888–, 1
Mathews, Blance Dingley, d. 1932, 1
McCollin, Frances, 1892–1960, 1,2
McGill, Josephine, 1877–1919, 1
McPartland, Marian Margaret Turner Page, 1918–1986, 2
Merrick, Mrs. C., fl. 1930s, 1
Meyer, Lucy Jane Rider, 1849–1972, 2
Miller, Anne Langdon, 1908–, 2
Mitchell, Mae, 1
Montana, Patsy, 1914–, 1,2
Moore, Luella Lockwood, fl. 1940s, 1
Moore, Mary Carr, 1873–1957, 1
Morse, Anna Justina, 1893–, 2
Murden, Eliza Crawly, 1790–1851, 2
Nichols, Alberta, 1
Niemark, Ilza, fl. 1920s, 1
Noyes-Greene, Edith Rowena, 1875–, 1
O'Hara, Mary, 1
Oliveros, Pauline, 1932–, 2
Orth, Lizette E., d. 1913, 1
Osgood, Marion, fl. 1940s, 1
Osser, Edna, 1919–, 1
Owen, Julia D., fl. 1940s, 1
Paldi, Mari, fl. 1940s, 1
Pattison, Lee Marion, 1890–, 2
Pease, Jessie L., fl. 1940s, 1
Perkins, Emily Swan, 1866–1941, 2
Petkere, Bernice, 1906–, 1
Pettit, Laura Mildred Tanner, 1895–, 2
Peycke, Frieda, 1
Phillips, Burrill, 1907–, 2

Phippen, Laud German, fl. 1940s, 1
Pinkard, Edna Belle, 1892–, 1
Pitts, Carol Marhoff, 1888–, 1
Polk, Grace Porterfield, fl. 1940s, 1
Pollock, Muriel, fl. 1930s, 1
Porter, Ruth Stephens, fl. 1940s, 1
Powers, Ada Weigel, fl. 1940s, 1
Pray, Ada Jordan, fl. 1940s, 1
Prentice, Marion, fl. 1910s, 1
Preston, Matilee Loeb, fl. 1940s, 1
Price, Florence Beatrice Smith, 1888–1953, 1,2
Ralston, F. Marion, fl. 1940s, 1
Rapoport, Ruth, 1900–1935, 1
Rebe, Louise Christine, fl. 1940s, 1
Remick, Bertha, fl. 1940s, 1
Rich, Gladys, 1893–, 1
Richter, Ada, 1944–, 1
Richter, Marga, 1926–, 2
Risher, Anna Priscilla, 1875–, 1
Ritter, Irene Marschand, fl. 1940s, 1
Rive-King, Julia, 1854–1937, 1,2
Robyn, Louise, 1878–1949, 1
Rodgers, Irene, fl. 1940s, 1
Rodgers, Mary, 1931–, 1
Rohrer, Gertrude Martin, fl. 1940s, 1
Roma, Caro, 1866–1937, 1
Ronell, Ann, 1910–, 2
Roobenian, Amber, 1905–, 1
Roosevelt, Emily, 1893–, 1
Ross, Gertrude, fl. 1940s, 1
Rubin, Ruth Rosenblatt, 1898–1953, 2
Runcie, Constance Faunt le Roy, 1836–1911, 1,2
Ryckoff, Lalla, fl. 1940s, 1
Ryder, Theodora Sturkow, 1876–, 1
Salter, Mary Turner, 1856–1938, 1,2
Sanders, Alma M., 1882–1923, 1
Schaeffer, Mary, 1
Schmitt, Susan, fl. 1940s, 1
Schumann, Meta, fl. 1940s, 1
Schuyler, Philippa Duke, 1931–1967, 1
Seaver, Blanche Ebert, 1891–, 1
Seay, Virginia, 1922–, 1
Sheldon, Lillian Taitt, 1865–1925, 1
Siddall, Louise, d. 1935, 1
Silberta, Rhea, 1900–, 1
Simms, Alice D., 1917–, 1
Simpson, Elizabeth, fl. 1940s, 1
Smith, Anita, 1922–, 1
Smith, Eleanor, 1858–1942, 1
Smith, Ella May, 1860–1934, 1

Composers, Peruvian
  Monk, Meredith, 1942–, 2
Composers, Polish
  Badarzewska, Thekla, 1834–1861, 2
  Baroni-Cavalcabo, Julie von, fl.
    1800s, 1
  Knapp, Phoebe Palmer, 1839–1908, 2
  Szymanowska, Marja Agata, 1790–
    1831, 1
Composers, Roman
  Caccia, 1759–, 1
Composers, Russian
  Boyarska, Rivka, fl. 1960s, 2
  Bronsart, Ingeborg von, 1840–1913, 1
  Makarova, Nina P., 2
  Rapoport, Eda, 1900–, 1
  Saidaminova, Diloram, 1944–, 2
  Schultz-Adaievsky, Ella von, 1846–
    1926, 1
  Uslovolskaya, Galina, 2
Composers, Scottish
  Hopekirk, Helen, 1856–1945, 1,2
  Musgrave, Thea, 1928–, 2
  Nairne, Carolina(e) Oliphant, Baron-
    ess, 1766–1845, 1,2
Composers, Swedish
  Andree, Elfrida, 1844–1929, 1
Composers, Venezuelan
  Carreno, Teresa, 1853–1917, 1,2
Composers, Welsh
  Beaumesnil, Henriette Adelaide Vil-
    lard, 1748–1803, 1
  Davies, Llewela, fl. 1890s, 1
  Williams, Frances, 1
Composers, West Indian
  Armatrading, Joan, 1950–, 2
Compton brothers—Mother
  Compton, Otelia Katherine Aug-
    sperger, 1859–1944, 1,2
Compton, Edward—Spouse
  Bateman, Virginia, 1853–1940, 2
Compton, Fay—Mother
  Bateman, Virginia, 1853–1940, 2
Computer scientists
    See also
    Systems analysts
  Avram, Henriette D., fl. 1970s, 2
  Davis, Ruth M., 2
  Hopper, Grace Murray, 1906–, 2
  Watson, Vera, d. 1878, 2
Concannon*
  MacDermott, Una, fl. 1500s, 1
Concert managers
  Hughes, Adella Prentis, 1869–1950, 2
  Olney, Dorothy McGrayne, fl.
    1930s, 1

Concubines
  Chao Yun, fl. 1080s, 1
  Chen Fei, Pearl, fl. 1880s, 1
  Hsi, Tzw, 1835–1908, 2
  Hsiang Fei, fl. 1750s, 1
  Li, Mistress, fl. 1600s, 1
  Pao Ssu, fl. 490s, 1
  T'a Chi, 1
  Wang Ch'Iang, fl.33s BC, 1
  Yang, Kuei-Fei, 718–, 1
Conductors (Music)
  Anderson, Eva, 2
  Bond, Victoria, 1949–, 2
  Boulanger, Lili (Juliette Marie Olga),
    1893–1918, 1,2
  Boulanger, Nadia Juliette, 1887–
    1979, 1,2
  Branscombe, Gena, 1881–1977, 1,2
  Brico, Antonia, 1902–, 1,2
  Bristol, Margaret, 1
  Caldwell, Sarah, 1928–, 2
  Calloway, Blanche, 1902–1978, 1,2
  Capers, Valerie, fl. 1970s, 2
  Chazel, Mrs., fl. 1700s, 1
  Crane, Ruth, fl. 1920s, 2
  Davenport-Engberg, Mary, fl. 1920s,
    2
  Dessoff, Margarethe, 1874–1944, 2
  Dudarova, Veronica, fl. 1960s, 2
  Engberg, Mary Davenport, 1830–, 1
  Folville, Juliette, 1870–1946, 1
  Harland, Lizzie, fl. 1880s, 1
  Harris, Margaret, 1943–, 2
  Hartline, Mary, 1926–, 1
  Hillis, Margaret Eleanor, 1921–, 1,2
  Jessye, Eva, 1895–, 1,2
  Kolb, Barbara Anne, 1939–, 2
  Kullmer, Ann, 1917–, 1
  Kuyper, Elizabeth, 1877–, 1
  Leginska, Ethel Liggins, 1886–1970,
    1,2
  McCollin, Frances, 1892–1960, 1,2
  Musgrave, Thea, 1928–, 2
  Nichols, Caroline B., fl. 1880s, 2
  Osgood, Marion, fl. 1940s, 1
  Perry, Julia, 1927–, 2
  Petrides, Frederique, 2
  Pitts, Carol Marhoff, 1888–, 1
  Queler, Eve (Robin), 1936–, 2
  Riddick, Kathleen, d. 1973, 2
  Risher, Anna Priscilla, 1875–, 1
  Ronell, Ann, 1910–, 2
  Somogi, Judith, 1941–, 2
  Stair, Patty, 1869–1926, 1,2

Studer, Carmen, fl. 1940s, 1
Sundstrom, Ebba, fl. 1920s, 2
Welge, Gladys, fl. 1930s, 1
Confederate government officials
  Darby, Mary, 2
Confederate hospital
  Hopkins, Juliet Ann Opie, 1818–
    1890, 2
Confederate rebel fighter
  Hart, Nancy, fl. 1860s, 2
Congress for Neighborhood Women
  Peterson, Jan, fl. 1960s, 2
Congresswomen
  Abzug, Bella Savitzsky, 1920–, 2
  Andrews, Elizabeth B., 1911–, 2
  Baker, Irene B., 2
  Berry, Rachel B. Allen, 1859–, 2
  Blitch, Iris Faircloth, 1912–, 1,2
  Boggs, Corinne (Lindy), 1916–, 2
  Boland, Veronica B., 1899–, 2
  Bolton, Frances Payne Bingham,
    1885–1977, 1,2
  Bosone, Reva Beck, 1895–, 1,2
  Buchanan, Vera D., 1902–1955, 2
  Byron, Katharine Edgar, 1902–1976,
    1,2
  Chisholm, Shirley, 1923–, 2
  Church, Marguerite Stitt, 1892–, 1,2
  Clarke, Marian Williams, 1880–1952,
    1,2
  Craig, Minnie, 2
  Douglas, Emily Taft, 1899–, 1,2
  Douglas, Helen Mary Gahagan,
    1909–1980, 1,2
  Dwyer, Florence P., 1902–1976, 1,2
  Eslick, Willa B., 1879–1961, 1,2
  Farrington, (Mary) Elizabeth Pruett,
    1898–1984, 1,2
  Fenwick, Millicent Vernon Ham-
    mond, 1910–, 2
  Ferraro, Geraldine Anne, 1935–, 2
  Ffost, Gracie, d. 1965, 2
  Fischer, Helen, fl. 1950s, 2
  Frazier, Maude, 1881–1963, 2
  Fulmer, Willa L., 1884–1968, 1,2
  Gasque, Elizabeth (Bessie) Hawley,
    1,2
  Gibbs, Florence Reville, 1890–1964,
    1,2
  Granahan, Kathryn Elizabeth
    O'Hay, 1896–, 1,2
  Green, Edith Starrett, 1910–1987, 1,2
  Greenway, Isabella, d. 1935, 1,2
  Griffiths, Martha Wright, 1912–, 1,2

  Hansen, Julia Butler, 1,2
  Harden, Mrs. Cecil Murray, 1894–,
    1,2
  Heckler, Margaret Mary O'Shaug-
    nessy, 1932–, 1,2
  Hicks, Louise Day, 1919–, 2
  Holt, Marjorie Sewell, 1920–, 2
  Holtzman, Elizabeth, 1941–, 2
  Honeyman, Nan Wood, d. 1970, 1,2
  Huck, Winnifred Sprague Mason,
    1882–1936, 1,2
  Jenckes, Virginia Ellis, 1882–1975, 1,2
  Jordan, Barbara (Charline), 1936–, 2
  Kahn, Florence Prag, 1866–1948, 1,2
  Kee, Elizabeth Frazier, 1899–1975,
    1,2
  Kelly, Edna Flannery, 1906–, 1,2
  Kempfer, Hannah Jensen, 1830–
    1943, 2
  Keys, Martha, 1930–, 2
  Knutson, Coya, 1912–, 1,2
  Kryszak, Mary Olszewski, 1875–
    1945, 2
  Langley, Katherine, 1883–1948, 1,2
  Luce, Clare Booth, 1903–1987, 1,2
  Lusk, Georgia Lee, 1893–1971, 1,2
  Mankin, Helen Douglas, 1894–1956,
    1,2
  May, Catherine Dean, 1914–, 1,2
  McCarthy, Kathryn O'Loughlin,
    1894–1952, 1,2
  McMillan, Clara G., 1894–1957, 1,2
  Mikulski, Barbara Ann, 1936–, 2
  Mink, Patsy Takemoto, 1927–, 1,2
  Noble, Elaine, 1944–, 2
  Nolan, Mae Ella Hunt, 1886–, 1,2
  Norrell, Catherine Dorris, 1901–, 1,2
  Norton, Mary Teresa Hopkins, 1875–
    1959, 1,2
  O'Day, Caroline Goodwin Love,
    1875–1943, 1,2
  Ochoa, Elisa, fl. 1940s, 2
  Oldfield, Pearl Peden, 1876–1962, 1,2
  Owen, Ruth Bryan, 1895–1954, 1,2
  Pfost, Gracie Bowers, 1906–1965, 1,2
  Pratt, Jane, 1902–, 2
  Pratt, Ruth Sears Baker, 1877–1965,
    1,2
  Rankin, Jeannette Pickering, 1880–
    1973, 1,2
  Reece, Louise Goff, 1899–1970, 1,2
  Reid, Charlotte Thompson, 1913–,
    1,2
  Riley, Corinne Boyd, 1894–, 2

Robertson, Alice Mary, 1854–1931, 1,2
Rogers, Edith Nourse, 1881–1960, 1,2
Sandler, Bernice, 1928–, 2
Schroeder, Patricia, 1940–, 2
Simms, Ruth Hanna McCormick, 1880–1944, 1,2
Simpson, Edna Oakes, 1891–, 2
Somerville, Nellie Nuggent, 1863–1952, 2
St. George, Katharine, 1896–1983, 1,2
Stanley, Winifred C., 1909–, 1,2
Sullivan, Leonor Alice Kretzer, 1903–, 1,2
Sumner, Jessie, 1909–, 1,2
Thomas, Lera M., 1893–, 2
Thompson, Ruth, 1887–1970, 1,2
Weis, Jessica McCullough, 1901–1963, 1,2
Wingro, Effiegene L., 1883–1962, 1,2
Woodhouse, Margaret Chase Going, 1890–1984, 1,2
Woodward, Ellen Sullivan, 1887–1971, 2
Connecticut
Driscoll, Margaret Connors, 1915–, 2
Grasso, Ella Tambussi, 1919–1981, 1,2
Levinson, Sara Sherman, 1886–, 2
Roosevelt, Edith Kermit Carow, 1861–1948, 1,2
Silliman, Mary Fish, 1736–1804, 1,2
Stow, Freelove Baldwin, 1728–, 1,2
Stowe, Harriet Elizabeth Beecher, 1811–1896, 1,2
Trumbull, Faith Robinson, 1718–1780, 1,2
Varga, Julia Kotel, 1889–, 2
Willard, Emma C. Hart, 1787–1870, 1,2
Conrad IV—Spouse
Margaret, Queen, 2
Conservationists
See also
Ecologists
Environmentalists
Bingham, Millicent Todd, 1880–1968, 1,2
Dunlap, Louise, fl. 1970s, 2
Edge, Rosalie Barrow, 1877–1962, 1
Heller, Barbara, fl. 1970s, 2
Koupal, Joyce, fl. 1970s, 2
Labudde, Wilhelmine Diefentaeler, 1880–1955, 2

Leopold, Estella Bergere, 1927–, 2
McCrackin, Josephine Woempner Clifford, 1838–1920, 2
Morton, Caroline Joy French, 1833–1881, 2
Nelson, Wanda, fl. 1970s, 2
Reeves, Maud Celeste Colmer, 1886–, 2
Strong, Harriet Williams Russell, 1844–1929, 2
Westenberger, Jane, 2
Willard, Beatrice, 1926–, 2
Yarn, Jane, 1925–, 2
Constable, John—Family
Constable, Anne, 1768–1854, 2
Constable, Mary, 1781–1865, 2
Constantin, Ernst—Spouse
Weimar, Anna Amalia, 1739–1807, 1
Constantine V—Daughter
Irene, 752–803, 1,2
Constantine the Great—Mother
Helena, Flavia Julia, 247–328, 1,2
Constantine the Great—Niece
Constantia, Augusta, d.c. 354, 1
Constantius III—Spouse
Faustina, Maxima, m. 360, 1
Galla, d. 350, 1
Theodora, m. 293, 1
Construction artists
Saar, Betye, 1926–, 2
Consul—Aunt
Sulpicia, fl. 186BC, 1
Consultants
See also
Business consultants
Employment consultants
Museum consultants
Political consultants
Tax consultants
Theatrical consultants
Travel consultants
Wedding consultants
Follett, Mary Parker, 1868–1933, 2
Galvin-Lewis, Jane, fl. 1960s, 2
Goodrich, Edna L., 2
Harper, Beverly, 1942–, 2
Matthews, Alva T., fl. 1970s, 2
Parker, Bettina, fl. 1960s, 2
Schain, Josephine, 1
Sklover, Theodora K., 1938–, 2
Taylor, Peggy Hammond, fl. 1930s, 1
Wolfe, Deborah Cannon Partridge, 1916–, 1
Consumer Action Network
Goldman, Ilene, 2

Consumerists
Brady, Mildred Edie, 1906–1965, 2
Campbell, Persia Crawford, 1898–1974, 2
Foreman, Carol Tucker, 1938–, 2
Furness, Betty (Elizabeth Mary), 1916–, 1,2
Goldman, Ilene, 2
Karpatkin, Rhoda Hendrick, 1930–, 2
Kyrk, Hazel, 1886–1957, 2
Peterson, Esther Eggertsen, 1906–, 1,2
Redford, Lola van Wagenen, 1938–, 2
Roberts, Eirlys, fl. 1950s, 2
Rosa, Maria Isabel Carmelo, fl. 1970s, 2
Sullivan, Leonor Alice Kretzer, 1903–, 1,2
Contest winners
Schneider, Deborah, fl. 1950s, 2
Cookbook authors
Becker, Marion Rombauer, 2
Benoit, Jehane, fl. 1950s, 2
Bertholle, Louisette (Comtesse de Naleche), 2
De Spain, June, fl. 1970s, 2
Farmer, Fannie Merritt, 1857–1915, 1,2
Glasse, Hannah, fl. 1720s, 2
Haines, Edith Kay, fl. 1930s, 1
Johnston, Myrna, fl. 1930s, 2
Randolph, Mary Randolph, 1762–1828, 2
Rorer, Sarah Tyson Heston, 1849–1937, 2
Terhune, Mary Virginia Hawes, 1830–1922, 1,2
Cooke, Anthony—Daughter
Burghley, Mildred Cooke, 2
Cooke, John Henry—Friend
Cooke, Kate Walsh, d. 1903, 1
Cooke, Sir Anthony—Daughter
Burleigh, Mildred Cooke Cecil, Lady, d. 1589, 1
Cooks
See also
Bakers
Frozen food pioneer
Arp, Leslie, fl. 1970s, 2
Beeton, Isabella Mary Mayson, 1836–1865, 1,2
Bowman, Sarah A., 1912–1866, 2
Child, Julia McWilliams, 1912–, 1,2
Corson, Juliet, 1841–1897, 1,2

Dutrumble, Gloria, fl. 1970s, 2
Fischbacher, Simone (Simca) S.R.M., 1904–, 2
Fisher, Mary Frances Kennedy, 1908–, 1,2
Leslie, Eliza (Elizabeth), 1787–1858, 1,2
Lewis, Edna, fl. 1970s, 2
Lucas, Mrs. Dione Narona Margaris Wilson, 1909–, 1
Niles, Kathryn, fl. 1950s, 2
Paddleford, Clementine Haskin, 1900–1967, 1,2
Revelle, Carrie Caroline Milligan, 1880–1965, 2
Rombauer, Irma von Starkloff, 1877–1962, 1,2
Smith, Lucille Bishop, 1892–, 2
Coolidge, Calvin—Mother
Coolidge, Victoria Moor, 1846–1885, 2
Coolidge, Calvin—Spouse
Coolidge, Grace Anna Goodhue, 1879–1957, 1,2
Coombs, Leslie—Mother
Richardson, Sarah, fl. 1700s, 1
Coriolanus—Mother
Veturia, fl.400sBC, 1
Coriolanus—Spouse
Volumnia, fl.400sBC, 1
Cormac—Spouse
Eithne, Princess, fl. 840s, 1
Cornelia—Mother
Aemilia, Tertia, 169–200BC, 1,2
Cornetists
Preston, Matilee Loeb, fl. 1940s, 1
Correspondents
Alving, Barbara, 2
Ames, Mary E. Clemmer, 1831–1884, 1,2
Angelo, Bonnie, 2
Bacon, Dorothy, 2
Briggs, Emily Pomona Edson, 1830–1910, 2
Denny, Anne, 2
Dunnigan, Alice Allison, 1906–, 1,2
Field, Kate, 1838–1896, 1,2
Liber, Nadine, fl. 1970s, 2
McLendon, Winzola, fl. 1970s, 2
Voipio, Anni, fl. 1940s, 2
Cortes, Hernando—Consort
Malinche, 1504–1528, 2
Cosell, Howard—Spouse
Cosell, Emmy, fl. 1970s, 2

Crafts writers
  Slivka, Rose, fl. 1950s, 2
Crane, Stephen—Daughter
  Crane, Cheryl, 1944–, 2
Crates—Spouse
  Hipparchia, 2
Cree Indians
  Sainte-Marie, Buffie (Beverly),
    1940–, 2
Creek Indian Colony Advisor
  Murgrove, Mary, fl. 1740s, 2
Creek Indians
  Francis, Milly, 1802–1848, 2
  Harjo, Joy, 1951–, 2
  Sullivan, Elizabeth, fl. 1970s, 2
Cremation Society
  Hart, Alice Marion (Mrs. Ernest),
    1872–, 2
Criminals
  See also
  Assassins and murders
  Bandit queen
  Blackmailers
  Cattle rustlers
  Counterfeiters
  Gangsters
  Hijackers
  Imposters
  Outlaws
  Perjurors
  Pirantes
  Vagrants
  Vigilantes
  War criminals
  Arrington, Marie Dean, 2
  Barclay, Polly, 2
  Barker, Arizona Clark "Ma", 1871–
    1935, 2
  Barker, Kate "Ma", 1872–1935, 2
  Bathory, Elizabeth, 1560–1614, 1,2
  Bender, Katie, fl. 1870s, 2
  Borden, Lizzie Andrew, 1860–1927,
    2
  Botkin, Gordelia, 1854–1910, 2
  Bracey, Joan, 1640–1685, 2
  Bravo, Florence, m. 1875, 1
  Brinvilliers, Margurite Marie D'Au-
    bray, Marquise de, 1630–1676, 1,2
  Butterfield, Jane, fl. 1770s, 2
  Chadwick, Cassi I., 1857–1907, 2
  Coffin, Miriam, 1723–, 2
  Corday, Charlotte (Marie Anne
    Charlotte Corday D'Armont),
    1768–1798, 1,2

Cox, Jane Cannon, fl. 1870s, 1
Dale, Elizabeth, fl. 1830s, 2
Dixon, Margaret, fl. 1728s, 2
Dohrn, Bernadine Rae, 1942–, 2
Dunn, Rose, 1878–, 1
Eisemann-Schier, Ruth, fl. 1960s, 2
Elena the Butcher, 2
Esther, Queen "Crazy", fl. 1770s, 2
Frith, Molly, 1589–1663, 2
Fromme, Lynette Alice (Squeaky),
  1948–, 2
Fulgate, Carili Ann, 1943–, 2
Grammont, Duchess of, fl. 1700s, 1
Greene, Anne, 1628–, 2
Gunness, Belle, 1860–1908, 2
Hall, Camilla, 1944–1974, 2
Harris, Emily Schwartz, 1947–, 2
Ivie, Theodosia, 1623–1686, 1
Juanita, d. 1851, 2
Judd, Winnie Ruth McKissell, 1905–,
  2
Kelly, Catherine, 2
Le Neve, Ethel, 1883–1967, 2
Leverson, Sarah Rachel, 1806–1888, 1
Mandelbaum, Frederika "Marm",
  1818–1889, 2
Manning, Mrs., 1821–1849, 1
Monvoisin, Catherine, d. 1680, 2
Moore, Sara Jane, 1930–, 2
Motte, Jeanne, Comtesse de la, 1756–
  1791, 2
Olah, Susi, 1869–1929, 2
Osborne, Ethel Florence Eliot, fl.
  1800s, 1
Pau, Elena, 2
Perkins, Josephine Amelia, fl. 1830s,
  2
Perrers, Alice, d. 1400, 1
Petronia Justa, 79, 2
Place, Etta, 2
Poillon, Charlotte, fl. 1900s, 2
Poillon, Katherine, fl. 1900s, 2
Power, Katherine Ann, 1949–, 2
Russ, Mary Carolina, fl. 1770s, 2
Saxe, Susan Edith, 1950–, 2
Silver, Frances "Frankie" Stuart, d.
  1833, 2
Smith, Madeleine-Hamilton, 1835–
  1928, 1,2
Snyder, Ruth Brown, 1895–1928, 2
Soltysik, Patricia, 1949–1974, 2
Somerset, Frances Howard Carr,
  1594–1632, 1
Starr, Belle Shirley, 1848–1889, 1,2

Webb, Jane, d. 1740, 1
Wilson, Sarah, 1750–, 1,2
Criminologists
    Glueck, Eleanor Touroff, 1898–1972,
    1,2
    Touroff, Eleanor, 1898–1972, 2
Criswell, Wallis Amos—Mother
    Criswell, Anna Currie, 2
Critics
    See also
        Art critics
        Dance critics
        Drama critics
        Fashion critics
        Food critics
        Literary critics
        Motion picture critics
        Music critics
        Newspaper critics
        Television critics
        Textbook critics
    Arvede, Barine, pseud., 1840–1908, 1
    Baer, Leone Cass, fl. 1930s, 1
    Barnes, Margaret Ayer, 1886–1967,
    1,2
    Bauer, Marion Eugenie, 1887–1955,
    1,2
    Becker, May Lamberton, 1873–1958,
    1
    Bree, Germaine, 1907–, 2
    Brophy, Brigid, 1929–, 2
    Byatt, A. S. (Antonia Susan), 1936–,
    2
    Coleridge, Mary Elizabeth, 1861–
    1907, 2
    Deutsch, Babette, 1895–, 1,2
    Drabble, Margaret, 1939–, 2
    Gerrish-Jones, Abbie, 1863–1929, 1
    Gillott, Jacky, 1939–, 2
    Gilmore, Elizabeth McCabe, 1874–, 1
    Gippius, Zinaida, 1869–1945, 2
    Gluck, Barbara Elisabeth, 1812–
    1894, 1
    Gordon, Caroline, 1895–1981, 1,2
    Govan, Christine Noble, 1898–, 1
    Hardwick, Elizabeth, 1916–, 2
    Isaacs, Edith Juliet Rich, 1878–1956,
    2
    Laski, Marghanita, 1915–, 1,2
    Lippmann, Julie Mathilde, d. 1952, 1
    Lowell, Amy, 1874–1925, 1
    Lowell, May Lawrence, 1874–1925, 2
    MacAulay, Rose, 1881–1958, 2
    McCarthy, Mary Therese, 1912–, 1,2

    Moore, Honor, fl. 1970s, 2
    Moore, Marianne Craig, 1887–1972,
    1,2
    Murray, Michele, 1934–1974, 2
    Oates, Joyce Carol, 1938–, 2
    Olsen, Tillie, 1913–, 2
    Pardo-Bazan, Emilia, 1851–1921, 1,2
    Raine, Kathleen (Jessie), 1908–, 2
    Reeve, Clara, 1729–1807, 1,2
    Rich, Adrienne Cecile, 1929–, 2
    Riding, Laura, 1901–, 1,2
    Rinser, Luise, 1911–, 2
    Rittenhouse, Jessie Bell, 1869–1948,
    1,2
    Rourke, Constance Mayfield, 1885–
    1941, 1,2
    Sarraute, Nathalie, 1900–, 1,2
    Seacombe, Mrs. Charles M., fl.
    1930s, 1
    Sitwell, Edith, Dame, 1887–1964, 1,2
    Sontag, Susan, 1933–, 2
    Spark, Muriel Sarah Camberg, 1918–,
    2
    Stael (Stael-Holstein), Anne Louise
    Germaine Necker, 1766–1817, 1,2
    Tracey, Cateau Stegeman, fl. 1940s, 1
    Underhill, Harriette, d. 1928, 1
    Wilder, Jessie, fl. 1930s, 1
    Wood, Virginia, 1882–1941, 2
Crockett, David—Mother-in-law
    Finley, Jean, 2
Cromwell, Oliver—Mother
    Cromwell, Elizabeth, 1554–1654, 2
Crook, George—Spouse
    Crook, Mrs. George, fl. 1860s, 2
Croquet players
    Steel, Dorothy Dyne, 1884–1965, 2
Cross country skiers
    Rockwell, Martha, fl. 1960s, 2
Crow Creek Sioux
    Lynn, Elizabeth Cook, 1930–, 2
Crusade for Christ
    Fain, Barbara Hancock, 2
Cryptologists
    Budenbach, Mary H., fl. 1960s, 2
Crystallographers
    Karle, Isabella L., fl. 1970s, 2
    Lonsdale, Kathleen, 1903–1971, 2
Cult leaders
    Craigin, Mary, fl. 1840s, 1
Curran, Richard—Daughter
    Curran, Sarah, 1783–1806, 1
Custer, George—Spouse
    Custer, Elizabeth Bacon, 1842–1933,
    1,2

Cyclists
  See also
    Motorcyclists
  Burton, Beryl, fl. 1950s, 2
  Novara, Sue, fl. 1970s, 2
  Peppler, Mary Jo, 1944–, 2
  Robinson, Jean, 1934–, 2
  Young, Sheila, 1950–, 2
Cyclotron researchers
  Johnson, Kristen, 2
Cytologists
  Lewis, Margaret, 1881–, 1

D

D'Albret, Jeanne—Daughter
  Bourbon, Catherine de, 1559–1604, 2
D'Estoubion—Spouse
  Sartre, Marquese de, 2
DAR
  Harrison, Caroline Lavinia Scott,
    1832–1892, 1,2
DAR—Founders
  Darling, Flora Adams, 1840–1910,
    1,2
  Desha, Mary, d. 1910, 1,2
  Walworth, Ellen Hardin, 1832–1915,
    1,2
  Washington, Eugenia, d. 1900, 1,2
DNA researchers
  Franklin, Rosalind Elsie, 1920–1958,
    2
  Schweber, Miriam, fl. 1970s, 2
  Singer, Maxine F., fl. 1970s, 2
Dairy farmers
  Catela, Joan Segal, fl. 1970s, 2
  Hanson, Jeanne, 2
  O'Leary, Catherine, fl. 1870s, 2
  Pickett, Anne, fl. 1830s, 2
Dakota Indians
  Deloria, Ella Cara, 1888–1971, 2
Dalrymple, Hugh—Spouse
  Eliot, Grace Dalrymple, 1754–1823, 1
Dana, John Cotton—Spouse
  Watson, Sarah, 2
Dance critics
  Cassidy, Claudia, 1905–, 1
Dance directors
  Newmar, Julie, 1935–, 1
Dance hall owners
  Hensley, Josephine, 1844–, 2
Dance teachers
  Dominique, Madame, 2
  Murray, Kathryn, 1906–, 1,2

Shridharani, Shrimati, 2
Souther, Marguerite, fl. 1940s, 1
Vacani, Madame, fl. 1910s, 2
Wigman, Mary, 1886–1973, 1,2
Dance therapists
  Chace, Marian, 1896–1970, 2
Dancers
  See also
    Ballet dancers
    Choreographers
    Folk dancers
    Topless dancers
    Western dancers
  Algeranova, Claudie, 1924–, 1
  Allan, Maud, 1879–, 1
  Amaya, Carmen, 1913–1963, 1,2
  Angelou, Maya, 1928–, 2
  Argentinita, (Encaracion Lopez),
    1905–1945, 1,2
  Argyll, Pearl, 1910–1948, 1
  Astaire, Adele, 1898–1981, 1,2
  Atunez, Fernanda, 2
  Azuma, Tokuho, 1910–, 1,2
  Baker, Carroll, 1931–, 1,2
  Baker, Josephine, 1906–1975, 1,2
  Bedells, Phyllis, 1893–, 1
  Bemis, Lalu Lathoy "China Polly",
    1853–1933, 1,2
  Bonehill, Bessie, fl. 1800s, 1
  Bremer, Lucille, 1923–, 2
  Bricktop (Ada Smith), 1895–, 1
  Brooks, Louise, 1906–1985, 2
  Broughton, Phyllis, 1862–1926, 1
  Carmencita, 2
  Castle, Irene Foote, 1893–1969, 1,2
  Celeste (Celeste-Elliot), Celine,
    1815–1882, 1
  Champion, Marge Celeste (Belcher),
    1923–, 1,2
  Charisse, Cyd, 1921–, 1,2
  Chase, Barrie, 1934–, 1
  Childs, Lucinda, 1940–, 2
  Clarke, Shirley, 1927–, 2
  Clayton, Bessie, d. 1948, 1
  Clifford, Camille, m. 1906, 1
  Collins, Lottie, 1866–1910, 2
  Cooke, Kate Walsh, d. 1903, 1
  Corio, Ann, 1
  Cullberg, Birgit, 1908–, 2
  Dazie, Mademoiselle, fl. 1910s, 1
  De Koven, Jean, d. 1937, 2
  De Marco, Renee, fl. 1940s, 1
  DeLavallade, Carmen, 1931–, 1
  DeMille, Agnes George, 1905–, 1,2

Neagle, Anna, Dame, 1904–, 1,2
Nesbit, Evelyn, 1884–1967, 1,2
Newmar, Julie, 1935–, 1
Nissen, Greta, 1906–, 1,2
No-Fru, fl. 1200s, 1
North, Sheree, 1932–, 1
Nurmi, Maila, 1921–, 2
Osata, Sono, 1919–, 1
Paige, Janis, 1923–, 1
Patterson, Nan, 1882–, 1
Pavlova, Anna, 1881–1931, 1,2
Peers, Joan, 1911–, 2
Pennington, Ann, 1893–1971, 2
Perrine, Valerie, 1943–, 2
Pickard, Mae, m. 1914, 1
Pointing, Audrey, m. 1933, 1
Polite, Carlene Hatcher, 1932–, 2
Powell, Eleanor, 1913–1982, 1,2
Previn, Dory Langan, 1929–, 2
Price, Ruth, 1938–, 2
Primus, Pearl, 1919–, 1,2
Provine, Dorothy, 1937–, 1,2
Prowse, Juliet, 1936–, 1,2
Rand, Sally, 1904–1979, 1,2
Raye, Martha, 1916–, 1,2
Reinking, Ann, 1941–, 2
Reynolds, Jane Louisa, d. 1907, 1
Richards, Rosa Coates, fl. 1930s, 1
Riefenstahl, Leni (Berta Helene
    Amalia), 1902–, 2
Rivera, Chita, 1933–, 1,2
Robinson, Edna Mae Holly, 1
Rogers, Ginger, 1911–, 1,2
Rolfe, Bari, 1916–, 2
Rubinstein, Ida, 1895–1960, 1
Salome, fl. 100 AD, 1,2
San Juan, Olga, 1927–, 2
Shannon, Peggy, 1907–1941, 1,2
Shelley, Gladys, 1918–, 1,2
Shridharani, Sundari, 2
Sinclair, Guinivere, m. 1925, 1
Singleton, Penny "Blondie", 1935–, 2
Smith, Kate Walsh Fitzroy, d. 1903, 1
Snow, Anna Rablen, 1861–, 1,2
Sokolova, Lydia, fl. 1920s, 1
Souray, Eleanor, m. 1910, 1
St. Denis, Ruth, 1877–1968, 1,2
Stagg, Mary, 1710–1730, 1,2
Strangeways, Susan Fox, m. 1764, 1
Stuyvesant, Elizabeth, 1910–1970, 2
Suratt, Valeska, fl. 1910s, 1
Sweeney, Genevieve Evelyn, fl.
    1930s, 1
Tan Eyck, Melissa, fl. 1910s, 1

Tcherkassky, Marianna, 1952–, 2
Thompson, Lydia, 1836–1908, 1,2
Tibbetts, Irene Lyons, 1883–1973, 2
Trefilova, Vera, fl. 1900s, 1
Van Cleve, Edith, fl. 1930s, 1
Van Hamel, Martine, 1945–, 2
Vanderbilt, Gertrude, 1889–1960, 1,2
Vera-Ellen, (Vera-Ellen Rohe), 1926–
    1981, 1,2
Verchinana, Nina, fl. 1930s, 1
Verdon, Gwen, 1925–, 1,2
Wailes, Marylin, fl. 1920s, 1
Walker, Cindy, 2
Washinton, Fredi, 1903–, 2
Whitney, Eleanore, 1914–, 2

Dante Alighieri—Friend
    Beatrice Portinari, 1266–1290, 1
Darby, John—Spouse
    Darby, Joan, fl. 1700s, 1
Darwin, Charles—Granddaughter
    Cornford, Frances Crofts Darwin,
        1886–1960, 2
    Raverst, Gwen Darwin, 1885–1957,
        1,2
Darwin, Charles—Mother
    Darwin, Suzannah Wedgwood, d.
        1817, 2
Darwin, Charles—Spouse
    Darwin, Emma Wedgwood, 2
Data processors
    See
    Computer scientists
Daughters of the American Revolution
    See
    DAR
David, King—Spouse
    Bathsheba, 1040–1015, 1,2
David—Daughter
    Tamar, 1
David—Granddaughter
    Mahalath, 1
David—Sister
    Abigail, 1
David—Spouse
    Ahinoam, 1
Davis, Jefferson—Benefactor
    Dorsey, Sarah Anne Ellis, 1829–
        1879, 1,2
Davis, Jefferson—Daughter
    Davis, Winnie (Varina Anne), 1864–,
        2
Davis, Jefferson—Spouse
    Davis, Varina Anne Banks Howell,
        1826–1906, 1,2

Davis, Sammy—Spouse
  Davis, Altovise, 1947–, 2
De Bourbon, C. F.—Spouse
  Marie-Caroline Ferdinande Louise,
    Duchess de Berry, 1798–1870, 1
De Gaulle, Charles—Mother
  De Gaulle, Jeanne Maillot-Delannoy,
    d. 1940, 2
De Gaulle, Charles—Spouse
  De Gaulle, Yvonne Vendroux, 1900–,
    1
De Master, Douglas—Spouse
  Thomas, Jeanette, fl. 1970s, 2
De Moss, Arthur—Spouse
  De Moss, Nancy, 2
De Sade, Marquis—Mother
  Carman, Marie Elenore Maille de, fl.
    1730s, 2
De Soto, Hernando—Daughter
  De Soto, Sara, 2
De Soto, Hernando—Expedition
  Hinestrosa, Francisca, d. 1541, 1,2
De Stael, Madame—Daughter
  Necker, Germaine, fl. 1700s, 1
Deacons
  Eustochium, fl. 386, 2
  Fedde, Elizabeth, 1850–1921, 1,2
  Harman, Belle Carter, fl. 1920s, 2
  Marcela, 325–420, 1,2
  Paula, 347–404, 1,2
  Swanson, Katrina, 2
Deaf
  Howey, Ella Mae, fl. 1950s, 1
  Keller, Helen Adams, 1880–1968, 1,2
  O'Neil, Kitty, 1948–, 2
Deaf education
  Fuller, (Sarah) Margaret, 1810–1850,
    1,2
  Garrett, Emma, 1846–1893, 2
  Garrett, Mary Smith, 1839–1925, 2
  Joiner, Enfield, d. 1965, 2
  Rogers, Harriet Burbank, 1834–1919,
    2
  Yale, Caroline Ardelia, 1848–1933, 2
Deaf mute
  Bridgman, Laura Dewey, 1829–1889,
    1,2
  Cogswell, Alice, fl. 1800s, 1
Dean, John—Spouse
  Dean, Maureen E. Kane, 1946–, 2
Debutantes
  Harriman, Mary, fl. 1900s, 2
  Jacob, Mary Phelps, fl. 1910s, 2
  Salaman, Peggy, fl. 1930s, 2

Tiarks, Henrietta, fl. 1950s, 2
  Whigham, Margaret, fl. 1930s, 2
Defendant in unusual law case
  Sykes, Gloria, fl. 1970s, 2
Delaware
  Boggs, Lettie Vaughn, 1885–1971, 2
  Buchanan, Mary Madaline, 1908–, 2
  Davis, Vera Gibridge, 1894–, 2
  Ehinger, Aline N., 1891–, 2
  Frear, Esther Schaner, 1909–, 2
  Lewis, Mary Caulk, 1880–, 2
  Mayer, Bessie Bruce, 1890–, 2
  O'Neill, Margaret Moffett, 1900–, 2
  Ridgely, Mabel LLoyd, 1872–1957, 2
  Speakman, Margorie Willoughby,
    1890–, 2
Delaware Indians
  Freeman, Indian Hannah, 1730–
    1802, 2
Demeter—Daughter
  Persephone, 2
Democratic National Committee
  Bush, Dorothy Vredenburgh, fl.
    1950s, 2
Demographers
  Hagood, Margaret Lloyd Jarman,
    1907–1963, 2
  Taeuber, Irene Barnes, 1906–1974, 2
Dentists
  Abelson, Josephine May, fl. 1930s, 1
  Berger, Hulda E., fl. 1930s, 1
  Bruenn, Anna Rosa, fl. 1930s, 1
  Gardner, Trixie, fl. 1950s, 2
  Harwood, Fanny, 1889–1973, 2
  Henin, Marie-Louise, 1898–1944, 2
  Kelner, Sophie, fl. 1930s, 1
  Kohlhepp, Evelyn Marie, fl. 1930s, 1
  Pagelson, Henriette, fl. 1860s, 2
  Sigmond, Anna, fl. 1920s, 1
  Sinkford, Jeanne Craig, fl. 1960s, 2
  Taylor, Lucy Beaman Hobbs, 1833–
    1910, 1,2
Department store executives
  LaForge, Margaret Getchell, 1841–
    1880, 2
  Michelson, Gertrude G., fl. 1940s, 2
Derby, Richard—Spouse
  Derby, Martha Coffin, 1783–1832, 2
Dermatologists
  Zaidens, Sadie Helene, fl. 1930s, 1
Designers
  See also
    Carpet designers
    China designers

Fashion designers
Furniture designers
Doll designers
Industrial designers
Interior designers
Jewelry designers
Lighting designers
Scenic designers
Stoneware design
Tapestry designers
Textile designers
Austin, Inez, 2
Beilenson, Edna, 1909–1981, 2
Bergmann, Ava, fl. 1970s, 2
Blondin, Catharine F., fl. 1930s, 1
Brosnan, Mary, fl. 1930s, 1
Brummer, Eva, 1901–, 2
Castaing, Madeleine, 2
Churchill, Eleanor Franzen, fl. 1900s, 2
Cook, Nancy, fl. 1930s, 1
Diamond, Freda, fl. 1950s, 2
Finelli, Ivonne (Sivone), 2
French, Annie, 1872–1965, 2
Fry, Laura Ann, 1857–1943, 2
Greenaway, Kate (Catherine), 1846–1901, 1,2
Honeywell, Annette, 1904–, 1
Horn, Carol, 1938–, 2
Hoyt, Peggy, fl. 1930s, 1
Hulbert, Katherine Allmond, fl. 1900s, 1
Hyde, Helen, 1,2
Ilvessalo, Kirsti, 1920–, 2
Jacob, Mary Phelps, fl. 1910s, 2
Johansson-Pape, Lisa, 1907–, 2
Koehler, Florence, 1861–1944, 2
Korsmo, Grete Prytz, 1917–, 2
MacBeth, Ann, 1875–1948, 2
Macdonald, Frances, 1874–1921, 2
Macdonald, Margaret R. S. W., 1865–1933, 2
Newbery, Jessie Rowat, fl. 1880s, 2
Newill, Mary J., 1860–1947, 2
O'Kane, Helen Marguerite, fl. 1900s, 2
Oakley, Violet, 1874–1961, 1
Paskauskaite, Lili, fl. 1960s, 2
Raeburn, Agnes, R. S. W., 1872–1955, 2
Rice, Laura W., fl. 1930s, 1
Rikki (Rikki Kilsdonk), 2
Siimes, Aune, 1909–, 2
Still, Nancy, 1926–, 2

Tuumi, Raija, 1923–, 2
Twomey, Kathleen, 1914–, 1
Van der Wal, Franki, fl. 1950s, 1
Detectives
Abreu, Lucille, fl. 1970s, 2
Burke, Kathy, fl. 1960s, 2
Fritz, Barbara, 2
Owen, Marie, fl. 1890s, 2
Sullivan, Mary Agnes, 1879–1950, 1
Taylor, Winifred, 2
Dexter*
Greenleaf, Ann, fl. 1790s, 1
Diarists
A.M.B., Miss, fl. 1860s, 1
Agnes, fl. 1820s, 1
Alden, Esther, c. 1847, 1
Almy, Mary Gould, 1735–1808, 2
Andrews, Eliza Frances, 1840–1932, 1,2
Arnold, Mary Ellen, fl. 1860s, 1
Bashkirtseff/Bashkirtsev, Marie Constantinova, 1859–1884, 1,2
Bates, Mrs. D. B., fl. 1850s, 1,2
Biddle, Adele, 2
Bowne, Eliza Southgate, 1783–1809, 1,2
Brandt, Alice, fl. 1893, 2
Brooks, Mary Frances, fl. 1860s, 1
Burney, Fanny, 1752–1840, 1,2
Byson, Mary, fl. 1860s, 1
Cahal, Mary, fl. 1860s, 1
Carr, Emily, 1871–1945, 1,2
Cary, Constance, fl. 1860s, 1
Chesnut, Mary Boykin Miller, 1823–1886, 1,2
Clifford, Anna Rawle, 1757–1858, 2
Collis, Septima, fl. 1890s, 2
Cramer, Vrow, 1655–, 2
Cumming, Kate, 1835–1909, 1,2
Custer, Elizabeth Bacon, 1842–1933, 1,2
Davis, Varina Anne Banks Howell, 1826–1906, 1,2
Dawson, Sarah Morgan, 1841–, 1
De Jesus, Carolina Maria, fl. 1970s, 2
Dostoevsky, Anna, 1846–1918, 2
Drinker, Elizabeth Sandwith, 1734–1807, 1,2
Dunlap, Kate, fl. 1860s, 2
Edmondson, Belle, fl. 1860s, 1
Edwards, Esther, d. 1756, 2
Ferguson, Jane Young, fl. 1770s, 2
Field, Joanna, pseud., 1905–, 2
Fiennes, Celia, 1662–1741, 1,2

Waters, Lydia, fl. 1850s, 1,2
White, Tryphena, fl. 1800s, 1
Wilcox, Mrs. G. Griffin, fl. 1860s, 1
Wilkinson, Eliza Yonge, fl. 1770s, 1,2
Winslow, Anna Green, fl. 1770s, 1,2
Wister, Sarah, 1761–1804, 1,2
Woolf, (Adeline) Virginia (Stephen), 1882–1941, 1,2
Wordsworth, Dorothy, 1771–1855, 1,2
Yarnall, Anna, 1844–, 2
Diarists (Counterfeit)
Whitely, Opel, fl. 1920s, 2
Dibri—Daughter
Shelomith, 1
Dickens, Charles—Friend
Ternan, Ellen, 2
Dickens, Charles—Mother
Dickens, Elizabeth Barrow, d. 1863, 2
Dickens, Charles—Sister-in-law
Hogarth, Georgina, fl. 1840s, 2
Dickens, Charles—Spouse
Dickens, Catherine Hogarth, fl. 1830s, 2
Dickinson, Emily—Sister
Dickinson, Lavinia, fl. 1840s, 1
Dieticians
See
Nutritionists
Didius Severus Julianus—Spouse
Manlia Scantilla, fl. 130s, 1
Dimond, Tony—Spouse
Dimond, Dorothea, fl. 1930s, 2
Diocletian—Spouse
Prisca (Serena), fl. 310s, 1
Diplomats
See also
Secretaries of state
Diplomats, American
Anderson, (Helen) Eugenie More, 1909–, 1,2
Armstrong, Anne Legendre, 1927–, 2
Black, Shirley Temple, 1928–, 2
Carter, Susan Shirley, fl. 1960s, 2
Chambers, Anne Cox, fl. 1970s, 2
Harriman, Florence Jaffray Hurst, 1870–1967, 1,2
Harris, Patricia Roberts, 1924–1985, 1,2
Lord, Mary Stimson Pillsbury, 1,2
Mesta, Perle Skirvan (Skirvin), 1893–1975, 1,2
Olmstead, Mary S., 1919–, 2

Owen, Ruth Bryan, 1895–1954, 1,2
Ridgeway, Rozanne L., fl. 1970s, 2
Smythe, Mabel Murphy, fl. 1970s, 2
White, Katharine Elkus, 1906–1985, 1,2
Wilkowski, Jean, 1919–, 2
Willis, Frances Elizabeth, 1899–, 1,2
Diplomats, Australian
Dobson, Ruth, fl. 1970s, 2
King, Maris, 2
Rankin, Anabelle, Dame, fl. 1970s, 2
Diplomats, Austrian
Kottauer, Helene, 1410–1470, 1
Diplomats, Brazilian
Castro e Silva de Vinvenzi, Maria de Lourdes, fl. 1970s, 2
Diplomats, Byzantine
Dalassena, Anna, d. 1105, 1
Diplomats, Colombian
Crovo, Maria Elena Jimenez de, 1935–, 2
Cuevas Cancino, Esmerelda Arboleda de, fl. 1960s, 2
Diplomats, Danish
Begtrup, Bodil Andreasen, 1903–, 1,2
Diplomats, English
Salt, Barbara, fl. 1950s, 2
Warburton, A. M., fl. 1970s, 2
Diplomats, Finnish
Forsman, Eeva-Kristina, fl. 1950s, 2
Diplomats, German
Hutten, Margarete, 2
Lieven, Dorothea, 1784–1857, 1,2
Diplomats, Hungarian
Zrini, Ilona (Helen), 1643–1703, 1,2
Diplomats, Indian
Menon, Mrs. K. Rukmini, fl. 1970s, 2
Pandit, Vijaya Lakshmi, 1900–, 1,2
Diplomats, Indonesian
Rusad, Laili, fl. 1950s, 2
Diplomats, Italian
Sforza, Caterina, 1463–1509, 1,2
Diplomats, Jordanian
Hlass, Laurice, 2
Diplomats, Lithuanian
Petkevikaite, Gabriele, 1861–1943, 1
Diplomats, Pakistani
Ali Kahn, Begum Liaquat, 2
Diplomats, Paraguayan
Vallejo, Isabel Arr, fl. 1940s, 2
Diplomats, Russian
Kollontay, Alexandra Mikhailovna, 1872–1952, 1,2
Diplomats, Swedish
Myrdal, Alva Reimer, 1902–, 1,2
Rossel, Agda, 1910–, 1,2

Diplomats, Ugandan
  Olowo, Bernadette, fl. 1970s, 2
Diplomats, Venezuelan
  Gramcko, Ida, fl. 1940s, 2
Disraeli, Benjamin—Spouse
  Beaconsfield, Mary Anne Evans Dis-
    raeli, 1792–1872, 1
Divers
  Chandler, Jennifer, fl. 1970s, 2
  Coleman, Georgia, 1912–1940, 2
  Draves, Vicki Manalo, 1924–, 1
  Engel-Kramer, Ingrid, fl. 1960s, 2
  Gestring, Marjorie, 1923–, 2
  Hanson, Norma, fl. 1970s, 2
  Johansson, Greta, 2
  King, Maxine, 1943–, 2
  McCormick, Patricia Keller, 1930–,
    1,2
  McIngvale, Cynthia Potter, fl. 1970s,
    2
  Poynton, Dorothy, 1915–, 2
  Riggin, Aileen, 2
Divorcee
  Perkins, Mary Fitch Wescott, d.
    1894, 2
Doctors
  See
  Physicians and surgeons
Dodge, Horace—Spouse
  Dodge, Gregg Sherwood, 1923–, 1
Dog fanciers
  Bonaparte, Mrs. Jerome Napoleon, fl.
    1930s, 1
  Patterson, Elizabeth (Bonaparte),
    1785–1879, 1,2
Dog owners
  Murphy, Mary, d. 1979, 2
Dog specialists
  Miller, Daisy Orr, fl. 1930s, 1
Dog trainers
  Jewett, Mildred, 1
  Smith, Eleanor, fl. 1860s, 1
Dole, Robert J.—Spouse
  Dole, Elizabeth Hanford, 1936–, 2
  Dole, Phyllis Holden, 2
Doll makers
  Alexander, Madame Beatrice, 1895–,
    1
  Cochran, Dewees, 1902–, 1
  O'Neill, Rose Cecil, 1874–1944, 1,2
  Sherman, Florence A., fl. 1930s, 1
Domitia Lepida—Sister
  Domitia, fl. 40s, 1
Domitian—Mother
  Domitilla, d. 90s, 1

Domitian—Spouse
  Domitia Longina, fl. 70s, 1
Domnina, Saint—Friend
  Theonilla, fl. 200s, 1
Donatus—Daughter
  Ursula, d.238/451, 1
Donner party
  Breen, Margaret, fl. 1840s, 1,2
  Covilland, Mary Murphy, 2
  Reed, Margaret, fl. 1840s, 1,2
Dostoevsky, Fyodor—Spouse
  Dostoevsky, Anna, 1846–1918, 2
Douglas, Kirk—Spouse
  Douglas, Anne, fl. 1970s, 2
Douglas, Stephan—Spouse
  Douglas, Adele Cutts, 1835–1899, 2
Douglass, Frederick—Spouse
  Douglass, Anna Murray, m. 1840, 1
Douglass, Sarah Hallam—Niece
  Hallam, Sarah, fl. 1760s, 1
Dow, Laurence—Spouse
  Dow, Peggy, fl. 1800s, 2
Dowsers
  Penrose, Evelyn, 2
Dragoons
  Figuer, Therese, 1798–1812, 2
Drama critics
  Barker, E. Frye, fl. 1910s, 1
  Cassidy, Claudia, 1905–, 1
  Crist, Judith Klein, 1922–, 2
  Gilder, Jeannette Leonard, 1849–
    1916, 1,2
  Gilder, Rosamond, 1,2
  Hieronymous, Clara W., fl. 1950s, 2
  Holmes, Ann, fl. 1970s, 2
  Leslie, Amy, 1855–1939, 1,2
  Oliver, Edith, fl. 1960s, 2
  Syse, Glenna, fl. 1950s, 2
  Winer, Linda, fl. 1970s, 2
Drama teachers
  Coit, Dorothy, 1889–, 1
  Conti, Italia, 1873–1946, 1,2
  Krause, Alvina, 1893–1981, 2
  Leontovich, Eugenie, 1894–, 2
  Manner, Jane, d. 1943, 1
  McGauley, Minna Hoppe, fl. 1920s, 1
  McLean, Margaret, fl. 1930s, 1
  Moore, Anne, fl. 1930s, 1
  Morgan, Anna, 1851–1936, 2
  Robinson-Duff, Frances, fl. 1930s, 1
  Stenholm, Katherine, fl. 1950s, 2
  Wolter, Annett, fl. 1930s, 1
Dramatic artists
  McBrown, Gertrude P., fl. 1970s, 2

Mowatt, Anna Cora Ogden, 1819–1870, 1,2
Mumford, Ethel Watts, d. 1940, 1
Murray, Judith Sargent Stevens, 1751–1820, 1,2
Mygatt, Tracy Dickinson, fl. 1930s, 1
Nichols, Anne, 1892–1966, 1,2
Norman, Marsha Williams, 1947–, 2
Olcott, Rita, fl. 1930s, 1
Owens, Rochelle, 1936–, 2
Parker, Lottie Blair, d. 1937, 1
Peabody, Josephine Preston, 1874–1922, 1,2
Perelman, Laura, fl. 1930s, 1
Phelps, Pauline, fl. 1910s, 1
Phillips, Anita, fl. 1930s, 1
Rinehart, Mary Roberts, 1876–1958, 1,2
Ritchie, Anna Cora O. Mowatt, 1819–1870, 1
Rouverol, Aurania, 1885–1955, 1
Sears, Zelda, 1873–, 1
Shange, Ntozake, 1948–, 2
Short, Marion, fl. 1910s, 1
Sifton, Claire, 1898–, 1
Sinclair, Jo, pseud., 1913–, 1,2
Stanley, Martha, 1879–, 1
Starling, Lynn, 1893–, 1
Steele, Norma Mitchell Talbot, m. 1932, 1
Stephens, Nan Bagby, 1892–, 1
Terry, Megan, 1932–, 2
Tewkesbury, Joan, 1936–, 2
Thane, Elswythe, 1900–, 1,2
Thompson, Charlotte, fl. 1910s, 1
Tonkonogy, Gertrude, 1908–, 1
Treadwell, Sophie, 1890–1970, 1,2
Unger, Gladys Buchanan, d. 1940, 1
Vollmer, Lula, 1898–1955, 1,2
Warren, Mercy Otis, 1728–1814, 1,2
Wasserstein, Wendy, 1950–, 2
Waters, Marianne, 1906–, 1
Watkins, Maurine Dallas, 1900–, 1
Weiman, Rita, 1889–1954, 1
West, Mae, 1892–1980, 1,2
Winer, Lucy, fl. 1970s, 2
Young, Rida Johnson, 1869–1926, 1,2
Dramatists, Austrian
Grazie, Marie Eugenie Dell, 1864–1931, 1
Dramatists, English
Anspach, Elizabeth Berkeley, 1750–1828, 1
Anthony, C. L., pseud., 1896–, 1,2

Bagnold, Enid Algerine, 1889–1981, 1,2
Banks, Lynne Reid, 1929–, 2
Behn, Aphra, 1640–1689, 1,2
Cavendish, Margaret, Duchess of Newcastle, 1624–1674, 1
Centlivre, Susanna, 1667–1723, 1,2
Charke, Charlotte Cibber, fl. 1710s, 1
Christie, Agatha (Mary Clarissa) Miller, Dame, 1891–1976, 1,2
Churchill, Caryl, 1938–, 2
Cockburn, Catharine Trotter, 1679–1749, 1
Cowley, Hannah Parkhurst, 1743–1809, 1,2
Dane, Clemence, pseud., 1887–1965, 1,2
Delafield, E. M. (Edmee Monica), 1890–1943, 1,2
Delaney, Shelagh, 1939–, 1,2
Du Maurier, Daphne, Lady Browning, 1907–, 1,2
Griffith, Elizabeth, 1730–1793, 1
Harwood, Isabella, 1840–1888, 2
Hatton, Ann Julia (Kemble) Curtis, 1757–, 2
Haywood, Eliza Fowler, 1693–1756, 1,2
Inchbald, Elizabeth Simpson, 1753–1821, 1,2
Jennings, Gertrude E., 1877–1958, 1
Jesse, Frynwid Tennyson, d. 1958, 1
Kemble, Fanny (Frances Anne), 1809–1893, 1,2
Kennedy, Margaret, 1896–1967, 1,2
Lee, Sophia, 1750–1824, 1
Long, Gabrielle Margaret Vere Campbell, 1888–1952, 1
Manley, Mary de la Riviere, 1663–1724, 1,2
More, Hannah, 1745–1833, 1,2
Newcastle, Margaret Cavendish, Duchess of, 1624–1694, 1,2
Pix, Mary Griffith, 1666–1720, 1,2
Rowson, Susanna Haswell, 1762–1824, 1,2
Sayers, Dorothy Leigh, 1893–1957, 1,2
Smedley, Constance, 1881–1941, 1
Trotter, Catherine, 1679–1749, 1,2
Webster, Augusta Davies, 1837–1894, 1
Weldon, Fay, fl. 1970s, 2
Wiseman, Jane, fl. 1700s, 1

Woolf, (Adeline) Virginia (Stephen), 1882–1941, 1,2

Dramatists, French
Duveyrier, Anne Honore Joseph, 1787–1865, 1
Gay, Delphine, 1804–1835, 1,2
Sagan, Francoise, pseud., 1935–, 1,2

Dramatists, German
Birch-Pfeiffer, Charlotte Karoline, 1793–1868, 1
Fleisser, Marieleuse, 1901–1974, 2
Klink, Gertrud Schotz, 1902–, 1,2
Langgasser, Elisabeth, 1899–1950, 2
Rosmer, Ernst (Elsa Bernstein), fl. 1800s, 1
Rostwitha (Hrosvitha), 935–1000, 1,2
Sachs, Nelly Leone, 1891–1970, 1,2

Dramatists, Hungarian
Artner, Marie Therese "Theone", 1772–1829, 1
Orczy, Emmuska, 1865–1947, 1,2
Spewack, Bella Cohen, 1899–, 1,2

Dramatists, Indochinese
Duras, Marguerite Donnadieu, 1914–, 1,2

Dramatists, Irish
Gregory, (Isabella) Augusta Persse, 1852–1932, 1,2

Dramatists, Latvian
Peksen, Marija, 1845–1903, 1

Dramatists, Polish
Nalkowska, Zofia, 1884–1954, 2
Zapolska, Gabryela, 1860–1921, 1

Dramatists, Puerto Rican
Benitez, Maria Bibiana, 1783–, 1

Dramatists, Russian
Flint, Eva Kay, 1902–, 1
Panova, Vera, 1905–1973, 2
Sarraute, Nathalie, 1900–, 1,2

Dramatists, Scottish
MacKintosh, Elizabeth, 1896–1952, 1
Tey, Josephine, pseud., 1897–1952, 2

Dramatists, South African
Lessing, Doris May, 1919–, 1,2
Millin, Sarah Gertrude Liebson, 1889–1968, 1,2

Dramatists, Swedish
Edgren, Anne Charlotte Leffler, 1849–1892, 1

Dramatists, Welsh
Royde-Smith, Naomi Gwladys, 1875–1964, 1,2

Draughtsmen
Gillette, Martha Taylor, fl. 1930s, 1
Lamme, Cornelie, 2

Palmer, Frances "Fanny" Lora Bond, 1812–1876, 2

Dress reformers
Hasbrouck, Lydia Sayer, 1827–1910, 2
Smith, Elizabeth Gerrit, fl. 1850s, 2

Dressmakers
Cahill, Mary, fl. 1740s, 1
Keckley, Elizabeth, 1818–1907, 2
Woods, Mary A., fl. 1910s, 1

Drummers
Dodgion, Dottie (Dorothy) Giamo, 1929–, 2
Hopkins, Linda, 1925–, 2
Oliphant, Grassella, 1929–, 2

Drusus, Marcus Livius—Sister
Livia, fl. 91 BC, 1

Drusus, Nero Claudius—Spouse
Antonia Minor, 36BC–37AD, 1

Duchess of Cambridge
Fitz, Mrs. George, d. 1890, 1

Duchess of Lorraine
Elizabeth of Lorraine, 1676–1744, 1

Duchess of Saxe-Weimar
Anna Amalia, 1739–1807, 1

Duchesses
Alba, Maria del Pilar Rosario, Cayenta Fitz-James Stuart y Silva, 1762–1802, 2
Ancaster, Mary, Duchess, d. 1793, 2
Beauharnais, Stephanie de, 1789–, 1
Birute, fl. 1300s, 1
Charlotte, Grand Duchess of Luxembourg, 1896–1985, 2
Cromartie, Ann, Countess of, 1829–1888, 1

Dude wranglers
Fergusson, Erna (Emma), 1888–1964, 1,2

Dudley, Robert—Spouse
Robsart, Amy, 1532–1560, 1,2

Duke, Doris—Mother
Duke, Nanaline Holt Inman, m. 1907, 1

Dumas, Alexander—Inspiration
Du Plessis, Marie Alice Bradford, 1824–1847, 1,2

Dunbar, Paul Lawrence—Mother
Dunbar, Matilda J., 1848–1934, 1

Duncombe—Spouse
Highmore, Susanna Highmore, 1730–1812, 2

Durant, Will—Spouse
Durant, Ariel K., 1898–1981, 2

E

Eaton, Major—Spouse
Eaton, Margaret (Peggy) O'Neale,
1799–1879, 1,2
O'Neal, Margaret, m. 1916, 1
Eccentrics
Batchelor, Emma, fl. 1900s, 1
Batchelor, Rosa, fl. 1900s, 1
Batchelor, Rosanna, d. 1942, 1
Butler, Eleanor, Lady, 1745–1829, 1
Colby, Mary Colgate, d. 1938, 1
Coogan, Harriet Gardiner Lynch,
1861–1947, 1
Coogan, Jessie, fl. 1930s, 1
Emerson, Mary Moody, 1774–1863,
1,2
Herzog, Beatrice, d. 1934, 1
Herzog, Helene, d. 1945, 1
Hubbard, Ann, 1
Jordan, Mrs. Jesse, fl. 1940s, 1
Leary, Anna, 1
Leary, Louise, 1
O'Grady, Dorothy Pamela, fl. 1940s,
1
Phyfe, Mrs. Duncan, d. 1944, 1
Ponsonby, Sarah, 1745–1831, 1
Powers, Mary Bullock, 1878–1948, 1
Romero family, fl. 1870s, 1
Shaw, Mrs. Stoddard, fl. 1950s, 1
Thorn, Emily, 1865–, 1
Thornton, Alice Wandesford, 1626–,
1
Tredwell, Gertrude, 1840–1933, 1
Wendell, Ella Von Echtel, d. 1931, 1,2
Wendell family, fl. 1900s, 1
West, Sandra Ilene, 1904–1977, 2
Wilks, Hetty Sylvia Green, 1871–
1951, 1
Winchester, Sarah Pardee, 1837–
1922, 2
Wood, Mary Elizabeth, 1870–1950, 1
Eclipse chasers
Sigler, Marcy, fl. 1960s, 2
Ecologists
Ishumure, Michiko, fl. 1950s, 2
Komarkova, Vera, 2
Morgan, Ann Haven, 1882–1966, 2
Willard, Beatrice, 1926–, 2

Economists
See also
Labor economists
Political economists
Housing economists
Alexander, Ruth, 1
Allen, Donna, fl. 1970s, 2
Baker, Elizabeth Bradford Faulkner,
1885–, 1
Balch, Emily Greene, 1867–1961, 1,2
Bernheim, Nicole, fl. 1970s, 2
Berry, Harriet Morehead, 1877–
1940, 2
Bitterman, Kathleen Studdar, 1916–,
2
Burns, Eveline Mabel, 1900–, 1
Campbell, Persia Crawford, 1898–
1974, 2
Coman, Katharine, 1857–1915, 1,2
Dewson, Mary Williams (Molly),
1874–1962, 1,2
Dublin, Mary, fl. 1930s, 1
Dulles, Eleanor Lansing, 1895–, 1
Freudenthal, Elsbeth Estelle, 1902–
1953, 1
Gilman, Charlotte Perkins Stetson,
1860–1935, 1,2
Gilson, Mary Barnett, 1877–, 1
Hammond, Barbara Bradby, gr.
1895, 1
Hulse, Anne Elizabeth, fl. 1930s, 1
Jackson, Barbara Ward, 1914–1981, 1
Johnson, Gloria T., fl. 1950s, 2
Kellor, Frances Alice, 1873–1952, 1,2
Keyserling, Mary Dublin, fl. 1930s, 2
Khe-Tagurova, Tamara, 2
Litvinenko, Lydia, fl. 1970s, 2
Lloyd, Cynthia B., 2
Luxemburg, Rosa, 1870–1919, 1,2
Meredith, Virginia, 1848–1936, 2
Newcomer, Mabel, 1891–, 1
Pace, Norma, 1923–, 2
Peixotto, Jessica Blanche, 1864–1941,
2
Pierson, Gail, 1941–, 2
Reagan, Barbara B., fl. 1970s, 2
Rivlin, Alice Mitchell, 1931–, 2
Robins, Margaret Dreier, 1868–1945,
1,2
Slater, Courtenay, 1934–, 2
Soss, Wilma Porter, 1902–, 1
Ushakova, Yelizveta, fl. 1940s, 2
Ward, Barbara Mary, 1914–1981, 1,2
Webb, Beatrice Potter, 1858–1943, 1,2

Whitman, Marina von Neumann, 1935–, 2
Wickens, Aryness Joy, 1901–, 1
Woodhouse, Margaret Chase Going, 1890–1984, 1,2
Wootton, Barbara Frances, 1897–, 1,2
Edison, Thomas—Mother
Edison, Nancy Elliott, 1810–1871, 1,2
Edison, Thomas—Spouse
Edison, Mina Miller, 1865–1947, 2
Editors
   See also
   Art editors
   Fashion editors
   Magazine editors
   Motion picture editors
   Music editors
   Newspaper editors
   Photography editors
   Poetry editors
   Puzzle editors
   Radio editors
   Television arts editors
   Television editors
Adam, Juliette Lamber, 1836–1936, 1,2
Adams, Elizabeth Kemper, 1872–1948, 1
Ahern, Mary Eileen, 1860–1938, 1,2
Aikens, Amanda L., 1833–1892, 1
Allen, Martha Frances, 1906–, 1,2
Ames, Elinor, fl. 1930s, 1
Andrews, Eliza Frances, 1840–1932, 1,2
Applegarth, Margaret Tyson, 1886–, 1
Archer, Alma, fl. 1930s, 1
Arman de Caillavet, Leontine Charlotte Lippman, 1844–1910, 1
Avary, Myrta Lockett, fl. 1910s, 1,2
Aw Sian, Sally, 1931–, 2
Babcock, Lucille, fl. 1930s, 1
Baggett, Helen M., fl. 1930s, 1
Barclay, Dorothy, 1921–, 2
Barratt, Louise Bascom, fl. 1930s, 1
Barrows, Katharine Isabel Hayes Chapin, 1845–1913, 1,2
Bass, Charlotte Spears, 1880–1969, 2
Bates, Mary E., d. 1956, 1
Bauer, Marion Eugenie, 1887–1955, 1,2
Becker, May Lamberton, 1873–1958, 1

Beeby, Nell V., 1896–1957, 1
Beilenson, Edna, 1909–1981, 2
Bellon, Yannick, fl. 1940s, 2
Benjamin, Louise Paine, fl. 1930s, 1
Bennett, Eve, fl. 1930s, 1
Berman, Avis, 2
Bernard, Jessie, 1903–, 2
Bevans, Gladys Huntington, fl. 1930s, 1
Bitker, Marjorie, 1901–, 2
Blackburn, Helen, 1842–1903, 1,2
Blavatsky, Helena Hahn Petrovna, 1831–1891, 1,2
Bodichon, Barbara Leigh-Smith, 1827–1891, 1,2
Boucherett, (Emilia) Jessie, 1825–1905, 1,2
Brady, Mildred Edie, 1906–1965, 2
Brastow, Virginia, 1872–1952, 1
Brewster, Cora Belle, 1859–, 1
Briney, Nancy Wells, 1911–, 1
Bromley, Dorothy Dunbar, 1896–, 1
Brooke, Frances Moore, 1724–1789, 1,2
Brown, Katharine, fl. 1930s, 1
Brown, Zaidee Mabel, 1875–1950, 1
Browne, Nina Eliza, 1860–, 1
Bruce, Elizabeth M., fl. 1880s, 1
Bryan, Mary Edwards, 1838–1913, 1,2
Buchanan, Anna Elizabeth, 1836–, 1
Buchanan, Annabel Morris, 1888–, 1,2
Buchanan, Mary Elizabeth, fl. 1930s, 1
Buckmaster, Henrietta, 1909–1983, 1,2
Buell, Sarah, fl. 1820s, 1
Bulkeley, Christy, fl. 1970s, 2
Bunting, Mary Ingraham, 1910–, 1,2
Burke, B. Ellen, 1850–, 1
Burnett, Hallie Southgate, 1908–, 1
Burnham, Mary, 1881–, 1
Caldwell, Mira, fl. 1870s, 1
Campbell, Ruth Elizabeth, fl. 1930s, 1
Carbine, Patricia, fl. 1970s, 2
Carpenter, Mary, 1807–1877, 2
Carper, Elsie, fl. 1970s, 2
Carraway, Gertrude Sprague, 1896–, 1
Carter, Ernestine, 2
Cauer, Minna, 1841–1922, 1,2
Cervantes, Lorna Dee, 1934–, 2

Mitford, Nancy Freman, 1907–1973, 1,2
Moir, Phyllis, fl. 1930s, 1
Molloy, Emma, 1839–, 1
Monroe, Harriet, 1860–1936, 1,2
Montgomery, Carrie Frances Judd, 1858–, 1
Montgomery, Vaida, 1888–1959, 2
Moody, Helen Waterson, 1860–, 1
Moore, Alma Chestnut, fl. 1930s, 1
Moore, Honor, fl. 1970s, 2
Moore, Marianne Craig, 1887–1972, 1,2
Morton, Elizabeth Homer, 1903–, 1
Moss, Elizabeth (Bettye) Murphy, fl. 1940s, 2
Neal, Alice B., m. 1946, 1
Nevier, Leona, fl. 1950s, 2
Nicholson, Eliza Jane Poitevent Holbrook, 1849–1896, 1,2
Nicholson, Margaret, 1904–, 1
Northcott, Kaye, fl. 1970s, 2
O'Mahoney, Katherine A., fl. 1910s, 1
O'Neill, Lois Decker, fl. 1940s, 2
Onassis, Jacqueline Bouvier Kennedy, 1929–, 2
Onis, Harriet (Vivian Wishnief) de, 1899–1969, 1,2
Ovens, Florence Jane, fl. 1930s, 1
Palmer, Caroline L., fl. 1930s, 1
Palmer, Sophia F., d. 1920, 1
Parker, Eleanor R., 1874–, 1
Patterson, Alicia (Alicia Guggenheim), 1906–1963, 1,2
Patterson, Flora W., 1847–, 1
Pauley, Gay, fl. 1970s, 2
Paxon, Marjorie, fl. 1940s, 2
Paxton, Jean Gregory, fl. 1930s, 1
Payne, Winona Wilcox, 1865–1949, 1
Pennock, Grace Lavinia, fl. 1930s, 1
Pennock, Meta, fl. 1930s, 1
Peyser, Ethel R., fl. 1910s, 1
Phillips, Frances Lucas, fl. 1930s, 1
Pickering, Ruth, 1920–1970, 2
Pinney, Jean Burrows, fl. 1930s, 1
Pool, Mary Jane, fl. 1940s, 2
Porter, Catherine, fl. 1920s, 1
Porter, Charlotte Endymion, 1857–1942, 1,2
Poulssn, Ann Emile, 1853–1939, 1
Prang, Mary Amelia Dana Hicks, 1836–1927, 1,2
Pritchard, Esther Tuttle, 1840–, 1

Ratchford, Fannie Elizabeth, 1887–, 1
Rathbone, Josephine Adams, 1856–1941, 1,2
Ratliff, Beulah Amidon, fl. 1930s, 1
Rawson, Eleanor S., fl. 1970s, 2
Raynal, Jackie, fl. 1960s, 2
Restivo, Sally Jo, fl. 1970s, 2
Rhondda, Margaret Haig Thomas, 1883–1958, 1
Richardson, Ellen A., 1845–1911, 1
Richardson, Florence, fl. 1920s, 1
Riding, Laura, 1901–, 1,2
Rittenhouse, Jessie Bell, 1869–1948, 1,2
Roberts, Mary Fanton, d. 1956, 1
Roberts, Mary May, 1877–1959, 1,2
Robinson, Abbie C. B., 1828–, 1
Roland, Jeanne Manon Philipon, 1754–1793, 1,2
Romanelli, Elaine, fl. 1970s, 2
Ross, Pat, 2
Rothrock, Mary Utopia, 1890–, 1
Ryan, Patricia, 2
Saal, Rollene, fl. 1970s, 2
Salmenhaara, Kyllikki, 1915–, 2
Salminen, Leena, fl. 1970s, 2
Samoilova, Natasha (Concurdia), 1876–, 2
Sangster, Margaret Elizabeth Munson, 1838–1912, 1,2
Sawyer, Caroline Mehitable Fisher, 1812–1894, 1,2
Schmitt, Gladys Leonore, 1909–1972, 1,2
Schoff, Hannah Kent, 1853–1940, 1,2
Sellers, Marie, fl. 1930s, 1
Shadiyeva, Taijikhan, fl. 1920s, 2
Sheehy, Gail Henion, 1937–, 2
Sherwood, Katharine "Kate" Margaret Brownlee, 1841–1914, 1,2
Shinn, Milicent Washburn, 1858–1940, 1,2
Sloan, Margaret, 2
Slott, Molly, 1896–1967, 1
Smith, Charlotte Ann, fl. 1930s, 1
Smith, Hazel Brannon, 1914–, 2
Smith, Helen Evertson, 1839–, 1
Smith, Lillian Eugenia, 1897–1966, 1,2
Snow, Carmel White, 1890–1961, 1
Soliman, Patricia, fl. 1960s, 2
Soltesova, Elena Marothy, 1855–, 1
Squires, Delphine Anderson, 1868–, 2
Stephens, Ann(a) Sophia Winterbotham, 1810–1886, 1,2

Anderson, Alyce E., 2
Andrews, Jane, 1833–1887, 1,2
Angela Merici, Saint, 1474–1540, 1,2
Anguiano, Lupe, 1929–, 2
Arbuthnot, May Hill, 1884–1969, 2
Arendt, Hanna, 1906–1975, 1,2
Arnold, Sarah Louise, 1859–, 1
Astell, Mary, 1666–1731, 1,2
Atkins, Mary, 1817–1882, 1,2
Atwood, Elizabeth Gordon, 1882–, 1
Aull, Elizabeth, fl. 1860s, 2
Babcock, Martha Cross, 1814–1873, 2
Bailey, Jean Iris Murdock, 1918–, 1
Baker, Elizabeth Bradford Faulkner,
    1885–, 1
Baker, Katharine Lee, 1859–1929, 2
Baldwin, Mary, fl. 1840s, 2
Barbauld, Anna Laetitia, 1743–1825,
    1,2
Barker, Mary Cornelia, 1879–1963, 2
Barker, Tommie Dora, 1888–, 1
Barnes, Mary Downing Sheldon,
    1850–1898, 2
Barrett, Janie Porter, 1865–1948, 1,2
Bates, Katherine Lee, 1859–1929, 1,2
Bauer, Clara, d. 1912, 2
Beale, Dorothea, 1831–1906, 1,2
Beam, Lura, 1887–, 1
Beaufort, Margaret, 1443–1509, 1,2
Beecher, Catherine Esther, 1800–
    1878, 1,2
Bellini [Billini], Maria Nicolasa,
    1839–1903, 1
Benedict, Ruth Fulton, 1887–1947,
    1,2
Benitez, Helena Z., fl. 1930s, 2
Berry, Martha McChesney, 1866–
    1942, 1,2
Bertola, Mariana, fl. 1920s, 1
Bethune, Mary McLeod, 1875–1955,
    1,2
Bevier, Isabel, 1860–1942, 1,2
Bildersee, Adele, fl. 1930s, 1
Bingham, Millicent Todd, 1880–1968,
    1,2
Blake, Florence G., 1907–, 1
Blake, Katherine Devereaux, 1857–
    1950, 1
Blanchard, Hazel Ann, 1920–, 1
Blanding, Sarah Gibson, 1898–1985,
    1,2
Bliss, Anna Elvira, 1843–1925, 2
Bliss, Ethel House, 1880–1946, 1
Blunt, Katharine, 1876–1954, 1,2

Boehringer, Cora Louise, fl. 1920s, 1
Bond, Elizabeth Powell, 1841–, 1
Booth, Almida, fl. 1880s, 1
Borchardt, Selma Munter, 1895–
    1968, 2
Bourgeoys, Marguerite, fl. 1850s, 2
Bowne, Eliza Southgate, 1783–1809,
    1,2
Brackett, Anna Callender, 1836–
    1911, 2
Bradley, Amy Morris, 1823–1904, 1,2
Bragdon, Helen Dalton, 1895–, 1
Breckinridge, Sophonisba Preston,
    1866–1948, 2
Bridgman, Eliza Jane Gillet, 1805–
    1871, 2
Brown, Charlotte Eugenia Hawkins,
    1883–1961, 1,2
Brown, Esther Lucile, fl. 1940s, 1
Brown, Hallie Quinn, 1849–1949, 1,2
Brown, Ina Corinne, fl. 1950s, 1
Brown, Winifred, fl. 1930s, 1
Browne, Rose Butler, 2
Brownson, Josephine Van Dyke,
    1880–1942, 1,2
Bruce, Alice Moore, d. 1951, 1
Bryan, Anna E., 1858–1901, 2
Bryant, Sophie, 1850–1922, 1
Burgess, Elizabeth Chamberlain,
    1877–1949, 1
Burns, Eveline Mabel, 1900–, 1
Burroughs, Nannie Helen, 1878–
    1961, 1,2
Burrows, Christine Mary Elizabeth,
    1872–1959, 1
Buss, Frances Mary, 1827–1894, 1,2
Butler, Clarissa, fl. 1880s, 1
Calahan, Mary A., d. 1906, 1,2
Caldwell, Sarah Campbell, 1903–, 1
Cam, Helen Maud, 1885–1968, 1
Campan, (Jeanne Louise) Henriette
    Genet, 1753–1822, 1,2
Carden, Mae, fl. 1930s, 1
Carey, Ocean Daily, fl. 1930s, 1
Carnegie, Dorothy Reeder Price,
    1912–, 1
Carpenter, Caroline A., fl. 1870s, 1
Carpenter, Mary, 1807–1877, 2
Carroll, Consolata, pseud., 1892–, 1
Carson, Luella Clay, 1856–, 1
Case, Adelaide Teague, 1887–1948, 2
Cassidy, Mary Q., fl. 1930s, 1
Cauer, Minna, 1841–1922, 1,2
Center, Stella Stewart, 1878–, 1

Chall, Jeanne S., fl. 1970s, 2
Chamberlin, Georgia Louise, 1862–1943, 1
Chandler, Anna Curtis, fl. 1910s, 1
Chandor, Valentine, fl. 1920s, 1
Chapin, Alice Delafield, fl. 1930s, 1
Chapin, Mary E., fl. 1870s, 1
Chase, Mary Ellen, 1887–1983, 1,2
Clapp, Margaret Antoinette, 1910–1974, 1,2
Clark, Septima Poinsette, 1898–, 2
Cleveland, Emeline Horton, 1829–1878, 1,2
Clough, Anne Jemima, 1820–1892, 1,2
Cobbs, Susan Parker, fl. 1950s, 1
Colgan, Eleanor, fl. 1900s, 1
Collver, Nathalia S., fl. 1930s, 1
Coman, Katharine, 1857–1915, 1,2
Comstock, Anna Botsford, 1854–1930, 1,2
Cone, Helen Gray, 1859–1934, 1
Cook, Alice Hanson, 2
Cook, Iva Dean, fl. 1970s, 2
Cooke, Flora Juliette, 1864–1953, 2
Cooper, Anna Julia Haywood, 1859–1964, 2
Coppin, Fanny Marion Jackson, 1837–1913, 1,2
Cori, Gerty Theresa Radnitz, 1896–1957, 1,2
Cornell, Sophia S., 1875–, 1
Corson, Juliet, 1841–1897, 1,2
Cosgrave, Jessica Gerretson Finch, d. 1949, 1
Costello, Delores, fl. 1960s, 2
Cotton, Elizabeth Avery, 1872–, 2
Cowles, Betsey Mix, 1810–1876, 2
Coxe, Margaret, fl. 1870s, 1
Coyle, Grace Longwell, 1892–1962, 2
Crandall, Almira, fl. 1830s, 1
Crandall, Prudence, 1803–1890, 1,2
Crawford, Gretchen C., fl. 1930s, 1
Crocker, Lucretia, 1829–1886, 1,2
Cronkhite, Bernice Brown, 2
Crowley, Pauline Shoemaker, 1879–1960, 2
Cullis, Winifred Clara, 1875–1956, 1
Curtis, Georgina Pell, 1859–1922, 1
Cushman, Beulah, fl. 1950s, 1
Darbishire, Helen, gr. 1903, 1
Davies, Emily, 1830–1921, 1,2
Davies, Sarah Emily, 1830–1921, 1
De Kooning, Elaine Marie Catherine, 1920–, 2

Dean, Rebecca Pennell, 1821–1890, 1
Densford, Katharine Jane, 1890–, 1
Dewey, (Hattie) Alice Chipman, 1858–1927, 2
Dickerman, Marion, fl. 1930s, 1
Dickey, Sarah Ann, 1838–1904, 2
Dickinson, Mary Lowe, 1839–1914, 1
Dodge, Grace Hoadley, 1856–1914, 1,2
Dolz, Luisa Maria, 1854–, 1
Dopp, Katherine Elizabeth, 1863–, 1
Dorsey, Susan Almira Miller, 1857–1946, 2
Dorsey, Susan M., 1845–1919, 1
Douglass, Mabel Smith, 1877–1933, 2
Downing, Eleanor, fl. 1930s, 1
Doyle, Sarah Elizabeth, 1830–1922, 2
Drexel, Mary Katharine, Mother, 1858–1955, 1,2
Dunlop, Florence S., d. 1963, 1
Dye, Marie, 1891–, 1
Edgeworth, Maria, 1767–1849, 1,2
Elliott, Harriet Wiseman, 1884–1947, 1,2
Erdman, Loula Grace, 1
Faithfull, Lilian Mary, gr. 1887, 1
Farnell, Vera, gr. 1914, 1
Farnham, Mary Frances, fl. 1880s, 1
Farwell, Beatrice, fl. 1970s, 2
Fauset, Jessie Redmon, 1884–1961, 1,2
Fearnall, Ida W., 1877–1947, 2
Fenimore-Cooper, Susan de Lancey, 1857–1940, 1
Ferguson, Abbie Park, 1837–1919, 2
Fickert, Augusta, 1855–1910, 1
Field, Mary, 1876–1968, 2
Fisher, Welthy Blakesley Honsinger, 1879–1980, 1,2
Fisk, Sara Ellen, 1886–1976, 2
Fiske, Catherine, fl. 1814, 1
Fliedner, Frederica, 1800–1842, 1
Flowers, Emma Payne, 1892–, 2
Ford, Elinor Rita, Sister, 1931–, 2
Foster, Bertha M., fl. 1940s, 1
Foster, Fay, 1886–1960, 1,2
Fox, Emma Augusta, 1847–, 2
Frame, Alice Seymour Browne, 1878–1941, 2
Frazier, Maude, 1881–1963, 2
Freeman, Agnes Suiter, 1843–1931, 2
Freeman, Alice Elvira, 1855–, 1
Fries, Constance, fl. 1930s, 1
Fry, Sara Margery, fl. 1930s, 1

Eisenhower, Dwight D.—Mother
    Eisenhower, Ida Elizabeth Stover,
        1862–1946, 1,2
Eisenhower, Dwight D.—Spouse
    Eisenhower, Mamie Geneva Doud,
        1896–1979, 1,2
Eisenhower, John—Spouse
    Eisenhower, Barbara Jean, 1926–, 1
Electress of Hanover
    Sophia, 1630–1714, 1,2
Electress of Saxony
    Maria Antonia Walpurgis, 1724–
        1780, 1
Electric industries
    See
        Electronics industries
Electrical engineers
    See also
        Radio engineers
        Television engineers
    Clarke, Edith, 1883–1959, 1,2
    Dresselhaus, Mildred S., 1930–, 2
    Hicks, Beatrice Alice, 1919–, 1,2
    Peden, Irene Carswell, fl. 1970s, 2
    Resnik, Judith A., 1948–1986, 2
    Rockwell, Mabel MacFerran, 1902–, 1
    Soulsby, Elsie MacGill, gr. 1927, 1
    Townsend, Marjorie Rhodes, 1930–, 2
Electronics industries
    McAfee, Naomi J., 2
    Olson, Edith, 1
    Volodina, Maria, fl. 1960s, 2
    White, Ruth, 1914–1969, 2
Eliah—Daughter
    Abihail, 1
Ellsworth, Oliver—Spouse
    Ellsworth, Abigail Wolcott, 1756–
        1818, 1,2
Embroiderers
    Bitters, Jean Ray Laury, 1928–, 2
    Blencowe, Agnes, 2
    Burden, Elizabeth, fl. 1870s, 2
    Burne-Jones, Georgiana, fl. 1860s, 2
    Faulkner, Kate, d. 1898, 2
    Faulkner, Lucy, fl. 1860s, 2
    Hart, Alice Marion (Mrs. Ernest),
        1872–, 2
    Holiday, Catherine, 2
    Holmes, Mrs. Oliver Wendell, Jr, 2
    Hoyt, Mrs. William S., 2
    Johnson, Florence, fl. 1890s, 2
    Linwood, Mary, 1755–1845, 1,2
    MacBeth, Ann, 1875–1948, 2
    Macdonald, Frances, 1874–1921, 2

Macdonald, Margaret R. S. W., 1865–
    1933, 2
Miller, Ellen, 2
Morris, Jane Burden, fl. 1970s, 2
Morris, May, 1862–1938, 1,2
Newbery, Jessie Rowat, fl. 1880s, 2
Newill, Mary J., 1860–1947, 2
Powell, Louise Lessore, 1910–1930, 2
Rudder, Madame de, fl. 1890s, 1
Wardle, Elizabeth Wardle, 1834–
    1902, 2
Wheeler, Dora, fl. 1850s, 2
Whiting, Margaret C., fl. 1890s, 2
Yeats, Elizabeth Corbe, 1,2
Yeats, Lily, 2
Embryologists
    Harvey, Ethel Browne, 1885–1965, 2
    Pythias, 380–320, 2
    Rudnick, Dorothea, 1907–, 1
Emerson, Ralph W.—Aunt
    Emerson, Mary Moody, 1774–1863,
        1,2
Employment agents
    Clarke, Alva J., fl. 1930s, 1
    Dodd, Carolyn G., fl. 1930s, 1
    Geyselman, Mrs, fl. 1880s, 2
Employment consultants
    Murray, Evelyn, fl. 1940s, 1
Empresses
    Agrippina I, The Elder, 13BC–
        33AD, 1,2
    Alexandra Feodorovna, 1872–1918,
        1,2
    Ann of Savoy, 1320–1353, 1
    Ann, consort of Alexius II (Agnes of
        France), d. 1220, 1
    Anna Ivanova (Ioannova), 1693–
        1740, 1,2
    Anne of Savoy, 1320–1353, 1,2
    Augusta Marie Louise Katharina,
        1811–1890, 1
    Augusta Victoria, 1858–1921, 1
    Bonaparte, Josephine, 1763–1814, 2
    Caesonia, Milonia, fl. 30–40, 1
    Carlotta, Marie Charlotte Amelie,
        1840–1927, 1
    Catherine I, 1684–1727, 1,2
    Catherine II (the Great), 1729–1796,
        1,2
    Constance of Hohenstaufen, d. 1313,
        1
    Constance of Sicily, 1152–1198, 1
    Constantia, d.c. 330, 1
    Crispilla, Quintia, fl. 200s, 1

Enamellers
Copeland, Elizabeth E., fl. 1970s, 2
Dawson, Edith Robinson, fl. 1890s, 2
De Court, Suzanne, fl. 1600, 2
Fisher, Kate, 2
France, Georgina Cave, 1868–1934, 2
Gay, Patty, fl. 1890s, 2
Hart, May, 2
Lalique, Rene, 1860–1945, 2
Mills, Ernestine Evans Bell, 1871–
1959, 2
Moron, Theresa Concordia, 1725–
1806, 1
Munson, Julia, fl. 1890s, 2
Stabler, Phoebe, fl. 1900s, 2
Encyclopedists
Philista, 2
Endocrinologists
Finkler, Rita V., 1888–, 1
Ramey, Estelle, 2
Russell, Jane Anne, 1911–1967, 2
Engineers
See also
Aeronautic engineers
Bridge builders
Chemical engineers
Civil engineers
Electrical engineers
Environmental engineers
Flight engineers
Hydraulic engineers
Industrial engineers
Mechanical engineers
Nuclear engineers
Rocket engineers
Structural engineers
Tracking engineers
Andriamanjato, Rahantavolo, 2
Belashova, Alla, fl. 1970s, 2
Belkin, Sophia, fl. 1960s, 2
Dennis, Olive Wetzel, 1885–1957, 1
Duignan-Woods, Eileen, fl. 1970s, 2
Faget, Maxine A., 1
Fitzroy, Nancy D., fl. 1970s, 2
Fletcher, Ann, fl. 1970s, 2
Flugge-Lotz, Irmgard, 1903–1974, 2
Gillette, Martha Taylor, fl. 1930s, 1
Haslett, Caroline, Dame, 1895–1957,
1
Hoff, Madeline, fl. 1930s, 1
Hopper, Grace Murray, 1906–, 2
Howard-Lock, Helen E., 2
Johnson, Barbara Crawford, fl.
1940s, 2

Kellems, Vivien, 1896–1975, 1,2
Levicheva, Valentina, fl. 1840s, 2
Matthews, Alva T., fl. 1970s, 2
Meyer, Editha Paula Chartkoff,
1903–, 1
Nasriddinova, Yadgar, 1920–, 2
Ovchinnikova, Alexandra, fl. 1960s, 2
Pennington, Mary Engle, 1897–1952,
1,2
Pfeiffer, Jane Cahill, 1932–, 2
Quick, Hazel Irene, gr. 1915, 1
Reilly, Jeanne Lennox, 1942–, 2
Savitskaya, Svetlana "Sveta", 1948–, 2
Sink, (Mary) Virginia, 1913–, 1
Telkes, Mari(a) de, 1900–, 1,2
Widnall, Sheila E., fl. 1970s, 2
Winans, Ann, 1828–, 2
Yevdokimova, Alla, fl. 1970s, 2
Engravers
Burne-Jones, Georgiana, fl. 1860s, 2
Facius, Angelika, 1806–1887, 1
Hyde, Helen, 1,2
Koker, Anna Marie de, fl. 1600s, 1
Lamme, Cornelie, 2
Mantegna, Andrea, 1431–1506, 2
Merian, Maria Sibylla, 1647–1717, 1,2
Ostroumova-Lebedeva, Anna Pe-
trovna, 1871–1955, 2
Passe (or Paas), Madeleine van de,
1570–, 1
Questier, Catherine, fl. 1650s, 1
Watson, Caroline, 1760–1814, 2
Entertainers
See also
Actors
Circus performers
Comedians
Dancers
Magicians
Mimes
Radio performers
Singers
Television performers
Ventriloquists
Bellina, Madonna, fl. 1500s, 2
Bess, Mina, 2
Carne, Judy, 1939–, 2
Dietrich, Marlene, 1901–, 1,2
Diller, Phyllis Driver, 1917–, 1,2
Duncan, Vivian, 1902–, 1,2
Farina, Mimi, 1945–, 2
Fears, Peggy, 1906–, 2
Foxe, Fanne, 1936–, 2
French, Callie, fl. 1870s, 2

Harper, Ethel, 1904–1979, 2
Jordan, Marian Driscoll (Molly
   McGee), 1897–1961, 1,2
Jorgensen, Christine, 1926–, 1,2
Rand, Sally, 1904–1979, 1,2
Thompson, Kay, 1911–, 1,2
Tucker, Sophie Kalish, 1884–1966,
   1,2
Entomologists
  Auten, Mary, 1898–, 1
  Branch, Hazel E., fl. 1918, 1
  Braun, Annette Frances, 1884–, 1
  Broadbent, Bessie May, 1895–, 1
  Cheesman, Evelyn, 1881–1969, 2
  Colcord, Mabel, 1872–, 1
  Conant, Helen S., 1839–1899, 1
  Faber, Betty Lane, 2
  Fernald, M. E., 1839–1919, 1
  Johnson, Dorothy B., fl. 1930s, 1
  McCracken, Mary Isabel, fl. 1930s, 1
  McDaniel, Eugenia I., 1884–, 1
  Merian, Maria Sibylla, 1647–1717, 1,2
  Mosher, Edna, fl. 1930s, 1
  Murtfeldt, Mary E., 1848–1913, 1
  Ormerod, Eleanor Anne, 1828–1901,
    1
  Palmer, Miriam A., fl. 1910s, 1
  Patch, Edith Marion, 1876–1954, 1
  Payne, Nelle Maria de Cottrell,
    1900–, 1
  Slosson, Anne Trumbull, 1838–1926,
    1
  Smith, Emily Adella, fl. 1880s, 1
Environmental engineers
  Schupak, Lenore H., fl. 1970s, 2
Environmentalists
  Blum, Barbara Davis, fl. 1970s, 2
  Braun, Emma Lucy, 1889–1971, 2
  Callaway, Virginia Hand, 1900–, 2
  Carson, Rachel Louise, 1907–1964,
    1,2
  Carthan, Hattie, 1900–, 2
  Conover, Catherine Mellon, 1936–, 2
  Dedrick, Claire, fl. 1970s, 2
  Weiner, Ruth, fl. 1960s, 2
Epicurus—Mistress
  Leontium, fl.340sBC, 1
Epidemiologists
  Broome, Claire, 1946–, 2
  Horstmann, Dorothy Millicent,
    1911–, 1,2
  MacDonald, Eleanor, 2
Equal Rights Advisors
  Schenk, Lynn A., fl. 1970s, 2

Equal Rights Amendment
  Rachlin, Marjorie B., fl. 1950s, 2
  Schlafly, Phyllis Stewart, 1924–, 2
Equestrians
  Aspinwall, Nan Jane, fl. 1910s, 2
  Kusner, Kathy, 1940–, 2
  Lisenhoff, Liselott, fl. 1970s, 2
  Moore, Anne, fl. 1970s, 2
  Stuckelberger, Christine, fl. 1970s, 2
  Tissot, Janou, fl. 1960s, 2
Eric II—Daughter
  Margaret (3), 1283–1290, 1,2
Ernest I—Consort
  Louise, Duchess of Saxe-Coburg—
    Gotha, 1800–1831, 1
Esalen Institute
  Lederman, Janet, 2
Esau—Spouse
  Adah, 1
  Mahalath, 1
Eskimoes
  Lorna, fl. 1970s, 2
  Reindeer, Mary, 2
Essayists
  Adams, Hannah, 1755–1831, 1,2
  Agoult, Marie Catherine Sophie Flav-
    igny de, 1805–1876, 1,2
  Agreda, Maria de (Maria Fernandez
    Coronel), 1602–1664, 1
  Barber, Margaret Fairless, 1869–
    1901, 2
  Bedford, Sybille, 1911–, 2
  Bowen, Catherine (Shober) Drinker,
    1897–1903, 1,2
  Burge, Dolly Sumner Lunt, 1817–, 1
  Chapone, Hester Mulso, 1727–1801,
    1,2
  Colby, Nathalie Sedgwick, 1875–
    1942, 1
  Cowden-Clarke, Mary Victoria,
    1809–1898, 1,2
  Craigie, Pearl Mary Teresa, 1867–
    1906, 1,2
  Didion, Joan, 1934–, 2
  Dutt, Toru, 1856–1877, 1,2
  Fisher, Dorothy Canfield, 1879–
    1958, 1,2
  Fuller, (Sarah) Margaret, 1810–1850,
    1,2
  Gerould, Katherine Elizabeth Fuller-
    ton, 1879–1944, 1,2
  Gethin, Grace Norton, 1676–1697, 1
  Guiney, Louise Imogen, 1861–1920,
    2

Hall, Sarah Ewing, 1761–1830, 1
Hardwick, Elizabeth, 1916–, 2
Hunt, Helen Fiske, 1830–1885, 1
Ingelow, Jean, 1820–1897, 1,2
Jackson, Helen Maria Hunt Fiske, 1830–1885, 1,2
Janeway, Elizabeth Hall, 1913–, 1,2
Jewsbury, Maria Jane, 1800–1833, 1,2
Lamb, Caroline, Lady, 1785–1828, 1,2
Lazarus, Emma, 1849–1887, 2
Martin, Anne Henrietta, 1875–1951, 2
Meynell, Alice Christ(a)na Gertrude Thompson, 1847–1922, 1,2
Monroe, Anne Shannon, 1877–1942, 1
Pfeiffer, Emily Jane, 1827–1890, 2
Repplier, Agnes, 1855–1950, 1,2
Russell, Elizabeth Mary Annette Beauchamp, Countess von Arnim, 1866–1941, 1
Sanborn, Katherine Abbot, 1939–1917, 1
Schelling, Karoline, 1763–1809, 1
Talbot, Catherine, 1720–1770, 1,2
Whitman, Sarah Helen Power, 1803–1878, 2
Woolf, (Adeline) Virginia (Stephen), 1882–1941, 1,2
Essex, Earl of—Cousin
Vernon, Elizabeth, fl. 1590s, 1
Etchers
Dillaye, Blanche, d. 1931, 1
Fontana, Veronica, 1576–, 1
Goldthwaite, Anne Wilson, 1875–1944, 1,2
Hopkins, Edna Boies, 1878–, 1
Hyde, Helen, 1,2
Kirmse, Marguerite, 1885–1954, 1
Koker, Anna Marie de, fl. 1600s, 1
Lewis, Jane Mary Dealy, fl. 1900s, 1
Merritt, Anna Lea, 1844–1930, 1,2
Moran, Mary Nimmo, 1842–1899, 1,2
Ryerson, Margery Austen, 1896–, 1
Sirani, Elisabetta, 1638–1665, 1,2
Stevens, Helen B., 1878–, 1
Ethnologists
See also
Anthropologists
Folklorists
Bates, Daisy Hunt O'Dwyer, 1861–1951, 1

Emerson, Ellen Russell, 1837–1907, 2
Fletcher, Alice Cunningham, 1838–1923, 1,2
Kingsley, Mary Henrietta, 1862–1900, 1,2
Marriott, Alice Lee, 1910–, 1
Owen, Mary Alicia, 1858–, 1,2
Smith, Erminne Adele Platt, 1836–1886, 1,2
Stevenson, Matilda Coxe Evans, 1849–1915, 1,2
Van Lawick-Goodall, Jane, Baroness, 1934–, 1,2
Ethnomusicologists
Densmore, Frances Theresa, 1867–1957, 1,2
Kinney, Esi Sylvia, fl. 1960s, 2
Etiquette authorities
Moore, Clara Sophia Jessup, 1824–1899, 1,2
Post, Emily Price, 1873–1960, 1,2
Sherwood, Mary Elizabeth Wilson, 1826–1903, 1,2
Vanderbilt, Amy, 1908–1974, 1,2
Etolin—Spouse
Etolin, Margaret, fl. 1840s, 2
Euthanasia activists
Russell, Olive Ruth, fl. 1970s, 2
Evangelists
Jones, Mary C., 1842–, 1
Kempe, Margery, 1373–1440, 1,2
Kuhlman, Kathryn, 1907–1967, 2
Livermore, Harriet, 1788–1868, 1,2
McPherson, Aimee Semple, 1890–1944, 1,2
Meech, Jeannette du Bois, 1835–, 1
Paisley, Mary Neale, fl. 1750s, 1
Palmer, Phoebe Worrall, 1807–1874, 1,2
Phillips, Catherine Payton, 1727–1794, 1
Prosser, Anna Weed, 1866–, 1
Smith, Amanda Berry, 1837–1915, 1,2
Smith, Hannah Whitall, 1832–1911, 1,2
Stapleton, Ruth Carter, 1929–1983, 2
Van Cott, Margaret Ann Newton, 1830–1914, 1,2
Walter, Mary Jane, fl. 1910s, 1
Executioners
Shakhovskaya, Eugenie, Princess, 2
Executives
See
Business executives

Department store executives
Fashion executives
Mail order executives
Motion picture executives
Newspaper executives
Radio executives
Sales executives
Television executives
Experts
See
Art experts
Aviation experts
Childbirth experts
Etiquette authorities
Fashion experts
Fingerprint experts
Health experts
Housing experts
Puzzle experts
Explorers
See also
Bottanical explorers
Adams, Harriet Chalmers, 1875–
1937, 1,2
Akeley, Delia Denning, 1865–1970,
1,2
Akeley, Mary Lee Jobe, 1878–1966,
1,2
Baker, Lady Samuel, fl. 1830s, 1
Bishop, Isabella Lucy Bird, 1831–
1904, 1,2
Boyd, Louise Arner, 1887–1972, 1,2
Bradley, Mary Hastings, fl. 1940s, 1
Brown, Lilian Mabel Alice Roussel,
1883–1946, 1
Cheesman, Evelyn, 1881–1969, 2
Coudreau, Octavie, fl. 1890s, 1
David-Neal, Alexandra, 1868–1969, 2
Dixie, Florence Caroline Douglas,
Lady, 1857–1905, 1,2
Ellis, Mina A., fl. 1900s, 1
Fowler-Billings, Katharine, 1902–, 1
Gillespie, Marian, fl. 1930s, 1
Harkness, Mrs. William, fl. 1930s, 1
Harris, Jane Davenport, fl. 1930s, 1
Harrison, Marguerite, 1879–1960, 2
Hinestrosa, Francisca, d. 1541, 1,2
Johnson, Osa Helen Leighty, 1894–
1953, 1,2
Kingsley, Mary Henrietta, 1862–
1900, 1,2
Niles, Blair Rice, 1887–1959, 1
Peck, Annie Smith, 1850–1935, 1,2
Pratt, Gladys Lynwall, fl. 1930s, 1

Seton, Grace Gallatin, 1872–1959, 1,2
Simpson, Myrtle Lillias, 1931–, 2
Singer, Ava Hamilton, fl. 1930s, 1
Stanhope, Hester Lucy, Lady, 1776–
1839, 1,2
Stark, Freya Madeline, 1893–, 1,2
Workman, Fanny Bullock, 1859–
1925, 1,2
Exporters and importers
Ford, Gertrude H., fl. 1930s, 1
Grant, Mrs. Sueton, fl. 1740s, 1
Eye specialists
Marguerite of Naples, fl. 1414, 2
Read, Lady, fl. 1710s, 2
Zerline of Frankfurt am Main, fl.
1420s, 2
Eyeglass designers
Sanders, Altina, fl. 1940s, 2
Ezra—Daughter
Miriam, 1

F

FBI agents
Miller, Marion, 1862–, 2
Factory workers
Chernikovsky, Molly, fl. 1920s, 2
Ghulamili, Razia, 2
Hasanovitz, Elizabeth, 2
Sheppard, Peggy, fl. 1950s, 2
Faience artists
Watt, Linnie, 1875–1890, 2
Fain, John—Spouse
Fain, Barbara Hancock, 2
Faith healers
Kuhlman, Kathryn, 1907–1967, 2
Moreno, Victoria, 1957–, 2
Falasha (Black Jews)
Judith, d. 977, 2
Falk, Peter—Spouse
Falk, Shera Danese, fl. 1970s, 2
False messiah
Joseph, Daughter of, 2
Farm leaders
Furber, Jackie, 2
Mayo, Mary Anne Bryant, 1845–
1903, 2
Sewell, Edna Belle Scott, 1881–1967, 2
Farmers
See also
Agriculturists
Dairy farmers
Food industry

Hog farmers
Plantation owners
Clay, Mrs. Cassius, 1815–, 2
Coffin, Mrs. Peter, fl. 1770s, 1,2
Croucher, Lorena, fl. 1970s, 2
Davis, Elaine, 2
Gillett sisters, fl. 1860s, 1
Howell, Catherine, fl. 1970s, 2
Keene, Betty, fl. 1940s, 2
Knutsson, Ann-Marie, fl. 1970s, 2
Mueller, Darlene, fl. 1970s, 2
Riker, Janette, 1,2
Smiley, Julie, fl. 1960s, 2
Wallace, Florence Richardson, 1875–, 2

Farouk, King—Spouse
Farida, 1921–, 1
Sadek, Narriman, 1934–, 1
Fashion agents
See
Model and fashion agents
Fashion critics
Colburn, Joan, fl. 1930s, 1
Fashion designers
Adri, fl. 1970s, 2
Ashley, Grace, fl. 1930s, 1
Baitman, Rasmar, fl. 1970s, 2
Ben Joseph, Rojy, fl. 1960s, 2
Bennani, Rabea, 2
Bennett, Eve, fl. 1930s, 1
Bergery, Bettina Jones, fl. 1930s, 2
Bernard, Madame Marie, fl. 1930s, 1
Boulanger, Louise, 2
Brenner, Eleanor, 2
Byers, Margaretta, 1901–, 1
Callot sisters, 2
Campbell, Jeanne Sanford, 1
Carbone, Paula, fl. 1960s, 2
Carnegie, E. Hattie, 1889–1956, 1,2
Casas, Martha, fl. 1970s, 2
Cashin, Bonnie, 1915–, 1,2
Champcommunal, Elspeth, 2
Chanel, Gabrielle Bonheur "Coco", 1883–1971, 1,2
Chapman, Ceil, 1912–, 1
Close, Elizabeth Stuart, fl. 1930s, 1
Cole, Dollie, 2
Cole, Helen D., fl. 1930s, 1
Connolly, Sybil, 1921–, 1,2
Cookman, Helen Cramp, fl. 1930s, 1
Copeland, Jo, 1903–, 1
D'Estreillis, Baroness, fl. 1930s, 1
Dache, Lilly, 1904–, 1,2
Davis, Tobe Collier, 1893–, 1

Davis, Vicki, fl. 1970s, 2
De la Falaise, Maxime, fl. 1950s, 2
Dolson, Hildegarde, fl. 1930s, 1
Donnelly, Nell Quinlan, 1889–, 2
Donner, Vyvyan, fl. 1930s, 1
Eiseman, Florence, 1899–, 2
Fitzgerald, Pegeen, 1910–, 1
Fogarty, Anne, 1919–1980, 1,2
Frankfurt, Elsie, 1918–, 1
Gartner, Louise Frankfurt, 1
Gerrard, Mady, 2
Gill, Ardash, 2
Gill, Surjit, fl. 1970s, 2
Gimbel, Sophie, 1902–, 1
Gres, Alix (Gre), Madam, 1899–, 2
Groult, Nicole, 2
Haddad, Claire, fl. 1960s, 2
Hardwick, (Cathy) Kathy, 1934–, 2
Harp, Holly, fl. 1960s, 2
Harris, Sharon, 2
Hawes, Elizabeth, 1903–1971, 1,2
Head, Edith, 1898–1981, 1,2
Hicks, Ami Mali, fl. 1890s, 1
Holley, Bertha Delbert, fl. 1930s, 1
Holmes, Marion, 2
Hulanicki, Barbara, fl. 1900s, 2
Irene, 1907–1962, 1,2
Ito, Sumako, fl. 1970s, 2
Johnson, Bets(e)y, 1942–, 2
Karan, Donna, 1948–1974, 2
Karasz, Mariska, 1898–1960, 2
Karinska, Barbara, 1886–, 2
Keckley, Elizabeth, 1818–1907, 2
Kidder, Priscilla, fl. 1930s, 2
King, Muriel, 1901–1977, 1,2
Klein, Anne, 1923–1974, 2
Kops, Margot De Bruyn, fl. 1930s, 1
Lanvin, Jeanne, Madame, 1867–1946, 1,2
Le Grange, Ann, fl. 1930s, 1
Lee, Helen, fl. 1970s, 1,2
Leithersdorf, Fini, 1906–, 2
Leser, Tina, 1911–, 1,2
Lewis, Mary, 1897–, 1
Logan, Charlotte, fl. 1930s, 1
Lowe, Ann, 1898–1981, 2
Majors, Beverly, 1951–, 2
Malsin, Lane Bryant, 1879–1951, 1,2
Mara, Clara, 2
Marusia, 1918–, 1
Maxwell, Vera Huppe, 1901–, 2
McCardell, Claire, 1905–1958, 1,2
McFadden, Mary Josephine, 1938–, 2
Mikeladze, Ketto, fl. 1920s, 1

Cari, Teresa, fl. 1890s, 2
Carlen, Emilie Smite, 1807–1892, 1
Carlisle, Rosalind Frances Stanley
  Howard, Countess of 1845–1921, 1
Catt, Carrie Chapman Lane, 1859–
  1947, 1,2
Cauer, Minna, 1841–1922, 1,2
Chace, Elizabeth Buffum, 1806–
  1899, 2
Chamberlain, Hope Summerell, 2
Chapman, Maria Weston, 1806–1885,
  1,2
Chapone, Hester Mulso, 1727–1801,
  1,2
Chesler, Phyllis, 2
Chessman, Andrea, 2
Chicago, Judy, 1939–, 2
Christine de Pisan, 1363–1431, 1,2
Churchill, Caroline N., 1833–, 2
Claflin, Roxanna (Roxie), fl. 1850s,
  1,2
Claflin, Tennessee, 1846–1923, 1,2
Clarenback, Kathryn, 1920–, 2
Clay, Laura, 1849–1911, 1,2
Coe, Emma Robinson, fl. 1850s, 1
Cole, Miriam M., fl. 1870s, 1
Collett(e), Camilla Wergeland, 1813–
  1895, 2
Cooperperson, Ellen, fl. 1970s, 2
Corbin, Hannah Lee, 1728–, 2
Cott, Nancy F., 1780–1835, 2
Cowles, Betsey Mix, 1810–1876, 2
Craig, May, 1889–1975, 2
Crandall, Prudence, 1803–1890, 1,2
Crocker, Hannah Mather, 1752–
  1829, 1,2
Croly, Jane Cunningham, 1829–
  1901, 1,2
Cullis, Winifred Clara, 1875–1956, 1
Cupps, Anita, 1948–, 2
Cutler, Hannah Maria Conant Tracy,
  1815–1896, 1,2
Dall, Caroline Wells Healey, 1822–
  1912, 1,2
Daly, Mary, fl. 1970s, 2
Davies, Emily, 1830–1921, 1,2
Davies, Sarah Emily, 1830–1921, 1
Davis, Nancy L., fl. 1960s, 2
Davis, Paulina Wright, 1813–1876, 1,2
Davis, Susan, fl. 1970s, 2
Davison, Emily, d. 1913, 2
De Crow, Karen L., 1938–, 2
De Ford, Miriam Allen, 2
De Pauw, Linda Grant, fl. 1960s, 2

Denison, Flora M., 1867–1921, 2
Denning, Ann Eliza Webb Young,
  1844–1908, 2
Densmore, Dana, fl. 1970s, 2
Deutsch, Helen, 2
Dezso, Terry, 1931–, 2
Diner, Helen, pseud., 2
Dixie, Florence Caroline Douglas,
  Lady, 1857–1905, 1,2
Dixon, Marlene, 2
Dock, Lavinia Lloyd, 1858–1956, 1,2
Dolz, Luisa Maria, 1854–, 1
Donovan, Frances, fl. 1900s, 2
Dorr, Rheta Childe, 1866–1948, 1,2
Draper, Muriel Gurdon Sanders,
  1886–1952, 1
Dubrey, Ana Roque de, 1853–, 2
Dubrow, Marcia, 2
Dunbar, Roxanne, fl. 1970s, 2
Duniway, Abigail Jane Scott, 1834–
  1915, 1,2
Duprey, Ana Roque de, 1853–, 2
Durant, Pauline, fl. 1870s, 2
Durlach, Theresa Mayer, fl. 1930s, 1
Dwight, Minnie Ryan, 1873–1957, 2
Eastman, Crystal, 1881–1928, 2
Edey, Birdsall Otis, 1852–1940, 1
Edgeworth, Maria, 1767–1849, 1,2
Edwards, Henrietta, 1849–1933, 1
Enoki, Miswo, fl. 1970s, 2
Fabbri, Tecla, 2
Fairbank, Janet Ayer, 1878–1951, 1
Faithfull, Emily, 1835–1895, 1,2
Farnham, Eliza Wood Burhans, 1815–
  1864, 1,2
Farnham, Marynia L. Foot, 1899–
  1979, 2
Fasteau, Brenda Sue Feigen, 2
Fawcett, Millicent Garrett, 1847–
  1929, 1,2
Ferguson, Renee, 2
Ferrin, Mary Upton, 1810–1881, 2
Fibiger, Mathilde, 1830–1871, 1
Fickert, Augusta, 1855–1910, 1
Figes, Eva, 1932–, 2
Filosofova, Anna, 2
Firestone, Shulamita, fl. 1970s, 2
Flowers, Ruth, 2
Foltz, Clara Shortridge, 1849–4934, 2
Forbes, Dorothy (Dolly) Murray, fl.
  1740s, 2
Frankfort, Ellen, 2
Franklin, Martha, fl. 1910s, 2
Freeman, Jo, 1946–, 2

Parker, Alice, 1864–, 1
Parlby, Irene, 1878–1965, 1,2
Pauker, Ana Rabinsohn, 1894–1960, 1,2
Paul, Alice, 1885–1977, 1,2
Peck, Annie Smith, 1850–1935, 1,2
Peter, Sarah Worthington King, 1800–1877, 2
Peterson, Esther Eggertsen, 1906–, 1,2
Phillips, Lena Madesin, 1881–1955, 1,2
Picton-Turbervill, Edith, 1872–1960, 1
Pier, Kate Hamilton, 1845–1925, 1,2
Pilpel, Harriet Fleischl, 2
Plath, Sylvia, 1932–1963, 2
Pollitzer, Anita Lily, 1894–1975, 2
Popelin, Marie, 1846–1913, 2
Post, Amalia Barney Simons, m. 1864, 1
Pottker, Janice, 2
Pruette, Lorine Livingston, 1876–, 1,2
Purdue, Connie, fl. 1950s, 2
Quitsland, Sonia, fl. 1970s, 2
Rachlin, Marjorie B., fl. 1950s, 2
Radcliffe, Mary, 2
Ramey, Estelle, 2
Ramsay, Martha Laurens, 1759–1811, 1,2
Rankin, Jeannette Pickering, 1880–1973, 1,2
Rashed, Samia Sadeek, fl. 1970s, 2
Reid, Elizabeth Ann, fl. 1970s, 2
Remy, Nahida, 2
Retzius, Anna, 1841–1924, 1
Reuter, Gabriele, 1859–1941, 1
Reuther, Rosemary Radford, fl. 1970s, 2
Rhondda, Margaret Haig Thomas, 1883–1958, 1
Rich, Adrienne Cecile, 1929–, 2
Richards, Janet Elizabeth Hosmer, d. 1948, 1
Riesel, Yetta, fl. 1970s, 2
Roberts, Sylvia, fl. 1960s, 2
Robertson, Mary Imogene, 1906–1948, 1,2
Robinson, Harriet Jane Hanson, 1825–1911, 1,2
Rodman, Henrietta, 2
Rodriguez, Rosalinda, 1948–, 2
Rogers, Annie Mary Anne Henley, 1856–1927, 1

Ronchi, Vittoria Nuti, fl. 1950s, 2
Rose, Ellen Alida, 1843–, 1
Rose, Ernestine Louise Siismondi Potowski, 1809–1882, 1,2
Rosenberg, Sheli, 2
Rosenthal, Anna Heller, 1872–1941, 2
Rossi, Alice S., 2
Rossner, Judith, 1935–, 2
Rothenberg, Sheribel, fl. 1970s, 2
Rowbotham, Sheila, fl. 1970s, 2
Ruffin, Josephine St. Pierre, 1843–1924, 1,2
Runeberg, Fredrika, 1807–1879, 1
Saadawi, Nawal el, 1930–, 2
Sadat, Jihan, 1933–, 2
Salomon, Alice, 1872–1948, 2
Samoilova, Natasha (Concurdia), 1876–, 2
Sandler, Bernice, 1928–, 2
Sanford, Maria Louise, 1836–1920, 2
Schapiro, Miriam, 1923–, 2
Schein, Virginia, 2
Schenk, Lynn A., fl. 1970s, 2
Schneiderman, Rose, 1882–1972, 1,2
Schreiner, Olive, 1855–1920, 1,2
Schurman, Anna Maria von, 1607–1678, 1,2
Schwimmer, Rosika, 1877–1948, 2
Scott, Ann (London), 1929–1975, 2
Scott, Catherine Amy Dawson, 1863–1934, 1
Scott, Masha, fl. 1940s, 2
Scott, Rose, 1847–1925, 1
Scott-Maxwell, Florida, 1893–, 2
Seaman, Barbara, 2
Searing, Annie Eliza Pidgeon, 1857–1942, 1
Seton, Cynthia Propper, fl. 1970s, 2
Seton, Grace Gallatin, 1872–1959, 1,2
Severance, Carolina Maria Seymour, 1820–1914, 1,2
Sewall, May Eliza Wright, 1844–1920, 1,2
Shadiyeva, Taijikhan, fl. 1920s, 2
Shaffer, Deborah, fl. 1970s, 2
Shafik, Doris Ahmad, 1919–, 1
Sharawi, Mrs. Huda, 2
Sharp, Evelyn, 1869–1955, 1
Shaw, Mary G., 1860–1929, 1,2
Sheppard, Katharine, 1848–1934, 2
Slesinger, Tess, 1905–1945, 1,2
Sloan, Margaret, 2
Smith, Abby Hadassah, 1797–1878, 2
Smith, Doris, fl. 1910s, 1

Smith, Hannah Whitall, 1832–1911, 1,2
Smith, Jane Norman, 1874–1953, 1
Smith, Julia Evelina, 1792–1886, 2
Smith, Lillian Eugenia, 1897–1966, 1,2
Smith, Zephania Hollister, 1840–1870, 2
Smyth, Ethel Mary, Dame, 1858–1944, 1,2
Snowden, Ethel, 1881–1951, 1
Sochen, June, fl. 1970s, 2
Soemario, Roesial, fl. 1950s, 2
Somerville, Nellie Nuggent, 1863–1952, 2
Spencer, Cornelia Phillips, 1825–1908, 2
Stanton, Elizabeth Cady, 1815–1902, 1,2
Stasova, Helena, 1873–1966, 2
Stearns, Sarah Burger, 1836–, 1
Steinem, Gloria, 1934–, 2
Stern, Marjorie Hefter, fl. 1970s, 2
Sternburg, Janet, fl. 1970s, 2
Stevens, Alzina Parsons, 1844–1900, 1,2
Stone, Lucinda Hinsdale, 1814–1900, 1,2
Stone, Lucy, 1818–1893, 1,2
Stopes, Marie Charlotte Carmichael, 1880–1959, 1,2
Strickland, S. E., fl. 1870s, 1
Suleimanova, Khadycha, fl. 1960s, 2
Summerskill, Edith Clara, Baroness, 1901–1980, 1,2
Sun Yat-Sen, Chingling Soong, 1830–1981, 1,2
Svetla, Karolina Rottova, 1830–1899, 1
Svetlanova, E., 2
Swanwick, Anna, 1813–1897, 1,2
Swisshelm, Jane Grey Cannon, 1815–1884, 1,2
Syfers, Judy, 2
Tarbell, Ida Minerva, 1857–1944, 1,2
Taub, Nadine, fl. 1970s, 2
Tax, Meredith, fl. 1970s, 2
Taylor, Kathleen DeVere, fl. 1930s, 1
Taylor, Mary, 1817–1893, 2
Taylor, Susan Lucy Barry, 1807–1881, 1
Terrell, Mary Eliza Church, 1863–1954, 1,2
Terry, Megan, 1932–, 2

Thomas, Martha Carey, 1857–1935, 1,2
Thurber, Louise Lockwood, fl. 1930s, 1
Tinker, Irene, fl. 1940s, 2
Tobias, Sheila, fl. 1930s, 2
Tobolowsky, Hermine D., fl. 1950s, 1
Tonaillon, Christiane, 1878–1928, 1
Tristan, Flora, 1803–1844, 1,2
Trout, Grace Wilbur, d. 1955, 1
Truth, Sojourner, 1797–1883, 1,2
Tsin, King, d. 1907, 2
Tuley, Cathy, 1950–, 2
Tully, Mary Jean, fl. 1970s, 2
Umphreville, Lucina, fl. 1830s, 1
Upton, Harriet Taylor, 1853–1945, 1,2
Valesh, Eva McDonald, 1866–, 1
Van Hoosen, Bertha, 1863–1952, 1,2
Van Horn, Edith, 1923–, 2
Van Ness, Marcia Burns, 1782–1832, 1,2
Vanderbilt, Alva Ertskin Smith Belmont Hazard, 1853–1933, 1,2
Veres, Hermine Beniczky, 1815–1895, 1
Vernon, Mabel, 1883–1975, 2
Volkenstein, Liudmilla, 2
Wallace, Zerelda Gray Sanders, 1817–1901, 1,2
Wells, Emmeline Blanch Woodward, 1828–1921, 2
Wells-Barnett, Ida Bell, 1862–1931, 2
Werfel, Alma Mahler Gropius, 1879–1964, 2
West, Rebecca, Dame, pseud., 1892–1983, 1,2
Wheeler, Anna Doyle, 1785–, 1
Whitney, Anne, 1821–1915, 1,2
Whitton, Charlotte Elizabeth, 1896–1975, 1,2
Wilkinson, Eliza Yonge, fl. 1770s, 1,2
Wilkinson, Ellen Cicely, 1891–1947, 1,2
Willard, Emma C. Hart, 1787–1870, 1,2
Willard, Frances Elizabeth Caroline, 1839–1898, 1,2
Williams, Fannie Barrier, 1855–1944, 2
Willis, Olympia Brown, 1835–1926, 1
Wilson, Justina Leavitt, fl. 1930s, 1
Winans, Ann, 1828–, 2
Winer, Lucy, fl. 1970s, 2

Wold, Emma, 1871–1950, 2
Woodhull, Victoria Claflin, 1838–
1927, 1,2
Wright, Frances, 1795–1852, 1,2
Wright, Martha Coffin Pelham, 1806–
1875, 1,2
Wyckoff, Elizabeth Porter, 2
Yankova, Zoya, 2
Young, Ann Eliza Webb, 1844–1908,
1,2
Young, Rose Emmet, 1869–1941, 1
Zetkin, Clara Eissner, 1857–1933, 1,2
Fencers
Belova, Elena, 2
Cramer, Beth, fl. 1970s, 2
De Tuscan, Bela, fl. 1930s, 1
Elek, Ilona, 2
Geisler, Lisa, 1954–, 2
Mayer, Helena (Helene), 1911–1963,
2
Muller-Preiss, Ellen, 2
Pugliese, Julia Jones, fl. 1930s, 2
Rejto-Sagine, Ildiko, 2
Schacher-Elek, Ilona, 1930–1950, 2
Ujaki-Rejito, Ildiko, 1937–, 2
Ferdinand I—Consort
Maria, fl. 1920s, 1
Marie Alexandria Victoria, 1875–
1938, 1,2
Ferrer Colony
Ferm, Elizabeth, 1857–1944, 2
Ferry pilots
Rees, Rosemary, fl. 1940s, 1,2
Fiber artists
Meredith, Dorothy L., 1906–, 2
Fillmore, Millard—Daughter
Fillmore, (Mary) Abigail Powers,
1832–1854, 1,2
Fillmore, Millard—Mother
Fillmore, Phoebe Millard, 1780–
1831, 1,2
Fillmore, Millard—Spouse
Fillmore, Abigail Powers, 1798–1853,
1
Fillmore, Caroline Carmichael McIn-
tosh, d. 1881, 1
Filmmakers
Adato, Perry Miller, 2
Amir, Aziza, fl. 1920s, 2
Andersen, Yvonne, fl. 1960s, 2
Anderson, Erica Kellner Collier,
1914–1976, 1,2
Anderson, Madeline, fl. 1960s, 2
Arnold, Eve, fl. 1970s, 2

Bachner, Annette, fl. 1940s, 2
Bachrach, Dora, fl. 1970s, 2
Beeson, Coni, fl. 1970s, 2
Bertozzi, Patricia, fl. 1970s, 2
Beveridge, Hortense, fl. 1950s, 2
Booth, Sheila, 1928–, 2
Bostan, Elizabeth, fl. 1960s, 2
Brandon, Liane, fl. 1970s, 2
Broyde, Ruth, fl. 1970s, 2
Brumberg, Zenajeda, fl. 1960s, 2
Cavani, Liliana, 2
Child, Abigail, fl. 1970s, 2
Chinlund, Phyllis Johnson, fl. 1970s,
2
Chopra, Joyce, fl. 1970s, 2
Compton, Juleen, fl. 1970s, 2
Coolidge, Martha, fl. 1960s, 2
Couzin, Sharon, fl. 1970s, 2
Cox, Nell, 2
Dansereau, Mireille, fl. 1960s, 2
De Hirsch, Storm, fl. 1960s, 2
Debi, Arundhati, fl. 1960s, 2
Demetrakas, Johanna, fl. 1970s, 2
Dey, Manju, 2
Duras, Marguerite Donnadieu,
1914–, 1,2
Field, Mary, 1876–1968, 2
Finch, Kaye, 2
Firestone, Cinda, fl. 1970s, 2
Fischer, Lynn Conner, fl. 1970s, 2
Flack, Luise, 1910–1914, 2
Fox, Beryl, fl. 1960s, 2
Godmillow, Jill, fl. 1960s, 2
Gould, Diana, fl. 1960s, 2
Greenfield, Amy, fl. 1970s, 2
Gregory, Mollie, fl. 1970s, 2
Halleck, Deedee, fl. 1960s, 2
Harriton, Maria, fl. 1960s, 2
Hartley, Elda, fl. 1970s, 2
Hodes, Roberta, fl. 1970s, 2
Hoelscher, Jean, fl. 1970s, 2
Hoffman-Uddgrew, Anna, fl. 1910s,
2
Horvath, Joan, fl. 1960s, 2
Hubley, Faith Elliott, 1924–, 2
Hultin, Jill, fl. 1960s, 2
Hunter, Marian, fl. 1970s, 2
Irvine, Louva Elizabeth, fl. 1960s, 2
Isaacs, Barbara, fl. 1960s, 2
Jakubowska, Wanda, 2
Jassim, Linda, fl. 1970s, 2
Johnson, Karen, fl. 1960s, 2
Johnson, Osa Helen Leighty, 1894–
1953, 1,2

First bloomer wearer
  Smith, Elizabeth Gerrit, fl. 1850s, 2
First builder of little theater
  De Ponte, Roza Solomon, 2
First child to die in car accident
  Kahlert, Marion Ooletia, d. 1904, 2
First co-ed
  Blount, Barbara, fl. 1800s, 2
First female servant in Virginia
  Burras, Anne, 1608–, 2
First ovariotomy patient
  Crawford, Jane Todd, d. 1842, 2
First person buried in pet cemetery
  Kopp, Lillian, 1909–1978, 2
First shopkeeper
  Goose, Mrs., fl. 1640s, 1,2
First test tube baby
  Brown, Louise, 1978–, 2
First white girl born in New England
  Alden, Elizabeth Alden, 1623–1717, 2
First woman voter
  Swain, Louisa Ann, 1800–, 1,2
Fitzgerald, Edward—Spouse
  Barton, Lucy, 2
Fitzgerald, F. Scott—Mother
  Fitzgerald, Mollie McQuillan, 1860–, 2
Fitzgerald, F. Scott—Spouse
  Fitzgerald, Zelda Sayre, 1900–1948, 2
Flaccus, Quintus Fulvius—Spouse
  Sulpicia, fl. 390s, 1
Flag makers
  Godare, Madam, fl. 1770s, 2
  Pickersgill, Caroline, fl. 1818s, 1
  Pickersgill, Mary Young, fl. 1810s, 2
  Ross, Betsy Griscom, 1752–1836, 1,2
  Snyder, Lillian, fl. 1870s, 2
  Troutman, Joanna, d. 1880, 2
  Winborne, Rebecca M., d. 1918, 2
  Woods, Mary A., fl. 1910s, 1
Flaubert, Gustave—Inspiration
  Delamare, Delphine Couturier, 1822–1848, 1,2
Fleming, Sir John—Spouse
  Lascelles, Mrs. Edwin, 1732–1813, 2
Flight attendants
  Barrios, Marie Jeanne, fl. 1920s, 1
  Church, Ellen, 1905–, 1,2
  Dale, Maureen, fl. 1960s, 1
  Davis, Bun, fl. 1930s, 1
  Ferret, Monique, fl. 1960s, 1
  Granger, Nellie, fl. 1930s, 1
  Heitz, Margaret, fl. 1960s, 1
  Hurley, Marie Louise, fl. 1950s, 1

  Keene, Mona, fl. 1930s, 1
  Kellet, Charlotte, 1
  Kommer, Jayne, fl. 1950s, 1
  Lohorra, Cora, 1
  Mody, Perin, fl. 1960s, 1
  O'Connor, Mary, fl. 1930s, 1
  Olsen, Mae, 1
  Peck, Willie, fl. 1930s, 1
  Salway, Ray, fl. 1940s, 1
  Wharton, Frankie, fl. 1930s, 1
  Zeller, Joan, fl. 1950s, 1
Flight crews
  See also
    Pilots
  Cravens, Penelope, fl. 1970s, 2
  Crawford, Connie, fl. 1930s, 1
  Jenner, Chrystie, 1950–, 2
  Marshall, Ellen Church, 1905–1965, 2
  Mott, Del R., fl. 1970s, 2
  Robertson, Marion G. (Pat), 1930–, 2
  Rueck, Kelly, 2
  Ryden, Hope, 2
  Smith, Ida Van, fl. 1960s, 2
Flight engineers
  Holley, Jane, 2
Flight instructors
  Cavis, Helen, fl. 1930s, 1
  Erickson, Barbara Jane, fl. 1930s, 1,2
  Farr, Virginia, fl. 1930s, 1
  Gipson, Elsie, fl. 1930s, 1
  Hager, Carol, fl. 1930s, 1
  Hallady, Bessie G., fl. 1930s, 1
  Harmon, Ruth J., fl. 1930s, 1
  Jorgensen, Evelyn, 1
  Kilgore, Evelyn, fl. 1930s, 1
  Lennox, Peggy, fl. 1930s, 1
  Mallette, Dorothy, 1
  McElroy, Lenore, fl. 1930s, 1
  Monasterio, Lillian, fl. 1930s, 1
  Omlie, Phoebe Jane Fairgrave, 1902–1975, 1,2
  Plant, Jane, fl. 1930s, 1
  Robinson, Pearle Thurber, 1
  Scharr, Adela Rick, fl. 1930s, 1
  Spirito, Yolanda, fl. 1930s, 1
  Stilson, Ruth, fl. 1930s, 1
  Thomas, Patricia, fl. 1930s, 1
Flight school owners
  Burke, Marion E., fl. 1950s, 1
Florida
  Bedell, Harriet, fl. 1910s, 2
  Bethune, Mary McLeod, 1875–1955, 1,2
  Dozier, Beverly Fisher, 1933–, 2

King, Louisa Boyd Yeomans, 1863–
1848, 2
Loudon, Jane Webb, 1807–1858, 1
Lumpkin, Mary B. T., fl. 1890s, 2
Maynard, Catherine, fl. 1850s, 2
Pearce, "Mistress", 1907–1627, 1
Riggs, Mary, 1818–1852, 1
Rockley, Alicia-Margaret Amherst,
1941–, 1
Willmot, Ellen, d. 1932, 2
Gardening writers
King, Louisa Boyd Yeomans, 1863–
1948, 2
Garfield, James A.—Mother
Ballou, Eliza-, 1
Garfield, Eliza Ballou, 1801–1888, 1,2
Garfield, James A.—Spouse
Garfield, Lucretia Rudolph, 1832–
1918, 1,2
Garibaldi, Giuseppe—Mother
Garibaldi, Rosa Raimondi, 1770–
1852, 2
Gaspard de Coligny—Daughter
Coligny, Louise de, 1555–1620, 2
Gatty, Alfred—Spouse
Gatty, Margaret Scott "Aunt Judy",
1807–1873, 2
Gelon—Daughter
Harmonia, fl. 470BC, 1
Gelston, David—Spouse
Gelston, Phoebe Mitchell, 1740–
1811, 2
Gem cutters
Dorsch, Susanna Maria, 1701–, 2
Schwindel, Rosa Elizabeth, 2
Genealogists
Abbe, Elizabeth, 1950–, 2
Adams, Enid Eleanor, 1909–, 2
Adams, Marilyn L., 1931–, 2
Adkins, Wilma, 1941, 2
Aitken, Barbara B., 1938–, 2
Ames, Agnes H., 1916–, 2
Anderson, Alloa C., 1900–, 2
Anderson, Audentia Smith, 1872–, 1
Anderson, Janet H., 1920–, 2
Ashton, Sharron Standifer, 1940–, 2
Atzberger, Christina Marie, 1947–, 2
Audin, Margaret, 1926–, 2
Bailey, Rosalie Fellows, 1908–, 2
Barekman, June Beverly Terry,
1915–, 2
Baumann, Louise Bloom, 1922–, 2
Beevers, Jane E., 1927–, 2
Bell, Carol Willsey, 1939–, 2

Bentley, Elizabeth Petty, 1945–, 2
Berry, Lois M., 1911–, 2
Beverly, Trevia Wooster, 1931–, 2
Bland, Doris Ellen, 1934–, 2
Blumhagen, Helen M., 1922–, 2
Boczon, Mary Ann, 1941–, 2
Bodziony, Gill Tod, 1953–, 2
Bohle, Georgia, 1916–, 2
Boling, Yvette Guillot, 1938–, 2
Botts, Virgina M., 1904–, 2
Bowerman, Myreline Elizabeth,
1921–, 2
Bowers, Doris Roney, 1928–, 2
Bowersox, Jerry Sue Gray, 1944–, 2
Bowman, Myreline Elizabeth, 1921–,
2
Briggs, Ruth Ella, 1911–, 2
Brooks, Agnes McVeigh, 1922–, 2
Brown, Barbara J., 1921–, 2
Brubaker, Joan Bake, 1931–, 2
Bryan, Patricia J., 1946–, 2
Bubb, Ella L., 1907–, 2
Budd, Anne Dallas, 1935–, 2
Bumpus, Bettie McShane, 1935–, 2
Burns, Loretta Elliott, 1928–, 2
Bushman, Katherine Gentry, 1919–,
2
Callard, Carole Crawford, 1941–, 2
Callum, Agnes Kane, 1925–, 2
Caraher-Manning, Doreen, 1929–, 2
Carousso, Dorothee Hughes, 1909–,
2
Carpenter, Mildred Carver, fl. 1930s,
1
Cavanaugh, Karen Byers, 1946–, 2
Chadwell, Patricia Ann, 1943–, 2
Chadwick, Nancy Gaillard, 1924–, 2
Chaston, Gloria Duncan, 1920–, 2
Childs, Marleta Marie, 1946–, 2
Chisholm, Donna Gagnier, 1942–, 2
Christensen, Fern Breakenridge,
1923–, 2
Christopher, Jeannette May, 1920–, 2
Chudleigh, Norma Lane, 1938–, 2
Church, Carol R., 1877–1954, 2
Clark, Carmen Ercell, 1914–, 2
Clark, Marie Taylor, 1933–, 2
Coderre, Anita Mary, 1921–, 2
Collins, Carolyn H., 1929–, 2
Colwell, Stella, 1944–, 2
Combs, Mary Lou, 1940–, 2
Cornell, Nancy Jones, 1936–, 2
Corry, Ruth L., 1920–, 2
Cox, E. Evelyn, 1936–, 2

Crickard, Madeline W., 1916–, 2
Crone, Marie Luise, 1949–, 2
Crump, Mary Ruth, 1921–, 2
Culbreth, Blanche Waldrop, 1919–, 2
Cullar, W. Clytes, 1920–, 2
Curtis, Mary Barnett, 1924–, 2
Darlington, Jane Eaglesfield, 1928–, 2
Davidson, Flora, 1924–, 2
Davis, Rosalie Edith, 1931–, 2
De Filipps, Marsha L., 1947–, 2
De Haven, Mabel, 1896–, 2
DeLay, Marie Long, 1905–, 2
Dehn, Dorothy Harriet, 1916–, 2
Dieterle, Diane, 1939–, 2
Dietrich, Martha Jane, 1916–, 2
Donnelly, Mary Louise, 1927–, 2
Doswell, Thelma Esther, 1921–, 2
Douthit, Ruth Long, 1909–, 2
Drake, Margaret Johnson, 1914–, 2
Dryden, Ruth Tamm, 1923–, 2
Duncan, Marilyn Arend, 1930–, 2
Eakle, Arlene H., 1936–, 2
Eastwood, Elizabeth C., 1910–, 2
Eichholz, Alice, 1942–, 2
Elliott, Colleen Morse, 1927–, 2
Elliott, Wendy L., 1939–, 2
Ericson, Carolyn Reeves, 1931–, 2
Eubank, Mildred Olevia, 1895–, 2
Fahy, Margaret Cheadle, 1902–, 2
Faler, June H., 2
Fay, Mary S., 1915–, 2
Finch, Jean Haynes, 1935–, 2
Fitzgerald, Ruth Coder, 1944–, 2
Floyd, Elizabeth Ardery, 1917–, 2
Forbes, Amanda Crawford, 1920–, 2
Forsyth, Alice Daly, 1917–, 2
Foster, Margaret, 1931–, 2
Fraustein, Rebah Morgan, 1905–, 2
Frederick, Nancy Gubb, 1925–, 2
Frendlich, Sharon Lee, fl. 1970s, 2
Gaar, Patricia A., 1926–, 2
Gaines, Patricia E., 1939–, 2
Gentry, Emma Gene Seale, 1939–, 2
Gillis, Irene Stampley, 1918–, 2
Glover, Anna, fl. 1870s, 1
Godfrey, Marie H., 1920–, 2
Grasse, Patricia A., 1944–, 2
Green, Mae Ruth, 1921–, 2
Gregath, Ann Cochrane, 1926–, 2
Gregory, Patricia Ann McConnaughay, 1925–, 2
Griffith, Dorothy Amburgey, 1924–, 2
Grimes, Marilla R., 1924–, 2

Habelman, E Carolyn, 1941–, 2
Haddock, Janet Egelston, 1933–, 2
Hainley, Lynda (Lynne) Lee, 1951–, 2
Hamilton, Von Gail, 1928–, 2
Hammersmith, Mary Powell, 1920–, 2
Hancocks, Elizabeth, 1927–, 2
Hansen, Darlene F. N., 1924–, 2
Hanson, Margery Day, 1903–, 2
Harpur, V. Lorraine, 1923–, 2
Harriss, Helen L., 1911–, 2
Harrod, Mildred Dixon, 1906–, 2
Harshman, Lida Flint, 1900–, 2
Harvey, Mazie Manson, 1902–, 2
Haun, Weynette Parks, 1926–, 2
Heiss, Phyllis M., 1922–, 2
Hemperley, Marion R., 1923–, 2
Henry, Jeanne Hand, 1921–, 2
Henry, Mary Helen, 1948–, 2
Hensen, Joyce B., 1933–, 2
Higdon, Bettina Pearson, 1920–, 2
Hill, Barbara L., 1943–, 2
Hills, Daphne Anne, 1938–, 2
Hinton, Rose Marie B., 1928–, 2
Hitselberger, Mary Eleanor Fitz Hugh, 1931–, 2
Hodge, Harriet Woodbury, 1916–, 2
Hoelle, Edith E., 1925–, 2
Hook, Charlene, 1935–, 2
Horn, Peggy Grubb, 1916–, 2
Hotaling, Donna Reid, 1932–, 2
Hunt, E. Virginia, 1931–, 2
Ingman, Mary Frances Gilbert, 1923–, 2
Inman, Gloria Kay Vandiver, 1939–, 2
Ireland, Norma Olin, 1907–, 1,2
Ison, Judith G., 1930–, 2
Jackson, Evelyn Jean Seyphers, 1927–, 2
Jacobsen, Phebe R., 1922–, 2
Jarvis, Grace Hemrick, 1917–, 2
Jaussi, Laureen Richardon, 1934–, 2
Jeanson, Beverly Forrest, 1938–, 2
Jehn, Janet B., 1928–, 2
Johnson, Arta P., 1921–, 2
Johnson, Phyllis Walker, 1922–, 2
Jones, Orlo Louise, 1929–, 2
Joyner, Peggy Shomo, 1928–, 2
Kay, Mary Alma, 1930–, 2
Keffer, Marion Christena, 1911–, 2
Kieffer, Elizabeth Clarke, 1899–, 2
King, Helen L., 1925–, 2
King, Martha Eheart, 1923–, 2
Kinsey, Margaret B., 1920–, 2

Kirk, Clarie McCay, 1928–, 2
Klingman, Eloise Clark, 1908–, 2
Krusell, Cynthia Hagar, 1929–, 2
Kucera, Zdenka, 1916–, 2
Kupillas, Mary Martin, 1912–, 2
LaBarre de Raillicourt, Maria Teresa Candela y Sapieha, 2
Lacy, Ruby, 1922–, 2
Lane, Frances Corry, 1910–, 2
Lane, Hassie Olivia, 1909–, 2
Lantz, Emily Emerson, fl. 1900s, 1
Larson, Jean A., 1941–, 2
Lawrence-Dow, Elizabeth Carr, 1916–, 2
Leary, Helen F. M., 1935–, 2
Lichliter, Asselia S., 1912–, 2
Linder, Anna Dorsey, 1911–, 2
Linn, Jo White, 1930–, 2
Livingston, Mildred Ruth, 1918–, 2
Livingston, Virginia Pope, 1907–, 2
Lo Buglio, Rudecinda Ann, 1934–, 2
Lower, Dorothy M., 1914–, 2
Ludlow, Inger P., 1930–, 2
Luther-Schafer, Vivian, fl. 1930s, 2
Madison, Barbara Snyder, 1942–, 2
Magnusson, Lora Wilkins, fl. 1960s, 2
Manley, Myra del (Hodson), 1952–, 2
Manuel, Janet D., 1935–, 2
Marks, Lillian Bayly, 1914–, 2
Marshall, Lucy, Carlile, 1930–, 2
Mast, Lois Ann, 1951–, 2
McAllister, Annabelle Cox, 1904–, 2
McCurdy, Mary Burton Derrickson, 1908–, 2
McLane, Bobbie Jones, 1927–, 2
McMillion, Lynn C., 1934–, 2
Meadows, Mary W., 1918–, 2
Merriman, Brenda, 1940–, 2
Metzger, Joyce Owen, 1934–, 2
Meyer, Mary Keysor, 1919–, 2
Miller, Carolynne L., 1929–, 2
Miller, Cynthia Ann, 1935–, 2
Miller, Margaret Hardwick, 1910–, 2
Millman, Dorothy K., 1922–, 2
Mills, Elizabeth Shown, 1944–, 2
Milner, Anita Cheek, 1936–, 2
Mittelstaedt-Krubaseck, Carla, 1912–, 2
Monk, Arliss Shaffer, 1921–, 2
Moore, Caroline T., 1907–, 2
Moorhouse, B-Ann, 2
Morris, Ellen Thorne, 1944–, 2
Morris, Jean Sanswenbaugher, 1927–, 2

Morris, Louise Elizabeth Burton, 1905–, 2
Mossong, Verna Elaine, 1925–, 2
Moulton, Joy Wade, 1928–, 2
Mowrer, Rita Schive, 1927–, 2
Myers, Margaret Elizabeth, 1925–, 2
Myers, Mary Eleanor, 1905–, 2
Neal, Lois Smathers, 1912–, 2
Neet, Nazle Boss, 1921–, 2
Nesbitt, Virginia Bell, 1909–, 2
Newhard, Malinda E. E., 1943–, 2
Newsome, Elizabeth Pritchard, 1907–, 2
Nichols, Elizabeth L., 1937–, 2
Nichols, Joann H., 1930–, 2
Nimmo, Sylvia Lee, 1937–, 2
Novak, Lucile Kaufmann, 1929–, 2
O'Brien, Bayne Palmer, 1920–, 2
Ogle, Sandra K., 1943–, 2
Olmsted, Virginia L., 1916–, 2
Overton, Julie M., 1939–, 2
Parker, Nancy L., 1931–, 2
Pattinson, Penelope Mary, 1944–, 2
Paul, Dorothy H., 1922–, 2
Paxton, Darlene Steffa Ward, 1917–, 2
Pealer, Ruth M. Griswold, m. 1869, 1
Pearlman, Agnes Branch, 1922–, 2
Penrose, Maryly Barton, 1938–, 2
Pinches, Rosemary Vivian, 1929–, 2
Potter, Dorothy Williams, 1937–, 2
Powner, I. Florence, 1938–, 2
Presley, Cloie, 1922–, 2
Pullen, Doris Evelyn, 1920–, 2
Quigg-Lennox, Naomi M., 1921–, 2
Quigley, Maud, 1900–, 2
Rademacher, Carol Sims, 1928–, 2
Radewald, Bette Miller, 1931–, 2
Reeve, Vera, 1910–, 2
Reeves, Emma Barrett, 1901–, 2
Reid, Judith P., 1945–, 2
Reisinger, Joy A., 1934–, 2
Rentmeister, Jean R., 1935–, 2
Richards, Mary Fallon, 1920–, 2
Ridlen, Colleen Alice, 1926–, 2
Robinson, Mona Dean, 1928–, 2
Rose, Christine, 1935–, 2
Ross, Margaret, 1922–, 2
Schiffman, Carol Mehr, 1928–, 2
Schreiner-Yantis, Nerti, 1930–, 2
Schwartz, Mary E., 1940–, 2
Seibel, Ruth Robinson, 1907–, 2
Seitz, Beatrice West, 1912–, 2
Sencevicky, Lorraine Cowles, 1926–, 2

Seubold, Helen Winters, 1921–, 2
Shaw, Aurora C., 1913–, 2
Sherman, Ruth Wilder, 1929–, 2
Sherwood, Dorothy C., 1923–, 2
Shuler, Beverly Sloan, 1927–, 2
Simon, Margaret Miller, 1922–, 2
Simpson, Elizabeth, 1923–, 2
Sinko, Peggy Tuck, 1949–, 2
Sisson, Sarah Martha, 1942–, 2
Sistler, Barbara J., 1942–, 2
Slezak, Eva, 1946–, 2
Smallwood, LaViece Moore, 1935–, 2
Snedden, Barbara A., 1926–, 2
Speakman, Mary N., 1920–, 2
Starin, Mary Elizabeth, fl. 1950s, 2
Starrett, Marion H., 1930–, 2
Straney, Shirley Garton, 2
Stryker-Rodda, Harriet, 1905–, 2
Stuart, Donna Valley, 1927–, 2
Sween, Jane C., 1931–, 2
Swift, Betty J., 1922–, 2
Talley, Fay Stainbrook, 1916–, 2
Tally-Frost, E. Stephenie, 1917–, 2
Thompson, Katherine W., 1910–, 2
Thorsell, Elisabeth, 1945–, 2
Thurston, Jean Merrill, 1939–, 2
Tonkin, Muriel, 1918–, 2
Townsend, Edna Waugh, 1908–, 2
Tregillis, Helen Cox, 1944–, 2
Turk, Marion G., 1914–, 2
Turner, L. Patton, 1912–, 2
Turner, Shirley J., fl. 1950s, 2
Versailles, Elizabeth Starr, 1909–, 2
Wagstaff, Ann T., 1939–, 2
Walter, Alice Granberry, 1908–, 2
Warren, Judy, 1942–, 2
Warren, Mary (Claire) Bondurant, 1930–, 2
Watson, Lilian D., 1932–, 2
Watts, Dorothy Chambers, 1911–, 2
Weeks, Jennie N., 1902–, 2
Wegner, Sandra DeFore, 1938–, 2
Weikel, Sally Ann, 1930–, 2
Wellauer, Maralyn Ann, 1949–, 2
Wellhouse, (Mary) Ann Walcher, 1928–, 2
Wester, June Hart, 1924–, 2
Wheeler, Geraldine Hartshorn, 1918–, 2
White, Elizabeth Pearson, 1914–, 2
Whitehead, Lenore R., 1917–, 2
Whitley, Edythe Johns Rucker, 1900–, 2
Wilcox, Shirley Langdon, 1942–, 2

Wiles, Marie Davis, 1912–, 2
Wilson, Shirley B., 1937–, 2
Windham, Margaret Leonard, 1924–, 2
Wingo, Elizabeth B., 1907–, 2
Wood, Anne Higgins, 1917–, 2
Wood, Christine Knox, 1923–, 2
Wood, Virginia Steele, fl. 1950s, 2
Woodward, Neil Sachse, 1920–, 2
Worley, Ramona Ann Cameron, 1933–, 2
Worthing, Ruth Shaw, 1904–, 2
Wynne, Frances Holloway, 1932–, 2
General Federation of Women's Clubs
Decker, Sarah Sophia Chase Platt, 1852–1912, 2
Ozbirn, Catherine Freeman, 1900–1974, 1,2
Geneticists
Bakhtadze, Kseniya Yermolayevna, 1899–, 1
Macklin, Madge Thurlow, 1893–1962, 2
McClintock, Barbara, 1902–, 2
Mintz, Beatrice, 1921–, 2
Ronchi, Vittoria Nuti, fl. 1950s, 2
Russell, Elizabeth Shull, 1913–, 1,2
Sager, Ruth, 1918–, 1,2
Stevens, Nettie Maria, 1861–1912, 2
Turner, Helen Newton, 2
Genoscientists
Schwarzer, Theresa F., fl. 1970s, 2
Geochemists
Cashman, Katherine, fl. 1970s, 2
Jones, Lois Marilyn, 1934–, 2
Lindsay, Kay, fl. 1960s, 2
Saru-Hashi, Katsuko, 2
Geodesists
Lehmann, Inge, 1888–, 1,2
Geographers
See also
Explorers
Bingham, Millicent Todd, 1880–1968, 1,2
Boyd, Louise Arner, 1887–1972, 1,2
Myers, Sarah Kerr, 1940–, 2
Newbigen, Marion, d. 1934, 1
Semple, Ellen Churchill, 1863–1932, 1,2
Seton, Grace Gallatin, 1872–1959, 1,2
Singer, Ava Hamilton, fl. 1930s, 1
Stirling, Marion, fl. 1940s, 2
Geologists
See also
Geochemists

Baden-Powell, Olive St. Claire, Lady, 1889–1977, 1,2
Choate, Anne Hyde, fl. 1920s, 1
Kimball, Inez B., fl. 1940s, 2
Layton, Olivia Cameron Higgins, 1898–1975, 1,2
Low, Juliette Magill Kinzie Gordon, 1860–1927, 1,2
Rippin, Jane Parker Deeter, 1882–1953, 2
Scott, Gloria Dean, 1938–, 2
Girl Scouts, Philippines
Escoda, Josefa Lianes, 1898–1945, 2
Gladstone, William—Spouse
Gladstone, Catherine Glynne, 1813–1900, 1
Glass designers
Nyman, Gunnel, 1909–1948, 2
Persson-Melin, Signe, fl. 1950s, 2
Glass engravers
Block, Joanna, 1650–1715, 2
Visscher, Anna, 1583–1651, 1,2
Visscher, Maria, 1595–1649, 2
Glass painters and stainers
Cowles, Genevieve Almeda, 1871–, 1
Cowles, Maud Alice, 1871–1905, 1
Geddes, Wilhelmina Margaret, 1887–1955, 2
Lowndes, Mary, fl. 1890s, 2
Macdonald, Frances, 1874–1921, 2
Macdonald, Margaret R. S. W., 1865–1933, 2
Newill, Mary J., 1860–1947, 2
Purser, Sarah, fl. 1900s, 2
Tillinghast, Mary Elizabeth, d. 1912, 1
Whall, Veronica, 1887–, 2
Willet, Anna Lee, 1867–1943, 1
Woodward, Alice Bolingbroke, 1862–, 1,2
Glassmakers
Backstrom, Monica, 2
Brandt, Asa, 2
Lundin, Ingeborg, 1921–, 2
Morales-Schildt, Mona, fl. 1960s, 2
Wareff, Ann, fl. 1960s, 2
Glassman*
King, Evelyn "Champagne", 1960–, 2
Glenn, John—Spouse
Glenn, Annie, 2
Glider pilots
Allen, Naomi, fl. 1950s, 1
Bennis, Virginia, fl. 1940s, 1
Bevins, Mrs. Okey, d. 1942, 1

Brunton, Laura May, fl. 1930s, 1
Burns, Anne, fl. 1950s, 1,2
Downsbrough, Margaret, fl. 1950s, 1
Du Pont, Allaire, fl. 1930s, 1
Eaton, Genevieve, d. 1942, 1
Fletcher, Evelyn, fl. 1930s, 1
Hastings, Margaret, fl. 1960s, 1
Holderman, Dorothy, fl. 1930s, 1
Loufek, Betty, fl. 1940s, 1
Majewska, Pelagie, fl. 1960s, 1
Modilbowska, Wanda, fl. 1930s, 1
Montgomery, Helen Marie, 1911–, 1
Nicks, Diana, fl. 1960s, 1
Price, Joan Meakin, fl. 1930s, 1
Reitsch, Hanna, 1912–, 1,2
Welch, Ann, fl. 1930s, 1
Woodward, Betsy, fl. 1950s, 1
Goat herders
Armer, Margaret McEvey Reid, d. 1933, 2
Goddesses
Aphrodite, 2
Archippe, fl. 100BC, 2
Artemis, 2
Atalanta, 2
Athena, 2
Bona Dea, 2
Ceres, 2
Demeter, 2
Fortuna, 2
Hera, 2
Hygeia, 2
Isis, 2500– BC, 2
Magna Mater, 2
Nikandre, 660 BC, 2
Panacea, 2
Persephone, 2
Vesta, 2
Goethe, Johann Wolfgang von—Friend
Buff, Charlotte, 1752–1828, 1
Willemer, Marianne von Jung, 1784–1869, 1
Goethe, Johann Wolfgang von—Mother
Goethe, Katherina Elisabeth Textor von, 1731–1808, 1,2
Textor, Katherine Elizabeth, fl. 1720s, 1
Gold miner's wife
O'Farrell, Mary Ann Chapman, fl. 1860s, 2
Gold players
Alcott, Amy, 1956–, 2
Gold rush
Arthur, Dolly, 1919–1975, 2
Berry, Ethel Bush, fl. 1890s, 2

Carmack, Katie, fl. 1890s, 2
Klondike Kate, 1881–1957, 2
Pullen, Harriet Smith, 1859–1947, 2
Walsh, Mollie, d. 1902, 2
White, Josephine, 1873–1956, 2
Goldsmiths
Courtauld, Louisa Perina, 2
Deard(s), Mary, fl. 1700s, 2
Foote, Anne, fl. 1750s, 2
Godfrey, Elizabeth, fl. 1741s, 2
Goldsworthy—Spouse
Goldsworthy, Phillipia Vanbrugh, 1716–1777, 1
Golfers
Abbot, Margaret, fl. 1900s, 2
Baugh, Laura, 1955–, 2
Berg, Patricia Jane, 1918–, 1,2
Bertolaccini, Silvia, fl. 1970s, 2
Blalock, Jane, 1945–, 2
Bradley, Pat, fl. 1970s, 2
Brown, Mrs. Charles S., fl. 1890s, 1,2
Burke, Mrs. F., fl. 1940s, 2
Carner, Joanne Gunderson, 1939–, 2
Collett, Glenna, 1903–, 1,2
Cummings, Edith, fl. 1920s, 1
Curtis, Harriot S., fl. 1900s, 2
Curtis, Margaret, fl. 1900s, 2
Dod, Charlotte, 1871–1960, 2
Drivers, Mrs. W., fl. 1940s, 2
Fishwick, Diana Lesley, 1911–, 1
Hagge, Marlene, fl. 1970s, 2
Higuchi, Chako, fl. 1970s, 2
Jessen, Ruth, 1937–, 2
Leitch, Charlotte Cecilia Pitcairn, 1890–, 1
Little, Sally, fl. 1970s, 2
Lopez, Nancy, 1957–, 2
Mann, Carol, 1941–, 2
Martin, Kathy, 2
Martin, Mrs. A. E. "Paddy", fl. 1960s, 2
Merchant, Marjorie, 2
Morgan, Wanda, fl. 1920s, 2
Palmer, Sandra, 1941–, 2
Parry, Lily, fl. 1970s, 2
Press, Sue, fl. 1970s, 2
Rankin, Judy Torluermke, 1945–, 2
Rawls, Betsy, 2
Robie, Marie, fl. 1940s, 2
Russell, Lise Ann, fl. 1970s, 2
Scott, Margaret, Lady, fl. 1890s, 2
Stack, Carol, fl. 1970s, 2
Suggs, Louise, 1923–, 1,2
Thompson, Susan, fl. 1970s, 2

Tourischeva, Ludmilla, 1952–, 2
Vare, Glenna Collett, 1903–, 1,2
Venker, Mary, fl. 1970s, 2
Wethered, Joyce, 1901–, 1,2
Whitworth, Kathy, 1939–, 2
Wilson, Enid, 1910–, 1
Wright, Mickey (Mary Kathryn), 1935–, 1,2
Zaharias, (Babe) Mildred Didrikson, 1914–1956, 1,2
Gordianus III—Spouse
Tranquillina, Turia Sabina, fl. 230s, 1
Gordianus, the Elder—Spouse
Orestilia, Fabia, fl. 150s, 1
Gordon, George—Mother
Byron, Catherine Gordon, 2
Gospel singers
Jackson, Mahalia, 1911–1972, 1,2
Nevins, Natalie, 1943–, 2
Williams, Marion, 1927–, 2
Gough, John B.—Mother
Gough, Jane, 1817–1834, 1
Gould, Elliott—Spouse
Bogart, Jenney, 2
Gould, George Jay—Spouse
Gould, Edith M. Kingdom, d. 1921, 1
Gould, Sam—Daughter
Castellane, Anna Gould, Marquise de, 1876–1961, 1
Talleyrand-Perigord, Anna Gould, Duchess de, 1876–1961, 1,2
Governesses
Ashley, Katherine, d. 1565, 1
Bicknell, Anna, fl. 1852, 1
Callcott, Maria, Lady, 1
Cavell, Edith Louisa, 1865–1915, 1,2
Clairmont, Claire, 1798–1879, 1,2
Crawford, Miss, fl. 1880s, 1
Cumming, Henrietta, fl. 1780s, 1
Davison, Edith, fl. 1900s, 1
Eagar, Miss, fl. 1890s, 1
Elstob, Elizabeth, 1683–1765, 1,2
Fellows, Mary, 1868–1941, 1
Graham, Maria, 1785–1843, 2
Hamblyn, Mistress, fl. 1576, 1
Leonowens, Anna Harriette Crawford, 1834–1915, 1,2
Lott, Emmeline, fl. 1890s, 1
Mangnall, Richmal, 1769–1820, 1
Mary of Chatillon, fl. 1300, 2
May, Miss, fl. 1890s, 1
Murray, Mrs., fl. 1600s, 1
Panton, Sally, fl. 1770s, 2
Sharpe, Miss, fl. 1780s, 1

Swynford, Catherine, Duchess of
Lancaster, 1350–1403, 1,2
Trimmer, Selina, 1765–1829, 1
Walker, Jane, fl. 1940s, 1
Weeton, Ellen, 1776–, 1
White, Miss, fl. 1840s, 1
Woolley, Ann (Hannah?), fl. 1650s,
1,2
Government employees, American
Dulles, Eleanor Lansing, 1895–, 1
Graffenried, (Mary) Clare de, 1849–
1921, 1,2
Hickey, Margaret A., 1902–, 1
Kelly, Margaret V., fl. 1900s, 1
Lacy, Mary Goodwin, 1875–1962, 1
Le Hand, Marguerite "Missy", 1898–
1944, 1,2
Leonard, Mrs. Willard A., fl. 1860s, 1
Rathbone (Rathbun), Mary Jane,
1860–, 1
Shattuck, Harriette Lucy Robinson,
1850–, 1
Tully, Grace, 1900–, 2
White, Nettie L., fl. 1870s, 1
Wright, Rebecca, m. 1871, 1
Government employees, Australian
Evalt, Elizabeth, 2
Government employees, English
Llewellyn-Smith, Elizabeth, 2
Government employees, Israeli
Aloni, Shulamit, 2
Government employees, Zambian
Konie, Gwendoline, 1938–, 2
Government officials, African
N'kanza, Lusibu Z., 2
Government officials, American
See also
Congresswomen
County officials
Municipal officials
Senators
State officials
Abbott, Elizabeth M. Griffin, 1845–
1941, 2
Abbott, Grace, 1878–1939, 1,2
Ackroyd, Margaret F. O'Connor, fl.
1920s, 1
Adams, Eva Bertrand, 1908–, 1
Adkins, Bertha Sheppard, 1906–
1983, 1,2
Alpern, Anita F., fl. 1970s, 2
Anderson, Bette B., 1929–, 2
Anderson, Mary, 1872–1964, 1,2
Armstrong, Anne Legendre, 1927–, 2

Austin, Margretta Stroup, 1907–, 1
Babcock, Barbara Ellen, 2
Bailar, Barbara A., 2
Bailey, Consuelo Northrop, 1899–, 1
Banister, Marion Glass, 1875–1951, 2
Banuelos, Romana Acosta, 1925–, 2
Baumgartner, Leona, 1902–, 1
Beard, Dita Davis, 1918–, 2
Benson, Lucy Wilson, 1927–, 2
Bentley, Helen Delich, 1923–, 2
Bernstein, Bernice Lotwin, 2
Bernstein, Jody, 2
Berry, Mary Frances, 1938–, 2
Bethune, Mary McLeod, 1875–1955,
1,2
Beyer, Clara Mortenson, 1892–, 2
Bingham, Eula, fl. 1950s, 2
Bitterman, Kathleen Studdar, 1916–,
2
Blair, Emily Newell, 1877–1951, 2
Blum, Barbara Davis, fl. 1970s, 2
Brooks, Mary T., fl. 1960s, 1
Brown, Virginia Mae, 1923–, 2
Brunauer, Esther Delia Caukin,
1901–1959, 1,2
Carpenter, Mrs. Leslie, 1920–, 1
Carter, Mary E., fl. 1970s, 2
Chatham, Lois Albro, fl. 1970s, 2
Chayes, Antonia Handler, 1929–, 2
Christman, Elizabeth, 1891–1975, 1,2
Clapp, Margaret Antoinette, 1910–
1974, 1,2
Clapper, Olive Ewing, 1896–1968, 2
Clark, Georgia Neese, 1900–, 1,2
Clark, Joan, fl. 1940s, 2
Clauss, Carin Ann, fl. 1950s, 2
Claybrook, Joan, 1937–, 2
Coffin, Jo, 1880–1943, 2
Davenport, Joan M., fl. 1970s, 2
Dawson, Mimi Weyforth, 1944–, 2
Denning, Bernardine Newsom,
1930–, 2
Derian, Patricia (Pat), 1929–, 2
Diamondstein, Barbaralee, 2
Dole, Elizabeth Hanford, 1936–, 2
Donlon, Mary Honor, 1894–1977,
1,2
Douglas, Diana, Lady, 1943–, 2
Douglas, Jane "Jennie", 2
Edelstein, Susan, fl. 1970s, 2
Edson, Katherine Philips, 1870–
1933, 2
Eldridge, Marie D., 1926–, 2
Eliot, Martha May, 1891–1978, 1,2

Elliott, Harriet Wiseman, 1884–1947, 1,2
Falco, Malthea, 1944–, 2
Fennell, Dorothy I., 1916–1977, 2
Foreman, Carol Tucker, 1938–, 2
Fraser, Arvonne S., 1925–, 2
Furness, Betty (Elizabeth Mary), 1916–, 1,2
Gage, Gloria, fl. 1930s, 1
Gardener, Helen Hamilton, 1853–1925, 1,2
Gibby, Mabel Kunce, fl. 1960s, 2
Gorsuch, Anne (McGill), 1942–, 2
Grant, Julia L., 1936–, 2
Greenberger, Marcia D., 1946–, 2
Gunderson, Barbara Bates, m. 1941, 1
Hanks, Nancy, 1927–1983, 2
Harriman, Florence Jaffray Hurst, 1870–1967, 1,2
Heller, Barbara, fl. 1970s, 2
Hennock, Frieda Barkin, 1904–1960, 1,2
Herman, Alexis M., 1947–, 2
Hermann, Mildred R., 1891–, 2
Hernandez, Aileen Clarke, 1926–, 2
Herrick, Elinore Morehouse, 1895–1964, 1,2
Hills, Carla Anderson, 1934–, 2
Hobby, Oveta Culp, 1905–, 1,2
Hoey, Jane Margueretta, 1892–1968, 1,2
Hoffman, Anna Marie Rosenberg Lederer, 1902–1983, 2
Hornbeck, Bernice M., 2
Howard, Katherine Montague Graham, 1898–, 1
Howorth, Lucy Somerville, 1895–, 1,2
Hufstedler, Shirley Ann Mount, 1925–, 2
Humphrey, Helen Florence, 1909–1963, 1
Jacobson, Dorothy H., fl. 1960s, 2
Johnson, Thomasina Walker, 1911–, 1,2
Jones, Mary Gardiner, 1921–, 2
Kamm, Linda Heller, fl. 1970s, 2
Karmel, Roberta S., 1937–, 2
Kelsey, Frances Oldham, 1914–, 1,2
Keyserling, Mary Dublin, fl. 1930s, 2
King, Marguerite Cooper, 2
Kinney, Stephanie Smith, fl. 1970s, 2
Knauer, Virginia Harrington Wright, 1915–, 2

Knight, Frances Gladys, 1905–, 1,2
Koontz, Elizabeth Duncan, 1919–, 1,2
Kreps, Juanita Morris, 1921–, 2
LaDame, Mary, 1885–, 2
LaFontant, Jewel Stradford, fl. 1970s, 2
Laise, Carol C., fl. 1960s, 2
Lathrop, Julia Clifford, 1858–1932, 1,2
Lawton, Esther C., fl. 1930s, 2
Lenroot, Katharine Fredrica, 1891–, 1,2
Leopold, Alice Koller, 1909–, 1,2
Louchheim, Katie Scofield, 1903–, 1
Magrabi, Frances M., fl. 1970s, 2
Margolin, Bessie, 1930–1970, 2
Marin, Ludmilla, fl. 1940s, 2
Martinez, Arbella, fl. 1950s, 2
McAlister, Dorothy, 1900–, 2
McArthur, Henrietta Duncan, 1945–, 2
McConnell, Beatrice, 1894–, 2
McGee, Anita Newcomb, 1864–1940, 1,2
McIver, Pearl, 1893–, 1,2
McKenna, Margaret, fl. 1970s, 2
McMillin, Lucille Foster, 1870–1949, 1,2
Miller, Emma Guffey, 1874–1970, 1,2
Miller, Frieda Segelke, 1890–1973, 1,2
Molony, Winifred D., fl. 1940s, 2
Morio, Winifred (Peggy), fl. 1970s, 2
Morton, Azie T., 2
Morton, Patricia, fl. 1970s, 2
Murphy, Betty Southard, 1929–, 2
Murray, Florence Kerins, 1916–, 2
Myerson, Bess, 1924–, 1,2
Norton, Eleanor Holmes, 1937–, 2
Oettinger, Katherine Brownell, 1903–, 1
Omlie, Phoebe Jane Fairgrave, 1902–1975, 1,2
Patterson, Hanna Jane, 1879–1937, 2
Perkins, Frances, 1882–1965, 1,2
Peterson, Esther Eggertsen, 1906–, 1,2
Pfeiffer, Jane Cahill, 1932–, 2
Plank, Rosine, fl. 1970s, 2
Plunkett, Margaret L., 2
Porter, Elsa A., 1928–, 2
Poulain, Simone A., fl. 1950s, 2
Priest, Inez Baber, d. 1973, 2
Priest, Ivy Maud Baker, 1905–1975, 1,2

Ray, Dixy Lee, 1914–, 1,2
Rees, Mina S., 1902–, 1,2
Rivlin, Alice Mitchell, 1931–, 2
Robins, Eva, fl. 1970s, 2
Robinson, Dollie Lowther, fl. 1950s, 2
Roche, Josephine Aspinwall, 1886–1976, 1,2
Rose, Mary Davies Swartz, 1874–1941, 1,2
Rosenberg, Anna Marie, 1902–, 1
Sanders, Marion K., 1905–, 2
Schneider, Alma Kittredge, 1901–, 1
Sechler, Susan, fl. 1970s, 2
Shalala, Donna Edna, 1941–, 2
Shanahan, Eileen, fl. 1970s, 2
Sherman, Mary Belle King, 1802–1935, 2
Shipley, Ruth Bielaski, 1855–1966, 1
Shotwell, Odette, fl. 1960s, 2
Simpson, Joanne, fl. 1960s, 2
Slater, Courtenay, 1934–, 2
Smith, Elizabeth Rudel, 1911–, 1
Smith, Hilda Worthington, 1888–, 2
Spain, Jayne, 1941–, 2
Spindler, Pearl G., fl. 1940s, 2
Stanley, Louise, 1883–1954, 2
Starbuck, Dorothy L., fl. 1940s, 2
Stiebeling, Hazel Katherine, 1896–, 1
Stovall, Thelma, 1919–, 2
Stratton, Dorothy Constance, 1899–, 1,2
Sturtevant, Brereton, 1921–, 2
Stutman, Judith C., fl. 1970s, 2
Styers, Aleta, fl. 1960s, 2
Swartz, Maud(e) O'Farrell, 1879–1937, 2
Switzer, Mary Elizabeth, 1900–1971, 1,2
Synder (S), Nancy, fl. 1970s, 2
Tabankin, Margery Ann, fl. 1970s, 2
Takeda, Marguerite Hu, fl. 1970s, 2
Taylor, Charlotte, fl. 1970s, 2
Thoben, Patricia Joan, 1933–1977, 2
Thomson, Thyra Godfrey, 1916–, 2
Townsend, Marjorie Rhodes, 1930–, 2
Tuchman, Jessica, 2
Van Cleve, Ruth G., fl. 1970s, 2
Wald, Patricia M., 1928–, 2
Wallace, Joan S., fl. 1970s, 2
Watson, Barbara M., 1918–, 2
Weber, Enid W., fl. 1970s, 2
Weddington, Sarah Ragle, 1945–, 2
Weinstock, Anna, 2

Westenberger, Jane, 2
Westphal, Jeanne, fl. 1970s, 2
Wexler, Anne, 1930–, 2
Wheaton, Anne Williams, 1892–1977, 1,2
White, Margita Eklund, 1937–, 2
White, Sue Shelton, 1887–1943, 2
Wickens, Aryness Joy, 1901–, 1
Widnall, Sheila E., fl. 1970s, 2
Willebrandt, Mabel Walker, 1889–1963, 1,2
Wolfe, Carolyn, 1890–, 2
Woodbury, Helen Laura Sumner, 1876–1933, 2
Woodsmall, Ruth Frances, 1883–1963, 1,2
Woodward, Ellen Sullivan, 1887–1971, 2
Woolsey, Suzanne, 2
Government officials, Australian
Guilfoyle, Margaret Georgina Constance, 1926–, 2
Radford, Gail, 1941–, 2
Rehor, Grete, 1910–, 2
Reid, Elizabeth Ann, fl. 1970s, 2
Government officials, Austrian
Firnberg, Hertha, 1909–, 2
Karl, Elfriede, 1933–, 2
Government officials, Bhutan
Wangchuck, Dechhen Wang-mo, 2
Government officials, Canadian
Fairclough, Ellen, 1905–, 1
Gelber, Sylvia M., 2
Holden, Joyce, fl. 1970s, 2
Lamarsh, Judy, 1924–1980, 1,2
Lapointe, Renaude, 1912–, 2
Sinclair, Adelaide Helen Grant MacDonald, 1900–1982, 1,2
Whitton, Charlotte Elizabeth, 1896–1975, 1,2
Wilson, Cairine, fl. 1930s, 2
Government officials, Chinese
Sun Yat-Sen, Chingling Soong, 1830–1981, 1,2
Government officials, Colombian
Cuevas Cancino, Esmerelda Arboleda de, fl. 1960s, 2
Government officials, Danish
Bjerregaard, Mrs. Ritt, fl. 1970s, 2
Gredal, Eva, fl. 1970s, 2
Ostergaard, Lise, fl. 1970s, 2
Stallknecht, Kirsten, 1937–, 2
Government officials, Ecuadorian
Robalino, Isabel, 2

Goya, Francisco—Mother
  Goya, Gracia Lucientes, 2
Gracchi—Mother
  Cornelia, fl. 169BC, 1,2
Graham, Billy—Mother
  Graham, Morrow, 1892–, 2
Graham, Billy—Spouse
  Graham, Ruth, 2
Grand Duchesses
  Charlotte Aldegonde Elise, 1919–
    1964, 1
  Marie, 1890–1958, 1
  Marie Adelaide, 1894–1924, 1
Grand Duke of Baden—Spouse
  Stephanie de Beauharnais, Grand
    Duchess of Baden, 1789–1860, 1
Grant, Frederick Dent—Spouse
  Honore, Ida Marie, m. 1874, 1
Grant, Ulysses S.—Daughter
  Grant, Nellie, fl. 1870s, 1,2
  Sartoris, Ellen Grant, 1857–, 1
Grant, Ulysses S.—Mother
  Grant, Hannah Simpson, 1798–1883,
    1,2
Grant, Ulysses S.—Spouse
  Grant, Julia Dent, 1826–1902, 1,2
Graphic artists
  Akhvlediani, Elena Dmitrievna,
    1901–, 2
  Brown, Kay, 2
  Carrillo, Graciela, fl. 1970s, 2
  De Bretteville, Sheila, 2
  Forrester, Patricia Tobacco, fl. 1970s,
    2
  Kollwitz, Kathe Schmidt, 1867–1945,
    1,2
  Mechenen, Ida Van, fl. 1400s, 2
  Negrin, Sue, fl. 1970s, 2
  Paskauskaite, Lili, fl. 1960s, 2
  Paurin, Phyllis Belle, fl. 1970s, 2
  Schwalb, Susan, 1944–, 2
  Skiles, Jacqueline, fl. 1970s, 2
  Slesin, Aviva, fl. 1970s, 2
  Urbach, Lily, fl. 1970s, 2
  Wayne, June, 1918–, 2
Graphologists
  Downey, June, 2
  Lewinson, Thea Stein, fl. 1930s, 1
  Spencer, Shirley, 1897–, 1
Green, Hetty—Daughter
  Wilks, Hetty Sylvia Green, 1871–
    1951, 1
Green, Jonas—Spouse
  Hoof, Ann(e) Catherine, d. 1775, 2

Greenback labor party
  Todd, Marion Marsh, 1841–, 2
Greene, Thomas—Daughter
  Hubbard, Mary Greene, 1734–1808,
    2
Gregory the Divine—Mother
  Nonna, 329–374, 1
Gregory the Great—Mother
  Silva, fl. 540s, 1
Gregroy of Utrecht—Mother
  Adela, d. 735, 1
Grenfell, Wilfred—Spouse
  Grenfell, Anne MacClanahan, d.
    1938, 1
Grey Panthers
  Kuhn, Margaret E., 1905–, 2
Grillparzer, Franz—Friend
  Frolich, Katherina, 1800–1879, 1
Grimaldi, Anthony I.—Daughter
  Hippolyte, Louise, m. 1715, 1
Grocery trade
  Moorland (Morland), Jane, fl. 1760s,
    1
  Sheaffe, Susannah Child, fl. 1770s, 1
Gruening, Ernest—Spouse
  Gruening, Dorothy, fl. 1930s, 2
Guidance counselors
  Harris, Ruth Bates, fl. 1960s, 2
  Riley, Ranny, 2
Guides
  Sacajawea, 1786–1812, 1,2
Guitarists
  Allen, Rosalie, 1924–, 2
  Armatrading, Joan, 1950–, 2
  Bowes, Margie, 1941–, 2
  Carson, Martha, 1921–, 2
  Carson, Sally (Bonnie Lou), 1926–, 2
  Collins, Judy Marjorie, 1939–, 2
  Cooper, Wilma Lee (Leary), 1921–, 2
  Cotten, Elizabeth (Libra), 1893–, 2
  Cummins, Betty (Foley), 1923–, 2
  Dane, Barbara, 1927–, 2
  Donnell-Vogt, Radka, fl. 1950s, 2
  Ford, Mary, 1924–1977, 1,2
  Gentry, Bobbie Lee, 1942–, 2
  Gooding, Cynthia, 1924–, 2
  Grimes, Anne (Laylin), 1912–, 2
  Harden, Arleen, 1945–, 2
  Maddox, Rose, 1926–, 2
  Osborne, Mary, 1921–, 2
  Purim, Flora, 1942–, 2
  Raitt, Bonnie, 1949–, 2
  Sainte-Marie, Buffie (Beverly),
    1940–, 2

Snow, Phoebe Laub, 1952–, 2
Tharpe, Rosetta, Sister, 1921–1973, 2
Wells, Kitty, 1919–, 2
Williams, Mary Lou, 1910–1981, 1,2
Wynette, Tammy, 1942–, 2
Gunnery
   Foster, Marjorie, 1894–1974, 2
   Vito, Mary de, fl. 1970s, 2
Gymnasts
   See also
      Child gymnasts
   Avener, Judi, fl. 1970s, 2
   Botscharova, Nina, fl. 1950s, 2
   Caslavska-Oklozil, Vera, 1942–, 2
   Comanici, Nadia, 1961–, 2
   Grossfield, Muriel Davis, 1941–, 2
   Janz, Karin, fl. 1970s, 2
   Kallio, Elin Waenerberg, 1859–1927,
      1
   Keleti, Agnes, fl. 1950s, 2
   Kim, Nelli, 1957–, 2
   Korbut, Olga, 1955–, 2
   Latynina, Larissa Semyonova, 1935–,
      2
   Lyon, Lisa, 2
   Metheny, Linda Jo, fl. 1960s, 2
   Peters, Mary, 1939–, 2
   Pierce, Roxanne, 2
   Rice, Joan Moore, 1954–, 2
   Rigby, Cathy, 1952–, 2
   Schroth, Clara, fl. 1940s, 2
   Schuckman, Karen, fl. 1970s, 2
   Tourischeva, Ludmilla, 1952–, 2
   Turischeva, Ludmilla, 1952–, 2
Gynecologists
   Barringer, Emily Dunning, 1876–
      1961, 2
   Barrington, Emily Dunning, 1876–
      1961, 1
   Chinnatamby, Siva, fl. 1950s, 2
   Cleopatra, fl. 100s, 2
   Dickins, Helen Octavia, 1900–, 2
   Hirsch, Jeanne, 1917–, 2
   Hirsch, Jenny, 1829–1902, 2
   Hirsch, Lolly, 1941–, 2
   Hurdon, Elizabeth, 1868–1941, 1,2
   Kazhanova, Dr., 2
   Kleegman, Sophie Josephine, 1900–
      1971, 1,2
   Levine, Lena, 1903–1965, 2
   Potter, Marion Craig, fl. 1930s, 1
   Scharlieb, Mary Ann Dacomb Bird,
      1845–1930, 1
   Storch, Marcia, 1933–, 2
   Warner, Marie Pichel, fl. 1930s, 1

Gypsies
   Amaya, Carmen, 1913–1963, 1,2
   Mitchell, Kelly, 1868–1915, 2
   Sauer, Marie Elizabeth, fl. 1700s, 2

H

Hadassah founder
   Szold, Henrietta, 1860–1945, 1,2
Hadrian—Spouse
   Sabina, Vibia, d. 138, 1
Hairdressers
   Carita, Maria, 1918–1978, 2
   Ryan, Harriet, fl. 1790s, 1
Haldane, Lord—Mother
   Sanderson, Elizabeth, 1825–1925, 1
Halket, Lady—Mother
   Murray, Mrs., fl. 1600s, 1
Hall, John—Mother
   Symonds, Rebekah, fl. 1660s, 2
Hall, Lyman—Spouse
   Hall, Abigail Burr, d. 1753, 1
   Hall, Mary, fl. 1750s, 1
Hallmark Cards founder
   Hall, Joyce Clyde, 1891–, 2
Hamilton, Alexander—Friend
   Reynolds, Maria, fl. 1790s, 1
   Ridley, Catharine Livingston, fl.
      1770s, 1
Hamilton, Alexander—Spouse
   Hamilton, Elizabeth Schuyler, 1757–
      1854, 1,2
   Hamilton, Rachel Faucett, 1729–, 1
Hammerton*
   Tree, Helen Maude, 1863–, 1
Hancock, John—Aunt
   Hancock, Lydia, fl. 1770s, 1
Hancock, John—Spouse
   Hancock, Dorothy Quincy, 1750–
      1828, 1,2
Handicapables
   Caliguiri, Nadine, 2
Handicapped
   See also
      Blind
      Deaf
   Biffin, Sarah, 1784–1850, 1
   Dalager, Betsy, 1852–, 2
   Lester, Margaret, 1938–, 2
   Peters, Kim, fl. 1970s, 2
   Robertson, Nan, 2
   Rosenbaum, Ruth Broemmer, 1945–,
      2
   Thoben, Patricia Joan, 1933–1977, 2

Handicapped children
  Foster, Edith, 1914–, 2
  Giles, Mrs Arnett, 1901–, 2
Handmaiden
  Hagar, 1,2
Handwriting experts
  See
  Graphologists
Hanks, Dennis—Spouse
  Johnston, Elizabeth, m. 1821, 1
Hanks, Lucy—Mother
  Hanks, Lucy, d. 1825, 1
Hanks, Lucy—Sister
  Sparrow, Elizabeth Hanks, 1771–
  1818, 1
Harding, Warren G.—Friend
  Britton, Nan, 2
Harding, Warren G.—Mother
  Harding, Phoebe Elizabeth Dicker-
  son, 1843–1920, 1,2
Harding, Warren G.—Spouse
  Harding, Florence King, 1860–1924,
  1,2
Hardy, Duffus—Daughter
  Hardy, Isa Duffus, fl. 1890s, 1
Hari, Mata—Daughter
  MacLeod, Banda, d. 1950, 2
Harness racing
  Farber, Bea, 1940–, 2
Harpists
  Ashby, Dorothy Jeanne, 1932–, 2
  Burford, Beatrice, fl. 1930s, 1
  Dilling, Mildred, fl. 1920s, 1
  Goosens, Sidonie, 1894–, 2
  Ives, Cora Semmes, fl. 1860s, 2
  Khuwyt, 1950 BC, 1
  Lehwalder, Heidi, 1950–, 2
  Lowe, Marie, fl. 1840s, 1
  MacAlindon, Mary, fl. 1700s, 1
  Marquardt, Alexandria, 1866–1942, 1
  Miller, Marie, fl. 1910s, 1
  Mooney, Rose, fl. 1700s, 1
  Morgan, Maud, 1864–1941, 1
  Reed, Susan Karen, 1927–, 2
  Spohr, Dorette Scheidler, fl. 1790s, 1
Harpsichordists
  Ehlers, Alice, 1890–, 1,2
  Gerson-Kiwi, Edith, 1
  La Guerre, Elisabeth-Claude Jacquet
  de, 1664–1727, 2
  Lalandi, Lina, 2
  Landowska, Wanda Louis, 1877–
  1959, 1,2
  Marlowe, Sylvia, 1908–, 1

Pelton-Jones, Frances, fl. 1940s, 1
Pessl, Yella, fl. 1930s, 1
Roesgen-Champion, Marguerite,
  1894–, 1
Tureck, Rosalyn, 1914–, 1,2
Harrison, Benjamin—Daughter
  McKee, Mary Harrison, 1858–1930, 1
Harrison, Benjamin—Mother
  Harrison, Elizabeth E. Irwin, 1810–
  1850, 1,2
Harrison, Benjamin—Spouse
  Harrison, Caroline Lavinia Scott,
  1832–1892, 1,2
Harrison, William Henry—Hostess
  Findlay, Jane, fl. 1840s, 1
Harrison, William Henry—Mother
  Harrison, Elizabeth Bassett, 1730–
  1792, 1,2
Harrison, William Henry—Spouse
  Harrison, Anna Symmes, 1775–1864,
  1,2
  Harrison, Mary Scott Lord Dimmick,
  1858–1949, 1,2
Hasdrubal—Daughter
  Sophonisba, d. 203 BC, 1
Hasidic Jews
  Eidele, 2
Hastings, Warren—Spouse
  Hastings, Anna Maria Apollonia,
  1747–1837, 1
Hat industry
  See
  Milliners
Hawaii
  Abreu, Lucille, fl. 1970s, 2
  Bishop, Bernice Pauahi, 1831–1884, 2
  Damon, Mary Happer, 1858–, 2
  Emma, 1836–1885, 1,2
  Hanakaulani-o-kamamalu, 1843–, 2
  Helvin, Marie, fl. 1970s, 2
  Judd, Laura Fish, 1804–, 2
  Kaahumanu, Elizabeth, 1772–1832, 2
  Kaleleonalani, Emma, 1835–1875, 1
  Kamanalu, Victoria, d. 1824, 1
  Kapiolani, 1781–1841, 2
  Kapiolani, 1834–1899, 1
  Kapule, Deborah, d. 1853, 2
  Kekuiapoiwa II, fl. 1900s, 2
  Keopuolani, 2
  Kinau, High Chieftess, 2
  Kudaka, Geraldine, 1951–, 2
  Lifelike, Miriam, 1851–1887, 1
  Lilioukalani, Lydia Kamekeha, 1838–
  1917, 1,2

Okumura, Katsu, d. 1942, 2
Pauahi, Bernice, 1831–, 2
Richards, Mary Atherton, 1869–, 2
Tokunaga, Laura, 1950–, 2
Hawks, Frank—Spouse
  Bowie, Edith Hawks, fl. 1920s, 1
Hawthorne, Nathaniel—Daughter
  Lathrop, Rose Hawthorne, 1851–
  1926, 1,2
Hawthorne, Nathaniel—Spouse
  Hawthorne, Sophia Amelia Peabody,
  1809–1871, 2
Hayes, Rutherford B.—Mother
  Hayes, Sophia Birchard, 1792–1866,
  1,2
Hayes, Rutherford B.—Niece
  Platt, Emily, d. 1922, 1
Hayes, Rutherford B.—Spouse
  Hayes, Lucy Ware Webb, 1831–1889,
  1,2
Healers
  Maurice, Mrs., fl. 1840s, 1
  Wheeler, Edith, 2
Health care services
  Ferebee, Dorothy, fl. 1920s, 2
Health experts
  Bernie, Rose L., fl. 1930s, 1
  Bragg, Mabel Caroline, 1870–1945, 1
Health food authors
  Chase, Alice, d. 1974, 2
Health workers
  Anderson, Elda Emma, 1899–1961, 2
  Clark, Mamie Phipps, 1917–, 2
  Downer, Carol, fl. 1970s, 2
  Gagne, Betty, 1923–, 2
  Metzelthin, Pearl Violetta, 1894–
  1947, 1
  Nichols, Mary Grove, 1810–1884, 2
  Williamson, Pauline Brooks, fl.
  1930s, 1
  Yonge, Charlotte Mary, 1823–1901,
  1,2
Hearn, Lafcadio—Translator
  Japanese woman, 1866–1900, 2
Hearst, William Randolph—Spouse
  Hearst, Millicent Willson, 1859–
  1951, 1,2
Hebrew Trade Council
  August, Rebecca, 1883–, 2
Hector—Mother
  Hecuba, 2
Hector—Spouse
  Andromache, 2
Hedylus—Mother
  Hedyle, fl. 260BC, 1

Heile Selassi I—Spouse
  Menen (Manin), Waizaro (Waizero),
  1891–1962, 1,2
Heine—Mistress
  Mirat, Mathilde (Madame Heine),
  1818–1883, 1
Heiresses
  Alexander, Margaret "Daisy", d.
  1939, 2
  Barnsdall, Louise Alice, 1882–1946, 2
  Bonynge, Virginia, m. 1894, 1
  Caldwell, Mary Gwendolin, Marquise
  of Montriers-Merinville, 1863–
  1909, 1,2
  Castellane, Anna Gould, Marquise
  de, 1876–1961, 1
  Chamberlain, Jeannie, 1865–, 1
  Cromartie, Ann, Countess of, 1829–
  1888, 1
  Curzon of Kedleston, Mary Victoria
  Leiter, 1868–1906, 1,2
  De Miramion, Madame, 1629–1694, 1
  Dodge, Delphine, fl. 1930s, 1
  Duke, Doris, 1912–, 1,2
  Frazier, Brenda Diana Dudd, 1921–,
  1,2
  Gaines, Myra Clark, 1805–1885, 1,2
  Garner, Florence, m. 1891, 1
  Goelet, May Wilson, Duchess of Rox-
  burgh(e), fl. 1910s, 1,2
  Gordon-Cumming, Florence Garner,
  d. 1922, 1
  Hearst, Patricia Campbell, 1954–, 2
  Hill, Sarah Althea, d. 1937, 1
  Huntingdon, Helen, 1950–, 1
  Hutton, Barbara, 1912–1979, 1,2
  Inaga, Consuelo, d. 1909, 1
  Ives, Elizabeth Cabot, m. 1876, 1
  Leiter, Mary Victoria, d. 1906, 1
  Manchester, Helena Zimmerman, fl.
  1930s, 1
  Marlborough, Consuelo Vanderbilt,
  1877–1964, 1
  Marlborough, Lily Hammersley, d.
  1909, 1
  McCormick, Mary Ann Hall, 1
  Merriweather, Marjorie, 1946–1973, 2
  Mundeville, Maude de, fl. 1140s, 1
  Newberry, Julia, 1853–1876, 1,2
  Onassis, Christina, 1950–, 2
  Paget, Mary Fiske Stevens, 1853–
  1919, 1
  Percy, Elizabeth, 1666–1722, 1
  Picot, Eugenia, fl. 1170s, 1

Heroes
See also
Child heroes
Ackland, Harriet Christina, Henrietta, Lady, 1750–1818, 1,2
Agnes of Dunbar (Black Agnes), 1312–1369, 1
Agostina, the maid of Saragossa, 1788–1857, 1
Alison, Isabel of Perth, d. 1681, 1
Allen, Maria, fl. 1770s, 1
Almeida, Brites de, d.c. 1386, 1
Ambler, Mary, fl. 1850s, 2
Appolonia, Jagiello, 1825–, 1
Arria, the elder, d. 42, 1,2
Aylward, Gladys, 1903–1970, 1,2
Bache, Sarah, d. 1798, 1
Bailey, Ann "Mad Ann", 1742–1825, 1,2
Ballard, Emily, fl. 1830s, 1
Bankes, Mary Hawtrey, Lady, d. 1661, 1
Barrett, Meliscent, fl. 1770s, 1,2
Batherick, Mother, fl. 1800s, 2
Baylis, Lilian Mary, 1874–1937, 1,2
Beckham, Mrs., fl. 1770s, 1
Bernauer, Agnes, d. 1435, 1
Bieloverskaia, Maria, fl. 1910s, 1
Boadicea, d. 62, 1,2
Bolling, Susanna, 2
Botssi, Despo, fl. 1700s, 1
Bouboulina, Laskarina, 1783–1825, 1
Bozarth, Elizabeth (Experience), fl. 1770s, 1,2
Bradford, Mary, fl. 1860s, 1
Bradford, Susan, 1846–, 1,2
Breen, Margaret, fl. 1840s, 1,2
Brevard, Mrs., fl. 1770s, 1
Brown, Mary Buckman, 1740–1824, 1
Brownell, Kady, 1842–, 1
Brusselmans, Anne, 2
Bryant, Mary Broad, fl. 1790s, 1
Buchanan, Sally Ridley, 1750–, 2
Buckles, Tanja, fl. 1960s, 2
Burgh (or Burgo), Honora de, fl. 1680s, 1
Camacho, Maria de Luz, 1
Candelaria, Andrea, fl. 1830s, 2
"Captain Molly", 1751–1800, 1
Carroll, Anna Ella, 1815–1893, 1,2
Champion, Deborah, 1753–, 1,2
Channing, Mrs., fl. 1770s, 1
Chapin, Hannah, fl. 1700s, 1

Chipeta, 1842–1880, 1,2
Cloelia, 94 BC-, 2
Cochrane, Grizel, fl. 1600s, 1
Cook, Jesse, fl. 1790s, 1
Cook, Miss, fl. 1700s, 1
Cook, Mrs. Hosea, fl. 1790s, 1
Cooper, Mildred (Milly), fl. 1810s, 2
Corbin, Margaret Cochran "Captain Molly", 1751–1800, 1,2
Cox, Lucy Ann, fl. 1860s, 1
Cromartie, Hazel M., fl. 1960s, 2
Curran, Sarah, 1783–1806, 1
Dabertin, Rita, 1936–, 2
Darling, Grace Horsley, 1815–1842, 1,2
Darragh (Darrah), Lydia Barrington, 1728–1789, 1,2
Davis, Ann Scott, 1801–1891, 1
Dervorgilla, d. 1193, 1
Devalet, Germaine, 1898–1945, 2
Dickerson, Suzanna, fl. 1830s, 1,2
Dillard, Mrs., fl. 1770s, 1
Dimitrova, Anastasie, 1856–1894, 1
Dimitrova, Lilyana Nikolova, 1918–1944, 1,2
Doane, Rose E., 1933–1967, 2
Dokken, Julia C., 1947–, 2
Dorion, Marie, 1786–1850, 1,2
Duperrault, Terry Jo, 1950–, 1
Duston (Dustin), Hannah, 1657–1736, 1,2
Edgar, Rachel, fl. 1770s, 1
Elizabeth, 1890–1945, 1
Ellet, Mary, 1779–, 1
Elliott, Ann, 1762–1848, 1
Endreson, Guri, fl. 1860s, 2
Fannia, 2
Fitzgerald, Cathelyn, d. 1604, 1
Fitzgerald, Eleanor, m. 1538, 1
Fitzgerald, Elizabeth, 1528–1589, 1
Fitzgerald, Margaret, d. 1542, 1
Fontes, Cynthia, fl. 1970s, 2
Ford, Antonia, fl. 1860s, 1,2
Fowler, Kate, fl. 1780s, 2
Francis, Milly, 1802–1848, 2
Frank, Anne, 1929–1945, 1,2
Fraser, Mrs. Alexander, fl. 1890s, 1
French, Emma, fl. 1880s, 2
Frietschie, Barbara, 1766–1862, 1,2
Garibaldi, Anita, 1821–1894, 2
Garibaldi, Anita Riveira de Silva, 1807–1849, 1
Gaston, Esther, fl. 1770s, 1,2
Gaylord, Katherine Cole, 1745–1840, 1

Ramus, Anna Kolbjors, 1665–1736, 1
Ranee of Jhansi (Lakshmi Bai), 1822–1857, 1
Reyes, Mercedes Abrego de, 1785–, 1
Rivers, Mary M., fl. 1960s, 2
Rivet, Elise, 1890–1945, 1
Robbins, Nancy, fl. 1790s, 1
Roberts, June E., fl. 1960s, 2
Rodriguez, Gloria, fl. 1960s, 2
Rogers, Mary, fl. 1890s, 1
Rooke, Sarah J., 1908–, 2
Roper, Margaret More, 1505–1544, 1,2
Roshone, Edna, fl. 1960s, 2
Roussilon, Alice, 2
Rubens, Maria, 1
Russell, Lenie, fl. 1860s, 1
Russell, Tillie, fl. 1860s, 1
Saish, Maureen, 1
Salavarrieta, Policarpa "La Pola", 1
Sandes, Flora, fl. 1910s, 1,2
Saragossa (Saragoza), Augustina, 1786–1857, 1,2
Schidlowskaia, Olga, fl. 1910s, 1
Semmer, Marcelle, fl. 1910s, 1
Senesh, Hannah, 1921–1944, 1,2
Sharp, Reta R., fl. 1970s, 2
Sheads, Carrie, fl. 1860s, 1
Shelley, Kate, 1866–1912, 2
Shover, Felicia Lee Carey Thornton, fl. 1860s, 1
Silcott, Jane, 1842–1895, 1,2
Simms, Sarah Dickinson, fl. 1770s, 1
Sims, Isabella, fl. 1770s, 1
Slocum(b), Mary Hooks (Polly), 1760–1836, 1,2
Smart, Susannah Barnett, 1761–, 1
Smirnoff, Zoe, fl. 1910s, 1
Sorrells, Connie M., fl. 1960s, 2
Spalding, Mrs., fl. 1770s, 1
Starr, Belle Shirley, 1848–1889, 1,2
Starr, Mrs. Harold, fl. 1920s, 1
Stuart, Flora Cooke, fl. 1860s, 1
Tanaquil, 2
Tao Suranari, fl. 1820s, 1
Tchankova, Iordanka, fl. 1940s, 1
Tcherniawaka, Glustchenko, fl. 1910s, 1
Threritz, Emily Geiger, 1760–, 1
Thuliez, Louise, 2
Titlow, Effie, fl. 1860s, 1
Toombs, Mrs. Robert, fl. 1860s, 2
Turchin, Nadine, 1826–1904, 1
Turner, Kerenhappuch, fl. 1780s, 2

Tusnelda, fl. 9, 1
Tynes, Mary Elizabeth, fl. 1860s, 1,2
Vata, Shkurte Pal, 1952–1967, 2
Vercheres, Madeleine de, 1678–1747, 1
Veturia, fl.400sBC, 1
Vicario, Maria Leona, 1787–1842, 1
Viscario, Leona, d. 1842, 1
Volumnia, fl.400sBC, 1
Vrooman, Angelica, fl. 1770s, 1
Wanda, Queen, fl. 730s, 1
Warner, Jemima, fl. 1770s, 1,2
Wenonah, fl. 1800s, 2
Whitall, Ann, fl. 1770s, 2
Whitney, Ann, d. 1867, 2
Windsor, Mary Catherine, 1830–1914, 1
Wright, Mrs. David, fl. 1770s, 1
Wright, Prudence Cumings, 1739–1823, 1
Wright, Rebecca, m. 1871, 1
Zellers, Christine, fl. 1740s, 1
Heroes (Fiction)
John, Madame, 2
Heston, Charlton—Spouse
  Heston, Lydia, 2
Heywood, Oliver—Mother
  Heywood, Mrs., fl. 1600s, 1
Hezron—Spouse
  Abiah, 1
Highway beautifier
  Honeyman, Jessie M., d. 1948, 2
Hijackers
  Khaled, Leila, fl. 1970s, 2
Hill, Edward—Spouse
  Hill, Jane, 1934–, 2
Hirohito, Prince—Friend
  Shoda, Michiko, 1935–, 1
Histologists
  Pythias, 380–320, 2
Historians
  See also
    Antiquarians
    Archeologists
    Art historians
    Classicists
    Genealogists
    Iconographers
    Labor historians
    Medievalists
    Orientalists
  Abel, Annie, 1873–1947, 2
  Adams, Hannah, 1755–1831, 1,2
  Ady, Cecilia Mary, d. 1958, 1

Palfrey sisters, fl. 1860s, 1
Palmerston, Emily Mary Lamb,
 Lady, 1787–1869, 1
Peyster, Mrs. D. E., m. 1935, 1
Pickens, Lucy Petway Holcombe,
 1832–1899, 1,2
Portland, Margaret Harley, fl. 1730s,
 1
Proxmire, Ellen, 2
Purbeck, Frances Coke Villiers, d.
 1645, 1
Queensberry, Catherine Hyde,
 Duchess, d. 1977, 1,2
Raunall, Sarah, fl. 1760s, 1
Schuyler, Catherine van Renssalaer,
 1733–1803, 1,2
Sharington, Olive, d. 1651, 1
Shirley, Frances, 1707–, 1
Smith, Margaret Bayard Harrison,
 1778–1844, 1,2
Speyer, Ellin Leslie Prince Lowery,
 1849–1921, 2
Sunderland, Dorothy Sidney, m.
 1639, 1
Talbot, Elizabeth, Countess of
 Shrewsbury, 1518–1608, 1
Tubman, Emily H., 1794–1885, 1
Welch, Mrs. E. Sohier, fl. 1930s, 1
Westmeath, Lady, fl. 1850s, 1
Widener, Ella H. Pancoast, d. 1929, 1
Widener, Josephine "Fifi", fl. 1920s,
 1
Hostilianus—Spouse
 Orbiana, Barbia, fl. 200s, 1
Hotel owners and managers
 See also
  Boardinghouse owners
  Marriott Hotels
  Restaurateurs
  Tavern keepers
 Ballard, Mary, fl. 1755, 1
 Bowman, Sarah A., 1912–1866, 2
 Brown, Hannah, fl. 1770s, 1,2
 Cashman, Nellie, 1851–1925, 2
 Cockrell, Sarah, fl. 1850s, 2
 Crawford, Lucy, fl. 1840s, 2
 Crosnier, Madame, 2
 Eberly, Angelina B., d. 1860, 1,2
 Eliott, Rebekah Ward, fl. 1930s, 1
 Elliot, Rebekah Ward, fl. 1930s, 1
 Engle, Mary, fl. 1810s, 1
 Grant, Bridget, 1831–1923, 1
 Grossinger, Jennie, 1892–1972, 1,2
 Heiman, Gertrude, fl. 1930s, 1

Hudson, Hester, d. 1796, 1
Ivaikina, Claudia, fl. 1970s, 2
Khourey, Nadia el, 2
Knight, Sarah Kemble, 1666–1727,
 1,2
Kramer, Maria, fl. 1930s, 1
Laxalt, Theresa Alpetche, fl. 1920s, 2
Lewis, Rosa Overden, 1867–1952, 1,2
Lloyd, Nita, 2
Love, Ann, d. 1858, 2
Mann, Pamela, d. 1840, 1,2
Marriott, Elizabeth, d. 1755, 1
Murat, Catherine (Katrina), 1824–
 1910, 2
Orchard, Sadie, 1863–1943, 2
Pullen, Harriet Smith, 1859–1947, 2
Reid, Margaret E., 1846–1923, 1
Roberts, Widow, fl. 1740s, 1
Sproat, Florantha Thompson, 1811–,
 1
Stevens, Marieta, fl. 1850s, 2
Walker, Elizabeth, fl. 1800s, 2
Wilson, Luzena Stanley, fl. 1840s, 2
Withy, Mary, d. 1810, 1
Houdini, Harry—Spouse
 Houdini, Beatrice (Bess), 2
Housewives Association
 Huq, Tayyeba, 1921–, 2
Housing economists
 Wood, Edith Elmer, 1871–1945, 1,2
Housing experts
 Rosenman, Dorothy Reuben, 1900–,
 1
Housing reformers
 Dinwiddie, Emily Wayland, 1879–
 1949, 2
 Simkhovitch, Mary Melinda Kings-
 bury, 1867–1951, 1,2
Houston, Sam—Cousin
 Hamilton, Narcissa, fl. 1830s, 1
Houston, Sam—Friend
 Barker, Widow, fl. 1830s, 1
 Eberly, Angelina B., d. 1860, 1,2
 Irion, Anna Raguet, 1819–1883, 1
 O'Neal, Margaret, m. 1916, 1
Houston, Sam—Godmother
 Sterne, Eva Rosine Ruff, 1810–, 1
Houston, Sam—Mother
 Houston, Elizabeth Paxton, 1765–
 1831, 1
Houston, Sam—Mother-in-law
 Lea, Nancy Lea, 2
Houston, Sam—Spouse
 Houston, Eliza Allen, d. 1862, 1
 Houston, Margaret Moffett Lea,
 1819–1867, 1,2

Lea, Margaret Moffette, d. 1867, 1
Rogers, Tiana, d. 1838, 1
Howard, Cordelia—Mother
    Howard, Caroline Emily Fox, 1829–
    1908, 2
Howland, John—Spouse
    Howland, Elizabeth Tilley, 1606–
    1687, 1
Hsi Tsung—Mother
    K'o, Lady, fl. 1620s, 1
Hsien Feng—Concubine
    Hsi, Tzw, 1835–1908, 2
Huggins, William—Spouse
    Huggins, Margaret Lindsay, 1848–
    1915, 1
Hughes, Howard—Spouse
    Hughes, Jean Peters, 1926–, 2
Hugo, Victor—Mother
    Hugo, Sophie Trebuchet, d. 1821, 1
    Trebuchet, Sophie, 1778–1821, 1
Hugo, Victor—Spouse
    Hugo, Adele Foucher, 1806–1868, 1
Hull House
    Starr, Ellen Gates, 1859–1940, 2
Humanitarians
    Abbott, Helen Probst, fl. 1930s, 1
    Abreu de Estevez, Marta, 1845–1909,
    1
    Adams, Helen Balfour, 1848–1948, 1
    Addams, Jane, 1860–1935, 1,2
    Alden, Cynthia May Westover, 1862–
    1931, 1,2
    Arenal de Garcia Carrasco, Dona
    Conception, 1820–1893, 1
    Baker, Delphine P., 1828–, 1
    Barker, Mrs. Stephen, fl. 1860s, 1
    Biddle, Mary Duke, 1887–1960, 1
    Bigelow, Mrs. R. M., fl. 1860s, 1
    Blackwell, Alice Stone, 1857–1950,
    1,2
    Borg, Madeleine Beer, 1878–1956, 1
    Brackenridge, M. Eleanor, fl. 1890s, 1
    Bradford, Charlotte, fl. 1860s, 1
    Brady, Mary A., 1821–1864, 1
    Brandstrom, Elsa, 1888–1948, 1
    Brayton, Mary Clark, fl. 1860s, 1
    Bryce, Elizabeth Marion, 1853–1939,
    1
    Bucklin, Sophronia, fl. 1860s, 1
    Burson, Josephine Wainman, fl.
    1940s, 2
    Cadwise, Mrs. David, fl. 1800s, 1
    Campbell, Valeria, fl. 1860s, 1
    Carey, Emma Forbes, 1833–, 1

Clapp, Anna L., fl. 1860s, 1
Coffey, Phyllis C., fl. 1930s, 1
Colby, Marie F., fl. 1930s, 1
Colt, Henrietta L. Peckham, 1812–, 1
Concepcion, Arenal, 1820–1893, 1
Conger, Mrs. Al, fl. 1900s, 1
Couzzins, Adaline, fl. 1860s, 1
Currey, Louise Sevier, 1903–, 2
Cushman, Emma, 1862–, 1
Davis, Mrs. G. T. M., fl. 1860s, 1
De Miramion, Madame, 1629–1694, 1
De Ponce de Leon, Dona Ines, 1475–
    1515, 1
Derricotte, Juliette, 1897–1931, 2
Dooly, Ismay, d. 1921, 1
Doremus, Sarah Platt Haines, 1802–
    1877, 1,2
Draper, Muriel Gurdon Sanders,
    1886–1952, 1
Dreier, Ethel E., fl. 1920s, 1
Drexel, Mary Katharine, Mother,
    1858–1955, 1,2
Dublin, Mary, fl. 1930s, 1
Dunn, Hilda S., fl. 1930s, 1
Eddy, Olive Tyndale, fl. 1930s, 1
Emrick, Jeanette Wallace, 1878–, 1
Fenn, Mrs. Curtis T., fl. 1860s, 1
Forbes, Arethusa L., fl. 1860s, 1
Frajoso de Rivera, Bernardina, 1800–
    1863, 1
George, Mrs. E. E., fl. 1860s, 1
Gottlieb, Bessie, 1891–1972, 2
Greble, Susan Virginia, fl. 1860s, 1
Grier, Maria C., fl. 1860s, 1
Griffin, Josephine R., fl. 1860s, 1
Hackely, Emma Azalia Smith, 1867–
    1923, 2
Hackley, Emma Azalia, 1867–1922, 1
Hallowell, Mrs. M. M., fl. 1860s, 1
Harlan, Mrs. James, m. 1845/6, 1
Harriman, Grace Carley, 1873–1950,
    1
Harris, Eliza, fl. 1860s, 1
Harris, Mrs. John, fl. 1860s, 1
Hartman, May Weisser, 1900–, 1
Hirsch, Clara de, Baroness, 1833–
    1899, 1
Hitz, Ann, fl. 1860s, 1
Hoge, Mrs. A. H., 1811–1890, 1
Holden, Miriam Young, fl. 1930s, 1
Hosmer, Mrs. O. E., fl. 1860s, 1
Hunton, Hazel, fl. 1930s, 1
Ingersoll, Marion Crary, fl. 1930s, 1
Johnson, Kate Burr, 1881–, 2

White, Edith Hamilton, fl. 1930s, 1
White, Rhoda Elizabeth Waterman, fl. 1830s, 1
Wittenmyer, Annie Turner, 1827–1900, 1,2
Woerishoffer, Anna, 2
Wood, Edith Elmer, 1871–1945, 1,2
Woodbury, Anna Lowell, fl. 1870s, 1
Woolsey, Jane Stuart, fl. 1860s, 1
Wrede, Mathilda, 1864–1929, 1
Wright, Mrs. Crafts J., fl. 1860s, 1
Humorists
    See also
    Cartoonists
Bacon, Josephine Dodge Daskam, 1876–1961, 1
Beard, Miriam, fl. 1920s, 1
Best, Molly, fl. 1920s, 1
Cooper, Jilly, 1937–, 2
Dodge, Mary Abigail, 1833–1896, 1,2
Eastman, Elaine Goodale, 1863–1953, 1
Gould, Lois, 1937–, 2
Holley, Marietta, 1836–1926, 1,2
Howe, Helen (Allen), 1905–1875, 1,2
Kerr, Jean Collins, 1923–, 1,2
Lebowitz, Frances Ann, 1950–, 2
Leslie, Eliza (Elizabeth), 1787–1858, 1,2
Parker, Dorothy Rothschild, 1893–1967, 1,2
Skinner, Cornelia Otis, 1901–1979, 1,2
Whitcher, Frances Miriam Berry, 1811–1852, 1,2
Hunters
Maxwell, Martha A., 2
Huntington, Collis P.—Spouse
Huntington, Elizabeth T Stoddard, d. 1883, 2
Huntley, Chet—Mother
Huntley, Blanche Tatham, 1893–, 2
Hussein, King—Consort
Halaby, Elizabeth (Lisa), 1951–, 2
Hussein, King—Spouse
Dina Abdul Hamid, 1928–, 1
Hyde, Edward—Daughter
York, Anne, 1637–1671, 1
Hydraulic engineers
Tretiakova, Oktiabrina, 2
Hydrographic researchers
Bernasconi, Irene, fl. 1960s, 2
Caria, Maria Adela, fl. 1960s, 2
Fontes, Elena M., fl. 1960s, 2
Pujals, Carmen, fl. 1960s, 2

Hydrological researchers
Whitmore, Joan, 2
Hygienists
Phillips, Carolyn F., 2
Hymnists
Adams, Sarah Fowler, 1805–1848, 1,2
Akerman, Lucy Evelina Metcalf, 1816–1874, 2
Bates, Katherine Lee, 1859–1929, 1,2
Baxter, Lydia, 1809–1874, 2
Breck, Carrie Ellis, 1855–1934, 1,2
Brock, Blanche Kerr, 1888–, 1
Brown, Phoebe Hinsdale, 1783–1861, 2
Buell, Harriett Eugenia (Peck), 1834–1910, 2
Carney, Julia Abigail (Fletcher), 1823–1908, 2
Cary, Alice, 1820–1871, 1,2
Cary, Phoebe, 1824–1871, 1,2
Clayton, Edith, 1897–, 2
Collier, Mary Ann, 1810–1866, 2
Cook, Martha Ann (Woodbridge), 1807–1884, 2
Copenhaver, Laura (Scherer), 1868–1940, 2
Crosby, Frances "Fanny" Jane, 1820–1916, 1,2
Cuninggim, Maud Merrimon, 1874–, 2
Dana, Mary Stanley Bunce Palmer, 1810–1883, 2
Dorr, Julia Caroline Ripley, 1825–1913, 1,2
Elliott, Charlotte, 1789–1871, 1
Esling, Catherine Harbison, 1812–1897, 2
Follen, Eliza Lee Cabot, 1787–1860, 1,2
Gates, Ellen Huntington, 1835–1920, 2
Gilman, Caroline Howard, 1794–1888, 1,2
Gould, Hannah Flagg, 1789–1865, 1,2
Hale, Mary Whitwell, 1810–1862, 1,2
Halverson, Frances Ridley, fl. 1870s, 1
Havergal, Frances Ridley, 1836–1879, 1
Hawks, Annie Sherwood, 1835–1918, 1,2
Hearne, Mary, 1834–1909, 2
Hutchinson, Abigail (Abby) Jemima, 1829–1892, 1,2

Meredith, Virginia, 1848–1936, 2
Porter, Gene Stratton, 1862–1924, 1,2
Rabb, Kate Milner, 1866–1937, 2
Slocum, Frances "Maconaquah",
  1773–1847, 1,2
Wallace, Zerelda Gray Sanders, 1817–
  1901, 1,2
Industrial designers
  Eddy, Lillian E., 1902–1966, 1
Industrial engineers
  Gilbreth, Lillian Moller, 1878–1972,
  1,2
Industrialists
  Beech, Olive Ann Mellor, 1903–, 1,2
  Gridley, Mary Putnam, 2
  Kellems, Vivien, 1896–1975, 1,2
  Knox, Rose Markward, 1857–1950,
  1,2
  Lukens, Rebecca Webb Pennock,
  1794–1854, 1,2
  Roche, Josephine Aspinwall, 1886–
  1976, 1,2
  Warringer, June, fl. 1960s, 2
  Wohlers, Jeanne, 2
Infanta
  Isabella of Austria, Clara E., 1566–
  1633, 1
Informers
  Gordon, Vivian, d. 1931, 2
Innocent X—Niece
  Olympia Maldachini, fl. 1600s, 1
Inspiration for Evangeline
  Labiche, Emmeline, 2
Insurance
  Adsit, Nancy H., 1825–, 1
  Ann, Judith, 2
  Archibald, Lil(l)iana, 2
  Brandwein, Gerturde, fl. 1930s, 1
  Burtnett, Florissa, 1936–, 2
  Ellis, Patricia A., fl. 1970s, 2
  Ford, Kathryn, fl. 1930s, 1
  Hamberger, Margot, 2
  Olsen, Leonora Emelie, fl. 1930s, 1
  Paul, Nora Vincent, fl. 1930s, 1
  Procope, Ernesta G., fl. 1970s, 2
  Rodgers, Elizabeth Flynn, 1847–
  1939, 2
Interior designers
  See also
  White House decorators
  Baggett, Helen M., fl. 1930s, 1
  Bayes, Jessie, 1890–1934, 2
  Brown, Eleanor McMillen Stack-
  strom, fl. 1920s, 1,2

Cumming, Rose Stuart, fl. 1930s, 1
Daggett, Helen M., fl. 1930s, 1
Davis, Louisa J., fl. 1890s, 2
De Wolfe, Elsie, Lady Mendl, 1856–
  1950, 2
Devereaux, Margaret Green, fl.
  1920s, 1
Diamond, Freda, fl. 1950s, 2
Dodd, Carolyn G., fl. 1930s, 1
Draper, Dorothy (Tuckerman), 1889–
  1969, 1,2
Fairman, Agnes Rowe, fl. 1930s, 1
Garrett sisters, 2
Hall, Marian Wells, fl. 1930s, 1
Hamill, Virginia, fl. 1930s, 1
Kahane, Melanie, 1911–, 2
Knoll-Bassett, Florence Schust, fl.
  1970s, 2
Lee, Frances E., fl. 1870s, 2
Lewis, Esther, fl.1870–s, 2
Lewis, Ethel, fl. 1930s, 1
Lewis, Florence E., d. 1917, 2
Malino, Emily, 2
Maugham, Syrie, 1879–1955, 2
McClelland, Nancy, 1877–1959, 2
McCluskey, Ellen Lehman, fl. 1970s,
  1,2
Mendl, Lady, 1865–1960, 1
Miller, Gladys, fl. 1930s, 1
Murdock, Louise Caldwell, 1858–
  1915, 2
Radziwill, Lee Bouvier, Princess,
  1933–, 1,2
Rense, Paige, 1933–, 2
Roman, Mae, fl. 1930s, 1
Sabin, Pauline Morton, 1887–1955,
  1,2
Shatford, Vera V., fl. 1930s, 1
Sullivan, Marie, fl. 1930s, 1
Wheeler, Candace Thurber, 1827–
  1923, 1,2
Wheeler, Dora, fl. 1850s, 2
Wood, Ruby Ross, fl. 1910s, 1
International Association of School Li-
  brarians
  Lowrie, Jean Elizabeth, 1918–, 2
Internal flame
  Reeser, Mary Hardy, d. 1951, 2
International Association of Machinists
  Holden, Joyce, fl. 1970s, 2
International Merchandizing Associ-
  ation
  Schoenberg, Patricia, fl. 1960s, 2
Interpreters
  Montour, Catherine, Madame, 1684–
  1752, 1,2

Stoothoff, Saartze Kierstede von Borsum, d. 1693, 1

Inventors
Agnes, Maria Gaetana, 1718–1799, 1
Alden, Cynthia May Westover, 1862–1931, 1,2
Allison, Emma, fl. 1880s, 1
Andrassy, Stella (Countess), 2
Baker, Betsey Metcalf, fl. 1790s, 2
Barton, Kate, fl. 1870s, 1
Bassani, Signora, fl. 1800s, 1
Blanchard, Helen Augusta, fl. 1870s, 1
Bottomshaw, Mrs., fl. 1746, 1
Chang, Marguerite Shue-Wen, fl. 1970s, 2
Demorest, Ellen Curtis, 1824–1898, 2
Dennis, Olive Wetzel, 1885–1957, 1
Denton, Isabel, 2
Ducoudray, Madame, fl. 1700s, 1
Glover, Sarah Ann, 1785–1867, 1,2
Greene, Catherine, 1731–1794, 1
Horn, Debi, fl. 1970s, 2
Johnson, Lucy, 1789–1867, 1
Jones, Amanda Theodosia, 1835–1914, 2
Kies, Mary Dixon, 1752–, 1,2
Knight, Margaret E., 1838–1914, 1,2
Lazarenko, Natalita Iosafovna, 1911–, 1
Lefebre, Madame, fl. 1850s, 1
Logan, Charlotte, fl. 1930s, 1
Masters, Sybilla, d. 1720, 1,2
Miller, Elizabeth Smith, 1822–1911, 1,2
Muller, Gertrude Agnes, 1887–1954, 2
Palmer, Bernice, fl. 1940s, 1
Rodger, Augusta M., fl. 1870s, 1
Rodgers, Dorothy, 1909–, 2
Saunders, Mary A., 1849–, 1
Sawyer, Lucy, fl. 1870s, 1
Schroeder, Becky, fl. 1970s, 2
Scovil, Cora, fl. 1930s, 1
Slater, Hannah, fl. 1820s, 2
Smith, Quincy, fl. 1940s, 1
Stearns, Betsey Ann Goward, 1830–, 1
Stearns, Mary Beth, d. 1973, 2
Welles, Sophia Woodhouse, fl. 1820s, 2
Woodhouse, Sophia, fl. 1810s, 1,2
Investment advisers
Howard, Lulu Smith, fl. 1930s, 1
Muir, Gloria Ludwig, fl. 1940s, 2

Wagle, Asha, 1944–, 2
Walsh, Julia M., fl. 1940s, 2
Investment trust founders
Kaplan, Monique, fl. 1970s, 2
Iowa
Bloomer, Amelia Jenks, 1818–1894, 1,2
Boyd, Mamie Alexander, 1876–1973, 2
Cowles, Florence Call, 1861–1950, 2
Crowell, Grace Noll, 1877–1969, 1,2
Eisenhower, Ida Elizabeth Stover, 1862–1946, 1,2
Eitzen, Sarah Block, 1840–1917, 2
Harlan, Ann, 1824–1884, 2
Hillis, Cora Bussey, 1858–1924, 2
Houghton, Dorothy Deemer, 1890–1972, 1,2
Kalawequois, d. 1837, 2
Menninger, Flora Knisely, 1863–1945, 2
Nevins, Martha Griffith, 1860–, 2
Sayre, Ruth Buxton, 1896–, 2
Shambraugh, Jessie Field, 1881–1971, 2
Smith, Martha Kergan, 1824–1918, 2
Smith, Mary Louise, 1914–, 2
Swensson, Alma Christine Lind, 1859–1939, 2
White, Mary Ann Hatten, 1830–1924, 2
Whittenmyer, Annie Turner, 1827–1858, 2
Wollman, Betty Kohn, 1836–, 2
Iron and steel industry
Guest, Charlotte Elizabeth Bertie, Lady, 1812–1875, 1,2
Halascsak, Bonnie, 1943–, 2
Lukens, Rebecca Webb Pennock, 1794–1854, 1,2
Irving, Washington—Friend
Hoffman, Matilda, 2
Isaac—Spouse
Rebecca (Rebekah), 1,2
Israel
Silverman, Ida, 1882–1973, 2

J

Jackson, Andrew—Daughter-in-law
Jackson, Emily Donelson, fl. 1800s, 1
Jackson, Andrew—Mother
Hutchinson, Elizabeth, fl. 1750s, 1
Jackson, Elizabeth Hutchinson, fl. 1770s, 1,2

Jackson, Andrew—Niece
Donelson, Emily Jackson, fl. 1800s, 1
Jackson, Andrew—Spouse
Jackson, Rachel Donelson Robards,
1767–1828, 1,2
Yorke, Sarah, m. 1831, 1
Jacob—Spouse
Rachel, 1,2
Jagger, Mick—Spouse
Jagger, Bianca, 1945–, 2
Jahan, Shah—Spouse
Mahal, Mumtaz, 1593–1630, 1
Mumtaz-Mahal (Mumtaza Zemani),
1592–1631, 1,2
James I—Mother
Mary Stuart, Queen of Scots, 1542–
1587, 1,2
James II—Consort
Mary Beatrice, "Mary of Modena",
1658–1718, 1,2
James II—Spouse
Mary of Gueldres, 2
James III—Spouse
Clementina, m. 1719, 1
James IV (Scotland)—Consort
Margaret (4), 1489–1541, 1,2
James V—Spouse
Guise, Mary, 1515–1560, 2
Mary of Guise (Mary of Lorraine),
1515–1560, 1
James, Duke of York—Mistress
Churchill, Arabella, 1648–1730, 2
James, Henry—Mother
James, Mary Robertson Walsh, 1810–
1882, 1,2
James, Henry—Sister
James, Ada, 1876–1952, 2
James, Alice, 1848–1892, 2
James, Jesse—Mother
James, Zerelda Cole, fl. 1800s, 2
James, William—Mother
James, Mary Robertson Walsh, 1810–
1882, 1,2
James, William—Sister
James, Ada, 1876–1952, 2
James, Alice, 1848–1892, 2
James—Mother
Salome of Bethsaide, 1,2
Japan
Denton, Mary Florence, 1857–1947, 2
Jarvis, Anna M.—Mother
Jarvis, Anna Marie Reeves, 1836–
1905, 2
Jay, John—Spouse
Jay, Sarah (Sally) Livingston Van
Brugh, 1757–1802, 1,2

Jazz pianists
Akiyoshi, Toshiko, 1929–, 2
Alsop, Olive "Inez", 1905–, 2
Armstrong, Lil Hardin, 1898–1971, 2
Bown, Patricia Anne (Patti), 1931–, 2
Capers, Valerie, fl. 1970s, 2
Carlisle, Una Mae, 1918–1956, 2
Carroll, Barbara, 1925–, 2
Jazz singers
Alix, May, 1904–, 1,2
Babs, Alice, 1924–, 2
Bridgewater, Denise (Dee Dee),
1950–, 2
Brown, Ada, 1889–1950, 2
Brown, Norma E., fl. 1950s, 2
Brown, Olive, 1922–, 2
Brown, Ruth, 1928–, 2
Calloway, Blanche, 1902–1978, 1,2
Jefferson, Thomas—Daughter
Jefferson, Mary, fl. 1770s, 1
Randolph, Martha Jefferson, 1772–
1836, 1,2
Jefferson, Thomas—Friend
Burwell, Rebecca, fl. 1800s, 1
Hemings, Sally, 1773–1835, 2
Jefferson, Thomas—Mother
Jefferson, Jane Randolph, 1720–1776,
1,2
Jefferson, Thomas—Spouse
Jefferson, Martha Wayles, 1748–
1782, 1,2
Jehiel—Spouse
Maachah, 1
Jenner, Bruce—Spouse
Jenner, Chrystie, 1950–, 2
Jephthah—Daughter
Sheilah, 1
Jesus Christ—Mother
Mary, 1,2
Jet car racing
Breedlove, Lee, fl. 1960s, 2
Jet pilots
Mary Aquinas, Sister, fl. 1950s, 1
Jewelers
Bishop, Gwendolyn, 2
Courtauld, Louisa Perina, 2
Foote, Anne, fl. 1750s, 2
France, Georgina Cave, 1868–1934, 2
Gaskin, Georgina Cave France, 2
Gay, Patty, fl. 1890s, 2
Godfrey, Elizabeth, fl. 1741s, 2
Hart, May, 2
Koehler, Florence, 1861–1944, 2
McLeish, Annie, 2

John III (Sweden)—Spouse
Jagellonica, Katarina, d. 1583, 2
John of Gaunt—Spouse
Swynford, Catherine, Duchess of
Lancaster, 1350–1403, 1,2
John the Baptist—Mother
Elizabeth, 1,2
John the Fearless—Daughter
Bedford, Anne, 1402–1430, 1,2
John, Duke of Bedford—Spouse
Bedford, Anne, 1402–1430, 1,2
John—Mother
Salome of Bethsaide, 1,2
Johnson, Andrew—Daughter
Patterson, Martha Johnson, 1828–, 1
Johnson, Andrew—Mother
Johnson, Mary McDonough, fl.
1790s, 1,2
Johnson, Andrew—Spouse
Johnson, Eliza McArdle, 1810–1876,
1,2
Johnson, Isaac—Spouse
Johnson, Ar(a)bella, Lady, d. 1630,
1,2
Johnson, Jack—Mother-in-law
Falconet, Mrs. Cameron, 2
Johnson, Lyndon B.—Daughter
Nugent, Luci Baines Johnson, 1947–,
1,2
Robb, Lynda Bird Johnson, 2
Johnson, Lyndon B.—Mother
Johnson, Rebekah Baines, 1881–
1958, 2
Johnson, Lyndon B.—Spouse
Johnson, "Lady Bird" Claudia Alta
Taylor, 1912–, 1,2
Johnson, Samuel—Friend
Piozzi, Hester Lynch Thrale Salus-
bury, 1741–1821, 1,2
Johnson, Samuel—Spouse
Porter, Tetty, fl. 1700s, 2
Johnson, Thomas Jennings—Spouse
Johnson, Elizabeth Russell, 2
Johnson, Wallace—Mother
Johnson, Josephine, 2
Johnson, Wallace—Spouse
Johnson, Alma, 2
Jolson, Al—Mother
Yoelson, Naomi Cantor, d. 1895, 2
Jordon, David Starr—Spouse
Jordan, Jessie Knight, 1866–, 1
Jordon, John—Daughter
Newton, Mary, fl. 1770s, 1
Joseph II—Daughter
Nora Elizabeth, 1

Joseph—Sister-in-law
Mary, 1
Journalists
See also
Columnists
Court reporters
Editors
Foreign correspondents
Magazine reporters
Newspaper correspondents
Newspaper editors
Newspaper publishers
Newspaper reporters
Police reporters
Press agents
Radio commentators
Radio newscasters
Reporters
Sportswriters
Television commentators
Television newscasters
Television reporters
War correspondents
Washington correspondents
Abrams, Norma, fl. 1920s, 1
Adams, Mildred, fl. 1930s, 1
Alden, Cynthia May Westover, 1862–
1931, 1,2
Aldrich, Mildred, d. 1928, 1
Alexander, Shana Ager, 1925–, 2
Allison, Margaret, fl. 1940s, 2
Anderson, Katherine Watson, fl.
1930s, 1
Anspacher, Carolyn, d. 1979, 2
Applegate, Roberta, fl. 1950s, 2
Arne, Sigrid, 1
Austin, Kay, fl. 1930s, 1
Baer, Leone Cass, fl. 1930s, 1
Bailey, Margaret L., 1812–, 1
Ball, Isabel Worrell, 1855–, 1
Banks, Elizabeth L., 1870–1938, 1,2
Barclay, Dorothy, 1921–, 2
Barker, Ama, fl. 1922, 1
Barnes, Djuna, 1892–1982, 2
Bartimus, Tad, fl. 1970s, 2
Bartlett, Alice Elinor, 1848–1920, 1
Bartlett, Dorothy D., fl. 1920s, 1
Baskins, Ada, fl. 1970s, 2
Battelle, Phyllis, 1
Beale, Betty, 1912–, 1,2
Bean, Theodora, d. 1926, 1
Beatty, Bessie, 1886–1947, 1
Beck, Joan, fl. 1960s, 2
Becker, May Lamberton, 1873–1958,
1

Beckley, Zoe, fl. 1910s, 1,2
Bedell, Sally, 1948–, 2
Beloff, Leah Norah, fl. 1940s, 1,2
Benjamin, Anna, d. 1902, 2
Bentley, Helen Delich, 1923–, 2
Bergengren, Anna Farquhar, 1865–, 1
Bernard, Jacqueline, 1921–, 2
Bernheim, Nicole, fl. 1970s, 2
Best, Molly, fl. 1920s, 1
Bevans, Gladys Huntington, fl. 1930s, 1
Biggs, Caroline Ashurst, 1840–1889, 2
Birkhead, May, fl. 1927, 1
Bitker, Marjorie, 1901–, 2
Black, Winifred Sweet, 1863–1936, 1,2
Blackburn, Victoria Grace "Fan-Fan", d. 1928, 1
Blake, Doris, 1
Blanc, Marie Therese, 1840–1907, 1
Blanshard, Julia, d. 1934, 1
Bloor, Ella Reeve, 1862–1951, 2
Bly, Nellie, pseud., 1867–1892, 1,2
Boardman, Frances, fl. 1930s, 1
Boehringer, Cora Louise, fl. 1920s, 1
Boissevain, Inez Milholland, 1886–1916, 1,2
Bonney, (Mabel) Therese, 1894–1978, 1,2
Booker, Edna Lee, 1
Booth, Mary Louise, 1831–1889, 1,2
Bowles, Mrs. A. Lincoln, fl. 1900s, 1
Boyd, Mamie Alexander, 1876–1973, 2
Boyd, Pattie, fl. 1900s, 2
Brady, Mildred Edie, 1906–1965, 2
Brastow, Virginia, 1872–1952, 1
Briggs, Mary Blatchley, 1846–, 1
Brinkley, Nell, 1888–1944, 1
Bristow, Gwen, 1903–1980, 1,2
Brockman, Zoe Kincaid, 1893–, 1
Brody, Catharine, fl. 1920s, 1,2
Bromley, Dorothy Dunbar, 1896–, 1
Brophy, Brigid, 1929–, 2
Brown, Caro, fl. 1950s, 2
Brown, Nancy, 1869–1948, 1,2
Bryan, Mary Edwards, 1838–1913, 1,2
Bryant, Louise, m. 1923, 1
Bryant, Louise, 1890–1936, 2
Bugbee, Emma, 1888–1981, 1,2
Burgos, Julia De, 1914–1953, 2
Burke, Mildred, fl. 1930s, 1

Burr, Kate, fl. 1930s, 1
Burros, Marian, fl. 1970s, 2
Butcher, Fanny, 1888–, 1
Butts, Mrs., fl. 1880s, 1
Byers, Ruth, fl. 1910s, 1
Cameron, Kate, fl. 1930s, 1
Carpenter, Liz, 1920–, 2
Cartwright, Marguerite, fl. 1950s, 2
Cary, Mary Ann Shadd, 1823–1893, 1,2
Cass, Erna W., fl. 1930s, 1
Cather, Willa Sibert, 1873–1947, 1,2
Cattell, Hettie, fl. 1930s, 1
Cazneau, Jane Maria Eliza McManus Storms, 1807–1878, 2
Chandler, Dorothy Buffum, 1901–, 1,2
Chase, Mary Coyle, 1907–1981, 1,2
Chung, Connie, 1946–, 2
Churchill, Bonnie, 1937–, 1
Churchill, Caroline N., 1833–, 2
Churchill, Reba, 1934–, 1
Clemens, Mazie E., d. 1952, 1
Clements, Hall-Kane, fl. 1930s, 1
Coggins, Caroline, fl. 1930s, 1
Coit, Margaret Louise, 1919–, 1
Colby, Anita, 1914–, 1,2
Cole, Miriam M., fl. 1870s, 1
Collins, Gail, fl. 1970s, 2
Colvin, Mrs. A.S., 2
Coman, Martha, d. 1959, 1,2
Conn, Canary, 1949–, 2
Connor, Marcia, fl. 1930s, 1
Cooper, Jilly, 1937–, 2
Cotes, Sarah Jeannette, 1862–, 1
Couch, Hilda Juanita, fl. 1930s, 1
Cover, Juel Reed, 1
Cowan, Ruth Baldwin, 1
Cowden-Clarke, Mary Victoria, 1809–1898, 1,2
Cowles, Virgina Spencer, 1912–1983, 1,2
Craft, Mabel, fl. 1890s, 1
Craig, Elizabeth May Adams, 1888–1975, 1,2
Cramer, Harriet Laura Barker, 1848–1922, 1
Croly, Jane Cunningham, 1829–1901, 1,2
Crovo, Maria Elena Jimenez de, 1935–, 2
Curtis, Charlotte Murray, 1930–1987, 2
Dalrymple, Martha, fl. 1920s, 1

Harpman, Julia, fl. 1920s, 1,2
Harriman, Florence Jaffray Hurst, 1870–1967, 1,2
Harris, Julia, 1875–, 2
Harrison, Dorothy Ann, fl. 1930s, 1
Harrison, Marjorie, fl. 1920s, 1
Havener, Helen, fl. 1900s, 1
Haywood, Eliza Fowler, 1693–1756, 1,2
Hector, Annie French, 1825–1902, 1,2
Heini, Maija Liisa, fl. 1970s, 2
Heiskell, Marian, fl. 1970s, 2
Heloise, 1919–, 1
Hemingway, Mary Welsh, 1908–, 1,2
Henry, Alice, 1857–1943, 2
Herdman, Ramona, fl. 1920s, 1
Herrick, Genevieve Forbes, 1894–, 1,2
Hickock, Lorena A., 1893–1908, 1,2
Hill, Edith Knight, fl. 1920s, 1
Hind, (Ella) Cora, 1861–1942, 1,2
Hirst, Anne, fl. 1930s, 1
Hoey, Frances, 1830–1908, 2
Hooten, Elvira, fl. 1930s, 1
Hopkins, Jenny Lind, d. 1925, 1
Hornaday, Mary F., fl. 1920s, 1
Hostetter, Helen, fl. 1910s, 2
Hoult, Norah, 1898–, 1,2
Howar, Barbara, 1914–, 2
Howard, Lisa, 1930–1965, 2
Huber, Antje, 1924–, 2
Huck, Winnifred Sprague Mason, 1882–1936, 1,2
Hughes, Alice, fl. 1930s, 1
Hull, Peggy, fl. 1910s, 1,2
Hultin, Tekla, fl. 1890s, 2
Humphrey, Mary, fl. 1920s, 1
Hunt, Nancy, 1927–, 2
Huxtable, Ada Louise Landman, 1921–, 2
Irons, Evelyn, gr. 1921, 1
Irwin, Inez Lenore Haynes Gillmore, 1873–1970, 1,2
Jaburkova, Jozka Palaeckova, 1896–1942, 2
Jacobs, Leonebel, fl. 1930s, 1
Jacobson, Pauline, fl. 1920s, 1
James, Bessie, fl. 1910s, 1
James, Jean, fl. 1930s, 2
James, Winifred Lewellin, 1876–1941, 1
Jemison, Alice Mae Lee, 1901–1964, 2
Jewsbury, Geraldine Endsor, 1812–1880, 1,2

Johaneson, Bland, fl. 1930s, 1
Johnson, Nancy Cummings, 1818–1892, 1
Jones, Adelaide H., fl. 1950s, 2
Jones, Emily Beatrix Coursolles, 1893–, 1
Jones, Lee, fl. 1940s, 2
Jones, Ruth E., fl. 1930s, 1
Jordan, Elizabeth Garver, 1865–1947, 1,2
Joy, Sally, fl. 1870s, 1,2
Jurney, Dorothy, 1909–, 2
Katznelson, Rachel, fl. 1910s, 2
Kaufman, Beatrice Bakrow, fl. 1920s, 1
Keating, Isabelle, fl. 1930s, 1
Keating, Micheline, fl. 1920s, 1
Keen, Betty, fl. 1950s, 2
Kelley, Gertrude, 1882–1955, 1
Kellogg, Elenore, d. 1935, 1
Kelly, Elizabeth, fl. 1910s, 1
Kelly, Florence Finch, 1858–1939, 1,2
Kempton, Sally, 1943–, 2
Kenyon, Nellie, fl. 1950s, 2
Kerr, Adelaide, fl. 1930s, 1
Kerrigan, Louise Edie, fl. 1970s, 2
Kilgallen, Dorothy, 1913–1965, 1,2
Kimball, Alice Mary, fl. 1910s, 2
King, Elizabeth, 1889–1973, 2
King, Fay, fl. 1910s, 1
King, Mary, fl. 1920s, 1
Kirkland, Caroline Matilda Stansbury, 1801–1864, 1,2
Kirkpatrick, Helen Paull, 1909–, 1,2
Kohler, Ruth, d. 1953, 2
Krout, Mary Hannah, 1857–1927, 1
Kuhn, Irene Corbally, 1900–, 1,2
Kuusinen, Hertta (Elina), 1904–1974, 1,2
Landon, Letitia Elizabeth, 1802–1838, 1,2
Lane, Gertrude Battles, 1874–1941, 1,2
Lane, Margaret, 1907–, 1
Lane, Rose Wilder, 1867–1957, 1
Lantz, Emily Emerson, fl. 1900s, 1
Lapointe, Renaude, 1912–, 2
Lassen, Lulu, 1899–, 2
Lauferty, Lilian, 1887–1958, 1
Laut, Agnes Christina, 1871–1936, 1
Lawrence, Mary Viola Tingley, d. 1931, 1
Leatherbee, Mary, 2
Lee, Rosamund, fl. 1930s, 1

Leffler, Dorothy, fl. 1940s, 2
Leslie, Amy, 1855–1939, 1,2
Lewis, Lillian Alberta, 2
Lilly, Doris, 1926–, 1
Lindsay, Malvina, fl. 1930s, 1
Linton, Elizabeth Eliza Lynn, 1822–
1898, 1,2
Littledale, Clara Savage, 1891–1956,
1,2
Loeb, Sophie Irene Simon, 1876–
1929, 1,2
Logan, Jacqueline, 1901–, 1,2
Logan, Olive, 1839–1909, 1,2
Lombard, Helen Carusi, 1905–, 1
Long, Tania, 1913–, 1,2
Lowe, Corinne Martin, 1882–1952, 1
Lynahan, Gertrude, fl. 1920s, 1
MacDougall, Sally, fl. 1930s, 1
MacDowell, Anne Elizabeth, 1826–
1901, 1,2
Mahnkey, Mary Elizabeth, fl. 1930s,
1
Mahoney, Mary, fl. 1920s, 1
Mallon, Winifred, 1879–1954, 1
Malloy, (Marie) Louise, d. 1947, 1
Mandigo, Pauline Eggleston, 1892–
1956, 1
Mannes, Marya, 1904–, 1,2
Mannin, Ethel Edith, 1900–1978, 1,2
Manning, Olivia, 1914–, 2
Mansfield, Katherine, pseud., 1888–
1923, 1,2
Marble, Anna, fl. 1900s, 1
Marshall, Marguerite Moers, 1887–
1964, 1
Marshall, Paule, 1929–, 2
Martineau, Harriet, 1802–1876, 1,2
Martyn, Marguerite, fl. 1930s, 1
Marzolf, Marion, 2
Maule, Frances, fl. 1930s, 1
Mayo, Katherine, 1867–1940, 1,2
McBride, Mary Margaret, 1899–
1976, 1,2
McCarthy, Julia, fl. 1920s, 1
McCarthy, Mary Therese, 1912–, 1,2
McClendon, Sarah, 1913–, 1,2
McClung, Mary J., fl. 1930s, 1
McCormick, Anne Elizabeth O'Hare,
1881–1954, 1,2
McCormick, Elsie, 1894–1962, 1
McCrackin, Josphine, 1846–, 1
McCullar, Bernice Brown, 1905–
1975, 2
McDonald, Lucile Saunders, 1898–, 1

McDowell, Rachel Kollock, 1880–
1949, 1
McElliott, Martha, fl. 1930s, 1
McGrory, Mary, 1918–, 2
McKernan, Maureen, fl. 1920s, 1
McLaughlin, Kathleen, fl. 1920s, 1
McWilliams, Margaret, 1875–1952, 1
Means, Marianne Hansen, 1934–, 2
Mears, Marjorie, fl. 1920s, 1
Meherin, Elenore, fl. 1910s, 1
Mehle, Aileen, 1,2
Meloney, Marie Mattingly, 1878–
1943, 1,2
Meyer, Agnes Elizabeth Ernst, 1887–
1970, 1,2
Miller, Emily Clark Huntington,
1833–1913, 1,2
Miller, Hope Ridings, 190?–, 1
Miller, Sadie Kneller, d. 1920, 1
Mitchell, Milly Benett, fl. 1920s, 1
Montgomery, Ruth Shick, 1912–, 1
Moody, Helen Waterson, 1860–, 1
Moore, Sarah, fl. 1910s, 1
Morgan, Maria "Middy", 1828–1898,
1,2
Morris, Jan James, 1927–, 2
Morris, Mildred, fl. 1930s, 1
Mortimer, Penelope Ruth Fletcher,
1918–, 2
Mosby, Aline, fl. 1960s, 2
Mossell, Mrs. N. F., fl. 1890s, 2
Mowrer, Lilian Thomson, 1
Mozley, Anne, 1809–1891, 2
Mugglebee, Ruth, fl. 1930s, 1
Murray, Joan, fl. 1960s, 2
Mydans, Shelley Smith, 1915–, 1
Nicholson, Eliza Jane Poitevent Hol-
brook, 1849–1896, 1,2
Northcott, Kaye, fl. 1970s, 2
O'Hagan, Anne, fl. 1930s, 1
Ohl, Maud Andrews, 1862–, 1
Olds, Jessie Gouds, fl. 1930s, 1
Olson, Lynne, fl. 1970s, 2
Orem, Donna M., fl. 1970s, 2
Orr, Flora, fl. 1920s, 1
Ottenberg, Miriam, 2
Owen, Marjorie Lewis, 2
Packard, Eleanor, 1905–1972, 1,2
Paddleford, Clementine Haskin,
1900–1967, 1,2
Palmer, Gretta Brooker, 1905–1953, 1
Park, Ruth, 1920–, 1
Parkin, Molly, 1932–, 2
Parsons, Mary L., fl. 1910s, 1

Stanley, Imogene, fl. 1920s, 1
Stephens, Ann(a) Sophia Winterbo-
  tham, 1810–1886, 1,2
Stevens, Alzina Parsons, 1844–1900,
  1,2
Stevenson, Fay, 1895–, 1
Stockton, Louise, 1839–1914, 1
Stone, Verlinda Cotton Burdette
  Boughton, fl. 1650s, 1
Strong, Anna Louise, 1885–1970, 1,2
Strong, Betsy, fl. 1930s, 1
Susong, Edith O'Keefe, fl. 1910s, 2
Suttner, Bertha, Baroness von, 1843–
  1914, 1,2
Sweet, Ada Celeste, 1853–1928, 1
Swisshelm, Jane Grey Cannon, 1815–
  1884, 1,2
Switzer, Marguerite Birdelle, fl.
  1890s, 1
Tabouis, Genevieve R. Le Quesne,
  1892–, 1
Taft, Mary, fl. 1920s, 1
Talmey, Allene, 1902–, 1,2
Taney, Mary Florence, 1861–, 1
Tankersley, Ruth McCormick, 1
Tarbell, Ida Minerva, 1857–1944, 1,2
Taylor, Alva, fl. 1920s, 1
Teichner, Miriam, fl. 1910s, 1
Terrington, Lady, m. 1927, 1
Thackerey, Dorothy Schiff, 1903–, 1
Thomas, Clara Chaplin, fl. 1920s, 1
Thomas, Helen, 1920–, 2
Thompson, Dorothy, 1893–1961, 1,2
Tighe, Dixie, 1905–1946, 1
Timothy, Ann Donovan, 1727–1792,
  1,2
Tinee, Mae, fl. 1920s, 1
Titayana, fl. 1930s, 2
Tomara, Sonia, 1897–, 1,2
Torre, Marie, 1924–, 1,2
Treadwell, Sophie, 1890–1970, 1,2
Trivulzio, Cristina Belgiojoso, 1808–
  1871, 1
Troup, Augusta Lewis, 1848–1920, 2
Tuchman, Barbara Mayer Wertheim,
  1912–, 1,2
Tufty, Esther van Wagoner, 2
Turner, Frances, fl. 1930s, 1
Tweedie, Ethel Brilliana, d. 1940, 1
Underhill, Harriette, d. 1928, 1
Utley, Freda, 1898–1978, 1,2
Valesh, Eva McDonald, 1866–, 1
Van Doren, Irita Bradford, 1891–
  1966, 1,2

Van Horne, Harriet, 1920–, 1,2
Vanderbilt, Amy, 1908–1974, 1,2
Vedres, Nicole, fl. 1940s, 2
Vitary, Laura, fl. 1930s, 1
Von Kettler, Wanda, fl. 1930s, 1
Vorse, Mary Heaton Marvin, 1874–
  1966, 1,2
Vreeland, Diana Dalziel, 1903–, 1,2
Waite, Catherine van Valkenburg,
  1829–1913, 2
Wallace, Lila Bell Acheson, 1889–
  1984, 1,2
Walter, Cornelia Wells, 1913–1898, 2
Walters, Barbara, 1931–, 2
Wasilewska, Wanda, 1905–1964, 1
Wason, Betty, 1912–, 1,2
Waterhouse, Helen, fl. 1930s, 1
Watts, Mary, fl. 1920s, 1
Wayne, Pinky, fl. 1829s, 1
Weekes, Marie, fl. 1920s, 1
Weick, Louise, fl. 1930s, 1
Wells, Charlotte Fowler, 1814–1901,
  1,2
Wells-Barnett, Ida Bell, 1862–1931, 2
West, Mary Allen, fl. 1870s, 1
West, Rebecca, Dame, pseud., 1892–
  1983, 1,2
Wetmore, Elizabeth Bisland, 1863–, 1
Wheaton, Anne Williams, 1892–
  1977, 1,2
Whitcomb, Mildred E., gr. 1919, 1
White, Antonia, 1899–, 2
Whitehouse, Mary, 1910–, 2
Whiting, (Emily) Lilian, 1847–1942,
  1,2
Whitton, Charlotte Elizabeth, 1896–
  1975, 1,2
Wight, Estella, 1874–1955, 1
Wilcox, Ella Wheeler, 1850–1919, 1,2
Wilcox, Molly Warren, fl. 1930s, 1
Wille, Lois, 1931–, 2
Wilson, Bess M., fl. 1930s, 1
Wilson, Louisa, fl. 1920s, 1
Winn, Marcia, fl. 1930s, 1
Winslow, Thyra Samter, 1893–1961,
  1,2
Winter, Ella, 1898–1980, 1,2
Witherspoon, Naomi Long, gr. 1945,
  1
Wood, Minnie Lee, fl. 1840s, 1
Woodward, Emily, fl. 1920s, 1
Wooley, Edna K., fl. 1900s, 1
Worden, Helen, 1896–, 1
Young, Marguerite, fl. 1930s, 1

Young, Marian "Martha Deane", 1908–1973, 1,2
Zuckerkandl, Berta, 1863–1945, 2
Judges
See also
Supreme Court Justices
Adams, Annette Abbott, 1877–1956, 1,2
Allen, Florence Ellinwood, 1884–1966, 1,2
Amsterdam, Birdie, 1902–, 1
Arguas, Margarita, fl. 1920s, 2
Armstrong, Joan, 1942–, 2
Barron, Jennie Loitman, 1891–1969, 2
Bartelme, Mary Margaret, 1866–1954, 1,2
Bigler-Enggenberger, Margrit, fl. 1970s, 2
Bird, Rose Elizabeth, 1936–, 2
Bolin, Jane Matilda, 1908–, 1,2
Brill, Jeannette Goodman, 1888–1964, 1
Burns, Ellen B., 2
Chandy, Anna, 1905–, 1,2
Cline, Genevieve Rose, 1878–1959, 1,2
Coleman, Mary Stallings, 1914–, 2
Deborah, 1,2
Deiz, Mercedes F., 1917–, 2
Donlon, Mary Honor, 1894–1977, 1,2
Driscoll, Margaret Connors, 1915–, 2
Ginsburg, Ruth Bader, 1933–, 2
Green, Joyce H., fl. 1970s, 2
Harron, Marion Janet, 1903–, 1
Heilbron, Rose, fl. 1940s, 2
Hufstedler, Shirley Ann Mount, 1925–, 2
Hughes, Sara Tilghman, 1896–1985, 1,2
Jiagge, Annie, 1914–, 2
Kennedy, Cornelia, fl. 1970s, 2
Kenyon, Dorothy, 1888–1972, 1,2
Kessler, Gladys, fl. 1970s, 2
Kinnear, Helen Alice, 1894–, 1
Kroesen, J. H., fl. 1950s, 2
Kross, Anna Moskowitz, 1891–1979, 1,2
Lane, Elizabeth, Dame, fl. 1940s, 2
Lawson, Marjorie, 2
Lee Tai-Young, fl. 1950s, 2
Lopez, Natividad, 1914–, 2
Manning, Julia, fl. 1970s, 2

Marshall, Merna, fl. 1960s, 2
Matthews, Burnita Shelton, 1894–, 1
Mibuchi, Jochiko, fl. 1970s, 2
Miller, Blanche Funk, 1910–1920, 2
Motley, Constance Baker, 1921–, 1,2
Murphy, Charlotte P., fl. 1950s, 2
Murphy, Emily, 1868–1933, 1,2
Murray, Florence Kerins, 1916–, 2
Neethling, Leonora, 2
Nieland, Gerda Kuger, 2
Niemeyer, Gisela, fl. 1970s, 2
O'Connor, Sandra Day, 1930–, 2
Paderson, Inger, fl. 1970s, 2
Pedersen, Helga, fl. 1950s, 2
Phile of Priene, 200 B.C., 2
Polier, Justine Wise, 1903–, 2
Rabeno, Georgette, fl. 1960s, 2
Schaeffer, Margaret G., fl. 1970s, 2
Scott, Irene Feagin, fl. 1960s, 2
Sellers, Kathryn, 1870–1939, 1
Selmer, Ragnihild, fl. 1970s, 2
Sharp, Susie Marshall, 1907–, 2
Shi Liang, fl. 1950s, 2
Slaughter, Constance "Connie" Tona, fl. 1960s, 2
Stout, Juanita Kidd, 1919–, 1
Sumner, Jessie, 1909–, 1,2
Tucker, Bertha Fain, 1899–, 1
Weinshienk, Zita, 1933–, 2
Yekaterina, Irina, fl. 1950s, 2
Judo
Braziel, Maureen, fl. 1970s, 2
Pierce, Diane, fl. 1970s, 2
Julia Maesa—Daughter
Julia Soemias, fl. 200s, 1
Julia Mamaea—Mother
Julia Maesa, fl. 217, 1,2
Junior League
Harriman, Mary, fl. 1900s, 2
Henderson, Nathalie, d. 1934, 2
Londa, Jeweldean (Dean) Jones, fl. 1950s, 2
Rumsey, Mary Harriman, 1881–1934, 2
Junot, Andoche—Spouse
Junot, Laure Permon, 1784–1838, 1
Jury foreman
Graf, Louise Spinner, fl. 1950s, 2
Justices of the peace
Hobbs, Amelia, fl. 1870s, 1
Miller, Blanche Funk, 1910–1920, 2
Stevens, Mary E., fl. 1870s, 1

Juvenile court reform
Schoff, Hannah Kent, 1853–1940, 1,2

K

Kahn, Aga—Spouse
Khan, Begum Liaquat Ali, 1
Kamehameha II—Spouse
Kamanalu, Victoria, d. 1824, 1
Kamehameha IV—Consort
Emma, 1836–1885, 1,2
Kansas
Croucher, Lorena, fl. 1970s, 2
Keats, John—Friend
Brawne, Fanny, fl. 1800s, 2
Keller, Helen—Teacher
Sullivan, Anne, 1866–1936, 1,2
Kennedy, Jacqueline—Mother
Auchincloss, Janet Lee Bouvier,
1908–, 1
Kennedy, John F.—Mother
Kennedy, Rose Fitzgerald, 1890–
1995, 1,2
Kennedy, John F.—Spouse
Kennedy, Jacqueline Lee Bouvier,
1929–, 1
Onassis, Jacqueline Bouvier Kennedy,
1929–, 2
Kennedy, Joseph—Daughter
Smith, Jean Kennedy, 1928–, 1
Kennedy, Robert—Mother
Kennedy, Rose Fitzgerald, 1890–
1995, 1,2
Kennedy, Robert—Spouse
Kennedy, Ethel Skakel, 1928–, 1,2
Kent, Elihu—Spouse
Kent, Sibbil Dwight, 1744–1822, 1
Kentucky
Bendl, Gerta, 2
Bryant, Ruth Flowers, 1917–, 2
Clement, Emma Clarissa Williams,
1874–1952, 1,2
Egbert, Ercell Jan, 1895–, 2
Foster, Edith, 1914–, 2
Hite, Mabel Bradbury, 1909–, 2
Jackson, Abbie Clement, fl. 1940s, 2
Kirksey, Lucile Hicks, 1904–, 2
Morgan, Hannah, fl. 1970s, 2
Richardson, Sarah, fl. 1700s, 1
Smith, Beulah Morgan, fl. 1930s, 2
Stovall, Thelma, 1919–, 2

Khan, Husain—Spouse
Petral, fl. 1400s, 1
Khruschev, Nikita—Spouse
Khruschev, Nina Petrovna, 1900–, 1
Kilmer, Joyce—Spouse
Kilmer, Aline, 1888–1941, 1
Kindergarten teachers
Blaker, Eliza Ann Cooper, 1854–
1926, 2
Blow, Susan Elizabeth, 1843–1916, 2
Bryan, Anna E., 1858–1901, 2
Cooper, Sarah Brown Ingersoll,
1835–1896, 2
Frankenburg, Caroline Louisa, 2
Harrison, Elizabeth, 1849–1927, 2
Hill, Mildred J., 1859–1916, 1,2
Hill, Patty Smith, 1868–1946, 1,2
Kraus-Boelte, Maria, 1836–1918, 2
Laws, Annie, 1855–1927, 2
Marenholtz-Bulow, Bertha von, d.
1893, 2
Marwedel, Emma Jacobina Christi-
ana, 1818–1893, 2
Peabody, Elizabeth Palmer, 1804–
1894, 1,2
Putnam, Alice Harvey Whiting,
1841–1919, 2
Ramabai, Sarasvati Pandita, 1858–
1922, 1,2
Ronge, Bertha, 2
Ronge, Johan, fl. 1890s, 2
Rydelius, Edit V., 1903–, 2
Schurz, Margarethe Meyer, 1832–
1876, 1,2
Shaw, Mrs. Quincy A., fl. 1870s, 1
Temple, Alice, 1871–1946, 2
Wheelock, Lucy, 1857–1946, 2
Wiggin, Kate Douglas Smith, 1856–
1923, 1,2
King, Alan—Spouse
King, Jeanette, 1930–, 2
King, James—Mother
King, Anne, 2
King, Martin Luther, Jr.—Mother
King, Alberta Christine "Mamma"
Williams, 1904–1974, 2
"King of Bourges"—Mother-in-law
Aragon, Yolande of, 2
Kingsley, Charles—Daughter
Harrison, Mary St. Leger, 1
Kipling, Rudyard—Spouse
Kipling, Caroline Starr Balestier,
1865–1939, 1

Knox, Henry—Spouse
Knox, Mrs., fl. 1789s, 2
Knox, John—Follower
Locke, Anne, 2
Knox, John—Spouse
Bowes, Marjory, 2
Koussevitzky, Serge—Spouse
Koussevitzky, Olga Naumoff, 1881–1942, 1
Krupp, Friedrich Alfred—Spouse
Krupp von Bohien und Halbach, Bertha, 1886–1957, 2
Kumeyaay Indians
Cuero, Delfina, 2
Kung, H. H.—Spouse
Kung, Eling Soong Hsiang-Hsi, fl. 1900s, 1

L

LaFollette, Robert M.—Spouse
LaFollette, Belle Case, 1859–1931, 1,2
Labor economists
Dickason, Gladys Marie, 1903–1971, 2
Tanner, Lucretia Dewey, fl. 1960s, 2
Wolfson, Theresa, 1897–1972, 2
Labor educators
Coit, Eleanor G., 1894–1976, 2
McLaren, Louise Leonard, 1885–1968, 2
Labor historians
Woodbury, Helen Laura Sumner, 1876–1933, 2
Labor leaders
Abramowitz, Bessie, 1888–, 2
Agrebi, Saida, 1945–, 2
Anderson, Mary, 1872–1964, 1,2
Anderson, Mary Reid MacArthur, 1880–1921, 1,2
Bagley, Sarah G., 1806–, 1,2
Bambace, Angela, 1898–1975, 2
Barker, Mary Cornelia, 1879–1963, 2
Barnum, Gertrude, 1866–1948, 2
Barry, Leonora Marie Kearney, 1849–1930, 2
Behrens, Edna, fl. 1940s, 2
Bellanca, Dorothy Jacobs, 1894–1946, 2
Bengtsson, Anny, 1918–, 2
Berry, Suzanne, 2
Bloor, Ella Reeve, 1862–1951, 2

Bondfield, Margaret Grace, 1873–1953, 1,2
Borchardt, Selma Munter, 1895–1968, 2
Braut, Bessy, fl. 1910s, 2
Caldwell, Shirley, 2
Cari, Teresa, fl. 1890s, 2
Carlsson, Britt, fl. 1960s, 2
Carr, Shirley, 2
Castle, Barbara Ann Betts, 1911–, 1,2
Christensen, Ethyn, 2
Christman, Elizabeth, 1891–1975, 1,2
Chupak, Lydia, fl. 1970s, 2
Cohn, Fannia Mary, 1885–1962, 2
Collins, Jennie C., 1828–1887, 1,2
Conboy, Sara Agnes McLaughlin, 1870–1928, 2
Cronin, Margaret, 2
Curry, Diane Sutherland, 1939–, 2
Dailey, Thelma, fl. 1950s, 2
Davis, Caroline Dawson, 1
Dickason, Gladys Marie, 1903–1971, 2
Dubrow, Evelyn, fl. 1970s, 2
Dunham, Dana, 2
Ellickson, Katherine Pollak, fl. 1930s, 2
Fabbri, Tecla, 2
Figueroa, Ana, 1907–1970, 1,2
Flynn, Elizabeth Gurley, 1830–1964, 1,2
Fuchs, Anke, fl. 1970s, 2
Gee, Virginia, fl. 1970s, 2
Glenn, Elinor Marshall, 1915–, 2
Goodin, Joan M., 1934–, 2
Haener, Dorothy, 1917–, 2
Hager, Francie "Granny", fl. 1970s, 2
Haley, Margaret Angela, 1861–1939, 2
Haman, Kato, 1884–1936, 2
Henry, Alice, 1857–1943, 2
Herman, Alexis M., 1947–, 2
Herrick, Elinore Morehouse, 1895–1964, 1,2
Hillman, Bessie Abramowitz, 1889–1970, 2
Hillman, Ponsie Barclay, fl. 1960s, 2
Hoffman, Anna Marie Rosenberg Lederer, 1902–1983, 2
Holleran, Susan Ellen, 1941–, 2
Holm, Birte Roll, 1941–, 2
Honeycutt, Pamela, fl. 1970s, 2
Horenson, Belle, 2
Hulett, Josephine, fl. 1970s, 2

Johnson, Gloria T., fl. 1950s, 2
Jones, Mary Harris (Mother Jones), 1830–1930, 1,2
Kalinina, Antonina, fl. 1970s, 2
Keegan, Esther, fl. 1860s, 2
Koltoi, Anna, 1891–1944, 1,2
Kornbluh, Joyce, fl. 1940s, 2
Kovnator, Rachel, fl. 1910s, 2
Kristensen, Ruth, fl. 1970s, 2
Laguiller, Ariette, 1940–, 2
Lazurkina, Dora, 2
Leijon, Anna-Greta, 2
Leininger, Burldene, fl. 1930s, 2
Lonergan, Anna, fl. 1930s, 1
Lopes, Maria, fl. 1890s, 2
Loughlin, Anne, 1894–, 1
Madar, Olga M., fl. 1940s, 2
Magee, Elizabeth Stewart, 1889–, 1
Maimunkova, Anna Krusteva, 1879–1925, 2
Maloney, Elizabeth, 1910–1920, 2
Marot, Helen, 1865–1940, 1,2
Martin, Marion E., 1900–, 2
Masaryk, Charlotte Garrigue, 1850–1923, 1
Mason, Lucy Randolph, 1882–1959, 2
Maupin, Joyce, 1914–, 2
McCaughan, Cynthia, 1928–, 2
McConnell, Beatrice, 1894–, 2
McCreery, Marie Maud Leonard, 1883–1938, 2
Mee, Cassis Ward, 1848–, 1
Miller, Jean, fl. 1970s, 2
Miller, Joyce D., 1928–, 2
Morio, Winifred (Peggy), fl. 1970s, 2
Moriyama, Mayumi, 1927–, 2
Mullaney, Kate, fl. 1860s, 2
Murphy, Betty Southard, 1929–, 2
Nelson, Anne H., 1925–, 2
Newman, Pauline M., 1891–, 1,2
Newman, Sarah H., 1907–, 2
Nikolayeva, Claudia, 1893–, 2
Nikolova, Iordanka Georgieva, 1911–1944, 2
Norwood, Elizabeth C., fl. 1950s, 2
Nowicki, Stella, fl. 1970s, 2
Nussbaum, Karen, 1950–, 2
O'Reilly, Leonora, 1870–1927, 2
O'Sullivan, Mary Kenney, 1864–1943, 2
Parent, Madeleine, 1918–, 2
Parker, Julia Sarsfield O'Connor, 1890–1972, 2
Pesotta, Rose, 1896–1965, 2

Popp, Adelheid, 1869–1939, 2
Preli, Sorine A., 2
Rachlin, Marjorie B., fl. 1950s, 2
Rayl, Hannah Jo, fl. 1970s, 2
Reed, Carolyn Coulter, 1939–, 2
Reilly, Jeanne Lennox, 1942–, 2
Riesel, Yetta, fl. 1970s, 2
Robb, Isabel Adams Hampton, 1860–1910, 1,2
Robbins, Margaret Dreier, fl. 1900s, 1,2
Roberts, Lillian, 1929–, 2
Robinson, Dollie Lowther, fl. 1950s, 2
Roche, Josephine Aspinwall, 1886–1976, 1,2
Rodgers, Elizabeth Flynn, 1847–1939, 2
Rodionova, Aleandra, fl. 1910s, 2
Rosenberg, Anna Marie, 1902–, 1
Sabia, Laura, fl. 1970s, 2
Sain, Dorothy M., fl. 1970s, 2
Samoilova, Natasha (Concurdia), 1876–, 2
Sarabhai, Anusuya(ben), 1885–, 1,2
Schneiderman, Rose, 1882–1972, 1,2
Schwartz, Sydnee M., 1941–, 2
Sellins, Fannie Mooney, 1872–1919, 2
Sender, Toni, 1888–, 1
Simchak, Morag McLeod, 1914–, 2
Smith, Mary Mattie, fl. 1970s, 2
Spindler, Pearl G., fl. 1940s, 2
Stallknecht, Kirsten, 1937–, 2
Stellman, Jeanne M., fl. 1970s, 2
Stern, Marjorie Hefter, fl. 1970s, 2
Stevens, Alzina Parsons, 1844–1900, 1,2
Swartz, Maud(e) O'Farrell, 1879–1937, 2
Taka, Toyoko, 1925–, 2
Takahashi, Hisako, 1927–, 2
Troisgros, Simone, 1904–, 2
Troup, Augusta Lewis, 1848–1920, 2
Turner, Doris, 2
Van Kleeck, Mary Abby, 1893–1972, 1,2
Wade, Betsy, 1929–, 2
Wanngard, Hanna, 1892–, 2
Weber, Enid W., fl. 1970s, 2
Wilkinson, Ellen Cicely, 1891–1947, 1,2
Wolfgang, Myra Komaroff, 1914–1976, 2
Wyatt, Addie L., 1924–, 2

Bosone, Reva Beck, 1895–, 1,2
Boves, Josefina, 1
Bozzidini, Bettisia, fl. 1239s, 2
Bradwell, Myra Colby, 1831–1894, 1,2
Braman, Ella Frances, 1850–, 1
Brochester, Ruth, fl. 1930s, 1
Brown, Rowine Hayes, 2
Brown, Virginia Mae, 1923–, 2
Burlingame, Lettie L., gr. 1886, 1
Butler, Sally, 1891–, 1
Calderini, Novella, fl. 1349, 2
Carpenter, Mrs. Philip, fl. 1900s, 1
Carter, Eunice Hunton, 1899–1970, 2
Cary, Mary Ann Shadd, 1823–1893, 1,2
Chauvin, Mademoiselle, fl. 1880s, 1
Chayes, Antonia Handler, 1929–, 2
Clark, Mary Chase, fl. 1920s, 1
Cline, Genevieve Rose, 1878–1959, 1,2
Coe, Emma Robinson, fl. 1850s, 1
Comb, Helen, fl. 1870s, 1
Couzins, Phoebe Wilson, 1839–1913, 1,2
Crampe, Michiko Ito, 1947–, 2
Daniel, Alice, 2
Davis, Frances, fl. 1970s, 2
Davis, Minerva M., fl. 1930s, 1
Davis, Nancy L., fl. 1960s, 2
De Sasallow, Olga Nunez, fl. 1950s, 2
Densen-Gerber, Judianne, 1934–, 2
Dilhan, Jeanne Chauvin, 1862–1926, 2
Douglas, Judith Hyams S., 2
Eastman, Hope, fl. 1970s, 2
Edelman, Marian Wright, 1939–, 2
Farenthold, Frances (Sissy), 1926–, 2
Fasteau, Brenda Sue Feigen, 2
Feingold, Pauline, fl. 1970s, 2
Field, Pauline O., fl. 1930s, 1
Foltz, Clara Shortridge, 1849–4934, 2
Forbes, Carol, 1913–, 2
Foster, Judith Ellen Horton, 1840–1910, 1,2
Frooks, Dorothy, fl. 1930s, 1
Gates, Margaret, 2
Gaudron, Mary, 1943–, 2
Gevers, Marie, 2
Gillett, Emma Millinda, 1852–1927, 2
Ginossar, Rosa, 1890–, 2
Glantzberg, Pinckney L., fl. 1920s, 1
Goodell, (Rhoda) Lavinia, fl. 1870s, 1,2

Goodman, Emily Jane, 1940–, 2
Gordon, Laura de Force, 1838–1904, 1,2
Gozzadini, Betisia (Bettisia), d. 1249, 1,2
Greene, Mary Anne, fl. 1890s, 1
Griffiths, Martha Wright, 1912–, 1,2
Gupta, Ruth Church, fl. 1950s, 2
Haddock, Emma, fl. 1870s, 1
Hall, Lydia S., fl. 1870s, 1
Hamburger, Bessie Snow, 1880–1952, 1
Hames, Marjie Pitts, fl. 1960s, 2
Harris, Patricia Roberts, 1924–1985, 1,2
Hart, Janet, fl. 1970s, 2
Hauser, Rita, 1934–, 2
Heilbron, Rose, fl. 1940s, 2
Helmer, Bessie Bradwell, 1858–1927, 1,2
Hennock, Frieda Barkin, 1904–1960, 1,2
Hermann, Mildred R., 1891–, 2
Hernandez, Aileen Clarke, 1926–, 2
Herrick, Mary Elizabeth, fl. 1870s, 1
Hicks, Louise Day, 1919–, 2
Hobby, Oveta Culp, 1905–, 1,2
Hoffman, Anna Marie Rosenberg Lederer, 1902–1983, 2
Holton, Tabitha, d. 1886, 2
Holtzmann, Fanny, fl. 1920s, 1
Hopkins, Julia B., 1
Hubbard, Emma, fl. 1870s, 1
Hughes, Sara Tilghman, 1896–1985, 1,2
Hulett, Alta M., 1854–1877, 1
Humphrey, Helen Florence, 1909–1963, 1
Isnard, Margueritte, 2
James, Mona, fl. 1930s, 2
Jones, Mary Gardiner, 1921–, 2
Jordan, Barbara (Charline), 1936–, 2
Kamm, Linda Heller, fl. 1970s, 2
Karmel, Roberta S., 1937–, 2
Karpatkin, Rhoda Hendrick, 1930–, 2
Kay, Herma Hill, 1934–, 2
Kempin, Emile, fl. 1880s, 1
Kemprin-Spyri, Emilie, 1853–1901, 2
Kennedy, Florynce, 1916–, 2
Kenyon, Dorothy, 1888–1972, 1,2
Kepley, Ada H., gr. 1870, 1
Kessler, Gladys, fl. 1970s, 2
Kilgore, Carrie Burnham, 1836–1909, 1,2

King, Carol Weiss, 1895–1952, 1,2
Knowles, Ella, 1870–, 1,2
Knowles, Marjorie Fine, fl. 1960s, 2
Krupsak, Mary Ann(e), 1932–, 2
LaFontant, Jewel Stradford, fl. 1970s, 2
Lamarsh, Judy, 1924–1980, 1,2
Lamy, Paule, 2
Lathen, Emma, pseud., 1929–, 2
Lathrop, Mary Florence, 1865–1951, 1
Laughlin, Gail, 1868–1952, 2
Law, Sylvia, fl. 1970s, 2
Lawton, Mary Cecilia, fl. 1960s, 2
LeBlanc, Nancy E., 2
Lee, Dorothy McCullough, 1901–, 1
Lee Tai-Young, fl. 1950s, 2
Lewinson, Ruth, fl. 1920s, 1
Lippner, Sally Nemerover, fl. 1930s, 1
Lipschitz, Sylvia Steinberg, fl. 1930s, 1
Lockwood, Belva Ann Bennett Mc-
  Nall, 1830–1917, 1,2
Luff, Ellen, 2
Magoon, Mary E., fl. 1860s, 1
Mankin, Helen Douglas, 1894–1956, 1,2
Manoochehrian, Mehran-Guiz, 2
Manoppo, Ani, fl. 1940s, 2
Mansfield, Arabella Babb "Belle",
  1846–1911, 1,2
Marlatt, Frances Knoche, fl. 1930s, 1
Marshall, Merna, fl. 1960s, 2
Martinez, Vilma S., 1943–, 2
McCullough, Catharine Gouger
  Waugh, 1862–1945, 2
McDannel, Lucy C., fl. 1930s, 1
McKenna, Margaret, fl. 1970s, 2
McLean, Sheila Avrin, 2
McNall, Mrs. B. A., fl. 1860s, 1
Mentschikoff, Soia, 1915–, 2
Mihopoulou, Maria, fl. 1970s, 2
Miller, Mary E., 1864–, 1
Mink, Patsy Takemoto, 1927–, 1,2
Mirenburg, Mary, fl. 1930s, 1
Mulliner, Gabrielle, fl. 1920s, 1
Murphy, Betty Southard, 1929–, 2
Murphy, Charlotte P., fl. 1950s, 2
Murray, Pauli, 1910–, 2
Murrell, Ethel Ernest, 1909–, 1
Mushkat, Marion, fl. 1940s, 2
Mussey, Ellen Spencer, 1850–1936, 1,2
Nash, Clara Holmes Hapgood,
  1839–, 1

Normanton, Helena, 1883–1957, 2
Norton, Eleanor Holmes, 1937–, 2
O'Crowley, Irene Rutherford, fl. 1930s, 1
O'Hair, Madalyn Murray, 1919–, 2
Olivarez, Graciela, fl. 1970s, 2
Olmsted, Sophia Amson, fl. 1930s, 1
Owens, Elisabeth, fl. 1940s, 2
Palmer, Hazel, 1903–, 1
Parker, Alice, 1864–, 1
Paul, Alice, 1885–1977, 1,2
Peters, Ellen Ash, fl. 1960s, 2
Phillips, Lena Madesin, 1881–1955, 1,2
Phillips, Velvalea, 1925–, 1
Picker, Jane Moody, 1930–1970, 2
Pier, Kate Hamilton, 1845–1925, 1,2
Pilpel, Harriet Fleischl, 2
Plummer, Edna Covert, fl. 1910s, 1
Popelin, Marie, 1846–1913, 2
Preiskel, Barbara Scott, 2
Rabb, Harriet, fl. 1960s, 2
Raggio, Louise Ballerstedt, fl. 1970s, 2
Ranson, Ruth, fl. 1910s, 1
Rashed, Samia Sadeek, fl. 1970s, 2
Rateb, Aisha, fl. 1970s, 2
Ray, Charlotte E., 1850–1911, 1,2
Rembaugh, Bertha, 1876–1950, 1
Renson, Marcelle, fl. 1920s, 2
Richards, Suzanne, fl. 1970s, 2
Ricker, Marilla Marks Young, 1840–
  1920, 1,2
Roberts, Sylvia, fl. 1960s, 2
Robinson-Sawtelle, Lelia, d. 1891, 1
Rock, Lillian, fl. 1920s, 1
Roebling, Emily Warren, 1843–1903, 1
Rosenberg, Anna Marie, 1902–, 1
Rosenberg, Sheli, 2
Rothenberg, Rose, fl. 1930s, 1
Rothenberg, Sheribel, fl. 1970s, 2
Ryssdal, Signe, 2
Sampson, Edith Spurlock, 1901–
  1979, 1,2
Santaella, Irma, fl. 1960s, 2
Sarraute, Nathalie, 1900–, 1,2
Sawyer, Ada Lewis, d. 1911, 2
Scheuer, Laura, 2
Schmitt, Edwienne, fl. 1930s, 1
Schreiber-Favre, Nelly, fl. 1900s, 2
Schwartz, Bertha, fl. 1930s, 1
Schwartz, Helene, fl. 1970s, 2
Scott, Irene Feagin, fl. 1960s, 2

Couzzins, Adaline, fl. 1860s, 1
Cunningham, Kate Richards O'Hare, 1877–1948, 1,2
Curie, Eve, 1904–, 1,2
Cutler, Hannah Maria Conant Tracy, 1815–1896, 1,2
Davis, Mary Fenn, 1824–1886, 2
De Forest, Jane O., fl. 1880s, 1
De Kroyft, Susan Helen Aldrich, 1818–1915, 1
De Voe, Emma Smith, 2
Dean, Vera Micheles, 1903–1972, 1,2
Delaney, Adelaide Margaret, 1875–, 1
Dowd, Mary Hickey, 1866–, 1
Drummond, Sarah Prescott, fl. 1670s, 1,2
Eastman, Mary F., fl. 1880s, 1
Emrick, Jeanette Wallace, 1878–, 1
Fair, Ethel Marion, 1884–, 1
Flanner, Janet, 1892–1978, 1,2
Flintham, Lydia Stirling, fl. 1780s, 1
Follett, Mary Parker, 1868–1933, 2
Forbes, (Joan) Rosita, 1893–, 1
Foster, Abigail Kelley, 1810–1887, 1,2
French, Anna Densmore, fl. 1870s, 1
Fryberger, Agnes Moore, 1868–, 1
Gage, Matilda Joslyn, 1826–1898, 1,2
Gardner, Anna, fl. 1770s, 1
Gasaway, Alice Elizabeth, fl. 1930s, 1
Gerson-Kiwi, Edith, 1
Goessmann, Helena Theresa, fl. 1890s, 1
Gordon, Laura de Force, 1838–1904, 1,2
Gozzadini, Betisia (Bettisia), d. 1249, 1,2
Graves, Mary H., fl. 1870s, 1
Greenwalt, Mary Elizabeth Hallock, 1871–1950, 1
Grove, Mary, fl. 1830s, 1
Gruenberg, Sidonie Matsner, 1881–1974, 1,2
Hall, Addye Yeargain, fl. 1940s, 1
Hall, Ruth Julia, fl. 1920s, 1
Harbert, Lizzie Boynton, m. 1870, 1
Hardin, Pablita Velarde, 1918–, 2
Hardy, Kay, 1902–, 1
Harman, Elizabeth, gr. 1930, 1
Harper, Frances Ellen Watkins, 1825–1911, 1,2
Hartin, Deborah, 1933–, 2
Hasdew, Julia, 1869–1888, 1
Hastings, Caroline E., fl. 1870s, 1

Housman, Rosalie Louise, 1888–1949, 1
Howey, Ella Mae, fl. 1950s, 1
Huss, Hildegarde Hoffman, fl. 1940s, 1
Jenkins, Helen P., fl. 1880s, 1
Jenkins, Lydia A., fl. 1850s, 1
Johnston, Frances Benjamin, 1864–1952, 1,2
Johnstone, Margaret Blair, 1913–, 1
Jones, Jane Elizabeth Hitchcock, 1813–1896, 1,2
Kelley, Marion Booth, fl. 1930s, 1
Kilmer, Aline, 1888–1941, 1
Kingsbury, Elizabeth A., fl. 1880s, 1
Kinkead, Elizabeth Shelby, fl. 1900s, 1
Kohut, Rebekah Bettelheim, 1864–1951, 1,2
Lawrence, Jeanette, fl. 1930s, 1
Lease, Mary Elizabeth Clyens, 1850–1933, 1,2
Logan, Olive, 1839–1909, 1,2
Loud, Hulda Barker, 1844–, 1
Lozier, Jennie de la, m. 1872, 1
Lund, Charlotte, 1870–1951, 1
Lyman, Mrs. Walter C., fl. 1880s, 1
Mandola, Carol M., fl. 1930s, 1
Mann, Erika, 1905–1969, 1,2
Marble, Annie Russell, 1864–, 1
Marryat, Florence, 1838–1899, 1,2
Marshall, Paule, 1929–, 2
McCabe, Lida Rose, 1895–1938, 1
McClurg, Virginia Donaghe, fl. 1920s, 1
Mears, Helen, 1900–, 1
Mee, Cassis Ward, 1848–, 1
Meeker, Rose, 2
Miller, Anna Jenness, 1884–, 1
Miller, Harriet Mann, 1831–1918, 1,2
Miller, Nellie Burget, 1875–, 1
Misch, Mrs. Ceasar, fl. 1910s, 1
Moir, Phyllis, fl. 1930s, 1
Monroe, Anne Shannon, 1877–1942, 1
Mowrer, Lilian Thomson, 1
Murdoch, Jean Iris, 1919–, 1,2
O'Mahoney, Katherine A., fl. 1910s, 1
Oberdorfer, Anne Faulkner, fl. 1940s, 1
Orth, Jane Davis, fl. 1920s, 1
Palencia, Isabel de, 1881–, 1
Pattee, Alida Francis, d. 1942, 1

Bradshaw, Lillian Moore, 1915–, 2
Brode, Mildred Hooker, 1900–, 1
Brown, Alberta Louise, 1894–, 1
Brown, Zaidee Mabel, 1875–1950, 1
Browne, Nina Eliza, 1860–, 1
Burke, Mildred, fl. 1930s, 1
Burnham, Mary, 1881–, 1
Carr, Deborah Edith Wallbridge, 1854–, 1
Cheney, Frances Neel, 1906–, 1
Colcord, Mabel, 1872–, 1
Coleman, Ann, 1872–, 2
Coleridge, Sara(h) Henry, 1802–1852, 1,2
Colwell, Eileen Hilda, 1904–, 1
Coolbrith, Ina Donna, 1841–1928, 2
Countryman, Gratia Alta, 1866–1953, 1
Crawford, Phyllis, 1899–, 1
Culver, Essae Martha, 1
Dickerson, Una Reilly, 1881–, 2
Doren, Electra Collins, 1861–1927, 1,2
Doyle, Agnes Catherine, fl. 1900s, 1
Dunham, (Bertha) Mabel, 1881–, 1
Eastman, Linda Anne, 1867–1963, 1,2
Eastman, Mary Huse, 1879–1963, 1
Elmendorf, Theresa Hubbell West, 1855–1932, 1
Estes, Eleanor Ruth Rosenfeld, 1906–, 1,2
Evans, Orrena Louise, fl. 1910s, 1
Fair, Ethel Marion, 1884–, 1
Fairchild, (Mary) Salome Cutler, 1855–1921, 1,2
Farnell, Vera, gr. 1914, 1
Fay, Lucy Ella, 1875–1963, 1
Flexner, Jennie Maas, 1882–1944, 1,2
Freeman, Marilla Waite, 1
Fuller, Margaret Hartwell, 1904–, 1
Furbeck, Mary Elizabeth, fl. 1920s, 1
Fyan, Loleta Dawson, 1894–, 1
Gaver, Mary Virginia, 1906–, 1
Giffin, Etta Josselyn, 1863–1932, 1
Graham, Aubry Lee, fl. 1930s, 1
Gray, Elizabeth Janet, 1902–, 1,2
Greene, Belle da Costa, 1883–1950, 2
Gscheidle, Gertrude E., 1905–, 1
Guerrier, Edith, 1870–, 1
Gunterman, Bertha Lisette, fl. 1910s, 1
Haines, Helen Elizabeth, 1872–1961, 1,2
Haskell, Parola, fl. 1870s, 1

Hazeltine, Mary Emogene, 1868–1949, 1,2
Hewins, Caroline Maria, 1846–1926, 1,2
Holmes, Jeanne M., 1922–, 2
Ireland, Norma Olin, 1907–, 1,2
Irwin, Helen, fl. 1950s, 1
Isom, Mary Frances, 1865–1920, 1,2
James, Hannah Packard, 1835–1903, 1
Jamison, Evelyn Mary, gr. 1901, 1
Jenkins, Essie Cynthia, fl. 1960s, 2
Jewett, Alice L., fl. 1920s, 1
Jones, Clara Araminta Stanton, 1913–, 2
Jones, Virginia Lacy, 1914–, 1
Keck, Lucile Liebermann, 1898–, 1
Kelly, Patsy, fl. 1930s, 1
Kinder, Katharine Louise, 1912–, 1
King, Patricia Miller, fl. 1970s, 2
Klahre, Ethel Susan, 1905–, 1
Kroeger, Alice Bertha, 1864–1909, 1,2
Kucera, Zdenka, 1916–, 2
Lacy, Mary Goodwin, 1875–1962, 1
Laich, Katherine (Wilhelmina Schlegel), 1910–, 2
Larsen, Nella, 1893–1964, 2
Lee, Mollie Huston, 1907–, 2
Lindem, Selma Marie, fl. 1930s, 1
Lodge, Eleanor Constance, 1869–1936, 1
Loeber, L. Elsa, fl. 1930s, 1
Logasa, Hannah, 1879–, 1
Lord, Isabel Ely, fl. 1930s, 1
Lowrie, Jean Elizabeth, 1918–, 2
Ludington, Flora Belle, 1898–, 1
MacGregor, Ellen, 1906–, 1
MacKaye, Julia Josphine Gunther, fl. 1890s, 1
Macrum, Adeline, fl. 1930s, 1
Major, Kathleen, gr. 1928, 1
Manley, Marian C., 1892–, 1
Martin, Allie Beth, 1914–1976, 2
Massee, May, 1881–1966, 2
Meixell, Louise Granville, fl. 1930s, 1
Miller, Anna, 2
Miner, Dorothy Eugenia, 1904–1973, 2
Morsch, Lucile M., 1906–1972, 1,2
Morton, Elizabeth Homer, 1903–, 1
Morton, Florrinell Frances, 1904–, 1
Mowat, Angus, 1892–, 1
Mudge, Isador(e) Gilbert, 1875–1957, 2

M

Maids of honor
  Blagg, Henrietta Maria, m. 1675, 1
  Bloomfield, Georgiana, Lady, 1822–1905, 1
  Clayton, Charlotte Dyve, d. 1742, 1
  Cowper, Mary Claverling, Lady, 1685–1723, 1
  Farrington, Mary, fl. 1730s, 1
  Fitton, Mary, fl. 1600s, 1
  Hawes, Frances Ann, 1713–1788, 1
  Hervey, Mary Lepell, 1700–1768, 1
  Hobart, Miss, fl. 1600s, 1
  Howe, Sophia, d. 1726, 1
  Hyde, Catherine, d. 1777, 1
  Jeffreys, Henrietta Louisa, Countess of, d. 1761, 1
  Killigrew (Killegrew), Anne, 1660–1685, 1,2
  Lepell, Mary, 1700–1768, 1
  Lightfoot, Hannah, 1730–, 1
  Meadows, Margaret, fl. 1720s, 1
  Montespan, Francoise Athenaise Rochechouart, 1641–1707, 1,2
  Parry, Blanche, d. 1589, 1
  Price, Goditha, fl. 1600s, 1
  Thynne, Frances, d. 1754, 1
Mail order executives
  Keene, Betty, fl. 1940s, 2
Maine
  Brann, Martha Cobb, 1882–1961, 2
  Chase, Carrie Matilda Murray, 1876–, 2
  Eckstorm, Fannie Pearson Hardy, 1865–1946, 2
  Emerson, Mary Moody, 1774–1863, 1,2
  Gilley, Hannah Lurvey, fl. 1820s, 2
  Goon, Toy Len Chin, 1,2
  Jacataqua, fl. 1770s, 2
  Jones, Sybil, 1808–1877, 1,2
  Laughlin, Gail, 1868–1952, 2
  Richards, Laura Elizabeth Howe Ward, 1850–1943, 1,2
  Washburn, Patty Benjamin, 1792–, 2
  Whittier, Hannah Clough, fl. 1770s, 2
  Wood, Sally Sayward Bearall Keating, 1759–1854, 2
Maksoutoff, Dimitrii Petr—Spouse
  Maksoutoff, Mariia, fl. 1860s, 2
Malcolm, King—Spouse
  Margaret (1), 1048–1093, 1,2
Malcolm—Daughter
  Mary of Atholl, 1085–, 1
Male impersonators
  See
    Passing women

Management consultants
  See
    Business consultants
Managers
  Mannion, Madeleine Gosman, fl. 1930s, 1
  Showalter, Edna Blanche, fl. 1940s, 1
Mannequin maker
  Roostein, Adel, fl. 1970s, 2
Manoah—Spouse
  Manoah's wife, 1
Mansfield, Mike—Spouse
  Mansfield, Maureen, 2
Manufacturers
  Baird, Jacqueline Davis, 1931–, 2
  Bishop, Hazel Gladys, 1906–, 1,2
  Boit, Elizabeth Eaton, 1849–1932, 2
  Boucher, Constance, 2
  Brumell, Stella, 2
  Crathorne, Mary, fl. 1760s, 1
  Davis, Hannah, d. 1863, 1,2
  Donnelly, Nell Quinlan, 1889–, 2
  Franklin, Elizabeth, fl. 1750s, 1
  Gazley, Martha, fl. 1730s, 1
  Hall, Joyce Clyde, 1891–, 2
  Jackson, Mary, fl. 1740s, 1,2
  Kitchin, Hannah Chapman, m. 1751, 1
  Metcalf, Betsey, fl. 1790s, 2
  Mitchell, Gillian, 2
  Nutt, Anna Rutter Savage, 1686–1760, 1
  Pollock, Elsie Frankfurt, 2
  Rosenthal, Ida Cohen, 1889–1973, 2
Mao Tse-Tung—Spouse
  Chiang Ching, 1913–, 2
Marathon runners
  Switzer, Katherine V., 1946–, 2
  Ullyot, Joan, 2
Marcos, Ferdinand—Spouse
  Marcos, Imelda Romualdez, 1931–, 1,2
Marguerite—Daughter
  Albret, Jeanne d', 1528–1572, 1,2
Marimba players
  Stubbs, Ruth, 2
Marine Corps officers
  Bane, Mary E., 2
  Barton, Ivy, 2
  Brewer, Margaret A., 2
  Daly, Lillian O'Malley, fl. 1940s, 2
  Ferguson, Martrese Thek, fl. 1940s, 2
  Hamblet, Julia E., 1916–, 1,2
  Lenz, Anne A., fl. 1940s, 2

Marx brothers—Mother
  Marx, Minnie Schoenberg, 1860–
  1929, 2
Marx, Karl—Daughter
  Marx-Aveling, Eleanor, fl. 1880s, 1,2
Marx, Karl—Mother
  Marx, Henrietta Pressburg, d. 1863, 2
Marx, Karl—Spouse
  Marx, Jenny von Westphalen, 1814–
  1881, 1,2
Marxists
  Laguiller, Ariette, 1940–, 2
Mary (Biblical)—Mother
  Anne, 1
Mary (Biblical)—Sister
  Martha, 1,2
Mary Knoll Sister of St. Dominic
  Rogers, Mary Joseph, Mother, 1882–
  1955, 2
Mary had a little lamb
  Sawyer, Mary, 2
Mary, Queen—Mother
  Teck, Mary Adelaide, Duchess of,
  1833–, 1
Maryland
  Boone, Maggie Augusta, 1867–, 2
  Brent, Margaret, 1600–1671, 1,2
  Carroll, Molly (Mary) Darnall, 1747–
  1782, 1,2
  Graham, Mary Ann, 2
  Lamb, Anne Cecilia, 1865–1948, 2
  Lincoln, Nancy Hanks, 1783–1818,
  1,2
  Nicholson, Rebecca Lloyd, fl. 1860s,
  2
  Norman, Julie Bowie, 1889–, 2
  Nuthead, Dinah, 1695, 1,2
  Revelle, Carrie Caroline Milligan,
  1880–1965, 2
  Trott, Edna Ruby Louise, 1920–, 2
Masons
  Leger, Elizabeth Saint, 1693–, 1
Massachusetts
  Adams, Abigail Smith, 1744–1818,
  1,2
  Barron, Jennie Loitman, 1891–1969, 2
  Dwight, Minnie Ryan, 1873–1957, 2
  Jasper, Teresa (Tessie), 1893–, 2
  Kennedy, Rose Fitzgerald, 1890–
  1995, 1,2
  Livermore, Mary Ashton Rice, 1820–
  1905, 1,2
  Mitchell, Lucy Miller, fl. 1900s, 2
  Noble, Elaine, 1944–, 2

Shih, Hsio-Yen, 1934–, 2
Shih, Nellie Y. Y., 1903–, 2
Stoneman, Abigail, 1760–1777, 2
Zulalian, Rose Donabedian, 1895–
  1972, 2
Matadors
  See
  Bullfighters
Mathematicians
  See also
  Statisticians
  Agnes, Maria Gaetana, 1718–1799, 1
  Agnesi, Maria Gaetana, 1718–1799,
  1,2
  Bailar, Barbara A., 2
  Borromeo, Clelia Grillo, fl. 1700s, 1
  Breteuil, Emilie de, Marquise du Cha-
  telet, 1706–1749, 2
  Butler, Margaret, 2
  Chatelet, Gabrielle Emilie le Tonnel-
  eve, 1706–1749, 1,2
  Christina of Hesse, 1578–1658, 2
  Davis, Ruth M., 2
  Devi, Shakuntala, 2
  Fischer, Charlotte F., 2
  Flugge-Lotz, Irmgard, 1903–1974, 2
  Geiringer, Hilda, 1893–1973, 1,2
  Germain, Sophie, 1776–1841, 1,2
  Herschel, Caroline Lucretia, 1750–
  1848, 1,2
  Hickock, Hannah Hadassah, fl.
  1840s, 2
  Hopper, Grace Murray, 1906–, 2
  Hypatia, 370–415, 1,2
  Katsurada, Yoshi, fl. 1950s, 2
  Keldysh, Lyudmila Vseyolodovna,
  1904–, 2
  Keller, Evelyn Fox, 1936–, 2
  Kovalevski, Sonya, 1850–1891, 1,2
  Lelong-Ferrand, Jacqueline, fl.
  1930s, 2
  Lepaute, Nicole R., 1723–1788, 1
  Luchins, Edith H., 2
  Maria di Novella, fl. 1200s, 2
  Matthews, Alva T., fl. 1970s, 2
  Meitner, Lise, 1878–1968, 1,2
  Neumann, Hanna, d. 1971, 2
  Noether, Emmy (Amalie), 1882–
  1935, 2
  Novella, Maria di, fl. 1200s, 2
  Pastori, Maria, fl. 1950s, 2
  Rees, Mina S., 1902–, 1,2
  Sartre, Marquese de, 2
  Scott, Charlotte Angas, 1858–1931,
  1,2

Mineralogists
  Beausoleil, Martine, Baroness De, 1602–1640, 1
  Homer, Ella, fl. 1870s, 1
Mining industry
  Braeunlich, Sophia, 1860–, 1
  Cashman, Nellie, 1851–1925, 2
  Franklin, Cora, fl. 1890s, 2
  Martin, Martha, pseud., fl. 1970s, 2
  McCourt, Augusta, 1834–1935, 2
  McCourt, Baby Doe, 1854–1935, 2
  Messenger-Harris, Beverly, fl. 1970s, 2
  Messer, Daisy, fl. 1970s, 2
  Miller, Jean, fl. 1970s, 2
  O'Bryan, Mollie, 2
  Ricket, Mrs. Townsend, 2
  Smith, Betty Messer, fl. 1970s, 2
  Tabor, Augusta Pierce, 1833–1895, 1,2
  Tabor, Elizabeth Honduel McCourt, 1854–1935, 1,2
  Wimmer, Elizabeth Jane, fl. 1840s, 2
Mink ranchers
  Wustenburg, Phyllis, fl. 1970s, 2
Minnesota
  Devney, Verona Stubbs, 1916–, 2
  Fuller, Phebe Sutherland, 1860–1917, 2
  Hetteen, Mor Johnson "Betty", 1861–, 2
  Parson, Lillian Bendeka, 1896–, 2
  Stageberg, Susie W., 1877–1961, 2
  Tibbetts, Irene Lyons, 1883–1973, 2
  Van Cleve, Charlotte Clark, 1819–1907, 2
  Whipple, Cornelia Wright, 1816–1890, 2
  Wolff, Mabel Olson, 1895–, 2
  Wood, Julia Amanda Sargent, 1825–1903, 2
Missionaries
  Alumbaugh, Goldie P., 1920–1950, 1
  Atherton, Eva Havens, fl. 1920s, 1
  Austin, Ann, d. 1665, 1,2
  Austin, Belinda, fl. 1879, 2
  Aylward, Gladys, 1903–1970, 1,2
  Baker, Lelia Barber, fl. 1930s, 1
  Baldwin, Mary Briscoe, 1811–1877, 1
  Barger, Myrtle King, fl. 1910s, 1
  Barron, Marjorie Wilson, m. 1952, 1
  Bateman, Georgia, fl. 1920s, 1
  Bateman, Martha, fl. 1930s, 1
  Bedell, Harriet, fl. 1910s, 2

  Bennett, Belle Harris, 1852–1922, 2
  Bennett, Mary Katharine Jones, 1864–1950, 2
  Benton, Loanza Goulding, fl. 1860s, 1,2
  Berkeley, Sister Xavier, 1861–1944, 1
  Berry, Martia L. Davis, 1844–, 1
  Bingham, Jemima, m. 1769, 1
  Bizalion, Anne Catherine, 2
  Blackburn, Katherine, fl. 1900s, 1
  Bompas, Charlotte Selina Cox, 1830–1917, 1
  Bowers, Gladys Irene, m. 1944, 1
  Boyer, Beatrice Alexander, m. 1919, 1
  Brady, Elizabeth Patton, fl. 1880s, 2
  Bridgman, Eliza Jane Gillet, 1805–1871, 2
  Brinton, Mary Williams, fl. 1940s, 1
  Burton, Emma, 1844–1927, 1
  Butler, Mrs. William, fl. 1850s, 1
  Byerlee, Victoria Ann, fl. 1920s, 1
  Cameron, Donaldina Mackenzie, 1869–1968, 2
  Cardwell, Sue Webb, fl. 1940s, 1
  Carvajal, Luisa de, 1568–1614, 1
  Case, Alice Montague, 1870–, 1
  Catchings, Rose, 1925–, 2
  Chatfield, Ena Lyle Brown, m. 1932, 1
  Chevers, Sarah, fl. 1650s, 1
  Clarke, Virginia, fl. 1920s, 1
  Clement, Annie W., fl. 1850s, 1
  Cloud, Elizabeth Roe, fl. 1950s, 1,2
  Coates, Ruth Keezel, fl. 1940s, 1
  Cobble, Alice Dunning, fl. 1930s, 1
  Coillard, Christina, 1829–1891, 1
  Coleman, Alice Blanchard Merriam, 1858–1936, 1,2
  Comstock, Sarah Davis, fl. 1830s, 1
  Coombs, Lucinda, gr. 1873, 1
  Coppin, Fanny Marion Jackson, 1837–1913, 1,2
  Cort, Mabel Gibson, fl. 1915, 1
  Crosse, Mary Fisher Bayley, 1624–1690, 1
  Culbertson, Belle Caldwell, 1857–, 1
  Cuppy, Vera Grace Negley, fl. 1940s, 1
  Dade, Barbara Bates, m. 1941, 1
  Damon, Mary Happer, 1858–, 2
  Danser, Fanny Root, fl. 1930s, 1
  Davis, Jane Totah, fl. 1940s, 1,2
  Davis, Julia Margaret Hubman, m. 1948, 1

Davis, Newell Trimble, fl. 1920s, 1
Day, Emma V., 1853–1894, 1
Declan, Mother, 1
Denton, Mary Florence, 1857–1947, 2
Devore, Ella, 1849–1920, 1
Dewhirst, Susan Lucretia, 1876–, 1
Dix, Ruth, 2
Dodson, Wilma Joy Livingston, m. 1950, 1
Doremus, Sarah Platt Haines, 1802–1877, 1,2
Douglas, Alice May, 1865–, 1
Drexel, Mary Katharine, Mother, 1858–1955, 1,2
Duchesne, Rose Philippine, 1769–1852, 1,2
Dwight, Elizabeth Baker, 1808–, 1
Dye, Mrs. Royal J., d. 1951, 1
Eccles, Mrs. George E., fl. 1920s, 1
Edwards, Edna Eck, fl. 1900s, 1
Edwards, Ruth Hamilton, fl. 1940s, 1
Eldred, Edith Lillia Byers, d. 1912, 1
Eliot, Ann(e) Mountfort, d. 1687, 2
Evans, Katherine, fl. 1650s, 1
Everett, Seraphina Haynes, d. 1856, 2
Ewing, Ella Campbell, fl. 1900s, 1
Faris, Bessie Homan, m. 1901, 1
Farrar, Cynthia, 1795–1862, 2
Fay, Lydia Mary, fl. 1850s, 1
Feller, Henrietta, 1800–1868, 1
Fisher, Mary, 1623–1698, 1,2
Fisher, Welthy Blakesley Honsinger, 1879–1980, 1,2
Fiske, Fidelia, 1816–1864, 1,2
Frame, Alice Seymour Browne, 1878–1941, 2
Frost, Helen, 2
Frymire, Josephine, fl. 1910s, 1
Fulton, Mary Hannah, 1854–1927, 2
Goodrich, Frances Louisa, 1856–1944, 1,2
Gulick, Alice Winfield Gordon, 2
Haines, Sarah Platt, 1842–, 1
Hall, Rosetta Sherwood, 1865–1951, 2
Hall, Susan Webb, 1850–1922, 2
Harris, Ula Moulton, m. 1946, 1
Havens, Mary Sue McDonald, fl. 1920s, 1
Hayden, Mary Bridget, Mother, 1814–1890, 2
Haygood, Laura Askew, 1845–1900, 2
Heck, Barbara Ruckle, 1737–1804, 1,2

Hedges, Lillie Bowyer, fl. 1910s, 1
Heimer, Ruth Loretta Duggins, m. 1948, 1
Henderson, Allison Jamison, m. 1939, 1
Hensey, Alice Ferrin, d. 1950, 1
Hill, Frances Maria Mulligan, 1799–1884, 1,2
Hixon, Evalyn Willard, fl. 1930s, 1
Hobgood, Tabitha Aldersen, m. 1916, 1
Holder, Myrtle Avery, fl. 1910s, 1
Holt, Maggie Winifred Mair, m. 1927, 1
Horner, Marjorie Crittenden, m. 1938, 1
Horton, Constance Smith, fl. 1930s, 1
Houston, Jessie W., 1900–, 2
Howard, Meta, fl. 1880s, 2
Huntley, Amelia Elmore, 1844–, 1
Hurt, Ambra Halsey, m. 1916, 1
Ingalls, Murilla Baker, m. 1850, 1
Jaggard, Annella, d. 1918, 1
Jaggard, Wilhelmina Zoe Smith, fl. 1910s, 1
James, Annie P., 1825–, 1
Johnson, Ava Dale Plummer, m. 1949, 1
Johnson, Eva Marie, fl. 1940s, 1
Johnston, Lillian Proefrock, d. 1946, 1
Jones, Mrs., fl. 1820s, 1
Jones, Sybil, 1808–1877, 1,2
Jones, Wanda, 2
Joseph Calasanctius, 1860–1946, 1
Judd, Laura Fish, 1804–, 2
Judson, Ann Hasseltine, 1789–1826, 1,2
Judson, Emily Chubbuck, 1817–1854, 1,2
Judson, Sarah Hall Boardman, 1803–1845, 1,2
Keister, Lillie Resler, 1851–, 1
Kellogg, Fanny, fl. 1870s, 2
Kirkland, Jerusha Bingham, m. 1769, 1
Kollock, Florence E., 1848–, 1
Kreamer, Mary Elizabeth, fl. 1960s, 2
Kugler, Anna Sarah, 1856–1930, 1,2
Layton, Jessie Trunkey, d. 1934, 1
Lea, Mrs. Frank T., m. 1896, 1
Learned, Grace Utter, fl. 1920s, 1
Leavitt, Mary Greenleaf Clement, 1830–1912, 2

Lewis, Lillian Callis, fl. 1940s, 1
Livingstone, Mary Moffat, 1820–1862, 1
Lyth, Mrs. R. B., d. 1890, 1
Mackenzie, Jean Kenyon, 1874–1936, 2
Macomber, Eleanor, 1801–1840, 1
Maria Alvarez, Mother, fl. 1900s, 1
Maria Gratia, Mother, fl. 1920s, 1
Marie Suzanne, fl. 1900s, 1
Marietta, 1
Marshman, Hannah, 1767–1847, 1
McBeth, Susan Law, 1830–1893, 2
McCracken, Faith A., fl. 1920s, 1
McCune, Vesta Marie, d. 1938, 1
McFarland, Amanda, 1837–1898, 1,2
McMillan, Hazel Fern, fl. 1940s, 1
McMillan, Lucile Short, m. 1946, 1
Meeker, Eleanor Richardson, fl. 1830s, 1
Mendoza, Luisa de Carvajal y, 1568–1614, 2
Miller, Susan Lincoln Tolman, 1825–1912, 2
Mills, Susan Lincoln Tolman, 1821–1912, 1,2
Miner, Sarah Luella, 1861–1935, 2
Mitchell, Hattie Poley, fl. 1920s, 1
Mitchell, Rebecca Brown, 1834–1908, 1
Moffat, Mary Smith, 1795–1871, 1
Moon, Bessie Huntington, fl. 1900s, 1
Moon, Lottie Digges, 1840–1912, 1,2
Mosher, Edith Apperson, fl. 1910s, 1
Mossell, Mary Ella, 1853–1886, 1
Murray, Marjorie, fl. 1960s, 2
Musgrave, Ruth, fl. 1910s, 1
Newell, Harriet Atwood, 1793–1812, 1,2
Newman, Angelia Louise French Thurston Kilgore, 1837–1910, 1,2
Noah, Myrtle Whaley, fl. 1920s, 1
Okama, Mrs. Kyoko, fl. 1930s, 1
Olford, Bessie Santmire, 1893–, 2
Ost, Ruth Elin, 1886–1953, 2
Page, Fannie Pender, 1870–1942, 1
Paget, Della Mae Dale, fl. 1940s, 1
Parmalee, Ruth A., fl. 1920s, 1
Patrick, Mary Mills, 1850–1940, 1,2
Paul, Tillie, fl. 1950s, 2
Paula, Mother, fl. 1910s, 1
Peabody, Lucy Whitehead McGill Waterbury, 1861–1949, 2
Pearson, Evelyn Utter, fl. 1910s, 1

Perreton, Francoise, fl. 1840s, 1
Picton-Turbervill, Edith, 1872–1960, 1
Pitt, Rosa Parks, 1873–1959, 1
Poole, Edna, fl. 1930s, 1
Prosser, Anna Weed, 1866–, 1
Quinn, Edel, 1907–1944, 1
Ramabai, Sarasvati Pandita, 1858–1922, 1,2
Rankin, Melinda, 1811–1888, 1
Reed, Mary, 1854–1943, 1,2
Riggs, Mary, 1818–1852, 1
Roberts, Jewell Elizabeth Owen, m. 1934, 1
Robertson, Anne Eliza Worchester, 1820–1905, 2
Rogers, Emma Winner, fl. 1910s, 1
Rosalita, Sister, fl. 1940s, 1
Ross, Mabel Hughes, m. 1929, 1
Ross, Myrta Pearson, m. 1917, 1
Rowe, Lucretia Olin, 1896–, 1
Russell, Lois Hasselvander, m. 1920, 1
Scudder, Ida Sophia, 1870–1960, 1,2
Seymour, Agnes Rogers, fl. 1940s, 1
Shaw, Margaret Elizabeth, fl. 1940s, 1
Shoemaker, Gertrude Mae, fl. 1920s, 1
Shuck, Henrietta, 1817–1844, 1
Slessor, Mary, 1848–1915, 1,2
Smith, Amanda Berry, 1837–1915, 1,2
Smith, Elizabeth Baker, fl. 1920s, 1
Smith, Helen, 1840–1891, 1
Smith, Lulu Gestis, fl. 1910s, 1
Smith, Mary "Sis" Hopkins, fl. 1900s, 1
Smith, Myrtle Lee, fl. 1820s, 1
Smith, Sarah L. Huntington, 1802–, 1
Snipes, Esther Wacknitz, fl. 1920s, 1
Spalding, Eliza Hart, 1807–1851, 1,2
Stam, Elizabeth, 1906–, 1
Stober, Buena Rose, fl. 1920s, 1
Stoddard, Harriet B., d. 1848, 1
Stone, Anna, d. 1905, 1
Talcott, Eliza, 1836–1911, 2
Thoburn, Isabella, 1840–1901, 1,2
Thurston, Lucy G., 1795–1876, 1
Thurston, Matilda Smyrell Calder, 1875–1958, 2
Tillery, Merle Gulley, fl. 1940s, 1
Underwood, Lillias Stirling Horton, 1851–1921, 1,2
Van Lennep, Mary Elizabeth, 1821–, 1

Hiroko, fl. 1960s, 2
Hunt, Marsha (Marcia Virginia), 1917–, 2
Hutton, Lauren, 1943–, 2
Jones, Candy, 1925–, 1
Joyce, Brenda, 1916–, 2
Keeler, Christine, 1942–, 2
Kelly, Nancy, 1921–, 1,2
Koopman, Toto, fl. 1930s, 2
Leigh, Dorian, 1919–, 1,2
Levine, Beth, fl. 1940s, 2
Lucky, 2
Luna, Donyvale, 1925–1979, 2
MacGraw, Ali, 1939–, 2
Miller, Lee, 1920–1930, 2
Mitchell, Sharon, 2
Muthe, Madame, 2
Newton, Zoe, fl. 1950s, 2
Nilsson, Anna Q., 1888–1974, 2
Paolozzi, Christina, 1939–, 1
Parker, Suzy, 1933–, 1,2
Peretti, Elsa, 1940–, 2
Phryne, 400 BC, 1,2
Pickford, Kaylan, 2
Prue, Edwina, 2
Ramsey, Caroline, 2
Reno, Terry, fl. 1970s, 2
Robinson, Edna Mae Holly, 1
Russell, Jane (Ernestine Jane Geraldine), 1921–, 1,2
Sebastian, Dorothy, 1903–1957, 2
Shepherd, Cybill, 1950–, 2
Shields, Brooke, 1965–, 2
Shrimpton, Jean Rosemary, 1942–, 2
Simpson, Sloan, 1917–, 2
Slick, Grace Wing, 1939–, 2
Smith, Jaclyn, 1947–, 2
Stone, Pauline, fl. 1950s, 2
Sumurun, fl. 1920s, 2
Sundstrom, Anne-Marie, fl. 1960s, 1
Tashman, Lilyan, 1899–1934, 2
Taylor, (Ida) Estelle, 1899–1958, 1,2
Thom, Mrs. Douglas, m. 1919, 1
Tidmarsh, Christine, 2
Tiegs, Cheryl, 1947–, 2
Twiggy (Leslie Hornby), 1949–, 1,2
Valadon, Suzanne, 1865–1940, 2
Verushka, 1943–, 2
Victoire, fl. 1950s, 2
Weaver, Marjorie, 1913–, 2
Welch, Barbara, fl. 1940s, 1
Worth, Marie, 2
Wyman, Jane, 1914–, 1,2
Modoc Indians
Winema, 1836–1920, 2

Mohammad—Spouse
Khadija, 556–619, 1
Mohammed's harem
Zaynab, fl. 1500s, 2
Mohammed—Daughter
Fatima, 606–663, 1,2
Molecular biologists
Haschemeyer, Audrey, 1936–, 2
Jacox, Marilyn E., fl. 1970s, 2
Long, Sharon, 1951–, 2
Moliere—Spouse
Bejart, Armande Gresinde Claire Elizabeth, 1642–1700, 1,2
Molina, Trujillo—Mother
Trujillo, Angelita, 1939–, 1
Monasteries
Arethusa of Antioch, fl. 300s, 2
Mondale, Walter—Spouse
Mondale, Joan Adams, 1930–, 2
Monologists
Cooke, Marjorie Benton, 1876–1920, 1
Draper, Ruth, 1884–1956, 1,2
Harris, Arlene, 1898–, 1
Skinner, Cornelia Otis, 1901–1979, 1,2
Monroe, James—Daughter
Gouverneur, Maria Hester Monroe, 1802–1850, 1
Hay, Eliza Monroe, 1787–, 1
Monroe, Maria Hester, m. 1820, 1
Monroe, James—Mother
Monroe, Eliza Jones, 1747–, 1,2
Monroe, James—Spouse
Monroe, Elizabeth Kortright, 1768–1830, 2
Monroe, Marilyn—Mother
Hogan, Gladys, 2
Montagu, John—Mistress
Ray, Martha, 1779–, 1
Montague, David—Spouse
Cadwalader, Frances, Lady Erskine, 1781–1843, 2
Montana
Alderson, Nannie Tiffany, 1860–1946, 1,2
Dahl, Anna Boe, 1892–, 2
Davey, Mary Rogers, 1877–, 2
Fearnall, Ida W., 1877–1947, 2
Harman, Belle Carter, fl. 1920s, 2
Huntley, Blanche Tatham, 1893–, 2
Kaiser, Edna Fay, 1872–1962, 2
Nevins, Tish, fl. 1890s, 2
Rankin, Olive Pickering, 1854–, 2

Sacajawea, 1786–1812, 1,2
Turpin, Ella Wheeler, 1876–, 2
Valiton, Mary Rae, 1863–1946, 2
Montresor, John—Spouse
  Montresor, Frances Tucker, fl. 1770s, 2
Moralists
  Gethin, Grace Norton, 1676–1697, 1
  Martineau, Harriet, 1802–1876, 1,2
Moravian leaders
  Nitschmann, Anna, fl. 1740s, 2
More, Sir Thomas—Daughter
  Roper, Margaret More, 1505–1544, 1,2
Mormon leaders
  Anderson, Audentia Smith, 1872–, 1
  Cannon, Martha (Mattie) Hughes, 2
  Corey, Melissa, 2
  Cutler, Virginia, 1905–, 2
  Gates, Susa Young, 1856–1933, 1,2
  Hammond, Mary Dilworth, fl. 1860s, 2
  Kimball, Ellen Saunders, 2
  Lyman, Amy Brown, 1872–1959, 1,2
  Mott, Eliza Ann Middaugh, fl. 1880s, 2
  Shipp, Ellis Reynolds, 1847–1933, 2
  Smith, Emma Hale, 1804–1879, 1,2
  Snow, Eliza Roxey, 1804–1887, 1,2
  Spafford, Belle Smith, 1895–1982, 2
  Stenhouse, Fanny, 2
  Young, Harriet Page Wheeler Decker, fl. 1840s, 2
Moses—Mother
  Jochebed, 1,2
Moses—Sister
  Miriam, 1
Mostel, Zero—Spouse
  Mostel, Kate (Katherine) Cecilia Harkin, 2
Mother Goose
  Vergoose, Elizabeth Foster, 1648–1752, 2
Mother of 69 children
  Scheinberg, Mrs. Bernard, 1854–1911, 2
Mother of Methodism
  Heck, Barbara Ruckle, 1737–1804, 1,2
  Wesley, Susanna Annesley, 1669–1742, 1,2
Mother of Thanksgiving
  Hale, Sarah Josepha Buell, 1788–1879, 1,2

Mother of an inventor
  Marcel, Madame, 1830–1875, 1
Mother of famous sons
  Duncan, Anne, fl. 1800, 2
  Marshall, Mary Randolph Keith, 1737–1809, 2
Mother of seven martyrs
  Hannah, 1
Mother's Day
  Jarvis, Anna M., 1864–1948, 2
Mothers
  Chapman, Marion, fl. 1930s, 2
  Rosenkowitz, Sue, 2
  Vassilet, Mrs. Fyodor, 1816–1872, 2
Mothers of prominent men
  Adams, Susanna Boylston, 1709–1797, 1,2
  Adela, d. 735, 1
  Agrippina, The Younger, 15–59, 1,2
  Andersen, Anne Marie, 1767–1834, 1,2
  Anderson, Mabel, 1886–, 2
  Anthusa, 307–407, 1
  Aquitain, Elenor d', 1122–1204, 1
  Armstrong, Mary Ann, fl. 1800s, 2
  Arnold, Hannah, 2
  Arouet, Marie Marguerite Damard, 2
  Arsinoe, 200–300BC, 1
  Arthur, Malvina Stone, 1802–1869, 1,2
  Ashworth, Mrs., fl. 1860s, 1
  Aurela, d. 54 BC, 1
  Autriche, Anne D', 1601–1666, 1
  Bach, Elisabeth Laemmerhirt, 1644–1694, 2
  Balfour, Margaret Isabella, fl. 1800s, 1
  Baline, Leah, 2
  Ballou, Eliza–, 1
  Banu, Valide, Nur, Sultana, d. 1583, 2
  Barrie, Margaret Ogilvy, d. 1895, 1
  Bateman, Virginia, 1853–1940, 2
  Bathsheba, 1040–1015, 1,2
  Beecher, Roxanna Foote, d. 1816, 1
  Beethoven, Maria Magdelena van, 1746–1787, 2
  Bell, Eliza Grace Symonds, 1809–1897, 2
  Belshazzar's mother, 1
  Bernardone, Sister Pica, fl. 1200s, 1
  Bolivar, Maria Concepcion Placios y Vianco, 1759–1792, 2
  Bonaparte, Maria Letizia Ramolino, 1750–1836, 1,2
  Booth, Mary Ann Holmes, 2

Sanderson, Elizabeth, 1825–1925, 1
Servilia, fl. 80sBC, 1
Shakespeare, Mary Arden, 1538–
1608, 1,2
Shaw, Bessie Gurley, 2
Silva, fl. 540s, 1
Smith, Maude E., 2
Snell, Sarah, fl. 1780s, 1
Sobieski, Maria Clementina, d. 1735,
1
Sophia Charlotte, 1668–1705, 1
Sophia of Mechlenburg, 2
Spock, Mildred Stoughton, 1876–
1968, 2
Sterne, Agnes, d. 1759, 2
Stevenson, Margaret Isabella Balfour,
1829–1897, 1
Stolberg Wernigerode, Juliana van,
1506–1580, 1
Stuart, Mary Horton, 1842–1925, 1
Symonds, Rebekah, fl. 1660s, 2
Taft, Louisa Maria Torrey, 1828–
1907, 1,2
Tamar, 1
Taylor, Sarah Strother, 1760–1822,
1,2
Textor, Katherine Elizabeth, fl.
1720s, 1
Thaw, Mrs. William, 2
Theoctista, 740–801, 1
Theodota, fl. 900s, 1
Thompson, Hannah, 2
Tiy, 1400 BC, 1
Tolstoy, Marya Nikolayevna Volkon-
skaya, d. 1830, 2
Tracy, Carrie Brown, d. 1942, 2
Trebuchet, Sophie, 1778–1821, 1
Trujillo, Angelita, 1939–, 1
Truman, Martha Ellen Young, 1852–
1947, 2
Tyler, Mary Armistead, 1761–1797,
1,2
Van Buren, Maria Hoes Van Alen,
1747–1818, 1,2
Van Gogh, Anna Cornelia Carbentus,
1819–, 2
Van Rijn, Neeltjen Willemdochter van
Suydtbrouck,1750–1640, 2
Vasseur, Marie le, 1674–1767, 2
Veturia, fl.400sBC, 1
Wallace, Susan Binney, fl. 1810s, 1
Washington, Mary Ball, 1707–1789,
1,2
Washington, Mrs., fl. 1840s, 1

Wellesley, Anne Hill, Lady Morning-
ton, 1743–, 2
Wells, Faith McCain, d. 1961, 2
Wesley, Susanna Annesley, 1669–
1742, 1,2
Whistler, Anna Matilda McNeill,
1804–1881, 1,2
White, Mary Ann Hatten, 1830–
1924, 2
Wiedemann, Sarah Anna, fl. 1810s, 1
Wilde, Jane Francesca Elgee, 1824–
1896, 1,2
Willard, Mary Thompson Hill,
1805–, 1
Wilson, Janet Woodrow, fl. 1840s, 1
Wilson, Jessie Woodrow, 1826–1888,
1,2
Winslow, Phebe Horrox, 1760–, 1
Wright, Susan Catherine, 1831–1889,
1,2
Yoelson, Naomi Cantor, d. 1895, 2

Mothers of prominent women
Aemilia, Tertia, 169–200BC, 1,2
Agrippina I, The Elder, 13BC–
33AD, 1,2
Alcott, Abigail (Abba) May, 1800–
1877, 1,2
Anne, 1
Austen, Cassandra, 1729–1827, 2
Ball, Widow Johnson (Mrs. Joseph),
fl. 1700s, 1
Bronte, Maria Branwell, 1783–1821, 2
Cady, Margaret Livingston, 2
Chase, Carrie Matilda Murray,
1876–, 2
Churchill, Frances, Duchess of Marl-
borough, d. 1899, 2
Colette, Adele-Eugenie-Sidonie, d.
1912, 2
Domitia Lepida, d. 53, 1
Duke, Nanaline Holt Inman, m.
1907, 1
Fonteyn, Hilda Acheson, 1894–, 2
Gabor, Jolie, 1896–, 1
Gustafsson, Anna, 2
Hanks, Lucy, d. 1825, 1
Jarvis, Anna Marie Reeves, 1836–
1905, 2
Julia Maesa, fl. 217, 1,2
Latouche, Mrs., fl. 1800s, 1
Loubet, Mrs., fl. 1820s, 1
Lowe, Marie, fl. 1840s, 1
Lyon, Jemima Shepherd, 1789, 2
Maachah, 1

Mabovitz, Bluma, d. 1951, 2
Maria Theresa, 1717–1780, 1,2
Markham, Elizabeth Winchell,
   1852–, 2
Martindale, Louisa, 1839–1914, 1
McBride, Elizabeth Craig, fl. 1890s, 1
Murray, Mrs., fl. 1600s, 1
Nightingale, Frances (Fanny) Smith,
   1788–1880, 2
Pavlova, Lyobov Fedorovna, 1849–, 2
Payne, Mary Cales, 2
Power, Mrs. Nicholas, 2
Roosevelt, Anna Hall, 1863–1892, 2
Smith, Elizabeth Quincy, 1722–1775,
   1
Smith, Polly, fl. 1860s, 1
Soong, Kwei-Tseng Ni, 1869–1931, 1
Stevenson, Margaret, fl. 1740s, 1
Stone, Hannah, 2
Sydenstricker, Caroline Stulting,
   1892–, 2
Talmadge, Margaret, fl. 1900s, 1
Teck, Mary Adelaide, Duchess of,
   1833–, 1
Victoire, Duchess of Kent, 1786–, 2
Mothers of the year
Diehl, Dena Shelby, fl. 1940s, 1
Engdahl, Olga Pauline Pearson,
   1896–, 1
Gillis, Pearl(e) Owens, 1888–, 1,2
Goon, Toy Len Chin, 1,2
Gray, Mrs. Carl, fl. 1940s, 1
Murray, Mrs. Frederick, fl. 1940s, 1
Phillips, Mrs. John, fl. 1940s, 1
Sibley, Mrs. Harper, fl. 1940s, 1
Thomson, Mrs. Alexander, fl. 1940s,
   1
Motion picture authors
Anhalt, Edna, 2
Baldwin, Ruth Ann, fl. 1910s, 2
Berg, Gertrude, 1899–1966, 1,2
Bergere, Ouida, d. 1974, 2
Blache, Simone, fl. 1970s, 2
Bute, Mary Ellen, fl. 1930s, 2
Chapple, Wendy Wood, fl. 1970s, 2
Cunard, Grace, 1894–1967, 2
Didion, Joan, 1934–, 2
Duras, Marguerite Donnadieu,
   1914–, 1,2
Eastman, Carole, fl. 1970s, 2
Fairfax, Marion, 2
Findlay, Roberta, 2
Gafford, Charlotte, fl. 1970s, 2
Gilliatt, Penelope Ann Douglas,
   1924–, 2

Glyn, Elinor Sutherland, 1864–1943,
   1,2
Goodrich, Frances, 1891–1984, 1,2
Gordon, Ruth, 1896–1985, 1,2
Harrison, Joan Mary, 1908–, 1,2
Katz, Gloria, 1943–, 2
Kelly, Mary Pat, fl. 1970s, 2
Loos, Anita, 1893–1981, 1,2
Marion, Frances, 1887–1973, 1,2
Mathis, June, 2
Murfin, Jane, fl. 1920s, 2
O'Hara, Mary Alsop Sturevasa,
   1885–1980, 2
Perry, Eleanor Bayer, 1914–1981, 2
Reville, Alma, 1879–1982, 2
Shipman, Nell, 1892–, 2
St. Johns, Adela Rogers, 1894–, 1,2
Szemes, Marianne, fl. 1960s, 2
Tewkesbury, Joan, 1936–, 2
Tuchok, Wanda, 2
Vinograskaya, Katerina, fl. 1920s, 2
Wicker, Ireene, 1905–, 1,2
Wilson, Jane, fl. 1970s, 2
Motion picture critics
Barry, Iris Sylvia Crump, 1895–
   1969, 2
Chester (Chesler), Phyllis, 2
Crist, Judith Klein, 1922–, 2
Gilliatt, Penelope Ann Douglas,
   1924–, 2
Kael, Pauline, 1919–, 2
Starr, Cecile, 1921–, 1
Motion picture directors
   See also
   Filmmakers
Arzner, Dorothy, 1900–1979, 2
Audrey, Jacqueline, 1908–, 2
Bachvarova, Radka, fl. 1960s, 2
Baldwin, Ruth Ann, fl. 1910s, 2
Bellon, Yannick, fl. 1940s, 2
Bertsch, Marguerite, fl. 1910s, 2
Blache, Alice Guy, 1873–1968, 2
Blackton, Paula, fl. 1910s, 2
Booker, Sue, fl. 1960s, 2
Bower, Holly, 2
Box, Muriel, fl. 1940s, 2
Boyadgieva, Lada, fl. 1940s, 2
Brandt, Yanna Kroyt, 1933–, 2
Brumberg, Valentina, fl. 1960s, 2
Burrill, Chris, fl. 1970s, 2
Bute, Mary Ellen, fl. 1930s, 2
Chapple, Wendy Wood, fl. 1970s, 2
Chytilova, Vera, 1929–, 2
Clarke, Shirley, 1927–, 2

Colson-Malleville, Marie, fl. 1930s, 2
Cox, Nell, 2
Cunard, Grace, 1894–1967, 2
Elek, Judit, 2
Epstein, Marie, fl. 1930s, 2
Espert, Nuria, 1938–, 2
Fairfax, Marion, 2
Fatima, Begum, 2
Ferchiou, Sofia, fl. 1960s, 2
Findlay, Roberta, 2
Fiske, Minnie Maddern, 1865–1932, 1,2
Friedman, Bonnie, 2
Gaudard, Lucette, fl. 1930s, 2
Henning-Jensen, Astrid, fl. 1940s, 2
Hovmand, Annelise, fl. 1950s, 2
Ivers, Julia Crawford, fl. 1910s, 2
Kaaresalo-Kasari, Ella, fl. 1970s, 2
Kaplan, Nelly, fl. 1950s, 2
Kelly, Mary Pat, fl. 1970s, 2
Kernochan, Sarah, fl. 1970s, 2
Kopple, Barbara J., 1946–, 2
Lee, Auriol, 1880–1941, 1
Loden, Barbara, 1932–1980, 2
Lupino, Ida, 1918–, 1,2
Macpherson, Jeanie, d. 1946, 2
Madison, Cleo, d. 1964, 2
Marion, Frances, 1887–1973, 1,2
McVey, Lucille, 1890–1925, 2
Meszaros, Marta, fl. 1960s, 2
Murfin, Jane, fl. 1920s, 2
Musidora, d. 1957, 2
Nordstrom, Frances, fl. 1920s, 2
O'Fredericks, Alice, fl. 1950s, 2
Orkin, Ruth, fl. 1950s, 2
Pakhmutova, A. N., fl. 1970s, 2
Park, Ida May, d. 1954, 2
Parker, Claire, fl. 1930s, 2
Parker, Francine, fl. 1970s, 2
Peragine, Frances, 2
Petelska, Eva, fl. 1950s, 2
Pickett, Elizabeth, 1910–1920, 2
Poirier, Anne-Claire, fl. 1960s, 2
Poplavskaya, Irina, fl. 1970s, 2
Preobrazhenskaya, Olga, 1871–, 1,2
Razeto, Stella, 2
Reid, Dorothy Davenport, 1895–, 2
Severson, Anne, fl. 1970s, 2
Shih Mei, 2
Shipman, Nell, 1892–, 2
Stonehouse, Ruth, 1894–1941, 2
Sutherland, Efua, 1924–, 2
Szemes, Marianne, fl. 1960s, 2
Tanaka, Kinuyo, 2

Terry, Alice, fl. 1920s, 2
Trintignant, Nadine Marquand, fl. 1960s, 2
Varda, Agnes, 1928–, 2
Vas, Judit, fl. 1960s, 2
Wang Ping, fl. 1950s, 2
Warrenton, Lule, d. 1932, 2
Weber, Lois, 1881–1939, 2
Weill, Claudia, 1947–, 2
Williams, Kathlyn, fl. 1910s, 2
Wilson, Elsie Jane, d. 1965, 2
Wilson, Margery, 1891–, 2
Zetterling, Mai Elizabeth, 1925–, 2
Zheljazova, Binka, fl. 1960s, 2
Motion picture editors
Allen, Dede, 1923–, 2
Bank, Mirra, fl. 1970s, 2
Bauchens, Anne, 1881–1967, 2
Bonsignori, Mili, fl. 1950s, 2
Booth, Margaret, fl. 1920s, 2
Burrill, Chris, fl. 1970s, 2
Coates, Anne V., fl. 1960s, 2
Connell, Thelma, fl. 1950s, 2
Fowler, Marjorie, fl. 1940s, 2
Friedman, Bonnie, 2
Lawrence, Viola, d. 1973, 2
McLean, Barbara R., 1930–1950, 2
Morra, Irene, 1913–, 2
Newman, Eve, fl. 1960s, 2
Renoir, Marguerite, fl. 1930s, 2
Roland, Rita, fl. 1960s, 2
Sargent, Peggy, 2
Shih Mei, 2
Slesin, Aviva, fl. 1970s, 2
Spencer, Dorothy, 1930–1960, 2
Thomson, Pat, fl. 1970s, 2
Tod, Dorothy, fl. 1960s, 2
Trintignant, Nadine Marquand, fl. 1960s, 2
Tual, Denise Piazza, fl. 1920s, 2
Valentine, Carla, 2
Warren, Eda, fl. 1920s, 2
Motion picture executives
Brown, Katharine, fl. 1930s, 1
Fields, Verna, 1918–, 2
Grew, Agnes Mengel, fl. 1930s, 1
Lansing, Sherry Lee, 1944–, 2
McCurdy, Jean H., 1949–, 2
Prieskel, Barbara Scott, 2
Townsend, Claire, 1952–, 2
Motion picture industry
Barbe, Victoria, fl. 1970s, 2
Firestone, Elizabeth, fl. 1940s, 2
Oelman, Ruth, fl. 1920s, 2
Weinstein, Paula, 2

Motion picture photographers
  Aviv, Nurith, fl. 1970s, 2
  Burrill, Chris, fl. 1970s, 2
  Deitch, Donna, fl. 1970s, 2
  Friedman, Bonnie, 2
  Wang, Juliana, fl. 1970s, 2
Motion picture producers
  Barskaya, M., fl. 1930s, 2
  Bodard, Mag, fl. 1960s, 2
  Box, Muriel, fl. 1940s, 2
  Brandt, Yanna Kroyt, 1933–, 2
  Bute, Mary Ellen, fl. 1930s, 2
  Cox, Nell, 2
  Deren, Maya, 1922–1961, 2
  Dougherty, Ariel, fl. 1960s, 2
  Douglas, Pamela, fl. 1970s, 2
  Dulac, Germaine, 1882–1942, 2
  Ferchiou, Sofia, fl. 1960s, 2
  Fiske, Minnie Maddern, 1865–1932,
    1,2
  Harrison, Joan Mary, 1908–, 1,2
  Heller, Roz, 2
  Johnson, Osa Helen Leighty, 1894–
    1953, 1,2
  Kaaresalo-Kasari, Ella, fl. 1970s, 2
  Kopple, Barbara J., 1946–, 2
  LeVine, Deborah Joy, 1952–, 2
  Lee, Auriol, 1880–1941, 1
  Moore, Mary Tyler, 1937–, 1,2
  Nedeva, Zlatina, 1877–1941, 1,2
  Parsons, Harriet Oettinger, 1906–
    1983, 1,2
  Patton, Jessie Maple, fl. 1970s, 2
  Roos, Barbara, fl. 1970s, 2
  Thornton, Naomi, 1935–, 2
  Turner, Florence E., 1888–1946, 1,2
  Van Upp, Virginia, fl. 1940s, 2
  Weill, Claudia, 1947–, 2
  Weinstein, Hannah, fl. 1950s, 2
Motion picture technicians
  Ronnel, Ann, fl. 1940s, 2
  Smirnova, M. N., 2
Motley, John Lothrop—Daughter
  Harcourt, Elizabeth Cabot Motley, d.
    1928, 1
Motorcyclists
  Ball, Florrie, fl. 1970s, 2
  Fish, Sue (Flying Fish), 2
  McGee, Mary, fl. 1970s, 2
Mott, Lucretia—Sister
  Wright, Martha Coffin Pelham, 1806–
    1875, 1,2
Mountain women
  Chandler, Artie, fl. 1970s, 2
  Chandler, Marie Wilson, fl. 1970s, 2

Dalton, Shirley, fl. 1970s, 2
Kincaid, Nancy, fl. 1970s, 2
Rector, Ellen, fl. 1970s, 2
Redmund, Donna, fl. 1970s, 2
Reece, Florence, fl. 1970s, 2
Smith, Betty Messer, fl. 1970s, 2
Smith, Della Mae, fl. 1970s, 2
Summerhour, Shirley, fl. 1970s, 2
Tiller, Katherine, fl. 1970s, 2
Watson, Myra, fl. 1970s, 2
Wilson, Wyoming, fl. 1970s, 2
Woodie, Effie, fl. 1970s, 2
Mountaineers
  Anderson, Alyce E., 2
  Anderson, Junita, 1890–, 2
  Barnard, Tissayac, 1878–, 1
  Bayley, Gertrude Arthur, fl. 1860s, 1
  Blum, Arlene, fl. 1970s, 2
  Brodt, Helen, d. 1908, 2
  Burr, Frances, fl. 1930s, 1
  Carrington, Karin, fl. 1970s, 2
  Engelhard, Georgia, fl. 1940s, 1
  Firey, Joan, d. 1980, 2
  Fuller, Fay, fl. 1890s, 2
  Gombu, Rita, 2
  Holmes, Julia, fl. 1850s, 2
  Keen, Dora, 1871–, 1,2
  Komarkova, Vera, 2
  Kramar, Piro, 2
  Miller, Irene Beardsley, 2
  Morton, Patricia, fl. 1970s, 2
  Peck, Annie Smith, 1850–1935, 1,2
  Phantog, Mrs., fl. 1970s, 2
  Ratcliff, Bernice, fl. 1970s, 2
  Rutkiewicz, Wanda, fl. 1970s, 2
  Tabei, Junko, 1940–, 2
  Taylor, Dyanna, 2
  Tews, Christy, 2
  Vickers, Julia, fl. 1970s, 2
  Watson, Vera, d. 1878, 2
  Welton, Caroline J., 1842–1884, 2
  Workman, Fanny Bullock, 1859–
    1925, 1,2
Mowhawk Indians
  Johnson, Emily Pauline, 1861–1913,
    1,2
  Tekakwitha, Kateri, 1656–1680, 1,2
Mozart, Wolfgang Amadeus—Mother
  Mozart, Anna Maria, 1720–1778, 1,2
Mozart, Wolfgang Amadeus—Daughter
  Mozart, Maria Anna (Nannerl), 1751–
    1829, 1,2
Muchmore, Harold—Spouse
  Muchmore, Donna, fl. 1970s, 2

Beck, Anne Landsbury, 1
Becker, Angela, 1
Bicking, Ada Elizabeth, d. 1953, 1
Bilbro, (Anne) Mathilde, fl. 1910s, 1
Bixby, Allene K., d. 1947, 1
Blake, Dorothy Gaynor, fl. 1940s, 1
Boulanger, Lili (Juliette Marie Olga), 1893–1918, 1,2
Boulanger, Nadia Juliette, 1887–1979, 1,2
Boyd, Anna Tomlinson, 1879–, 1
Brambilla, Marietta Cassano D'Adda, 1807–1875, 1
Briggs, Cora S., 1
Bright, Dora Estella, 1863–, 1
Broughton, Julia, 1
Brower, Harriette, 1869–1928, 1
Bugbee, L. A., d. 1917, 1
Burkhard, Julia L., 1
Burns, Annelu, 1889–1942, 1
Carpara, Clara H., fl. 1930s, 1
Chase, Helen Frances, fl. 1930s, 1
Clark, Frances Eliot, 1860–1958, 1,2
Clark, Mary Gail, 1914–, 1
Coit, Lottie Ellsworth, fl. 1940s, 1
Copeland, Bernice Rose, fl. 1940s, 1
Copp, Evelyn Fletcher, d. 1945, 1
Copp, Laura Remick, d. 1934, 1
Cornish, Nellie C., fl. 1910s, 1
Cramm, Helen L., d. 1939, 1
Crane, Julia E., 1855–1923, 1
Crosby, Marie, fl. 1940s, 1
Crowell, Annie L., fl. 1930s, 1
Davis, Fay Simmons, d. 1942, 1
Diller, Angela (Mary Angelica), 1877–1968, 1,2
Dodge, Mary Hewes, fl. 1940s, 1
Dunning, Carre Louise, 1860–1929, 1
Erb, Mae-Aileen Gerhart, fl. 1940s, 1
Figuero, Carmen Sanakia de, 1882–, 2
Flagg, Marion, fl. 1930s, 1
Fletcher-Copp, Evelyn, d. 1944, 1
Fryberger, Agnes Moore, 1868–, 1
Glenn, Mabelle, fl. 1940s, 1
Glover, Sarah Ann, 1785–1867, 1,2
Gober, Belle Biard, fl. 1940s, 1
Goff, Anna Chandler, fl. 1940s, 1
Grondahl, Agathe Backer, 1847–1907, 1
Gulesian, Grace Warner, 1884–, 1
Haake, Gail Martin, 1884–, 1
Hahn, Emilie, 1891–1971, 2
Hammond, Fanny Reed, fl. 1940s, 1
Holst, Marie Seuel, fl. 1940s, 1

Hopson, Elizabeth Louise, fl. 1915s, 1
Hudson, Octavia, fl. 1940s, 1
Huebner, Ilse, fl. 1940s, 1
Hunt, Arabella, d. 1705, 1
Huss, Hildegarde Hoffman, fl. 1940s, 1
Inskeep, Alice Carey, fl. 1940s, 1
Jenkins, Cora W., 1870–1947, 1
Kelley, Mrs. Edgar Stillman, fl. 1910s, 1
Kimmel, Carol Karraker, 1917–, 2
Knouss, Isabelle G., fl. 1940s, 1
Kotzschmar, Mrs. Hermann, 1853–, 1
Lang, Edith, fl. 1940s, 1
Leonard, Florence, fl. 1940s, 1
Lewing, Adele, 1866–1943, 1
Lhevinne, Rosina L., 1880–1976, 1,2
Liszniewska, Marguerite Melville, fl. 1940s, 1
Luboschutz, Lea, 1887–1965, 1,2
MacChesney, Norma Gertrude, 1876–, 1
Mannes, Clara Damrosch, 1869–1948, 1,2
Marshall, Harriet Gibbs, fl. 1900s, 1
Mathews, Blance Dingley, d. 1932, 1
Murray, Charlotte Wallace, m. 1915, 1
Noyes-Greene, Edith Rowena, 1875–, 1
Owen, Julia D., fl. 1940s, 1
Paldi, Mari, fl. 1940s, 1
Patterson, Elizabeth Kelso, fl. 1940s, 1
Patti, Carlotta, 1840–1889, 1
Peterson, Edna Gunnar, fl. 1940s, 1
Peycke, Frieda, 1
Phippen, Laud German, fl. 1940s, 1
Prentice, Marion, fl. 1910s, 1
Ralston, F. Marion, fl. 1940s, 1
Ramann, Lina, 1833–1912, 1
Risher, Anna Priscilla, 1875–, 1
Robyn, Louise, 1878–1949, 1
Ross, Margaret Wheeler, d. 1953, 1
Ruta, Gilda, fl. 1930s, 1
Ryan, Mary P. Van Buren, fl. 1930s, 1
Ryder, Theodora Sturkow, 1876–, 1
Samaroff, Olga Hickenlooper, 1882–1948, 1,2
Seymour, Harriet Ayer, 1876–1944, 1
Showalter, Edna Blanche, fl. 1940s, 1
Simpson, Elizabeth, fl. 1940s, 1
Smith, Ella May, 1860–1934, 1

N

NATO Women's Conference
  Gould, Patricia, fl. 1970s, 2
  Kor, Serefnur, 2
  Thomas, Waltraud, 2
  Tiryakioglu, Guler, 2
NOW
  Banville, Anne, 2
  Clarenback, Kathryn, 1920–, 2
  Friedan, Betty, 1921–, 2
  Shields, Laurie, fl. 1970s, 2
  Smeal, Eleanor Marie Cutri, 1939–, 2
  Sommers, Tish, 2
  Steinem, Gloria, 1934–, 2
  Tully, Mary Jean, fl. 1970s, 2
Nahor—Daughter
  Maachah, 1
Nala—Spouse
  Damayanti, Princess, 1
Namer of city
  Rumsey, Mary Ann, fl. 1820s, 1,2
Napoleon I—Mistress
  Walewska, Marie, Countess, 1787–
    1817, 1,2
Napoleon I—Spouse
  Josephine de Baucharnais, 1763–
    1814, 1,2
  Marie Louise, 1791–1847, 2
Napoleon III—Mistress
  Howard, Harriet, 1823–1865, 1
Napoleon III—Spouse
  Eugenie, Marie Eugenie de Montijo
    de Guzman, 1826–1920, 1,2
Nasser, Gamal Abdel—Spouse
  Nasser, Tahia Mahmoud, 1923–, 1
National Aeronautics and Space Admin-
    istration
  See
  NASA
National Association for the Advance-
    ment of Colored People
  See
  NAACP
National Federation of Business and
    Professional Women's Clubs
  Phillips, Lena Madesin, 1881–1955,
    1,2
National Council of Churches
  Gibbes, Emilly, 2
  Lowry, Edith Elizabeth, 1897–1970,
    2
National Council of Jewish Women
  American, Sadie, 1862–1944, 1,2
  Solomon, Hannah Greenbaum, 1858–
    1942, 2

National Council of Negro Women
  Height, Dorothy Irene, 1912–, 2
National Council of Women
  Parsons, Rose Peabody, 1891–1985,
    1,2
National Labor Relations Board
  Allen, Natalie Pannes, fl. 1970s, 2
National League of Cities
  Lamphere, Phyllis Lee Hagmore, 2
National Organization for Women
  See
  NOW
National Volunteer Award winners
  Dawson, Barbara Joan, fl. 1960s, 2
Native American benefactors
  Newcomb, Franc Johnson, 1887–
    1970, 2
Native American collectors
  Seargeant, Mary Elizabeth, 1855–
    1921, 2
Native American educators
  Gilbert, Madonna, 1937–, 2
  Robertson, Alice Mary, 1854–1931,
    1,2
  Wilson, Florence, fl. 1840s, 2
Native American languages
  Elliott, Maud, 1854–1948, 2
  Elliott, Maud(e) Howe, 1854–1948, 2
Native American leaders
  Aliquippa, fl. 1750s, 2
  Allen, Betsy, fl. 1830s, 2
  Angeline, d. 1836, 2
  Aza-ya-man-ka-win, 1788–1873, 2
  Bailey, Ann "Mad Ann", 1742–1825,
    1,2
  Bennett, Kay, fl. 1920s, 2
  Blackfoot Indian wife, fl. 1935, 2
  Bosomworth, Mary Musgrove Mat-
    thews, 1700–1760, 1,2
  Brant, Mary (Molly), 1736–1796, 2
  Campbell, Janet, 1947–, 2
  Carmack, Katie, fl. 1890s, 2
  Cateechee, 2
  Chiltosky, Charlotte Hornbuckle,
    1868–1936, 2
  Chipeta, 1842–1880, 1,2
  Clarke, Helen, 2
  Cooper, Polly, fl. 1770s, 2
  Dat-so-la-lee, 1835–1925, 2
  Deer, Ada, 1935–, 2
  Deluvina, 1848–, 2
  Desai, Anita, 1937–, 2
  Esther, Queen "Crazy", fl. 1770s, 2
  Grinnell, Josephine, 2

Comstock, Anna Botsford, 1854–
1930, 1,2
Green, Charlotte Hilton, 1889–, 1
Lulham, Rosalie Blanche Jermaine,
1872–1934, 1
Maxwell, Martha A., 2
Merian, Maria Sibylla, 1647–1717, 1,2
North, Marianne, 1830–1890, 1,2
Porter, Gene Stratton, 1862–1924, 1,2
Rathbone (Rathbun), Mary Jane,
1860–, 1
Royer, Clemence Augustine, 1830–
1902, 1
Sandrart, Esther Barbara von, 1651–
1729, 2
Searls, Fanny, 1851–1939, 1
Shattuck, Lydia White, 1822–1889, 2
Shaw, Ellen Eddy, fl. 1930s, 1
Treat, Mary, 1830–, 1
Walcott, Mary Morris Vaux, 1860–
1940, 2
Weston, Elizabeth, fl. 1600s, 2
Nature writers
Butler, Lorine Letcher, fl. 1930s, 1
Doubleday, Neltje Blanchan de Graff,
1865–1918, 2
Stanwood, Cordelia, 1865–1958, 2
Wright, Mabel Osgood, 1859–1934,
1,2
Navajo Indians
Francisco, Nia, 1952–, 2
Wauneka, Annie Dodge, 1910–, 2
Naval officers, American
Byerly, Kathleen, 2
Feldman, Peggy, 2
Gardner, Elsa, fl. 1930s, 1
Garner, Nancy R., 2
Hinman, Katherine, fl. 1970s, 2
Hopper, Grace Murray, 1906–, 2
Kuhn, Lucille R., fl. 1950s, 2
Latsch, Bonnie, 2
McKee, Fran, fl. 1950s, 2
Rainey, Rachel, fl. 1970s, 2
Smith, Dody Wilson, fl. 1940s, 2
Stephens, Sue, fl. 1970s, 2
Stoll, Alice, fl. 1960s, 2
Stratton, Dorothy Constance, 1899–,
1,2
Tomsuden, Ruth, fl. 1970s, 2
Wilde, Louise Kathleen, 1910–, 1
Navigators
Burgess, Hannah Rebecca Crowell,
1835–, 1
Converse, Mary Parker, 1872–1961, 2
Fairweather, Margie, fl. 1940s, 1

Navy nurses, American
Bowman, J. Beatrice, gr. 1922, 1
Dauser, Sue Sophia, 1888–, 1,2
Duerke, Alene Bertha, 1920–, 2
Higslee, Lenah S., fl. 1910s, 1
Navy physicians and surgeons
Voge, Victoria, fl. 1970s, 2
Willoughby, Frances Lois, fl. 1940s, 2
Navy pilots
Allen, Barbara, 2
Alverson, Lee Ruth, 2
Baumgartner, Ann, 2
Hancock, Joy Bright, 1898–, 1,2
Kokes, Carol L., fl. 1970s, 2
Neuffer, Judith Ann, fl. 1970s, 2
Nazi victims
Benario-Prestes, Olga, 1908–1942, 2
Eisenblatter, Charlotte, 1903–1944, 2
Eisenschneider, Elvira, 1924–, 1,2
Frank, Anne, 1929–1945, 1,2
Harnack, Mildred Fish, 1902–1943,
1,2
Hermann, Liselotte, 1909–1938, 2
Lindner, Hertha, 1920–1943, 2
Niederkirchner, Kathe (Katja), 1909–
1959, 2
Sedlackova, Marie, 2
Nearchos—Daughter
Aristarete, 2
Nebraska
Abbott, Elizabeth M. Griffin, 1845–
1941, 2
Abel, Hazel Hempel, 1888–1966, 1,2
Aldrich, Bess Genevra Streeter, 1881–
1954, 1,2
Bryan, Mary Elizabeth Baird, 1861–
1930, 2
Fulstone, Mary Hill, 1892–, 2
Gray, Lenora Dennis, 1873–1957, 2
Hasebroock, Margaret Elizabeth, 2
Hurst, Sadie Dotson, 1857–1951, 2
Joslyn, Sarah Hannah Selleck, 1851–
1940, 2
La Flesche, Mary Gale, 1826–1909, 2
Morton, Caroline Joy French, 1833–
1881, 2
Pound, Laura Biddlecombe, 1841–
1928, 2
Needleworkers
Crabb, Mary, fl. 1730s, 1
Ducray, Anne, fl. 1760s, 1
East, Henrietta Maria, fl. 1760s, 1
Gazley, Martha, fl. 1730s, 1
Harbeson, Georgiana Brown, 1894–
1980, 1,2

Hobdy, Ann F., fl. 1930s, 1
Jones, Anne Scotton, fl. 1750s, 1
Karasz, Mariska, 1898–1960, 2
Lancaster, Sarah, fl. 1730s, 1
Linwood, Mary, 1755–1845, 1,2
Lucar, Elizabeth, d. 1537, 1
Maines, Rachel, fl. 1970s, 2
Massari, Luigia, 1810–, 1
Post, Parthenia A., fl. 1880s, 1
Stone, Elizabeth, fl. 1840s, 2
Whichelo, Nellie, fl. 1890s, 2
Wilson, Erica, 2
Nehru, Jawaharlal—Sister
Nehru, Vijaya Lakshmi, 1
Nelson, Horatio—Mistress
Hamilton, Emma Lyon, Lady, 1761–
1815, 1,2
Nelson, Horatio—Mother
Nelson, Catherine Suckling, 1726–
1768, 2
Nero—Friend
Acte, Claudia, fl. 50–60, 1
Nero—Mother
Agrippina, The Younger, 15–59, 1,2
Nero—Spouse
Poppaea Sabina, the younger, d. 65, 1
Sabina, Poppaea, d. 65, 1
Nesbit, Evelyn—Mother
Nesbit, Mrs. Winifield, 2
Neurobiologists
Levi-Montalcini, Rita, fl. 1950s, 2
Neuroimmunologists
Bulloch, Karen, 1945–, 2
Neurologists
Ball, Erna D., fl. 1930s, 1
Ellington, Kathryn, 2
Nevada
Blair, Minnie Nichols, 1886–, 2
Davis, Nellie Verrill, 1844–, 2
Dickerson, Una Reilly, 1881–, 2
Eldridge, Mary Agnes Prowse,
1896–, 2
Laxalt, Theresa Alpetche, fl. 1920s, 2
Ronzone, Bertha Bishop, 1895–, 2
Squires, Delphine Anderson, 1868–, 2
Stewart, Helen Jane Wiser, 1854–
1926, 2
New Hampshire
Cilley, Elsie, 2
Copp, Dolly Emery, fl. 1830s, 2
Duston (Dustin), Hannah, 1657–
1736, 1,2
Eastman, Mary Butler, d. 1837, 2
Eddy, Mary Baker, 1821–1910, 1,2

Hale, Sarah Josepha Buell, 1788–
1879, 1,2
Johnson, Suzanna Willard H., 1730–
1810, 2
Pierce, Jane Means Appleton, 1806–
1863, 1,2
Sanborn, Katherine Abbot, 1939–
1917, 1
Stark, Elizabeth Page (Molly), 1736–
1814, 1,2
Thaxter, Celia Laighton, 1835–1894,
1,2
New Jersey
Buck, Bertha Ann Stanley, 1913–, 2
Caldwell, Hannah Ogden, 1737–
1780, 2
Garron, Etta R. Small, 1887–, 2
Minnis, Margaret Kitchens, 1921–, 2
Morris, Margaret Hill, 1737–1816, 1,2
Reeve, Virginia Watson, 1885–, 2
Stone, Lucy, 1818–1893, 1,2
White, Margaret Davis Fisher, 1874–,
2
New Mexico
Bear, Grace Tharpe, 1868–1959, 2
Charles, Bula Ward, 1887–1974, 2
Hardin, Pablita Velarde, 1918–, 2
Hosford, Jessie Wiegand, 1882–, 2
Huning, Ernestine Franke, 1845–
1923, 2
Jaramillo, Cleofas Martinez, 1877–
1956, 2
Martinez, Maria Montoya, 1887–
1980, 2
Neff, Francine Irving, 1925–, 2
Newcomb, Franc Johnson, 1887–
1970, 2
Perrault, Jesusita Acosta, 1872–1960,
2
New Orleans preservationists
Werlein, Elizabeth Thomas, 1883–
1946, 2
New York
Hayes, Helen, 1900–, 1,2
Luce, Clare Booth, 1903–1987, 1,2
Moses, Anna Mary Robertson
(Grandma Moses), 1860–1961, 1,2
Motley, Constance Baker, 1921–, 1,2
Pierce, Jessie Webster, 1892–, 2
Prendergast, Mehitabel Wing, 1738–,
2
Schechter, Mathilde Roth, 1859–
1924, 2
Seton, Elizabeth Ann Bayley
"Mother", 1774–1821, 1,2

Nixon, Richard—Spouse
  Nixon, Patricia Thelma Catherine
    Ryan, 1912–, 2
  Nixon, Thelma Ryan "Pat", 1913–
    1993, 1
Nkruman, Kwame—Spouse
  Nkrumah, Fathia Halim Ritzk,
    1931–, 1
Noblewomen
  Anjou, Marguerite d', 1429–1482, 1,2
  Borgia, Lucrezia, Duchess of Ferrara,
    1480–1519, 1,2
  Cenci, Beatrice, 1577–1599, 1,2
  Hudavent, fl. 1200s, 1
Nonagenarian
  Martin, May, 1870–, 2
Nordica, Lillian—Sister
  Norton, Amanda Allen, fl. 1920s, 2
Norris, Frank—Spouse
  Black, Jeannette, 1878–1952, 2
North American Indian Association
  Cox, Marie, fl. 1970s, 2
North American Indian Women's Asso-
  ciation
  Fate, Mary Jane, 2
North American Treaty Organization
  See
  NATO
North Carolina
  Caldwell, Margaret Hood, fl. 1940s, 2
  Chiltosky, Charlotte Hornbuckle,
    1868–1936, 2
  Johnson, Kate Burr, 1881–, 2
  Latham, Maude Moore, 1871–, 2
  Lee, Mollie Huston, 1907–, 2
  McKimmon, Jane Simpson, 1867–, 2
  Pfohl, Bessie Whittington, 1881–, 2
  Sloop, Mary T Martin, 1873–1962,
    1,2
  Spencer, Cornelia Phillips, 1825–
    1908, 2
  Weil, Mina Rosenthal, 1859–, 2
North Dakota
  Burkhart, Anna K. Miller, 1868–, 2
  Crowley, Pauline Shoemaker, 1879–
    1960, 2
  Hall, Ina Beauchamp, 1905–, 2
  Hall, Susan Webb, 1850–1922, 2
  Herseth, Clara Nelson, 1884–1947, 2
  Kindred, Anna D. Dersheimer, 1836–
    1937, 2
  Lunney, Jessie Mae Wenck, 1870–
    1961, 2
  Nevens, Mary McNamara, 1872–
    1965, 2
  Slaughter, Linda, 1843–, 2

Notaries public
  Conise, Annette, fl. 1870s, 1
Noted law case defendant
  Teebay, Susan, fl. 1970s, 2
Noted mausoleum
  Hansell, Leila Davidson, d. 1915, 2
Noted perfect wife
  Davis, Sarah, 2
Noted well water donor
  Winchester, Lydia and Elizabeth, fl.
    1880s, 2
Notorious woman
  Digby, Venetia, 1600–1633, 1
Novelists, American
  Abbott, Eleanor Hallowell, 1872–
    1958, 1,2
  Abbott, Jane Ludlow Drake, 1881–, 1
  Adler, Renata, 1938–, 2
  Albrand, Martha, 1911–, 1,2
  Alcott, Louisa May, 1832–1888, 1,2
  Aldrich, Annie Reeve, 1866–1892, 1
  Aldrich, Bess Genevra Streeter, 1881–
    1954, 1,2
  Aldrich, Darragh, fl. 1940s, 2
  Allis, Marguerite, 1887–1958, 1
  Alther, Lisa, 1944–, 2
  Andrews, Mary Raymond Shipman,
    1860–1936, 1,2
  Anthony, Evelyn, pseud., 1928–, 2
  Arnow, Harriet Louise Simpson,
    1908–, 1,2
  Atherton, Gertrude Franklin Horn,
    1857–1948, 1,2
  Atkinson, Eleanor Stackhouse, 1863–
    1942, 1,2
  Austin, Jane Goodwin, 1831–1894, 1
  Austin, Mary Hunter, 1868–1934, 1,2
  Bailey, Temple, d. 1953, 1
  Baker, Dorothy Dodds, 1907–1968,
    1,2
  Baldwin, Faith Cuthrell, 1893–1978,
    1,2
  Banks, Nancy Huston, 1850–, 1
  Banning, Margaret Culkin, 1891–
    1982, 1,2
  Barnes, Carman Neal, 1912–, 1
  Barnes, Djuna, 1892–1982, 2
  Barr, Amelia Edith Huddleston,
    1831–1919, 1,2
  Bartley, Nalbro, 1888–, 1
  Beattie, Ann, 1947–, 2
  Bengis, Ingrid, fl. 1970s, 2
  Benson, Sally Smith, 1900–1972, 1,2
  Birstein, Ann, fl. 1970s, 2

Bleecker, Ann(a) Eliza, 1752–1783, 1,2
Blume, Judy Sussman, 1938–, 2
Boley, Jean, 1914–, 1
Borden, Lucille Papin, 1873–, 1
Bowles, Jane Sydney, 1917–1973, 2
Boyle, Kay, 1902–, 1,2
Boylston, Helen Dore, 1895–1984, 1,2
Brackett, Leigh, 1915–1978, 2
Bristow, Gwen, 1903–1980, 1,2
Brooks, Gwendolyn, 1917–, 1,2
Brown, Katharine Holland, fl. 1900s, 1
Brown, Rita Mae, 2
Brownell, Gertrude Hall, 1863–, 1
Buck, Pearl Sydenstricker, 1892–1973, 1,2
Burnham, Clara Louise, d. 1927, 1
Burt, Katharine Newlin, 1882–, 1,2
Calisher, Hortense, 1911–, 2
Carman, Dorothy Walworth, 1900–, 1
Carroll, Gladys Hasty, 1904–, 1,2
Caspary, Vera, 1904–1987, 1,2
Cather, Willa Sibert, 1873–1947, 1,2
Catherwood, Mary Hartwell, 1847–1902, 1,2
Cavannah, Betty (Betsy Allen), 1909–, 1
Chapman, Mary Hamilton Isley, 1865–, 1
Chase, Mary Ellen, 1887–1983, 1,2
Chopin, Kate O'Flaherty, 1851–1904, 2
Clare, Ada, pseud., 1836–1874, 2
Cleghorn, Sarah Northcliff, 1876–1959, 1,2
Coatesworth, Elizabeth Jane, 1893–, 1,2
Cockrell, Marian, 1909–, 1
Colby, Nathalie Sedgwick, 1875–1942, 1
Comstock, Harriet, 1860–, 1
Craigie, Pearl Mary Teresa, 1867–1906, 1,2
Cullinan, Elizabeth, fl. 1950s, 2
Cummins, Maria Susanna, 1827–1866, 1
Dalton, Jane Martin, d. 1879, 2
Daly, Elizabeth, 1879–1967, 2
Dargan, Olive Tilford, 1869–1968, 1,2
Davenport, Marcia, 1903–, 1,2

Daviess, Maria Thompson, 1872–1924, 1
Davis, Dorothy Salisbury, 1916–, 2
Deal, Babs H., 1929–, 2
Deland, Margaret Wade, 1857–1945, 1,2
Denison, Mary Ann Andrews, 1826–1911, 2
Desai, Anita, 1937–, 2
Deutsch, Babette, 1895–, 1,2
Didion, Joan, 1934–, 2
Doolittle, Hilda, 1886–1961, 1,2
Dorsey, Anna Hanson McKenney, 1815–1896, 1
Douglas, Ellen Hope, pseud., 1921–, 2
Du Jardin, Rosamond Neal, 1902–1963, 1,2
Dundy, Elaine, 1927–, 2
Dupuy, Eliza Ann, 1814–1880, 2
Eastman, Elizabeth, 1905–, 1
Eastman, Julia Arabella, 1837–1911, 1
Eberhart, Mignon Good, 1899–, 2
Elliott, Sarah Barnwell, 1848–1928, 2
Erskine, Dorothy, 1906–, 1
Ertz, Susan, 1894–, 1
Evans, Augusta Jane, 1835–1909, 1,2
Faralla, Dana, 1909–, 1
Farnham, Mateel Howe, m. 1910, 1
Fauset, Jessie Redmon, 1884–1961, 1,2
Ferber, Edna, 1887–1968, 1,2
Field, Rachel Lyman, 1894–1942, 1,2
Fielding, Sarah, 1710–1768, 1,2
Fisher, Dorothy Canfield, 1879–1958, 1,2
Flebbe, Beulah Marie Dix, 1876–, 1
Fletcher, Inglis Clark, 1879–1969, 1,2
Forbes, Esther, 1894–1967, 1,2
Foster, Hannah Webster, 1758–1840, 1,2
Freeman, Mary Eleanor Wilkins, 1852–1930, 1,2
French, Marilyn, 2
Frost, Frances Mary, 1905–1959, 1,2
Fuller, Iola, 1906–, 1
Fuller, Margaret, 1872–, 1
Furnas, Marthedith, 1904–, 1
Gates, Susa Young, 1856–1933, 1,2
Gellhorn, Martha, 1908–, 1,2
Gerould, Katherine Elizabeth Fullerton, 1879–1944, 1,2
Gibbs, Willa, 1917–, 1
Gilman, Dorothy, pseud., 1923–, 2

Praed, Rosa Caroline Mackworth,
1851–1935, 1
Prichard, Katharine Susannah, 1884–
1972, 1,2
Pym, Barbara, 1913–, 2
Richardson, Henrietta, 1870–1946,
1,2
Richardson, Henry Handel, pseud.,
1870–1946, 2
Ross, Ida Alena, 1855–, 1
Russell, Elizabeth Mary Annette
Beauchamp, Countess von Arnim,
1866–1941, 1
Stead, Christina Ellen, 1902–1983, 1,2
Novelists, Austrian
Aichinger, Ilse, 1921–, 2
Bachmann, Ingeborg, 1926–1973, 2
Baum, Vicki, 1896–1960, 1,2
Ebner-Eschenbach, Marie Von, Bar-
oness, 1830–1916, 1,2
Pichler, Karoline von Greiner, 1769–
1843, 1
Novelists, Belgian
Yourcenar, Marguerite, 1903–1987,
1,2
Novelists, Bohemian
Konig, Barbara, 1925–, 2
Novelists, Canadian
Archibald, Edith Jesse, 1854–, 1
Atwood, Margaret Eleanor Killian,
1939–, 2
Blais, Marie Claire, 2
Campbell, Grace MacLennan Grant,
1895–1963, 1
Cape, Judith, fl. 1940s, 1
Chapman, Ethel, fl. 1920s, 1
De La Roche, Mazo, 1885–1961, 1,2
Eaton, Evelyn Sybil Mary, 1902–, 1
Engel, Marian, fl. 1970s, 2
Gallant, Mavis, 1922–, 2
Graham, Gwethalyn, 1913–1965, 1
Hamilton, Cicely Viets Dakin, 1837–
1909, 2
Keith, Marion, 1876–, 1
Laurence, Margaret, 1926–, 2
MacDonald, Lucy Maude Montgom-
ery, 1874–1942, 1
Mackay, Isabel Ecclestone Macpher-
son, 1875–1928, 1
Millar, Margaret Storm, 1915–, 1,2
Montgomery, Lucy Maud, 1874–
1942, 1
Roy, Gabrielle, 1909–, 2
Tomkinson, Grace, fl. 1940s, 1
Tovell, Ruth Massey, 1889–, 1

Novelists, Chilean
Chacon, Rosario Orrego de, 1834–
1879, 1
Novelists, Chinese
Han Suyin, 1917–, 1,2
Novelists, Cuban
Zambrana, Luisa Perez de, 1835–
1922, 1
Novelists, Czechoslovakian
Marothy-Soltesova, Elena, 1855–
1938, 2
Nemcova, Bozena, 1820–1882, 1,2
Novelists, Danish
Michaelis, Karin, 1872–1950, 1,2
Novelists, Dutch
Ammers-Ku(e)ller, Johanna van,
1884–, 2
Bosboom-Toussaint, Anna Louise
Geertruida, 1812–1886, 1
Deken, Agatha (Aagji), 1741–1804,
1,2
Wolff, Elisabeth, 1738–1804, 2
Novelists, Egyptian
Saadawi, Nawal el, 1930–, 2
Novelists, English
Aguilar, Grace, 1816–1847, 1,2
Albanesi, Madame M. Henderson, fl.
1900s, 1
Anderson, Stella Benson, 1892–1933,
2
Andrews, Lucilla, 2
Anthony, C. L., pseud., 1896–, 1,2
Askew, Alice J. de C., d. 1917, 1
Austen, Jane, 1775–1817, 1,2
Ayres, Ruby Mildred, 1883–1955, 1,2
Bagnold, Enid Algerine, 1889–1981,
1,2
Baillie-Saunders, Margaret Elsie
Crowther, 1873–1949, 1
Bainbridge, Beryl, 1934–, 2
Banks, Isabella Varley Linnaeus,
1821–1897, 1,2
Banks, Lynne Reid, 1929–, 2
Barclay, Florence Louisa Charles-
worth, 1862–1921, 1,2
Barker, A. L., 1918–, 2
Barker, Jane, fl. 1715, 1,2
Bawden, Nina, 1925–, 2
Bayly, Ada Ellen, 1857–1903, 1,2
Beck, Lily Adams, d. 1931, 1
Behn, Aphra, 1640–1689, 1,2
Belloc, Marie Adelaide, 1868–, 1
Benson, Stella, 1892–1933, 1,2
Bentham-Edwards, Matilda, 1836–
1919, 2

Bentley, Phyllis Eleanor, 1894–, 1,2
Bloom, Ursula, 1898–, 2
Blower, Elizabeth, 1763–, 1
Boileau, Ethel, Lady, 1882–1942, 1
Bottome, Phyllis, 1864–1963, 1,2
Braddon, Mary Elizabeth Maxwell, 1837–1915, 1,2
Brand, Christianna, 1907–, 2
Bray, Anna Eliza Kempe, 1790–1883, 1
Brittain, Vera Mary, 1893–1970, 1,2
Bronte, Anne, 1820–1849, 1,2
Bronte, Charlotte, 1816–1855, 1,2
Bronte, Emily Jane, 1818–1848, 1,2
Broughton, Rhoda, 1840–1920, 1,2
Bryher (Bryer), pseud., 1894–, 2
Burnett, Frances Eliza Hodgson, 1849–1924, 1,2
Burney, Fanny, 1752–1840, 1,2
Butler, Gwendoline, 1922–, 2
Byatt, A. S. (Antonia Susan), 1936–, 2
Caird, (Alice) Mona, 1855–1932, 1,2
Caldwell, Taylor, 1900–1985, 1,2
Cambridge, Ada, 1844–1926, 2
Carey, Rosa Nouchette, 1840–1909, 2
Carter, Angela, 1940–, 2
Cartland, Barbara Hamilton, 1901–, 2
Charles, Elizabeth Rundle, 1828–1896, 1,2
Chatterton, Georgiana, Lady, 1806–1876, 2
Cholmondeley, Mary, 1859–1925, 1,2
Christie, Agatha (Mary Clarissa) Miller, Dame, 1891–1976, 1,2
Clay, Bertha M, pseud., 1836–1884, 1
Clifford, Lucy Lane, d. 1929, 1
Clive, Caroline Meyse-Wigley, 1801–1875, 2
Coleridge, Mary Elizabeth, 1861–1907, 2
Collins, Jackie, 1939–, 2
Collyer, Mary Mitchell, 1716–1762, 2
Compton-Burnett, Ivy, 1892–1969, 1,2
Conlon, Kathleen, 1943–, 2
Cookson, Catherine, 2
Cooper, Jilly, 1937–, 2
Corelli, Marie, pseud., 1854–1924, 1,2
Cost, March, d. 1973, 1,2
Cowden-Clarke, Mary Victoria, 1809–1898, 1,2

Craik, Dinah Maria Mulock, 1826–1887, 1,2
Craik, Georgiana, 1831–, 2
Crowe, Catherine Stevens, 1800–1876, 1,2
Curie, Mary, 1843–1905, 2
Danby, Frank, pseud., 1863–1916, 1
Dane, Clemence, pseud., 1887–1965, 1,2
Darcy, Clare, 2
Davys, Mary, fl. 1750s, 1
Delafield, E. M. (Edmee Monica), 1890–1943, 1,2
Dell, Ethel M., fl. 1939, 1
Dickens, Monica Enid, 1915–, 2
Diver, Katherine Maud Marshall, 1867–1945, 1,2
Dixie, Florence Caroline Douglas, Lady, 1857–1905, 1,2
Drabble, Margaret, 1939–, 2
Du Maurier, Daphne, Lady Browning, 1907–, 1,2
Duffy, Maureen, 1933–, 2
Dunn, Nell, 1936–, 2
Eden, Emily, 1797–1869, 1
Edwards, Amelia Ann Blanford, 1831–1892, 1,2
Eliot, George, pseud., 1819–1880, 1,2
Ellis, Sarah, 1810–1872, 2
Evans, Margaret, 2
Faithfull, Emily, 1835–1895, 1,2
Feinstein, Elaine, 1930–, 2
Ferrars, Elizabeth X., pseud., 1907–, 2
Fleming, Joan, 1908–, 2
Forster, Margaret, 1938–, 2
Fothergill, Jessie, 1851–1891, 1,2
Fowler, Ellen Thorneycroft, 1860–1929, 2
France, Marie de, fl. 1170s, 1
Frankau, Pamela, 1907–1967, 1,2
Fullerton, Georgiana Charlotte, Lady, 1812–1885, 1,2
Fulton, Mary, fl. 1910s, 1
Gaskell, Elizabeth Cleghorn Stevenson, 1810–1865, 1,2
Gibbons, Stella Dorothea, 1902–, 2
Gilliatt, Penelope Ann Douglas, 1924–, 2
Gillott, Jacky, 1939–, 2
Glyn, Elinor Sutherland, 1864–1943, 1,2
Godden, Rumer, pseud., 1907–, 1,2
Gore, Catherine Grace Frances Moody, 1799–1861, 1,2

Goudge, Elizabeth, 1900–1984, 1,2
Gray, Maxwell, 1847–1923, 1,2
Griffith, Elizabeth, 1730–1793, 1
Gunning, Susannah Minifie, 1740–
1800, 1
Hall, (Marguerite) Radclyffe, 1886–
1943, 1,2
Hansford-Johnson, Pamela, 1912–, 2
Hardwick, Mollie, 2
Harker, Lizzie Allen Watson, 1863–
1933, 1
Harraden, Beatrice, 1864–1936, 1,2
Harris, Elizabeth F. S., 1822–1852, 2
Harwood, Isabella, 1840–1888, 2
Hays, Mary, 1759–1843, 1,2
Haywood, Eliza Fowler, 1693–1756,
1,2
Heyer, Georgette, 1902–1974, 2
Hill, Susan, 1942–, 2
Hodge, Jane Aiken, 1917–, 2
Hodgman, Helen, 2
Holme, Constance, 1881–1955, 2
Holtby, Winifred, 1898–1935, 1,2
Howard, Elizabeth Jane, 1923–, 2
Howatch, Susan, 1940–, 2
Hoyt, Alva, fl. 1950s, 1
Hunt, Isobel Violet, 1866–1942, 2
Hunt, Violet, 1866–1942, 1,2
Huth, Angela, 1938–, 2
Inchbald, Elizabeth Simpson, 1753–
1821, 1,2
Ingelow, Jean, 1820–1897, 1,2
Irwin, Margaret, 2
Jacob, Naomi Ellington, 1884–1964, 2
James, P(hyllis) Dorothy, 1920–, 2
Jameson, (Margaret) Storm, 1891–,
1,2
Jesse, Frynwid Tennyson, d. 1958, 1
Jewsbury, Geraldine Endsor, 1812–
1880, 1,2
Johnson, Pamela Hansford, 1912–
1981, 1,2
Kavan, Anna (Helen Edmonds),
1901–1968, 2
Kaye, Mary Margaret, 1909–, 2
Kaye-Smith, Sheila, 1887–1956, 1,2
Kelly, Mary, 1927–, 2
Kennedy, Margaret, 1896–1967, 1,2
King, Alice, 1839–1894, 2
Kingsley, Mary, 1852–1931, 2
Lamb, Caroline, Lady, 1785–1828,
1,2
Landon, Letitia Elizabeth, 1802–
1838, 1,2

Laski, Marghanita, 1915–, 1,2
Lee, Harriet, 1757–1851, 1
Lee, Sophia, 1750–1824, 1
Lee, Vernon, pseud., 1856–1935, 1,2
Lehmann, Rosamund Nina, 1901–,
1,2
Leverson, Ada, 1862–1933, 2
Linton, Elizabeth Eliza Lynn, 1822–
1898, 1,2
Lofts, Norah Robinson, 1904–1983, 2
Long, Gabrielle Margaret Vere Camp-
bell, 1888–1952, 1
Lorrimer, Claire, 2
MacAulay, Rose, 1881–1958, 2
MacNaughton, Sarah, d. 1916, 1
Macaulay, Emily Rose, 1881–1958, 1
Macquoid, Katharine Sarah, 1824–
1917, 2
Manley, Mary de la Riviere, 1663–
1724, 1,2
Mann, Jessica, 1937–, 2
Mannin, Ethel Edith, 1900–1978, 1,2
Manning, Anne, 1807–1879, 1,2
Manning, Olivia, 1914–, 2
Marryat, Florence, 1838–1899, 1,2
Marshall, Emma, 1830–1899, 2
Mayo, Isabella Fyrie, 1843–, 2
Mayor, Flora Macdonald, 1872–
1932, 2
Meade, L. T., 1854–1914, 2
Meynell, Viola, 1896–1956, 1,2
Mirrlees, Hope, fl. 1910s, 1
Mitchell, Gladys, 1901–, 2
Mitford, Mary Russell, 1787–1855,
1,2
Mitford, Nancy Freman, 1907–1973,
1,2
Mortimer, Penelope Ruth Fletcher,
1918–, 2
Newman, Andrea, 1938–, 2
Noel, Augusta, Lady, 1838–1902, 2
Norton, Caroline Elizabeth Sarah
Sheridan, 1808–1877, 1,2
Norton, Mrs., 1827–1877, 1
Opie, Amelia Alderson, 1769–1853,
1,2
Ouida (pseud.), 1,2
Pardoe, Julia S. H., 1806–1862, 2
Pargeter, Edith, 1913–, 2
Parkin, Molly, 1932–, 2
Parr, Harriet, 1828–1900, 2
Perrin, Alice, 1867–1934, 1,2
Phillpotts, Eden, 1862–1960, 2
Plaidy, Jean, 1906–, 2

Plantin, Arabella, fl. 1720s, 1
Porter, Jane, 1776–1850, 1,2
Pratz, Claire de, fl. 1900s, 1
Prescott, Hilda Francis Margaret, 1896–1972, 1,2
Price, Eugenia, fl. 1950s, 1
Quin, Ann, 2
Radcliffe, Ann Ward, 1764–1823, 1,2
Rash, Doreen Wallace, gr. 1919, 1
Read, Miss, pseud., 2
Reeve, Clara, 1729–1807, 1,2
Reeves, Amber, fl. 1910s, 1
Reeves, Helen Mathers, 1853–1920, 2
Renault, Mary, pseud., 1905–1983, 1,2
Rendell, Ruth, 1930–, 2
Richardson, Dorothy Miller, 1872–1957, 1,2
Ritchie, Anne Isabella Thackeray, 1837–1919, 1
Robins, Denise, 1897–, 2
Robinson, Emma, 1814–1890, 2
Rowson, Susanna Haswell, 1762–1824, 1,2
Ruck, Berta, 1878–, 1
Sackville-West, Victoria Mary, 1892–1962, 1,2
Savage, Ethel Dell, 1881–1939, 2
Sayers, Dorothy Leigh, 1893–1957, 1,2
Sergeant, Adeline, 1851–1904, 1,2
Seton, Anya Chase, 1916–, 1,2
Sewell, Elizabeth Missing, 1815–1906, 2
Seymour, Beatrice Kean Stapleton, d. 1955, 1
Shelley, Mary Wollstonecraft Godwin, 1797–1851, 1,2
Sheppard, Elizabeth Sara, 1830–1862, 1,2
Sidgwick, Ethel, 1877–, 1
Sidhwa, Bapsi, 2
Simpson, Helen de Guerry, 1897–1940, 1
Sinclair, Mary (May), 1863–1946, 1,2
Smedley, Menella Bute, 1820–1877, 2
Smith, Charlotte Turner, 1749–1806, 1,2
Smith, Eleanor Armor, m. 1745, 1
Smith, Eleanor Furneaux, Lady, 1902–1945, 1
Smith, Stevie (Florence Margaret), 1902–1971, 2
Soldene, Emily, 1845–1912, 1

Spender, Lily, 1835–1896, 1
Stannard, Henrietta Eliza Vaughn Palmer, 1856–1911, 1
Steel, Flora Annie Webster, 1847–1929, 1,2
Stern, Gladys Bronwyn, 1890–1973, 1,2
Stewart, Mary Florence Elinor Rainbow, 1916–, 2
Stretton, Julia Cecilia Collinston Dewinton, 1812–1878, 1,2
Stubbs, Jean, 1926–, 2
Taylor, Elizabeth Coles, 1912–1975, 1,2
Tennant, Emma, 1937–, 2
Thirkell, Angela Margaret Mackail, 1890–1961, 1,2
Thompson, Flora, 1877–1947, 2
Thompson, Sylvia Elizabeth, 1902–, 1
Tonna, Charlotte Elizabeth Browne, 1790–1846, 2
Trollope, Frances Milton, 1780–1863, 1,2
Veley, Margaret, 1843–1887, 2
Weamys, Anne, fl. 1650s, 1
Webb, Mary Gladys Meredith, 1881–1927, 1,2
Webling, Peggy, fl. 1900s, 1
Weldon, Fay, fl. 1970s, 2
White, Antonia, 1899–, 2
Williams, Helen Marie, 1762–1827, 1,2
Wood, Ellen Price, 1814–1887, 1,2
Wood, Emma Caroline, 1802–1879, 2
Wood, Virginia, 1882–1941, 2
Woods, Margaret Louisa Bradley, 1856–1945, 1,2
Woolf, (Adeline) Virginia (Stephen), 1882–1941, 1,2
Yonge, Charlotte Mary, 1823–1901, 1,2
Yorke, Margaret, pseud., 1924–, 2

Novelists, French

Agoult, Marie Catherine Sophie Flavigny de, 1805–1876, 1,2
Audoux, Marguerite, 1863–1937, 1,2
Audry, Colette, fl. 1940s, 1
Beauvoir, Simone Lucie Ernestine Maria Bertrand de, 1908–1986, 1,2
Beck, Beatrix, 1914–, 1
Bertin, Celia, 1921–, 1
Blanc, Marie Therese, 1840–1907, 1
Bourniquel, Camille, 1918–, 1
Colette, Sidonie Gabrielle Claudine, 1873–1954, 1,2

O'Brien, Edna, 1930–, 2
O'Brien, Kate, 1897–1974, 1,2
Riddell, Charlotte Eliza Lawson
  Cowan, 1832–1906, 1,2
Ross, Amanda McKettrick, 1861–
  1939, 2
Sadlier, Mary Anne Madden, 1820–
  1903, 1,2
Sheridan, Frances Chamberlaine,
  1724–1766, 1,2
Somerville, Edith Anna Oenone,
  1858–1949, 1,2
Voynich, Ethel Lilian, 1864–1960, 2
West, Rebecca, Dame, pseud., 1892–
  1983, 1,2
Novelists, Italian
  Deledda, Grazia, 1875–1936, 1,2
  Ginzburg, Natalia, fl. 1960s, 2
  Morante, Elsa, 1918–, 2
  Serao, Matilda, 1856–1927, 1
Novelists, Japanese
  Murasaki Shikibu, Lady Murasaki,
    978–1030, 2
Novelists, New Zealand
  Ashton-Warner, Sylvia, 1908–1978, 2
  Frame, Janet, 1924–, 2
  Hyde, Robin, 2
  Mansfield, Katherine, pseud., 1888–
    1923, 1,2
  Marsh, Edith Ngaio, Dame, 1899–
    1982, 1,2
Novelists, Norwegian
  Collett(e), Camilla Wergeland, 1813–
    1895, 2
  Ostenso, Martha, 1900–1963, 1,2
  Sandel, Cora, 1880–1974, 2
  Undset, Sigrid, 1832–1949, 1,2
Novelists, Polish
  Zapolska, Gabryela, 1860–1921, 1
Novelists, Romanian
  Vacarescu, Helene, 1866–1947, 2
Novelists, Russian
  Chukovskaya, Lydia, fl. 1930s, 2
  Federova, Nina, 1895–, 1,2
  Gippius, Zinaida, 1869–1945, 2
  Kobyljanska, Olga, 1863–1942, 1
  Krudener, Barbara Juliane von
    Vietinghoff, 1764–1824, 1,2
  Panova, Vera, 1905–1973, 2
  Rand, Ayn, 1905–1982, 1,2
  Sarraute, Nathalie, 1900–, 1,2
  Scott, Natalie Anderson, 1906–, 1
  Serebriakova, Galina, 1905–, 2
  Triolet, Elsa, 1896–1970, 1,2

Novelists, Scottish
  Brunton, Mary, 1778–1818, 2
  Carswell, Catherine MacFarlane Rox-
    burgh, 1879–1946, 1,2
  Craig, Isa, 1831–1903, 2
  Davie, Elspeth, 2
  Dunnett, Dorothy, 1923–, 2
  Ferrier, Susan Edmonstone, 1782–
    1854, 1,2
  Findlater, Jane Helen, 1866–1946, 1
  Gordon, Katherine, 2
  Hawker, Mary Elizabeth, 1848–
    1908, 2
  Humphreys, Mrs. Desmond, 1860–
    1938, 2
  MacInnes, Helen Clark, 1907–1985,
    1,2
  MacKintosh, Elizabeth, 1896–1952, 1
  Mitchison, Naomi Margaret Haldane,
    1897–1964, 1,2
  Oliphant, Margaret Wilson, 1828–
    1897, 2
  Peck, Winifred Frances Knox, gr.
    1904, 1
  Ross, Ishbel, 1897–1975, 1,2
  Sinclair, Catherine, 1800–1864, 2
  Spark, Muriel Sarah Camberg, 1918–,
    2
  Tey, Josephine, pseud., 1897–1952, 2
  Walford, Lucy Bethia Colquhoun,
    1845–1915, 1,2
Novelists, South African
  Drummond, June, 1923–, 2
  Goquiiolay-Arellano, Remidios,
    1911–, 2
  Gordimer, Nadine, 1923–, 1,2
  Lessing, Doris May, 1919–, 1,2
  Lewis, Ethelreda, 189?–1946, 1
  Millin, Sarah Gertrude Liebson,
    1889–1968, 1,2
  Schreiner, Olive, 1855–1920, 1,2
  Wilson, Ethel Davis, 1888–1980, 2
Novelists, Spanish
  Arenal de Garcia Carrasco, Dona
    Conception, 1820–1893, 1
  Castro, Rosalie de, 1837–1885, 1,2
  Laforet, Carmen, fl. 1940s, 2
  Pardo-Bazan, Emilia, 1851–1921, 1,2
Novelists, Swedish
  Boye, Karin, 1900–1941, 2
  Bremer, Frederika, 1801–1865, 1,2
  Carlen, Emilie Smite, 1807–1892, 1
  Edgren, Anne Charlotte Leffler,
    1849–1892, 1

Lagerlof, Selma Ottiniana Louisa, 1858–1940, 1,2
Wahloo, Per, 1926–1975, 2
Novelists, Tasmanian
Lyttleton, Doris Jean, 1873–1945, 1
Ward, Mary Augusta Arnold, 1851–1920, 2
Ward, Mrs. Humphrey, 1851–1920, 2
Novelists, Welsh
Laing, Dilys Bennett, 1906–1960, 2
Rhys, Jean, 1894–1979, 2
Roberts, Kate, 1891–, 2
Royde-Smith, Naomi Gwladys, 1875–1964, 1,2
Rubens, Bernice, 1927–, 2
Nuclear engineers
Libby, Leona M., fl. 1940s, 2
Nuclear Information Center
Maskewitz, Betty F., fl. 1960s, 2
Nuclear physicists
Capo, Mary Ann, fl. 1950s, 2
Carter, Virginia L., 1936–, 2
Hansen, Luisa Fernandes, 2
Meitner, Lise, 1878–1968, 1,2
Way, Katherine, 1903–, 2
Wu, Chien-Shiung, 1912–, 1,2
Yalow, Rosalyn Sussman, 1921–, 2
Nun's Coalition
Donnelly, Dorothy, Sister, 2
Nuns
See also
Abbesses
Specific orders
Agreda, Maria de (Maria Fernandez Coronel), 1602–1664, 1
Aikenhead, Sister Mary, 1787–1858, 1
Alacoque, Marguerite Maria, 1647–1690, 1
Alardine Gasquiere, Sister, fl. 1450s, 2
Alcoforado, Marianna, 1640–1723, 1
Aloysia, Sister, fl. 1840s, 1
Angela Merici, Saint, 1474–1540, 1,2
Anna Marie, Sister, fl. 1930s, 1
Antonia O.S.D. Fischer, 1849–, 1
Arguello, Concha Maria de Concepcion, 1791–1857, 1,2
Auguste, Phillipe, 1164–1225, 1
Ava, Frau, fl. 1100s, 1
Beatrix D'Este, d. 1262, 1
Benizelos, Philothey, fl. 1650s, 1
Berners, Dame Juliana, 1388–, 1
Bertels, Thomas More, Sister, 2
Billiart, Julie, Blessed, 1751–1816, 1

Bizalion, Anne Catherine, 2
Boillet, Colette, 1381–1447, 2
Bonzel, Mother Mary Theresia, 1830–1905, 1
Borgia, Mary Borgia, fl. 1930s, 1
Bresoles, Judith de, d. 1673, 2
Buhse, Sheila, Sister, fl. 1970s, 2
Butler, Marie Joseph, 1860–1940, 2
Butler, Sally, fl. 1970s, 2
Cahoon, Mary Odile, fl. 1970s, 2
Cannon, Harriet Starr, 1823–1896, 2
Carl, Mary, fl. 1970s, 2
Carroll, Elizabeth, 2
Caspary, Anita, 2
Cecelia, 2
Celeste, Maria, Sister, d. 1642, 1
Chapellin, Emilia, Mother, 1858–1890, 1
Christy, Mary Rose, 2
Clara (Clare) of Assisi, 1193–1253, 1,2
Clara Isabella Fornari, 1697–1744, 1
Clarke, Mary Frances, Mother, 1803–1887, 1,2
Claudia, Mother Superior, 2
Clement, Alice, fl. 1200s, 1
Connelly, Cornelia Augusta, 1809–1879, 1,2
Coston, Carol, 1935–, 2
Crescentia, Sister, fl. 1960s, 1
Cruz, Sor Juana Ines de la, 1651–1695, 2
Cunegunde, d. 1040, 1,2
D'Youville, Marie Marguerite, 1701–1771, 1,2
Daigler, Jeremy, 2
Deckers, Jeanne, 1933–, 2
Declan, Mother, 1
Dempsey, Mary Joseph, 1856–1939, 2
Dominica, Mary, d. 1857, 2
Donella, 2
Donnelly, Dorothy, Sister, 2
Duchesne, Rose Philippine, 1769–1852, 1,2
Durocher, Mary Rose, Mother, 1811–1868, 1
Egan, Jogues, 1918–, 2
Elizabeth, 1890–1945, 1
Emmerich, Anna Katharina, 1774–1824, 1,2
Ende, 2
Etheria (Aetheria), 2
Eutropia McMahon, Mother, fl. 1900s, 1

Romuald, Mary, 1895–, 2
Rosalita, Sister, fl. 1940s, 1
Rostwitha (Hrosvitha), 935–1000, 1,2
Russell, Mary Baptist, Mother, 1829–1898, 2
Saint Augustine, Mother, fl. 1830s, 1
Salis, Giugone, d. 1470, 1
Santa Francesca Romana, 1384–1440, 1
Schervier, Frances, 1819–1876, 1
Schwager, Virginia, fl. 1940s, 2
Segale, Blandina, Sister, 1850–, 2
Sinclair, Margaret, 1900–1925, 1
Sister A of Santa Marta, fl. 1500s, 2
Sister of the Beguines of Fl.., fl. 1340s, 1
Spalding, Catherine, Mother, 1793–1858, 1,2
St. Damien, Sister, 1
St. Remi, Sister, 1
Stanislaus, Sister, fl. 1800s, 1
Stein, Edith, 1891–1942, 1,2
Stevens, Georgia Lydia, Mother, 1870–1946, 1,2
Teresa, M. Imelda, 1862–, 1
Teresa, Mother (1), 1910–, 2
Theresa of Lisieux, 1873–1897, 1,2
Theresa of the Cross Chevrel, fl. 1830s, 1
Thomas Aquinas, Sister, 1884–1957, 1
Tranchepain de Saint Augustin., Marie de, Sister, d. 1733, 1
Ursula of Munsterberg, 1491–1534, 2
Van Rensselaer, Euphemia, 1840–, 1
Veronica, M., fl. 1960s, 1
Veronica Giuliani, Saint, 1660–1697, 1,2
Virginia, Sister, 1575–1650, 1
Wexler, Jacqueline Grennan, 1926–, 2
Whateley, Anne, Sister, 1561–1600, 1,2
Youville, Marie Marguerite Dufrus de la Gesmerais, 1701–1771, 1,2
Yu Hsuan-Chi, d. 870, 1
Nurse corps organizer
McGee, Anita Newcomb, 1864–1940, 1,2
Nurses
   See also
   Air Force nurses
   Army nurses
   Civil War nurses
   Midwives
   Navy nurses

Public health nurses
Acca Laurentia, 634 BC, 1
Aikenhead, Sister Mary, 1787–1858, 1
Alardine Gasquiere, Sister, fl. 1450s, 2
Angela Merici, Saint, 1474–1540, 1,2
Auguste, Phillipe, 1164–1225, 1
Ayers, Lucy C., 1865–, 1
Baggallay, Olive, fl. 1930s, 1
Baker, Bessie, fl. 1920s, 1
Bari-Dussot, Comtesse "Mlle. Petite", fl. 1914, 1
Barton, Clara Harlowe, 1821–1912, 1,2
Beard, Mary, 1875–1946, 1
Beckford, Lydia C., 1703–1804, 1
Beeby, Nell V., 1896–1957, 1
Behrens, Edna, fl. 1940s, 2
Belmont, Eleanor Elise Robson, 1879–1979, 1,2
Benjamin, Sarah Matthews, 1744–1861, 1
Berg, Eva, 2
Bickerdyke, Mary Ann Ball "Mother", 1817–1901, 1,2
Bihet, Mille., fl. 1950s, 1
Birchard, Dora E., 1
Biscot, Jeanne Arras, 1601–1664, 1,2
Blake, Florence G., 1907–, 1
Boardman, Mabel Thorp, 1860–1946, 1,2
Bois-Berenger, Madame de, fl. 1700s, 1
Bolton, Frances Payne Bingham, 1885–1977, 1,2
Bonzel, Mother Mary Theresia, 1830–1905, 1
Borden, Helen, fl. 1870s, 1
Bradley, Amy Morris, 1823–1904, 1,2
Breckinridge, Mary, 1877–1965, 1,2
Bresoles, Judith de, d. 1673, 2
Brewster, Mary, 2
Brinton, Mary Williams, fl. 1940s, 1
Brockway, Marion T., fl. 1900s, 1
Brown, Esther Lucile, fl. 1940s, 1
Browne, Charlotte, fl. 1750s, 1
Browne, Dame Sidney Jane, 1850–1941, 1
Buckel, Cloe Annette, 1833–1912, 2
Burgess, Elizabeth Chamberlain, 1877–1949, 1
Butler, Ida Fatio, 1868–1949, 1
Cannon, Ida Maud, 1877–1916, 2
Cannon, Martha (Mattie) Hughes, 2

Johnson, Florence Merriam, fl.
1910s, 1
Jones, Agnes Elizabeth, 1832–1868, 1
Jordan, Alice Boyer, fl. 1930s, 1
Joy, Helen N., fl. 1920s, 1
Kantorovich, Leah, fl. 1970s, 2
Karll, Agnes, 1872–1927, 1
Kasper, Catharine, fl. 1810s, 1
Keller, Florence, 1900–, 2
Keller, Manelva Wylie, fl. 1900s, 1
Kempner, Mary Jean, 1
Kenny, Elizabeth, 1886–1952, 1,2
Kildare, Brigid of, 453–523, 1
Kimball, Martha Gertrude, 1840–
1894, 1
Kimber, Diana Clifford, d. 1928, 1
Kingsley, Mary Henrietta, 1862–
1900, 1,2
La Motte, Ellen Newbold, 1873–
1961, 1
Lally, Grace, 1
Lane, Anna Maria, fl. 1770s, 2
Lathrop, Rose Hawthorne, 1851–
1926, 1,2
Lawler, Elsie M., fl. 1900s, 1
Le Gras, Louise, 1591–1660, 1,2
Lees, Dacre, fl. 1870s, 1
Leete, Harriet L., d. 1927, 1
Leonard, Vera, 2
Levertov, Denise, 1923–, 2
Linthicum, Barbara, 2
Livingston, Nora Gertrude, 1847–
1927, 1
Logan, Laura R., fl. 1920s, 1
Loveridge, Emily L., 1860–, 1
Lynch, Joseph, Mother, fl. 1860s, 1
Maass, Clara Louise, 1876–1901, 1,2
MacAuley, Catherine, 1787–1841, 1
MacDonald, V. May, fl. 1920s, 1
MacLeod, Charlotte, gr. 1891, 1
Mahoney, Mary Eliza, 1845–1926,
1,2
Mance, Jeanne, 1606–0673, 1,2
Mannerheim, Sophie, 1863–1928, 1
Marcela, 325–420, 1,2
Margaret of Meteola, 1287–1320, 1
Maria Gratia, Mother, fl. 1920s, 1
Maria Kristina, 1911–, 1
Marianne, Sister, fl. 1900s, 1
Mason, Biddy "Grandma", 1818–
1891, 1,2
Mayo, Edith Graham, fl. 1930s, 1,2
McInsaac, Isabel, 1858–1914, 1
Meirs, Linda, fl. 1910s, 1

Mellinchamp, Julia St. Lo, d. 1939, 1
Melun, Madamoiselle de, d. 1679, 2
Miller, Elizabeth, d. 1940, 1
Miller, Mable, fl. 1930s, 2
Mons Tessa, fl. 1200s, 2
Muchmore, Donna, fl. 1970s, 2
Muller, Eliza, d. 1876, 2
Muse, Maude B., fl. 1920s, 1
Neff, Mary, fl. 1690s, 1,2
Nice, Mrs., 1622, 2
Nienhuys, Janna, m. 1937, 1
Nightingale, Florence, 1820–1910,
1,2
Noyes, Clara Dutton, 1869–1936, 1,2
O'Connell, Anthony, Sister, 1814–
1897, 2
O'Donnell, Mary Agnes, d. 1938, 1
O'Driscoll, Hannah, 1892–, 1
O'Hara, Dolores B., 1935–, 1
Ohlson, Agnes, fl. 1950s, 1
Olsen, Mae, 1
Osborn, Mrs. William Church, fl.
1870s, 1
Osburn, Lucy, 1837–1891, 1
Ott, Elsie S., 1
Ott, Frances M., fl. 1890s, 1
Paget, Lady Arthur, 1865–1919, 1
Palmer, Sophia F., d. 1920, 1
Pennock, Meta, fl. 1930s, 1
Petry, Lucile, 1903–, 1
Pope, Amy Elizabeth, fl. 1890s, 1
Porter, Elizabeth Kerr, 1894–, 1
Pringle, Angelique Lucille, 1846–
1920, 1
Prochazka, Anne, 1897–, 1
Radegonde, 518–587, 1,2
Randolph, Anne Dillon, fl. 1920s, 1
Reichardt, Gertrude, fl. 1800s, 1
Riddle, Estelle Massey, 1903–, 1
Robb, Isabel Adams Hampton, 1860–
1910, 1,2
Roberts, Mary May, 1877–1959, 1,2
Robinson, Mary, fl. 1850s, 1
Romuald, Mary, 1895–, 2
Russell, Martha M., fl. 1910s, 1
Salis, Giugone, d. 1470, 1
Sandes, Flora, fl. 1910s, 1,2
Schervier, Frances, 1819–1876, 1
Sciffi, Clare Dei, 1194–1253, 1
Selassie, Tsahai Haile, 1919–1942, 1
Sellew, Gladys, 1887–, 1
Seymour, Louise, fl. 1890s, 1
Shaw, Flora Madeline, gr. 1896, 1
Shaw, Margaret Elizabeth, fl. 1940s, 1

Sieveking, Amalie, 1794–1859, 1
Simpson, Cora E., fl. 1900s, 1
Sirch, Margaret Frances, fl. 1920s, 1
Sister of the Beguines of Fl.., fl.
    1340s, 1
Sleeper, Ruth, 1899–, 1
Smellie, Elizabeth, fl. 1910s, 1
Smith, Alice Maud, fl. 1920s, 2
Smith, Mary Heathman "Granny", 2
Snively, Mary Agnes, d. 1933, 1
Stanislaus, Sister, fl. 1800s, 1
Stimson, Julia Catherine, 1881–1948,
    1,2
Stinetorf, Louise, fl. 1950s, 1
Strong, Rebecca Thorogood, 1843–
    1944, 1
Stroup, Leora, fl. 1940s, 1
Sutliffe, Irene, d. 1936, 1
Swope, Ethel, fl. 1930s, 1
Talcott, Eliza, 1836–1911, 2
Taylor, Effie J., fl. 1920s, 1
Taylor, Euphemia J., fl. 1900s, 1
Taylor, Rebecca, fl. 1800s, 1
Thoms, Adah B. Samuels, 1863–
    1943, 1,2
Tracy, Susan E., d. 1928, 1
Tucker, Lucy Dougherty, fl. 1770s, 1
Turner, Kerenhappuch, fl. 1780s, 2
Ubaldina of Pisa, Sister, fl. 1100s, 2
Unwin, Mary, 1724–1796, 1,2
Upjohn, Elizabeth P., 1876–1910, 1
Vail, Stella Boothe, fl. 1910s, 1
Van Blarcom, Carolyn Conant, 1879–
    1960, 1,2
Van Rensselaer, Euphemia, 1840–, 1
Vigri, Caterina da (Catherine of Bolo-
    gna), 1413–1463, 1,2
Wald, Lillian D., 1867–1940, 1,2
Warne, Margaret Vliet "Aunt Peggy",
    1751–1840, 1,2
Warr, Emma Louise, 1847–1937, 1
Way, Amanda M., 1828–1914, 1,2
Weeks-Shaw, Clara, fl. 1800s, 1
Whitmore, Mrs. Thomas, fl. 1760s,
    1,2
Whyte, Edna Gardner, fl. 1930s, 1
Williams, Rachel, 1840–1908, 1
Wilson, Maude H. Mellish, d. 1933, 1
Wolf, Anna D., fl. 1930s, 1
Zabriskie, Louise G., 1864–1963, 1
Zaleska, Katherina, 1919–, 2
Zimmerman, Anne, fl. 1970s, 2
Nursing educators
Maxwell, Anna Caroline, 1851–1929,
    1,2

Nutting, Mary Adelaide, 1858–1948,
    1,2
Powell, Louise Mathilde, 1871–1943,
    2
Richards, Linda Ann, 1841–1930, 1,2
Stewart, Isabel Maitland, 1878–1963,
    1,2
Nursing homes
Graham, Mary Belle Gleamons, fl.
    1970s, 2
Nut museums
Tashjian, Elizabeth, fl. 1930s, 2
Nutritionists
Barber, Mary Isabel, 1887–1963, 1
Blunt, Katharine, 1876–1954, 1,2
Cave, Jessie King, 1897–, 2
Christian, Angela, 2
Cooper, Lenna Frances, fl. 1930s, 1
Davis, Adelle, 1904–1974, 2
Delafield, Ann, fl. 1930s, 1
Dye, Marie, 1891–, 1
Elsom, Katharine O'Shea, 1903–, 1
Farmer, Fannie Merritt, 1857–1915,
    1,2
Flager, Alicia Mayre, fl. 1930s, 1
Fougeret, Madame, 2
Frankelstein, Beatrice, fl. 1960s, 1
George, Susan, fl. 1970s, 2
Gilmore, Marion Sprague, fl. 1930s, 1
Goldsmith, Grace Arabell, 1904–
    1975, 2
Gonzalez, Nancie Loudon, fl. 1970s,
    2
Graves, Lulu Grace, 1874–1949, 1
Hager, Alice Mayre, fl. 1930s, 1
Hentschel-Guernth, Dorothea,
    1749–, 2
Lappe, Frances Moore, 1944–, 2
MacLeod, Grace, 1878–1962, 1
Metzelthin, Pearl Violetta, 1894–
    1947, 1
Morgan, Agnes Fay, 1884–1968, 1,2
Pattee, Alida Francis, d. 1942, 1
Raymond, Marilyn A., fl. 1970s, 2
Richards, Ellen Henrietta Swallow,
    1842–1911, 1,2
Roberts, Lydia Jane, 1879–1965, 2
Rorer, Sarah Tyson Heston, 1849–
    1937, 2
Rose, Mary Davies Swartz, 1874–
    1941, 1,2
Santos, Jocelina, 1956–, 2
Stern, Frances, 1873–1947, 2
Strahan, Elsie T., fl. 1920s, 1

Streeter, Virginia, 2
Swallow, Ellen, 1842–1911, 1
Wheeler, Ruth, 1877–1948, 2
Wittenmyer, Annie Turner, 1827–
1900, 1,2

O

O'Connor, Carroll—Spouse
O'Connor, Nancy, 1931–, 2
O'Neill, Eugene—Spouse
O'Neill, Carlotta Montery Hazel
Tharsing, 1888–1970, 2
Obolensky, Prince—Spouse
Obolensky, Alice Astor, m. 1924, 1
Obstetricians
Adelmota, Princess of Carrara, fl.
1300s, 2
Angiolina of Padua, 2
Boivin, (Marie) Anne Victoire Gillain,
1773–1841, 1,2
Cellier, Elizabeth, fl. 1642, 2
Chantal, Jeanne Francois Fremiot,
1574–1641, 1,2
Chinnatamby, Siva, fl. 1950s, 2
Costa (Coste), Blanche Marie de, fl.
1566, 2
Cramer, Vrow, 1655–, 2
Daniel, Annie Sturges, 1858–1944, 2
Dickins, Helen Octavia, 1900–, 2
Donne, Maria Delle, 1776–1842, 1,2
Duges, Marie Louise, 1769–1821, 2
Duges, Marie-Jonet, 1730–1797, 2
Durocher, Marie Josefina, 1809–
1895, 1
Edwards, Lena Frances, 1900–, 1
Eleanora, Duchess of Mantua, 2
Ferebee, Dorothy, fl. 1920s, 2
Kaltenbeiner, Victorine, 2
Kazhanova, Dr., 2
Kleegman, Sophie Josephine, 1900–
1971, 1,2
Leboursier, Angelique Marguerite
DuCourdray, 1712–1789, 2
Mears, Martha, 2
Morata, Fulvia of Ferrara, 2
Petraccini, Maria, fl. 1780s, 2
Saxtorph, Matthias, 1740–1800, 2
Siebold, Charlotte von, 1761–1859,
1,2
Siebold, Regina Joseph Henning von,
1761–, 2

Siegemundin, Justine(a) Dittrichin,
1645–1705, 2
Stephen, Margaret, fl. 1790s, 2
Storch, Marcia, 1933–, 2
Trotula of Salerno, fl. 1000s, 1,2
Van Hoosen, Bertha, 1863–1952, 1,2
Warne, Margaret Vliet "Aunt Peggy",
1751–1840, 1,2
Occultists
Halpir, Salomee Anne, 1719–1786,
1,2
Turbeville, Sarah, fl. 1700s, 2
Occupational therapists
Fish, Marjorie, fl. 1930s, 1
Slagle, Eleanor Clarke, 1872–1942, 2
Oceanographers
Bunce, Elizabeth T., fl. 1940s, 2
Clark, Eugenie, 1922–, 1,2
Earle, Sylvia A., 1935–, 2
Joye, Judy, fl. 1970s, 2
Kleinova, Maria V., fl. 1950s, 2
Octavian—Daughter
Julia, fl. 13 BC, 1
Octogenarians
Bloom, Sara, 1900–, 2
Huntington, Hallie, 1898–, 2
Oculists
Ulricha de Foschua, 2
Odysseus—Spouse
Penelope, 67 AD, 1,2
Offa—Spouse
Cynethryth, 757–796, 1
Ohio
Brown, Martha (Mattie) McLellan,
1838–1916, 1,2
Cave, Jessie King, 1897–, 2
Compton, Otelia Katherine Augs-
perger, 1859–1944, 1,2
Cooper, Martha Kinney, 1874–, 2
Hayes, Lucy Ware Webb, 1831–1889,
1,2
Mock, Jerrie Fredritz, 1925–, 2
Poling, Lillian Diebold, 1880–, 2
Rickoff, Rebecca Davis, fl. 1870s, 2
Sheridan, Mary, 1810–, 2
Solomon, Margaret Grey "Mother
Solomon", 1815–1890, 2
Thomson, Mary Moore Dabney,
1887–, 2
Zwick, Florence, 1894–, 2
Okanogon Indians
Mourning Dove "Hum-Ishu-Ma",
1888–1936, 2
Oklahoma
Hall, Ruby Hibler, 1912–, 2
Metcalf, Augusta J. C., 1871–, 2

Gadski, Johanna, 1872–1932, 1,2
Galli-Curci, Amelita, 1882–1963, 1,2
Garden, Mary, 1877–1967, 1,2
Garrison, Mabel, 1888–1963, 1,2
Gates, Emma Lucy, 1880–, 2
Gay, Maria, 1879–1943, 1,2
Gerville-Reache, Jeanne, 1882–1915, 1,2
Giannini, Dusolina, 1902–, 1,2
Gluck, Alma, 1884–1938, 1,2
Grisi, Giulia, 1,2
Guden, Hilde, 1917–, 1,2
Hamlin, Anna, 1902–, 2
Harper, Heather, 1930–, 2
Hauk (Hauck), Minnie, 1851–1929, 1,2
Hempel, Frieda, 1885–1955, 1,2
Henders, Harriet, 1904–1972, 1,2
Hoeppel, Elizabeth, fl. 1930s, 2
Homer, Louise Dilworth Beatty, 1871–1947, 1,2
Horne, Marilyn B., 1934–, 1,2
Hunt, Marsha (Marcia Virginia), 1917–, 2
Hunter, Rita, 1933–, 2
Ingram, Frances, 1883–, 1,2
Janowitz, Gundula, 1937–, 2
Jarboro, Caterina (Yarborough), 1903–, 1,2
Jepson, Helen, 1906–, 1,2
Jeritza, Maria, Baronness von Popper, 1887–, 1,2
Jurinac, Sena, 1921–, 1,2
Kanawa, Kiri Te, 1944–, 2
Kappel, Gertrude, 1884–1971, 1,2
Kellogg, Clara Louise, 1842–1916, 1,2
Kirsten, Dorothy, 1917–, 1,2
Klafsky, Katharina, 1855–1896, 1,2
Korjus, Miliza, 1900–1980, 2
Kronold, Selma, 1861–1920, 1,2
Kurt, Melanie, 1880–1941, 1,2
Kurtz, Selma, 1874–1933, 1,2
Lawrence, Marjorie, 1908–1979, 1,2
Lear, Evelyn Shulman, 1929–, 2
Lehmann, Lilli, 1848–1929, 1,2
Lehmann, Lotte, 1886–1976, 1,2
Leslie, Amy, 1855–1939, 1,2
Lewis, Jessica, 1890–1972, 2
Lewis, May, 1900–1941, 2
Liebling, Estelle, 1880–1970, 1,2
Lind, Jenny, 1820–1887, 1,2
Lindsey, Claudia, fl. 1970s, 2
Lipkowska, Lydia, 1882–1955, 1,2

Lorengar, Pilar, 1928–, 2
Ludwig, Christa, 1932–, 2
Macbeth, Florence, 1891–, 1,2
Madeira, Jean Browning, 1918–1972, 1,2
Manski, Dorothee, 1895–1967, 1,2
Mario, Queen(a) Tillotson, 1896–1951, 1,2
Marton, Eva, 1943–, 2
Mason, Edith Barnes, 1893–1973, 1,2
Massey, Ilona, 1912–1974, 1,2
Mathis, Edith, 1938–, 2
Matzenauer, Margarete, 1881–1963, 1,2
Mazarin, Mariette, 1874–1953, 1,2
Meisle, Kathryn, 1895–1970, 1,2
Melba, Nellie, Dame, 1859–1931, 1,2
Melis, Carmen, 1885–1967, 1,2
Milnes, Sherrill, 1935–, 2
Minton, Yvonne, 1938–, 2
Modl, Martha, 1912–, 1,2
Moffo, Anna, 1932–, 1,2
Moore, Grace, 1898–1947, 1,2
Mueller, Maria, 1898–1958, 1
Muller, Maria, 1898–1958, 2
Munsel, Patricia, 1925–, 1,2
Muzio, Claudia, 1889–1936, 1,2
Nau, Maria Dolores Benedicta Josefina, 1818–1891, 1,2
Nevada, Emma Wixom, 1859–1940, 1,2
Nielson, Alice, 1876–1943, 1,2
Nilsson, Christine, 1843–1921, 1,2
Nilsson, (Marta) Birgit, 1918–, 1,2
Nordica, Lillian, pseud, 1857–1914, 1,2
Norena, Eide (Kaja Hansen Eide), 1884–, 1,2
Norman, Jessye, 1945–, 2
Ober, Margarette, 1,2
Olivero, Magda, 1913–, 2
Onegin, Sigrid, 1889–1943, 1,2
Pasta, Giuditta Negri, 1798–1865, 1,2
Paton, Mary Anne, 1802–1864, 1,2
Patti, Adelina (Adela Joana Maria), 1843–1919, 1,2
Peters, Roberta, 1930–, 1,2
Phillipps, Adelaide, 1833–1882, 1,2
Pons, Lily Alice Josephine, 1904–1976, 1,2
Ponselle, Rose Melba, 1897–1981, 1,2
Popova, Katya Asenova, 1924–1966, 2
Popp, Lucia, 1939–, 2

Prentiss, Narcissa, 1808–, 2
Riker, Janette, 1,2
Organic chemists
    Hahn, Dorothy Anna, 1876–1950, 2
Organists
    Adams, Carrie B., 1859–1940, 1
    Albani, Emma Lajeunesse, 1847–
      1930, 1,2
    Andree, Elfrida, 1844–1929, 1
    Bartholomew, Ann S. Mounsey,
      1811–1891, 1
    Beardsley, Caroline Lattin, 1860–
      1944, 2
    Biresak, Thusnelda, 1
    Bixby, Allene K., d. 1947, 1
    Briel, Marie, 1896–, 2
    Briggs, Cora S., 1
    Broughton, Julia, 1
    Calegari, Cornelia, 1644–, 1
    Coci, Claire, fl. 1930s, 1
    Couperin, Celeste, 1793–1860, 2
    Crowe, Bonita, fl. 1940s, 1
    Dickerman, Julia Elida, 1859–, 1
    Downey, Mary E., fl. 1940s, 1
    Eakin, Vero O., 1900–, 1
    Farmer, Bess "Miss Bess", 1919–, 2
    Foster, Bertha M., fl. 1940s, 1
    Foster, Fay, 1886–1960, 1,2
    Garron, Etta R. Small, 1887–, 2
    Genet, Marianne, fl. 1900s, 1
    Goodrich, Florence, fl. 1940s, 1
    Hall, Ruth Julia, fl. 1920s, 1
    Hatch, Edith, 1884–, 1
    Hill, Mildred J., 1859–1916, 1,2
    Hopkins, Linda, 1925–, 2
    Jewitt, Jessie Mae, fl. 1940s, 1
    Lang, Edith, fl. 1940s, 1
    Lewis, Allie May, 1859–1930, 2
    Lockwood, Charlotte, fl. 1940s, 1,2
    Moore, Caroline Rudy, 1943–, 2
    Ostinelli, Sophie Henriette Hewitt, d.
      1846, 2
    Patterson, Annie Wilson, 1868–1934,
      1
    Pelton-Jones, Frances, fl. 1940s, 1
    Perfield, Effa Ellis, fl. 1940s, 1
    Pollock, Muriel, fl. 1930s, 1
    Raymond, Carrie B., fl. 1880s, 2
    Risher, Anna Priscilla, 1875–, 1
    Ritter, Irene Marschand, fl. 1940s, 1
    Roobenian, Amber, 1905–, 1
    Schaeffer, Mary, 1
    Sheldon, Lillian Taitt, 1865–1925, 1
    Smith, Ella May, 1860–1934, 1

Smith, Ethel, 1910–, 2
    Smith, Georgina, fl. 1930s, 1
    Stair, Patty, 1869–1926, 1,2
    Stairs, Louise E., 1892–, 1,2
    Stirling, Elizabeth, 1819–1895, 1,2
    Vannah, Kate, 1855–1933, 1
    Wallace, Sippie, 1898–1926, 2
    Westbrook, Helen Searles, 1898–, 1
Organization officials
    Achelis, Elisabeth, 1
    Adams, Abby, fl. 1910s, 1
    Ahlgren, Mildred Carlson, 1902–, 1
    Allen, Martha Frances, 1906–, 1,2
    Anderson, Constance Myers, 1898–,
      1
    Beck, Mildred Buchwalder, 1914–, 1
    Blalock, Ruby Wooten, 1905–, 1
    Blanchard, Hazel Ann, 1920–, 1
    Bowron, Elizabeth Moore, fl. 1890s,
      1
    Boynton, Helen Mason, m. 1871, 1
    Bragdon, Helen Dalton, 1895–, 1
    Breckinridge, Aida de Acosta, 1884–
      1962, 1,2
    Brode, Mildred Hooker, 1900–, 1
    Buchanan, Mrs. Robert, fl. 1890s, 1
    Buck, Dorothea Dutcher, 1887–, 1
    Bushnell, Sophie Walker Hyndshaw,
      m. 1878, 1
    Butler, Sally, 1891–, 1
    Caldwell, Sarah Campbell, 1903–, 1
    Carraway, Gertrude Sprague, 1896–,
      1
    Cass, Melnea, 2
    Chapman, Helen Louise Busch,
      1904–, 1
    Colvin, Mamie White, 1883–1955, 1
    Conkling, Julia Catherine, 1827–
      1893, 1
    Cowan, Minna Galbraith, 1
    Crosman, Mrs. J. Heron, fl. 1900s, 1
    Culver, Essae Martha, 1
    Daniels, Grace Baird, fl. 1950s, 1
    De Reimer, Emily True, fl. 1900s, 1
    Dickens, Marguerite, fl. 1870s, 1
    Dickey, Jane K., fl. 1930s, 1
    Diehl, Frances White, 1888–, 1
    Dye, Marie, 1891–, 1
    Edey, Birdsall Otis, 1852–1940, 1
    Fate, Mary Jane, 2
    Ferguson, Harriet Rankin, 1888–
      1966, 1
    Fuller, Margaret Hartwell, 1904–, 1
    Fyan, Loleta Dawson, 1894–, 1

Lewis, Grace Anna, 1821–, 1
Miller, Harriet Mann, 1831–1918, 1,2
Naumburg, Elsie Margaret, fl. 1930s, 1
Nice, Margaret Morse, 1883–1974, 2
Owen, Juliette, d. 1943, 2
Stanwood, Cordelia, 1865–1958, 2
Orphans
　Gray, Mary Alice Smith, 2
　Smith, Mary Alice, fl. 1800s, 2
Orr*
　Leon, Leonie, d. 1906, 1
Orthopedic surgeons
　Stimson, Barbara Bartlett, 1898–, 1
Osteopaths
　Traver, Ethel K., fl. 1930s, 1
Oswald, Lee Harvey—Spouse
　Oswald, Marina Nikolaevna, 1942–, 1,2
Otho—Spouse
　Poppaea Sabina, the elder, fl. 30s, 1
Ottawa Indians
　Juneau, Josette, 2
Otto I—Mother
　Matilda (Maud), 895–968, 1
Outlaws
　Hart, Pearl, 1872–1925, 1,2
　Parker, Bonnie, 1910–1934, 2
　Starr, Belle Shirley, 1848–1889, 1,2

P

PEO
　See
　　Philanthropic Educational Organization
PTA
　Leonard, Lucille Putnam, 1895–, 1,2
　Stapleton, Bessie Lackey, 1861–, 2
Paasikivi, Juho Kusti—Spouse
　Paasikivi, Alli, fl. 1940s, 1
Paca, William—Spouse
　Paca, Anne Harrison, d. 1780, 1,2
Pacifists
　Andrews, Fannie Fern Phillips, 1867–1950, 2
　Bailey, Hannah Clark Johnston, 1839–1923, 1,2
　Corrigan, Mairead, 1944–, 2
　Dennett, Mary Coffin Ware, 1872–1947, 2
　Dudley, Helena Stuart, 1858–1932, 1,2

Eastman, Crystal, 1881–1928, 2
Hooper, Jessie Annette Jack, 1865–1935, 2
Hughan, Jessie Wallace, 1875–1955, 1,2
Hull, Hannah Hallowell Clothier, 1872–1958, 2
LaFollette, Belle Case, 1859–1931, 1,2
Mead, Lucia True Ames, 1856–1936, 2
Nhat Chi Mai, d. 1967, 2
Popelin, Marie, 1846–1913, 2
Rankin, Jeannette Pickering, 1880–1973, 1,2
Schwimmer, Rosika, 1877–1948, 2
Suttner, Bertha, Baroness von, 1843–1914, 1,2
Vernon, Mabel, 1883–1975, 2
Williams, Betty Smyth, 1943–, 2
Wilson, Dagmar, 1916–, 2
Paetus, A Caecina—Spouse
　Arria, the elder, d. 42, 1,2
Painters
　See also
　　China painters
　　Ceramic painters
　　Sand painters
Painters, Alsatian
　Rebay, Hilla, 1890–1967, 2
Painters, American
　Abbatt, Agnes Dean, 1847–1917, 1
　Ahrens, Ellen Wetherald, 1859–, 1
　Alf, Martha, fl. 1970s, 2
　Ayhens, Olive Madora, fl. 1970s, 2
　Aylong, Helene, fl. 1970s, 2
　Aylward, Ida, fl. 1930s, 1
　Baber, Alice, fl. 1970s, 2
　Bacon, Peggy, 1895–, 1,2
　Baer, Jo, fl. 1970s, 2
　Baker, Elizabeth Goudy, 1860–1927, 1
　Baker, Ellen Kendall, d. 1913, 1
　Baker, Martha Susan, 1871–1911, 1
　Baldwin, Edith Ella, fl. 1890s, 1
　Barchus, Eliza, fl. 1880s, 2
　Bartlett, Jennifer, 1941–, 2
　Baxter, Martha Wheeler, 1869–, 1
　Bayliss, Lillian, 1875–, 1
　Beaux, Cecilia, 1855–1942, 1,2
　Beck, Carol H, 1859–1908, 1
　Beck, Margit, fl. 1970s, 2
　Beck, Rosemarie, 1923–, 2
　Beckinton, Alice, 1868–, 1

Beek, Alice D. Engley, 1876–, 1,2
Belcher, Hilda, 1881–1963, 1
Benbridge, Letitia Sage, 1770–1787, 1
Bennich, Agathe, fl. 1970s, 2
Berman, Ariane R., fl. 1970s, 2
Bett, Mum, fl. 1810s, 2
Black, Jinny, fl. 1970s, 2
Blackshear, Sue, fl. 1970s, 2
Blaine, Nell, 1922–, 2
Blum, June, fl. 1970s, 2
Blumenschein, Mary Shepard Greene, 1869–, 1
Bonsall, Elizabeth Fearne, 1861–, 1
Bonsall, Mary M., fl. 1900s, 1
Boott, Elizabeth, fl. 1870s, 1
Bouguereau, Elizabeth Jane, 1851–1922, 1,2
Brenner, Susan, 2
Bridges, Fidelia, 1834–1923, 1,2
Brooks, Romaine, 1874–1970, 2
Brown, Agnes, fl. 1920s, 1
Brown, Joan, fl. 1970s, 2
Browne, Matilda, 1869–, 1
Brumer, Miriam, fl. 1970s, 2
Burton, Marie, 2
Cadwalader-Guild, Emma Marie, 1843–, 1
Campbell, Helena E. Ogden, fl. 1930s, 1
Campbell, Timothea, 2
Carlson, Cynthia, 1942–, 2
Caroompas, Carole, fl. 1970s, 2
Cassatt, Mary Stevenson, 1844–1926, 1,2
Castoro, Rosemarie, fl. 1970s, 2
Cathcart, Marjorie, 2
Chase, Adelaide Cole, 1868–, 1
Chase, Doris, 1923–, 2
Chase, Doris, 1923–, 2
Cherry, Emma Robinson, 1859–, 1
Chicago, Judy, 1939–, 2
Clarke, Sarah, 1808–1896, 1
Clement, Ethel, 1874–, 1
Coe, Ethel Louise, 1
Cohen, Katherine M., 1859–1914, 1
Cole, Jessie Duncan Savage, 1858–1940, 1
Cole, Max, fl. 1970s, 2
Coman, Charlotte Buel, 1833–1924, 1
Cooper, Emma Lampert, d. 1920, 1
Corse, Mary, fl. 1970s, 2
Coudert, Amalia Kussner, 1876–1932, 1,2
Cowles, Fleur Fenton, 1910–, 2

Cowles, Genevieve Almeda, 1871–, 1
Cowles, Maud Alice, 1871–1905, 1
Cox, Louise Howland King, 1865–1945, 1
Crile, Susan, fl. 1970s, 2
Crump, Iris, fl. 1970s, 2
Davies, Maria Thompson, fl. 1920s, 2
De Feo, Jay, 1929–, 2
De Haas, Alice Preble Tucker, fl. 1900s, 1
De Kay, Helena, fl. 1870s, 1
De Kooning, Elaine Marie Catherine, 1920–, 2
De Mooning, Elaine, fl. 1970s, 2
Dewing, Maria Richards, 1845–1927, 1
Dillaye, Blanche, d. 1931, 1
Dodd, Lois, 1927–, 2
Dodson, Betty, fl. 1970s, 2
Dodson, Sarah Paxton Ball, 1847–1906, 1
Dorosh, Daria, 2
Drexler, Rosalyn, 1922–, 2
Drouet, Bessie Clarke, 1879–1940, 1
Edelson, Mary Beth, fl. 1970s, 2
Edgerly, Mira, 1879–, 1
Emerson, Sybil, 1895–, 1
Engel, Sylvette, fl. 1950s, 2
Enters, Angna, 1907–, 1,2
Eyre, Elizabeth, fl. 1920s, 1
Fassett, Cornelia Adele Strong, 1831–1898, 1,2
Febland, Harriet, 2
Flack, Audrey, 1931–, 2
Ford, Lauren, 1891–, 1
Frankenthaler, Helen, 1928–, 1,2
Fuerst, Shirley M., fl. 1960s, 2
Fuller, Lucia Fairchild, 1870–1924, 1,2
Gablik, Suzi, fl. 1970s, 2
Gag, Wanda Hazel, 1893–1946, 1,2
Galloway, Susan Moss, 2
Genth, Lillian Matilde, 1876–1953, 1
Gillespie, Dorothy, fl. 1970s, 2
Golden, Eunice, fl. 1970s, 2
Goldsmith, Deborah, 1808–1836, 1
Goodrich, Eliza, fl. 1950s, 2
Greene, Mary Shepard, fl. 1900s, 1
Grossman, Nancy, 1940–, 2
Hale, Ellen Day, 1855–, 1
Hall, Ann(e), 1792–1863, 1,2
Hall, Susan, fl. 1970s, 2
Hardin, Pablita Velarde, 1918–, 2
Hardy, Anna Eliza, 1839–1934, 2

Perkins, Sarah, 1771–1831, 2
Perrault, I. Marie, fl. 1910s, 1
Perry, Clara Greenleaf, fl. 1900s, 1
Perry, Lillia Cabot, 1848–1933, 1,2
Peterson, Jane, 1876–1965, 1,2
Phul, Anna Maria von, 1786–1823, 2
Picard, Lil, fl. 1970s, 2
Pindell, Howardina, 1943–, 2
Pinney, Eunice Griswold, 1770–
    1849, 1,2
Platt, Aletha Hill, 1861–1932, 1
Prellwitz, Edith Mitchell, 1865–, 1
Putnam, Sarah Goold, fl. 1900s, 1
Rand, Ellen Gertrude Emmet, 1875–
    1941, 1,2
Redfield, Heloise Giullou, 1883–, 1
Remington, Deborah, 1930–, 2
Rhonie, Aline, 1909–, 1
Richards, Anna Mary, 1870–, 1
Richert, Shirley, fl. 1970s, 2
Ringgold, Faith, 1930–, 2
Ripley, Lucy Fairfield Perkins, d.
    1949, 1
Roberts, Mary, d. 1761, 1,2
Robinson, Imogene Morell, fl. 1870s,
    1
Robinson, Irene Bowen, 1891–, 1
Roser, C. E., fl. 1970s, 2
Rothenberg, Susan, 1945–, 2
Rush, Olive, fl. 1930s, 2
Ryan, Anne, 1889–1954, 2
Ryerson, Margery Austen, 1896–, 1
Sage, Kay Linn, 1898–1963, 2
Sawyer, Janet, fl. 1970s, 2
Schille, Alice, 1
Scott, Emily Maria Spaford, 1832–
    1915, 1
Sears, Sarah C., fl. 1890s, 1
Semmel, Jean, fl. 1970s, 2
Serena, fl. 1970s, 2
Sewell, Amanda Brewster, d. 1926, 1
Shaw, Annie Cornelia, 1852–1887, 1
Sherwood, Rosina Emmett, 1854–,
    1,2
Shrimpton, Ada M., fl. 1900s, 1
Sleigh, Sylvia, fl. 1970s, 2
Sloane, Patricia, fl. 1970s, 2
Smith, Isabel Elizabeth, 1845–1938, 1
Smith, Jessie Wilcox, 1863–1935, 1,2
Smith, Letta Crapo, 1862–1921, 1
Smith, Pamela Coleman, 1877–, 2
Snowden, Mary, fl. 1970s, 2
Snyder, Joan, 1940–, 2
Southwick, Elsie Whitmore, fl.
    1920s, 1

Spencer, Lily Martin, 1822–1902, 1,2
Spero, Nancy, 1926–, 2
Stacey, Anna Lee, fl. 1900s, 1
Stanton, Lucy May, 1875–1931, 1
Stebbins, Emma, 1815–1852, 1,2
Steckel, Anita, fl. 1970s, 2
Stein, Pat, fl. 1970s, 2
Stettheimer, Florine, 1871–1944, 2
Stevens, May, 1924–, 2
Strider, Marjorie, fl. 1970s, 2
Stumm, Maud, fl. 1900s, 1
Swope, Kate, fl. 1880s, 1
Tanning, Dorothea, 1910–, 2
Thayer, Theodora W., 1868–1905, 1
Thomas, Alma W., 1891–1978, 2
Thomas, Clara Fargo, fl. 1930s, 1
Thurber, Caroline Nettleton, fl.
    1890s, 1
Tibbles, Suzette "Bright Eyes" La
    Flesche, 1854–1903, 2
Tillinghast, Mary Elizabeth, d. 1912,
    1
Turner, Helen M., 1858–, 1
Turpin, Ella Wheeler, 1876–, 2
Van der Veer, Miss, fl. 1900s, 1
Walter, Martha, fl. 1930s, 1
Waters, Sadie P., 1869–1900, 1
Watkins, Susan, 1875–, 1
Webb, Aileen Osborn, 1892–1979,
    1,2
Weir, Irene, 1862–1944, 2
Welch, Mabel R., 1871–1959, 1
Wentworth, Cecile de, 1853–1933, 1,2
Wheeler, Dora, fl. 1850s, 2
Wheeler, Janet D., fl. 1900s, 1
Whitman, Sarah de St. Crix, 1842–
    1904, 1
Wilding, Faith, fl. 1970s, 2
Williams, Mary Lyde Hicks, fl.
    1900s, 2
Willson, Mary Ann, 1810–1825, 1,2
Wilson, Jane, fl. 1970s, 2
Woodbury, Marcia Oakes, 1865–
    1913, 1
Woodward, Dewing, 1856–1950, 1
Wright, M. Louise Wood, 1865–, 1

Painters, Australian
  Gould, Elizabeth Coxen, 1804–1841,
    1

Painters, Austrian
  Beernaerts, Euphrosine, fl. 1870s, 1
  Began, Luise Parmentier, m. 1877, 1
  Blau-Lang, Tina, 1845–1916, 1,2
  Egner, Marie, fl. 1890s, 1

Painters, English
  Airy, Anna, 1882–, 1
  Austen, Winifred, fl. 1900s, 1
  Bainbridge, Beryl, 1934–, 2
  Bayes, Jessie, 1890–1934, 2
  Beale, Mary, 1632–1697, 1,2
  Beauclerk, Diana, 1734–1808, 2
  Bell, Vanessa, 1879–1961, 1,2
  Biffin, Sarah, 1784–1850, 1
  Bowen, Lota, fl. 1890s, 1
  Butler, Elizabeth Southerden Thompson, Lady, 1850–1933, 1,2
  Cameron, Margaret, 2
  Carlisle, Anne, d. 1680, 1
  Carpenter, Margaret Sarah Geddes, 1793–1872, 1,2
  Charretie, Anna Maria, 1819–1875, 1
  Cookesley, Margaret Murray, fl. 1890s, 1
  Dawson, Edith Robinson, fl. 1890s, 2
  De Morgan, Evelyn Pickering, fl. 1870s, 1,2
  Earl, Maud, fl. 1880s, 1
  Fanner, Alice, 2
  Foord, J., fl. 1900s, 1
  Forbes, Mrs. E. Stanhope, 2
  Fortescue-Brickdale, (Mary) Eleanor, 1872–1945, 1,2
  French, Annie, 1872–1965, 2
  Garnett, Eve, fl. 1940s, 1
  Gere, Margaret, 1878–1965, 2
  Gloag, Isobel Lilian, fl. 1900s, 1
  Green, Florence Topping, 1882–1945, 1
  Hall, Edna Clarke, Lady, 1881–, 2
  Heathcote, Millicent, fl. 1960s, 2
  Hereford, Laura, 1831–1870, 1,2
  Hogarth, Mary, fl. 1900s, 1
  Hotham, Amelia, 2
  How, Beatrice, 2
  John, Gwen, 1876–1938, 2
  Jopling-Rowe, Louise, 1843–1923, 1
  Kemp-Welch, Lucy Elizabeth, 1869–1958, 1,2
  Killigrew (Killegrew), Anne, 1660–1685, 1,2
  Knight, Laura Johnson, Dame, 1877–1970, 1,2
  Lewis, Florence E., d. 1917, 2
  Lewis, Jane Mary Dealy, fl. 1900s, 1
  Louise, Caroline Alberta, Duchess of Argyll, 1849–1939, 1
  MacGregor, Jessie, fl. 1900s, 1
  Manly, Alice Elfrida, fl. 1900s, 1

  Martineau, Edith, fl. 1900s, 1
  Massey, Gertrude, 1868–, 1
  McCrossnan, Mary, fl. 1900s, 1
  McIan, Fanny, 2
  Montagu-Douglas-Scott, Alice, 1901–, 1
  Montalba, Clara, 1842–1929, 1
  Mott, Alice, fl. 1900s, 1
  Murray, Elizabeth, fl. 1900s, 1
  Nicholls, Rhoda Holmes, 1854–1930, 1,2
  Nichols, Catherine Maude, fl. 1900s, 1
  Normand, Henrietta Rae, 1859–1928, 1
  North, Marianne, 1830–1890, 1,2
  Payne, Edith Gere, 1875–1959, 2
  Perugini, Caterina E. Dickens, 1839–1929, 1
  Porter, Thea, fl. 1960s, 2
  Raeburn, Agnes, R. S. W., 1872–1955, 2
  Read, Catherine, d. 1786, 2
  Reynolds, Frances, 1729–1807, 2
  Riley, Bridget Louise, 1931–, 2
  Sartain, Emily, 1841–1927, 1,2
  Sharples, Rolinda, 1794–1838, 2
  Sharples (Sharplales), Ellen Wallace, 1769–1849, 2
  Sjoo, Monica, fl. 1970s, 2
  Spurr, Gertrude E., fl. 1900s, 1
  Stanley, Dorothy, fl. 1900s, 1
  Stevens, Mary, fl. 1900s, 1
  Taylor, Elizabeth V., fl. 1890s, 1
  Thompson, Margaret, 2
  Traquair, Phoebe Anna Moss, 1852–1936, 2
  Ward, Henrietta Mary Ada, 1832–1924, 1
  Waterford, Louisa, Lady, 1818–1891, 2
  Watts, Mary, 2
  White, Florence, fl. 1890s, 1
  Wright, Ethel, fl. 1890s, 1
  Youngman, A. M., 2
Painters, Finnish
  Brummer, Eva, 1901–, 2
  Thesleff, Ellen, 2
Painters, Flemish
  Teerlinc, Levina, 1520–1576, 2
  Van Hemessen, Caterina, 1528–, 2
Painters, French
  Abbema, Louise, 1858–1927, 1
  Achille-Fould, Georges, 1865–, 1

Hoffman-Tedesco, Giulia, 1850–, 1
Hormuth-Kallmorgen, Margarete,
    1858–1916, 1
Kalckreuth, Maria, 1857–1897, 1
Kendell, Marie von, 1838–, 1
Knobloch, Gertrude, 1867–, 1
Kollwitz, Kathe Schmidt, 1867–1945,
    1,2
Kroener, Magda, fl. 1890s, 1
Kuntze, Martha, 1849–, 1
Lepsius, Sabina, fl. 1900s, 1
Liscewska, Anna Dorothea, 1722–
    1782, 2
Liszewska, Anna Rosina, 1716–1783,
    1
Liszewska-Therbusch, Anna Doro-
    thea, 1721–1782, 1,2
Lutmer, Emmy, 1859–, 1
Mach, Hildegarde von, fl. 1900s, 1
Massolein, Ann, 1848–, 1
Mathilde Caroline, 1813–1863, 1
Mengs, Anna Maria, 1751–1790, 1
Milbacher, Louise von, 1845–, 1
Modersohn-Becker, Paula, 1876–
    1907, 1,2
Moron, Theresa Concordia, 1725–
    1806, 1
Moser, Mary, 1744–1819, 2
Moser, Mary, 1744–1819, 2
Munter, Gabriele, 1877–1962, 2
O'Connell, Frederique Emilie Au-
    guste Meine, 1823–1885, 1
Paczka-Wagner, Cornelis, 1864–, 1
Parlaghy, Vilma, Princess Lwoff,
    1863–, 1,2
Penicke, Clara, 1818–1849, 1
Peters, Anna, 1843–1926, 1
Popert, Charlotte, 1848–, 1
Popp, Babette, 1800–1840, 1
Poppe-Luderitz, Elizabeth, 1858–, 1
Prestel, Ursula Magdalena, 1777–
    1845, 1
Preuschen, Hemine von Schmidt,
    1857–, 1
Puehn, Sophie, 1864–, 1
Puyroche-Wagner, Elise, 1828–1895,
    1
Raab, Doris, 1851–, 1
Reinhardt, Sophie, 1775–1843, 1
Remy, Marie, 1829–, 1
Reuter, Elizabeth, 1853–, 1
Rupprecht, Tini, 1868–, 1
Salles, Adelheid, 1825–1890, 1
Schaefer, Maria, 1854–, 1

Schleh, Anna, 1833–, 1
Schmitt-Schenkh, Maria, 1837–, 1
Seidler, Caroline Luise, 1786–1866, 1
Stocks, Minna, 1846–, 1
Stokes, Marianne(a), fl. 1880s, 1,2
Therbusdi, Anna D. Liszewska,
    1722–1782, 1
Treu, Katharina, 1742–1811, 1
Volkmar, Antonie Elizabeth Caecilia,
    1827–, 1
Wagner, Maria Dorothea Dietrich,
    1728–1792, 1
Waldau, Martarethe, 1860–, 1
Wolff, Betty, fl. 1890s, 1

Painters, Greek
Aristarete, 2
Calypso, 2
Helena, fl.300sBC, 1
Laya, fl.100sBC, 1,2
Thamyris, fl.400sBC, 1

Painters, Hungarian
Boemm, Ritta, fl. 1890s, 1
Herman, Hermine von, 1857–, 1
Kaerling, Henriette, 1832–, 1
Konek, Ida, 1856–, 1

Painters, Indian
Sher-Gill, Amrita, 1913–1941, 2

Painters, Irish
Butler, Mildred Anne, 1858–, 1
Cosway, Maria Cecilia Louise Had-
    field, 1759–1838, 1,2
French, Jane Kathleen, fl. 1900s, 1
Gleeson, Evelyn, fl. 1900s, 1
Greatorex, Eliza Pratt, 1820–1897,
    1,2
Johnston, Henrietta Deering, 1670–
    1729, 1,2
Peyat, Mary, fl. 1750s, 1

Painters, Israeli
Yoresh, Abigail, 1908–, 2

Painters, Italian
Alippi-Fabretti, Quirina, 1849–, 1
Anguisciola, Lucia, d. 1565, 1
Anguissola, Sofonisba, 1532–1625,
    1,2
Benato-Beltrami, Elizabeth, fl.
    1850s, 1
Biondi, Nicola, 1866–, 1
Bompiani-Battaglia, Clelia, 1847–, 1
Bortolan, Rosa, fl. 1840s, 1
Borzino, Leopoldina, fl. 1880s, 1
Bozzino, Candida Luigia, 1853–, 1
Carriera, Rosalba, 1675–1757, 1,2
Conath, Estelline, fl. 1500s, 1

Corazzi, Giulitta, 1866–, 1
Correlli, Clementina, 1840–, 1
De Angelis, Clotilde, fl. 1870s, 1
Dina, Elisa, fl. 1880s, 1
Dionigi, Mariana Candidi, 1756–
  1826, 2
Fontana, Lavinia, 1552–1614, 1,2
Gaggiotti-Richards, Emma, 1825–
  1912, 1
Galli, Emira, fl. 1880s, 1
Gentileschi, Artemisia, 1593–1653,
  1,2
Ginassi, Catterina, 1590–, 1
Helena, Flavia Julia, 247–328, 1,2
Hoffmann, Felicitas, d. 1760, 1
Joris, Agnese, 1
Kirchsberg, Ernestine von, 1867–, 1
Kondelka, Pauline von, 1806–1840, 1
Lama, Guilia, 1685–1753, 2
Licata-Faccioli, Orsola, 1826–, 1
Locatelli, Maria Caterina, d. 1723, 1
Longhi, Barbara, 1552–1638, 1,2
Mackubin, Florence, 1861–1918, 1
Magliani, Francesca, 1845–, 1
Mantegna, Andrea, 1431–1506, 2
Marcovigi, Clementina, fl. 1800s, 1
Mariani, Virginia, 1824–, 1
Massari, Luigia, 1810–, 1
Mathilde, 1820–1904, 1
Modigliani, Corinna, fl. 1890s, 1
Moldura, Lilla, fl. 1900s, 1
Moretto, Emma, fl. 1870s, 1
Nelli, Plautilla, 1523–1588, 1,2
Nobili, Elena, fl. 1890s, 1
Occioni, Lucilla Marzolo, fl. 1900s, 1
Osenga, Giuseppina, fl. 1900s, 1
Pascoli, Luigia, fl. 1870s, 1
Pazzi, Maria Maddalena Caterina del,
  1566–1607, 1
Pellegrino, Itala, 1865–, 1
Perelli, Lida, fl. 1880s, 1
Pillini, Margherita, fl. 1880s, 1
Pinto-Sezzi, Ida, fl. 1880s, 1
Radovska, Annetta, fl. 1880s, 1
Rijutine, Elisa, fl. 1890s, 1
Robusti, Marietta, 1560–1590, 1,2
Rodiana, Honorata (Onorata), d.
  1472, 1,2
Romani, Juana, 1869–1890, 1
Rosa, Aniella di, 1613–1649, 1
Rossi, Properzia di, 1490–1530, 1,2
Seydelmann, Apollonie, 1768–1840, 1
Sirani, Elisabetta, 1638–1665, 1,2
Sister A of Santa Marta, fl. 1500s, 2

Sister B of Santa Marta, fl. 1500, 2
Spano, Mario, 1843–, 1
Spilimberg, Irene di, 1540–, 1
Sues, Lea, fl. 1890s, 1
Viani, Maria, 1670–1711, 1
Vigri, Caterina da (Catherine of Bolo-
  gna), 1413–1463, 1,2
Painters, Japanese
  Katsura Yukiko, 1913–, 2
  O'Tama-Chiovara, fl. 1900s, 1
Painters, Latvian
  Davidova-Medene, Lea, 1921–, 2
Painters, Lithuanian
  Cvirkiene, Marija, 1912–, 2
  Mingilaite, Brone, 1919–, 2
  Shimshi, Siona, 1939–, 2
Painters, Mexican
  Izquierdo, Maria, 1904–, 1
  Jones, Frida, 1910–1954, 2
  Kahlo, Frida, 1910–1954, 1,2
  Rosa, Dona (Rosa Real de Nieto), fl.
    1950s, 2
Painters, Moravian
  Flesch-Brunnengen, Luma von,
    1856–, 1
Painters, New Zealand
  Sutherland-Hunter, Mary Young, 1,2
Painters, Norwegian
  Aarestrup, Marie Helene, 1829–, 1
  Backer-Grondahl, Agatha, 1847–
    1907, 1
  Dietrichsen, Mathilde Bonneire,
    1847–, 1
  Kielland, Kitty, 1843–1914, 1
Painters, Polish
  Bilinska, Anna, 1858–1893, 1
  Friedrichson, Ernestine, 1824–1892, 1
  Jerichau-Baumann, Elizabeth, 1817–
    1881, 1
Painters, Puerto Rican
  Martinez, Maria Cadilla de, 1886–
    1951, 2
Painters, Roman
  Bricci (or Brizio), Plautilla, fl. 1600s,
    1
  Iaia of Kyzikos, 2
  Regis, Emma, fl. 1900s, 1
Painters, Romanian
  Deschly, Irene, fl. 1900s, 1
Painters, Russian
  Adamova, Eugenia Mikhailovna,
    1913–, 2
  Akhvlediani, Elena Dmitrievna,
    1901–, 2

Bashkirtseff/Bashkirtsev, Marie Constantinova, 1859–1884, 1,2
Boznanska, Olga de, fl. 1860s, 1,2
Daneshvar, Julia Prokofyena, 1912–, 2
Foulques, Elisa, fl. 1880s, 1
Katiliute, Marcei, 1913–, 2
Kovalevakaia, Zinaida Mikhailovna, 1902–, 2
Lieb, Nina, 2
Magalashvili, Ketevana Konstantinova, 1894–1973, 2
Mamedova, 2
Muuga, Leili Adamovna, 1922–, 2
Popova, Liubov Serbeevna, 1889–1924, 2
Shoumatoff, Elizabeth Avinoff, 1888–1980, 2
Suprun, Kseniya, 2
Wirth, Anna Marie, 1846–, 1
Yablonskaya, Tatiana, 1917–, 2
Painters, Scottish
Arnold, Annie R. Merrylees, fl. 1900s, 1
Dunnett, Dorothy, 1923–, 2
Kay, Katherine, fl. 1900s, 1
King, Jessie Marion, 1875–1949, 1,2
Laing, Mrs. J. G., fl. 1900s, 1
Moran, Mary Nimmo, 1842–1899, 1,2
Perman, Louise E., fl. 1900s, 1
Redpath, Anne, 1895–, 1
Walker, Ethel, 1867–1951, 1
Walton, Cecile, 1891–, 1
Painters, Serbian
Petrovic, Nadezda, 1873–1915, 2
Painters, Sicilian
Rocco, Lili Rosalia, fl. 1880s, 1
Painters, Silesian
Bloch, Madame Elisa, 1848–, 1
Wiegmann, Marie Elizabeth Hanche, 1826–1893, 1
Painters, South American
Freedman, Deborah, 1947–, 2
Painters, Spanish
Abarca, Marie de, d. 1656, 1
Banuelos, Antonia de, fl. 1870s, 1,2
Barrantes Manuel de Aragon, Maria del Carmen, fl. 1810s, 1
Bourbon, Infanta dona Paz de, 2
Crespo de Reignon, Asuncion, fl. 1840s, 1
De Ayala, Josefa, 1630–1684, 2
Garrido y Agudo, Maria de la Soledad, fl. 1870s, 1

Gasso y Vidal, Leopolda, fl. 1870s, 1
Gessler de Lacroix, Alejandrena, fl. 1880s, 1
Gonzalez, Ines, fl. 1840s, 1
Martin de Campo, Victoria, fl. 1840s, 1
Nicolau y Parody, Teresa, fl. 1900s, 1
Rodriguez de Toro, Luisa, fl. 1850s, 1
Serrano y Bartolome, Joaquina, fl. 1870s, 1
Urrutia de Urmeneta, Ana Gertrudis de, 1812–1850, 1
Weis, Rosario, fl. 1820s, 1
Painters, Swedish
Adelsparre, Sophie Albertine, 1808–1862, 1
Bauck, Jeanna Maria Charlotte, 1840–, 1,2
Frumerie, Agnes de, 1861–, 1
Kayser, Ebba, 1846–, 1
Lindegren, Amalia, 1814–1891, 1
Pasch, Ulricke Friederika, 1735–1796, 1
Pauli, Hanna Hirsch, fl. 1880s, 1
Stading, Evelina, 1803–1829, 1
Painters, Swiss
Athes-Perrelet, Louise, fl. 1880s, 1
Boissonnas, Madame Caroline Sordet, fl. 1890s, 1
Breslau, (Marie) Louisa Catherine, 1856–1927, 1,2
Fries, Anna, 1827–, 1
Golay, Mary, fl. 1890s, 1
Kauffmann, Angelica, 1741–1807, 1,2
Massip, Marguerite, fl. 1900s, 1
Merian, Maria Sibylla, 1647–1717, 1,2
Niederhausen, Sophie, fl. 1890s, 1
Rapin, Aimee, 1869–, 1
Rappard, Clara von, 1857–, 1
Rath, Henriette, 1772–1856, 1
Redmond, Frieda Voelter, fl. 1890s, 1
Roederstein, Ottilie, 2
Taeber-Arp, Sophie, 1889–1943, 2
Tauber-Arp, Sophie, 1889–1943, 2
Waser, Anna, 1679–1713, 1,2
Wasser, Anna, 1676–1713, 1,2
Wegmann, Bertha, 1847–, 1
Painters, Welsh
Williams, Margaret Lindsay, d. 1960, 1
Painters, Yugoslavian
Barilli-Pavlovic, Milena, 1909–1945, 2
Loewenthal, Anka, 1853–, 1

Paiute Indians
Hopkins, Sarah Winnemucca, 1844–1891, 2
Winnemucca, Sarah, 1844–1891, 2
Paleontologists
Anning, Mary, 1799–1847, 1,2
Askin, Rosemary, 1949–, 2
Edinger, Tilly, 1897–1967, 2
Gardner, Julia Anna, 1882–1960, 2
Goldring, Winifred, 1888–1971, 2
Hyman, Libbie Henrietta, 1888–1969, 1,2
Jordan, Louise, 1908–, 1
Kablick, Josephine, 1787–, 1
Leopold, Estella Bergere, 1927–, 2
Stopes, Marie Charlotte Carmichael, 1880–1959, 1,2
Palmer, Potter—Spouse
Palmer, Bertha Honore, 1849–1918, 1,2
Parachutists
Abrescia, Donna, fl. 1960s, 1
Borden, Sylvia, 1899–, 1
Broadwick, Georgia (Tiny), 1893–1978, 1,2
Collin, Mademoiselle, fl. 1920s, 1
Cook, Edith Maud, d. 1910, 2
Ferguson, Edna, fl. 1920s, 1
Garnerin, Elisa, fl. 1790s, 1
Graham, Margaret, fl. 1850s, 1
Gray, Adeline, fl. 1940s, 1
Hilsz, Maryse, 1903–1946, 1,2
Jourjon, Yvonne, fl. 1930s, 1
June, Miss, fl. 1910s, 1
Komissarova, O., fl. 1960s, 2
Ledbetter, Marie, fl. 1970s, 2
MacFarland, Irene, fl. 1920s, 1
Macdonald, Ada, fl. 1890s, 1
Paulus, Kathe, fl. 1880s, 1
Pointevin, Madame, fl. 1800s, 1
Rogner, Arveta, fl. 1920s, 1
Smith, Hilder Florentina, fl. 1910s, 1
Smith, Jacqueline, fl. 1970s, 2
Switlik, Lottie, 1
Parent and Teacher Association
See
PTA
Parents Without Partners
Bernard, Jacqueline, 1921–, 2
Parkman, Francis—Sister
Parkman, Eliza W. S., d. 1905, 1
Parliamentarian
Lewis, Mary Burr, 2
Parton*
Lafayette, Anastasie de Noailles, d. 1807, 1

Party girl
Rice-Davies, Many, 1944–, 2
Pascal, Louis—Sister
Perier, Jacqueline, fl. 1630s, 1
Passing women
Agnodice of Greece, fl. 300BC, 2
Barry, James (Miranda), 1793–1865, 1,2
Blalock, Malinda (Sam), fl. 1860s, 2
Bordereau, Renee, fl. 1790s, 2
Bracey, Joan, 1640–1685, 2
Cavanagh, Kit, 1607–1739, 2
Clarke, Amy, 1,2
Compton, Lizzie, 2
Craft, Ellen, 1826–1897, 1,2
Edmonds, (Sarah) Emma E., 1841–1898, 1,2
Eranso, Catalina, 1592–1650, 1,2
Guerin, Elsa Jane Forest, d. 1879, 2
Jean, Petit, 2
K'uo Ch'un Ch'ing, fl. 1940s, 2
Malpass, Barbara Ann, fl. 1950s, 2
Monahan, Johanna, fl. 1860s, 2
Parkhurst, Charlotte, 1812–1870, 2
Read, Mary M., 1680–1721, 1,2
Sampson, Deborah, 1760–1827, 1,2
Snell, Hannah, 1723–1792, 2
St. Clair, Sally, fl. 1770s, 2
Thomas, Vivia, d. 1870, 2
Velazquez, Loretta Janeta, 1838–1897, 1,2
Walker, Mary Edwards, 1832–1919, 1,2
Pasteur, Louis—Spouse
Pasteur, Mrs. Louis, fl. 1830s, 1
Patent holders
See
Child patent holders
Pathologists
Andersen, Dorothy Hansine, 1901–1963, 2
Cone, Claribel, 1864–1929, 2
De Witt, Lydia Maria Adams, 1859–1928, 2
Frenkel-Brunswik, Else, 1908–1958, 2
Hurdon, Elizabeth, 1868–1941, 1,2
L'Esperance, Elise Depew Strang, 1878–1959, 1,2
Marmorston, Jessie, fl. 1930s, 1
McClintock, Barbara, 1902–, 2
McGill, Caroline, 1900–1930, 2
Patterson, Flora W., 1847–, 1
Pearce, Louise, 1885–1959, 1,2

Patriots, Indian
  Naipu, Sarojini, 1879–1949, 1,2
  Padmini of Chitore, fl. 1300s, 1
Patriots, Irish
  Gonne, Maude, 1865–1953, 1,2
  Inghin Dubh, fl. 1500s, 1
  Markievicz, Constance Gorebooth,
    Countess de, 1868–1927, 1,2
  O'Connell, Mary, 1775–1836, 1
  O'Conor, Finola, d. 1493, 1
  O'Doherty, Rosa, 1590–, 1
  O'Donnell, Finola O'Brien, d. 1528,
    1
  O'Donnell, Mary (alias Stuart), fl.
    1600s, 1
  O'Donnell, Nuala, fl. 1600s, 1
  O'Neill, Catherine, fl. 1600s, 1
  O'Sullivan, Johanna MacSwiney, fl.
    1585, 1
  O'Toole, Rosa, fl. 1580s, 1
  Tyrrell, Catherine, fl. 1640s, 1
Patriots, Italian
  Belgiojoso, Cristina, 1808–1871, 1
Patriots, Latvian
  Ziglevice, Elza, 1898–1919, 1
Patriots, Liberian
  Newport, Matilda, fl. 1820s, 1
Patriots, Lithuanian
  Zimantas, Julija, 1845–1921, 1
Patriots, Mexican
  La Malinche, O. Dona Marina,
    1519–, 1
  Ortiz de Dominguez, Josefa, 1773–
    1829, 1
  Vicario, Maria Leona, 1787–1842, 1
  Viscario, Leona, d. 1842, 1
Patriots, Peruvian
  Bellido, Maria Parado de Andrea, d.
    1882, 1
Patriots, Polish
  Wanda, Queen, fl. 730s, 1
Patriots, Portuguese
  Almeida, Brites de, d.c. 1386, 1
  Gouveia, Joana de, fl. 1300s, 1
Patriots, Puerto Rican
  Braceti, Mariana, fl. 1868, 1
Patriots, Romanian
  Doamna, Maria, fl. 1300s, 1
  Golescu, Zinca, 1790–1878, 1
Patriots, Russian
  Melnik, Marite, 1
Patriots, Scottish
  Brux, Lady, fl. 1500s, 1
  Cunningham, Eliza Bertrand, 1788–,
    2

Lauderdale, Elizabeth Murray, d.
  1697, 1
Schaw, Janet, fl. 1770s, 2
Patriots, Sri Lankan
  Dharmapala, Anarhharika, 1864–, 1
Patriots, Uruguayan
  Artigas de Ferreira, Rosalie, 1809–
    1891, 1
  Monterrosso de Lavalleja, Ana, 1791–
    1853, 1
Patrons of the arts
  See also
    Astronomy patrons
    Aviation patrons
    Native American benefactor
  Anderson, Margaret Caroline, 1890–
    1973, 2
  Asquith, Cynthia Mary Evelyn,
    Lady, 2
  Barney, Natalie Clifford, 1876–1972,
    2
  Beach, Sylvia Woodbridge, 1887–
    1962, 2
  Buccleuch and Monmouth, Anne,
    Duchess of, 1651–1732, 1
  Carter, Artie Mason, 1
  Cone, Etta, 1866–, 2
  Coolidge, Elizabeth Penn Sprague,
    1864–1953, 1,2
  Cunard, Maud Alice Burke, Lady,
    1872–1948, 1,2
  Dreier, Katherine Sophie, 1877–1952,
    2
  Eglinton, Susannah Kennedy, d.
    1780, 1
  Evans, Anne, 1869–1941, 1
  Fisher, Emma Roderick, fl. 1940s, 1
  Geoffrin, Marie Therese Rodet, 1669–
    1757, 1
  Gordon, Jane, 1749–1812, 1
  Greffulhe, Elisabeth, d. 1952, 1
  Grimaldi, Jeanne, 1596–1620, 1
  Griswold, Florence, 1851–1937, 2
  Guggenheim, Minnie, 1882–1966, 1
  Guggenheim, Peggy "Marguerite",
    1898–1979, 1,2
  Harkness, Rebekah West, 1915–1982,
    2
  Horniman, Annie Elizabeth Freder-
    ika, 1860–1937, 1,2
  Howard, Minnie Frances, 1872–, 1,2
  Huntington, Anna Vaughn Hyatt,
    1876–1973, 1,2
  Jolas, Maria, 2

Pelving—Mistress
  Delbo, Helvig, d. 1944, 1
Penn, William—Spouse
  Penn, Gulielma Maria Springett,
    1644–1694, 1,2
  Penn, Hannah Callowhill, 1671–
    1726, 1,2
Penney, James Cash—Mother
  Penney, Mary Frances Paxton, 1
Pennsylvania
  Bowen, Catherine (Shober) Drinker,
    1897–1903, 1,2
  Buck, Pearl Sydenstricker, 1892–
    1973, 1,2
  "Captain Molly", 1751–1800, 1
  Corbin, Margaret Cochran "Captain
    Molly", 1751–1800, 1,2
  Lane, Harriet, 1830–1903, 1,2
  Mead, Margaret, 1901–1978, 1,2
  Mott, Lucretia Coffin, 1793–1880,
    1,2
  Patrick, Ruth, 1907–, 2
  Price, Maybelle K., 1887–1973, 2
  Ross, Betsy Griscom, 1752–1836, 1,2
  Sturgis, Katherine Boucet, 1903–, 2
Penologists
  Barrows, Katharine Isabel Hayes
    Chapin, 1845–1913, 1,2
  Davis, Katharine Bement, 1860–
    1935, 1,2
  Grenfell, Helen Loring, 1868–, 1
  Van Waters, Miriam, 1887–1974, 1,2
Pentatheletes
  Pollak, Burglinde, fl. 1970s, 2
  Swift, Gina, fl. 1970s, 2
  Wilms, Eva, fl. 1970s, 2
Pepys, Samuel—Spouse
  Pepys, Elizabeth St. Michel, 1,2
Percussionists
  Dudziak, Urszula, 1943–, 2
  Evans, Sue, 1951–, 2
  Purim, Flora, 1942–, 2
Percy, Charles H.—Daughter
  Case, Valerie Percy, d. 1966, 2
Perfectionists
  Craigin, Mary, fl. 1840s, 1
Pericles—Spouse
  Aspasia of Miletus, 470–410BC, 1,2
Perjurors
  Canning, Elizabeth, 1734–1773, 1,2
Peron, Juan—Spouse
  Peron, Isabel (Maria Estela Martinez
    de), 1931–, 2
  Peron, Maria Eva (Evita) Duarte de,
    1919–1952, 1,2

Perry, Commodore—Daughter
  Belmont, Caroline Slidell Perry, fl.
    1850s, 1,2
Personnel directors
  Boyd, Marion, fl. 1930s, 1
  Carr, Charlotte E., 1890–1957, 1
  Diehl, Mary, fl. 1930s, 1
  Doty, Katharine S., fl. 1930s, 1
  Edwards, Lottie, fl. 1930s, 1
  Grandstaff, Grace M., fl. 1930s, 1
  Hickey, Margaret A., 1902–, 1
  Holland, Clara Helena, fl. 1930s, 1
  Hudson, Hortense Imboden, fl.
    1930s, 1
  Hyde, Helen Smith, fl. 1930s, 1
  Kretschmar, Alice Anne, fl. 1930s, 1
  Laslett, Dixie L., fl. 1930s, 1
  Leahy, Agnes Berkeley, fl. 1930s, 1
  McClung, Mary J., fl. 1930s, 1
  Sparks, Sarah, fl. 1930s, 1
  Westgate, Elizabeth, fl. 1930s, 1
Peruvian Indians
  Puyucahua, Micaela, fl. 1760s, 2
Peruvian bark discoverer
  Chinchon, Countess of, fl. 1660s, 2
Peter I—Daughter
  Elizabeth Petrovna, 1709–1762, 1,2
Peter I—Sister
  Sophia, 1657–1704, 1,2
Peter I—Spouse
  Maria Feodorovna, 1759–1828, 1,2
Petrarch—Friend
  Laura, 1308–1348, 1
Petroleum industry
  Cooper, Cameron, fl. 1790s, 2
  Vandegrift, Mary Hudson, fl. 1930s, 2
Petrov, Vladimir—Spouse
  Petrov, Yevdoklya, fl. 1950s, 1
Pharez—Mother
  Tamar, 1
Pharmacologists
  Byrd, Mary, fl. 1700s, 2
  Davis, Nelle, fl. 1930s, 1
  Enoki, Miswo, fl. 1970s, 2
  Feeney, Mary Ignatius, d. 1915, 1
  Hutton, "Mother", fl. 1700s, 2
  Jex-Blake, Sophie Louisa, 1840–1912,
    1,2
  Mankin, "Widow", fl. 1730s, 1,2
  Marshall, Elizabeth, fl. 1800s, 1
  Ruby, Ida Hall, 1867–, 1
  Tytler, Jane, fl. 1820s, 1
  Wahlman, Mary, fl. 1970s, 2
  Waterhouse, Jessie, fl. 1910s, 1

Phenix, Katharine Joan—Aunt
  Wiesner, Elizabeth, fl. 1970s, 2
Philanthropic Educational Organization
  Allen, Mary Stafford, 2
  Bird, Alice, 2
  Briggs, Hattie, 2
  Coffin, Alice Virginia, 2
  Pearson, Suela, 2
  Roads, Franc, 2
Philanthropists
  See also
  Patrons of the arts
Abbot, Sarah, fl. 1820s, 1,2
Abbott, Edith, 1876–1957, 1,2
Abrabanel, Benvenida, d. 1560, 2
Abreu de Estevez, Marta, 1845–1909,
  1
Acquillon, Duchess of, 1604–1675, 1
Aiguillon, Marie Madeleine de Wig-
  nerod du Pont de Courlay, Duchess
  of, 1604–1675, 1
Aikenhead, Sister Mary, 1787–1858, 1
Aikens, Amanda L., 1833–1892, 1
Alexander, Francesca, 1837–1917, 1,2
Alford, Joanna, fl. 1785, 1
Allen, Mary Gray, d. 1928, 1
Allen, Vivian Beaumont, d. 1962, 1
Ames, Fanny Baker, 1840–1931, 1,2
Anastasia, Saint, d. 303, 1
Anderson, Elizabeth Milbank, 1850–
  1921, 2
Anderson, Julia Taylor, d. 1842, 2
Andrews, Judith Walker, 1826–, 1
Armine, Mary, Lady, d. 1675, 2
Artigas de Ferreira, Rosalie, 1809–
  1891, 1
Athol, Katherine Marjory, 1874–
  1960, 1
Auerbach, Beatrice Fox, 1887–1968, 2
Aull, Elizabeth, fl. 1860s, 2
Bailey, Hannah Clark Johnston,
  1839–1923, 1,2
Balsan, Consuelo Vanderbilt, 1877–
  1964, 1,2
Baranamtarra, 1
Bari-Dussot, Comtesse "Mlle. Pe-
  tite", fl. 1914, 1
Barnard, Kate, 1875–1930, 1,2
Barnsdall, Alice, d. 1946, 2
Barnsdall, Louise Alice, 1882–1946, 2
Barrett, Kate Waller, 1857–1925, 1,2
Bay, Josephine Holt Perfect, 1900–
  1962, 1,2
Baylis, Lilian Mary, 1874–1937, 1,2

Belmont, Alva E. Smith, d. 1933, 1
Belmont, Eleanor Elise Robson,
  1879–1979, 1,2
Berry, Martha McChesney, 1866–
  1942, 1,2
Bethune, Joanna Graham, 1770–
  1860, 2
Biddle, Mary Duke, 1887–1960, 1
Bishop, Bernice Pauahi, 1831–1884, 2
Blaine, Anita Eugene McCormick,
  1866–1954, 2
Bliss, Lizzie Plummer, 1864–1931, 2
Bliss, Mrs. George, fl. 1890s, 1
Blood, Mrs. K. E., fl. 1910s, 1
Bodichon, Barbara Leigh-Smith,
  1827–1891, 1,2
Booth, Ellen Warren Scripps, 1863–
  1943, 2
Borluut, Isabella, d. 1443, 1
Bovey, Catharine, 1669–1726, 1
Bowen, Louise Haddock DeKoven,
  1859–1953, 1,2
Bradley, Lydia Moss, 1816–1908, 2
Brady, Mary A., 1821–1864, 1
Brittano, Susannah, d. 1764, 1
Bruce, Ailsa Mellon, 1901–1969, 2
Bruce, Catherine Wolfe, 1816–1900, 2
Buckingham, Kate Sturges, fl. 1920s,
  2
Bulette, Julia, 1832–1867, 1,2
Burdette-Coutts, Angela Georgina,
  Baroness, 1814–1906, 1,2
Burdick, Nellie Follis, fl. 1920s, 1
Cadwise, Mrs. David, fl. 1800s, 1
Caldwell, Mary Gwendolin, Marquise
  of Montriers-Merinville, 1863–
  1909, 1,2
Carnegie, Louise, 1857–1946, 2
Carpenter, Mary, 1807–1877, 2
Carse, Matilda Bradley, 1835–1917,
  1,2
Chanler, Margaret, fl. 1910s, 1
Chapman, Maria Weston, 1806–1885,
  1,2
Chase, Elizabeth B., fl. 1870s, 1
Cheney, Ednah Dow Littlehale,
  1824–1904, 1, 2
Chisholm, Caroline Jones, 1810–
  1877, 1
Clark, Susan Carrington, 1831–1895,
  1
Clifford, Anne, Countess of Dorset,
  1590–1676, 1,2
Cobbe, Frances Power, 1822–1904,
  1,2

Harkness, Mary Stillman, fl. 1930s, 1
Harkness, Rebekah West, 1915–1982, 2
Harriman, Mary Williamson Averill, 1851–1932, 1,2
Hartman, Mrs. Gustave, 1900–, 1
Hastings, Elizabeth, Lady, 1682–1739, 1
Haughery, Margaret Gaffney, 1813–1882, 1,2
Havemeyer, Louisine Waldron Elder, 1855–1929, 2
Hearst, Phoebe Apperson, 1842–1919, 1,2
Hemenway, Mary Porter Tileston, 1820–1894, 1,2
Henrotin, Ellen Martin, 1847–1922, 1,2
Hickey, Katherine Maloney, fl. 1860s, 2
Hill, Florence Davenport, 1829–1919, 1
Hirsch, Clara de, Baroness, 1833–1899, 1
Hoffman, Sarah C., 1742–, 1
Hoffman, Sophia C., fl. 1860s, 1
Hogg, Ima, 1882–1975, 2
Holt, Winifred, 1870–1945, 1,2
Hooker, Jeanette Annenberg, 1905–, 2
Horton, Mrs. John Miller, fl. 1880s, 1
Howland, Emily, 1827–1929, 2
Hunter, Mrs. M. A., fl. 1810s, 1
Huntington, Arabella Duval Yarrington Worsham, 1849–1924, 2
Huntington, Susan, 1791–, 1
Hutchison, Ida Jones Seymour, 1877–1950, 1
Ileana, Princess, fl. 1940s, 1
Jacobs, Frances, 1843–1892, 2
Jenkins, Helen Hartley, 1860–1934, 1,2
Johnson, Electa Amanda, 1838–, 1
Jones, Elizabeth Dickson, 1862–, 1
Jones, Irma Theoda, 1845–, 1
Joslyn, Sarah Hannah Selleck, 1851–1940, 2
Jovane, Josefa Jacoba, 1860–1929, 1
Keep, Mabel Hazlett, fl. 1930s, 1
Keyser, Agnes, 1853–, 1
Kimball, Martha Gertrude, 1840–1894, 1
King, Susan, 1,2
Kubie, Matilda Steinam, fl. 1930s, 1

Ladd, Kate Macy, 1863–1945, 2
Lasker, Mary Woodward, 1900–, 1,2
Lautz, Katherine Bardol, 1842–, 1
Lazarus, Emma, 1849–1887, 2
Le Gras, Louise, 1591–1660, 1,2
Ledyard, Mary, fl. 1770s, 1
Lee, Mary W., fl. 1860s, 1
Leonard, Cynthia H. Van Name, 1828–, 1
Levey, Ethel, 1881–1955, 1
Longyear, Mary Beecher, fl. 1900s, 2
Lopp, Clara Washington, fl. 1910s, 1
Lowden, Florence Pullman, 1868–, 1
Lowell, Josephine Shaw, 1843–1905, 1,2
Lum, Mary, d. 1815, 1
Lynde, Mary Elizabeth Blanchard, 1819–, 1
MacAuley, Catherine, 1787–1841, 1
Mahaut, Countess of Artois and of Burgundy, d. 1329, 1
Mance, Jeanne, 1606–1673, 1,2
Mann, Maria R., fl. 1860s, 1
Marlborough, Consuelo Vanderbilt, 1877–1964, 1
Martin, Mrs. Bradley, 2
Mather, Sarah Ann, 1820–, 1
McCormick, Edith Rockefeller, 1872–1932, 1,2
McCormick, Katharine Dexter, 1875–1967, 2
McCormick, Nettie Fowler, 1835–1923, 1,2
McDougall, Irene G., fl. 1930s, 1
McFadden, Margaret Bischell, m. 1890, 1
McGill, Sarah, fl. 1910s, 1
McNay, Marion Koogler, d. 1950, 2
McShane, Agnes, fl. 1910s, 1
Meagher, Katherine Kelly, m. 1907, 1
Mendenhall, Elizabeth S., fl. 1860s, 1
Mendesa, Gracia (Beatrice de Luna), 1510–1569, 1,2
Mercer, Margaret, 1792–1846, 1
Merrick, Mary Virginia, 1866–1955, 1
Meyer, Agnes Elizabeth Ernst, 1887–1970, 1,2
Michallet, Francoise, fl. 1700s, 1
Miliken, Mrs. D. A., fl. 1910s, 1
Minijima, Mrs. Kiyo, 1833–1919, 1
Miramion, Marie Bonneau, Madame de, 1629–1696, 1,2
Mitchell, Martha Reed, 1818–, 1
Montgomery, Leila Post, fl. 1920s, 2

Rand, Ayn, 1905–1982, 1,2
Reed, Elizabeth Armstrong, 1842–
1915, 1
Rodde, Dorothea von, 1770–1824, 2
Rorty, Amelia Oksenberg, 1932–, 2
Serina, Laura Cereta, 2
Sontag, Susan, 1933–, 2
Theano, fl. 540BC, 1
Trotter, Catherine, 1679–1749, 1,2
Weil, Simone, 1909–1943, 1,2
Well, Simone, 1903–1943, 2
Wilson, Margaret D., fl. 1960s, 2
Phips, Sir William—Spouse
Phips, Mary, Lady, 2
Photographers
  See also
  Motion picture photographers
  Aerial photographers
Abbott, Berenice, 1898–, 1,2
Adams, Marian Hooper, 1843–1885,
2
Akeley, Mary Lee Jobe, 1878–1966,
1,2
Anderson, Erica Kellner Collier,
1914–1976, 1,2
Arbus, Diane Nemerov, 1923–1971, 2
Arnold, Eve, fl. 1970s, 2
Astman, Barbara, fl. 1970s, 2
Austen, Alice, 1866–1952, 1,2
Bank, Mirra, fl. 1970s, 2
Bannister, Constance, 1919–, 1
Bartlett, Freude, fl. 1970s, 2
Bernhard, Ruth, 1905–, 2
Bonney, (Mabel) Therese, 1894–
1978, 1,2
Bourke-White, Margaret, 1905–1971,
1,2
Breckenridge, Mary Marvin, fl.
1930s, 1,2
Cameron, Evelyn Jephson, fl. 1910s,
2
Cameron, Julia, 1815–1879, 2
Chapelle, Georgette "Dickey"
Meyer, 1920–1965, 2
Chapple, Wendy Wood, fl. 1970s, 2
Child, Abigail, fl. 1970s, 2
Conner, Linda, fl. 1970s, 2
Conners (O'Conner), Martha, fl.
1970s, 2
Corpron, Carlotta M., 1901–, 2
Cunningham, Imogen, 1883–1976, 2
Dahl-Wolf, Louise, 1895–, 2
Dater, Judy, 1941–, 2
Davies, Maria Thompson, fl. 1920s, 2

Dorr, Nell, 1893–, 2
Frissell, Toni, 1907–, 1,2
Gillespie, Marian, fl. 1930s, 1
Gilpin, Laura, 1891–, 2
Groebli, Rene, 2
Hilscher-Wittgenstein, Herta, fl.
1970s, 2
Hudson, Henrietta, d. 1942, 1
Jacobi, Lotte J., 1896–, 1,2
Johnston, Frances Benjamin, 1864–
1952, 1,2
Kanaga, Consuelo, 1894–1978, 2
Kasebier, Gertrude Stanton, 1852–
1934, 2
Kendall, Nancy, fl. 1970s, 2
Korris, Risa, fl. 1970s, 2
Krementz, Jill, 1940–, 2
Lange, Dorothea Nutzhorn, 1895–
1965, 2
Lasley, Mrs. Clinton, fl. 1890s, 2
Leen, Nina, 2
Leonard, Joan, fl. 1970s, 2
Levitt, Helen, 1913–, 2
Light, Mary, fl. 1930s, 1
Logue, Joan, fl. 1970s, 2
Lyndon, Alice Atkinson, 1935–, 2
Mark, Mary Ellen, 1940–, 2
Martin, Jackie, 1903–, 1
Meitner-Graf, Lotte, d. 1974, 2
Michener, Diana, 1940–, 2
Miller, Sadie Kneller, d. 1920, 1
Modotti, Tina, 1886–, 2
Morgan, Barbara, 1900–, 2
Nettles, Bea, fl. 1970s, 2
Orkin, Ruth, fl. 1950s, 2
Phillipps, Angela, fl. 1970s, 2
Richards, Wynn, fl. 1930s, 1
Riefenstahl, Leni (Berta Helene
Amalia), 1902–, 2
Rothschild, Amalie, fl. 1970s, 2
Ryden, Hope, 2
Scully, Julia, fl. 1960s, 2
Seed, Suzanne, fl. 1970s, 2
Shannon, Julia, 2
Shipman, Nell, 1892–, 2
Sipprell, Clara, fl. 1920s, 1
Smith, Lela, fl. 1970s, 2
Stanwood, Cordelia, 1865–1958, 2
Stromsten, Amy, fl. 1960s, 2
Sundstrom, Anne-Marie, fl. 1960s, 1
Taylor, Dyanna, 2
Tucker, Anne, fl. 1970s, 2
Weber, Alicia, 1945–, 2
Wilson, Rosemary, fl. 1970s, 2

Beatrice of Savoy, fl. 1280s, 2
Bedell, Leila Gertrude, fl. 1860s, 1
Beilby, Elizabeth, fl. 1870s, 1
Bekhtereva, Natalie, fl. 1970s, 2
Bender, Lauretta, 1897–, 1
Bennett, Alice, 1851–1925, 1,2
Bentley, Inez A., fl. 1940s, 1
Berengaria, Queen, fl. 1200s, 1,2
Bernheim, Alice Rheinstein, fl.
  1930s, 1
Berthagyta, d. 616, 2
Bertola, Mariana, fl. 1920s, 1
Betts, Helen M., 1846–, 1
Bhatia, Sharju Pandit, 1907–, 2
Birch, Carroll, 1896–, 1
Blackwell, Elizabeth, 1821–1910, 1,2
Blackwell, Emily, 1826–1910, 1,2
Blake, Louisa Aldrich, fl. 1890s, 1
Blake, Sophia Jex, 1840–1912, 1
Blatchford, Ellen C., 1900–, 2
Bliss, Eleanor Albert, 1899–, 1
Bocker, Dorothy, fl. 1920s, 2
Borsarelli, Fernanda, 1904–, 2
Bovin, Madame Marie, fl. 1700s, 1
Bowles, Catherine, fl. 1720s, 2
Bradnox, Mary, fl. 1648, 1
Braestrup, Agnete Meinert, 1909–, 2
Branicka, Rosa, Countess, 2
Braunwald, Nina Starr, 1928–, 1,2
Brenk, Irene, 1902–, 2
Bres, Madeleine, fl. 1870s, 2
Brewster, Cora Belle, 1859–, 1
Broido, Mademoiselle, gr. 1903, 1
Bromall, Anna E., fl. 1880s, 1
Broomall, Anna Elizabeth, 1847–
  1931, 1,2
Brown, Charlotte Amanda Blake,
  1846–1910, 1,2
Brown, Dorothy Lavinia, fl. 1940s, 2
Brown, Dame Edith Mary, 1864–
  1956, 1
Brown, Edith P., fl. 1970s, 2
Brown, Rowine Hayes, 2
Bruch, Hilde, fl. 1930s, 1
Brundtland, Gro Harlem, 1939–, 2
Bruson, Mary Blackmar, fl. 1860s, 1
Bryant, Alice Gertrude, fl. 1890s, 2
Buckel, Cloe Annette, 1833–1912, 2
Budzinski-Tylicka, Justine, gr. 1900,
  1
Buerk, Minerva Smith, 1909–, 2
Butler, Mary Newport, fl. 1830s, 1
Buttelini, Marchesa, 2
Calderone, Mary Steichen, 1904–, 1,2

Caldicott, Helen, 1938–, 2
Calisch, Maria, Baronnes von, 1779–,
  2
Call, Emma Louise, fl. 1880s, 1
Carpegna, Countess of Rome, 2
Carroll, Delia Dixon, d. 1934, 2
Carvalho, Domitilia de, fl. 1950s, 1
Carvill, Maud, d. 1944, 2
Cass, E. Elizabeth, 1905–, 2
Castro-Carro sisters, fl. 1950s, 1
Cesniece-Freudenfelde, Zelma, 1892–
  1929, 1
Chang, Moon Gyung, 1904–, 2
Chard, Marie L., 1868–1938, 1
Chellier-Fumat, Mrs., fl. 1890s, 1
Chenoweth, Alice Drew, 1903–, 2
Chesser, Elizabeth Sloan, 1878–1940,
  1
Chilia, Elvira Rey, fl. 1940s, 1
Chinn, May E., 1896–1980, 2
Cilento, Phyllis, Lady, 1894–, 2
Clark(e), Nancy Talbot, 1825–1901,
  1,2
Clements, Fiona, 2
Cleveland, Emeline Horton, 1829–
  1878, 1,2
Colby, Sarah A., 1824–, 1
Cole, Rebecca, gr. 1867, 1
Comnena, Anna, 1083–1148, 1,2
Coombs, Lucinda, gr. 1873, 1
Corner, Beryl Dorothy, 1910–, 2
Correia, Elisa, gr. 1889, 1
Cowings, Patricia, 2
Culbert-Browne, Grace, fl. 1940s, 1
Cunningham, Gladys Story, 1895–, 2
Cushier, Elizabeth, 1837–1932, 1
Cushman, Beulah, fl. 1950s, 1
Cuthbert-Browne, Grace Johnston,
  1900–, 2
Cutler, Hannah Maria Conant Tracy,
  1815–1896, 1,2
Cutler, Mary M., fl. 1890s, 1
Dalai, Maria Jolanda Tosoni, 1901–, 2
Davey, Jean, fl. 1940s, 2
De Lange, Cornelia Catharina,
  1871–, 1
Del Mondo, Fe, 1911–, 1,2
Dengel, Anna Maria, 1892–1980, 2
Derscheid, Marie, gr. 1893, 1
Diblan, Makbule, fl. 1940s, 1
Dick, Gladys Rowena Henry, 1881–
  1963, 1,2
Dimock, Susan, 1847–1875, 1,2
Dodge, Eva F., 2

Hutchinson, Alice, fl. 1910s, 1
Ighodaro, Irene, fl. 1950s, 2
Inglis, Elsie Maud, 1864–1917, 1
Izrailovna, Evgenia, fl. 1970s, 2
Jackson, Mercy Ruggles Bisbe, 1802–1877, 1,2
Jacobi, Mary Corinna Putnam, 1842–1906, 1,2
Jacobs, Aletta, 1849–1929, 1,2
Jewell, Catherine Underwood, d. 1873, 1
Jex-Blake, Sophie Louisa, 1840–1912, 1,2
Jhirad, Jerusha, 1891–, 2
Jones, Harriet B., 1856–, 1
Jones, Margaret, d. 1648, 1,2
Jones, Sarah G., fl. 1860s, 1
Jordan, Sara Claudia Murray, 1884–1959, 1,2
Jorgensen-Krogh, Marie, gr. 1907, 1
Joshee, Anandibai, 1865–1887, 1,2
Joteyko, Josephine, gr. 1896, 1
Jourdain, Eleanor Frances, 1863–1942, 1,2
Julia Anicia, 472–, 2
Kachel, Malley, fl. 1970s, 2
Kagan, Helen(a), 1889–, 1,2
Kahn, Ida, fl. 1890s, 1
Kalapothakis, Minnie, gr. 1894, 1
Karpeles, Kate B., fl. 1930s, 1
Keller, Elizabeth C., 1873–, 1
Keller, Florence, 1900–, 2
Kelsey, Frances Oldham, 1914–, 1,2
Kemble, Fanny, fl. 1880s, 1
Kenealy, Arabella, fl. 1890s, 1
Kent, Leslie Swigart, fl. 1940s, 2
Keyes, Regina Flood, 1870–, 1
Kimball, Grace N., fl. 1920s, 1
King, Elizabeth, d. 1780, 2
Klein, Helena, 1885–, 2
Klumpke, Dorothea, fl. 1900s, 1
Klumpp, Margaret M., fl. 1930s, 1
Kovriga, Maria Dmitrievna, fl. 1930s, 1,2
Kramar, Piro, 2
Kubler-Ross, Elisabeth, 1926–, 2
Kugler, Anna Sarah, 1856–1930, 1,2
La Chappelle, Marie-Louise Duges, 1769–1821, 1,2
La Roe, Else K., fl. 1930s, 1
Lais, fl. 100s, 2
Lake, Anna Easton, d. 1899, 2
Lampl-de-Groot, Jeanne, 1895–, 2
Langsdorff, Toni von, 1884–, 2

Laouri, Tamara, 1900–, 2
Larsson, Elizabeth, 1895–, 2
Laurea Constatia Calenda, fl. 1423, 2
Lazarus, Hilda Mary, 1890–, 1,2
Lebedeva, Vera Pavlovna, 1881–, 1
Lee, Rebecca, fl. 1860s, 1,2
Leporin-Erxleben, Dorothea Christina, 1713–1762, 1,2
Levingstone, Mrs., fl. 1730s, 2
Li, Katherine Yuch-Yuin, 1911–, 1
Lind-Campbell, Hjordis, 1891–, 2
Lindsten-Thomasson, Marianne, 1909–, 2
Ljotchitch-Milochevitch, Draga, d. 1927, 1
Lloyd-Green, Lorna, 1910–, 2
Locatelli, Piera, gr. 1924, 1
Lodyjensky, Catherine, fl. 1940s, 2
Logan, Myra, 1908–1977, 2
Lollini, Clelia, fl. 1910s, 1
Lombroso-Ferrero, Gina, fl. 1900s, 1
Longshore, Hannah E. Myers, 1819–1902, 1,2
Lopez, Rita Lobato Velho, 1866–, 1
Lovejoy, Esther Clayson Pohl, 1870–1967, 1,2
Lozier, Clemence Sophia Harned, 1813–1888, 1,2
Lozier, Jennie de la, m. 1872, 1
Lubchenco, Portia, 1887–, 2
Luisi, Paulina, gr. 1908, 1
Lukens, Anna, 1844–, 1
Lummis, Dorothea, 1860–, 1
MacGuffie, Martha, fl. 1950s, 1
MacLeod, Enid, 1909–, 2
Macalpine, Ida, 1899–1974, 2
Mackay, Helen Marion MacPherson, 1891–, 1
Macklin, Madge Thurlow, 1893–1962, 2
Macrina, 2
Magno, Josephine, fl. 1970s, 2
Mahout, Countess of Artois, d. 1329, 2
Malahlele, Mary Susan, gr. 1947, 1
Manicatide, Elena, gr. 1900, 1
Marcet, Jane, 1769–1858, 1,2
Margaret, Queen, 2
Maria Hebrea, 2
Marmorston, Jessie, fl. 1930s, 1
Marshall, Clara, 1847–1931, 1,2
Mary Benedict, fl. 1960s, 1
Massey, Patricia, 1905–, 2
Mathison, Karoline, 1898–, 2

Mayo, Sara Tew, 1869–1930, 2
McAndrew, Helen Walker, fl. 1860s, 1
McCall, Annie, 1859–1949, 1
McConney, Florence, 1894–, 2
McGee, Anita Newcomb, 1864–1940, 1,2
McKinnon, Emily H. S., gr. 1896, 1
McLaren, Agnes, 1837–1913, 1
McMurchy, Helen, 1862–1953, 1
Mead, Kate Campbell, 1867–1941, 1
Mechthild of Magdeburg, 1210–1280, 1
Mechtild of (Hackedorn) Magdeburg, 2
Memmier, Ruth Lundeen, 1900–, 2
Mendenhall, Dorothy Reed, 1875–1964, 2
Mendoza-Guazon, Maria Paz, 1,2
Mergler, Marie Josepha, 1851–1901, 1,2
Merit, Ptah, 2700 BC, 2
Meriwether, Virginia, 1862–, 2
Meyling-Hylkema, Elisabeth, 1907–, 2
Mildmay, Grace Sherrington, 1552–1620, 2
Minoka-Hill, Lillie Rosa, 1876–1952, 2
Minuhin, Esther, fl. 1960s, 2
Mitchell, Elsie R., fl. 1920s, 1
Mix, Josephine B. Dexter, 1837–, 1
Miyaji, Kunie, 1891–, 2
Moffat, Agnes K., 1905–, 2
Montessori, Maria, 1870–1952, 1,2
Montoya, Matilde, gr. 1887, 1
Morani, Alma Dea, 1907–, 2
Morris, Margaret Hill, 1737–1816, 1,2
Morton, Rosalie Slaughter, 1876–, 1
Mosher, Clelia, 1863–, 1
Mosher, Eliza Maria, 1846–1928, 1,2
Moss, Emma Sadler, fl. 1950s, 2
Murray, Flora, fl. 1910s, 1
Murrell, Christine, 1874–1933, 2
Neal, Josephine Bickney, 1880–1955, 1
Necker, Suzanne Curchod, Madam, 1739–1794, 1,2
Nelson, Marjorie, fl. 1970s, 2
Nemir, Rosa Lee, 1905–, 2
Netrasiri, Khunying Cherdchalong, 1909–, 2
Newcomb, Kate Pelham, 1887–1956, 2

Nichols, Mary Sargeant Neal Gove, 1810–1884, 1,2
Niculescu, Medea P., fl. 1930s, 1
Nieh, Chung-en, 1907–, 2
Nielsen, Nielsine Mathilde, gr. 1855, 1
Noel, Suzanne, d. 1954, 2
Nolde, Helene Aldegonde, 1700–1790, 2
Norstrand, Lucille Joyce, fl. 1970s, 2
Nyswander, Marie E., 1919–, 1,2
Odilia (Otilla) of Hohenburg, fl. 700s, 1,2
Odlum, Doris, 1890–, 2
Ogino, G., fl. 1882s, 1
Ohnesorge, Lena, 1898–, 2
Olsen, Sandra, fl. 1970s, 2
Olympia of Antioch, fl. 390s, 2
Owens, Margaret, 1892–, 2
Pachaude, Leonard of Avignon, Dame, fl. 1600s, 2
Pak, Esther Kim, gr. 1900, 1
Palvanova, Bibi, 1920–, 2
Panayotatou, Alexandra, gr. 1896, 1
Panayotatou, Angelique, gr. 1896, 1
Paper, Ernestine, gr. 1877, 1
Parker, Valeria H., 1879–1959, 1
Parmalee, Ruth A., fl. 1920s, 1
Parrish, Rebecca, 1869–1952, 1
Parry, Angenette, fl. 1920s, 1
Parson, Lillian Bendeka, 1896–, 2
Pastori, Giuseppina, 1891–, 2
Pechey, Edith, fl. 1870s, 1
Perez, (Barahona) Ernestina, gr. 1887, 1
Peritz, Edith, fl. 1930s, 1
Perna of Fano, fl. 1460, 2
Perozo, Evangeline Rodriguez, gr. 1910, 1
Pettracini, Maria, fl. 1700s, 2
Philista, 2
Picotte, Susan La Flesche, 1865–1915, 2
Pinero, Dolores M., fl. 1940s, 1
Pirami, Edmea, 1899–, 2
Poli-Gardner, Madame, fl. 1930s, 1
Polydamna, 2
Possanner-Ehrenthal, Gabrielle, gr. 1893, 1
Potter, Ellen Culver, 1871–1958, 1
Potter, Marion Craig, fl. 1930s, 1
Potts, Anna M. Longshore, 1829–, 1
Pratt, Romania B., 2
Preston, Ann, 1813–1872, 1,2

Svartz, Nanna, 1890–, 2
Swain, Clara A., 1834–1910, 1,2
Szcawinska, Wanda, gr. 1902, 1
Takeuchi, Shigeyo, 1881–, 2
Taussig, Helen Brooke, 1898–1986, 1,2
Taylor, Esther, gr. 1872, 1
Tetsuo, Tamayo, 1888–, 2
Thelberg, Elizabeth B., 1860–1935, 1
Theodosia, Saint, 2
Thomas, Mary Frame Myers, 1816–1888, 1,2
Thompson, Mary Harris, 1829–1895, 1,2
Thorne, Isabel, fl. 1870s, 1
Tomasia, de Matteo de Castro Isiae, fl. 1300s, 2
Tomaszewiczowna, Anna, fl. 1870s, 2
Tonaillon, Christiane, 1878–1928, 1
Tracy, Martha, 1876–1942, 1,2
Travell, Janet Graeme, 1901–, 1,2
Tunnicliff, Ruth, 1876–1946, 1
Turner, Helen Newton, 2
Turpeinen, Kaisa, 1911–, 2
Tussenbroek, Catherine van, gr. 1880, 1
Ugon, Maria Armand, fl. 1910s, 1
Ullyot, Joan, 2
Underwood, Lillias Stirling Horton, 1851–1921, 1,2
Van Loon, Emily Lois, 1898–, 1
Vanderbilt, Clara, fl. 1970s, 2
Vaughan, Janet Maria, Dame, fl. 1940s, 1
Vejjabul, Pierra Hoon, 1909–, 1,2
Venkova, Tota, 1856–1921, 1
Vilar, Lola, 1900–, 2
Villa, Amelia Chopitea, d. 1942, 1,2
Vytilingam, Kamala Isreal, 1901–, 2
Wald, Lillian D., 1867–1940, 1,2
Walker, Gertrude A., d. 1928, 1
Walker, Mary Edwards, 1832–1919, 1,2
Wallin, Mathilda K., 1858–1955, 1
Warner, Estella Ford, 1891–, 1
Webster, Augusta, fl. 1950s, 1
Weiss, Soma, 1899–1942, 1
Welsh, Lilian, 1858–1938, 2
Widerstrom, Karolina, fl. 1880s, 1
Willets, Mary, 2
Williams, Anna May, 1896–, 1
Williams, Anna Wessels, 1863–1954, 2
Williams, Cicely D., 1893–, 1,2
Williams, Clara, fl. 1870s, 1

Williamson, Miriam Pierce, 1822–1890, 2
Willms, Emilie, fl. 1930s, 1
Winnocur, Perlina, fl. 1930s, 1
Withington, Alfreda, 1860–1951, 1
Wolcott, Laura, fl. 1850s, 2
Wong, Ah Mae, fl. 1920s, 1
Woodhouse, Eleanor, fl. 1610s, 2
Wright, Jane Cooke, 1919–, 1,2
Wright, Katharine, 1892–, 2
Wright, Phyllis, fl. 1970s, 2
Wright, Susanna, 1697–1784, 1,2
Wundt, Nora, 1895–, 2
Yarrow, Rachelle Slobodinsky, 1869–1946, 2
Yonis, Bathsheba, fl. 1910s, 1
Yoshioka, Yayoi, 1871–1959, 1,2
Zaidens, Sadie Helene, fl. 1930s, 1
Zaleska, Katherina, 1919–, 2
Zand, Nathalie, fl. 1930s, 1
Zay, Maria von, Baroness, fl. 1790s, 2
Physicists
   See also
   Astrophysicists
   Biophysicists
   Geophysicists
   Nuclear physicists
   Rocket engineers
   Solar physicists
   Surface physicists
Ancker-Johnson, Betsy, 2
Arete of Cyrene, fl. 370BC, 1
Ayrton, Hertha Marks, 1854–1923, 1,2
Bassi, Laura Maria Caterina, 1711–1778, 1,2
Blewett, M Hildred, fl. 1950s, 2
Blodgett, Katharine Burr, 1898–1979, 1,2
Byers, Nina, 2
Chatelet, Gabrielle Emilie le Tonnel-eve, 1706–1749, 1,2
Curie, Marie Sklodowska, 1867–1934, 1,2
Dreschhoff, Gisela, fl. 1970s, 2
Goldhaber, Gertrude Scharff, fl. 1970s, 2
Jackson, Shirley, 2
Johnson, Kristen, 2
Joliot-Curie, Irene, 1897–1956, 1,2
Kistiakowsky, Vera, 2
Lubkin, Gloria B., 2
Maltby, Margaret Eliza, 1860–1944, 1,2

Collins, Joyce, 1930–, 2
Collins, Judy Marjorie, 1939–, 2
Coltrane, Alice, 1937–, 2
Cook, May A., 1870–, 2
Coolidge, Elizabeth Penn Sprague, 1864–1953, 1,2
Coolidge, Peggy Stuart, 1913–1981, 2
Copp, Laura Remick, d. 1934, 1
Cortez, Leonora, fl. 1940s, 1
Cottlow, Augusta, 1878–1954, 1,2
Crawford-Seeger, Ruth Porter, 1901–1953, 1,2
Crowe, Bonita, fl. 1940s, 1
Crowell, Annie L., fl. 1930s, 1
Curtis, Natalie, 1875–1921, 1,2
Darre, Jeanne-Marie, 1905–, 1
Davies, Fanny, 1861–1934, 1
Davis, Fay Simmons, d. 1942, 1
De Cevee, Alice, 1904–, 1
De Horvath, Cecile, fl. 1940s, 1
De Larrocha, Alicia, 1923–, 2
Dearie, Blossom, 1926–, 2
Deppen, Jessie L., 1881–, 1
Dillon, Fannie Charles, 1881–1947, 1,2
Dlugoszewski, Lucia, 1931–, 2
Dodge, Mary Hewes, fl. 1940s, 1
Donald, Barbara Kay, 1942–, 2
Donegan, Dorothy, 1924–, 2
Dorfmann, Ania, 1899–, 1,2
Droucher, Sandra, fl. 1920s, 1
Duckwitz, Dorothy Miller, fl. 1920s, 1
Dungan, Olive, 1903–, 1
Dutton, Theodora, fl. 1940s, 1
Eakin, Vero O., 1900–, 1
Edwards, Clara, 1925–, 1
Eibenschutz, Ilona, 1872–, 1
Ertmann, Dorothea von, 1781–1849, 1
Essipov (or Essipoff), Annette, 1851–1914, 1
Europe, Mary L., fl. 1900s, 1
Fay, Amy, 1844–1928, 1,2
Fenstock, Belle, 1914–, 1
Field, Laura, fl. 1930s, 1
Fine, Vivian, 1913–, 1,2
Flack, Roberta, 1940–, 2
Fletcher, Polyxena, 2
Forster, Dorothy, 1884–1950, 1
Foster, Fay, 1886–1960, 1,2
Gainsborg, Lolita Cabrera, fl. 1910s, 1
Galajikian, Florence Grandland, 1900–, 1,2

George, Anna E., fl. 1920s, 1
Gere, Florence Parr, fl. 1940s, 1
Gerson-Kiwi, Edith, 1
Gest, Elizabeth, fl. 1940s, 1
Gillespie, Marian, 1889–1946, 1
Glen, Katherine, fl. 1940s, 1
Gober, Belle Biard, fl. 1940s, 1
Goddard, Arabella, 1836–1922, 1
Goodman, Lillian Rosedale, 1888–, 1
Goodson, Katherine, 1872–1958, 1
Goodwin, Amina Beatrice, 1867–1942, 1
Gradova, Gitta, 1904–, 1
Graham, Janet, 2
Graudan, Joanna Freudberg, 1
Greenwalt, Mary Elizabeth Hallock, 1871–1950, 1
Grever, Maria, 1894–1951, 1
Greville, Ursula, fl. 1940s, 1
Griswold, Henrietta Dippman, fl. 1940s, 1
Gulesian, Grace Warner, 1884–, 1
Haake, Gail Martin, 1884–, 1
Hagan, Helen Eugenia, 1893–1964, 1,2
Hall, Ruth Julia, fl. 1920s, 1
Hammond, Fanny Reed, fl. 1940s, 1
Harris, Margaret, 1943–, 2
Harrison, Hazel, 1881–1969, 1,2
Haskil, Clara, 1895–1960, 1
Hensel, Fanny Cecile Mendelssohn, 1805–1847, 1,2
Hess, Myra, Dame, 1890–1965, 1,2
Heyman, Katherine Ruth Willougby, 1877–1944, 1,2
Hier, Ethel Glenn, 1889–, 2
Higginbotham, Irene, 1918–, 1
Hill, Mildred J., 1859–1916, 1,2
Hipp, Jutta, 1925–, 2
Hoffman, Medora, fl. 1880s, 2
Holst, Marie Seuel, fl. 1940s, 1
Hood, Marguerite Vivian, fl. 1940s, 1
Hopekirk, Helen, 1856–1945, 1,2
Horn, Shirley, 1934–, 2
Horrocks, Amy Elsie, fl. 1890s, 1
Horvath, Cecile Ayres, 1889–, 2
Housman, Rosalie Louise, 1888–1949, 1
Howard, Fannie, 1885–, 2
Howe, Mary, 1882–1964, 1,2
Howell, Dorothy, 1898–, 1
Hudson, Octavia, fl. 1940s, 1
Huebner, Ilse, fl. 1940s, 1
Humby, Betty, fl. 1940s, 1

Iturbi, Amparo, 1898–, 1
Janotha, (Maria Cecilia) Nathalie, 1856–1932, 1
Jewitt, Jessie Mae, fl. 1940s, 1
Johnson, Rita, 1912–1965, 2
Jonas, Maryla, 1911–, 1
Joyce, Eileen, 1912–, 1
Kelley, Mrs. Edgar Stillman, fl. 1910s, 1
Kerr, Anita, 1927–, 2
Kerr, Muriel, 1911–, 1
Knouss, Isabelle G., fl. 1940s, 1
Korn, Clara Ann, fl. 1940s, 1
Kotzschmar, Mrs. Hermann, 1853–, 1
Kraus, Lili, 1905–, 2
La Croix, Aurore, fl. 1910s, 1
Landowska, Wanda Louis, 1877–1959, 1,2
Lara, Adelina de, 1872–, 1
Larrocha, Alicia de, 1923–, 1,2
Lawnhurst, Vee, 1905–, 1
Le Voe, Savy, 1906–1971, 2
LeBeau, Luise Adolpha, 1850–1927, 1,2
Lee, Julia, 1902–1958, 2
Leginska, Ethel Liggins, 1886–1970, 1,2
Leonard, Florence, fl. 1940s, 1
Lerner, Tina, 1889–, 1
Lev, Ray, 1912–, 1
Lewing, Adele, 1866–1943, 1
Lewis, Allie May, 1859–1930, 2
Lewyn, Helena, fl. 1940s, 1
Lhevinne, Rosina L., 1880–1976, 1,2
Lichtmann, Sina, fl. 1930s, 1
Liszniewska, Marguerite Melville, fl. 1940s, 1
Lorenzo, Ange, 1894–1971, 2
Lowe, Ruth, 1914–, 1
Lynn, Diana, 1926–1971, 1,2
Mana (Manna)-Zucca, Madame, pseud., 1894–, 1
Mannes, Clara Damrosch, 1869–1948, 1,2
Manning, Kathleen Lockhart, 1890–1951, 1
Marais, Miranda, 1912–, 1,2
Marschal-Loepke, Grace, fl. 1940s, 1
Martinez, Marianne von, 1774–1812, 1,2
Mason, Mary Knight, 1857–1956, 1
McManus, Jill, fl. 1970s, 2
McPartland, Marian Margaret Turner Page, 1918–1986, 2

McRae, Carmen, 1922–, 2
Menter, Sophie, 1846–1918, 1
Menuhin, Hephzibah, 1922–1981, 2
Menuhin, Kathleen, 2
Mero-Iron, Yolanda, 1877–1963, 1,2
Michael, Susie, 1
Mildner, Poldi Leopoldine, 1916–, 1,2
Monath, Hortense, 1903–1956, 1
Moore, Caroline Rudy, 1943–, 2
Moore, Luella Lockwood, fl. 1940s, 1
Morouges, Marie Bigot de, 1786–1820, 1
Nash, Frances, fl. 1940s, 1
Nemenoff, Genia, fl. 1930s, 1
Newcomb, Ethel, 1879–1959, 1,2
Ney, Elly, 1882–, 1,2
Nickerson, Camille L., fl. 1930s, 1
Norfleet, Helen, fl. 1940s, 1
Norton, Eunice, fl. 1930s, 1
Noyes-Greene, Edith Rowena, 1875–, 1
Ohe, Adele Aus der, 1865–1937, 1
Orth, Lizette E., d. 1913, 1
Ostermeyer, Micheline, 1923–, 2
Ottaway, Ruth Haller, fl. 1940s, 1
Pachler-Koschak, Marie Leopoldine, 1792–1855, 1
Paradis (Paradies), Maria Theresia von, 1759–1834, 1,2
Parke, Maria Hester, 1755–1822, 1
Pastorelli, France, 1
Pattison, Lee Marion, 1890–, 2
Paur, Maria Burger, 1862–1899, 2
Pease, Jessie L., fl. 1940s, 1
Pelton-Jones, Frances, fl. 1940s, 1
Peppercorn, Gertrude, fl. 1890s, 1
Peterson, Edna Gunnar, fl. 1940s, 1
Peycke, Frieda, 1
Phippen, Laud German, fl. 1940s, 1
Pierce, Billie, 1905–1974, 2
Pleyel, Marie Moke, 1811–1875, 1
Pollock, Muriel, fl. 1930s, 1
Postnikova, Victoria, fl. 1970s, 2
Powers, Ada Weigel, fl. 1940s, 1
Pray, Ada Jordan, fl. 1940s, 1
Price, Florence Beatrice Smith, 1888–1953, 1,2
Queler, Eve (Robin), 1936–, 2
Quimby, Helen Sherwood, 1870–, 2
Quinlan, Agnes Clune, d. 1949, 1
Ralston, F. Marion, fl. 1940s, 1
Rebe, Louise Christine, fl. 1940s, 1
Reisenberg, Nadia, Madame, 1904–, 1,2

Richter, Marga, 1926–, 2
Ritter, Irene Marschand, fl. 1940s, 1
Rive-King, Julia, 1854–1937, 1,2
Robinson, Carol, fl. 1930s, 1
Rockefeller, Martha Baird, 1895–1971, 2
Rodgers, Irene, fl. 1940s, 1
Ross, Gertrude, fl. 1940s, 1
Ross, Margaret Wheeler, d. 1953, 1
Rubin, Ruth Rosenblatt, 1898–1953, 2
Runcie, Constance Faunt le Roy, 1836–1911, 1,2
Rushen, Patrice Louise, 1954–, 2
Ruta, Gilda, fl. 1930s, 1
Ryckoff, Lalla, fl. 1940s, 1
Ryder, Theodora Sturkow, 1876–, 1
Sage, Florence, fl. 1940s, 1
Salzman, Pnina, 1922–, 1
Samaroff, Olga Hickenlooper, 1882–1948, 1,2
Schaeffer, Mary, 1
Scharrer, Irene, 1888–, 1
Schmitt, Susan, fl. 1940s, 1
Schnitzer, Germaine, 1888–, 1,2
Schultz-Adaievsky, Ella von, 1846–1926, 1
Schumann, Clara Josephine Wieck, 1819–1896, 1,2
Schuyler, Philippa Duke, 1931–1967, 1
Scott, Hazel Dorothy, 1920–1981, 1,2
Scott, Shirley, 1924–, 2
Showalter, Edna Blanche, fl. 1940s, 1
Simmons, Alberta, fl. 1920s, 1
Simmons, Lydia Avirit, 1883–1934, 1
Simone, Nina, 1933–, 1,2
Simpson, Elizabeth, fl. 1940s, 1
Slenczynski, Ruth, 1925–, 1,2
Smith, Elizabeth N., fl. 1800s, 1
Smith, Ella May, 1860–1934, 1
Smith, Julia, 1911–, 1,2
Snodgrass, Louise Harrison, fl. 1940s, 1
Sokolsky-Fried, Sara, 1896–, 1
Spencer, Eleanor, 1890–1973, 1,2
Spivey, Victoria, 1908–1976, 2
Steeb, Olga, d. 1942, 1
Stein, Nanette (Maria Anna), 1769–1833, 1,2
Stern, Lucie, 1913–1938, 1
Stewart, Dorothy M., 1891–1954, 1
Sturkow-Ryder, Theodora, fl. 1940s, 1

Suesse, Dana Nadine, 1911–, 1,2
Sutro, Ottile, fl. 1940s, 1
Sutro, Rose Laura, 1870–1957, 1,2
Swift, Kay, 1897–, 1,2
Szumowska, Antoinette, 1868–1938, 1,2
Szymanowska, Marja Agata, 1790–1831, 1
Tagliafero, Magda, fl. 1940s, 1
Tapper, Bertha Feiring, 1859–1915, 1,2
Tarbox, Frances, fl. 1940s, 1
Tauber, Doris, 1908–, 1
Taylor, Kate, 1949–, 2
Temple, Hope, pseud., d. 1938, 1
Terhune, Anice Stockton, fl. 1940s, 1
Thomas, Flora, fl. 1930s, 1
Tollefsen, Augusta Gould, 1885–1955, 1,2
Tracey, Cateau Stegeman, fl. 1940s, 1
Trautmann, Marie, 1846–1925, 1
Trumbull, Florence, fl. 1940s, 1
Tureck, Rosalyn, 1914–, 1,2
Unschuld, Marie von, fl. 1900s, 1
Vannah, Kate, 1855–1933, 1
Vaughan, Sarah Lois, 1924–, 1,2
Venable, Mary Elizabeth, d. 1926, 1
Vengerova, Isabelle, 1877–1956, 2
Verne, Adela, 1855–1952, 1
Verne, Mathilde, 1865–1936, 1
Virgil, Antha Minerva, d. 1939, 1
Voight, Henriette, 1808–1839, 1
Vronsky, Vitya, 1909–, 1
Wallace, Sippie, 1898–1926, 2
Ware, Harriet, 1877–1962, 1,2
Warren, Elinor Remick, 1905–, 1
Washington, Rachel M., fl. 1870s, 1
Watson, Frances Nash, 1890–1971, 2
Watson, Mabel Madison, fl. 1940s, 1
Wayne, Mabel, 1904–, 1,2
Wengerova, Isabella, fl. 1920s, 1
Wetche, Ludmila Vojackova, fl. 1940s, 1
Wieck, Marie, 1819–, 1
Williams, Jessica, 1948–, 2
Williams, Mary Lou, 1910–1981, 1,2
Wing, Helen, fl. 1940s, 1
Wollstein, Rose R., fl. 1940s, 1
Wood, Del, 2
Worth, Amy, 1888–, 1
Wright, Mary, d. 1874, 2
Wright, N. Louise, fl. 1940s, 1
Wurm, Mary, 1860–1938, 1
Wynette, Tammy, 1942–, 2

Zimmerman, Agnes, 1847–1925, 1
Zucca, Mana, 1891–, 1
Zumsteeg, Emilie, 1796–1857, 1
Piano teachers
 Hamilton, Anna Havermann, fl.
  1940s, 1
 Hatch, Edith, 1884–, 1
 Sutor, Adele, fl. 1940s, 1
Picasso, Pablo—Mother
 Lopez, Maria Picasso, 1860–, 2
Piccard, Jean—Spouse
 Piccard, Jeannette R., 1895–1981, 1,2
Piccolo players
 Humphrey, Barbara Ann (Bobbi),
  1950–, 2
Pierce, Franklin—Mother
 Pierce, Anne Kendrick, 1768–1838,
  1,2
Pierce, Franklin—Spouse
 Pierce, Jane Means Appleton, 1806–
  1863, 1,2
Pilate, Pontius—Spouse
 Claudia Procula, 1,2
Pilgrims
 Alden, Priscilla Mullins, 1604–1680,
  1,2
 Allerton, Fear Brewster, d. 1634, 1
 Allerton, Mary Norris, fl. 1600s, 1,2
 Allerton, Remember, 1614–1656, 1
 Billington, Helen, fl. 1600s, 1
 Bradford, Alice, 1590–1670, 1
 Bradford, Dorothy, 1597–1620, 1,2
 Brewster, Mary, 1569–1627, 1
 Carver, Katherine, fl. 1600s, 1
 Chilton, Susanna, 1634–1676, 1
 Cooke, Demaris Hopkins, m. 1647, 1
 Cooper, Humility, fl. 1600s, 1
 Dare, Eleanor White, fl. 1600s, 2
 Dare, Virginia, 1587–, 1,2
 Eaton, Sarah, fl. 1610s, 1
 Fuller, Bridget Lee, fl. 1635, 1,2
 Hopkins, Elizabeth, fl. 1600s, 1,2
 Howland, Elizabeth Tilley, 1606–
  1687, 1
 Minter, Desire, fl. 1600s, 1,2
 Standish, Barbara, d.c. 1659, 1
 Standish, Rose, d. 1620, 1
 Tilley, Ann, fl. 1600s, 1
 Tilley, Bridget, fl. 1600s, 1
 Warren, Elizabeth, 1583–1673, 1
 Winslow, Elizabeth Barker, d. 1621,
  1
 Winslow, Mary Chilton, 1608–1679,
  1,2

Winslow, Susanna Fuller White, d.
 1675, 1,2
Woodberry, Mary Dodge, fl. 1600s, 2
Pilots
 See also
 Air Force pilots
 Army pilots
 Astronauts
 Aviation experts
 Ballonists
 Child pilots
 Cosmonauts
 Ferry pilots
 Glider pilots
 Helicopter pilots
 Jet pilots
 Marine Corps pilots
 Navy pilots
 Stunt pilots
 Test pilots
 Acosts, Aida de, fl. 1900s, 1
 Adams, Clara, fl. 1920s, 1
 Aleksandrovna, Tamara, 2
 Atanassova, Maria, fl. 1950s, 2
 Auriol, Jacqueline Douet, 1917–, 1,2
 Bacon, Gertrude, 1874–1949, 1,2
 Bailey, Mary Westenra, Lady, 1890–
  1960, 1,2
 Barnato, Diana, fl. 1940s, 1,2
 Barnes, Florence Low "Pancho",
  1902–1975, 1,2
 Barr, Mary, fl. 1940s, 2
 Bastie, Maryse, 1898–1952, 1,2
 Batson, Nancy, fl. 1940s, 2
 Batten, Jean, 1910–, 1,2
 Bedford, Duchess of, 1866–1937, 1,2
 Beinhorn, Elly, fl. 1930s, 1,2
 Bennett, Betty, fl. 1950s, 2
 Bera, Frances, fl. 1950s, 1
 Besse, Nelli, fl. 1910s, 2
 Beverly, Pat, fl. 1940s, 2
 Bird, Nancy, fl. 1930s, 2
 Bixby, Diana, fl. 1940s, 1
 Blanc, Sophie, fl. 1890s, 2
 Boland, Adrienne, fl. 1910s, 1
 Bolland, Adrienne, fl. 1910s, 2
 Boselli, Elizabeth, fl. 1950s, 1
 Boswell, Florence, fl. 1940s, 1
 Boucher, Helene, d. 1934, 1
 Boyer, Lillian, fl. 1920s, 2
 Breckinridge, Aida de Acosta, 1884–
  1962, 1,2
 Brick, Katherine, fl. 1950s, 1
 Brown, Willa B., fl. 1930s, 1

Spicer, Dorothy, fl. 1930s, 1,2
Spooner, Winifred, d. 1933, 1,2
Sproull, Lillian R., fl. 1950s, 1
Stinson, Katharine, 1896–, 1,2
Stinson, Marjorie, 1896–, 1
Stites, Mabel M., fl. 1940s, 1
Strawbridge, Anne West, 1883–1941, 1
Stroup, Leora, fl. 1940s, 1
Sundstrom, Anne-Marie, fl. 1960s, 1
Surnachevskaya, Raya, fl. 1940s, 2
Tanner, Margo, fl. 1930s, 1
Taylor, Betty, 2
Tereshkova-Nikolayeva, Valentina, 1937–, 1,2
Thaden, Louise McPhetridge, 1905–, 1,2
Thompson, Myrtle Grey, fl. 1950s, 1
Thukral, Sarla, 1
Tier, Nancy Hopkins, fl. 1930s, 1
Tonkin, Lois Coots, fl. 1940s, 1
Trehawke-Davies, Eleanor J., d. 1915, 1
Trout, Evelyn, 1906–, 1
Ulanova, Lyubov, 2
Ulm, Mary Josephine, fl. 1930s, 1
Vokersz, Veronica, fl. 1940s, 1
Volkersz, Veronica, fl. 1940s, 2
Vollick, Eileen, fl. 1920s, 1
Wadsworth, Mary Ann, fl. 1930s, 1
Whyte, Edna Gardner, fl. 1930s, 1
Wilberforce, Marion, fl. 1940s, 2
Wilson, Mabel K., fl. 1930s, 1
Wotulanis, Barbara, fl. 1940s, 2
Yamshchikova, Olga, fl. 1930s, 2
Zelenko, Katherine I., fl. 1970s, 2
Pioneers
Ackley, Mary E., fl. 1850s, 2
Adams, Elizabeth, fl. 1600s, 2
Adkison, Harriet Brown, fl. 1900s, 1
Ah Lun, Mrs., d. 1883, 2
Alden, Priscilla Mullins, 1604–1680, 1,2
Alderson, Nannie Tiffany, 1860–1946, 1,2
Allen, Ann, fl. 1824, 1
Allen, Elizabeth, 1716–, 1
Aloysia, Sister, fl. 1840s, 1
Ames, Nabby Lee, 1771–, 1
Anderson, Audentia Smith, 1872–, 1
Anderson, Mrs., fl. 1800s, 1
Applegate, Melinda Miller, 1812–1887, 2
Arcane, Mrs. J.B., fl. 1840s, 1

Arguello, Concha Maria de Concepcion, 1791–1857, 1,2
Astell, Mary, 1666–1731, 1,2
Atkinson, Dorothy, 1892–, 1
Atkinson, Nellie, 1865–, 1
Aylett, Mary Macon, m. 1776, 1
Aza-ya-man-ka-win, 1788–1873, 2
Baird, Elizabeth, fl. 1840s, 2
Baker, Elizabeth Phoebe, 2
Baldwin, Tillie, 1888–1958, 1
Baldwin, Verona, fl. 1883, 1
Ball, Frances, fl. 1857, 1
Ballou, Mary, fl. 1850s, 2
Banfield, Mary, fl. 1850s, 1
Barber, Molly, fl. 1700s, 2
Barber, Mrs. Thomas W., fl. 1850s, 1
Barcelo, Gertrudis, d. 1869, 2
Barnard, Tissayac, 1878–, 1
Barnes, Jane, fl. 1810s, 1,2
Bartholomew, Elizabeth, 1749–1833, 1
Bartlett, Hanna Gray, d. 1807, 1
Bates, Mrs. D. B., fl. 1850s, 1,2
Bayley, Gertrude Arthur, fl. 1860s, 1
Behrins, Harriet Frances, 1830–, 2
Bemis, Lalu Lathoy "China Polly", 1853–1933, 1,2
Benedum, Caroline Southworth, 1869–1900, 2
Biddle, Ellen McGowan, fl. 1900s, 2
Birdseye, Clarissa Stein, 1834–, 2
Black, Clara Belle, fl. 1900s, 2
Blaine, Catherine, fl. 1850s, 2
Bledsoe, Katherine Montgomery, fl. 1800s,
Bledsoe, Mary, d. 1808, 1
Blennerhassett, Margaret Agnew, 1788–1892, 1
Bogaert, Sarah Rapelje Berber, 1625–1700, 1,2
Bonum, Elizabeth Johnson, fl. 1700s, 1
Boone, Jemima, 1792–, 1,2
Boone, Rebecca B., 1739–1813, 1,2
Boren, Louisa, fl. 1850s, 2
Bowers, Eilly Orrum, fl. 1850s, 1,2
Bowman, Sarah A., 1912–1866, 2
Boyd, Mrs. Orsemus Bronson, fl. 1860s, 2
Bozarth, Elizabeth (Experience), fl. 1770s, 1,2
Bradford, Mary D., d. 1943, 2
Brandt, Molly, fl. 1760s, 1
Braxton, Elizabeth Corbin, fl. 1770s, 1

Braxton, Judith Robinson, d. 1757, 1
Braxton, Mary Carter, fl. 1770s, 1
Braxton, Mrs., fl. 1840s, 1
Breckinridge, Mary Hopkins Cabell, fl. 1768, 1
Breen, Margaret, fl. 1840s, 1,2
Brett, Catherina, d. 1764, 1,2
Brett, Margaret, fl. 1730s, 1
Brewster, Patience, d. 1634, 1
Brier, Juliet, 2
Bristow, Susannah, 2
Brown, Frances Fowke, m. 1710, 1
Brown, Jane Gillespie, 1740–, 1
Brown, Maria "Grandmother", fl. 1800s, 1,2
Brown, Mary Anne Day, 1816–1844, 1
Brown, Tabitha Moffat, 1780–, 1,2
Bruce, Azealia, fl. 1880s, 1
Bulette, Julia, 1832–1867, 1,2
Bull, Eliza, fl. 1840s, 1
Burks, Amanda, fl. 1860s, 1
Burra (or Burroughs), Ann, fl. 1600s, 1
Byrd, Lucy Parke, c. 1704, 1
Cadwalader, Elizabeth Lloyd, fl. 1770s, 1
Cadwalader, Wilhelmina Bond, m. 1779, 1
Calamity Jane, (Martha Jane Canary), 1852–1903, 1,2
Callahan, Nancy "Granny Dollar", 1826–1931, 2
Callaway, Mary, fl. 1776, 2
Carpenter, Kate, fl. 1750s, 2
Carpenter, Mary, fl. 1600s, 1
Carrington, Margaret Irwin, d. 1867, 1
Carroll, Harriet Chew, fl. 1790s, 1
Carter, Mrs., fl. 1800s, 1
Carter sisters, fl. 1800s, 1
Cary, Mary Ann Shadd, 1823–1893, 1,2
Case, Alice Montague, 1870–, 1
Catherine, Sister, fl. 1840s, 1
Champion, Deborah, 1753–, 1,2
Chapin, Hannah, fl. 1700s, 1
Chapin, Lucy, fl. 1800s, 1
Chapin, Sylvia, fl. 1800s, 1
Chapman, Caroline, 1818–1876, 1,2
Chappel, Mrs., fl. 1760s, 1
Chase, Anne Baldwin, m. 1762, 1
Chase, Hannah Kilty, m. 1783, 1
Chase, Mary, fl. 1840s, 1

Chinn, Sarah Bryan, m. 1784, 1
Churchill, Caroline N., 1833–, 2
Clapp, Hannah, fl. 1860s, 2
Clappe (Clapp), Louise Amelia Knapp Smith, 1819–1906, 1,2
Clark, Charlotte A., fl. 1800s, 1
Clark, Isabella P., fl. 1870s, 1
Clendenin, Mrs., fl. 1760s, 1
Clyde, Mrs., fl. 1770s, 1,2
Cockrell, Sarah, fl. 1850s, 2
Coleman, Susan Lawrence, 1945–, 2
Collins, Libby Smith, 1844–1921, 1
Colt, Miriam, fl. 1850s, 2
Combs, Sarah Richardson, fl. 1800s, 1
Compton, Henria Packer, 1827–, 2
Comstock, Mrs., fl. 1800s, 1
Cook, Jesse, fl. 1790s, 1
Cook, Miss, fl. 1700s, 1
Cook, Mrs. Hosea, fl. 1790s, 1
Copp, Dolly Emery, fl. 1830s, 2
Corbin, Elizabeth T., fl. 1750s, 1
Cornelia, Sister, fl. 1840s, 1
Cranch, Mary, d. 1811, 1
Cranch, Mrs. Richard, fl. 1770s, 1
Crawford, Lucy, fl. 1840s, 2
Crippen, Abbie, 1860–, 1
Crippen, Effie Maude, 1868–, 1
Crippen, Fannie, 1806–, 1
Crippen, Kate, 1864–, 1
Crocker, Hannah Mather, 1752–1829, 1,2
Crockett, Elizabeth, d. 1860, 1
Cunningham, Ann Pamela, 1816–1875, 1,2
Cunningham, Mrs., fl. 1770s, 1
Curley, Kate, 2
Curry, Jennie Foster, d. 1948, 1
Custer, Elizabeth Bacon, 1842–1933, 1,2
Cutbert, Susan Stockton, fl. 1770s, 1
Dagget, Mrs., fl. 1780s, 1
Dalager, Betsy, 1852–, 2
Dalton, Mrs., fl. 1860s, 1
Dana, Elizabeth, 1751–, 1
Darling, Lucia, 2
Daviess, Mrs. Samuel, fl. 1780s, 1
Davis, Ann Scott, 1801–1891, 1
De Casa Yrujo, Sarah McKean, 1777–, 1
Degnan, Bridget Dixon, d. 1940, 1
Degnan, Mary Ellen, 1887–, 1
Denis, Mrs., fl. 1760s, 1
Denne, Elizabeth, fl. 1700s, 1

Mason, Mrs., fl. 1790s, 1
Maverick, Amias Thomson, fl. 1600s, 1
McCauley, Barbara, fl. 1870s, 1
McClure, Mary, fl. 1770s, 1,2
McDonald, Hannah "Aunt Mac", 1810–, 1
McKay, (Aunt) Lepha, 2
McMillan, Mary, fl. 1800s, 1
Meagher, Mary, 1855–, 1
Mendoza, Dona Ana de Zaldivar y, fl. 1500s, 1
Mercer, Isabella Gordon, m. 1767, 1
Merrill, Mrs. John, fl. 1770s, 1
Meyer, Elizabeth Stuart McCauley, 1866–1952, 1
Middleton, Mary Williams, d. 1761, 1
Miller, Harriet Emeline Phelps, 1891–1964, 2
"Minnie", fl. 1900s, 1
Monoghan, Josephine "Little Jo", d. 1903, 1
Montgomery, Janet Livingston, d. 1828, 1
Moor, Eunice Farnsworth, 1735–1822, 1
Moore, Huldah Traxler, fl. 1870s, 1
Moore, Kate, fl. 1850s, 1
Moore, Mary, 1777–1790, 1
More, Ellen, fl. 1600s, 1
Morgan, Abigail Bailey, 1736–1802, 1
Morgan, Henrietta Hunt, 1805–1891, 1
Morris, Deborah, d. 1800, 1
Morris, Esther Hobart McQuigg Slack, 1814–1902, 1,2
Morris, Mary Philipse, 1730–1825, 1
Morton, Anne Justis, m. 1745, 1
Moseley, Mrs., fl. 1890s, 1
Moulton, Hannah Lynch, m. 1779, 1
Moultrie, Elizabeth St. Julien, fl. 1770s, 1
Mullens, Alice, fl. 1600s, 1
Nash family, fl. 1640s, 1
Neal, Jean Frances, 1,2
Nearing, Helen Knothe, 1904–, 2
Neff, Isabella Eleanor, 1830–, 2
Newell, Harriet Atwood, 1793–1812, 1,2
Noble, Harriet L., fl. 1800s, 1
Noble, Mrs. Frank, fl. 1660s, 1
Norbertine, Sister, fl. 1840s, 1
Norris, Deborah, 1761–1839, 1
Nowell, Elizabeth Davis, fl. 1900s, 2

O'Farrell, Mary Ann Chapman, fl. 1860s, 2
Ogden, Mrs. Robert, fl. 1770s, 1
Ordway, Elizabeth, fl. 1870s, 2
Owen, Mrs. James, fl. 1790s, 1
Paddy, Elizabeth, 1641–, 2
Padishal, Madam, fl. 1800s, 2
Page, Julia, fl. 1800s, 1
Paine, Eliza Baker, m. 1795, 1
Park, Lucia Darling, fl. 1860s, 1
Parker, Cynthia Ann, 1827–1864, 1,2
Parker, Ruth, fl. 1770s, 1
Paybody, Elizabeth, fl. 1650s, 1
Payne, "Betsy" Johnson, fl. 1780s, 1
Pearson, Flora Engle, fl. 1860s, 1,2
Peck, Rosaline, 2
Pedersen, Gina, fl. 1890s, 2
Pentry, Mrs. Edward, fl. 1672, 1
Peregoyo, Mary Cochran, fl. 1880s, 1
Peterson, Miss, fl. 1840s, 1
Petkova, Baba Nedelia, 1826–1894, 1
Phillips, Abigail, m. 1769, 1
Phillips, Sarah Bowman, fl. 1850s, 2
Pico, Maria Antonia, fl. 1810s, 2
Plaisted, Emma, fl. 1890s, 2
Plassmann, Martha Edgerton, 1850–, 1
Pleasant, Mary Ellen "Mammy", 1814–1904, 1,2
Plummer, Electa Bryan, 1842–1912, 1
Plummer, Rachel, fl. 1830s, 1
Porter, Lavinia Honeyman, 2
Porter, Mrs., fl. 1780s, 1
Powell, Ann Murray, fl. 1770s, 2
Prendergast, Mehitabel Wing, 1738–, 2
Prentiss, Narcissa, 1808–, 2
Preston, Lizzie, fl. 1870s, 1
Preston, Margaret Wickliffe, 1819–, 1
Purcell, Polly Jane, 1842–, 2
Ragan, Mrs. John, fl. 1870s, 1
Ramsay, Margaret Jane, fl. 1750s, 1
Rankin, Jeannette Pickering, 1880–1973, 1,2
Rapelje, Cataline de Trice, 1624–, 1
Reed, Margaret, fl. 1840s, 1,2
Reed, Sarah, fl. 1840s, 1
Reed, Virginia, 1833–, 1
Richardson, Sarah, fl. 1700s, 1
Riker, Janette, 1,2
Robb, Louisa St. Clair, 1773–, 1
Robbins, Nancy, fl. 1790s, 1
Robertson, Ann Lewis, fl. 1770s, 1
Robertson, Charlotte Reeves, 1751–1814, 1

Jefferis, Marea Wood, fl. 1900s, 1
Jenney, Adeline, 1834–1968, 2
Johnson, Georgia Douglas, 1886–1967, 1,2
Jones, Kate E., fl. 1900s, 1
Jones, Sarah G., fl. 1860s, 1
Jong, Erica Mann, 1942–, 2
Jordan, Cornelia Jane Matthews, 1830–1898, 1
Jordan, June Meyer, 1936–, 2
Kandel, Lenore, 2
Kaufman, Shirley, 1923–, 2
Kenyon, Bernice, 1897–, 1
Kilmer, Aline, 1888–1941, 1
Kimball, Alice Mary, fl. 1910s, 2
Kingsbury, Elizabeth A., fl. 1880s, 1
Kizer, Carolyn, 1925–, 2
Kudaka, Geraldine, 1951–, 2
Kumin, Maxine Winokur, 1925–, 2
Kyger, Joanne, 1934–, 2
Larcom, Lucy, 1824–1893, 1,2
Lawrence, Elizabeth, fl. 1770s, 2
Lazarus, Emma, 1849–1887, 2
Le Cron, Helen Cowles, fl. 1920s, 1
Lee, Agnes, pseud., 1
Leitch, Mary Sinton Lewis, 1876–, 1
Levertov, Denise, 1923–, 2
Lewis, Estelle Anna Blanche, 1824–1880, 1
Lewis, Janet, 1899–, 2
Lifshin, Lyn, 2
Lindbergh, Anne Spencer Morrow, 1906–, 1,2
Livermore, Sarah White, 1789–1874, 1,2
Livingstone, Mabel, 1926–, 1
Lorde, Audre, 2
Lowe, Martha Perry, 1829–1902, 1
Lowell, Amy, 1874–1925, 1
Lowell, Maria White, 1821–1853, 2
Lowell, May Lawrence, 1874–1925, 2
Lucero, Judy, fl. 1970s, 2
Lucero-Trujillo, Marcela Christine, fl. 1970s, 2
MacDonald, Cynthia, 2
MacDougal, Violet, fl. 1920s, 1
Mace, Frances Lawton, 1836–, 1
Madeleva, Mary, Sister, 1887–1964, 1,2
Madgett, Naomi Long, 1923–, 2
Mandola, Carol M., fl. 1930s, 1
Mannix, Mary Ellen Walsh, 1846–1938, 1
Marie-Elise, 1950–, 2

Markham, Elizabeth Winchell, 1852–, 2
Marks, Jeannette (Augustus), 1875–1964, 1,2
Matthews, Frances Aymar, fl. 1910s, 1
Mayo, Sarah Edgarton, d. 1948, 1
McCord, Louisa Susannah Cheves, 1810–1879, 1,2
McElroy, Colleen, 1935–, 2
McGinley, Phyllis, 1905–1978, 1,2
McNeill, Louise, 2
McPherson, Sandra, 1943–, 2
Meigs, Mary Noel, fl. 1840s, 1
Merchant, Jane, 1919–, 1
Metzger, Deena, 1936–, 2
Miles, Anne, 1803–, 1
Miles, Ellen E., 1835–, 1
Miles, Josephine, 1911–, 2
Miles, Sarah E., 1807–, 1
Millay, Edna St. Vincent, 1892–1950, 1,2
Miller, May, fl. 1950s, 2
Miller, Nellie Burget, 1875–, 1
Miller, Vassar, 1924–, 2
Minnie, Memphis, 1900–, 2
Mitchell, Maria, 1818–1889, 1,2
Mitchell, Ruth Comfort, fl. 1900s, 1
Miyakawa, Kikuko, fl. 1930s, 1
Moise, Penina, 1797–1880, 1,2
Monroe, Harriet, 1860–1936, 1,2
Montgomery, Roselle Mercier, d. 1933, 1
Montgomery, Vaida, 1888–1959, 2
Moore, Julia A., 1847–1920, 2
Moore, Marianne Craig, 1887–1972, 1,2
Moore, Rosalie, 1910–, 2
Moreno, Victoria, 1957–, 2
Morgan, Angela, d. 1957, 1
Morton, Sarah Wentworth Apthorp, 1759–1846, 1,2
Moulton, Louise Chandler, 1835–1908, 1,2
Mueller, Lisel, 1924–, 2
Mugge, Mary Alice Pritchard Myers, 1895–, 2
Mullins, Edith, fl. 1930s, 1
Mumford, Ethel Watts, d. 1940, 1
Munday, Missouri Belle, 2
Murden, Eliza Crawly, 1790–1851, 2
Murray, Judith Sargent Stevens, 1751–1820, 1,2
Murray, Michele, 1934–1974, 2

Murray, Pauli, 1910–, 2
Nason, Emma Huntington, 1845–, 1
Nealis, Jean Ursula, fl. 1910s, 1
Nelson, Alice Dunbar, 1875–1935, 2
Newsome, Effie Lee, 1885–, 1
Nichols, Jeanette, fl. 1950s, 2
Nichols, Rebecca Shepard Reed, 1819–1903, 1
Nicholson, Martha Snell, 1886–1951, 1
Niedecker, Lorine, 1903–1970, 2
Norton, Grace Fallow, 1876–1926, 1
O'Malley, Sallie Margaret, 1862–, 1
Oates, Joyce Carol, 1938–, 2
Oberholtzer, Sara Louisa Vickers, 1841–1930, 1
Oliver, Sophia Helen, fl. 1811–, 1
Olmsted, Elizabeth Martha, 1825–, 1
Osgood, Frances Sargent Locke, 1811–1850, 1,2
Owens, Rochelle, 1936–, 2
Palmer, Anna Campbell, 1854–1928, 1
Palmer, Miriam, 1946–, 2
Pankhurst, Estelle Sylvia, 1882–1960, 1,2
Parker, Dorothy Rothschild, 1893–1967, 1,2
Pastan, Linda, 1932–, 2
Peabody, Josephine Preston, 1874–1922, 1,2
Piatt, Sarah Morgan Bryan, 1836–1919, 1,2
Piercy, Marge, 1936–, 2
Pierson, Lydia Jane, fl. 1840s, 1
Plath, Sylvia, 1932–1963, 2
Pomeroy, Genie Clark, 1867–, 1
Poole, Fannie Huntington Runnells, fl. 1910s, 1
Porter, Charlotte Endymion, 1857–1942, 1,2
Powers, Rose Mills, fl. 1920s, 1
Prentiss, Harriet Doan, fl. 1930s, 1
Preston, Margaret Junkin, 1820–1897, 1,2
Prosper, Joan Dareth, fl. 1920s, 1
Quick, Dorothy, 1895–1962, 1
Rainey, Gertrude Malissa Nix Pridgett "Ma", 1886–1939, 2
Ray, Henrietta Cordelia, 1849–1916, 1
Reese, Lizette Woodworth, 1856–1935, 1,2
Reese, Sarah T. Bolton, 2

Rich, Adrienne Cecile, 1929–, 2
Rich, Helen Hinsdale, 1827–, 1
Richards, Rosa Coates, fl. 1930s, 1
Richardson, Emily Tracey Y., 1863–1892, 1
Riding, Laura, 1901–, 1,2
Ripley, Mary A., 1831–, 1
Rittenhouse, Jessie Bell, 1869–1948, 1,2
Ritter, Margaret Tod, 1893–, 1
Robb, Elizabeth B., fl. 1930s, 1
Roberts, Elizabeth Madox, 1886–1941, 1,2
Robinson, Corinne Roosevelt, 1861–1933, 1
Robinson, Fannie Ruth, 1847–, 1
Robinson, Ophelia, 1897–, 1
Rude, Ellen Sargent, 1838–, 1
Rukeyser, Muriel, 1913–1980, 1,2
Sage, Kay Linn, 1898–1963, 2
Sampter, Jessie Ethel, 1883–1938, 2
Sanchez, Sonia, 1935–, 2
Sangster, Margaret Elizabeth Munson, 1838–1912, 1,2
Sarton, May, 1912–, 2
Sawyer, Caroline Mehitable Fisher, 1812–1894, 1,2
Schechter, Ruth Lisa, 1928–, 2
Scott, Ann (London), 1929–1975, 2
Scott, Evelyn D., 1893–1963, 1,2
Scott, Julia H., 1809–, 1
Scott, Mary, fl. 1770s, 1
Seifert, Marjorie Allen, fl. 1900s, 1
Sexton, Anne Gray Harvey, 1928–1974, 2
Shange, Ntozake, 1948–, 2
Sherwood, Katharine "Kate" Margaret Brownlee, 1841–1914, 1,2
Siegrist, Mary, 1881–1953, 1
Sigourney, Lydia Howard Huntley, 1791–1865, 1,2
Silko, Leslie Marmon, 1948–, 2
Sloan, Emily, 1910–1920, 2
Smart, Alice McGee, fl. 1950s, 1
Smith, Alice Maud, fl. 1920s, 2
Smith, Bessie (Elizabeth), 1894–1937, 1,2
Smith, Elizabeth Oakes Prince, 1806–1893, 1,2
Smith, Eveline Sherman, 1823–, 1
Smith, Helen Grace, 1865–, 1
Smith, Jessie Welborn, fl. 1900s, 1
Smith, L. Virginia, fl. 1850s, 1
Smith, Marion Couthouy, fl. 1920s, 1

Worthington, Jane T. Lomax, d. 1847, 1
Wright, Susanna, 1697–1784, 1,2
Wurdemann, Audrey May, 1911–1960, 1
Wylie, Elinor Morton Hoyt, 1885–1928, 1,2
Xelina, 1954–, 2
Young, Barbara, 1878–, 1
Young, Maude J. Fuller, 1826–1882, 2
Yvonne, fl. 1970s, 2
Poets, Arabian
　Al-Khansa, fl. 645s, 2
Poets, Argentine
　Storni, Alphonzina, 1892–1938, 1,2
Poets, Australian
　Dobson, Rosemary, 1920–, 2
　Harwood, Gwen, 1920–, 2
　Wickham, Anna, 1884–1947, 1,2
　Wright, Judith, 1915–, 2
　Wylie, Ida Alexis Boss, 1885–1959, 1,2
Poets, Austrian
　Ava, Frau, fl. 1100s, 1
　Bachmann, Ingeborg, 1926–1973, 2
　Grazie, Marie Eugenie Dell, 1864–1931, 1
Poets, Belgian
　Cammaerts, Emile, 1878–1953, 1
　Inez, Colette, 1931–, 2
Poets, Boccaccio*
　Cornificia, fl. 40sBC, 1
Poets, Bolivian
　Zamudio, Adela, 1854–1928, 2
Poets, Canadian
　Atwood, Margaret Eleanor Killian, 1939–, 2
　Avison, Margaret, 1918–, 2
　Crawford, Isabella, 1850–1887, 2
　Hebert, Anne, 1916–, 2
　Macpherson, Jay, 1932–, 2
　Pearce, Theodocia, 1894–1926, 1
Poets, Chicana
　Rivera, Marina, 1942–, 2
Poets, Chinese
　Chang, Diana, fl. 1950s, 2
　Chiang, Fay, 1952–, 2
　Chu Shu-Chen, 1126–1200, 1
　Hsing Tz'u Ching, fl. 1570s, 2
　Hsueh, Wu (Hsuen Su-Su), 1564–1637, 2
　Hsueh T'ao, fl. 760s, 2
　Li Ch'ing-Chao, 1081–, 1,2
　Ma Shou-chen, 1592–1628, 2

Mar, Laureen, 1953–, 2
Pan Chao (Ts'ao Taku), 45–115, 1,2
Ts'Ao Miao-Ch'ing, fl. 1300s, 2
Yu Hsuan-Chi, d. 870, 1
Yup, Paula, 1957–, 2
Poets, Cuban
　Avellaneda y Arteaga, Gertrudis Gomez, 1814–1873, 1
　Borrero, Juana, 1878–, 1
　Zambrana, Luisa Perez de, 1835–1922, 1
Poets, Czechoslovakian
　Krasnohorska, Elisa, pseud., 1847–, 1
　Nemcova, Bozena, 1820–1882, 1,2
Poets, Dominican Republic
　Henriquez, Salome Urena de, 1851–1899, 1
　Ovando, Leonor de, d. 1613, 1
　Urena de Henriquez, Salome, 1850–1897, 1
Poets, Dutch
　Deken, Agatha (Aagji), 1741–1804, 1,2
　Schurman, Anna Maria von, 1607–1678, 1,2
　Tesselschade, Maria, 1859–1649, 1
　Visscher, Anna, 1583–1651, 1,2
Poets, English
　Adams, Sarah Fowler, 1805–1848, 1,2
　Aguilar, Grace, 1816–1847, 1,2
　Bainbridge, Katherine, 1924–, 1
　Banks, Isabella Varley Linnaeus, 1821–1897, 1,2
　Barbauld, Anna Laetitia, 1743–1825, 1,2
　Barber, Margaret Fairless, 1869–1901, 2
　Battcock, Marjorie, 2
　Behn, Aphra, 1640–1689, 1,2
　Blind, Mathilde Cohen, 1841–1896, 1,2
　Boodson, Alison, 1925–, 2
　Booth, Evangeline Cory, 1865–1950, 1,2
　Bowles, Caroline, 1786–1854, 2
　Bronte, Emily Jane, 1818–1848, 1,2
　Browning, Elizabeth Barrett, 1806–1861, 1,2
　Caird, (Alice) Mona, 1855–1932, 1,2
　Carey, Elizabeth Tanfield, Lady, 1585–1639, 2
　Carter, Elizabeth, 1717–1806, 1,2
　Cavendish, Margaret, Duchess of Newcastle, 1624–1674, 1

Chapone, Hester Mulso, 1727–1801, 1,2

Charles, Elizabeth Rundle, 1828–1896, 1,2

Chudleigh, Elizabeth, 1720–1788, 1

Chudleigh, Mary, Lady, 1656–1701, 1

Cockburn, Catharine Trotter, 1679–1749, 1

Coleridge, Mary Elizabeth, 1861–1907, 2

Coleridge, Sara(h) Henry, 1802–1852, 1,2

Collins, Anne, fl. 1650s, 2

Cook, Eliza, 1818–1889, 1,2

Cornford, Frances Crofts Darwin, 1886–1960, 2

Cowley, Hannah Parkhurst, 1743–1809, 1,2

Daryush, Elizabeth Bridges, 1887–1977, 2

Drane, Augusta Theodosia, 1823–1894, 1

Elliott, Charlotte, 1789–1871, 1

Feinstein, Elaine, 1930–, 2

Field, Michael, pseud., 1846–1914, 2

Finch, Anne Kingsmill, Countess of Winchilsea, 1661–1720, 1,2

Foley, Helen, 1896–1938, 1

Fowler, Ellen Thorneycroft, 1860–1929, 2

Gibbons, Stella Dorothea, 1902–, 2

Greenwell, Dora, 1821–1882, 1,2

Havergal, Frances Ridley, 1836–1879, 1

Hemans, Felicia Dorothea Browne, 1793–1835, 1,2

Hickey, Emily, 1845–1924, 2

Ingelow, Jean, 1820–1897, 1,2

Jennings, Elizabeth, 1926–, 2

Jewsbury, Maria Jane, 1800–1833, 1,2

Kemble, Fanny (Frances Anne), 1809–1893, 1,2

Killigrew (Killegrew), Anne, 1660–1685, 1,2

Kingsmill, Anne, Lady Winchilsea, 1661–1720, 2

Landon, Letitia Elizabeth, 1802–1838, 1,2

Levy, Amy, 1861–1889, 2

Loy, Mina, 1882–1966, 2

Lucas, Margaret, Duchess of Newcastle, 1623–, 1

Lyon, Lilian Bowes, 1855–1949, 2

MacAulay, Rose, 1881–1958, 2

Mew, Charlotte Mary, 1869–1928, 1,2

Meynell, Alice Christ(a)na Gertrude Thompson, 1847–1922, 1,2

Mitford, Mary Russell, 1787–1855, 1,2

Montagu, Mary Wortley, Lady, 1689–1762, 1,2

Moore, Virginia, 1903–, 2

More, Hannah, 1745–1833, 1,2

Newcastle, Margaret Cavendish, Duchess of, 1624–1694, 1,2

Nicholson, Adela, 1865–1904, 2

Norton, Caroline Elizabeth Sarah Sheridan, 1808–1877, 1,2

Norton, Mrs., 1827–1877, 1

Nossis, fl. 200BC, 1

Pardoe, Julia S. H., 1806–1862, 2

Peirse, Juanita, 2

Pembroke, Mary Herbert Sidney, Countess of, 1561–1621, 1,2

Pfeiffer, Emily Jane, 1827–1890, 2

Philips, Katherine Fowler "Orinda", 1631–1664, 1,2

Pitter, Ruth, 1897–, 2

Procter, Adelaide Anne, 1825–1864, 1,2

Raine, Kathleen (Jessie), 1908–, 2

Ridler, Anne, 1912–, 2

Rossetti, Christina Georgina, 1830–1894, 1,2

Rowe, Elizabeth Singer, 1674–1737, 1,2

Sackville, Margaret, Lady, fl. 1910s, 1

Sackville-West, Victoria Mary, 1892–1962, 1,2

Seward, Anna, 1747–1809, 1,2

Shore, Louise, 1824–1895, 2

Sidney, Mary, 1555–1621, 1

Sitwell, Edith, Dame, 1887–1964, 1,2

Smedley, Menella Bute, 1820–1877, 2

Smith, Charlotte Turner, 1749–1806, 1,2

Smith, Stevie (Florence Margaret), 1902–1971, 2

Southey, Caroline Ann Bowles, 1786–1854, 1

Stuart-Wortley, Emmeline Charlotte Elizabeth Manners, Lady, 1806–1855, 1,2

Taylor, Jane, 1783–1824, 1,2

Trotter, Catherine, 1679–1749, 1,2

Underhill, Evelyn, 1875–1941, 1

Veley, Margaret, 1843–1887, 2
Webster, Augusta Davies, 1837–1894, 1
Wellesley, Dorothy, 1891–1956, 2
Weston, Elizabeth, fl. 1600s, 2
Wilder, Jessie, fl. 1930s, 1
Williams, Helen Marie, 1762–1827, 1,2
Williams, (Helen) Maria, 1762–1827, 1
Winchilsea, Elizabeth Finch, d. 1914, 1
Wroath (Wroth), Mary, Lady, 1586–1640, 1
Poets, Finnish
Salmela-Jarvinen, Martta, 1892–, 2
Poets, Flemish
Bijna (or Byns), Anna, 1494–1575, 1
Poets, French
Ackermann, Louise Victorine Choquet, 1813–1890, 1
Adam, Juliette Lamber, 1836–1936, 1,2
Albret, Jeanne d', 1528–1572, 1,2
Beauharnais, Marie Anne Francoise Mouchard, 1738–1813, 1
Bertin, Louise Angelique, 1805–1877, 1
Cheron(t), (Elizabeth) Sophie, 1648–1711, 1,2
Christine de Pisan, 1363–1431, 1,2
Colet, Louise Revoil, 1808–1876, 1,2
De Noailles, Marie-Laure, Vicomtesse, 2
Desbordes-Valmore, Marceline, 1786–1859, 1,2
Deshoulieres, Antoinette du Ligier, 1638–1694, 1
Giroud, Francoise, 1916–, 2
Krysinka, Marie, 2
Labe, Louise Charlin Perrin, 1524–1565, 1,2
Margaret of Navarre, 1492–1549, 1
Marguerite d'Angouleme of Nav., 1492–1549, 1
Marie de France, 1175–1190, 1,2
Noailles, Anna Brancovan, Comtesse de, 1876–1933, 2
Pisan, Christine de, 1364–1431, 1,2
Scuddery, Madeleine (Magdaleine) de, 1607–1701, 1,2
Tastu, Amable, Madame, 1798–1885, 2
Vivien, Renee Pauline Tarn, 1877–1909, 2

Poets, German
Ambrosius, Johanna, fl. 1800s, 1
Droste-Hulshoff, Annette Elisabeth Frelin von, 1797–1848, 1
Hellwig, Christina Regina, 2
Herrad(e) of Landsberg, d. 1195, 1,2
Hulshoff, Annette Von Droste, 1797–1848, 1
Karsch, Anna, 1722–1791, 2
Kaschnitz, Marie Luise, 1901–1974, 2
Klink, Gertrud Schotz, 1902–, 1,2
Langgasser, Elisabeth, 1899–1950, 2
Lioba, d. 779, 1
Martin, Martha, fl. 1930s, 1
Mechthild of Magdeburg, 1210–1280, 1
Mechtild of (Hackedorn) Magdeburg, 2
Reinig, Christa, 1926–, 2
Rostwitha (Hrosvitha), 935–1000, 1,2
Sachs, Nelly Leone, 1891–1970, 1,2
Poets, German/Icelandic
Novak, Helga, 1935–, 2
Poets, Ghanian
Sutherland, Efua, 1924–, 2
Poets, Greek
Amyte (Anicia), fl. 300BC, 2
Anyte of Tegea, fl.300 BC, 1,2
Cleobuline, fl. 570BC, 1,2
Corinna of Tanagro, fl. 490BC, 1,2
Erinna, fl.500sBC, 1,2
Hedyle, fl. 260BC, 1
Moero of Byzantium, fl.500 BC, 1
Myrtis, 2
Myrtis of Anthedon, fl.500sBC, 1
Parthenis, fl. 60, 1
Philaneis of Samos, fl. 270BC, 1
Praxilla, fl. 450BC, 1
Sappho, 600–580BC, 1,2
Telesilla, 51 BC, 1
Poets, Hungarian
Artner, Marie Therese "Theone", 1772–1829, 1
Papp-Vary, Sernea Sziklay, 1881–1923, 1
Poets, Indian
Bai, Mira, fl. 1500s, 1
Dutt, Toru, 1856–1877, 1,2
Mira Bai, fl. 1500s, 1
Naipu, Sarojini, 1879–1949, 1,2
Poets, Irish
Carmichael, Amy, fl. 1900s, 1
Gormlaith, d. 947, 1
Halvey, Margaret Mary Brophy, fl. 1880s, 1

Ukrainka, Lesya, pseud., 1872–1913, 1
Zaturenska, Marya, 1902–1982, 2
Poets, Scottish
  Adam, Jean, 1710–1765, 1
  Angus, Marion, 1866–1946, 2
  Baillie, Grizel (Grisell) Hume, Lady, 1665–1746, 1,2
  Baillie, Joanna, 1762–1851, 1,2
  Barnard, Anne Lindsay, Lady, 1750–1825, 2
  Blamire, Susanna, 1747–1794, 1
  Cockburn, Alison (Alicia), 1713–1794, 1,2
  Craig, Isa, 1831–1903, 2
  Cruikshank, Helen B., 1896–, 2
  Elliot, Jean, 1727–1805, 1
  Fleming, Marjory (Margaret), 1803–1811, 1,2
  Glover, Jean, 1758–1801, 1
  Hamilton, Janet, 1795–1873, 1
  Hume, Grisell, 1665–1746, 1
  Jacob, Mrs. Arthur Violet, fl. 1900s, 1
  Jacob, Violet, 1863–1946, 2
  Lindsay, Anne Barnard, 1750–1825, 1
  MacLeod, Mary, 1615–1706, 2
  Macpherson, Mary, 2
  Pagan, Isobel, 1741–1821, 1
  Simpson, Jane Cross, 1811–1886, 2
  Spark, Muriel Sarah Camberg, 1918–, 2
  Wardlaw, Elizabeth, Lady, 1677–1727, 1,2
  Washburn, Jean Linsey Bruce, 1838–1904, 1
Poets, South African
  Jonker, Ingrid, 1933–1965, 2
Poets, Spanish
  Castro, Rosalie de, 1837–1885, 1,2
  Kasmunah, fl. 1200s, 2
  Theresa of Avila, 1515–1582, 1,2
Poets, Swedish
  Fox, Siv Cedering, 1939–, 2
  Lenngren, Anna Malmstedt, 1754–1817, 1
  Nordenflycht, Hedwig Charlotte, 1718–1763, 1
Poets, Swiss
  Lagerlof, Selma Ottiniana Louisa, 1858–1940, 1,2
  Meylan, Elisabeth, 1937–, 2
Poets, Turkish
  Aristodama, fl. 218BC, 2

Poets, Uruguayan
  Augustine, Delmira, 1880–1914, 1
  Ibarbourou, Juana de, 1895–, 1
  Vaz Ferreira, Maria Eugenia, 1875–, 1
Poets, Venezuelan
  Caceres de Arismendi, Luisa, 1800–1866, 1
  Gramcko, Ida, fl. 1940s, 2
Poets, Welsh
  Laing, Dilys Bennett, 1906–1960, 2
  Owens, Vilda Sauvage, fl. 1900s, 1
  Puddicombe, Anne, 1836–1915, 2
Police
  See also
    Detectives
  Becke, Shirley, 2
  Blankenship, Betty, 2
  Boyle, Nina, 1863–1943, 2
  Cobb, Gail A., fl. 1970s, 2
  Coffal, Elizabeth, fl. 1960s, 2
  Damer-Dawson, Margaret, 2
  Fleysher, Ellen, 1944–, 2
  Green, Marty, fl. 1970s, 2
  Moore, Patti, fl. 1800s, 2
  O'Neill, Maggie, fl. 1970s, 2
  O'Reilly, Mary Boyle, 1873–, 1
  Renzullo, Vittoria, fl. 1970s, 2
  Robbins, Regina, 2
  Schimmel, Gertrude D. T., 1918–, 2
  Skillern, Daphne, 1928–, 2
  Stowe, Mary F., fl. 1970s, 2
  Tucker, Julia, 1939–, 2
  Uhnak, Dorothy, 1930–, 2
  Watkins, Elaine, 2
  Wells, Alice Stebbins, 2
Police reporters
  House, Toni, fl. 1970s, 2
Polio researchers
  Horstmann, Dorothy Millicent, 1911–, 1,2
Political cartoonists
  Rogers, Lou, 1920–1930, 2
Political consultants
  Costanza, Margaret (Midge), 1932–, 2
Political economists
  Martineau, Harriet, 1802–1876, 1,2
Political leaders, American
  Abbott, Daisy Rhea, fl. 1891–, 2
  Baxter, Annie White, m. 1888, 1,2
  Bellamy, Carol, 1942–, 2
  Bellamy, Mary Godot, 2
  Bendl, Gerta, 2
  Blair, Emily Newell, 1877–1951, 2
  Cannon, Isabella W., 1902–, 2

Political leaders, Hungarian
 Knur(r), Palne, 1889–1944, 1,2
 Koltoi, Anna, 1891–1944, 1,2
Political leaders, Indian
 Besant, Annie Wood, 1848–1933, 1,2
 Devi, Gayatri (Maharani of Jaipur),
 1919–, 2
 Jaipur, Maharani of, 1919–, 1
Political leaders, Irish
 De Valera, Sile, fl. 1970s, 2
 Markievicz, Constance Gorebooth,
 Countess de, 1868–1927, 1,2
Political leaders, Italian
 Este, Isabella d' Marchioness of Man-
 tua, 1474–1539, 1,2
 Farnesio, Isabel de, 1692–1766, 2
Political leaders, Peruvian
 Luz Gonzales del Valle v. de Marino,
 Maria, 1897–1969, 2
Political leaders, Philippine
 Marcos, Imelda Romualdez, 1931–,
 1,2
Political leaders, Puerto
 Almiroty, Maria Martinez de Perez,
 1889–, 2
Political leaders, Roman
 Hortensia, fl. 50 BC, 2
Political leaders, Russian
 Furtseva, Eketerina, 1909–, 1
 Kazhanova, Dr., 2
 Komarova, Domna, fl. 1970s, 2
 Nichipor, Alexandra, fl. 1970s, 2
 Rahimova, Ibodat, 2
 Stasova, Helena, 1873–1966, 2
 Zasulich, Vera, 1851–1919, 2
Political leaders, South Korean
 Yim, Louise, 1899–1977, 1,2
Political leaders, Vietnamese
 Ngo Dinh Nhu, Madam, 1910–1963,
 1,2
Political scientists
 Arendt, Hanna, 1906–1975, 1,2
 Hollingsworth, Mildred Harvey, fl.
 1930s, 1
 Wambuagh, Sarah, 1882–1955, 1,2
Political writers
 Carroll, Anna Ella, 1815–1893, 1,2
 Fitzgerald, Frances (Frankie), 1940–,
 2
Politicians
 Adkins, Bertha Sheppard, 1906–
 1983, 1,2
 Ashley, Grace Bosley, 1874–, 1
 Avary, Myrta Lockett, fl. 1910s, 1,2

Ballinger, Violet Margaret L. Hodg-
 son, gr. 1917, 1
Belmont, Alva E. Smith, d. 1933, 1
Borgia, Lucrezia, Duchess of Ferrara,
 1480–1519, 1,2
Boves, Josefina, 1
Brown, Laura A., 1874–1924, 1
Byrne, Catherine, 1897–, 1
Byrne, Doris I., fl. 1940s, 1
Byrne, Mabel, 1
Conkey, Elizabeth A. Loughran,
 1883–1963, 1
Cook, Nancy, fl. 1930s, 1
Cormier, Lucia, 1912–, 1
Crews, Julia Lesser, 1
Davie, Eugenie M. L., fl. 1930s, 1
Davie, May Preston, m. 1930, 1
Davis, Dorothy, 1922–, 1
Davis, Katherine McGrath, fl. 1950s,
 1
Diblan, Makbule, fl. 1940s, 1
Durlach, Theresa Mayer, fl. 1930s, 1
Earle, Genevieve Beavers, 1883–1956,
 1
Edwards, Henrietta, 1849–1933, 1
Edwards, India, 1895–, 1
Eve, Fanny Jean Turing, d. 1934, 1
Fortune, Jennie, 1895–, 1
Gordon, Jane, 1749–1812, 1
Hamilton, Mary Agnes Adamson,
 1883–, 1
Harman, Elizabeth, gr. 1930, 1
Hathaway, Maggie Smith, 1867–, 1
Haughland, Brynhild, 1905–, 1
Hay, Regina Deem, 1890–, 1
Hohenlohe-Waldenburg, Stefanie
 Richter, 1896–, 1
Hooper, Virginia Fite, 1917–, 1
Howard, Katherine Montague Gra-
 ham, 1898–, 1
Ibarruri, Dolores Gomez, 1895–, 1
Jones, Minona Stearns Fitts, 1855–, 1
Lawrence, Arabella Susan, 1871–
 1947, 1
Lee, Frances Marron, fl. 1950s, 1
Leese, Mary Elizabeth, 1853–, 1
Louchheim, Katie Scofield, 1903–, 1
Lowman, Mary D., 1842–, 1
Lyall, Beatrix Margaret, fl. 1890s, 1
Maime, Anne Louise Benedicte de
 Bourbon, 1676–1753, 1
Marchais, Madame du (Madame
 d'Anglivilliers), fl. 1700s, 1
Marie of Rohan, d. 1679, 1

Mayes, Rose Gorr, 1898–, 1
McCauley, Jane Hamilton, 1916–, 1
McClung, Nellie Mooney, 1874–
  1951, 1
McKinney, Louise, 1868–1933, 1
Murray, Esther Burke Higgins,
  1905–, 1
Phillips, Marion, 1881–1932, 1
Phillips, Velvalea, 1925–, 1
Price, Margaret Bayne, 1912–, 1
Reavis, Babs H., fl. 1930s, 1
Sunderland, Anne, Countess, fl.
  1690s, 1
Tree, Marietta, 1917–, 1
Tuttle, Florence Onertin, 1869–, 1
Velhagen, Millicent H., fl. 1920s, 1
Vredenburgh, Dorothy McElroy,
  1916–, 1
Wasilewska, Wanda, 1905–1964, 1
Williams, Clare, gr. 1931, 1
Polk, James K.—Mother
  Knox, Jane, fl. 1780s, 1
  Polk, Jane Knox, 1776–1852, 2
Polk, James K.—Spouse
  Polk, Sarah Childress, 1803–1891, 1,2
Polk, Lucius—Spouse
  Eastin, Mary, d. 1847, 1
Pollock, Channing—Spouse
  Marble, Anna, fl. 1900s, 1
Pompeius, Sextus—Mother
  Mucia, fl. 62 BC, 1
Pompey—Spouse
  Cornelia, d. 67 BC, 1
  Mucia, fl. 62 BC, 1
Ponce de Leon, Juan—Friend
  Dolores, Donna, fl. 1500s, 1
Pope, Alexander—Friend
  Blount, Martha, 1690–1762, 1
Popes
  Joan, fl. 853s, 1
Pork producers
  Van de Walle, Dee, fl. 1970s, 2
Port mistress
  Jenne, Crystal Snow, 2
Porter, Cole—Mother
  Porter, Kate Cole, d. 1952, 2
Portugal
  Catela, Joan Segal, fl. 1970s, 2
Posonby, Frederick—Daughter
  Lamb, Caroline, Lady, 1785–1828,
  1,2
Postal officials
  Aitchison, Beatrice, 1908–, 2
  Fields, Mary, 1832–1914, 2

Gentry, Ann Hawkins, 1791–1870, 2
Greenwood, Marie Chandler, 1901–,
  2
Robertson, Alice Mary, 1854–1931,
  1,2
Sharrer, Ethel V., fl. 1800s, 2
Slaughter, Linda, 1843–, 2
Wilson, Elizabeth Miller, fl. 1870s, 2
Potters
  Bailey, Henrietta, fl. 1900s, 2
  Banks, Eliza S., fl. 1870s, 2
  Barlow, Florence E., 1873–1909, 2
  Barlow, Hannah Bolton, 1870–1930,
    2
  Bespalova-Mikhaleva, Tamara Niko-
    laevna, fl. 1970s, 2
  Bessarabova, Natalia Nanovna,
    1895–, 2
  Billington, Dora, fl. 1900s, 2
  Bjorquist, Karin, 1927–, 2
  Bracquemond, Marie, fl. 1870s, 1
  Bringle, Cynthia, 2
  Bryk, Rut, 1916–, 2
  Charag-Zuntz, Hanna, 1915–, 2
  Dan'ko (Alekseenko), Natalia Iakov-
    levna, 1892–1942, 2
  Duckworth, Ruth, 1919–, 2
  Edwards, Emily J., d. 1876, 2
  Edwards, Louisa E., fl. 1870s, 2
  Eggers, Marie, 2
  Elenius, Elsa, 1897–, 2
  Frackleton, Susan Stuart Goodrich,
    1848–, 1,2
  Fry, Laura Ann, 1857–1943, 2
  Hagen, Alice Mary Egan, 1872–1972,
    2
  Holzer-Kjeuberb, Friedl, 1905–, 2
  Jacobus, Pauline, 1840–1930, 2
  Judd, Florence, 2
  Keepax, Mary, 2
  Krebs, Nathalie, 1895–, 2
  Kwali, Ladi, fl. 1950s, 2
  Lebedinskaia, Lidia Ivanovna, 1908–,
    2
  Lee, Frances E., fl. 1870s, 2
  Lewis, Esther, fl.1870–s, 2
  Lewis, Florence E., d. 1917, 2
  Lupton, Edith D., fl. 1870s, 2
  Martinez, Maria Montoya, 1887–
    1980, 2
  McLaughlin, Mary Louise M., 1847–
    1939, 1,2
  Mortimer, Ann, fl. 1960s, 2
  Muona, Toini, 1904–, 2

Nausicaa, 2
Nora Elizabeth, 1
Olga, d. 969, 1,2
Paley, Natalie, 1920–1930, 2
Paola, Donna Paola Margherita
  Maria, 1937–, 1
Pauahi, Bernice, 1831–, 2
Pocahontas, 1595–1617, 1,2
Radziwill, Catherine, 1
Roxana, d. 309 BC, 1
Sadako, 1885–1951, 1
Sayn-Wittgenstein, Carolyne, 1819–
  1887, 1
Sofia of Chotek, Princess of Hohen-
  burg, d. 1914, 1
Sooja Bae, fl. 1500s, 1
Sophia Dorothea Ulrike Alice, 1870–
  1932, 1
Talleyrand-Perigord, Catherine Noel
  Worlee Grand de, 1762–1835, 1
Thermouthis, fl.1500BC, 1
Thuringen, Elizabeth von, 1207–
  1231, 1
Tsahai, 1919–1942, 1
Victoria Alexandra Alice Mary,
  1897–, 1
Volkonsky, Marie Raevsky, 1806–
  1863, 1
Zita, 1892–1922, 1
Printers and printing
  See also
    Bookbinders and bookbinding
    Child printers
    Typographers
Aitken, Jane, 1764–1832, 1,2
Bailey, Lydia R., d. 1869, 1,2
Balle, Maria, d. 1940, 1
Bat Sheba (Verona), fl. 1594, 2
Beaufort, Margaret, 1443–1509, 1,2
Beilenson, Edna, 1909–1981, 2
Bird, Clementine, d. 1775, 1
Bonhomme, Yolande, fl. 1541, 1
Bradford, Cornelia Smith, d. 1772,
  1,2
Brodsky, Judith, 1923–, 2
Clark, Kathryn Haugh, fl. 1970s, 2
Coerr, S. DeRenne, fl. 1970s, 2
Colwell, Elizabeth, fl. 1910s, 1
Conat, Estellina, fl. 1496, 2
Connor, Emily E., fl. 1930s, 1
Craighton, Elizabeth, fl. 1720s, 1
Crouch, Mary, fl. 1780s, 1
Crough, Mary, 1740–1818, 2
Daniel, Emily, fl. 1880s, 2

Dickson, Mary, fl. 1820s, 1
Draper, Margaret Green, 1727–1807,
  1,2
Erickson, Melissa, fl. 1970s, 2
Evans, Margaret B., fl. 1940s, 1
Fishels, Riozl, fl. 1500s, 2
Flores, Dona Francisca, fl. 1720s, 1
Foster, Barbara, fl. 1970s, 2
Franklin, Ann Smith, 1696–1763, 1,2
Friedlander, Elizabeth, fl. 1950s, 1
Gela, fl. 1713, 2
Gentry, Helen, gr. 1922, 1
Gist, Malvina Black, 1842–, 1,2
Glover, Elizabeth, fl. 1630s, 1,2
Goddard, Anna, fl. 1770s, 1
Goddard, Mary Katherine, 1738–
  1816, 1,2
Goddard, Sarah Updike, 1700–1770,
  1,2
Goldthwaite, Anne Wilson, 1875–
  1944, 1,2
Goodridge, Sarah, 1788–1853, 2
Goudy, Bertha M., 1865–1935, 1
Green, Ann(e) Catherine Hoof,
  1720–1775, 1,2
Guillard, Charlotte, fl. 1500s, 1,2
Harrison, Margaret, fl. 1800s, 1
Hirsch, Fiola, fl. 1727, 2
Holt, Elizabeth Hunter, 1784–1785, 1
Hoof, Ann(e) Catherine, d. 1775, 2
Hoyle, Ethel, fl. 1950s, 1
Judel, Rachel, 2
Judel, Rebecca, 2
Kauffmann, Angelica, 1741–1807, 1,2
Kent, Corita, 1918–, 2
Kohen, Gutel, 1627–, 2
Kohlmeyer, Ida, 1912–, 2
Low, Esther, fl. 1810s, 1
Mallet, Elizabeth, fl. 1700s, 1,2
Mann, Elizabeth, d. 1954, 1
Margolis, Esther, fl. 1970s, 2
Maynard, Valerie, fl. 1970s, 2
Meiner, Annamarie, fl. 1930s, 1
Midwinter, Mrs., fl. 1710s, 1
Miller, August A., fl. 1870s, 1
Miller, Harriet Granger, fl. 1870s, 1
Molloy, Emma, 1839–, 1
Nasi, Reyna, fl. 1590s, 2
Nikolayeva, Claudia, 1893–, 2
Nuthead, Dinah, 1695, 1,2
Oswald, Elizabeth Holt, fl. 1790s, 1
Pissarro, Esther Bensusan, d. 1951, 2
Prideaux, Sarah T., 2
Richert, Shirley, fl. 1970s, 2

Rugerin, Anna, fl. 1480s, 1
Russel, Mrs. Ezekiel, fl. 1700s, 1
Russell, Penelope, fl. 1770s, 1
Russell, Sarah, fl. 1790s, 1
Shera, Florence B., fl. 1950s, 1
Shotoku, fl. 770, 1
Simon, Anna, fl. 1910s, 1
Sirani, Elisabetta, 1638–1665, 1,2
Smith, Cornelia, d. 1755, 1,2
Taylor, Elizabeth, fl. 1870s, 1
Tiktiner, Rebecca, d. 1550, 2
Timothy, Ann Donovan, 1727–1792, 1,2
Timothy, Elizabeth, 1700–1757, 1,2
Urbach, Lily, fl. 1970s, 2
Valesh, Eva McDonald, 1866–, 1
Van Orroer, Beatrice, fl. 1950s, 1
Vautrollier, Jeanne, fl. 1580s, 1
Viart, Guyonne, fl. 1500s, 1
Warde, Beatrice Lamberton, 1900–, 1
Weitbrecht, Oda, fl. 1910s, 1
Wellington, Margaret, fl. 1870s, 1
White, Callie, fl. 1870s, 1
Winthrop, Margaret, 1591–1647, 1,2
Yeats, Elizabeth Corbe, 1,2
Yeats, Lily, 2
Prison officials
  Harris, Mary Belle, 1874–1957, 2
  Kelly, Joanna Beadon, fl. 1950s, 1
Prison reformers
  Blair, Mrs. L. C., 2
  Cunningham, Kate Richards O'Hare, 1877–1948, 1,2
  Farnham, Eliza Wood Burhans, 1815–1864, 1,2
  Fry, Elizabeth Gurney, 1780–1845, 1,2
  Gilbert, Linda (Zelinda), 1847–1895, 1,2
  Hall, Emma Amelia, 1837–1884, 2
  Hodder, Jessie Donaldson, 1867–1931, 2
  Johnson, Ellen Cheney, 1829–1899, 2
  Robbins, Elizabeth Murray, d. 1853, 2
  Tutweiler, Julia Strudwick, 1841–1916, 1,2
  Van Waters, Miriam, 1887–1974, 1,2
Prisoners
  Mandela, Winnie, 1934–, 2
  Phillips, Eugenia Levy, fl. 1860s, 1,2
  Sikharane, Joyce, fl. 1970s, 2
Prithwi Raj.—Spouse
  Tara Bae, fl. 1500s, 1

Probus, Marcus Valerius—Spouse
  Procla, Julia, fl. 230s, 1
Prodigy
  Pascal, Jacqueline, 1625–1661, 1
Producers
  Berg, Ilene Amy, fl. 1970s, 2
  Cornell, Katharine, 1893–1974, 1,2
  Cowl, Jane Cowles, 1883–1950, 1,2
  Davis, Madelyn, 2
  Fichandler, Zelda, 1924–, 2
  Fisher, Doris, 1915–, 1
  Jones, Margo, 1912–1955, 2
  Kernochan, Sarah, fl. 1970s, 2
  Komisarjevskava, Vera, 1864–1910, 1
  Langner, Armina Marshall, 1898–, 1
  Littlewood, Joan, 1914–, 2
  O'Neil, Carolyn A., 1955–, 2
  Phillips, Elizabeth, fl. 1770s, 1
  Weber, Lois, 1881–1939, 2
  Webster, Margaret, 1905–1972, 1,2
  White, Ruth, 1914–1969, 2
Prohibition repeal
  Sabin, Pauline Morton, 1887–1955, 1,2
Prohibitionists
  Hurst, Sadie Dotson, 1857–1951, 2
Property managers
  Davenport, Elizabeth Wooley, fl. 1650s, 1,2
  Ferree, Mary Warenbuer, d. 1716, 1,2
Prophets
  Caecilia Metilla, "the good", fl. 90 BC, 1
  Deborah, 1,2
  Kahinah Dahiyah Dint Thaabita., 2
  Marat Guta, 2
  Miriam, 2
  Pythia, 900 BC, 2
  Sambathe (Sabbe), fl.100 BC, 2
  Shipton, Mother, 1486–1561, 1,2
  Southcott, Joanna, 1750–1814, 1,2
  Stanhope, Hester Lucy, Lady, 1776–1839, 1,2
Proprietors
  Pratt, Margaret, fl. 1740s, 1
  Prentice, Mrs. John, d. 1691, 1
Prostitutes
  Fernanda Fuentes, fl. 1960s, 2
  Hetzel, Barbara, fl. 1970s, 2
Proust, Marcel—Friend
  Chevigne, Laure de Sade, d. 1936, 1
Proust, Marcel—Mother
  Proust, Jeanne Weil, d. 1905, 2
Proxmire, Willis—Spouse
  Proxmire, Ellen, 2

Psellus, Michael—Mother
  Theodota, fl. 900s, 1
Psychiatrists
  See also
    Psychoanalysts
  Arkin, Frances S, fl. 1930s, 1
  Bender, Lauretta, 1897–, 1
  Farnham, Marynia L. Foot, 1899–
    1979, 2
  Fish, Barbara, fl. 1970s, 2
  Frankfort, Ellen, 2
  Fromm-Reichmann, Frieda, 1890–
    1957, 2
  Hinkle, Beatrice Moses, 1874–1953, 2
  Horney, Karen Daniels(s)on, 1885–
    1952, 1,2
  Kubler-Ross, Elisabeth, 1926–, 2
  Levine, Lena, 1903–1965, 2
  Nyswander, Marie E., 1919–, 1,2
  Ring, Barbara Taylor, 1879–1941, 1
  Saadawi, Nawal el, 1930–, 2
  Shainess, Natalie, 2
  Spurlock, Jeanne, fl. 1960s, 2
Psychics
  Dixon, Jeane L. Pinckert, 1918–, 2
  Hale, Tenny, 2
  Hughes, Irene, 2
  Jensen, Ann, 2
  Jourdain, Eleanor Frances, 1863–
    1942, 1,2
  Kinkade, Kebrina, 2
  Marks, Jandolin, 2
  Meyers, Ethel Johnson, 2
  Seton, Anya Chase, 1916–, 1,2
  Sotka, Kathy, 2
Psychoanalysts
  Andreas-Salome, Lou, 1861–1937,
    1,2
  Bonaparte, Marie, 1882–1962, 2
  Brunswick, Ruth Jane Mack, 1897–
    1946, 2
  Deutsch, Helen Rosenbach, 1884–
    1982, 2
  Dunbar, Helen Flanders, 1902–1959,
    2
  Fraiberg, Selma, 1918–1981, 2
  Freud, Anna, 1895–1982, 2
  Horney, Karen Daniels(s)on, 1885–
    1952, 1,2
  Klein, Margaret, fl. 1960s, 2
  Klein, Melanie, 1882–1960, 2
  Singer, June, 2
  Thompson, Clara (Mabel), 1893–
    1958, 2

Psychologists
  See also
    Child psychologists
  Abramson, Lyn, 1940–, 2
  Ames, Louise Bates, 1906–, 1
  Babcock, Harriet Sprague, d. 1952, 1
  Bronner, Augusta Fox, 1881–1966, 2
  Brothers, Joyce, 1927–, 1,2
  Buhler, Charlotte Bertha, 1893–
    1974, 2
  Calkins, Mary Whiton, 1863–1930,
    1,2
  Carrington, Karin, fl. 1970s, 2
  Chappelle, Mrs. B. F., 1897–, 1
  Chesler, Phyllis, 2
  Chester (Chesler), Phyllis, 2
  Confrin, Betsy, 2
  Curlee-Salisbury, Joan, 1930–, 2
  Dougherty, Dora Jean, 1921–, 1
  Downey, June Etta, 1875–1932, 2
  Eads, Laura Krieger, fl. 1920s, 1
  Ellison, Katherine White, fl. 1970s, 2
  Ferrero, Gina Lombroso, 1872–1944,
    1
  Field, Joanna, pseud., 1905–, 2
  Franklin, Christine Ladd, 1847–1930,
    1,2
  Gibson, Eleanor Jack, 1913–, 2
  Gilbreth, Lillian Moller, 1878–1972,
    1,2
  Goldsmith, C Elizabeth, fl. 1930s, 1
  Goodenough, Florence Laura, 1886–
    1959, 2
  Hollingsworth, Leta Anna, 1886–
    1939, 2
  Horner, Matina Souretis, 1939–, 2
  Johnson, Virginia Eshelman, 1925–, 2
  Joteyko, Josephine, gr. 1896, 1
  Kearney, Annette Gaines, 2
  Loftus, Beth, 2
  Lough, Orpha Maust, 1902–, 1
  Maccoby, Eleanor, 2
  Martin, Lillien Jane, 1851–1943, 1,2
  McBride, Katharine Elizabeth, 1904–
    1976, 1,2
  McHale, Kathryn, 1890–1956, 1
  Milnes-Walker, Nicolette, fl. 1970s, 2
  Muller-Schwarze, Christine, fl.
    1960s, 2
  Murdoch, Katharine, fl. 1920s, 1
  Oliver, Donna, fl. 1970s, 2
  Payton, Carolyn R., 2
  Pruette, Lorine Livingston, 1876–,
    1,2

Rand, Marie Gertrude, 1886–1970, 2
Ridenour, Nina, 1904–, 1
Robbins, Sara Franklin, fl. 1930s, 1
Russell, Olive Ruth, fl. 1970s, 2
Russo, Nancy Felipe, fl. 1970s, 2
Schacter, Frances, 2
Scott-Maxwell, Florida, 1893–, 2
Taft, Jessie, 1882–1960, 2
Valian, Virginia, 1942–, 2
Velimesis, Margery L., fl. 1940s, 2
Washburn, Margaret Floy, 1871–
1939, 2
Weill, Blanche C., fl. 1930s, 1
Weisstein, Naomi, 1939–, 2
Whitchurch, Anna K., fl. 1970s, 2
Wolfenstein, Martha, 1911–1976, 2
Woolley, Helen Bradford Thompson,
1874–1947, 2
Zeigarnik, Bluma, 2
Psychotherapists
Fromm-Reichmann, Frieda, 1890–
1957, 2
Ptolemy I—Daughter
Arsinoe, 316–271BC, 2
Ptolemy I—Mother
Arsinoe, 200–300BC, 1
Ptolemy II—Spouse
Arsinoe, 316–271BC, 2
Public health nurses
Arnstein, Margaret Gene, 1904–
1972, 2
Crandall, Ella Phillips, 1871–1938,
1,2
Fitzgerald, Alice, 1874–1962, 2
Gardner, Mary Sewall, 1871–1961,
1,2
Kmetz, Annette L., fl. 1930s, 1
McGarvah, Eleanor, fl. 1930s, 1
McIver, Pearl, 1893–, 1,2
Minnigerode, Lucy, 1871–1935, 1,2
Pambrun, Audra, 1929–, 2
Read, Katherine S., fl. 1930s, 1
Wales, Marguerite, fl. 1920s, 1
Public health officials
See also
Epidemiologists
Calderone, Mary Steichen, 1904–, 1,2
Clark, Mary Augusta, fl. 1930s, 1
Goldsmith, Grace Arabell, 1904–
1975, 2
Nightingale, Florence, 1820–1910,
1,2
Randall, Harriet Bulpitt, 1904–1975,
2
Williams, Cicely D., 1893–, 1,2

Public health workers
Baker, Sara Josephine, 1873–1945, 1,2
Benson, Marguerite, fl. 1930s, 1
Eliot, Martha May, 1891–1978, 1,2
Kmetz, Annette L., fl. 1930s, 1
Kutz, Sally, fl. 1930s, 1
Lebedeva, Vera Pavlovna, 1881–, 1
Parker, Valeria H., 1879–1959, 1
Pinney, Jean Burrows, fl. 1930s, 1
Potter, Ellen Culver, 1871–1958, 1
Warner, Estella Ford, 1891–, 1
Public opinion analysts
Arnold, Pauline, fl. 1910s, 1
Tovell, Billie, 2
Worcester, Dorothy F., fl. 1950s, 2
Public relations
See also
Press agents
Brodsky, Linda G., 2
Caine, Lynn, fl. 1970s, 2
Carpenter, Liz, 1920–, 2
Cazneau, Jane Maria Eliza McManus
Storms, 1807–1878, 2
Clarahan, Virg Binns, fl. 1930s, 1
Clawson, Carol, 2
Cott, Betty, 2
Crowne, Dorothy, fl. 1930s, 1
Fox, Muriel, fl. 1960s, 2
Gross, Miriam Zeller, fl. 1930s, 1
Humphrey, Mary, fl. 1920s, 1
Hunter, Barbara, fl. 1970s, 2
Levinsohn, Roann Kim, 1950–, 2
Livingstone, Beulah, 1886–1975, 2
Lobdell, Avis, fl. 1930s, 1
Mandigo, Pauline Eggleston, 1892–
1956, 1
McNeil, Dee Dee, fl. 1970s, 2
Mitchell, Lolly, fl. 1970s, 2
Reeves, Elizabeth, fl. 1920s, 2
Saunders, Hortense, fl. 1910s, 1
Schoonover, Jean Way, fl. 1950s, 2
Slator, Helen M., fl. 1930s, 1
Soss, Wilma Porter, 1902–, 1
Standish, Marian Eddy, fl. 1910s, 1
Thompson, Charlotte, fl. 1910s, 1
Wheaton, Anne Williams, 1892–
1977, 1,2
Winters, Midge, 1
Public welfare workers
Howard, Minnie Frances, 1872–, 1,2
Publicists
Arden, Sherry W., 2
Berlin, Kathy, fl. 1970s, 2
Clements, Hall-Kane, fl. 1930s, 1

Owen, Marjorie Lewis, 2
Parsons, Augustina, fl. 1820s, 1
Pattee, Alida Francis, d. 1942, 1
Medhill, Eleanor "Cissy" Patterson, 1884–1948, 2
Patterson, Eleanor "Cissy" Medill, 1881–1948, 1,2
Pugh, Esther, fl. 1880s, 1
Rawson, Eleanor S., fl. 1970s, 2
Remsen, Alice, 1896–, 1
Robichaud, Beryl, fl. 1940s, 2
Royall, Anne Newport, 1769–1854, 1,2
Rudrud, Judy L., 2
Russell, Sarah, fl. 1790s, 1
Saunders, Doris Evans, 1928–, 2
Scripps, Ellen Browning, 1836–1932, 1,2
Sharp, Jane, fl. 1670s, 2
Shaw, Carolyn Hagner, 1903–, 1
Smith, Robin B., fl. 1960s, 2
Soliman, Patricia, fl. 1960s, 2
Squires, Delphine Anderson, 1868–, 2
Susong, Edith O'Keefe, fl. 1910s, 2
Tapper, Joan, 1947–, 2
Thackerey, Dorothy Schiff, 1903–, 1
Thompson, Alice, 1
Vlachos, Eleni, 1911–, 2
Wallace, Mildred White, 1839–, 1
Ward, Maisie, 1889–1975, 1,2
Weekes, Marie, fl. 1920s, 1
Wells, Charlotte Fowler, 1814–1901, 1,2
Whitney, Joan, 1914–, 1
Wilcox, Molly Warren, fl. 1930s, 1
Wilde, Miriam Leslie, 1851–, 1
Winslow, Helen Maria, 1851–1938, 1
Wojciechowska, Maia Teresa, 1927–, 2
Pueblo Indians
Silko, Leslie Marmon, 1948–, 2
Velarde, Pablita, 1918–, 2
Puerto Rico
Dubrey, Ana Roque de, 1853–, 2
Mier, Isabel Alonso de, 1886–, 2
Romero, Josefina Barcelo de, 1901–, 2
Romeu, Marta Robert de, 1890–, 2
Timothee, Rosario Andraca de, 2
Tio, Lola Rodriquez de, 1853–, 2
Puerto Rico project
Brook, Marina, 1909–, 2
Puppeteers
Ackley, Edith Flack, fl. 1930s, 1
Baird, Cora Eisenberg, 1912–1967, 1
Lewis, Shari, 1934–, 1,2

Mokil, Sarah, fl. 1930s, 2
Oppenheimer, Lillian, 1898–, 2
Robu, Galina, fl. 1970s, 2
Purchasing agents
See also
Buyers
Gaddis, Edith, fl. 1920s, 1
Puritans
Edwards, Sarah Pierpont, 1710–1758, 2
Johnson, Ar(a)bella, Lady, d. 1630, 1,2
Martindale, Elizabeth Hall, fl. 1660s, 1
Poole (Pole), Elizabeth, 1599–1654, 1,2
Walling, Harriet, fl. 1680s, 1
Putnam, Israel—Mother
Perley, Elizabeth Porter Putnam, 1673–1746, 1
Puzzle editors
Farrar, Margaret Petherbridge, 1897–1967, 1,2
Puzzle experts
Kingsley, Elizabeth Seelman, 1872–1957, 2
Pythagoras—Spouse
Theano, fl. 540BC, 1

Q

Quadroons (Fiction)
John, Madame, 2
Quakers
Ambler, Mary, fl. 1850s, 2
Barnard, Hannah Jenkins, 1764–1825, 1,2
Blair, Hannah Millikan, 2
Bodley, Elizabeth Clark, fl. 1770s, 2
Comstock, Elizabeth Leslie Rous, 1815–1891, 1,2
Dilworth, Mary J., fl. 1840s, 2
Douglass, Sarah, fl. 1850s, 2
Douglass, Sarah Mapps Douglas, 1806–1882, 2
Drinker, Elizabeth Sandwith, 1734–1807, 1,2
Dyer, Mary, 1591–1660, 1,2
Fisher, Mary, 1623–1698, 1,2
Fry, Elizabeth Gurney, 1780–1845, 1,2
Griffitts, Hannah, 1727–1817, 2

Wilhelmina, Juliana Louise Emma
Marie, 1909–, 2
Zakutu, 700–650BC, 1
Zita, 1892–1922, 1
Quezon, Manual—Spouse
Quezon, Aurora Aragon, 1889–1949,
1
Quintuplets
Dionne sisters, 1934–, 1,2
Quirinus—Daughter
Balbina, fl. 100s, 1

R

Rabbi Meir—Spouse
Beruriah, fl. 1210s, 1,2
Rabbis
Feige, fl. 1750s, 2
Priesand, Sally, 1946–, 2
Rachel, Hannah, 1815–1892, 2
Sasso, Sandy, 1947–, 2
Tabick, Jacqueline, 1949–, 2
Werbermacher, Hannah Rachel,
1805–, 2
Rabin, Yitzhak—Spouse
Rabin, Mrs. Yitzhak, 2
Racquetball players
Steding, Peggy, fl. 1970s, 2
Radiation protection
Wood, Nan, fl. 1960s, 2
Radicals
Hopkins, Mary Alden, 1876–1960, 2
Jones, Mary Harris (Mother Jones),
1830–1930, 1,2
McAlmon, Victoria, 1910–1970, 2
Pissarro, Esther Bensusan, d. 1951, 2
Voynich, Ethel Lilian, 1864–1960, 2
Whitney, Charlotte Anita, 1867–
1955, 2
Radio advertising
Lyons, Josephine, fl. 1940s, 2
Nelson, Linnea J., 1920–1940, 2
Scanlan, Elenore, fl. 1930s, 2
Taylor, Joanne, fl. 1930s, 2
Radio announcers
Allen, Ida Bailey, fl. 1920s, 2
Dumon, Marte, 2
Flynn, Catherine, fl. 1930s, 1
Godwin, Natalie, 2
Greene, Gael, 2
Harris, Fran, fl. 1940s, 2
Hobby, Oveta Culp, 1905–, 1,2
Holden, Ann, fl. 1940s, 2

Howard, Besse(e), fl. 1940s, 2
Jackson, Jill, fl. 1940s, 2
Knutsson, Ann-Marie, fl. 1970s, 2
Kuhn, Irene Corbally, 1900–, 1,2
Laird, Ruth, fl. 1940s, 2
Laney, Mary, fl. 1970s, 2
Press, Tina, fl. 1970s, 2
Pryor, Sunny, 2
Radio authors
Aichinger, Ilse, 1921–, 2
Bachmann, Ingeborg, 1926–1973, 2
Bigart, Alice Weel, fl. 1940s, 2
Carrington, Elaine Sterne, 1892–
1958, 1,2
Hummert, Anne Schumacher, fl.
1930s, 1,2
Kent, Priscilla, fl. 1940s, 2
Mechtel, Angelika, 1943–, 2
Ogot, Grace, 2
Phillips, Irna, 1903–1973, 1,2
Snyder, Lucia, fl. 1940s, 2
Zuhorst, Mary, fl. 1940s, 2
Radio commentators
Alexander, Shana Ager, 1925–, 2
Ames, Adrienne, 1907–1947, 2
Broderick, Gertrude G., fl. 1940s, 2
Cravens, Kathryn, fl. 1930s, 1,2
Fitzgerald, Margaret, 1910–, 1
May, Catherine Dean, 1914–, 1,2
Radio directors
Anderson, Theodora D., 2
Briant, Nila Mack, fl. 1930s, 1
Chilton, Ruth, fl. 1920s, 2
Crane, Ruth, fl. 1920s, 2
Demorest, Charlotte, fl. 1940s, 2
Dewart, Janet, fl. 1970s, 2
Dick, Elsie, fl. 1940s, 2
Ellis, Caroline, fl. 1940s, 2
Harrison, Henriette K., fl. 1920s, 2
Hodgson, M. J., gr. 1941, 1
Johnsen, Grace M., fl. 1940s, 2
Leffler, Dorothy, fl. 1940s, 2
Mack, Nila, 1891–1953, 1,2
Markel, Hazel Kenyon, fl. 1940s, 2
Radio editors
Aloni, Shulamit, 2
Quigley, Janet, fl. 1950s, 1
Radio engineers
Kemble, Dorothy Ann, fl. 1930s, 2
Radio executives
Bradshaw, Dallas, fl. 1970s, 2
Brown, Mary Somerville, gr. 1925, 1
Brunson, Dorothy Edwards, fl.
1970s, 2

Radio producers
  Berg, Gertrude, 1899–1966, 1,2
  Bigart, Alice Weel, fl. 1940s, 2
  Franklin, Gladys, fl. 1940s, 2
  Hummert, Anne Schumacher, fl.
    1930s, 1,2
  Mack, Nila, 1891–1953, 1,2
  May, Catherine Dean, 1914–, 1,2
  Riger, Eleanor, 2
  Sanger, Eleanor N., 1930–1940, 2
  Searight, Patti, 1925–, 2
  Wadley, Ellen, fl. 1940s, 2
Radio program directors
  Aldrich, Darragh, fl. 1940s, 2
Radio researchers
  Peden, Irene Carswell, fl. 1970s, 2
Radiobiologists
  Stroud, F. Agness N., fl. 1970s, 2
Railroads
  Beechman, Marie A., fl. 1930s, 1
  Dennis, Olive Wetzel, 1885–1957, 1
  Head, Mary Johnston, fl. 1970s, 2
  Kelly, Ella Maynard, 1857–, 1
  Lobdell, Avis, fl. 1930s, 1
  Stuerm, Ruza Lukavaska, fl. 1930s, 1
  Thayer, Lizzie E. D., 1857–, 1
Rainbow, Edward—Mother
  Rainbow, Rachel Allen, fl. 1620s, 1
Rakoczi, George—Spouse
  Lorantffy, Susanna, 1600–1660, 1,2
Rama—Consort
  Sita, 1
Rama IX—Consort
  Sirikit Kitiyakara, 1932–, 1
Ramsay, Alexander—Sister
  Ramsay, Elizabeth, fl. 1720s, 1
Rana Sanga—Spouse
  Kurnarath, fl. 1500s, 1
Ranchers
  See also
    Cattle queen
    Dude wranglers
    Goat herders
    Mink ranchers
    Plantation owners
    Reindeer industry
    Sheep herders
  Ansolabehere, Mary Jean "Dolly", 2
  Austin, Sadie, fl. 1900s, 2
  Baker, Arcadia Bandini Stearns de,
    1825–1912, 2
  Brooks, Mary T., fl. 1960s, 1
  Cleaveland, Agnes Morley, fl. 1890s,
    2

Freeman, Agnes Suiter, 1843–1931, 2
  Heath, Mary, fl. 1930s, 2
  Heazle, Jean, d. 1949, 2
  Howard, Agnes, 2
  Kaiser, Edna Fay, 1872–1962, 2
  King, Henrietta Maria Morse Cham-
    berlain, 1832–1925, 2
  Knudsten, Molly Flagg, 2
  Lee, Frances Marron, fl. 1950s, 1
  Mann, Pamela, d. 1840, 1,2
  Marvel, Louise "Cattle lady", fl.
    1960s, 1
  Maxwell, Kate "Cattle Kate", fl.
    1880s, 1
  McCall, Dorothy Lawson, 1888–, 2
  Monahan, Johanna, fl. 1860s, 2
  Monoghan, Josephine "Little Jo", d.
    1903, 1
  Morris, Josie, d. 1964, 2
  Perkins, Carmen de, fl. 1960s, 2
  Rindge, May Knight, 1865–1941, 2
  Stewart, Helen Jane Wiser, 1854–
    1926, 2
  Taylor, Elizabeth, 2
  Taylor, Sally, fl. 1970s, 2
  Watson, Ella "Cattle Kate", 1862–
    1889, 1,2
Randolph, Jennings—Mother
  Randolph, Idell Bingman, 1876–
    1933, 2
Randulf the Sheriff—Daughter
  Avice, fl. 1155, 1
Rankin, Jeanette—Daughter
  Rankin, Olive Pickering, 1854–, 2
Rao, Manik—Daughter
  Korundevi, Princess, fl. 1407s, 1
Rape victims
  Massie, Thalia, 2
Rasputin—Daughter
  Rasputin, Maria, 1898–, 2
Rawson, Edward—Daughter
  Rawson, Rebecca, 1656–1692, 2
Rayburn, Sam—Spouse
  Rayburn, Metze Jones, 2
Read, Sir William—Spouse
  Read, Lady, fl. 1710s, 2
Reade, Charles—Friend
  Seymour, Laura, d. 1879, 1
Reagan, Ronald—Spouse
  Reagan, Nancy, 1921–, 2
Real estate business
  Bernie, Rose L., fl. 1930s, 1
  Blue, Virginia Neal, 1910–, 2
  Catlin, Ida, fl. 1930s, 1

Cincotta, Gale, 1930–, 2
Clarke, Helen, 2
Coffin, Mary, 2
Collins, Ellen, 1828–1913, 1,2
Colman, Julia, 1828–1909, 1,2
Coman, Katharine, 1857–1915, 1,2
Comstock, Elizabeth Leslie Rous, 1815–1891, 1,2
Cotton, Elizabeth Avery, 1872–, 2
Cowles, Betsey Mix, 1810–1876, 2
Cox, Hannah, 1796–1876, 1
Crandall, Prudence, 1803–1890, 1,2
Cunard, Nancy, 1896–1965, 2
Dall, Caroline Wells Healey, 1822–1912, 1,2
Dalton, Shirley, fl. 1970s, 2
Daniel, Annie Sturges, 1858–1944, 2
Danser, Fanny Root, fl. 1930s, 1
Darlington, Hannah, fl. 1870s, 1
Davies, Emily, 1830–1921, 1,2
Davis, Edith Smith, m. 1884, 1
Davis, Mary Fenn, 1824–1886, 2
Davis, Paulina Wright, 1813–1876, 1,2
Day, Dorothy, 1897–1980, 1,2
Decker, Sarah Sophia Chase Platt, 1852–1912, 2
Deer, Ada, 1935–, 2
Denison, Elsa, 1889–, 1
Dennett, Mary Coffin Ware, 1872–1947, 2
Despard, Charlotte, 1844–, 1
Diaz, Abby Morton, 1821–1904, 2
Dickinson, Anna Elizabeth, 1842–1932, 1,2
Diggs, Annie LaPorte, 1848–1916, 2
Dix, Dorothea Lynde, 1802–1887, 1,2
Dudley, Helena Stuart, 1858–1932, 1,2
Eastman, Crystal, 1881–1928, 2
Edson, Katherine Philips, 1870–1933, 2
Ellis, Margaret Dye, fl. 1870s, 1
Emery, Sarah Elizabeth Van de Vort, 1838–1895, 2
Emig, Lelia Dromgold, fl. 1890s, 1
Estelle, Helen G.H., fl. 1930s, 1
Estes, Hulduh, d. 1875, 1
Evans, Elizabeth Glendower, 1856–1937, 2
Farley, Harriet, 1813–1907, 2
Fayerweather, Sarah Harris, 1812–1878, 1,2
Foltz, Clara Shortridge, 1849–4934, 2
Foster, Abigail Kelley, 1810–1887, 1,2

Foster, Judith Ellen Horton, 1840–1910, 1,2
Fowler, Lydia Folger, 1822–1879, 1,2
Friedan, Betty, 1921–, 2
Fulbright, Roberta Waugh, 1875–1953, 2
Fuller, Minnie Ursula Oliver Scott Rutherford, 1868–1946, 2
Fuller, (Sarah) Margaret, 1810–1850, 1,2
Gage, Frances Dana Barker, 1808–1884, 1,2
Gardener, Helen Hamilton, 1853–1925, 1,2
Gerberding, Elizabeth, 1857–, 1
Gifford, Susan A., 1826–, 1
Gilman, Charlotte Perkins Stetson, 1860–1935, 1,2
Gilman, Elizabeth "Miss Lizzie", 1867–1950, 2
Godiva (Godgifu) Lady, 1040–1085, 1,2
Gordon, Anna Adams, 1853–1931, 1,2
Gordon, Kate M., 1861–1932, 2
Grandfield, Jennie McKee, m. 1885, 1
Greeley, Mary Y. C., fl. 1870s, 1
Greer, Mrs. Lester, fl. 1930s, 2
Grew, Mary, 1813–1896, 1,2
Grey, Jane Cannon, 1816–, 1
Griffing, Josephine Sophia White, 1814–1872, 1,2
Grimke, Charlotte L. Forten, 1838–1915, 1,2
Guest, Charlotte Elizabeth Bertie, Lady, 1812–1875, 1,2
Haley, Margaret Angela, 1861–1939, 2
Hamer, Fannie Lou Townsend, 1917–, 2
Hansen, Peggy Anne, fl. 1970s, 2
Harper, Frances Ellen Watkins, 1825–1911, 1,2
Hazard, Caroline, 1856–1945, 1,2
Henrotin, Ellen Martin, 1847–1922, 1,2
Herrick, Mary Elizabeth, fl. 1870s, 1
Hertz, Laura B., 1869–, 1
Heyrick, Elizabeth, fl. 1800s, 1
Hiles, Osia Jane, d. 1902, 2
Hill, Florence Davenport, 1829–1919, 1
Hill, Octavia, 1836–1912, 1,2
Hollingsworth, Mrs. S. L., fl. 1930s, 2

Hernandez, Francisca, 2
Hind Al-Hunud, fl. 400s, 1,2
Hopkins, Emma Curtis, 1853–1925, 2
Hutchinson, Anne Marbury, 1591–1643, 1,2
Jungreis, Esther, 1938–, 2
Lowry, Edith Elizabeth, 1897–1970, 2
Lubich, Chiara, fl. 1970s, 2
MacLeod, Dorothy Shaw, 1900–, 1
Maria of Hungary and Bohemia, 1505–1538, 2
Mathilde, 1046–1115, 1
Mayer, Bessie Bruce, 1890–, 2
Mechthild of Magdeburg, 1210–1280, 1
Medhavi, Ramabai Dongre, 1858–1922, 1,2
Mims, Sue Harper, m. 1866, 1
Mordecai, Rose, 1839–, 1
Pennington, Mary Proude Springett, d. 1682, 1
Ramsay, Regina, 2
Schrieck, Louise van der, Sister, 1813–1886, 1
Sforza, Bona, 2
Shapsnikoff, Antesia, 2
Stair, Lois Harkrider, 1923–1981, 2
Teresa, Mother (2), 1766–1846, 2
Theodelina, 568–628, 1
Watteville, Benigna Zinzendorf, 1725–1789, 1
Watteville, Henrietta Benigna Justine Zinzendorf von, 1725–1789, 2
Webb, Mary, 1881–1927, 1
Wells, Emmeline Blanch Woodward, 1828–1921, 2
White, Ellen Gould Harmon, 1827–1915, 1,2
Wicjck, Cornelia van Asch, fl. 1940s, 1
Wright, Lucy, fl. 1780s, 1
Wu Y-Fang, 1893–, 1
Young, Patricia, fl. 1970s, 2
Religious reformers
Campbell, Helen Stuart, 1839–1918, 2
Dirks, Lysken, m. 1549, 1
Ward, Mary Augusta Arnold, 1851–1920, 2
Religious scholars
Ima Shalom, fl. 70, 1,2
Religious workers
Abell, Mrs. Edwin F., fl. 1900s, 1
Ahok, Mrs., fl. 1890s, 1

Allen, Sarah, 1764–1849, 1
Ambrose, Alice, fl. 1660s, 1
Ashley, Mary Elliott, 1798–, 2
Barber, Jerusha, 1789–1860, 1
Battle, Laura Elizabeth Lee, 1855–, 1
Bishop, Mary Axtell, 1859–, 1
Blow, Mary Elizabeth Thomas, 1863–, 1
Bond, Rosalie B. De Sohns, 1843–, 1
Bottome, Margaret McDonald, 1827–1906, 2
Bowes, Elizabeth, 2
Brewster, Margaret, fl. 1670s, 1
Bright, Vonette, 2
Brown, Clara "Aunt", fl. 1850s, 2
Brown, J. Margarethe, fl. 1970s, 2
Bullock, Rebecca Burgess, 1886–, 2
Burghley, Mildred Cooke, 2
Casey, Margaret Elizabeth, 1874–, 1
Chizick, Sarah, fl. 1940s, 1
Clark, Mary, fl. 1650s, 1
Claudia, Mother Superior, 2
Clews, Mrs. James Blanchard, fl. 1910s, 1
Cobb, Zoe Desloge, 1850–, 1
Coleman, Ann, fl. 1660s, 1
Cooke, Katherine, Lady Killigrew, fl. 1750s, 2
Creemer, Lucy M., fl. 1870s, 1
Dancer, Alice, 1854–1944, 1
Darby, Mary Sargent, fl. 1700s, 1
Davis, Jane Totah, fl. 1940s, 1,2
Demjanovich, Miriam Teresa, 1901–1927, 1
Dienert, Millie, 2
Drake, Lucy R., fl. 1870s, 1
Drane, Augusta Theodosia, 1823–1894, 1
Elfstrom, Thelma, 2
Etzenhouser, Ida Pearson, 1872–1936, 1
Farmer, Hannah, fl. 1870s, 1
Ferguson, Catherine, 1749–1854, 1
Fitzgibbon, Irene, Sister, 1823–1896, 2
Galloway, Anne, fl. 1700s, 1
Gardner, Pearl, 1881–, 1
Goodrich, Nelle Chatburn, 1875–, 1
Green, Blanche Tucker, 1903–1949, 1
Guerin, Theodore, Mother, 1798–1856, 1,2
Haden, Charlyne E., 2
Hardin, Julia Carlin, fl. 1870s, 1
Harris, Elizabeth, fl. 1650s, 1

Barbara, fl. 200s, 1
Basilissa, d. 68, 1
Bathilda, d. c. 678, 1
Battia, Villana, fl. 1300s, 1
Beatrice, 303, 1
Beatrix D'Este, d. 1262, 1
Beatrix da Silva, 1424–1490, 1
Begga (or Begha), fl. 600s, 1
Belinda, 698, 1
Benincasa, Caterina, 1347–1380, 2
Benvenuta Bojani, fl. 1200s, 1
Bernadette of Lourdes, Saint, 1844–
    1879, 1,2
Bertha, d. 725, 1
Bertha, d. 500s, 1
Bertille, d.c. 705, 1
Bibiana (or Vivian), 1
Biro, Sari, fl. 1940s, 1
Bonita, fl. 900s, 1
Bonna, d. 1207, 1
Bonne D'Armagnac, Blessed, 1439–
    1462, 1
Bridget, Saint, of Scandinavia, 1302–
    1373, 1,2
Bridget (Brigid or Bride), 423–525, 2
Brigid, fl. 1400s, 1
Brigid of Kildare, 453–523, 1
Burgundofara of Fara, d. 667, 1
Cabrini, Frances Xavier, 1850–1917,
    1,2
Casilda, d. 1007, 1
Casilda, d. 458, 1
Catherine Laboure, 1806–1875, 1
Catherine dei Ricci, 1519–1589, 1
Catherine of Alexandria, d. 307, 1,2
Catherine of Bologna, 1413–1463, 1
Catherine of Genoa, 1447–1510, 2
Catherine of Siena, 1347–1380, 1,2
Catherine of Sweden, 1331–1380, 1
Cecilia, d.c. 230, 1
Chantal, Jeanne Francois Fremiot,
    1574–1641, 1,2
Christina of Stommeln, 1242–1313, 1
Christina the Astonishing,
    1150–1224,
Clara (Clare) of Assisi, 1193–1253,
    1,2
Clotilda (Clotilde), of Burgundy,
    475–545, 1,2
Colette, 1381–1447, 1
Columba of Sens, d.c. 374, 1
Constance, fl. 300s, 1
Constantia, Augusta, d.c. 354, 1
Cousin, Germaine, d. 1601, 1

Cunegund, Blessed Kinga, fl. 1000s, 1
Cuthburge, fl. 800s, 1
D'Amboise, Frances, Duchess of
    Brittany, 1447–1485, 1
Delphina, 1283–1360, 1
Denise, 234–250, 1
Devote, 286–304, 1
Diana of Andolo, d. 1236, 1
Domitilla, d. 90s, 1
Domnina, fl. 200s, 1
Dorothea (Dorothy of Montaw),
    1347–1394, 1
Dorothy, d. 311, 1
Dympna, fl. 800s, 1
Edith, 962–984, 1
Elizabeth of Aragon, 1271–1336, 2
Elizabeth of Hungary, 1207–1231, 1,2
Elizabeth of Portugal, 1271–1336, 1
Emily Bicchiere, 1238–1314, 1
Emma, d. 1050, 1
Etheldreda, Audrey, 630–679, 2
Eugenia, d. 258, 1
Eulalia dei Catalini, fl.300s, 1
Eulalia of Media, d. 303, 1
Euphrasia, d. 412, 1
Euphrasia Mary, 1796–1868, 1
Fabiola, d. 400, 1,2
Felicitas, fl. 138s, 1
Felicitas, d. 203, 1
Flavia, Domitilla, fl. 900s, 1
Flora of Cordova, d. 851, 1
Florentina, d. 600s, 1
Frances, 1384–1440, 1
Frideswide, d. 735, 1
Galgani, Gemma, Saint, 1878–1903,
    1,2
Galla, fl. 500s, 1
Genevieve, Saint, 422–512, 1,2
Genevieve of Brabant, fl. 700s, 1
Georgia (or Georgette), 1
Germaine, Saint, 1579–1601, 2
Gertrude of Nivelles, 626–659, 1
Gertrude the Great, 1256–1301, 1
Gertrude van der Oosten, d. 1358, 1
Gillian, 1340, 1
Gisela, d. 807, 1
Gisela (Gizella), Queen of Hungary,
    933–1095, 1,2
Gladys, fl. 400s, 1
Godelina, 1049–1070, 1
Goretti, Maria, 1800–1902, 1
Grace, 1
Gwen, fl. 587, 1
Hedwig, 1174–1243, 1

Helen of Skofde, fl. 1100s, 1
Helena, Flavia Julia, 247–328, 1,2
Hereswitha, d. 690, 1
Hilaria, d. 283, 1
Hilda of Whitby, 614–680, 1,2
Hildegarde of Bingen, 1098–1179, 2
Hiltrude, fl. 700s, 1
Hortulana, fl. 1200s, 1
Humbeline, fl. 1100s, 1
Hyacintha Mariscotti, 1585–1640, 1
Ida, 1040–1113, 1
Ida, fl. 760s, 1
Imelda, fl. 1330s, 1
Irene, fl. 600s, 1
Irmina, d. 708, 1
Ita, d. 570, 1
Jacoba, d. 1273, 1
Jane de Chantal, 1572–1641, 1
Jeanne Marie de Maille, 1332–1414, 1
Jeanne de Lestonac, 1556–1640, 1
Jeanne de Valois, 1464–1505, 1
Jeanne-Francoise de Chantal, 1575–1643, 1
Jennifer, fl. 512, 1
Joan of Arc, 1412–1431, 1,2
Joan of Valois, fl. 1500s, 1
Judith, fl. 800s, 1
Judith, d. 1260, 1
Julia, fl. 600s, 1
Julia of Rena, d. 1367, 1
Juliana, d. 305, 1
Juliana Falconieri, 1270–1340, 1
Julitta, d. 305, 1
Justa, d. 287, 1
Justina of Padua, fl. 900s, 1
Katherine, fl. 1378, 1
Kentigerna, fl. 700s, 1
Kunigunde, d. 1037, 1
Kyneburge, fl. 600s, 1
Laboure, Catherine, 1806–1876, 1
Le Gras, Louise, 1591–1660, 1,2
Lea, d. 383, 1
Leocadia, d. 303, 1
Lidwina, d. 1433, 1
Lioba, d. 779, 1
Loreto, Our Lady of, fl. 1200s, 1
Luceja, fl. 200s, 1
Lucia Filippini, 1672–1732, 1
Lucy, d. 303, 1
Lucy of Scotland, d. 1090, 1
Ludmilla, d. 927, 1
Lutgard, 1182–1246, 1
Macrina, fl. 200s, 1
Macrina the Younger, 327–379, 1

Maddalena of Canossa, 1774–1833, 1
Marcela, 325–420, 1,2
Marcellina, fl. 300s, 1
Margaret (1), 1048–1093, 1,2
Margaret Mary Alacoque, 1645–1690, 1
Margaret of Antioch, fl. 200s, 1
Margaret of Cortona, 1247–1297, 1
Margaret of Hungary, 1242–1271, 1,2
Margaret of Lorraine, 1463–1521, 1
Margaret of Savoy, fl. 1400s, 1
Margaret of Verona, d. 1395, 1
Maria Goretti, 1890–1902, 1
Maria Josepha Rosello, 1811–1880, 1
Maria Victoria Fornari, 1562–1617, 1
Maria of Cordova, d. 851, 1
Marie Christine of Savoy, 1812–, 1
Marie Clothilde, d. 1794, 1
Marie Madeleine Postel, 1746–1836, 1
Marie Therese De Soubiran, 1834–1899, 1
Martha, d. 270, 1
Martha, fl. 1400s, 1
Mary Bartholomew of Bagnesi, d. 1577, 1
Mary Bernard Soubirous, 1844–1879, 1
Mary Frances, 1715–1791, 1
Mary Magdelene de' Passi, 1566–1607, 1
Mary of Eqypt, d. 430, 1
Mary of Rome, d. 120, 1
Matilda (Maud), 895–968, 1
Maura, 1
Melania the Elder, d. 410, 1
Melania the Younger, 383–439, 1
Michaela, Mary Michael Dermaisieres, 1809–1865, 1
Michelina, Blessed, of Pesaro, 1300–1357, 1
Mildred, d. 700s, 1,2
Monica (Monnica), Saint, 333–387, 1,2
Natalia (or Samagotha), 1
Nataline, fl. 300s, 1
Nina (Christiana), fl. 300s, 1
Nymphia, fl. 200s, 1
Oda, of Odette, d. 713, 1
Odilia (Otilla) of Hohenburg, fl. 700s, 1,2
Olga, d. 969, 1,2
Olivia, fl. 800s, 1
Olympias, 360–410, 1,2
Opportuna, d. 770, 1

Lubkin, Gloria B., 2
Treat, Mary, 1830–, 1
Unzer, Johanna Charlotte of Altona, 1724–1782, 2
Scientists
    See also
    Agronomists
    Astronomers
    Bacteriologists
    Behavioral scientists
    Biologists
    Biophysicists
    Botanists
    Chemists
    Computer scientists
    Ecologists
    Embryologists
    Entomologists
    Geneticists
    Genoscientists
    Geochemists
    Geographers
    Geologists
    Geophysicists
    Inventors
    Limnologists
    Marine scientists
    Mathematicians
    Meteorologists
    Naturalists
    Neuroimmunologists
    Oceanographers
    Ornithologists
    Paleontologists
    Physicists
    Physiologists
    Researchers
    Seismologists
    Space scientists
    Toxicologists
    Zoologists
Anno, Kimiko, 2
Bayliss, Marguerite Farleigh, 1895–, 1
Clarke, Agnes Mary, 1842–1907, 2
Conwell, Esther M., 2
Cornero, Ellena Lucretia, 1646–1684, 2
Dedrick, Claire, fl. 1970s, 2
Halberg, Julia, 1956–, 2
Kochina, Pelagrya Yakovlevna, 1899–, 1
Li Hsiu-Chen, 2
Linton, Laura A., 1853–, 1
Maria Hebrea, 2

Miriam Micheal, Sister, fl. 1940s, 1
Peabody, Lucy Evelyn, 1865–, 1
Perey, Marguerite, 1909–1975, 1,2
Rumford, Marie Anne Pierrette Paulze Lavoisier,1758–1836, 1
Schalheimer, Marie Sophie Conring, fl. 1690s, 2
Seifert, Florence Barbara, 1897–, 1
Stearns, Mary Beth, d. 1973, 2
Thompson-Clewry, Pamela, fl. 1960s, 2
Yale, Caroline Ardelia, 1848–1933, 2
Scipio Africanus—Spouse
    Aemilia, Tertia, 169–200BC, 1,2
    Tertia Aemilia, fl. 230BC, 1
Scott, Winfield—Spouse
    Scott, Maria D. Mayo, d. 1866, 1
Scouts
    Bailey, Ann "Mad Ann", 1742–1825, 1,2
    Marks, Jane, 1
    Silcott, Jane, 1842–1895, 1,2
    Winnemucca, Sarah, 1844–1891, 2
Screenwriters
    See also
    Motion picture authors
    Akins, Zoe, 1886–1958, 1,2
    Allen, Jay Presson, fl. 1970s, 2
    Beranger, Clara, d. 1956, 1
    Crusinberry, Jane, fl. 1940s, 1
    Frings, Ketti Hartley, 1915–, 1
    Harbou, Thea Von, d. 1954, 2
    West, Claudine, 1884–1943, 1
Scribes
    Arwyller, Frommet, fl. 1400s, 2
    Benayahu, Miriam, fl. 1300s, 2
    Mansi, Paula Dei, fl. 1920s, 2
Scuba divers
    Brathcher, Twila, 2
    Garner, Nancy R., 2
Sculptors, American
    Abish, Cecile, fl. 1970s, 2
    Allen, Louise, fl. 1920s, 1
    Ames, Sarah Fisher, 1817–1901, 1
    Antin, Eleanor, 1935–, 2
    Arnold, Anne, fl. 1970s, 2
    Artel, Lili, fl. 1970s, 2
    Asawa, Ruth, fl. 1970s, 2
    Azara, Nancy, 2
    Ball, Caroline Peddle, 1889–, 1
    Ball, Ruth Norton, fl. 1920s, 1
    Bancroft, Hester, 1889–, 1
    Barnette, Anna Latham, d. 1948, 2
    Bartlett, Madeleine A., fl. 1920s, 1

Bas-Cohain, Rachel, fl. 1970s, 2
Bauermeister, Mary, fl. 1970s, 2
Baxter, Martha Wheeler, 1869–, 1
Benglis, Lynda, fl. 1970s, 2
Benton, Suzanne, fl. 1970s, 2
Beveridge, Kuhue, m. 1899, 1
Bice, Amy Hamada, fl. 1970s, 2
Blumenschein, Mary Shepard Greene, 1869–, 1
Boltz, Maude, fl. 1970s, 2
Bontecou, Lee, 1931–, 2
Bracken, Clio Hinton Huneker, 1870–1925, 1
Brackenridge, Marian, 1903–, 1
Brody, Sherry, fl. 1970s, 2
Browne, Matilda, 1869–, 1
Bruria, fl. 1970s, 2
Buchanan, Ella, d. 1951, 1
Bucher, Heidi, fl. 1970s, 2
Burroughs, Edith Woodman, 1871–1926, 1
Cadwalader-Guild, Emma Marie, 1843–, 1
Callery, Mary, 1903–, 1
Case, Lisa, fl. 1970s, 2
Castanis, Muriel, fl. 1970s, 2
Catlett, Elizabeth, fl. 1970s, 2
Chanler, Beatrice Ashley, 1875–1946, 1
Chapin, Cornielia Van A., fl. 1930s, 1
Chapline, Claudia, fl. 1970s, 2
Chase, Doris, 1923–, 2
Church, Angelica Schuyler, 1877–1954, 1,2
Cohen, Katherine M., 1859–1914, 1
Conkling, Mabel, 1871–, 1
Connor, Maureen, 2
Cook, Mary Elizabeth, 1881–, 1
Cooper, Alice, fl. 1920s, 1
Corbett, Gail Sherman, m. 1905, 1
Cox, Louise Howland King, 1865–1945, 1
Cox-McCormack, Nancy, 1885–, 1,2
Cresson, Margaret, 1889–, 1
Crosby, Katherine Van Rensellaer, 1897–, 1
Daggett, Maud, 1883–, 1
Davies, Maria Thompson, fl. 1920s, 2
Day, Worden, fl. 1970s, 2
Dillaye, Blanche, d. 1931, 1
Drouet, Bessie Clarke, 1879–1940, 1
Dubois, Yvonne Pene, fl. 1930a, 1
Eberle, Abastenia St. Leger, 1878–1942, 1,2

Eddy, Sarah James, 1851–, 1
Eyre, Luisa, 1872–1953, 1
Falkenstein, Clare, fl. 1970s, 2
Farnham, Sally James, 1876–1943, 1
Fenton, Beatrice, 1887–, 1
Foley, Margaret E., 1820–1877, 1,2
Frank, Mary, 1933–, 2
Fraser, Laura Gardin, 1889–, 1
Freedman, Faiya, 2
Freeman, Florence, 1836–1883, 1
Freeman, Phyllis, fl. 1970s, 2
Frishmuth, Harriet Whitney, 1880–, 1
Fry, Laura Ann, 1857–1943, 2
Fuller, Meta Vaux Warrick, 1877–1968, 1,2
Fuller, Sue, fl. 1970s, 2
Godwin, Frances Bryant, 1892–, 1
Graham, Cecelia B., fl. 1920s, 1
Graves, Nancy Stevenson, 1940–, 2
Greenwood, Gertrude B., fl. 1920s, 1
Gregory, Angela, 1903–, 1
Grimes, Frances, 1869–, 1
Grossman, Nancy, 1940–, 2
Guild, Emma Cadwalader, 1843–, 1
Hamlin, Genevieve Karr, 1896–, 1
Harkness, Rebekah West, 1915–1982, 2
Hartley, Edna, fl. 1970s, 2
Hawks, Rachel Marshall, 1879–, 1
Hawthorne, Mrs., fl. 1880s, 1
Heagney, Muriel, fl. 1920s, 2
Healey, Anne, fl. 1970s, 2
Hill, Clara, 2
Hodge, Lydia Herrick, 1889–, 1
Hoffman, Malvina Cornell, 1887–1966, 1,2
Hoffman, Virginia, fl. 1670s, 2
Hollister, Antoinette B., 1873–, 1
Holt, Winifred, 1870–1945, 1,2
Horowitz, Ida, fl. 1970s, 2
Hosmer, Harriet Goodhue, 1830–1908, 1,2
Howland, Edith, 1863–1949, 1
Hoxie, Vinnie Ream, 1847–1914, 1,2
Huntington, Anna Vaughn Hyatt, 1876–1973, 1,2
Huntington, Clara, 1878–, 1
Jackson, Hazel Brill, 1894–, 1
Jackson, May Howard, 1870–1930, 1
Jewett, Maude Sherwood, 1873–, 1
Johnson, Adelaide, 1847–1955, 1,2
Johnson, Grace Mott, 1882–, 1
Johnson, Marie, fl. 1970s, 2

Kaish, Luise, 2
Kantaroff, Maryon, fl. 1970s, 2
Katzen, Lila, 1932–, 2
Keeney, Ana, 1898–, 1
Kimball, Isabel Moore, 2
King, Marion P., 1894–, 1
Kinney, Belle, 1,2
Kisch, Gloria, fl. 1970s, 2
Kitson, Theo Alice Ruggles, 1871–
1932, 1
Kohn, Estelle Rumbold, fl. 1920s, 1
Ladd, Anna Coleman, 1878–1939, 1
Lamb, Ella Condie, fl. 1890s, 1
Lander, Louisa, 1826–, 1
Lane, Katherine Ward, 1899–, 1
Lathrop, Gertrude K., 1896–, 1
Lawson, Katherine Stewart, 1885–, 1
Lewis, Edmonia, 1845–1909, 1,2
Liedloff, Helen, fl. 1930s, 1
Longman, (Mary) Evelyn Beatrice,
1874–1934, 1
Lyndon, Alice Atkinson, 1935–, 2
MacDonald, Julie, fl. 1970s, 2
MacKinstry, Elizabeth, d. 1956, 1
MacLeary, Bonnie, 1892–, 1
MacNeil, Carol Brooks, 1871–, 1
Mackay, Frances I., 1906–, 1
Manning, Rosalie H., fl. 1910s, 1
Maxwell, Coralie DeLong, 1898–, 1
Maynard, Valerie, fl. 1970s, 2
Mayor, Harriet Hyatt, 1868–1934, 1
Mears, Helen Farnsworth, 1872–
1916, 1,2
Mellon, Eleanor M., 1894–, 1
Miles, Emily Winthrop, fl. 1920s, 1
Millar, Onnie, 1919–, 2
Moore, Mary E., fl. 1920s, 1
Mulroney, Regina Winifred, fl.
1920s, 1
Mundy, Ethel Frances, 1
Neal, Grace Pruden, 1876–, 1
Nelson, Emily, fl. 1970s, 2
Newman, Isadora, fl. 1930s, 1
Newman, Sophie, 2
Parsons, Edith Barretto Stevens,
1878–1956, 1
Peabody, Amelia, 1890–, 1
Peabody, Marian Lawrence, 1875–, 1
Pointer, Augusta L., 1898–, 1
Postgate, Margaret J., fl. 1920s, 1
Putnam, Brenda, 1889–, 1
Quiner, Joanna, 1796–1869, 1
Raboff, Fran, fl. 1970s, 2
Ratcliff, Mary-Curtis, fl. 1970s, 2

Richards, Myra Reynolds, fl. 1930s, 1
Ringgold, Faith, 1930–, 2
Ripley, Lucy Fairfield Perkins, d.
1949, 1
Rockburne, Dorothea, fl. 1970s, 2
Rosenthal, Rachel, fl. 1970s, 2
Sahler, Helen, 1877–1950, 1
Savage, Augusta Christine, 1892–
1962, 1,2
Scaravaglione, Concetta, 1900–1975,
2
Schwartz, Margaret, 1900–, 1
Scudder, Janet, 1869–1940, 1,2
Sherk, Bonnie, 2
Sherwood, Ruth, 1889–, 1
Smith, Barbara T., fl. 1970s, 2
St. Gaudens, Anetta Johnson, 1869–,
1
Stagg, Jessie A., fl. 1920s, 1
Stark, Shirley, fl. 1970s, 2
Stebbins, Emma, 1815–1852, 1,2
Stetson, Katherine Beecher, 1885–, 1
Stevens, Edith Barretto, 1878–, 1
Strider, Marjorie, fl. 1970s, 2
Strider, Nancy, fl. 1970s, 2
Talbot, Grace Helen, 1901–, 1
Tauch, Waldine, fl. 1920s, 1
Truitt, Anne, 1921–, 2
Turnbull, Ruth, 1912–, 1
Usher, Leila, fl. 1890s, 1
Vonnoh, Bessie Potter, 1872–1955, 1
Waggoner, Electra, fl. 1930s, 1
Walker, Nellie Verne, 1874–1973, 1,2
Ward, Miss E., fl. 1900s, 1
Wendt, Julia M. Bracken, 1871–, 1
Westcoast, Wanda, 2
Whitney, Anne, 1821–1915, 1,2
Whitney, Gertrude Vanderbilt, 1875–
1942, 1,2
Williams, Susan, fl. 1970s, 2
Wilson, May, fl. 1970s, 2
Wilson, Melva Beatrice, 1866–1921, 1
Wood, Caroline S., fl. 1900s, 1
Wright, Alice Morgan, 1881–, 1
Wright, Patience Lovell, 1725–1786,
1,2
Yandell, Enid, 1870–1934, 1,2
Yokoi, Rita, fl. 1970s, 2
Zoph, Fernanda, fl. 1970s, 2
Zucker, Barbara, fl. 1970s, 2
Sculptors, Austrian
Stix, Marguerite, 1907–1975, 2
Sculptors, Belgian
Hare, Jeannette R., 1848–, 1

Arnould, (Madeline) Sophie, 1744–1903, 1
Arral, Blanche, fl. 1910s, 1
Artot, Marguerite Josephine Desiree, 1835–1907, 1
Arville, Camille d', 1863–, 1
Ashby, Dorothy Jeanne, 1932–, 2
Athanasiu, Jean, 1885–1938, 1
Austral, Florence Wilson, 1894–, 1
Axman, Gladys, fl. 1930s, 1
Bach, Anna Magdalena Wulken, 1700–1760, 1
Baddeley, Sophia Snow, 1745–1786, 1
Baez, Joan, 1941–, 1,2
Baez, Mimi, 1945–, 2
Bailey, Mildred Rinker, 1903–1951, 2
Bailey, Pearl Mae, 1918–, 1,2
Baillie, Isobel, 1895–, 1
Baker, Belle, 1898–1957, 1
Baker, Bonnie "Wee", 1917–, 1,2
Baker, Josephine, 1906–1975, 1,2
Baker, Lavern, 1922–, 1
Ballard, Florence, 1943–1976, 2
Ballard, Kaye, 1926–, 1,2
Bancroft, Anne, 1931–, 1,2
Banks, Margaret, fl. 1910s, 1
Banti, Brigitta Giorgi, 1756–1806, 1
Barbieri, Fedora, 1919–, 1
Barnett, Clara Kathleen (Clara Doria pseud.), fl. 1850s, 1
Barrett, Emma, 1905–, 2
Bassey, Shirley, 1937–, 2
Batcheller, Mrs. Tryophosa Bates, 1878–, 1
Bates, Blanche Lyon, 1873–1941, 1,2
Batson, Flora Bergen, 1870–1906, 2
Bayes, Nora, 1880–1928, 1,2
Beaumesnil, Henriette Adelaide Villard, 1748–1803, 1
Bee, Molly, 1939–, 1,2
Beers, Evelyne Christine Sauer Andressen, 1925–, 2
Bellincioni, Gemma, 1864–1950, 1
Bellwood, Bessie, 1860–1896, 1,2
Belocca, Anna de, 1854–, 1
Bembo, Antonia, 1670–, 2
Bentley, Irene, 1870–1940, 1
Berganza, Teresa, 1935–, 1,2
Bergen, Flora Batson, 1870–1906, 1
Bergen, Polly, 1930–, 1,2
Bergengren, Anna Farquhar, 1865–, 1
Berger, Erna, 1900–, 1
Bernard, Caroline Richings, 1827–1882, 2

Biddulph, Jessie Catherine Vokes, 1851–1884, 1
Billington, Elizabeth Weichsel, 1768–1818, 1
Bilton, Belle, Countess of Clancarty, 1868–1906, 1
Bishop, Anna Riviere, 1810–1884, 1,2
Blair, Janet, 1921–, 1,2
Blake-Alverson, Margaret, 1836–1923, 2
Blakley, Ronee, 1946–, 2
Blauvert, Lillian Evans, 1873–1947, 2
Blegen, Judith, 1941–, 2
"Blossom Dearie", fl. 1950s, 2
Blyth, Ann(e), 1928–, 1,2
Bodanya, Natalie, fl. 1930s, 1
Bokor, Margit Wahl, 1909–1949, 1
Bonetti, Mary, 1902–, 1
Boone, Debbie, 1956–, 2
Bordoni, Faustina, 1700–1793, 1
Borkh, Inge, 1921–, 1
Bosio, Anigiolana, 1830–1859, 1
Boswell, Connee (Connie), 1907–1976, 1,2
Boswell, Martha, 1909–1958, 1
Boswell, Vet, fl. 1930s, 1
Boswell Sisters, fl. 1940s, 2
Boucicault, Agnes Robertson, 1833–1916, 1,2
Bovy, Vina, 1900–, 1
Bowers, Sarah Sedgwick, fl. 1850s, 1
Bowes, Margie, 1941–, 2
Boyer, Lucienne, fl. 1930s, 1
Braddock, Amelia, fl. 1930s, 1
Bradford, Clea Annah Ethell, 1936–, 2
Brambilla, Marietta Cassano D'Adda, 1807–1875, 1
Brandt, Marianne, 1842–1921, 1
Brema, Marie (Minny Fehrmann), 1856–1925, 1
Brett, Arabella, d. 1803, 2
Breval, Lucienne, 1869–1935, 1
Brewer, Theresa, 1931–, 1,2
Brice, Fanny Borach, 1891–1951, 1,2
Bricktop (Ada Smith), 1895–, 1
Bridewell, Carrie, 1879–1955, 1
Bristol, Margaret, 1
Brouwenstijn, Gre, 1915–, 1
Brown, Annie Williams, fl. 1940s, 1
Brown, Bonnie Gean, 1938–, 2
Brown, Jewel Hazel, 1937–, 2
Brown, Maxine, 1932–, 2
Browning, Lucielle, 1913–, 1

Curtin, Phyllis, 1922–, 1
Cuzzoni, Francesca, 1700–1770, 1
D'Aragona, Tullia, 1510–1556, 1,2
Dale, Clamma, 1948–, 2
Dalossy, Ellen, fl. 1920s, 1
Damari, Shoshana, 1922–, 1
Dane, Barbara, 1927–, 2
Darcel, Denise, 1925–, 1
Darclee, Hariclea, 1860–1939, 2
Davenport, Viola, fl. 1900s, 1
Davies, Cecilia, 1740–1836, 1
Davis, Agnes, fl. 1920s, 1
Davis, Betty Jack, 1932–1953, 2
Davis, Janette, 1
Davis, Jessie Bartlett, 1860–1905, 1,2
Davis, Vera Gibridge, 1894–, 2
Dawn, Hazel, fl. 1891–, 1,2
Day, Doris, 1924–, 1,2
Day, Edith, 1896–1971, 1,2
Daye, Irene, 1918–1971, 2
De Gaetani, Jan, 1933–, 2
De Haven, Gloria, 1926–, 2
De Leath, Vaughn, 1896–1943, 1
De Marco sisters, fl. 1930s, 1
De Reszke, Josephine, 1855–1891, 1
De Wolf sisters, fl. 1910s, 1
Dearie, Blossom, 1926–, 2
Deckers, Jeanne, 1933–, 2
Dee, Kiki, 1947–, 2
Della Chiesa, Vivian, 1915–, 1
Delna, Marie Ledan, 1875–1932, 1
Delpine, Margarita, fl. 1700s, 1
Demeur, Anne Arsene Charton,
  1842–1892, 1
Dereyne, Fay, fl. 1900s, 1
Desmond, Astra, fl. 1940s, 1
Dethridge, Luvena Wallace, fl. 1930s,
  1
Di Murska, Ilma, 1839–1889, 1
Dickenson, Jean, 1914–, 1
Dickey, Annamary, fl. 1930s, 1
Dietrich, Marlene, 1901–, 1,2
Divine, Grace, fl. 1920s, 1
Djanel, Lily, 1909–, 1
Dobbs, Mattiwilda, 1925–, 1
Doe, Doris, fl. 1930s, 1
Donalda, Pauline Mischa Leon, 1884–
  1970, 1,2
Donnelley, Frances, m. 1906, 1
Doria, Augusta, pseud., fl. 1900s, 1
Douglas, Helen Mary Gahagan,
  1909–1980, 1,2
Dragonette, Jessica, fl. 1920s, 1
Dresser, Marcia, fl. 1910s, 1

Drew, Doris, 1
Dudziak, Urszula, 1943–, 2
Dufau, Jennie, d. 1924, 1
Duprez, May Moore, fl. 1900s, 1
Durbin, Deanna, 1921–, 1,2
Dussek, Josepha Hambacher, 1754–
  1824, 1,2
Eadie, Noel, 1901–1950, 1
Earle, Virginia, 1873–, 1
Eddy, Sarah Hershey, m. 1879, 1
Eden, Irene, fl. 1940s, 1
Edvina, Marie Louise Lucienne Mar-
  tin, 1885–1948, 1
Edwards, Clara, 1925–, 1
Edwards, Joan, 1919–1981, 1,2
Eggerth, Martha, 1916–, 1
Elias, Rosalind, 1931–, 1
Eliot, (Mama) Cass, fl. 1940s, 2
Ellerman, Amy, 1888–1960, 1
Elliott, Victoria, 1922–, 1
Ellis, Anita, 1920–, 2
Elly, Ameling, 1938–, 2
Elzy, Ruby, 1910–1943, 1
Engel, Birgit, fl. 1920s, 1
Engle, Marie, 1860–, 1
Ennis, Ethel, 1934–, 2
Etting, Ruth, 1896–1978, 1,2
Europa, Madam, 2
Evans, Margie, 1941–, 2
Evanti, Lillian, 1
Fabray, Nanette, 1920–, 1,2
Falana, Lola, 1947–, 2
Falcon, Marie Cornelie, 1812–1897, 1
Farell, Marita, fl. 1930s, 1
Farina, Mimi, 1945–, 2
Farrell, Eileen, 1920–, 1,2
Faure, Jeanne, 1863–1950, 2
Faustina (Bordoni), 1693–1783, 1
Faye, Alice, 1915–, 1,2
Fellows, Edith, 1923–, 2
Fenn, Jean, 1930–, 1
Fenton, Lavinia Duchess of Bolton,
  1708–1769, 1,2
Ferrabini, Esther, fl. 1910s, 1
Fields, Gracie, Dame, 1898–1979, 1,2
Fisher, Bernice, 1889–, 1
Fisher, Clara, 1811–1898, 1,2
Fisher, Doris, 1915–, 1
Fisher, Susanne, fl. 1930s, 1
Fisher, Sylvia, m. 1953, 1
Fitzgerald, Ella, 1918–, 1,2
Fitzu, Anna, 1886–1967, 1
Flack, Roberta, 1940–, 2
Flahaut, Marianne, fl. 1900s, 1

Fleischer, Editha, 1898–, 1
Ford, Florrie Flanagan, 1876–1940, 1
Ford, Mary, 1924–1977, 1,2
Forde, Florrie, 1876–1940, 1,2
Forrest, Helen, 1917–, 2
Forrester, Maureen, 1931–, 1
Forsyth, Josephine, 1940–, 1
Fort, Cornelia, fl. 1940s, 1
Foster, Harriet, fl. 1940s, 1
Foster, Susanna, 1924–, 2
Fox, Ancella M., 1847–1920, 2
Fox, Della May, 1870–1913, 1,2
Francis, Connie, 1938–, 1,2
Franklin, Aretha, 1942–, 1,2
Franklin, Erma, 1940–, 2
Fraser, Marjorie Kennedy, 1857–
    1930, 1
Frazee, Jane, 1918–1985, 2
Freeman, Bettina, 1889–, 1
Freni, Mirella, 1935–, 2
Fricker, Sylvia, 1940–, 2
Friedlander, Thekla, 2
Friganza, Trixie, 1870–1955, 2
Frijsh, Povla, 1875–1960, 1
Froman, Jane, 1917–1980, 1,2
Funicello, Annette, 1942–, 1,2
Gaal, Franciska, 1904–, 2
Gabor, Eva, 1921–, 1,2
Gabrielli, Catarina, 1730–1796, 1
Gail-Garre, Edmee Sophia Garre,
    1775–1819, 1
Gall, Yvonne Irma, 1885–, 1
Galli-Campi, Amri, fl. 1920s, 1
Galli-Marie, Marie Celestine De
    L'Isle, 1840–1905, 1
Gantvoort, Mary Gretchen Morris,
    1894–1971, 2
Garcia, Maria-Felicita "Malibran",
    1808–1836, 1
Garland, Judy, 1922–1969, 1,2
Garrett, Betty, 1919–, 2
Garrigues, Malvina, 1825–1904, 1
Gates, Lucy, 1880–1951, 1
Gauthier, Eva, 1886–1958, 1,2
Gayle, Crystal, 1951–, 2
Gaynor, Gloria, 2
Geistinger, Marie, 1836–1904, 1
Genevieve (Ginger Auger), 1930–, 1
Gentle, Alice, 1888–1958, 1
Gentry, Bobbie Lee, 1942–, 2
George, Zelma Watson, 1903–, 1
Georgiou, Vilma, 1
Gerhardt, Elena, 1883–1961, 1
Gerster, Etelka, 1855–1920, 1

Gibbs, Georgia, 1
Gibson, Virginia, 1
Gilberto, Astrud, 1940–, 2
Gilman, Mabelle, fl. 1890s, 1
Ginster, Ria, 1898–, 1
Gitana, Gerti, 1887–1957, 1,2
Glade, Coe, 1906–, 1
Glaz, Herta, 1914–, 1
Gloria Jean, 1926–, 2
Golson, Florence, fl. 1940s, 1
Goltz, Christel, 1
Good, Dolly, 1915–1967, 2
Good, Millie (Mildred), 1913–, 2
Gooding, Cynthia, 1924–, 2
Goodman, Lillian Rosedale, 1888–, 1
Gordon, Cyrena Van, fl. 1930s, 1
Gordon, Jeanne, 1893–, 1
Gore, Lesley, 1946–, 2
Gorme, Eydie, 1931–, 1,2
Gorr, Rita, 1926–, 2
Grable, Betty, 1916–1973, 1,2
Grandi, Margherita, 1909–, 1
Grant, Gogi, fl. 1950s, 2
Grassini, Josephina Giuseppini,
    1773–1850, 1,2
Graupner, Catherine Hiluer, 1777–
    1821, 2
Gray, Dolores, 1930–, 1
Grayco, Helen, 1
Grayson, Kathryn, 1923–, 1,2
Grecco, Juliette, fl. 1940s, 2
Green, Ethel, fl. 1910s, 1
Greenfield, Elizabeth Taylor, 1808–
    1876, 1,2
Greer, Frances, 1
Grenville, Lillian Goertner, 1888–
    1928, 1,2
Grever, Maria, 1894–1951, 1
Greville, Ursula, fl. 1940s, 1
Grimes, Anne (Laylin), 1912–, 2
Grimes, Tammy Lee, 1934–, 1,2
Grippon, Eva, d. 1956, 1
Grove, Betty Ann, 1
Grummer, Elizabeth, 1
Gubrud, Irene, 1946–, 2
Guilbert, Yvette, 1867–1944, 1,2
Guilford, Nanette, 1906–, 1
Gutheil-Schoder, Marie, 1874–1935,
    1
Gye, Madame Albani, 1847–, 1
Hackely, Emma Azalia Smith, 1867–
    1923, 2
Hackeman, Vicki, fl. 1970s, 2
Hagar, Emily Stokes, fl. 1940s, 1

Hager, Mina, fl. 1940s, 1
Haines, Connie, 1923–, 1
Halban, Desi, 1
Hall, Adelaide, 1909–, 2
Hall, Connie, 1929–, 2
Hall, Josephine, fl. 1890s, 1
Hall, Juanita, 1913–1968, 1
Hall, Pauline, fl. 1870s, 1
Hall, Vera, 1905–1964, 2
Halstead, Margaret, fl. 1930s, 1
Hamilton, Nancy, 1908–, 1
Hammond, Joan, 1912–, 1
Hampton, Hope, fl. 1920s, 1
Hardelot, Guy D', 1858–1936, 1
Harden, Arleen, 1945–, 2
Harris, Barbara, 1935–, 1,2
Harris, Emmylou, 1948–, 2
Harris, Hettie, fl. 1930s, 1
Harry, Debbie, 1944–, 2
Harshaw, Margaret, 1912–, 1
Harvard, Sue, fl. 1920s, 1
Haver, June, 1926–, 2
Hawes, Bess Lomax, 1921–, 2
Hayden, Ethyl, fl. 1940s, 1
Hegamin, Lucille Nelson, 1897–1970, 2
Held, Anna, 1865–1918, 2
Hemingway, Clara Edwards, fl. 1940s, 1
Henderson, Florence, 1934–, 1,2
Henderson, Rosa Deschamps, 1896–1968, 2
Henschel, Lillian June Bailey, 1860–1901, 1,2
Hensler, Elsie, 1836–1929, 2
Hester, Carolyn, 1937–, 2
Hidalgo, Elvira de, fl. 1910s, 1
Hildegard, Hildegard Loretta Sell, 1906–, 1,2
Hill, Bertha "Chippie", 1905–1950, 2
Hill, Goldie, 1933–, 2
Hill, Jenny, 1850–1896, 1
Hines, Mimi, 1933–, 2
Hinkle, Florence, 1885–1933, 1
Hodgkinson, Mrs. John, 1770–1803, 1,2
Hoffmann, Emma, fl. 1910s, 1
Holiday, Billie, 1915–1959, 1,2
Holliday, Jennifer, 1960–, 2
Holm, Celeste, 1919–, 1,2
Holman, Libby, 1905–1971, 1,2
Holmes, Augusta Mary Anne, 1847–1903, 1,2
Hopkins, Linda, 1925–, 2

Horn, Shirley, 1934–, 2
Horne, Lena, 1917–, 1,2
Hotz, Mae Ebrey, fl. 1940s, 1
Howard, Kathleen, fl. 1900s, 1
Howe, Janet, fl. 1940s, 1
Humes, Helen, 1913–1981, 2
Hunt, Arabella, d. 1705, 1
Hunter, Alberta, 1895–1984, 2
Hunter, Louise, fl. 1940s, 1
Hurley, Laurel, 1927–, 1
Huss, Hildegarde Hoffman, fl. 1940s, 1
Hutchinson, Abigail (Abby) Jemima, 1829–1892, 1,2
Hutchinson, Elizabeth Chase, fl. 1870s, 1
Hutchinson, Viola, fl. 1800s, 1
Hutton, Betty, 1921–, 1,2
Hutton, Marion, 1919–, 2
Hyers, Anna Madah, 1854–1924, 1,2
Hyers, Emma Louise, 1853–1916, 1,2
Ian, Janis, 1950–, 2
Irwin, May, 1862–1938, 1,2
Ivogun, Maria, 1891–, 1
Jackson, Wanda, 1937–, 2
Jagger, Bianca, 1945–, 2
James, Joni, 1930–, 1
Jay, Penny, 1930–, 2
Jean, Norma Beasler, 1938–, 2
Jenkins, Florence Foster, 1865–1944, 1,2
Jerome, Maude Nugent, 1873–1958, 1,2
Jessner, Irene, 1910–, 1
Joan, Elsa, fl. 1900s, 1
Joel, Elsa, fl. 1900s, 1
Johnson, Christine, fl. 1940s, 1
Johnson, Judy, 1928–, 1
Jones, Etta, 1928–, 2
Jones, Grace, 1951–, 2
Jones, (Matilda) Sissieretta Joyner, 1868–1933, 1,2
Jones, Rickie Lee, 1955–, 2
Jones, Salena, 1930–, 2
Jones, Shirley, 1934–, 1,2
Joplin, Janis Lyn, 1943–1970, 2
Jordan, Mary, 1879–1961, 1
Jordan, Sheila, 1929–, 2
Juch, Emma Antonia Johanna, 1865–1930, 1,2
Kahn, Madeline Gail, 1942–, 2
Kallen, Kitty, fl. 1940s, 2
Kane, Helen, 1910–1966, 2
Kaschowska, Felicie, fl. 1890s, 1

Kaskas, Anna, 1910–, 1
Kay, Beatrice, fl. 1940s, 1,2
Kazan, Laine, 1942–, 2
Keator, Harriet Scudder, d. 1932, 1
Keeler, Ruby (Ethel), 1909–, 1,2
Keller, Greta, 1901–1977, 2
Kemble, Adelaide, 1814–1879, 1
Kemp, Barbara, 1883–1959, 1
Kennedy-Fraser, Marjory, 1857–1930, 1,2
Kerr, Anita, 1927–, 2
Khuwyt, 1950 BC, 1
King, Carol Klein, 1941–, 2
King, Morgana, 1930–, 2
King, Peggy, 1931–, 1
King, Teddi, d. 1977, 2
Kipnis, Hanna, 1910–, 1
Kirk, Lisa, 1925–, 1
Kitt, Eartha Mae, 1928–, 1,2
Klein, Miriam, 1937–, 2
Knight, Gladys Maria, 1944–, 2
Koenen, Tilly, 1873–1941, 1
Korolowicz, Jeanne, fl. 1900s, 1
Koshetz, Nina, 1894–, 1
Koulsoum, Oum, d. 1976, 2
Koyke, Hitzi, 1926–, 1
Kral, Irene, 1932–, 2
Krall, Heidi, fl. 1950s, 1
Krauss, Gabrielle, 1842–1906, 1
Kremer, Isa, 1887–1956, 1
Krog, Karin, 1937–, 2
Kurenko, Maria, fl. 1920s, 1
Kurz, Selma, 1875–1933, 1
L'Allemand, Pauline, 1862–, 1
La Camargo, 1710–1770, 1
La Maupin, Mille, fl. 1700s, 1
LaGrange, Anna De, 1825–1905, 1
Labelle, Patti, 1944–, 2
Labia, Maria, 1885–, 1
Ladd, Cheryl Stoppelmoor, 1950–, 2
Laine, Cleo (Clementine Dinah), 1927–, 2
Lamour, Dorothy, 1914–, 1,2
Landorf, Joyce, 2
Lane, Abbe, 1932–, 1,2
Lane, Priscilla, 1917–, 2
Lane, Rosemary, 1914–, 2
Langendorff, Frida, fl. 1900s, 1
Langford, Frances, 1913–, 1,2
Langley, Jane Pickens, fl. 1940s, 2
Langston, Marie Stone, fl. 1940s, 1
Larsen-Todsen, Nanny, 1884–, 1
Larson, Nicolette, 1952–, 2
Lashanska, Hulda, 1893–, 1

Lauper, Cyndi, 1953–, 2
Laurence, Katie, fl. 1890s, 1
Lawnhurst, Vee, 1905–, 1
Lawrence, Carol, 1934–, 1,2
Lawrence, Vicki, 1949–, 2
Lazzari, Carolina Antoinette, 1891–1946, 1
Le Voe, Savy, 1906–1971, 2
LeBlanc, Georgette, 1875–1941, 1
Lea, Barbara, fl. 1970s, 2
Lee, Aura, 1946–, 2
Lee, Barbara, fl. 1970s, 2
Lee, Brenda, 1939–, 1,2
Lee, Jeanne, 1939–, 2
Lee, Julia, 1902–1958, 2
Lee, Michele, 1942–, 2
Lee, Peggy, 1920–, 1,2
Lee, Rose, 1922–, 2
Leffler-Burkhardt, Madame, fl. 1890s, 1
Lehman, Evangeline, fl. 1940s, 1
Lehmann, Liza, 1862–1918, 1
Leider, Frida, 1888–, 1
Leigh, Adele, 1928–, 1
Lemnitz, Tiana, 1897–, 1
Lennox, Mary Anne Paton, d. 1864, 1
Lenya, Lotte, 1898–1981, 1,2
Leonard, Myrtle, fl. 1830s, 1
Leone, Maria, 1
Lerch, Louise, 1895–1967, 1
Lessing, Madge, fl. 1890s, 1
Leveroni, Elvira, fl. 1900s, 1
Lewis, Brenda, 1921–, 1
Lewis, Mary Sybil, 1900–1941, 1,2
Lewis, Monica, 1925–, 2
Lewis, Sarah Masten, d. 1931, 1
Lightner, Winnie, 1899–1961, 2
Lincoln, Abbey, 1930–, 2
Linley, Elizabeth, 1754–1792, 1
Lipton, Martha, 1
Lipton, Peggy, 1947–, 2
Litta, Marie von Elsner, 1856–1883, 2
Litvinne, Felia, 1860–1936, 1
Ljungberg, Gota, 1893–1955, 1
Lloyd, Marie, 1870–1922, 1,2
Lombardini-Sirmen, Maddalena, 1745–, 2
Lon, Alice, 1
London, Julie, 1926–, 1,2
Longet, Claudine Georgette, 1941–, 2
Lor, Denise, 1
Lorenzo, Ange, 1894–1971, 2
Loring, Gloria Jean, 1946–, 2
Loudon, Dorothy, 1933–, 2

Lowe, Marie, fl. 1840s, 1
Lubin, Germaine, 1890–, 1
Lucca, Pauline, 1841–1908, 1
Lucchese, Josephine, fl. 1920s, 1
Lulu Belle, 1913–, 2
Lunn, Louise Kirkby, 1873–1930, 1
Lussan, Zelie de, 1863–1949, 1,2
Lyne, Felice, 1891–1935, 1
Lynn, Cheryl, fl. 1970s, 2
Lynn, Judy, 1936–, 2
Lynn, Loretta Webb, 1935–, 2
MacArthur, Margaret Crowl, 1928–, 2
MacDonald, Jeannette, 1907–1965, 1,2
MacKenzie, Giselle, 1827–, 1,2
MacRae, Sheila Stephens, 1924–, 1,2
Machado, Lena, 1
Machat, Rivka, fl. 1920s, 1
Madden, Lotta, fl. 1940s, 1
Maddox, Rose, 1926–, 2
Makeba, Miriam, 1932–, 1,2
Malbin, Elaine, 1932–, 1
Maley, Florence Turner, 1927–, 1
Malibran, Maria Felicia Garcia, 1808–1836, 1
Mallinger, Mathilde Lichtenegger, 1847–1920, 1
Malone, Patty, 1853–1896, 2
Malten, Therese, 1855–1930, 1
Mana (Manna)-Zucca, Madame, pseud., 1894–, 1
Manchester, Melissa, 1951–, 2
Mandrell, Barbara, 1945–, 2
Manning, Kathleen Lockhart, 1890–1951, 1
Manski, Inge, 1913–, 1
Marais, Miranda, 1912–, 1,2
Marcel, Lucille Wasself, 1887–1921, 1
Marchesi, Blanche, 1864–1940, 1
Marchesi, Mathilde, 1826–1913, 1
Markan, Maria, fl. 1930s, 1
Marlowe, Marion, 1929–, 1,2
Marrs, Stella, 1932–, 2
Marryat, Florence, 1838–1899, 1,2
Marshall, Lois, 1924–, 1
Martin, Luci, 2
Martin, Mary, 1913–, 1,2
Martinez, Marianne von, 1774–1812, 1,2
Materna, Amelie, 1845–1918, 1
Mattfield, Marie, 1870–1927, 1
Maubourg, Jeanne, 1875–, 1,2
Maxwell, Margery, fl. 1910s, 1

May, Edna, 1878–1948, 1
Mayhew, Stella, 1875–1934, 2
Maynor (Mainor), Dorothy, 1910–, 1,2
Mayo, Mary, fl. 1950s, 2
McCormic, Mary, fl. 1940s, 1
McGuire, Dorothy, 1918–, 1,2
McGuire sisters, 1
McNair, Barbara, 1939–, 2
McNeil, Claudia, 1
McRae, Carmen, 1922–, 2
Megolastrata of Sparta, fl.600sBC, 1
Meitschik, Anna, 1875–1943, 1
Melanie, 1948–, 2
Melius, Luella, fl. 1940s, 1
Meller, Raquel, 1888–1962, 1
Melmoth, Charlotte, 1749–1823, 1,2
Mercer, Mabel, 1900–1984, 2
Merman, Ethel Agnes Zimmerman, 1908–1984, 1,2
Merrill, Helen, 1929–, 2
Merriman, Nan, 1
Merz-Tunner, Amelia, fl. 1920s, 1
Metzger-Latterman, Ottilie, fl. 1940s, 1
Meysenheym, Cornelie, 1849–1923, 1
Middleton, Velma, 1917–1961, 2
Midler, Bette, 1944–, 2
Milanov, Zinka Kune, 1906–, 1
Mildenburg, Anna von, 1872–1947, 1
Milder-Hauptmann, Pauline Anna, 1785–1838, 1
Miles, Lizzie, 1895–1963, 2
Miller, Elva Ruby Connes, 1908–, 2
Miller, Jody, 1941–, 2
Miller, Marilyn, 1898–1936, 1,2
Miller, Mildred, 1924–, 1
Mills, Florence, 1895–1927, 1,2
Mills, Vicki, 1934–, 1
Mingotti, Regina Valentini, 1721–1808, 1
Minnelli, Liza, 1946–, 2
Minnie, Memphis, 1900–, 2
Miranda, Carmen, 1909–1955, 1,2
Miranda, Salla, fl. 1900s, 1
Mistinguett, 1873–1956, 2
Mitchell, Abbie, 1884–1960, 1,2
Mitchell, Joni, 1943–, 2
Mitchell, Nellie Brown, fl. 1860s, 1
Mitchell, Priscilla, 1941–, 2
Mitzie, 1891–, 2
Miura, Tamaki, fl. 1910s, 1
Mock, Alice, fl. 1920s, 1
Molza, Tarquinia, 1542–1617, 1,2

Monk, Loes, 2
Monks, Victoria, 1894–1927, 1
Monroe, Lucy, 1907–, 1
Montana, Patsy, 1914–, 1,2
Montgomery, Melba Joyce, 1938–, 2
Monti-Gorsey, Lola, fl. 1930s, 1
Montserrat, Caballe, 1933–, 1
Moore, Caroline Rudy, 1943–, 2
Moore, Carrie, d. 1926, 1
Moore, Dorothy "Dottie" Louise
    Sutton, 1930–1967, 2
Moore, Mary, fl. 1930s, 1
Moore, Mary Carr, 1873–1957, 1
Moore, Melba, 1945–, 2
Moore, Monette, 1902–1962, 2
Morandi, Rosa, fl. 1810s, 1
Morena, Berta, 1878–1952, 1
Moreno, Rita, 1931–, 1,2
Morfova, Khristina Vasileva, 1889–
    1936, 2
Morgan, Billie, 1922–, 2
Morgan, Helen, 1900–1941, 2
Morgan, Jane, 1920–, 1,2
Morgan, Jaye P., 1929–, 1,2
Morgana, Nina, fl. 1920s, 1
Morison, Elsie, 1924–, 1
Morrisey, Marie, fl. 1940s, 1
Morse, Ella Mae, 1925–, 2
Moss, Mary Hissem de, fl. 1940s, 1
Moten, Etta, fl. 1930s, 1
Moylan, Marianne, 1932–, 1
Moylan, Peggy Joan, 1934–, 1
Muldaur, Maria Grazia Rosa Domen-
    ica D'Amato, 1942–, 2
Murray, Anne, 1945–, 2
Murray, Charlotte Wallace, m. 1915,
    1
Murska, Ilma di, 1835–1889, 1
Mysz, Gmeiner Lulu, 1876–1948, 1
Nadworney, Devora, 1924–, 1
Namara, Marguerite, fl. 1940s, 1
Narelle, Marie, 1874–1941, 1
Neff, Hildegarde, 1925–, 2
Neilsen, Alice, fl. 1910s, 1
Nelli, Herva, 1
Nelson, Harriet Hilliard, 1911–, 1,2
Nemeth, Maria, fl. 1930s, 1
Nevada, Mignon, 1887–, 1
Newton-John, Olivia, 1948–, 2
Nichols, Edith Elizabeth, fl. 1930s, 1
Nicholson, Martha Snell, 1886–1951,
    1
Nicks, Stevie, 1948–, 2
Niesen, Gertrude, 1910–1975, 1,2

Nikolaidi, Elena, 1910–, 1
No-Fru, fl. 1200s, 1
Noe, Emma, fl. 1940s, 1
Noni, Alda, 1920–, 1
Noria, Jana (Josephine Ludwig), fl.
    1910s, 1
Novello, Clara, 1818–1908, 2
Novello, Mary, 1818–1908, 2
Novotna, Jarmila, 1906–, 1
Nyro, Laura, 1949–, 2
O'Brien, Joan, 1936–, 1
O'Brien, Virginia, 1921–, 2
O'Bryant, Joan, 1923–, 2
O'Connell, Helen, 1920–, 1,2
O'Day, Anita, 1919–, 1,2
O'Dea, Anne Caldwell, 1867–1936,
    1,2
O'Neil, Dolores (Dodie), 2
Oakes, Betty, 1
Obratsova, Elena, 1939–, 2
Odetta (Odette), (Odetta Holmes Fel-
    ious Gordon), 1930–, 1,2
Oelheim, Helen, fl. 1930s, 1
Oerner, Inga, fl. 1910s, 1
Ohms, Elizabeth, 1896–, 1
Olay, Ruth, 1927–, 2
Olden, Margarete, fl. 1940s, 1
Oldmixon, Mrs. George, d. 1836, 1
Olheim, Helen Marion, fl. 1930s, 1
Olitzka, Rosa, 1873–1949, 1
Olszewska, Maria, 1892–, 1
Osborn-Hannah, Jane, 1873–1943, 1
Osborne, Mary, 1921–, 2
Osmond, Olive Marie, 1959–, 2
Ostinelli, Sophie Henriette Hewitt, d.
    1846, 2
Otero, Emma, fl. 1940s, 1
Owen, Julia D., fl. 1940s, 1
Owens, Bonnie, 1933–, 2
Page, Patti, 1927–, 1,2
Pallister, Esther Walters, 1872–, 2
Palmer, Bertha Louise Schantz,
    1881–, 2
Papas, Irene, 1926–, 2
Parepa-Rosa, Euphrosyne, 1836–
    1874, 1
Parke, Maria Hester, 1755–1822, 1
Parkinson, Elizabeth (Parkina), 1882–
    1922, 2
Parnell, Evelyn, fl. 1910s, 1
Parton, Dolly Rebecca, 1946–, 2
Pasquali, Bernice de, fl. 1900s, 1
Patey, Janet Monach, 1842–1894, 1
Patterson, Elizabeth Kelso, fl. 1940s,
    1

Patti, Carlotta, 1840–1889, 1
Patti-Brown, Anita, 1
Patton, Abby Hutchinson, 1829–, 1
Paulee, Mona, 1
Pauly, Rosa, 1905–, 1
Pavloska, Irene, 1889–1931, 1
Peaches, fl. 1970s, 2
Pearl, Minnie, 1912–, 2
Pennington, Lily May, 1917–, 2
Peralta, Angela, 1845–1883, 1
Peralta, Frances, d. 1933, 1
Persiani, Fanny Tacchinardi, 1812–
    1867, 1
Peschka-Leutner, Minna, 1839–1890,
    1
Peters, Bernadette, 1948–, 2
Peterson, Alma, fl. 1940s, 1
Peterson, May, d. 1952, 1
Petina, Irra, 1911–, 1
Phillips, Esther Mae Jones, 1935–
    1984, 2
Phillips, Michele, 1944–, 2
Phillips, Thea, fl. 1930s, 1
Piaf, Edith, 1915–1963, 1,2
Piccolomini, Maria, 1834–1899, 1
Pickens, Jane, 1
Pickens sisters, 2
Pinkert, Regina, fl. 1900s, 1
Pisaroni, Rosamunda Benedetta,
    1793–1872, 1
Pitzinger, Gertrude, 1906–, 1
Platt, Estelle Gertrude, fl. 1930s, 1
Poe, Elizabeth (Arnold) Hopkins,
    1787–1811, 1,2
Pointer sisters, 2
Polak, Jessamine, 1869–, 1
Polk, Grace Porterfield, fl. 1940s, 1
Polko, Elise Vogel, 1823–1899, 1
Pollak, Anna, 1915–, 1
Ponselle (Ponzillo), Carmela, 1892–,
    1
Potter, Marguerite, fl. 1930s, 1
Powell, Jane, 1929–, 1,2
Powell, Sue, fl. 1970s, 2
Powell, Virginia, d. 1959, 2
Pownall, Mary Ann, 1751–1796, 1,2
Previn, Dory Langan, 1929–, 2
Price, Ruth, 1938–, 2
Printemps, Yvonne, fl. 1910s, 1
Provine, Dorothy, 1937–, 1,2
Purim, Flora, 1942–, 2
Quatro, Susi, 1951–, 2
Quinn, Carmel, fl. 1930s, 1
Rainey, Gertrude Malissa Nix Prid-
    gett "Ma", 1886–1939, 2

Raisbeck, Rosina, 1918–, 1
Raitt, Bonnie, 1949–, 2
Ranczak, Hildegarde, fl. 1940s, 1
Rankin, Nell, 1926–, 1
Ravan, Genya, 1941–, 2
Ravogli, Guilia, 1860–, 1
Rawlinson, Mabel, 2
Ray, Martha, 1779–, 1
Raye, Martha, 1916–, 1,2
Raymond, Maud, fl. 1890s, 1
Raymondi, Lillian, fl. 1940s, 1
Rea, Virginia, fl. 1930s, 1
Redd, Elvria "Vi", 1930–, 2
Reddy, Helen, 1941–, 2
Redeker, Louise, 2
Redell, Emma, d. 1940, 1
Reed, Lucy, 1921–, 2
Reed, Susan Karen, 1927–, 2
Reese, Della, 1932–, 1,2
Reggiani, Hilde, 1914–, 1
Reicher-Kindermann, Hedwig, 1853–
    1883, 1
Reinhold, Eva, fl. 1900s, 1
Respighi, Elsa Olivieri Sangiacomo,
    1894–, 1
Reszke, Josephine de, 1855–1891, 1
Reuss-Belce, Luise, 1860–, 1
Reynolds, Debbie Marie Frances,
    1932–, 1,2
Reynolds, Libby Holman, fl. 1920s, 1
Reynolds, Malvina, 1900–1978, 2
Ribla, Gertrude, 1
Richards, Ann, 1935–, 2
Richmond, June, 1915–1962, 2
Rider-Kelsey, Corinne, 1880–1947,
    1,2
Rigal, Delia, 1923–, 1
Ring, Blanche, 1872–1961, 2
Rio, Anita, 1873–1971, 1,2
Riperton, Minnie, 1947–1979, 2
Ritchie, Jean, 1922–, 1,2
Rivera, Chita, 1933–, 1,2
Robinson, Anastasia, Countess of Pe-
    terborough, 1698–1755, 1
Roche, Mary Elizabeth, 1920–, 2
Rogers, Clara Kathleen Barnett,
    1844–1931, 1,2
Rogers, Dale Evans, 1912–, 1,2
Rogers, Ginger, 1911–, 1,2
Roggero, Margaret, 1
Roma, Caro, 1866–1937, 1
Roma, Lisa, fl. 1920s, 1
Romaine, Margaret, fl. 1910s, 1
Roman, Stella, fl. 1940s, 1

Ronstadt, Linda, 1946–, 2
Roobenian, Amber, 1905–, 1
Roosevelt, Blanche Tucker, 1853–1898, 2
Roosevelt, Emily, 1893–, 1
Rosell, Anne, fl. 1930s, 1
Ross, Annie, 1930–, 1,2
Ross, Beverly "Buddy" Morgan, 1914–, 2
Ross, Diana, 1944–, 2
Roth, Lillian, 1910–, 1,2
Roze, Marie Ponsin, 1846–1926, 1
Rudersdorff, Hermine, 1822–1882, 2
Runger, Gertrud, fl. 1940s, 1
Russell, Anne, 1911–, 1
Russell, Ella, 1864–1935, 1,2
Ryan, Mary P. Van Buren, fl. 1930s, 1
Sachs, Evelyn, 1924–, 1
Sack, Erna, 1908–, 1
Saint Huberty, Cecile Clavel, 1756–1812, 1
Sainte-Marie, Buffie (Beverly), 1940–, 2
Sainton-Dolby, Charlotte Helen, 1821–1885, 1
Salter, Mary Turner, 1856–1938, 1,2
Saltzman-Stevens, Minnie, 1878–, 1
Salvini-Donatelli, Fanny, fl. 1900s, 1
Sammis-MacDermid, Sibyl, fl. 1940s, 1
Saroya, Bianca, fl. 1910s, 1
Sartoris, Adelaide Kemble, 1814–1879, 1
Sasa, Marie-Constance, 1838–1907, 1
Saville, Frances, 1862–1935, 1
Sayao, Bidu, 1906–, 1
Scalchi, Sofia, 1850–1922, 1
Schechner-Waagen, Nanette, 1806–1860, 1
Scheff, Fritzi, 1879–1954, 1,2
Scheider, May, fl. 1900s, 1
Schlamme, Martha, 1930–, 1
Schnorr von Carolsfield, Malwine, 1832–1904, 1
Schoene, Lotte, fl. 1930s, 1
Schroter, Corona von, 1751–1802, 1,2
Schumann, Meta, fl. 1940s, 1
Scio, Julie Angelique, 1768–1807, 1
Scotney, Evelyn, fl. 1910s, 1
Scott, Hazel Dorothy, 1920–1981, 1,2
Scott, Linda, fl. 1960s, 1
Scott, Malcomb (Maidie), fl. 1910s, 1
Seefried, Irmgard, 1919–, 1
Seeger, Margaret "Peggy", 1935–, 2

Seeley, Blossom, 1891–1974, 2
Seely, Marilyn Jeanne, 1940–, 2
Segal, Vivienne, 1897–, 2
Selika, Marie, fl. 1870s, 1
Shacklock, Constance, 1913–, 1
Sharlow, Myrna Docia, fl. 1940s, 1
Sharrock, Linda Chambers, 1949–, 2
Shaw, Marlena, 1944–, 2
Shaw, Wini, 1910–, 2
Shay, Dorothy, 1921–1978, 1,2
Sherwood, Roberta, 1913–, 1
Shore, Dinah (Frances "Fannie" Rose), 1917–, 1,2
Showalter, Edna Blanche, fl. 1940s, 1
Shuard, Amy, 1924–, 1
Shutta, Ethel, 1896–1976, 2
Silberta, Rhea, 1900–, 1
Simms, Ginny E., 1915–, 1
Simms, Lu Ann, 1932–, 1
Simon, Carly, 1945–, 2
Simone, Nina, 1933–, 1,2
Simpson, Valeria, 1946–, 2
Sims, Ginny (Virginia), 1916–, 2
Sinatra, Nancy, 1941–, 2
Singleton, Margaret "Margie" Louise, 1935–, 2
Singleton, Penny "Blondie", 1935–, 2
Sirmen, Maddalena Lombardini, 1735–, 1
Sladen, Victoria, 1910–, 1
Sledge sisters, fl. 1970s, 2
Slick, Grace Wing, 1939–, 2
Slobodskaya, Oda, 1
Smith, Bessie (Elizabeth), 1894–1937, 1,2
Smith, Clara, 1894–1935, 2
Smith, Connie, 1941–, 2
Smith, Ethel, 1921–, 2
Smith, Georgina, fl. 1930s, 1
Smith, Kate, 1909–1986, 1,2
Smith, Keely, 1932–, 1,2
Smith, Mamie Robinson, 1883–1946, 1,2
Smith, Maybelle, 1924–1972, 2
Smith, Patti, 1946–, 2
Snow, Anna Rablen, 1861–, 1,2
Snow, Phoebe Laub, 1952–, 2
Snow, Valaida, 1900–1956, 1
Soldene, Emily, 1845–1912, 1
Somigli, Franca, 1907–, 1
Sontag, Henriette, Countess Rossi, 1806–1854, 1
Sparkes, Leonora, fl. 1900s, 1
Sparrow, Arianna Cooley, fl. 1860s, 1

Speaks, Margaret, fl. 1930s, 1
Speaks, Oley, 1874–1948, 2
Speare, Dorothy, 1
Speer, Lena Brock "Mom", d. 1967, 2
Spies, Hermine, 1857–1893, 1
Spivey, Victoria, 1908–1976, 2
Springfield, Dusty, 1939–, 2
Stacy, Jess Alexandria, 1904–, 2
Stader, Maria, 1915–, 1
Stafford, Jo, 1918–, 1,2
Stamper, Mrs., fl. 1770s, 1
Stanley, Helen, 1889–, 1
Stanley, Kim, 1921–, 1,2
Starr, Kay, 1922–, 1,2
Staton, Dakota, 1932–, 2
Stearns, Agnes June, 1939–, 2
Stella, Antoinette, 1929–, 1
Stellman, Maxine, fl. 1940s, 1
Sten, Suzanne, fl. 1940s, 1
Stephens, Catherine, Countess of
   Essex, 1794–1832, 1
Sterling, Antoinette, 1850–1904, 1,2
Steuber, Lillian, fl. 1940s, 1
Stevens, Connie, 1938–, 1,2
Stewart, Amii, fl. 1970s, 2
Stignani, Ebe, 1907–, 1
Stoltz, Rosine, 1815–1903, 1
Stolz, Teresa, 1834–1902, 1
Stone, Virginia, fl. 1950s, 2
Storer, Maria, 1750–1795, 1,2
Storm, Gale, 1921–, 1,2
Strauss, Pauline de Ahma, m. 1894, 1
Streisand, Barbra Joan, 1942–, 1,2
Strepponi, Giuseppina, 1815–1897, 1
Stritch, Elaine, 1925–, 1,2
Strong, May A., fl. 1940s, 1
Strozzi, Barbara, 2
Studholme, Marion, 1
Sucher, Rosa Hasselbeck, 1849–1927,
   1
Sullam, Sara Coppia, 1590–1641, 2
Sullivan, Maxine, 1911–1987, 2
Sumac, Yma, 1927–, 1,2
Summer, Donna, 1948–, 2
Sundelius, Marie, 1915–, 1
Supervia, Conchita, 1899–1936, 1
Suzuki, Pat, 1931–, 1
Swan, Dottie, 1916–, 2
Swartz, Jeska, fl. 1910s, 1
Sylva, Marguerite, fl. 1940s, 1
Symons, Charlotte, fl. 1940s, 1
Syms, Sylvia, fl. 1940s, 2
Szantho, Enid, fl. 1930s, 1
Talbert, Florence Cole, fl. 1910s, 1

Tanguay, Eva, 1878–1947, 1,2
Tauber, Doris, 1908–, 1
Taylor, Eva, 1896–, 2
Taylor, Kate, 1949–, 2
Taylor, Koko, 1938–, 2
Temple, Madge, fl. 1930s, 1
Templeton, Fay, 1865–1939, 1,2
Tennille, Tony, 1943–, 2
Tennyson, Jean, fl. 1830s, 1
Tentoni, Rosa, fl. 1930s, 1
Teodorini, Elena, 1857–1926, 1,2
Ternina, Milka, 1863–1941, 1
Terrell, Rha, 2
Tesi, Vittoria, 1700–1775, 1
Tharpe, Rosetta, Sister, 1921–1973, 2
Thomas, Carla, 1942–, 2
Thompson, Kay, 1911–, 1,2
Thompson, Sue, 1926–, 2
Thursby, Emma Cecilia, 1857–1931,
   1,2
Tietjens, Theresa, 1831–1877, 1
Tiffany, Marie, fl. 1910s, 1
Tilton, Martha, 1915–, 2
Tofts, Katherine, 1680–1758, 1
Torpadie, Greta, fl. 1940s, 1
Tracey, Minnie, 1870–1929, 1
Trapp, Maria Augusta von, 1905–, 1,2
Travers, Mary Ellin, 1936–, 2
Trebelli, Zelia, 1838–1892, 1
Trentini, Emma, 1878–1959, 1
Treville, Yvonne de (Le Gierce),
   1881–1954, 1,2
Truman, Mary Margaret, 1924–, 1,2
Tsianini, Princess, fl. 1940s, 1
Tubb, Carrie, fl. 1920s, 1
Tucker, Sophie Kalish, 1884–1966,
   1,2
Tucker, Tanya, 1938–, 2
Tully, Alice, fl. 1940s, 1
Turner, Blanche, fl. 1950s, 1
Turner, Eva, 1892–, 1
Turner, Tina (Annie Mae) Bullock,
   1938–, 2
Turner-Maley, Florence, fl. 1940s, 1
Ugalde, Delphine, 1829–1910, 1
Uggams, Leslie, 1943–, 1,2
Ulmar, Geraldine, 1862–1932, 1
Unger, Caroline, 1803–1877, 1
Unger, Karoline, 1803–1877, 1
Urbanek, Carolyn, fl. 1930s, 1
Ursuleac, Viorica, 1899–, 1
Valda, Guilia, 1855–1925, 2
Valdi, Marguerite, fl. 1940s, 1
Valente, Caterina, 1932–, 1,2

Valleria, Alwina Schoening, 1848–
1925, 1,2
Valli, June, 1
Van Buren, Alicia Keisker, 1860–
1922, 1
Van Dresser, Marcia, 1880–1937, 1,2
Van Emden, Harriet, 1896–1953, 1
Van Kirk, Mary, fl. 1910s, 1
Van Vorst, Marie Louise, 1867–1936,
1,2
Van Zandt-Vanzini, Jennie, fl. 1860s,
1
Van der Veer, Nevada, fl. 1940s, 1
Vance, Eunice, fl. 1910s, 1
Vartenissian, Shakeh, fl. 1950s, 1
Vassenko, Xenia, fl. 1940s, 1
Vaughan, Sarah Lois, 1924–, 1,2
Vaupel, Ouise, fl. 1930s, 1
Verrett, Shirley, 1933–, 1,2
Vettori, Elda, fl. 1940s, 1
Viafora, Gina Ciaparelli, d. 1936, 1
Viardot-Garcia, Marie Felicitas, fl.
1920s, 1
Viardot-Garcia, Pauline, 1821–1910,
1
Vicarino, Regina, fl. 1940s, 1
Victoria, Vesta, 1873–1951, 1
Villani, Luisa, fl. 1900s, 1
Villiers, Vera de, fl. 1930s, 1
Vix, Genevieve, 1879–1939, 1
Vogl, Therese, 1845–, 1
Vokes, Victoria, 1853–1894, 1
Von Januschowsky, Georgine, 1859–
1914, 2
Votipka, Thelma, fl. 1920s, 1
Vreeland, Jeannette, d. 1939, 1
Vyvyan, Jennifer, 1925–, 1
Wagner, Erica von, 1890–, 1
Wagner, Johanna, 1826–1894, 1
Wain, Bea, fl. 1940s, 2
Wakefield, Henrietta, fl. 1900s, 1
Walker, Rachel, fl. 1910s, 1
Wallace, Mildred White, 1839–, 1
Wallace, Sippie, 1898–1926, 2
Walter, Rose, fl. 1940s, 1
Ward, Anita, 1957–, 2
Ward, Clara, 1924–1973, 2
Ward, Helen, fl. 1930s, 2
Warfield, Sandra, 1
Warren, Margie Ann, 1922–, 2
Warwick, (Marie) Dionne, 1941–, 2
Washington, Dinah, 1924–1963, 1,2
Waters, Crystal, fl. 1920s, 1
Waters, Ethel, 1900–1977, 1,2

Wayne, Frances, 1924–, 2
Wayne, Mabel, 1904–, 1,2
Wayne, Susan, 2
Weaver, Marjorie, 1913–, 2
Webb, June Ellen, 1934–, 2
Weber, Caroline Brandt von, fl.
1790s, 1
Weed, Marion, 1870–1947, 1
Weidt, Luci, Baronness von Urmenyi,
1880–1940, 1
Wells, Ardis Arlee, 1917–, 2
Wells, Kitty, 1919–, 2
Wells, Phradie, fl. 1920s, 1
Werner, Kay, 1918–, 1
Werner, Sue, 1918–, 1
West, Dorothy Marie, 1932–, 2
West, Mae, 1892–1980, 1,2
Wettergren, Gertrud, 1896–, 1
Wheatley, Julia, 1817–1875, 2
White, Portia, 1917–, 1
Whiting, Margaret, 1924–, 1,2
Whitney, Joan, 1914–, 1
Wicker, Ireene, 1905–, 1,2
Wickham, Florence, 1882–1962, 1
Wieder, Gertrud, fl. 1940s, 1
Wiley, Lee, 1915–1975, 2
Wilkins, Marie, fl. 1940s, 1
Williams, Camilla, 1
Williams, Chickie, 1919–, 2
Williams, Irene, fl. 1940s, 1
Wilson, Ann, 1950–, 2
Wilson, Dolores, fl. 1950s, 1
Wilson, Grace, 1890–1962, 2
Wilson, Julie, 1925–, 1
Wilson, Mary, 1943–, 2
Wilson, Mary K., 1927–, 2
Wilson, Nancy, 1937–, 1,2
Wilt, Marie, 1833–1891, 1
Winstone, Norma, 1941–, 2
Wittkowska, Marta, fl. 1910s, 1
Wood, Del, 1
Woods, Patricia Rudy, 1946–, 2
Wright, Cobina, Jr., 1921–, 1,2
Wright, Martha, 1926–, 1
Wright, Nancy, 1
Wright, Ruby, 1939–, 2
Wynette, Tammy, 1942–, 2
Wysor, Elizabeth, fl. 1930s, 1
Yaw, (Lark) Ellen Beach, 1868–1947,
2
Yohe, May, 1869–1938, 1
Yuro, Timi, fl. 1960s, 1
Zabella-Vrubel, Madame, fl. 1890s, 1
Zadek, Hilde, fl. 1940s, 1

Gilpin, Mrs. Henry D., fl. 1900s, 1
Goelet, May Wilson, Duchess of Roxburgh(e), fl. 1910s, 1,2
Gore, "Widow", fl. 1790s, 1
Hammond, Natalie Harris, m. 1881, 1
Hampton, Hope, 1901–, 1
Hervey, Mary Lepell, 1700–1768, 1
Hills, Mrs., fl. 1860s, 1
Hogg, Ima, 1882–1975, 2
Huntington, Mrs. Rudd, fl. 1900s, 1
Jay, Sarah (Sally) Livingston Van Brugh, 1757–1802, 1,2
King, Mary Alsop, fl. 1770s, 1
Laraguais, Duchess de, fl. 1740s, 1
Lay, Julia, fl. 1880s, 1
Le Vert, Octavia Celeste Walton, 1810–1877, 1,2
Leary, Anne, fl. 1910s, 1
Leavenworth, Mary, fl. 1880s, 1
Leonard, Anna Byford, 1843–, 1
Lepell, Mary, 1700–1768, 1
Leslie, Miriam Florence Folline Squier, 1836–1914, 1,2
Lewis, Eleanor Parke Custis, 1779–1852, 1
Lincoln, Jennie Gould, fl. 1910s, 1
Logan, Deborah Norris, 1761–1839, 1,2
Londonderry, Edith Helen Chaplin Vane-Tempest-Stewart, Marchioness of, 1878–1959, 1
Loring, Elizabeth Lloyd, fl. 1770s, 2
Lowden, Florence Pullman, 1868–, 1
Mancini, Hortense, 1646–1699, 1
McLean, Mrs. Louis, m. 1812, 1
Merrick, Mrs. Wickliffe, fl. 1910s, 1
Nevill, Dorothy, 1826–1913, 1
Olcott, Rita, fl. 1930s, 1
Otis, Eliza Henderson, 1796–1873, 1
Ouseley, Lady William Gore, m. 1829, 1
Paget, Lady Arthur, 1865–1919, 1
Paley, Barbara Cushing, 1917–, 1
Patterson, Martha Johnson, 1828–, 1
Platen, Countess von, fl. 1700s, 1
Provoost, Maria de Peyster Schrick Spratt, 1693–1760, 1
Rice, Mrs. Isaac L., fl. 1860s, 1
Ridgeway, Ann, d. 1857, 1
Routt, Eliza Franklin, 1852–, 1
Rudd, Susan, fl. 1700s, 1
Rush, Phoebe Ann Ridgway, 1797–1857, 1
Salisbury, Georgiana, d. 1899, 1

Shaw, Carolyn Hagner, 1903–, 1
Simpson, Martha Ritchie, fl. 1800s, 1
Smith, Margaret Bayard Harrison, 1778–1844, 1,2
Southwick, Charlotte Augusta, fl. 1850s, 1
Speed, Mrs. Joshua, fl. 1850s, 1
Stannard, Martha Pierce, fl. 1860s, 1
Stover, Mary, fl. 1850s, 1
Stranahan, Clara Harrison, m. 1879, 1
Stuart, Louisa, 1757–1851, 1
Swetchine, Anne Sophie Soymanov, 1782–1857, 1
Tencin, Claudine Alexandrine Guerin de, 1685–1749, 1
Tesselschade, Maria, 1859–1649, 1
Thompson, Sarah, Countess Rumford, d. 1852, 1
Twisleton, Ellen Dwight, 1829–1862, 1
Van Ness, Cornelia, m. 1831, 1
Vanderbilt, Alice Claypoole Gwynne, 1
Vanderbilt, Grace Wilson, d. 1953, 1
Waddell, Charlotte Augusta Southwick, fl. 1870s, 1
Waldegrave, Frances Elizabeth Anne, 1821–1879, 1
Wallace, Susan Arnold, 1830–1907, 1
Warren, Mrs. Fiske, fl. 1920s, 1
Williams, Katherine Breed, d. 1953, 1
Williams, Pamela, 1785–, 1
Wilson, Mrs. Stewart, fl. 1770s, 1
Winthrop, Elizabeth Temple, fl. 1780s, 1
Wright, Kate Semmes, fl. 1910s, 1
Social reformers
    See
    Reformers
Social welfare leaders
    See also
    Civic leaders
    Youth leaders
Ashley, Mary Elliott, 1798–, 2
Blakeslee, Myra Allen, 1888–1953, 1
Brown, Ida Prescott Bigelow Eldredge, 1864–1950, 1
Glenn, Mary (Willcox) Brown, 1869–1940, 1,2
Gordon, Jean Margaret, 1865–1931, 2
Haldane, Elizabeth Sanderson, 1862–1937, 1
Hartman, May Weisser, 1900–, 1
Hudlun, Ann Elizabeth, 1840–1914, 1

Socialists

Rockefeller, "Happy" Margaretta Fitler, 1926–, 1,2
Roosevelt, Anna Hall, 1863–1892, 2
Rosenwald, Augusta "Gussie" Nusbaum, fl. 1890s, 2
Russell, Rachel Wriothesley, Lady, 1636–1728, 1,2
Rutherfurd, Alice Morton, d. 1917, 2
Schaumberj, Emilie, fl. 1860s, 1,2
Singer, Winnaretta "Winnie", Princesse de P, 1865–1943, 2
Smith, Mrs. Joseph, fl. 1780s, 2
Spencer, Charlotte, 1769–1802, 2
Spencer, Lavinia, Countess, 1762–1831, 2
Stern, Edith Rosenwald, 1895–1980, 2
Stewart, Deborah M. Clenahan, 2
Stoddard, Mrs. Simeon, 2
Stotesbury, Lucretia (Eva) Bishop Roberts, 1865–1946, 1,2
Van Ness, Marcia Burns, 1782–1832, 1,2
Vanderbilt, Alva Ertskin Smith Belmont Hazard, 1853–1933, 1,2
Vaubrun, Marguerite Therese, Marquisse de, fl. 1970s, 2
Ward, Mrs. Dudley, fl. 1920s, 2
Ward, Sallie Downs, 1,2
Willoughby, Catherine, Duchess of Suffolk, 1519–1580, 2
Windsor, (Bessie) Wallis Warfield Simpson, 1896–1986, 1,2
Yarrington, Catherine, fl. 1860s, 2
Sociologists
Avary, Myrta Lockett, fl. 1910s, 1,2
Balch, Emily Greene, 1867–1961, 1,2
Belais, Diana, fl. 1900s, 1
Blanding, Sarah Gibson, 1898–1985, 1,2
Brown, Corinne Stubbs, 1849–, 1
Coolidge, Mary Elizabeth Burroughs Roberts, 1860–, 1
Davis, Maxine, 2
Diner, Helen, pseud., 2
Epstein, Cynthia Fuchs, fl. 1970s, 2
Ferrero, Gina Lombroso, 1872–1944, 1
George, Zelma Watson, 1903–, 1
Gerberding, Elizabeth, 1857–, 1
Goldmark, Josephine Clara, 1877–1950, 2
Graffenried, (Mary) Clare de, 1849–1921, 1,2
Hagood, Margaret Lloyd Jarman, 1907–1963, 2

Hesselgren, Kerstin, 1872–1962, 1
Hopkins, Mrs. Archibald, 1857–, 1
Hubbard, Ruth, fl. 1950s, 2
Jackson, Jacqueline J., fl. 1970s, 2
Keller, Suzanne, fl. 1970s, 2
Kingsbury, Susan Myra, 1870–1949, 2
Komarovsky, Mirra, 1906–, 1,2
Lee, Ruse Hum, 1904–1964, 2
Leonard, Anna Byford, 1843–, 1
Lynd, Helen Merrell, 1896–1982, 2
Maz, Veronica, fl. 1970s, 2
McKissick, Margaret Smith, fl. 1910s, 1
Monich, Zinaida, 2
Mulliner, Gabrielle, fl. 1920s, 1
Palmer, Mrs. A. M., fl. 1910s, 1
Pankratova, Anna, 1897–1957, 2
Parsons, Elsie Worthington Clews, 1875–1941, 1,2
Ridker, Carol, 2
Robbins, Margaret Dreier, fl. 1900s, 1,2
Rose, Martha Parmelee, 1834–, 1
Rossi, Alice S., 2
Russell, Diana E. H., 2
Schwartz, Pepper, 2
Smart, Alice McGee, fl. 1950s, 1
Stacy, Hollis, fl. 1970s, 2
Theodore, Athena, 2
Trivulzio, Cristina Belgiojoso, 1808–1871, 1
Wootton, Barbara Frances, 1897–, 1,2
Yankova, Zoya, 2
Socrates—Spouse
Xanthippe, fl.400sBC, 1
Softball players
Anderson, Jenny, fl. 1970s, 2
Davis, Maxine "Mickey", fl. 1970s, 2
Dobson, Margaret, 2
Joyce, Joan, 1940–, 2
Lopiano, Donna, fl. 1970s, 2
Ramsey, Lorene, fl. 1970s, 2
Tickey, Bertha Reabin, 1914–, 2
Welborn, Nancy, fl. 1970s, 2
Wilkinson, Dot, 2
Soil scientists
Anderson, Carol A., fl. 1970s, 2
Solar physicists
Prinz, Dianne, 2
Smith, Elske V. P., 2
Timothy, Adrienne F., fl. 1970s, 2
Solar power researchers
Telkes, Mari(a) de, 1900–, 1,2

Soldiers
See also
Air Force officers
Army officers
Marines
Navy officers
Warriors
Beauglie, Madame de, fl. 1700s, 1
Bieloverskaia, Maria, fl. 1910s, 1
Blalock, Malinda (Sam), fl. 1860s, 2
Blalock, Mrs. L. M., fl. 1860s, 1
Bochkaryova, fl. 1910s, 2
Bordereau, Jeanne, fl. 1700s, 1
Bridekirk, Lady, fl. 1500s, 1
Broulon, Angelique, 1722–1859, 2
Brownell, Kady, 1842–, 1
Brux, Lady, fl. 1500s, 1
Budwin, Florena, 2
Cavanagh, Kit, 1607–1739, 2
Ch'iu Chin, fl. 1900s, 1
Chang, Widow, d. 1931, 1
Chase, Mary Wood, 1868–, 1
Chase, Nelly M., fl. 1860s, 2
Clarke, Amy, 1,2
Compton, Lizzie, 2
Davies, Christian, 1667–1739, 1
Detzliffin, Anna Sophia, 1738–1776, 1
Eranso, Catalina, 1592–1650, 1,2
Feng Pao, fl. 590s, 1
Fernig, Felicite de, 1776–1831, 1
Fernig, Theophile de, 1779–1819, 1
Fief, Madame du, fl. 1790s, 1
Figueredo, Candelaria, 1852–1913, 1
Garibaldi, Anita Riviera de Silva, 1807–1849, 1
Goodridge, Ellen, fl. 1860s, 1
Isoltseva, Apollovna, fl. 1910s, 1
Johnstone, Lady, fl. 1300s, 1
K'uo Ch'un Ch'ing, fl. 1940s, 2
Kovshova, N. V., fl. 1940s, 1
Lawson, Deborah, fl. 1770s, 1
Lilliard, fl. 1540s, 1
MacIntosh, Anne, fl. 1740s, 1
Malko, Marfa, fl. 1910s, 1
Muscal, Ruth, fl. 1970s, 2
Patton, Mary, fl. 1770s, 2
Plater, Emilia, 1806–1831, 1
Polivanova, M. S., fl. 1940s, 1
Ranee of Jhansi (Lakshmi Bai), 1822–1857, 1
Read, Mary M., 1680–1721, 1,2
Rodiana, Honorata (Onorata), d. 1472, 1,2

Sampson, Deborah, 1760–1827, 1,2
Sandes, Flora, fl. 1910s, 1,2
Saragossa (Saragoza), Augustina, 1786–1857, 1,2
Schidlowskaia, Olga, fl. 1910s, 1
Seelye, Maria, fl. 1860s, 1
Sforza, Caterina, 1463–1509, 1,2
Shattuck, Mrs. Job, fl. 1770s, 1
Smirnoff, Zoe, fl. 1910s, 1
St. Clair, Sally, fl. 1770s, 2
Stover, Sarah, fl. 1860s, 1
Tcherniawaka, Glustchenko, fl. 1910s, 1
Thomas, Vivia, d. 1870, 2
Turchin, Nadine, 1826–1904, 1
Velazquez, Loretta Janeta, 1838–1897, 1,2
Ward, Nancy, 1738–1822, 2
Wellman, Louisa, fl. 1860s, 1
Welsh, Kit, 1667–1739, 2
Solomon—Mother
Bathsheba, 1040–1015, 1,2
Solomon—Spouse
Naamah, 1
Songwriters
See also
Hymnists
Lyricists
Angelou, Maya, 1928–, 2
Armatrading, Joan, 1950–, 2
Bai, Mira, fl. 1500s, 1
Baillie, Grizel (Grisell) Hume, Lady, 1665–1746, 1
Baillie, Joanna, 1762–1851, 1,2
Bainbridge, Katherine, 1924–, 1
Barnard, Anne Lindsay, Lady, 1750–1825, 2
Barnard, Charlotte Allington, 1830–1869, 2
Barnett, Alice, 1896–, 1,2
Blamire, Susanna, 1747–1794, 1
Bond, Carrie Jacobs, 1862–1946, 1,2
Bonelli, Mona Modini, 1903–, 1
Breck, Carrie Ellis, 1855–1934, 1,2
Bryant, Felice, 1925–, 1,2
Caldwell, Anne, 1867–1936, 2
Carroll, Georgia Lillian, 1914–, 2
Carson, Martha, 1921–, 2
Carter, June, 1929–, 2
Carter, Maybelle Addington, 1909–1978, 2
Cockburn, Alison (Alicia), 1713–1794, 1,2
Comden, Betty, 1915–, 1,2

Szabo, Violette, d. 1945, 1
Thompson, Sarah, d. 1909, 1
Van Lew, Elizabeth L. (Mrs. John),
1818–1900, 1,2
Van Lew, Mrs. John, fl. 1860s, 1
Vanhoutte, Marie-Leonie, fl. 1910s, 1
Velazquez, Loretta Janeta, 1838–
1897, 1,2
Wake, Nancy, fl. 1940s, 1
Walker, Mary Edwards, 1832–1919,
1,2
Windsor, Mary Catherine, 1830–
1914, 1
Witherington, Pearl, fl. 1940s, 1,2
Wolkoff, Anna, fl. 1940s, 1
Wu, Eva, fl. 1950s, 1
X, Hilda, fl. 1940s, 1
X, Myra, fl. 1940s, 1
Spinners
Gungabehn Majmundar, fl. 1930s, 1
McGinty, Anne, 2
Pepper, Mrs., fl. 1890s, 2
Spiritualists
    See also
    Mystics
    Occultists
Crandall, Mrs. L. R. G. "Margery",
fl. 1920s, 1
Davis, Mary Fenn, 1824–1886, 2
Fox, Ann Leah, 1818–1890, 2
Fox, Catherine, 1839–1892, 2
Fox, Katherine (Kate), 1839–1894,
1,2
Fox, Margaret, 1833–1893, 1,2
Fox sisters, fl. 1880s, 2
Jones, Amanda Theodosia, 1835–
1914, 2
Palladino, Eusapia, 1854–1918, 1
Piper, Lenore Evelina Simonds, 1859–
1950, 2
Whitman, Sarah Helen Power, 1803–
1878, 2
Spock, Benjamin—Mother
Spock, Mildred Stoughton, 1876–
1968, 2
Sports
    See also
    Archers
    Athletes
    Automobile racers
    Backgammon players
    Baseball club owners
    Baseball players
    Basketball players

Boats and boating
Bowlers
Boxers
Bullfighters
Canoeists
Checkers
Chess players
Croquet players
Cross country skiers
Cyclists
Divers
Dude wranglers
Equestrians
Fencers
Golfers
Gymnasts
Harness racing
Hockey coaches
Hockey players
Horse breeders
Horse trainers
Horsewomen
Hunters
Jockeys
Lacrosse players
Lawn tennis players
Luge
Marathon runners
Markswomen
Mountaineers
Pentathletes
Pocket billiards players
Racquetball players
Rodeo riders
Roller skaters
Rowers
Scuba divers
Skaters
Skiers
Softball players
Sportswomen
Squash racquets players
Surfers
Swimmers
Table tennis
Television sportscasters
Tennis players
Track athletes
Volleyball players
Walkers
Waterskiers
Weightlifters
Whitewater river running
Wrestlers
Yachting

Alcott, Amy, 1956–, 2
Bruce, Mrs. Victor, m. 1926, 1,2
Sportscasters
  See
  Television sportscasters
Sportswomen
  Donaldson, Elizabeth W., fl. 1930s, 1
  Drogheda, Kathleen, fl. 1910s, 1
  Mandel, Carola Panerai, 1
  Payson, Joan Whitney, 1903–1975,
    1,2
  Uzes, Duchess d', 1847–, 1
Sportswriters
  Kaine, Elinor, 1936–, 2
  Morris, Jeanne, 1935–, 2
  Rosellini, Lynn, 2
  Ryan, Joan, 2
  Stonger, Karol, fl. 1970s, 2
  Vinson-Owen, Maribel, d. 1961, 2
Squash racquets players
  Cogswell, Sue, fl. 1970s, 2
  McKay, Heather Pamela Blundell,
    1941–, 2
Stagecoach drivers
  Orchard, Sadie, 1863–1943, 2
  Parkhurst, Charlotte, 1812–1870, 2
Stalin, Josef—Daughter
  Alliluyeva, Svetlana Stalina, 1926–, 1
Stalin, Josef—Mother
  Dzhugashvili, Ekaterina Gheladze,
    1856–, 2
  Gheladze, Ekaterina, 1856–1937, 2
Stalin, Josef—Spouse
  Alliluyev, Nadya, 2
Standish, Miles—Spouse
  Standish, Barbara, d.c. 1659, 1
  Standish, Rose, d. 1620, 1
Stanton, Elizabeth Cady—Mother
  Cady, Margaret Livingston, 2
Stark, Robert—Daughter
  Stark, Freya Madeline, 1893–, 1,2
State legislators
  Fauset, Crystal Dreda Bird, 1893–
    1965, 2
  Laughlin, Gail, 1868–1952, 2
  Martin, Marion E., 1900–, 2
  Motley, Constance Baker, 1921–, 1,2
  Neuberger, Maurine Brown, 1907–,
    1,2
  Wilmarth, Mary Jane Howes, 1873–
    1935, 2
State officials
  Blue, Virginia Neal, 1910–, 2
  Drake, Marie, fl. 1910s, 2

Fortune, Jennie, 1895–, 1
Gandy, Evelyn, fl. 1940s, 2
Martinez, Vilma S., 1943–, 2
Statisticians
  Bitterman, Kathleen Studdar, 1916–,
    2
  Carr, Deborah Edith Wallbridge,
    1854–, 1
  Cox, Gertrude Mary, fl. 1950s, 2
  Geiringer, Hilda, 1893–1973, 1,2
  Graffenried, (Mary) Clare de, 1849–
    1921, 1,2
  Hagood, Margaret Lloyd Jarman,
    1907–1963, 2
  Rosenblatt, Joan Raup, fl. 1970s, 2
  Weisner, Dorothy E., fl. 1930s, 1
Statius—Spouse
  Claudia, fl. 900s, 1
Steamboat captains
  Daniels, Philomen, 1838–, 2
Steamboat passengers
  Barker, Sarah, fl. 1800s, 1
Steel engravers
  Wormly, Mrs., fl. 1870s, 1
Stein, Gertrude—Friend
  Toklas, Alice Babette, 1877–1967, 1,2
Steinbeck, John—Spouse
  Steinbeck, Elaine Scott, fl. 1950s, 2
Stenographers
  Barrows, Katharine Isabel Hayes
    Chapin, 1845–1913, 1,2
  Seymour, Mary Foot, 1846–1893, 2
  White, Nettie L., fl. 1870s, 1
  Wilson, Dorothy, 1909–, 2
Step Family Foundation
  Roosevelt, Ruth, fl. 1970s, 2
Stephen—Daughter
  Mary of Boulogne, 1136–1181, 1
Stephen I—Spouse
  Gisela (Gizella), Queen of Hungary,
    933–1095, 1,2
Stepovich, Michael—Spouse
  Stepovich, Matilda, fl. 1950s, 2
Sterne, Laurence—Mother
  Sterne, Agnes, d. 1759, 2
Sterne, Laurence—Spouse
  Sterne, Elizabeth Lumley, 2
Stevenson, Mary—Mother
  Stevenson, Margaret, fl. 1740s, 1
Stevenson, Robert Louis—Mother
  Balfour, Margaret Isabella, fl. 1800s, 1
  Stevenson, Margaret Isabella Balfour,
    1829–1897, 1
Stevenson, Robert Louis—Spouse
  Stevenson, Vandergrift Osbourne, 2

Dreier, Mary Elizabeth, 1875–1963, 2
Dubrey, Ana Roque de, 1853–, 2
Duffy, Mary, fl. 1900s, 2
Duniway, Abigail Jane Scott, 1834–1915, 1,2
Duprey, Ana Roque de, 1853–, 2
Elliott, Sarah Barnwell, 1848–1928, 2
Fawcett, Millicent Garrett, 1847–1929, 1,2
Field, Sara Bard, 1882–1974, 2
Gardner, Nannette, fl. 1870s, 2
Gellhorn, Edna Fischer, 1878–1970, 2
Gordon, Jean Margaret, 1865–1931, 2
Gordon, Kate M., 1861–1932, 2
Gougar, Helen Mar Jackson, 1843–1907, 1,2
Green, Emma Edwards, 1890–1942, 2
Greenwood, Grace, pseud., 1823–1904, 1,2
Grew, Mary, 1813–1896, 1,2
Griswold, Hattie, 2
Harper, Ida A. Husted, 1851–1931, 1,2
Havemeyer, Louisine Waldron Elder, 1855–1929, 2
Hay, Mary Garrett, 1857–1928, 1,2
Hebard, Grace Raymond, 1861–1936, 1,2
Holmes, Julia, fl. 1850s, 2
Hooker, Isabella Beecher, 1822–1907, 1,2
Hooper, Jessie Annette Jack, 1865–1935, 2
Hull, Hannah Hallowell Clothier, 1872–1958, 2
Hunt, Jane, 2
Hutton, May Arkwright, 1860–1915, 2
Ingham, Mary Hall, 1866–1937, 2
Irwin, Inez Lenore Haynes Gillmore, 1873–1970, 1,2
Jackson, Lottie Wilson, fl. 1890s, 2
Jacobs, Pattie Ruffner, 1875–1935, 2
Kearney, Belle, 1863–1939, 2
LaFollette, Belle Case, 1859–1931, 1,2
Laidlaw, Harriet Burton, 1873–1949, 1,2
Lampkin, Daisy Elizabeth Adams, 1883–1965, 2
Lewis, Elizabeth Langhorne, 1852–1946, 2
Livermore, Mary Ashton Rice, 1820–1905, 1,2

McCreery, Marie Maud Leonard, 1883–1938, 2
McCullough, Catharine Gouger Waugh, 1862–1945, 2
McWhirter, Luella Smith, 1859–, 2
Mead, Lucia True Ames, 1856–1936, 2
Meriwether, Elizabeth Avery, fl. 1870s, 2
Merrick, Caroline Elizabeth Thomas, 1825–1908, 2
Miller, Emma Guffey, 1874–1970, 1,2
Minor, Virginia Louisa, 1824–1894, 2
Moorhead, Ethel, 2
Morris, Esther Hobart McQuigg Slack, 1814–1902, 1,2
Morris, Lucy Smith, 1852–1935, 2
Nathan, Maud(e), 1862–1946, 2
Nevins, Martha Griffith, 1860–, 2
Nichols, Clarinda Howard, 1810–1885, 1,2
Pankhurst, Christabel, Dame, 1882–1960, 1,2
Pankhurst, Emmeline Goulden, 1858–1928, 1,2
Park, Maud May Wood, d. 1955, 1,2
Partridge, Mary, 2
Patterson, Hanna Jane, 1879–1937, 2
Paul, Alice, 1885–1977, 1,2
Pinchot, Cornelia Elizabeth Bryce, 1881–1960, 2
Pollitzer, Anita Lily, 1894–1975, 2
Pryer, Margaret, 1784–, 2
Pugh, Sarah, 1800–1884, 2
Ricker, Marilla Marks Young, 1840–1920, 1,2
Ridgely, Mabel LLoyd, 1872–1957, 2
Robins, Elizabeth, 1862–1952, 1,2
Robinson, Harriet Jane Hanson, 1825–1911, 1,2
Ruffner, Pattie Ruffner, 1875–1935, 2
Seton, Grace Gallatin, 1872–1959, 1,2
Sewall, May Eliza Wright, 1844–1920, 1,2
Shaw, Anna Howard, 1847–1919, 1,2
Sheppard, Katharine, 1848–1934, 2
Sherwin, Belle, 1868–1955, 2
Shyler, Nettie Rogers, 1862–1939, 2
Smith, Abby Hadassah, 1797–1878, 2
Smith, Julia Evelina, 1792–1886, 2
Smyth, Ethel Mary, Dame, 1858–1944, 1,2
Stanton, Elizabeth Cady, 1815–1902, 1,2

Steel, Flora Annie Webster, 1847–
1929, 1,2
Stewart, Eliza Daniel, 1816–1908, 2
Stone, Lucy, 1818–1893, 1,2
Thomas, Martha Carey, 1857–1935,
1,2
Thomas, Mary Frame Myers, 1816–
1888, 1,2
Turner, Eliza L. Sproat Randolf,
1826–1903, 2
Ueland, Clara Hampson, 1860–1927,
2
Valentine, Lila Hardaway Meade,
1865–1921, 2
Vanderbilt, Alva Ertskin Smith Bel-
mont Hazard, 1853–1933, 1,2
Vernon, Mabel, 1883–1975, 2
Verone, Maria, 2
Villard, Fanny Garrison, 1844–1928,
2
Waite, Catherine van Valkenburg,
1829–1913, 2
Way, Amanda M., 1828–1914, 1,2
Wells, Emmeline Blanch Woodward,
1828–1921, 2
Wells, Marguerite Milton, 1872–
1959, 2
White, Sue Shelton, 1887–1943, 2
Whitney, Charlotte Anita, 1867–
1955, 2
Williams, Sarah, fl. 1970s, 2
Wilson, Mary, fl. 1870s, 2
Wolstenholme-Elmy, Elizabeth C.,
1834–1918, 2
Youmans, Theodora Winton, fl.
1910s, 2
Younger, Maud, 1870–1936, 2
Sulia—Spouse
Valeria, 138–78 BC, 2
Sultan Sujah—Daughter
Aesha, fl. 1650s, 1
Sultanas
Sheger-ed-Dur, fl. 1250s, 1
Sun Yat-Sen—Spouse
Sun Yat-Sen, Chingling Soong, 1830–
1981, 1,2
Sunshine lady
Hansell, Leila Davidson, d. 1915, 2
Superintendent of schools
Miller, Anna, 2
Supreme Court Justices
O'Connor, Sandra Day, 1930–, 2
Suramarit, Norodom—Spouse
Kossamak Neariat Seray Vathana, fl.
1950s, 1

Surface physics
Whitaker, Ann, fl. 1970s, 2
Surfers
Hoffman, Joyce, fl. 1960s, 2
Oberg, Margo, 1955–, 2
Surrey, Earl of—Daughter
Howard, Jane, Lady, fl. 1547, 1
Surveyors
Bohannon, Grete M., 2
Sussex, Earl of—Spouse
Sussex, Eleanor, Countess of, d.
1666, 1
Susskind, David—Spouse
Susskind, Joyce, 1935–, 2
Swift, Jonathan—Friend
Johnson, Esther, 1681–1728, 1
Vanhomrigh, Esther, 1690–1723, 1
Swimmers
Anke, Hannelore, 2
Babashoff, Shirley, 1957–, 2
Bartz, Jenny, 1955–, 2
Bell, Marilyn, 1937–, 1
Belote, Melissa, 1956–, 2
Bleibtrey, Ethela, fl. 1920s, 2
Boyle, Charlotte, fl. 1910s, 2
Caulkins, Tracy, 1963–, 2
Chadwick, Florence, 1918–, 1,2
Corson, Millie Gade, fl. 1920s, 2
Cox, Lynne, 1952–, 2
Crapp, Lorraine, 1938–, 2
Cummings, Iris, fl. 1950s, 2
Cuneo, Ann Curtis, 1926–, 1
Curtis, Ann, 1926–, 1,2
De Varona, Donna, 1947–, 2
Dean, Penny, 1955–, 2
Durack, Fanny, fl. 1910s, 2
Ederle, Gertrude (Trudy) Caroline,
1906–, 1,2
Ender, Kornelia, 1958–, 2
Feldman, Peggy, 2
Fletcher, Jennie, 2
Fraser, Dawn, 1937–, 2
Galligan, Claire, 2
Genesko, Lynn, 1955–, 2
Gerstung, Martha, fl. 1910s, 2
Gleitz, Mercedes, 1901–, 1
Gould, Shane E., 1956–, 2
Holm, Eleanor, 1914–, 1,2
Hveger, Ragnhild, 1920–, 2
Kammersgard, Jenny, 2
Kellerman, Annette, 1888–1975, 1,2
Khairi, Abla Adel, 1960–, 2
Kirk, Henrietta, fl. 1920s, 1
Knache, Christiana, fl. 1970s, 2

Kok, Aagje, fl. 1960s, 2
Lackie, Ethel, fl. 1920s, 2
MacInnis, Nina, 1954–, 2
Madison, Helene, 1913–1970, 2
McCormick, Patricia Keller, 1930–, 1,2
Merki, Nancy Lees, 1926–, 1
Meyer, Debbie, 1952–, 2
Mores, Karen, 2
Nicholas, Cindy, 1958–, 2
Norelius, Martha, 1910–1955, 2
Nyad, Diana Sneed, 1949–, 2
Rawls, Katherine, fl. 1930s, 2
Richter, Ulrike, fl. 1970s, 2
Saltza, Chris von, 1944–, 1
Soule, Aileen Riggin, 1906–, 1
Stone, Virginia, fl. 1950s, 2
Stouder, Sharon, fl. 1960s, 2
Szekely, Eva, fl. 1940s, 2
Taylor, Stella, 1929–, 2
Turral, Jenny, 2
Von Saltza, Chris, 2
Wichman, Sharon, fl. 1960s, 2
Williams, Esther, 1913–, 1,2
Wylie, Wilhelmina, fl. 1910s, 2
Swinburne, John—Daughter
Crathorne, Isabel, 2
Swordsmen
La Maupin, Mille, fl. 1700s, 1
Symbolist
Krysinka, Marie, 2
Synthesizer
Dudziak, Urszula, 1943–, 2
Systems analysts
Hamilton, Margaret, 1936–, 2
Nelson, Ruth, fl. 1970s, 2
Szegli, Stephan—Supporter
Mezeo, Helena, fl. 1560s, 2

T

Table tennis
Rozenau, Angelica, fl. 1950s, 2
Tabor, Horace A.W.—Spouse
McCourt, Baby Doe, 1854–1935, 2
Tabor, Elizabeth Honduel McCourt, 1854–1935, 1,2
Taft, Robert—Spouse
Taft, Martha Wheaton Bowers, 1889–1958, 1
Taft, William Howard—Grandmother
Howard, Sarah, fl. 1800s, 1

Taft, William Howard—Mother
Taft, Louisa Maria Torrey, 1828–1907, 1,2
Taft, William Howard—Spouse
Taft, Helen Herron, 1861–1943, 1,2
Tailors
Baxter, Susan Phinney, fl. 1820s, 1
Taj Mahal—Inspiration
Mumtaz-Mahal (Mumtaza Zemani), 1592–1631, 1,2
Tallyrand, Charles Maurice—Friend
Courland, Dorothea of, fl. 1780s, 1
Talmadge, Constance—Mother
Talmadge, Margaret, fl. 1900s, 1
Talmai—Daughter
Maachah, 1
Tanners
Bell, Hannah Turpin, d. 1939, 2
Tapestry designers
Agnes of Meissen, Saint, fl. 1200s, 2
Albers, Anni, 1899–, 2
Halling, Else, 1899–, 2
Hernmarck, Helena B., 1941–, 2
Wheeler, Dora, fl. 1850s, 2
Zorach, Marguerite Thompson, 1887–1968, 2
Tarnower, Herman—Friend
Tryforos, Lynne, 1943–, 2
Tarquinius Priscus, Lucius—Spouse
Gaia Cyrilla, fl. 570BC, 1
Tatoo artists
Hull, Millie, 2
Tavern keepers
Dawson, Elizabeth, fl. 1770s, 2
Flanagan, Elizabeth, fl. 1770s, 2
Frankland, Agnes Surriage, Lady, 1726–1783, 2
Marshall, Susannah, fl. 1770s, 2
Stoneman, Abigail, 1760–1777, 2
Tax consultants
Graeff, Beryl, fl. 1970s, 2
Hopkins, Julia B., 1
Taxi drivers
King, Margaret, fl. 1970s, 2
Taxidermists
Maxwell, Martha A., 2
Taylor, Deems—Spouse
Kennedy, Mary, fl. 1920s, 1
Taylor, Zachary—Daughter
Dandridge, Elizabeth Taylor Bliss, 1824–1909, 1
Taylor, Zachary—Daughter
Taylor, Elizabeth, fl. 1820s, 1
Taylor, Zachary—Mother
Taylor, Sarah Strother, 1760–1822, 1,2

Clouse, Rose, 1865–, 2
Coates, Gloria, 1938–, 2
Coffey, Phyllis C., fl. 1930s, 1
Collins, Fannie B., d. 1950, 2
Comish, Hannah, fl. 1860s, 2
Cook, May A., 1870–, 2
Corr, Mary Bernadine, 1858–, 1
Costa (Coste), Blanche Marie de, fl. 1566, 2
Crane, Caroline Julia Bartlett, 1858–1935, 1,2
Crawford-Seeger, Ruth Porter, 1901–1953, 1,2
Crowley, Teresa M., fl. 1930s, 1
Culver, Helen, 1832–, 1
Cuninggim, Maud Merrimon, 1874–, 2
Daniels, Pamela, 1937–, 2
Darling, Lucia, 2
Davenport, Frances Gardiner, 1870–, 1
Davidson, Hannah Amelia, 1852–, 1
Davidson, Nora Fontaine Maury, fl. 1860s, 2
Dawes, Helen B. Palmer, m. 1890, 1
Dean, Vera Micheles, 1903–1972, 1,2
Deane, Margaret, 1831–, 1
Delafield, Ann, fl. 1930s, 1
Desai, Anita, 1937–, 2
Desha, Mary, d. 1910, 1,2
Dickerman, Julia Elida, 1859–, 1
Diddock, Marguerite La Flesche, 1862–1945, 2
Diehl, Mary, fl. 1930s, 1
Dillon, Fannie Charles, 1881–1947, 1,2
Dithridge, Rachel L., fl. 1930s, 1
Dix, Dorothea Lynde, 1802–1887, 1,2
Dlugoszewski, Lucia, 1931–, 2
Doggett, Kate Newell, 1827–1884, 1
Dommet, Mrs. John, fl. 1730s, 1
Donnelly, Lucy Martin, 1870–1948, 2
Douglass, Margaret, fl. 1850s, 2
Dow, Betsy, fl. 1830s, 1
Dowd, Mary Hickey, 1866–, 1
Duniway, Abigail Jane Scott, 1834–1915, 1,2
Dunlap, Kate, fl. 1860s, 2
Dyhrenfurth, Hettie, fl. 1930s, 1
Eads, Laura Krieger, fl. 1920s, 1
East, Elizabeth Ann Thompson, 1849–1901, 2
Eberhart, Nelle Richmond, 1871–1944, 1,2

Ehinger, Aline N., 1891–, 2
Eldridge, Mary Agnes Prowse, 1896–, 2
Ellis, Mehetable, fl. 1760s, 1
Emerson, Mary Moody, 1774–1863, 1,2
Emerson, Sybil, 1895–, 1
Erdman, Jean, 1917–, 2
Erskine, Madge Mercer, 1882–, 2
Estelle, Helen G.H., fl. 1930s, 1
Fairbank, Lorena King, 1874–, 2
Fetter, Ellen Cole, fl. 1930s, 1
Fine, Vivian, 1913–, 1,2
Fisher, Kay, fl. 1960s, 2
Fitzgerald, Alice, 1874–1962, 2
Fleming, Pamela S., 1943–, 2
Flowers, Ruth, 2
Flynt, Margery Hoar, d. 1687, 2
Forbes, Grace Springer, fl. 1930s, 1
Foutekova, Raina Pop Georgieva, 1856–1917, 1
Fox, Ancella M., 1847–1920, 2
Fox, Emma Augusta, 1847–, 2
Fraser, Matilda, fl. 1750s, 1
Frazier, Susan Elizabeth, 1864–1924, 1
Fuller, Bridget Lee, fl. 1635, 1,2
Gaidule, Paula, 1848–1925, 1
Garnet, Sarah J. Smith Thompson, 1831–1911, 1,2
Garnett, Mrs. James M., fl. 1820s, 1
Gazley, Martha, fl. 1730s, 1
Gervis, Ruth Streatfield, 1894–, 1
Gilman, Isabel Ambler, fl. 1900s, 2
Gilmore, Gladys Chase, fl. 1930s, 1
Goodrich, Edna L., 2
Goodrich, Frances Louisa, 1856–1944, 1
Graham, Martha, 1893–, 1,2
Gray, Elizabeth Janet, 1902–, 1,2
Green, Mary, fl. 1750s, 1
Grey, Jane Cannon, 1816–, 1
Griffith, Emily, 1880–1947, 2
Grollmuss, Maria, 1896–1944, 2
Gross, Miriam Zeller, fl. 1930s, 1
Grossman, Paula, 1919–, 2
Hall, Eleaine Goodale, 1863–, 1
Hall, Frances M., fl. 1880s, 1
Hammond, Mary Dilworth, fl. 1860s, 2
Hardy, Kay, 1902–, 1
Harriton, Maria, fl. 1960s, 2
Hathaway, Ann, fl. 1940s, 1
Hauser, Alice, fl. 1970s, 2

Hawes, Bess Lomax, 1921–, 2
Hearne, Mary, 1834–1909, 2
Hensel, Ruth, fl. 1930s, 1
Hentz, Caroline Lee Whiting, 1800–
  1856, 1,2
Hentz, Eta, fl. 1930s, 1
Herrad(e) of Landsberg, d. 1195, 1,2
Hicks, Margaret, 1858–1883, 1,2
Hicks, Margaret, fl. 1600s, 1
Hill, Evelyn Corthell, 1886–, 2
Hill, Mabel Wood, 1870–1954, 1,2
Hiller (Hillyer), Mrs., fl. 1740s, 1
Hixson, Jean, fl. 1950s, 1
Hoisington, May Folwell, 1894–, 1
Holton, Susan May, 1875–1951, 1
Hope, Patricia, fl. 1980s, 2
Howard, Floretta, 1
Howard, Ida Tinsley, fl. 1870s, 1
Hubbard, Emma, fl. 1870s, 1
Hughes, Josephine Brawley, fl.
  1870s, 2
Hulse, Anne Elizabeth, fl. 1930s, 1
Huntley, Elizabeth Maddox, 1
Huntley, Gertrude, fl. 1930s, 2
Hurlburt, Margaret, 1915–1947, 1
Hurley, Catherine, fl. 1800s, 1
Hurll, Estelle May, 1863–, 1
Hurston, Zora Neale, 1901–1960, 1,2
Ingalls, Mildred Dodge Jeremy,
  1911–, 1
Irvine, Theodora Ursula, fl. 1930s, 1
Isbell, Olive Mann, d. 1899, 2
Ivey, Jean Eichelberger, 1923–, 2
James, Dorothy, 1901–, 1,2
Jewell, Lucina, 1874, 2
Jones, Julia L., fl. 1890s, 1
Jones, Wanda, 2
Karlinsey, Edna Cathern, 1908–, 2
Karnes, Matilda Theresa, fl. 1900s, 1
Kartini, Raden Adjeng, 1879–1904, 1
Kellet, Charlotte, 1
Kelley, Catherine Bishop, 1853–
  1944, 1
Kelly-Gadol, Joan, fl. 1960s, 2
Kempin, Emile, fl. 1880s, 1
Kemprin-Spyri, Emilie, 1853–1901, 2
Kessel, Mary Hickman, fl. 1950s, 1
King, Julie Rive, 1857–, 1
Knight, Sarah Kemble, 1666–1727,
  1,2
Lacey, Margaret E, fl. 1900s, 1
Laidlaw, Harriet Burton, 1873–1949,
  1,2
Lascelles, Mary Madge, gr. 1822, 1

Leavitt, Mary Greenleaf Clement,
  1830–1912, 2
Lee, Jennette Barbour Perry, 1860–
  1951, 1
Leginska, Ethel Liggins, 1886–1970,
  1,2
Levertov, Denise, 1923–, 2
Lewyn, Helena, fl. 1940s, 1
Lipman, Miriam Hillman, fl. 1930s, 1
Lockwood, Charlotte, fl. 1940s, 1,2
Loeber, L. Elsa, fl. 1930s, 1
Lorimer, Emily M. Overend, gr.
  1906, 1
Lorimer, Hilda Lockhart, gr. 1896, 1
Lunney, Jessie Mae Wenck, 1870–
  1961, 2
Lynn, Meda C., fl. 1930s, 1
MacLeod, Grace, 1878–1962, 1
MacVay, Anna Pearl, fl. 1930s, 1
Macironi, Clara Angela, 1821–1895, 1
Magnusson, Lora Wilkins, fl. 1960s, 2
Maines, Rachel, fl. 1970s, 2
Mann, Maria R., fl. 1860s, 1
Marsh, Lucille, fl. 1930s, 1
Martin, May, 1870–, 2
Mary Julia, Sister, 1886–, 1
Matienzo, Carlota, 1881–1926, 1
Maulson, Hannah, fl. 1970s, 2
McAlmon, Victoria, 1910–1970, 2
McGillicuddy, Frances L., fl. 1970s, 2
McGowan, Elizabeth Blaney, fl.
  1910s, 1
McLane, Enid Stryker, 1896–, 2
Meeker, Eleanor Richardson, fl.
  1830s, 1
Meeker, Josephine, fl. 1870s, 1,2
Menges, Kay, 1912–, 2
Menninger, Flora Knisely, 1863–
  1945, 2
Michel, Clemence Louise, 1830–
  1905, 1,2
Miles, Ellen E., 1835–, 1
Millay, Ernestine Edith, 1896–, 2
Miller, Anna, 2
Miller, Bina West, 1858–1954, 2
Mills, Susan Lincoln Tolman, 1821–
  1912, 1,2
Mistral, Gabriela, 1889–1957, 1,2
Moats, Alice-Leone, 1910–, 1
Moberly, Winifred H., fl. 1910s, 1
Moll, Mary Penman, fl. 1880s, 2
Moore, Caroline Rudy, 1943–, 2
Moore, Lizzie, 1843–1915, 1
Moore, Luella Lockwood, fl. 1940s, 1

Mosher, Edith R., fl. 1900s, 1
Munro, Mary Isobel, gr. 1929, 1
Myrtis, 2
Najafi, Najmeh, fl. 1860s, 1
Nash, Alice Morrison, 1879–, 1
Nedeva, Zlatina, 1877–1941, 1,2
Nelson, Alice Dunbar, 1875–1935, 2
Nevens, Mary McNamara, 1872–1965, 2
Nevins, Martha Griffith, 1860–, 2
Newby, Ruby Warren, fl. 1930s, 1
Newcomb, Franc Johnson, 1887–1970, 2
Newman, Angelia Louise French Thurston Kilgore, 1837–1910, 1,2
Nixon, Thelma Ryan "Pat", 1913–1993, 1
Norman, Julie Bowie, 1889–, 2
Nutting, Mary Olivia, 1831–1910, 1
Olcott, Virginia, gr. 1909, 1
Ordway, Elizabeth, fl. 1870s, 2
Oslund, Anna Marie, 1891–, 2
Overstreet, Bonaro Wilkinson, fl. 1930s, 1
Owen, Grace, 2
Owen, Narcissa Chisholm, 1831–, 2
Page, Elizabeth Wittredge, d. 1845, 1
Page, Fannie Pender, 1870–1942, 1
Park, Lucia Darling, fl. 1860s, 1
Parker, Helen Almina, gr. 1885, 1
Parsons, Lucy, fl. 1840s, 2
Pater, Clara, fl. 1880s, 1
Patterson, Mary J., 1840–1894, 1
Paul, Tillie, fl. 1950s, 2
Paxton, Ethel, fl. 1930s, 1
Peake, Mary S., 1823–1862, 1
Pearce, Marcella Morgan, 1868–, 2
Pease, Jessie L., fl. 1940s, 1
Peterson, Jetret Stryker, 1895–, 2
Pettracini, Maria, fl. 1700s, 2
Piskova, Vela Arkhakova, 1889–1925, 2
Platt, Estelle Gertrude, fl. 1930s, 1
Pope, Mildred Katharine, gr. 1893, 1
Pray, Ada Jordan, fl. 1940s, 1
Pritchard, Esther Tuttle, 1840–, 1
Pugh, Sarah, 1800–1884, 2
Punelli, Dianne, fl. 1970s, 2
Putnam, Georgiana Frances, 1839–1914, 1
Quinlan, Agnes Clune, d. 1949, 1
Rabb, Kate Milner, 1866–1937, 2
Randolph, Virginia, 1874–1958, 1
Rasmussen, Franka, 1909–, 2

Ray, Charlotte E., 1850–1911, 1,2
Raymond, Sarah E., fl. 1870s, 1,2
Read, Miss, pseud., 2
Rebe, Louise Christine, fl. 1940s, 1
Reiss, Johana de Leeuw, 1932–, 2
Reynolds, Myra, 1853–1936, 2
Rhodes, Mrs., fl. 1720s, 1
Richards, Fannie M., 1840–1923, 1
Ringgold, Faith, 1930–, 2
Rinser, Luise, 1911–, 2
Ripley, Mary A., 1831–, 1
Ritter, Irene Marschand, fl. 1940s, 1
Robertson, Anne Eliza Worchester, 1820–1905, 2
Robinson, Ophelia, 1897–, 1
Rogers, Abigail Dodge, fl. 1790s, 1
Rogers, Mrs., fl. 1790s, 1
Rorer, Sarah Tyson Heston, 1849–1937, 2
Ruddick, Sara, 1935–, 2
Rudersdorff, Hermine, 1822–1882, 2
Rullann, Maria, fl. 1860s, 1
Russell, Mrs. E. J., fl. 1860s, 1
Russier, Gabrielle, d. 1969, 2
Salter, Mary Turner, 1856–1938, 1,2
Sammis-MacDermid, Sibyl, fl. 1940s, 1
Samuels, Margaret, fl. 1930s, 1
Sanborn, Katherine Abbot, 1839–1917, 1
Sandoz, Mari, 1896–1966, 1,2
Sartian, Harriet, d. 1957, 1
Sawyer, Helen Alton, 1
Saxl, Eva R., 1921–, 1
Schaefer, Mary Cherubin, 1886–, 2
Scharibrook, Elizabeth, fl. 1760s, 1
Schmitt, Gladys Leonore, 1909–1972, 1,2
Schmitt, Susan, fl. 1940s, 1
Schoonhoven, Helen Butterfield, 1869–, 1
Schulman, Pat, 2
Scott, Jeannette, 1864–, 1
Scott, Masha, fl. 1940s, 2
Sedode, Julia Barbara de Lama "Babla", 1858–, 2
Segale, Blandina, Sister, 1850–, 2
Seitz, Helen, fl. 1930s, 1
Severson, Anne, fl. 1970s, 2
Sibley, Mrs. Harper, fl. 1940s, 1
Siddall, Louise, d. 1935, 1
Sigea, Aloysia, fl. 1500s, 2
Skolow, Anna, 1915–, 2
Slade, Mary Bridges Canedy, 1826–1882, 2

Kilgore, Carrie Burnham, 1836–
  1909, 1,2
Nichols, Clarinda Howard, 1810–
  1885, 1,2
Story, Ann, 1742–1817, 1,2
Wallace, Florence Richardson, 1875–,
  2
Vespacian—Concubine
  Caenis, Antonia, fl. 50, 1
Veterinarians
  Bakarich, Alexandra C., fl. 1960s, 2
  Carlson, Lynne, fl. 1970s, 2
  Cust, Aileen, fl. 1960s, 2
  Hinson, Lois E., 1926–, 2
  Kennedy, Suzanne, 2
  Matikashvili, Nina, 2
  Miller, Janice, 1938–, 2
Vibrists
  Hyams, Marjorie (Margie), 1923–, 2
Vice presidential candidates
  Brehm, Mane Caroline, fl. 1920s, 2
  Carlson, Grace, fl. 1940s, 2
  Cozzini, Georgia, fl. 1960s, 2
  Ferraro, Geraldine Anne, 1935–, 2
  Gunderson, Genevieve, fl. 1970s, 2
  Stowe, Mary L., fl. 1890s, 2
  Weiss, Myra Tanner, fl. 1950s, 2
  Yezo, Ann Marie, fl. 1950s, 2
Victims
  See
    Freezing accident victims
    Murder victims
    Nazi victims
    Rape victims
Victoria, Queen—Cousin
  Di Gallotti, Stephanie, 1840–, 1
Victoria, Queen—Daughter
  Helena, 1846–1923, 1
  Louise, Caroline Alberta, Duchess of
    Argyll, 1849–1939, 1
  Louise, Princess of Great Britain,
    1848–1949, 2
Victoria, Queen—Mother
  Victoire, Duchess of Kent, 1786–, 2
Victorinus—Spouse
  Victoria, fl. 260s, 1
Video jockeys
  Blackwood, Nina, 2
  Quinn, Martha, 2
Vigilantes
  Collins, Libby Smith, 1844–1921, 1
  Foster, Annette Hotchkiss Dimsdale,
    1836–1874, 1
  Park, Lucia Darling, fl. 1860s, 1

Plummer, Electa Bryan, 1842–1912, 1
Sanders, Mrs. Wilbur, fl. 1910s, 1
Slade, Maria Virginia Dale, fl. 1860s,
  1
Villeroi, Marshal—Granddaughter
  Luxembourg, Marechale de, 1707–
    1787, 1
Violin teachers
  DeLay, Dorothy, 1917–, 2
Violincellists
  Becker, Grace, fl. 1940s, 1
  Modave, Jeanne, 1873–1953, 1
  Suggia, Guilhermina, 1888–1951, 1
  Yellin, Thelma, fl. 1930s, 1
Violinists
  Aranyi, Yelly d', 1895–, 1
  Bang, Maia, 1877–1940, 1,2
  Barstow, Vera, 1893–, 1
  Breton, Ruth, 1
  Burns, Annelu, 1889–1942, 1
  Bustabo, Guila, 1919–, 1
  Chemet, Rene, 1888–, 1
  Coit, Lottie Ellsworth, fl. 1940s, 1
  Dodge, Mary Hewes, fl. 1940s, 1
  Engberg, Mary Davenport, 1830–, 1
  Fachira, Adila d'Aranyi, 1888–, 1
  Folville, Juliette, 1870–1946, 1
  Fonaroff, Vera, fl. 1890s, 1
  Gampbel, Lilit, 2
  Given, Thelma, 1898–, 1
  Glenn, Carroll, 1922–, 1
  Gray-Lhevinne, Estelle, 1892–1933, 1
  Haendal, Ida, 2
  Hall, Marie, 1884–1956, 1
  Halle, Wilhelmina (Wilma) Maria
    Franziska Norman-Neruda, 1838–
    1911, 1,2
  Hansen, Cecilia, 1898–, 1,2
  Hathaway, Ann, fl. 1940s, 1
  Hilger, Elsa, fl. 1940s, 1
  Isakadze, Liana, 2
  Jackson, Leonora, 1878–, 1
  Kemper, Ruth, fl. 1920s, 1
  Klein, Evelyn Kaye, fl. 1930s, 2
  Kneisel, Marianne, 1897–1972, 2
  Kurt, Melanie, 1880–1941, 1,2
  Kuyper, Elizabeth, 1877–, 1
  Lachert, Hanna, 1944–, 2
  Lent, Sylvia, 1923–, 1
  Lombardini-Sirmen, Maddalena,
    1745–, 2
  Luboschutz, Lea, 1887–1965, 1,2
  MacKenzie, Giselle, 1827–, 1,2
  MacKinstry, Elizabeth, d. 1956, 1

Magnes, Frances, 1922–, 1
Mara, (Gertrude) Elizabeth Schmel-
    ing, 1749–1833, 1,2
Mead, Olive, fl. 1940s, 1
Menges, Isolde, 1893–, 1
Milanollo, Marie, 1832–1848, 1
Milanollo, Therese, 1827–1904, 1
Mitchell, Viola, 1911–, 1
Moodie, Alma, 1900–1943, 1
Morini, Erica, 1906–, 1,2
Nichols, Marie, 1879–1954, 1
Niemark, Ilza, fl. 1920s, 1
Nilsson, Christine, 1843–1921, 1,2
Okey, Maggie, fl. 1930s, 1
Osgood, Marion, fl. 1940s, 1
Parlow, Kathleen Mary, 1890–1963,
    1,2
Pernel, Orrea, fl. 1940s, 1
Petrides, Frederique, 2
Posselt, Ruth, 1916–, 1
Powell, Maud, 1868–1920, 1,2
Quimby, Helen Sherwood, 1870–, 2
Rubinstein, Erna, 1903–, 1
Senkrah, Arma Leorette Hoffman
    Harkness, 1864–1900, 1,2
Seydel, Irma, fl. 1940s, 1
Shuchari, Sadah, fl. 1920s, 1
Sirmen, Maddalena Lombardini,
    1735–, 1
Sittig, Margaret, fl. 1910s, 1
Skolnik, Jenny, 1869–, 1
Soldat, Marie, 1864–, 1
Solovieff, Miriam, 1921–, 1
Speyer, Leonora von Stosch, 1872–
    1956, 1,2
Stillings, Kemp, fl. 1930s, 1
Strinasacchi, Regina, 2
Suchari, Sadah, fl. 1920s, 1
Sundstrom, Ebba, fl. 1920s, 2
Tas, Helen Teschner, 1889–, 1
Torre, Marta de la, fl. 1940s, 1
Trix, Helen, 1892–1951, 1
Troendle, Theodora, fl. 1940s, 1
Tua, Teresina, 1866–1911, 1
Urso, Camilla, 1842–1902, 1,2
Von Reuter, Florizel, 1890–, 2
Ware, Helen, 1877–, 1,2
Warren, Margie Ann, 1922–, 2
White, Elise Fellows, 1873–, 1
Wietrowetz, Gabriele, 1866–1937, 1
Wing, Helen, fl. 1940s, 1
Winn, Edith L., d. 1933, 1
Zwilich, Ellen Taaffe, 1939–, 2

Virginia
    Burras, Anne, 1608–, 2
    Douglas, Laura Virginia O'Hanlon,
        1889–, 1
    Harrison, Elizabeth Bassett, 1730–
        1792, 1,2
    Jefferson, Jane Randolph, 1720–1776,
        1,2
    Lee, Anne Hill Carter, 1773–, 2
    Madison, Nellie (Nelly) Conway,
        1731–1829, 1,2
    Monroe, Eliza Jones, 1747–, 1,2
    Pocahontas, 1595–1617, 1,2
    Taylor, Sarah Strother, 1760–1822,
        1,2
    Tyler, Mary Armistead, 1761–1797,
        1,2
    Walker, Maggie Lena, 1867–1934, 1,2
    Wilson, Jessie Woodrow, 1826–1888,
        1,2
Virgins
    Cornelia, fl. 83, 1
Virologists
    Cooney, Marion, fl. 1970s, 2
Viscountess
    Conway, Anne Finch, 1631–, 1,2
Visionaries
    Barton, Elizabeth, 1506–1534, 1,2
    Bernadette of Lourdes, Saint, 1844–
        1879, 1,2
    Bourignon, Antoinette, 1616–1680, 1
    Emmerich, Anna Katharina, 1774–
        1824, 1,2
Vitellius, Aulus—Spouse
    Fundana, Galeria, fl. 20–60, 1
Vitellius, Lucius—Spouse
    Junia Calvina, fl. 48, 1
    Triaria, fl. 1–50, 1
Vladimir I—Spouse
    Anna, m. 988, 1
Vocational counselors
    Hatcher, Orie Latham, 1868–1946, 2
    Heywood, Anne, 1913–1961, 1
    Marshall, Florence M., fl. 1900s, 1
    Odencrantz, Louise Christine, fl.
        1930s, 1
Voice teachers
    Maley, Florence Turner, 1927–, 1
    Marchesi, Mathilde, 1826–1913, 1
    Nichols, Edith Elizabeth, fl. 1930s, 1
    Schoen-Rene, Anna Eugenie, 1864–
        1942, 1
    Seiler, Emma, 1821–1866, 1

Volleyball players
Fortner, Nancy Owen, fl. 1960s, 2
Peppler, Mary Jo, 1944–, 2
Ryskal, Inna, 1944–, 2
Voltaire, Francois—Mother
Arouet, Marie Marguerite Damard, 2
Voltaire, Francois—Niece
Denis, Louise Mignot, 1710–1790, 1
Volunteers
Elden, Genevieve, 2
Volunteers of America
Booth, Maud Ballington, 1865–1948, 1,2
Booth, Mrs. Ballington, 1865–1948, 2
Von Bismark, Otto—Mother
Bismarck, Louise Wilhemine Mencken von, 1790–, 2
Von Meck, Sonia—Mother
Meck, Nadezhda von, fl. 1880s, 2
Von Wrangell, Baron—Spouse
Von Wrangell, Baroness, fl. 1830s, 2
Voodoo
Laveau, Marie, fl. 1800s, 2
Leveau, Marie, 1827–, 2
Voters
Swain, Louisa Ann, 1800–, 1,2
Walker, Mary, fl. 1770s, 2
White, Mary Jarrett, fl. 1920s, 2

W

WAGE founder
Maupin, Joyce, 1914–, 2
WASP
Marsh, Clara Jo, fl. 1940s, 1
WASPS founder
Love, Nancy Harkness, 1914–, 1,2
WAVES
Hancock, Joy Bright, 1898–, 1,2
Horton, Mildred Helen McAfee, 1900–, 1
Kennedy, Dolores G., fl. 1940s, 2
McAfee, Mildred Helen, 1900–, 1,2
WCTU
Leavitt, Mary Greenleaf Clement, 1830–1912, 2
WOW founder
Janney, Mary Draper, fl. 1940s, 2
Wagner, Richard—Spouse
Wagner, Cosima, 1837–1930, 1,2
Wagner, Minna Planer, 1809–1866, 1
Waldo, Cornelius—Spouse
Waldo, Faith Savage, 1683–1760, 2

Waldo, Daniel—Spouse
Waldo, Rebecca Salisbury, 1731–1811, 2
Wales, George, Prince—Friend
Hertford, Isabella, Marchioness of, 1760–1834, 1,2
Waleski, Count—Spouse
Ricci, Anne-Marie de, 1820–1905, 1
Walkers
Benham, Gertrude, fl. 1900s, 2
Moore, Barbara, 1904–1977, 2
Weaver, Eula, 1889–, 2
Wallace, Horace Binney—Mother
Wallace, Susan Binney, fl. 1810s, 1
Walpole, Horace—Friend
Berry, Agnes, 1764–1862, 1
War correspondents
Chapelle, Georgette "Dickey" Meyer, 1920–1965, 2
Howard, Besse(e), fl. 1940s, 2
Kilgore, Margaret, fl. 1970s, 2
Trotta, Liz, 1937–, 2
War criminals
Grese, Irma, 1923–1945, 1,2
Koch, Ilse, 1907–1967, 1,2
War workers
See also
Civil War workers
Queen, Norma Yerger, fl. 1940s, 2
Salm-Salm, Agnes Elisabeth Winona LeClerq Joy, Princess, 1840–1912, 2
Ward, Artemas—Spouse
Ward, Sarah Trowbridge, 1724–1788, 1
Ward, Humphrey—Mother
Arnold, Julia Sorrell, fl. 1850s, 2
Ward, Humphrey—Spouse
Ward, Mary Augusta Arnold, 1851–1920, 2
Warriors
Hsieh-Ping-Ying, fl. 1920s, 1
Hua Mu-Lan, fl. 400s, 1
Kahinah Dahiyah Dint Thaabita., 2
Liu Tsui, fl. 1930s, 1
Pai Ku-Niang Pai, fl. 1930s, 1
Tremoulle, Charlotte de la, Countess of Derby, fl. 1640s, 1
Wetamoo, squaw sachem of Pocasset, fl. 1670s, 2
Washington
Agranoff, Shirley Haft, fl. 1930s, 2
Clark, Adelaide, 2
Cline, Minerva Jane Mayo, 1847–, 2

Anderson, Mary, 1872–1964, 1,2
Anderson, Mary Christofferson, d. 1928, 2
Babcock, Bernie, 1868–, 2
Bacon, Dorothy, 2
Bacon, Peggy, 1895–, 1,2
Bailey, Margaret Jewett, fl. 1850s, 2
Baird, Elizabeth, fl. 1840s, 2
Bambara, Toni Cade, fl. 1950s, 2
Barrett, Rona, 1934–, 2
Bauer, Catherine Krouse, 1905–1964, 2
Behrins, Harriet Frances, 1830–, 2
Bennett, Kay, fl. 1920s, 2
Benson, Margaret, fl. 1970s, 2
Berckman, Evelyn, 1900–, 1,2
Berkeley, Ellen Perry, 2
Berman, Avis, 2
Bernard, Jessie, 1903–, 2
Beveridge, Hortense, fl. 1950s, 2
Bixby-Smith, Sarah, fl. 1870s, 2
Bonner, Katherine, 1849–, 2
Boyce, Neith, d. 1951, 2
Brent, Linda, pseud., 2
Brown, Harriet Connor, 2
Buckley, Helen Dallam, 1899–, 2
Burroughs, Margaret, 1917–, 2
Cabeza de Baca, Fabiola, 1896–, 2
Caine, Lynn, fl. 1970s, 2
Callahan, Jean, fl. 1960s, 2
Camacho, Mathilde "Dita", 2
Campbell, Janet, 1947–, 2
Carter, Mary E., fl. 1970s, 2
Chessman, Andrea, 2
Chicago, Judy, 1939–, 2
Clark, Eleanor, 1913–, 2
Cook, Alice Hanson, 2
Cooper, Louise Field, 1905–, 1,2
Cott, Nancy F., 1780–1835, 2
Crawford, Lucy, fl. 1840s, 2
Curran, Pearl, 1883–1937, 2
Davidson, Sara, 1943–, 2
Davis, Madelyn, 2
De Ford, Miriam Allen, 2
Decter, Midge, 1927–, 2
Deutsch, Helen, 2
Dillon, Diane, 2
Dillon, Fannie Charles, 1881–1947, 1,2
Dunbar, Roxanne, fl. 1970s, 2
Eckstorm, Fannie Pearson Hardy, 1865–1946, 2
Edmiston, Susan, fl. 1970s, 2
Eisenhower, Julie Nixon, 1948–, 2

Fallis, Guadalupe Valdes, 1941–, 2
Fazan, Adrienne, fl. 1930s, 2
Feingold, Pauline, fl. 1970s, 2
Felton, Rebecca Ann Latimer, 1835–1930, 2
Ferguson, Renee, 2
Ferguson, Sarah, fl. 1970s, 2
Fermon, Nicole, fl. 1970s, 2
Fox, Ancella M., 1847–1920, 2
Frankfort, Ellen, 2
Fremont, Jessie Ann Benton, 1824–1902, 1,2
Garland, Phyl, fl. 1950s, 2
Gaynor, Jessie Lovel Smith, 1863–1921, 2
Gilbert, Susan, 2
Gilman, Dorothy, pseud., 1923–, 2
Goodman, Emily Jane, 1940–, 2
Gornick, Vivian, 2
Graves, Mrs. A. J., 2
Green, Mary W., 2
Greenebaum, Louise G., 2
Grosvenor, Verta Mae, 1939–, 2
Hague, Parthenia Antoinette, fl. 1860s, 2
Hall, Sharlot Mabridth, 1870–1943, 1,2
Hamilton, Eleanor, fl. 1970s, 2
Hayden, Julie, 1939–, 2
Hayward, Brooke, 1937–, 2
Healey, Caroline, fl. 1800s, 2
Helson, Ravenna, 2
Hennig, Margaret, 2
Henning, Margaret, fl. 1970s, 2
Hershey, Lenore, 1920–, 2
Hollander, Anne, fl. 1970s, 2
Holm, Jeanne M., fl. 1940s, 2
Hopkins, Sarah Winnemucca, 1844–1891, 2
Horner, Matina Souretis, 1939–, 2
Horowitz, Janice M., fl. 1970s, 2
Houston, Jessie W., 1900–, 2
Hughes, Elizabeth, fl. 1870s, 2
Ivins, Virginia Wilcox, 1827–, 2
Jacobs, Jane, 1916–, 2
Jacoby, Susan, fl. 1970s, 2
Jardim, Anne, fl. 1970s, 2
Jones, Adelaide H., fl. 1950s, 2
Jones, Gail (Gayl), 1949–, 1,2
Judd, Laura Fish, 1804–, 2
Keller, Evelyn Fox, 1936–, 2
Kempton, Sally, 1943–, 2
King, Coretta Scott, 1927–, 2
Klaben, Helen, 2

Klumpke, Anna Elizabeth, 1856–1942, 1,2
Knowlton, Helen Mary, 1832–1918, 2
Koedt, Anne, fl. 1960s, 2
Langhorne, Orra, fl. 1880s, 2
Lasoff, Anne, 1922–, 2
Latham, Maude Moore, 1871–, 2
Lebowitz, Frances Ann, 1950–, 2
Leigh, Carolyn, 1926–1983, 2
Logan, Martha Daniel(l), 1702–1779, 1,2
Logan, Mary Simmerson Cunningham, 1838–1923, 2
Long, Shelley, 2
Loring, Emilie Baker, d. 1951, 1,2
Lowe-Porter, Helen Tracy, 1876–1963, 2
Lunney, Jessie Mae Wenck, 1870–1961, 2
Lynn, Elizabeth Cook, 1930–, 2
Mainardi, Pat, fl. 1970s, 2
Marot, Helen, 1865–1940, 1,2
Marshall, (Sarah) Catherine Wood, 1914–1983, 1,2
Mason, Emily Virginia, 1815–1909, 1,2
Mathews, Mary McNair, fl. 1860s, 2
McLaughlin, Mary Louise M., 1847–1939, 1,2
McPherson, Myra, 1935–, 2
Miller, Jean Baker, fl. 1970s, 2
Miyasaki, Gail Y., 1949–, 2
Moreman, Grace E., fl. 1970s, 2
Mountain Wolf Woman, 1884–1960, 2
Mourning Dove "Hum-Ishu-Ma", 1888–1936, 2
Nowell, Elizabeth Davis, fl. 1900s, 2
O'Neill, Lois Decker, fl. 1940s, 2
Parsons, Harriet Oettinger, 1906–1983, 1,2
Pateman, Pat, 2
Peary, Jo, 2
Perez, Soledad, 2
Pickering, Ruth, 1920–1970, 2
Polite, Carlene Hatcher, 1932–, 2
Popkes, Opal Lee, 1920–, 2
Prowda, Judith G., fl. 1970s, 2
Romanelli, Elaine, fl. 1970s, 2
Roos, Barbara, fl. 1970s, 2
Roosevelt, Blanche Tucker, 1853–1898, 2
Roosevelt, Ruth, fl. 1970s, 2
Roth, Lillian, 1910–, 1,2
Schaefer, Mary Cherubin, 1886–, 2

Schein, Virginia, 2
Schimmel, Gertrude D. T., 1918–, 2
Schwartz, Helene, fl. 1970s, 2
Seifer, Nancy, 2
Sekaquaptewa, Jelen, 1898–, 2
Smith, Dody Wilson, fl. 1940s, 2
Starr, Eliza Allen, 1824–1901, 2
Stenhouse, Fanny, 2
Sternburg, Janet, fl. 1970s, 2
Stockham, Alice Bunker, fl. 1880s, 2
Stoughton, Louise, fl. 1870s, 2
Sullivan, Elizabeth, fl. 1970s, 2
Syfers, Judy, 2
Tax, Meredith, fl. 1970s, 2
Toklas, Alice Babette, 1877–1967, 1,2
Toscano, Carmen, 2
Trambley, Estela Portillo, 1936–, 2
Von Riedesel, Frederika, Baroness, fl. 1770s, 2
Williams, Elizabeth Whitney, fl. 1900s, 2
Wiser, Vivian, fl. 1950s, 2
Witke, Roxane, fl. 1970s, 2
Woodberry, Mary Dodge, fl. 1600s, 2
Writers, Asian-American
  Kaneko, Helen Aoki, 1919–, 2
Writers, Australian
  Dunne, Mary Chavelita, 1859–1945, 2
  Greer, Germaine, 1939–, 2
Writers, Austrian
  Adamson, Joy (Freiderike Victoria), 1910–1980, 1,2
  Pfeiffer, Ida Laura Reyer, 1797–1806, 1,2
Writers, Canadian
  Munro, Alice, 1931–, 2
Writers, Chicana
  Rivera, Marina, 1942–, 2
Writers, Chinese
  Berssenbrugge, Mei-Mei, 1947–, 2
  Chang, Diana, fl. 1950s, 2
  Kingston, Maxine Hong, 1940–, 2
  Sansan, fl. 1960s, 2
Writers, Croatian
  Brlic-Mazuranic, Ivana, 1874–1938, 2
  Jarnevic, Dragojla, 1812–1973, 2
Writers, Cuban
  Fletcher, Alice Cunningham, 1838–1923, 1,2
Writers, Czechoslovakian
  Podjavorinska, Ludmila, d. 1951, 2
Writers, Dutch
  Tinne, Alexandrina, 1835–1868, 1,2
Writers, Egyptian
  Said, Amina el, fl. 1970s, 2

Writers, Polish
  Dabrowska, Maria, 1889–1965, 2
Writers, Portuguese
  Barreno, Maria Isabel, 2
  Horta, Maria Teresa, fl. 1970s, 2
Writers, Puerto Rican
  Mier, Isabel Alonso de, 1886–, 2
Writers, Russian
  Boyarska, Rivka, fl. 1960s, 2
  Dean, Vera Micheles, 1903–1972, 1,2
  Emelianova, Helen, fl. 1970s, 2
  Hasanovitz, Elizabeth, 2
  Keldysh, Lyudmila Vseyolodovna,
    1904–, 1,2
  Kuznetsova, Larisa, 2
  Peruanskaya, Valeria, 2
  Stasova, Helena, 1873–1966, 2
  Svetlanova, E., 2
Writers, South African
  Jabavu, Nontanto "Noni", 1921–, 2
  Jonker, Ingrid, 1933–1965, 2
Writers, Spanish
  Castra, Ann de, fl. 1629, 2
  Egeria, Abbess, 2
  Teresa Spagnuola, pseud., 2
Writers, Swiss
  Necker, Suzanne Curchod, Madam,
    1739–1794, 1,2
  Sandoz, Henrietta, fl. 1880s, 2
Writers, Zambian
  Brown, Denise Scott, 1931–, 2
Wu—Consort
  Hsi Shih, fl. 485BC, 1
Wyandot Indian Cemetery
  Conley sisters, fl. 1910s, 2
Wyatt, Francis—Spouse
  Wyatt, Margaret, fl. 1620s, 2
Wyoming
  Downey, June, 2
  Dunnewald, Helen Bishop, 1891–, 2
  Hill, Evelyn Corthell, 1886–, 2
  Hill, Margaret Ohler, 2
  Leigh, Jenny, d. 1876, 2
  Moore, Vandi, 1912–, 2
  Morris, Esther Hobart McQuigg
    Slack, 1814–1902, 1,2
  Northen, Rebecca Tyson, 1910–, 2
  Ross, Nellie Tayloe, 1876–1977, 1,2
  Simpson, Margaret Burnett, 1874–
    1974, 2
  Stevens, Alice Hardie, 1900–, 2
  Thomson, Thyra Godfrey, 1916–, 2

Wythe, George—Friend
  Broadnax, Lydia, 2

X

X-ray technicians
  Ascheim, Elizabeth Fleishman, 1859–
    1905, 2

Y

YWCA
  Anderson, Eleanor Copenhaver, fl.
    1930s, 1
  Bowles, Eva Del Vakia, 1875–1943, 2
  Cratty, Mabel, 1868–1928, 2
  Cushman, Vera Charlotte Scott,
    1876–1946, 2
  Danner, Louise Rutledge, 1863–
    1943, 1
  Haynes, Elizabeth A. Ross, 1883–
    1953, 1,2
  Hunton, Addie D. Waites, 1875–
    1943, 2
  Mason, Lucy Randolph, 1882–1959, 2
  Simms, Daisy Florence, 1873–1923, 2
  Woodsmall, Ruth Frances, 1883–
    1963, 1,2
Yachting
  Allix, Martine, fl. 1970s, 2
  Choynowska-Liskiewicz, Krystyna,
    fl. 1970s, 2
  Davison, Ann(e), fl. 1950s, 2
  Francis, Clare, 1946–, 2
  Sites, Sharon, fl. 1960s, 2
Yanaovskii, Semyon Ivanov—Spouse
  Yanaovskii, Irina Baranof, fl. 1810s, 2
Yarmouth, Lord—Spouse
  Fagniani, Maria, 1711–1856, 1
Yodlers
  Carson, Sally (Bonnie Lou), 1926–, 2
Yoga teachers
  Kalso, Anna, fl. 1950s, 2
Young, Brigham—Spouse
  Young, Clarissa Decker, fl. 1840s, 2
Young Women's Christian Association
  See
  YWCA
Youth leaders
  Holbrook, Sabra Rollins, 1912–, 1

Geographic Index

433

Borluut, Isabella, 1
Bovy, Vina, 1
Brandt, Isabella, 1
Cammaerts, Emile, 1
Christina the Astonishing,
Claessens, Maria, 1
Colette, Adele-Eugenie-Sidonie, 2
Collart (Collaert), Marie, 1,2
Deckers, Jeanne, 2
Delacroix, Caroline, Baronness de
    Vaugham, 1
Derscheid, Marie, 1
Desislava, 1
Devalet, Germaine, 2
Dirks, Lysken, 1
Djanel, Lily, 1
Driessche, Therese Vande, 2
Dumon, Marte, 2
Elizabeth, 1
Flahaut, Marianne, 1
Folville, Juliette, 1
Fourment, Helena, 1,2
Gamond, Isabelle Gatti de, 2
Geefs, Fanny Isabelle Marie, 1
Genevieve of Brabant, 1
Gertrude of Nivelles, 1
Gevers, Marie, 2
Giovanna, Elisabetta Antonia Ro-
    mana Maria, 1
Gorr, Rita, 2
Hare, Jeannette R., 1
Hemessen, Catharina van, 2
Henin, Marie-Louise, 2
Hirsch, Clara de, Baroness, 1
Horebout, Susanna(e), 2
Joseph Calasanctius, 1
Josephine, Charlotte, 1
Kindt, Adele, 1
LaLaing, Marie-Christine de, 1
Lamy, Paule, 2
Malaise, Elizabeth, 2
Marie, 1
Marie Alicia, Sister, 1
Marie Christine de Lalaing, 1
Marie Clothilde, 1
Marie Jose, Charlotte Sophie Hen-
    riette Gabrielle, 1
Mary, Mother Mary of Jesus, 1
Mary Liliane, Princess of Rethy, 1
Mary of Oignies, 1
Mirat, Mathilde (Madame Heine), 1
Modave, Jeanne, 1
Oboussier, Helene, 2
Paola, Donna Paola Margherita
    Maria, 1

Peeters, Clara, 2
Petit, Gabrielle, 1
Petrides, Frederique, 2
Pharailda, 1
Popelin, Marie, 2
Reimacker-Legot, Marguerite de, 2
Renson, Marcelle, 2
Rubens, Maria, 1
Sasa, Marie-Constance, 1
Sylva, Marguerite, 1
Thuliez, Louise, 2
Tirlinks, Liewena, 1
Van Orroer, Beatrice, 1
Van Vooren, Monique, 1
Wandru, 1
Ykens, Catherine, 1
Yourcenar, Marguerite, 1,2
Belgium/France
Camargo, Marie Anne de Cupis de,
    1,2
Belgium/US
Bayer, Adele Parmentier, 2
Hepburn, Audrey, 1,2
Inez, Colette, 2
Von Furstenberg, Diane Simone Mi-
    chelle, 2
Bhutan
Wangchuck, Dechhen Wang-mo, 2
Biblical
Abi, 1
Abiah, 1
Abigail, 2
Abigail, 1
Abihail, 1
Abihail, 1
Abimelech, 1
Abishag, 1
Abital, 1
Achsah, 1
Adah, 1
Adah, 1
Ahinoam, 1
Ahinoam, 1
Ahlai, 1
Aholibah, 1
Aholibamah, 1
Anah, 1
Anna of Jerusalem, 1
Anne, 1
Aquila, 1
Asenath, 1
Atarah, 1
Athalia, 1
Azubah, 1

Azubah, 1
Baara, 1
Barzillai's daughter, 1
Bashemath, 1
Bassmath, 1
Bathemath, 1
Bathsheba, 1,2
Belshazzar's mother, 1
Bernice, 1
Bethel, Woman of, 1
Bethsabee, 1
Bilhah, 1
Bithiah, 1
Cain's wife, 1
Candace, 1
Chanaanite woman, 1
Chloe, 1
Claudia, 1
Claudia Procula, 1,2
Cleopas, wife of, 1
Cozbi, 1
Damaris, 1
Deborah, 1,2
Deborah, 1
Delilah, 1,2
Diana, 1
Dinah, 1
Dorcas (or Tabitha), 1,2
Eglah, 1
Elisha's mother, 1
Elisheba, 1
Elizabeth, 1,2
Endor, Witch of, 1
Eodias, 1
Ephah, 1
Ephrath, 1
Esther, 1,2
Eunice, 1,2
Eve, 1,2
Ezekiel's wife, 1
Gilead's wife, 1
Gomer, 1
Hadad's wife, 1
Hadassah, 1
Hagar, 1,2
Haggith, 1
Hammoleketh, 1
Hamutal, 1
Hannah, 2
Hannah, 1
Hannah, 1
Hazeleponi, 1
Helah, 1
Heph-Zibah, 1

Herodias, 1,2
Herodias's daughter, 1
Hiram's mother, 1
Hodesh, 1
Hodiah, 1
Hosea, wife of, 1
Huldah, 1
Hushim, 1
Ichabod's mother, 1
Isaiah's wife, 1
Jabez's mother, 1
Jael, 1
Jairus' daughter, 1
Jecholiah, 1
Jedidah, 1
Jehoaddan, 1
Jehosheba, 1
Jehudijah, 1
Jemima, 1
Jepthah's daughter, 1
Jeremiah's mother, 1
Jerioth, 1
Jeroboam's wife, 1
Jerusalem, woman of, 1
Jerusha, 1
Jezebel, 1,2
Joanna, 1
Joash of Judah, 1
Job's wife, 1,2
Jochebed, 1,2
Judah's wife, 1
Judith, 1
Julia, 1
Keturah, 1
Kezia, 1
Leah, 1,2
Lilith, 1
Lo-Ruhamah, 1
Lois, 1,2
Lot's wife, 1,2
Lydia, 1,2
Maachah, 1
Maachah, 1
Maachah, 1
Maachah, 1
Maachah, 1
Maachah, 1
Maachah, 1
Machabees, mother of, 1
Mahalah, 1
Mahalath, 1
Mahalath, 1
Manoah's wife, 1
Mara, 1

Elizabeth Stuart, 2
Elizabeth of Bohemia, 2
Esch, Mathilde, 1
Janauschek, Francesco (Fanny) Ro-
    mana Magdalena, 1,2
Kablick, Josephine, 1
Konig, Barbara, 2
Landau, Resel, 2
Ludmilla, 1
Maria of Hungary and Bohemia, 2
Poetting, Adrienne, 1
Stolz, Teresa, 1
Bohemia/US
Goldsmith, Sophia, 1
Bolivia
Villa, Amelia Chopitea, 1,2
Zamudio, Adela, 2
Brazil
Bonomi, Maria, 1
Brandt, Alice, 2
Bueno, Maria Ester Audion, 1,2
Cari, Teresa, 2
Castro e Silva de Vinvenzi, Maria de
    Lourdes, 2
D'Orleans, Isabel Braganza, 1
De Jesus, Carolina Maria, 2
Djanira, 1
Dulce, Sister, 1
Estrela, Maria Augusto Generoso, 1
Fabbri, Tecla, 2
Garibaldi, Anita, 2
Gilberto, Astrud, 2
Haydee, Marcia, 2
Horrocks, Amy Elsie, 1
Isabel d'Orleans, 1
Isabella of Brazil, 1
Jesus, Carolina Maria de, 2
Leopoldina, D. Maria, 1,2
Lopes, Maria, 2
Lopez, Rita Lobato Velho, 1
Lutz, Bertha, 2
Matarazzo, Maria Pia Esmerelda, 2
Motta Diniz, Francisca de, 2
Nizia Floresta, 1
Novaes, (Pinto) Guiomar, 1,2
Pinto, Apolonia, 1
Purim, Flora, 2
Queiroz, Carlotta Pereira de, 2
Quiteria de Jesus Medeiros, Maria, 1
Sayao, Bidu, 1
Vierra da Silva, Maria Helena, 1,2
Brazil/US
Bambace, Angela, 2
Dietrich, Martha Jane, 2

Bulgaria
Bachvarova, Radka, 2
Ben Joseph, Rojy, 2
Botyo, Ivanka Petrova, 2
Boudevska-Gantcheva, Adriana, 1
Boyadgieva, Lada, 2
Budevska, Adriana Kuncheva,
    pseud., 1,2
Dimitrova, Anastasie, 1
Dimitrova, Lilyana Nikolova, 1,2
Donnell-Vogt, Radka, 2
Filaretova, Iordana Kikolaeva, 1
Foutekova, Raina Pop Georgieva, 1
Georgieve, Raina, 2
Golovina, Anastasia, 1
Ionna, 2
Khristova, Ivanka, 2
Maimunkova, Anna Krusteva, 2
Marie-Louise, 2
Morfova, Khristina Vasileva, 2
Nedeva, Zlatina, 1,2
Nikolova, Iordanka Georgieva, 2
Obretenova, Tonka Tihovitza, 1
Pavlovich, Nikola, 1
Petkova, Baba Nedelia, 1
Petrova, Helen Assen, 1
Piskova, Vela Arkhakova, 2
Popova, Katya Asenova, 2
Simidtchieva, Ekaterina A., 1
Snezhina, Elena, 1,2
Tabakova, Tsvetana Borisova, 2
Tchankova, Iordanka, 1
Tocheva, Anastasia, 1
Venkova, Tota, 1
Zheljazova, Binka, 2
Bulgaria/US
Welitch, Ljuba, 1,2
Burgundy
Adelaide, Saint, 1
Burma
Aw Sian, Sally, 2
Daw Thein Tin, (Madam U Thant), 1
Luce, Daw Tee Tee, 2
Byzantia
Ann of Savoy, 1
Ann, consort of Alexius II (Agnes of
    France), 1
Anna Comnena, 1,2
Anne of Savoy, 1,2
Comnena, Anna, 1,2
Constance of Hohenstaufen, 1
Dalassena, Anna, 1
Ducas, Irene, 1
Irene, 1

Gay, Marion, 2
Gelber, Sylvia M., 2
Gillese, Eileen, 2
Gordon, Jeanne, 1
Graham, Gwethalyn, 1
Grayson, Ethel Vaughan Kirk, 1
Greene, Nancy Catherine, 2
Gullen, Augusta Stow, 1
Guyart, Marie de l'Incarnation, 1
Gye, Madame Albani, 1
Haddad, Claire, 2
Hagen, Alice Mary Egan, 2
Hamilton, Cicely Viets Dakin, 2
Hancocks, Elizabeth, 2
Harman, Eleanor, 2
Harmer, Bertha, 1
Harpur, V. Lorraine, 2
Harris, Arlene, 1
Harrison, Helen, 1
Hart, Pearl, 1,2
Hartman, Grace, 2
Havoc, June, 1,2
Hayden, Melissa, 1,2
Hebert, Anne, 2
Hind, (Ella) Cora, 1,2
Hines, Mimi, 2
Hogg, Helen Sawyer, 1
Hogg, Mary Eileen, 2
Holden, Joyce, 2
Hoodless, Adelaide Sophie Hunter, 1,2
Hopson, Elizabeth Louise, 1
Howard, Kathleen, 1
Howard-Lock, Helen E., 2
Jamieson, Nina Moore, 1
Jewett, Paulina, 2
Jones, Orlo Louise, 2
Kain, Karen Alexandria, 2
Keffer, Marion Christena, 2
Keith, Marion, 1
Kelly, Judith, 1
Kelton, Pert, 2
Kent, Barbara, 2
Kerr, Muriel, 1
Kimber, Diana Clifford, 1
King, Violet, 1
Kinnear, Helen Alice, 1
Lamarsh, Judy, 1,2
Lambart, Evelyn, 2
Lapointe, Renaude, 2
Laurence, Margaret, 2
Lillie, Beatrice, Lady Peel, 1,2
Lindgren, Mavis, 2
Littlewood, Margaret, 2

Livesay, Florence Hamilton Randal, 1
Livingston, Mildred Ruth, 2
MacDonald, Lucy Maude Montgomery, 1
MacDonald, V. May, 1
MacGill, Elsie Gregory, 1,2
MacKenzie, Giselle, 1,2
MacLeod, Charlotte, 1
MacLeod, Enid, 2
MacPhail, Agnes Campbell, 1,2
Macbeth, Madge Hamilton Lyons, 1
Mackay, Isabel Ecclestone Macpherson, 1
Macpherson, Jay, 2
Magill, Eileen, 1
Magnussen, Karen, 2
Mallette, Gertrude Ethel, 1
Mance, Jeanne, 1,2
Marriott, Adelaide, 2
Marshall, Lois, 1
Martin, Andrea, 2
McClung, Nellie Mooney, 1
McConney, Florence, 2
McGee, Pamela Jo Lee, 2
McKinney, Louise, 1
McMurchy, Helen, 1
McWilliams, Margaret, 1
Merriman, Brenda, 2
Milstead, Violet, 2
Mitchell, Christine, 2
Mitchell, Joni, 2
Moffat, Agnes K., 2
Mortimer, Ann, 2
Morton, Elizabeth Homer, 1
Mowat, Angus, 1
Munro, Alice, 2
Murphy, Emily, 1,2
Murray, Anne, 2
Murray, Marjorie, 2
Nadeau, Claudette, 2
Nelligan, Kate, 2
Nicholas, Cindy, 2
O'Hara, Catherine, 2
Orr, Marion, 1
Owens, Margaret, 2
Parent, Madeleine, 2
Parker, Cecilia, 2
Parlby, Irene, 1,2
Parlow, Kathleen Mary, 1,2
Paterson, Daphne, 1
Pavloska, Irene, 1
Peacocke, Elizabeth, 2
Pearce, Theodocia, 1
Pickthall, Marjorie Lowry Christie, 1

Wei Fu-Jen, 1
Wei Shuo, 2
Wen Shu, 2
Wong, Ah Mae, 1
Wu, Eva, 1
Wu Chao (Hou), 2
Wu Y-Fang, 1
Yang, Kuei-Fei, 1
Yang Mei-Tzu, 2
Yu Hsuan-Chi, 1
Yu Kuliang, 1

China/US
Bemis, Lalu Lathoy "China Polly", 1,2
Berssenbrugge, Mei-Mei, 2
Chang, Diana, 2
Chang, Marguerite Shue-Wen, 2
Chiang, Fay, 2
Gee, Virginia, 2
Goon, Toy Len Chin, 1,2
Kaneko, Helen Aoki, 2
Kingston, Maxine Hong, 2
Lee, Lucy, 2
Lee, Ruse Hum, 2
Mar, Laureen, 2
Shih, Hsio-Yen, 2
Sung, Betty Lee, 2
Tong, Kaity, 2
Wong, Anna May (Lu Tsong), 1,2
Wu, Chien-Shiung, 1,2
Yup, Paula, 2

Colombia
Acosta, Ofelia Uribe, 2
Beltrain, Manuel, 1
Califa, Amazon, 2
Crovo, Maria Elena Jimenez de, 2
Cruz, Manuelita de la, 1
Cuevas Cancino, Esmerelda Arboleda de, 2
De Amaral, Olga, 2
Florentina, 1
Francisco Josefa de la Concep., 1
Gomez, Josefa Acevedole, 1
Reyes, Mercedes Abrego de, 1
Samper, Gabriela, 2
Santa Maria, Manuela Sanz de, 1

Cook Island
Makea, Takau Ariki, 1

Corinth
Neaira, 2

Costa Rica
Castro de Barish, Emila, 2

Crete
Theano, 1

Croatia
Brlic-Mazuranic, Ivana, 2
Jarnevic, Dragojla, 2
Murska, Ilma di, 1
Ternina, Milka, 1

Croatia/US
Evanich, Manda, 2

Cuba
Abreu de Estevez, Marta, 1
Acosts, Aida de, 1
Alonso, Alicia, 1,2
Arencibia, Marta Abreu y, 1
Avellaneda y Arteaga, Gertrudis Gomez, 1
Betancourt, Ana, 1,2
Borrero, Juana, 1
Castro, Argez Lina Gonzales, 2
Chilia, Elvira Rey, 1
Dolz, Luisa Maria, 1
Espin, Vilma, 2
Figueredo, Candelaria, 1
Garcia Montes, Teresa, 1
Grajales, Mariana, 2
Otero, Emma, 1
Ryder, Jeannette, 1
Teurbe Tolon, Emilia, 1
Torre, Marta de la, 1
Zambrana, Luisa Perez de, 1

Cuba/US
Anderson, Bonnie Marie, 2
Breckinridge, Aida de Acosta, 1,2
Cruz, Celia, 2
Fletcher, Alice Cunningham, 1,2
Gonzalez, Luisa, 2
Mandel, Carola Panerai, 1

Cyprus
Corner, Caterina, 2

Czechoslovakia
Caslavska-Oklozil, Vera, 2
Cecelia, 2
Chytilova, Vera, 2
Clauss-Szarvady, Wilhelmine, 1
Connolly, Olga Fikotova, 2
Cori, Gerty Theresa Radnitz, 1,2
Dalossy, Ellen, 1
Destinn, Emily Kitti, 1,2
Dussek, Josepha Hambacher, 1,2
Fibingerova, Helena, 2
Fikotova, Olga, 2
Horakova, Milada, 1
Jaburkova, Jozka Palaeckova, 2
Kimbrell, Marketa, 2
Kirschner, Marie, 1
Kohen, Gutel, 2

Komlosi, Irma, 1
Kralova, Hana, 2
Krasnohorska, Elisa, pseud., 1
Kuderikova, Marie, 2
Kvapilova, Jana Kubesova, 1,2
Laukota, Herminie, 1
Marothy-Soltesova, Elena, 2
Masaryk, Charlotte Garrigue, 1
Mueller, Maria, 1
Muller, Maria, 2
Navritolova, Martina, 2
Nemcova, Bozena, 1,2
Novotna, Jarmila, 1
Pauly, Rosa, 1
Pitzinger, Gertrude, 1
Podjavorinska, Ludmila, 2
Popp, Lucia, 2
Raabeova, Hedvika, 2
Soltesova, Elena Marothy, 1
Stuerm, Ruza Lukavaska, 1
Svetla, Karolina Rottova, 1
Svobodova, Ruzena Capova, 1
Swanger, Ludmilla E., 1
Varsova, Terezia, 1
Wetche, Ludmila Vojackova, 1
Zanova, Aja, 1
Zatopkova, Dana Ingrova, 2
Czechoslovakia/US
Kucera, Zdenka, 2
Saxl, Eva R., 1
Schumann-Heink, Ernestine Rossler, 1,2
Slezak, Eva, 2
Denmark
Ahlmann, Lis, 2
Alexandra of Denmark, 1,2
Alexandrine, 1
Ammundsen, Esther, 2
Andersen, Anne Marie, 1,2
Anna Sophia, Princess of Denmark, 2
Anne-Marie, 1
Bang, Nina Henriette Wendeline, 1,2
Begtrup, Bodil Andreasen, 1,2
Bengtsson, Anny, 2
Bennedsen, Dorte, 2
Bjerregaard, Mrs. Ritt, 2
Braestrup, Agnete Meinert, 2
Caroline Matilda, 1
Clausen, Franciska, 2
Dinesen, Isak, pseud., 1,2
Dorothea, Queen, 2
Dragomir, 1
Fibiger, Mathilde, 1
Frijsh, Povla, 1

Frith, Inger, 2
Genee, Adeline, 1
Gjoe, Birgitte, 2
Grahn, Lucile, 1,2
Gredal, Eva, 2
Hardenberg, Anna, 2
Hasselriis, Else, 1
Heiberg, Johanne Louise Patges, 1
Henning-Jensen, Astrid, 2
Holm, Birte Roll, 2
Hovmand, Annelise, 2
Hveger, Ragnhild, 2
Ingrid, 1
Jensen, Ella, 2
Jensen, Fanny, 2
Jorgensen-Krogh, Marie, 1
Juliane Marie, 2
Kalso, Anna, 2
Kammersgard, Jenny, 2
Koch, Bodil, 2
Krebs, Nathalie, 2
Kristensen, Ruth, 2
Lassen, Lulu, 2
Lehmann, Inge, 1,2
Leth, Marie Gudme, 2
Ludlow, Inger P., 2
Margrethe, 1,2
Michaelis, Karin, 1,2
Moller, Agnes Slott, 1
Nielsen, Kay, 1
Nielsen, Nielsine Mathilde, 1
O'Fredericks, Alice, 2
Ostergaard, Lise, 2
Paderson, Inger, 2
Pedersen, Helga, 2
Rasmussen, Franka, 2
Saxtorph, Matthias, 2
Schanne, Margrethe, 1
Schnorr von Carolsfield, Malwine, 1
Soreff, Helen, 2
Staehr-Nielsen, Eva, 2
Stallknecht, Kirsten, 2
Trock, Paula, 2
Ulfeld, Lenora Christine, 1
Zahle, Nathalie, 1
Ziesnsis, Margaretta, 1
Denmark/US
Bulow, Karen, 2
Dominican Republic
Anacaona, 1
Bellini [Billini], Maria Nicolasa, 1
Bernardino, Minerva, 1
Duarte, Rosa, 1
Henriquez, Salome Urena de, 1

Ancaster, Mary, Duchess, 2
Anderson, Betty Harvie, 2
Anderson, Elizabeth Garrett, 1,2
Anderson, Emily, 2
Anderson, Lucy Philpot, 1
Anderson, Stella Benson, 2
Anderton, Margaret, 1
Andrews, Julie, 1,2
Andrews, Lucilla, 2
Aner, Kerstin, 2
Angel, Heather, 1,2
Angelus, Muriel, 1
Ann Medica, 2
Anne, 1,2
Anne, Countess of Sunderland, 1
Anne Elizabeth Alice Louise, 1,2
Anne Neville, 2
Anne of Cleves, 1,2
Anne of Denmark, 1,2
Anning, Mary, 1,2
Anspach, Elizabeth Berkeley, 1
Anthony, C. L., pseud., 1,2
Applebee, Constance, 2
Arber, Agnes, 2
Archer, Georgina, 2
Archer, Patricia, 2
Archibald, Lil(l)iana, 2
Argyll, Jane Warbuton, 1
Argyll, Pearl, 1
Armine, Mary, Lady, 2
Arnold, Polly, 1
Arundale, Sybil, 1
Arundel, Isabella, Countess of, 1
Ashbee, Agnes, 2
Ashbridge, Elizabeth, 1
Ashburton, Harriet Montagu Baring,
 1
Ashcroft, Peggy, Dame, 1,2
Ashford, Daisy, 2
Ashley, Katherine, 1
Ashley, Lady Sylvia, 1
Ashton, Elizabeth, 1
Ashwell, Lena Simson, Lady, 2
Ashworth, Mrs., 1
Askew, Alice J. de C., 1
Askew, Anne Byrd, 1,2
Asquith, Cynthia Mary Evelyn,
 Lady, 2
Astell, Mary, 1,2
Astor, Nancy Whitcher Langhorne,
 1,2
Athol, Katherine Marjory, 1
Aubin, Penelope, 1
Audin, Margaret, 2

Augusta, Duchess of Cambridge, 1
Augusta of Saxe-Coburg-Gartha, 1
Ault, Marie, 1
Aumale, Hawisa, 1
Aumale and Devon, Isabella de Forz,
 1
Austen, Anna, Lady, 2
Austen, Cassandra, 2
Austen, Jane, 1,2
Austen, Winifred, 1
Austin, Sarah, 1
Avice, 1
Avisa of Gloucester, 2
Aylward, Gladys, 1,2
Ayres, Gillian, 2
Ayres, Ruby Mildred, 1,2
Ayrton, Hertha Marks, 1,2
Ayrton, Matilda Chaplin, 1
Backster, Margery, 1
Bacon, Anne Cooke, 1,2
Bacon, Delia, 1,2
Bacon, Elizabeth Duke, 2
Bacon, Gertrude, 1,2
Bacon, Katherine, 1,2
Baddeley, Angela, 1
Baddeley, Hermione, 1,2
Baddeley, Sophia Snow, 1
Baden-Powell, Olive St. Claire,
 Lady, 1,2
Baggallay, Olive, 1
Bagnold, Enid Algerine, 1,2
Baillie-Saunders, Margaret Elsie
 Crowther, 1
Bainbridge, Beryl, 2
Bainbridge, Katherine, 1
Baird, Dorothea, 1
Baird, Irene, 1
Baissac, Lise de, 1
Baker, Frances, 1
Baker, Janet, Dame, 2
Baker, Katherine, 1
Baker, Lady Samuel, 1
Baker, Mary, 2
Baker, Mary, 1
Balfour, Betty, 1
Balfour, Margaret Ida, 1
Ball, Florrie, 2
Ballinger, Violet Margaret L. Hodg-
 son, 1
Bancroft, Marie Effie Wilton, Lady,
 1,2
Bankes, Mary Hawtrey, Lady, 1
Banks, Eliza S., 2
Banks, Isabella Varley Linnaeus, 1,2

Bruce-Clark, Effie, 2
Brumell, Stella, 2
Brunton, Louisa, Countess of Craven, 1
Brusselmans, Anne, 2
Bryant, Mary Broad, 1
Bryant, Sophie, 1
Bryce, Elizabeth Marion, 1
Bryher (Bryer), pseud., 2
Bubb, Ella L., 2
Bucge, 1
Buckingham, Duchess of, 2
Buckland, Mrs. Frank, 1
Buckrose, J. E., 1
Buller, Mary, 2
Bunford, Jane, 2
Bunyan, Elizabeth, 1
Burbidge, Eleanor Margaret, 2
Burden, Elizabeth, 2
Burdette-Coutts, Angela Georgina, Baroness, 1,2
Burgh, Elizabeth de, 1
Burghley, Mildred Cooke, 2
Burgoyne, Charlotte Stanley, 2
Burke, Marie, 1
Burleigh, Mildred Cooke Cecil, Lady, 1
Burne-Jones, Georgiana, 2
Burnet, Elizabeth, 1
Burnett, Frances Eliza Hodgson, 1,2
Burney, Fanny, 1,2
Burns, Anne, 1,2
Burns, Eveline Mabel, 1
Burrowes, M., 2
Burrows, Christine Mary Elizabeth, 1
Burton, Beryl, 2
Burton, Elaine, 2
Burton, Isabel Arundel, Lady, 1
Burton, Mrs. Francis, 2
Burton, Sybil, 2
Buss, Frances Mary, 1,2
Bute, Mary Wortley Montagu, 1
Butler, Charlotte, 1
Butler, Elizabeth Southerden Thompson, Lady, 1,2
Butler, Gwendoline, 2
Butler, Josephine Elizabeth, 1,2
Butler, Sydney Elizabeth Courtauld, 1
Butt, Clara, 1,2
Butterfield, Jane, 2
Byatt, A. S. (Antonia Susan), 2
Cadell, (Violet) Elizabeth, 1
Caird, (Alice) Mona, 1,2

Cairns, May Emily Finney, 1
Caldwell, Taylor, 1,2
Callaghan, Domini, 1
Callcott, Maria, Lady, 1
Calvert, Adelaide, 1
Cam, Helen Maud, 1
Cambridge, Ada, 2
Camden, Francis, 2
Cameron, Evelyn Jephson, 2
Cameron, Julia, 2
Cameron, Margaret, 2
Cameron, Mrs. Lovett, 1
Cameron, Shirley, 2
Cameron, Violet, 1
Campbell, Beatrice Stella Tanner, 2
Campbell, Charlotte, Lady, 1
Campbell, Margaret, 1
Campbell, Mrs. Patrick, 1
Campbell-Bannerman, Sarah Charlotte Bruce, 1
Cannan, Mary Ansell Barrie, 1
Canziani, Estella L. M., 1
Cappe, Catharine Harrison, 1
Cardew, Gloria, 2
Carey, Elizabeth Tanfield, Lady, 2
Carey, Rosa Nouchette, 2
Carlile, Joan, 2
Carlisle, Alexandra, 1
Carlisle, Anne, 1
Carlisle, Rosalind Frances Stanley Howard, Countess of, 1
Carne, Judy, 2
Carney, Kate, 1
Caroline of Anspach, Wilhelmina Carolina, 1,2
Caroline of Brunswick, Amelia Elizabeth Caroline, 1,2
Carpenter, Margaret Sarah Geddes, 1,2
Carpenter, Mary, 2
Carpenter, Mrs., 2
Carrington, Eva, Lade de Clifford, 1
Carroll, Madeleine, 1,2
Carter, Angela, 2
Carter, Elizabeth, 1,2
Cartland, Barbara Hamilton, 2
Cartwright, Julia, 1
Cary, Mary Rande, 1
Casalis, Jeanne de, 1
Castle, Barbara Ann Betts, 1,2
Catchpole, Margaret, 1
Catherine of Aragon, 1,2
Catherine of Braganza, 1,2
Catherine of Valois, 1,2

Catley, Anne, 1
Cavanagh, Kit, 2
Cave, Mrs. Walter, 2
Cavell, Edith Louisa, 1,2
Cavendish, Ada, 1
Cavendish, Margaret, Duchess of
  Newcastle, 1
Cazalet-Keir, Thelma, 2
Cellier, Elizabeth, 2
Centlivre, Susanna, 1,2
Chambers, Mrs. Lambert, 1
Champion de Crespigny, Rose, 1
Chantrey, Mrs., 1
Chaplin, Mrs. Charles Hill, 2
Chapman, Marion, 2
Chapone, Hester Mulso, 1,2
Chapone, Sally Kirkham (Sappho), 1
Charke, Charlotte Cibber, 1
Charles, Elizabeth Rundle, 1,2
Charles, Ethel, 2
Charlesworth, Maria Louisa, 1,2
Charlotte (Sophia) of Mecklen., 1,2
Charlotte Augusta, 1,2
Charques, Dorothy Taylor, 1
Charretie, Anna Maria, 1
Chatterton, Georgiana, Lady, 2
Chazel, Mrs., 1
Cheesman, Evelyn, 2
Chennevix, Mary, 2
Chesser, Elizabeth Sloan, 1
Chetwynd, Mrs. Henry, 1
Chevers, Sarah, 1
Cholmondeley, Mary, 1,2
Christie, Agatha (Mary Clarissa)
  Miller, Dame, 1,2
Christie, Julie, 1,2
Christina of Markyate, 2
Chudleigh, Elizabeth, 1
Chudleigh, Mary, Lady, 1
Churchill, Arabella, 2
Churchill, Caryl, 2
Churchill, Clementine Ogilvy Hozier
  Spencer, Lady, 1,2
Churchill, Frances, Duchess of Marl-
  borough, 2
Churchill, Odette Mary Celine
  Brailly Sansom, 1,2
Churchill, Sarah, Lady Audley, 1,2
Cibber, Charlotte, 2
Cibber, Susannah Maria, 1,2
Ciobotaru, Gillian Wise, 2
Clairmont, Claire, 1,2
Clare, Mary, 1
Clark, Petula, 2

Clarke, Mary Anne Thompson, 1,2
Clarke, Maude Violet, 1
Clay, Bertha M, pseud., 1
Clayden, Pauline, 1
Clayton, Charlotte Dyve, 1
Clement, Alice, 1
Clere, Elizabeth, 1
Clifford, Anne, Countess of Dorset,
  1,2
Clifford, Lucy Lane, 1
Clifford, Rosamund "fair Rosa-
  mund", 1
Clithorow, Margaret Middleton, 1
Clive, Caroline Meyse-Wigley, 2
Clough, Anne Jemima, 1,2
Clough, Prunella, 2
Coate, Mary, 1
Coates, Edith, 1
Coats, Alice M., 1
Cobden-Sanderson, Annie, 2
Cockburn, Catharine Trotter, 1
Coddington, Grace, 2
Coghill, Mrs. Henry, 1
Cogswell, Sue, 2
Cohen, Harriet, 1
Coke, Mary Campbell, 1
Coleman, Rebecca, 2
Coleridge, Mary Elizabeth, 2
Coleridge, Sara(h) Henry, 1,2
Colledge, Cecilia, 2
Collier, Constance Hardie, 1,2
Collins, Anne, 2
Collins, Jackie, 2
Collins, Jose, 1
Collins, Lottie, 2
Collyer, Mary Mitchell, 2
Colquhoun, Maureen Morfydd, 2
Colwell, Eileen Hilda, 1
Colwell, Stella, 2
Compton, Fay, 1
Compton-Burnett, Ivy, 1,2
Conlon, Kathleen, 2
Cons, Emma, 1,2
Constable, Anne, 2
Constable, Mary, 2
Conti, Italia, 1,2
Conway, Anne Finch, 1,2
Conyngham, Lady, 1
Cook, Edith Maud, 2
Cook, Eliza, 1,2
Cook, Sarah, 1
Cooke, Jean, 2
Cooke, Katherine, Lady Killigrew, 2
Cooke, Sarah, 1

Cookesley, Margaret Murray, 1
Cookson, Catherine, 2
Cooper, Charlotte, 2
Cooper, Diana, Lady, 1,2
Cooper, Gladys, Dame, 1,2
Cooper, Jilly, 2
Copley, Heather, 1
Corbeaux, Fanny, 1
Corbett, Leonora, 1
Corelli, Marie, pseud., 1,2
Corey, Catherine, 1
Corner, Beryl Dorothy, 2
Cornford, Frances Crofts Darwin, 2
Cornwallis, Caroline Frances, 1
Cost, March, 1,2
Cotton, Anne, 2
Courtauld, Louisa Perina, 2
Courtneidge, Cicely, 1,2
Courtney, Janet Hogarth, 1
Courtney, Kathleen, Dame, 1
Cousins, Mrs., 2
Coveney, Harriet, 1
Cowden-Clarke, Mary Victoria, 1,2
Cowie, Laura, 1
Cowley, Hannah Parkhurst, 1,2
Cowper, Mary Claverling, Lady, 1
Cox, Elizabeth, 1
Cox, Jane Cannon, 1
Cox, Margaret, 1
Crabbe, Sarah Elmy, 2
Craig, Edith, 1,2
Craik, Dinah Maria Mulock, 1,2
Craik, Georgiana, 2
Crapo, Joanna, 2
Crathorne, Isabel, 2
Crawford, Mimi, 1
Crawford, Miss, 1
Crescentia, Sister, 1
Crommelin, May, 1
Cromwell, Elizabeth, 2
Crosbie, Diana "Fawn" Viscountess, 2
Cross, Joan, 1
Crossley, Winifred, 1,2
Crowe, Catherine Stevens, 1,2
Crowe, Jocelyn, 1
Crowe, Sylvia, 2
Crowfoot, Dorothy Mary, 1
Cruger, Mrs. Douglas, 2
Cullis, Winifred Clara, 1
Cumberland, Anne, Duchess, 2
Cumming, Henrietta, 1
Cunard, Nancy, 2
Cunnliffe-Offeley, Mrs. Foster, 2

Curie, Mary, 2
Currer, Elizabeth, 1
Cust, Aileen, 2
Cuthburge, 1
Cutler, Kate, 1
Cynethryth, 1
D'Alvarez, Marguerite, 1,2
D'Arcy, Ella, 2
Dale, Margaret, 1
Dale, Maureen, 1
Damer, Anne Seymour Conway, 1,2
Damer-Dawson, Margaret, 2
Damm, Sheila Van, 2
Danby, Frank, pseud., 1
Dane, Clemence, pseud., 1,2
Daniel, Emily, 2
Darbishire, Helen, 1
Darby, Abiah Maude Sinclair, 1
Darby, Deborah, 1
Darby, Joan, 1
Darby, Mary Sargent, 1
Darcy, Clare, 2
Dare, Phyllis, 1
Dare, Zena, 1
Darling, Grace Horsley, 1,2
Darrell, Maisie, 1
Darwin, Emma Wedgwood, 2
Darwin, Suzannah Wedgwood, 2
Daryush, Elizabeth Bridges, 2
Davenant, Mrs. John, 1
Davenport, Hester, 1
Davenport, Jane, 1
Davenport, Mrs., 1
Davidson, Flora, 2
Davidson, Lady, 2
Davies, Cecilia, 1
Davies, Eleanor Audley, 1
Davies, Eleanor Trehawke, 1
Davies, Emily, 1,2
Davies, Fanny, 1
Davies, Mary "Moll", 1
Davies, Sarah Emily, 1
Davies, Trehawke, 2
Davis, Louisa J., 2
Davis (or Davies), Katherine, 1
Davison, Ann(e), 2
Davison, Edith, 1
Davison, Emily, 2
Davys, Mary, 1
Dawes, Kathleen, 1
Dawes, Sophia, 1
Dawn, 2
Dawson, Edith Robinson, 2
De Grey, Mabel, 2

King, Alice, 2
King, Anne, 2
Kingsford, Anne Bonus, 2
Kingsford, Florence, 2
Kingsley, Mary, 2
Kingsley, Mary Henrietta, 1,2
Kingsmill, Anne, Lady Winchilsea, 2
Kingston, Gertrude, 1
Kipling, Caroline Starr Balestier, 1
Knepp, Mary, 1,2
Knight, Ellis Cornelia, 1
Knight, Frances Maria, 1
Knight, Jill, 2
Knight, Laura Johnson, Dame, 1,2
Knight, Peggy, 1
Knox, Jean, 1
Kyneburge, 1
Labany, 2
Lacy, Harriette Deborah Lacy, 1
Laine, Cleo (Clementine Dinah), 2
Lamb, Caroline, Lady, 1,2
Lamb, Mary Ann, 1,2
Lanchester, Ella, 1
Lanchester, Elsa (or Ella), 1,2
Lander, Hilda Cowham, 1
Landon, Letitia Elizabeth, 1,2
Lane, Elizabeth, Dame, 2
Lane, Jane, 1
Lane, Margaret, 1
Lane, Sara, 1
Langtry, Lady de Bathe, 1
Langtry, Lillie Emilie Charlotte le
    Breton, 1,2
Lansbury, Angela Brigid, 1,2
Lara, Adelina de, 1
Lascelles, Mary Madge, 1
Lascelles, Mrs. Edwin, 2
Laski, Marghanita, 1,2
Latouche, Mrs., 1
Latouche, Rose, 1
Laurence, Katie, 1
Lawrence, Arabella Susan, 1
Lawrence, Gertrude, 1,2
Lawrence, Margery, 1
Lawrence, Susan, 2
Lawson, Lizzie, 2
Lawson, Mary, 1
Laye, Evelyn, 1,2
Le Blonde, Elizabeth Frances, 1
Le Neve, Ethel, 2
Leaf, Freydia, 1
Leakey, Mary Douglas, 2
Leapman, Edwina, 2
Lee, Auriol, 1

Lee, Frances E., 2
Lee, Harriet, 1
Lee, Mary Chudleigh, Lady, 2
Lee, Sophia, 1
Lee, Vernon, pseud., 1,2
Lees, Dacre, 1
Lehmann, Liza, 1
Lehmann, Rosamund Nina, 1,2
Leigh, Adele, 1
Leigh, Alice, 2
Leigh, Elinor, 1
Leigh, Vera, 1
Leigh, Vivien, 1,2
Leighton, Margaret, 1,2
Leinster, Jessie Smither Fitzgerald, 1
Leitch, Charlotte Cecilia Pitcairn, 1
Lemond, Margaret, 1
Lennox, Mary Anne Paton, 1
Lepell, Mary, 1
Lester, Muriel, 1
Lestor, Joan, 2
Leverson, Ada, 2
Leverson, Sarah Rachel, 1
Levett, Ada Elizabeth, 1
Levey, Ethel, 1
Levitt, Dorothy, 2
Levy, Amy, 2
Lewis, Florence E., 2
Lewis, Jane Mary Dealy, 1
Lewis, Mrs. Arthur, 1
Lewis, Rosa Overden, 1,2
Licoricia of Winchester, 2
Liddell, Alice, 2
Lightfoot, Hannah, 1
Ligonier, Penelope, Viscountess, 2
Lincoln, Margaret, Countess of, 1
Lind-af-Haageby, Emelie Augusta
    Louise, 1
Lindsay, Charlotte, 1
Line, Anne, 1
Linley, Elizabeth, 1
Linton, Elizabeth Eliza Lynn, 1,2
Linwood, Mary, 1,2
Lisle, Alice, Lady, 1,2
Little, Mrs. Archibald, 1
Littlewood, Joan, 2
Litton, Marie, 1
Lively, Penelope, 2
Llewellyn-Smith, Elizabeth, 2
Lloyd, Doris, 2
Lloyd, Marie, 1,2
Locke-King, Mrs., 2
Lockett, Alice, 1
Lockhart, Enid, 2

Moiseiwitsch, Tanya, 1
Monckton, Mary, Comtess of Cork and Orrey, 1
Monks, Victoria, 1
Montagu, Mary Wortley, Lady, 1,2
Montagu-Douglas-Scott, Alice, 1
Montague, Elizabeth Robinson, 1,2
Montalba, Clara, 1
Montefiore, Judith Cohen, Lady, 1,2
Montford, Eleanor de, 2
Moore, Anne, 2
Moore, Eva, 1
Moore, Mary, 1
Moore, Mona, 1
Moore, Virginia, 2
Moore-Guggisberg, Decima, Lady, 1
Moorhead, Ethel, 2
Mordan, Clara Evelyn, 1
Mordaunt, Elinor, 1
More, Hannah, 1,2
Morrell, Ottoline Violet Ann, Lady Cavendish, 2
Morris, Jan James, 2
Morris, Jane Burden, 2
Morris, Margaret, 2
Morris, Margaret, 1
Morris, May, 1,2
Mortimer, Alice, 2
Mortimer, Penelope Ruth Fletcher, 2
Morton-Sale, Isobel, 1
Moss, Marlow, 2
Mott, Alice, 1
Moulton, Sarah Barrett "Pinkie", 2
Mounsey, Ann Shepard, 1
Mountbatten of Burma, Edwina Cynthia Annette Ashley, 1
Mozley, Anne, 2
Mozley, Harriett, 2
Mudie, Rosemary, 1
Muilman, Teresia Constantia, 1
Muir, Florence Roma, 1
Muller, Mary, 2
Mulso, Hester, 2
Mundeville, Maude de, 1
Munro, Mary Isobel, 1
Murray, Alma, 1
Murray, Augusta, 1
Murray, Elizabeth, 1
Murray, Fanny, 1
Murray, Margaret Alice, 1,2
Murray, Mrs., 1
Murray, Rosalind, 1
Murray, Rosemary, 2
Murray, Stella Wolfe, 1

Murrell, Christine, 2
Myddleton, Jane Needham, 1
Nagle, Florence, 2
Napier, Sarah Lennox Bunbury, Lady, 1,2
Neagle, Anna, Dame, 1,2
Neilson, Julia, 1
Neilson, (Lilian) Adelaide, 1
Nelson, Catherine Suckling, 2
Nepean, Edith, 1
Nesbit, Edith, 1,2
Nesbitt, Cathleen (Mary), 1,2
Nethersole, Olga Isabel, 1
Nevill, Dorothy, 1
Neville, Anne, 1,2
Newbery, Jessie Rowat, 2
Newcastle, Margaret Cavendish, Duchess of, 1,2
Newill, Mary J., 2
Newman, Andrea, 2
Newmarch, Rosa Harriet, 1
Nicholls, Rhoda Holmes, 1,2
Nichols, Catherine Maude, 1
Nicholson, Adela, 1
Nightingale, Frances (Fanny) Smith, 2
Nihell, Elizabeth, 2
Nisbet, Noel Laura, 1
Nisbett, Louise Cranston, 1
Noel, Augusta, Lady, 2
Norman, Mrs. Henry, 2
Normand, Henrietta Rae, 1
Normanton, Helena, 2
Norris, Mrs., 1
North, Marianne, 1,2
Northampton, Aelfgifu of, 1
Norton, Caroline Elizabeth Sarah Sheridan, 1,2
Norton, Frances Freke, Lady, 1
Norton, Jemima, 1
Norton, Mrs., 1
Norton, Mrs., 1
Nossis, 1
Nottingham, Essex Finch, Coun., 2
Novello, Clara, 2
Novello, Mary, 2
Nugent, Maria, Lady, 1
Nuthall, Betty, 1
O'Brien, Nelly, 1
O'Casey, Eileen, 2
O'Grady, Dorothy Pamela, 1
O'Neill, Catherine, 2
Odlum, Doris, 2
Ogilvie, Mary Helen Macaulay, 1
Okey, Maggie, 1

Siddons, Sara "Sally" Kemble, 1,2
Sidgwick, Ethel, 1
Sidhwa, Bapsi, 2
Sidney, Frances, 1
Sidney, Mary, 1
Sieff, Rebecca, 2
Simmance, Eliza, 2
Simmons, Jean, 1,2
Simpson, Elizabeth, 2
Simpson, Helen de Guerry, 1
Sinclair, Guinivere, 1
Sinclair, Mary (May), 1,2
Sitwell, Edith, Dame, 1,2
Sjoo, Monica, 2
Skillern, Daphne, 2
Skipworth, Alison, 2
Slade, Barbara, 1
Slade, Elizabeth, 1
Slade, Madeleine, 1
Sladen, Victoria, 1
Slingsby, Mary Aldridge, 1
Smedley, Constance, 1
Smedley, Menella Bute, 2
Smith, Alice Mary, 1,2
Smith, Alys Pearsall, 2
Smith, Charlotte Turner, 1,2
Smith, Eleanor, 1
Smith, Eleanor Armor, 1
Smith, Eleanor Furneaux, Lady, 1
Smith, Jacqueline, 2
Smith, Kate Walsh Fitzroy, 1
Smith, Maggie, 2
Smith, Mary Ellen, 2
Smith, Mrs. Joseph, 2
Smith, Stevie (Florence Margaret), 2
Smyth, Ethel Mary, Dame, 1,2
Smythe, Pat, 2
Snell, Hannah, 2
Snowden, Ethel, 1
Sokolova, Lydia, 1
Soldene, Emily, 1
Somerset, Frances Howard Carr, 1
Somerset, Isabel, 1
Sophia Dorothea of Celle, 1,2
Souray, Eleanor, 1
Southcott, Joanna, 1,2
Southey, Caroline Ann Bowles, 1
Sowerby, Amy Millicent, 1
Sparkes, Catherine, 2
Sparkes, Leonora, 1
Spence, Geraldine, 1
Spencer, Caroline Elizabeth, Lady, 2
Spencer, Charlotte, 2
Spencer, Jean, 2

Spencer, Lavinia, Countess, 2
Spender, Lily, 1
Spens, Janet, 1
Spicer, Charlotte, 1
Spicer, Dorothy, 1,2
Spooner, Winifred, 1,2
Springfield, Dusty, 2
Spry, Constance, 1,2
Spurgeon, Caroline Frances Eleanor, 1
Spurr, Gertrude E., 1
Stabler, Phoebe, 2
Standring, Heather, 1
Stanhope, Hester Lucy, Lady, 1,2
Stanley, Dorothy, 1
Stannard, Henrietta Eliza Vaughn Palmer, 1
Stark, Freya Madeline, 1,2
Starkie, Enid M., 1
Steel, Dorothy Dyne, 2
Steel, Flora Annie Webster, 1,2
Steele, Anne, 1
Steen, Marguerite, 1,2
Stephen, Margaret, 2
Stephens, Anne, 1
Stephens, Catherine, Countess of Essex, 1
Stephenson, Frances, 2
Stephenson, Sarah, 1
Stern, Gladys Bronwyn, 1,2
Sterne, Agnes, 2
Sterne, Elizabeth Lumley, 2
Stevens, Jane, 2
Stevens, Mary, 1
Stevenson, Alice, 2
Stewart, Clara, 1
Stewart, Mary, 2
Stewart, Mary Florence Elinor Rainbow, 2
Stillman, Marie Spartali, 1
Stirling, Anna Marie Wilhelmina Pickering, 1
Stirling, Elizabeth, 1,2
Stirling, Mary Anne, 1
Stobart, Mabel Annie St. Clair, 1
Stockes, Mary D., 1
Stokes, Mrs., 2
Stone, Elizabeth, 2
Stone, Paulene, 2
Stone, Sarah, 2
Stopes, Charlotte Carmichael, 1
Stopes, Marie Charlotte Carmichael, 1,2
Storey, Sylvia, Countess Poulett, 1

Twining, Louise, 1
Twinning, Louisa, 2
Twyford, Mrs., 1
Tyler-Odham, Dorothy, 2
Underhill, Evelyn, 1
Unwin, Mary, 1,2
Unwin, Nora Spicer, 1
Uphill, Susana, 1
Vacani, Madame, 2
Valdi, Marguerite, 1
Van Brugh, Irene, Dame, 1,2
Van Lawick-Goodall, Jane, Baroness,
     1,2
Vanbrugh, Violet, 1
Vane, Anne, 1
Vanhomrigh, Esther, 1
Vaughan, Janet Maria, Dame, 1
Vaughan, Kate, 1
Vaughn, Theresa, 2
Vautrollier, Jeanne, 1
Veley, Margaret, 2
Verbruggen, Susanna Percival, 1
Verne, Adela, 1
Verne, Mathilde, 1
Vernon, Elizabeth, 1
Vestris, Lucia Elizabetta, Madame,
     1,2
Victoria, 1,2
Victoria, Vesta, 1
Victoria Alexandra Alice Mary, 1
Villiers, Barbara, 1,2
Vokersz, Veronica, 1
Vokes, Rosina, 1
Vokes, Victoria, 1
Vyvyan, Jennifer, 1
Waddell, Helen, 1
Wade, Sarah Virginia, 2
Wagle, Asha, 2
Wailes, Marylin, 1
Wakefield, Priscilla, 1
Wakely, Shelagh, 2
Waldegrave, Frances Elizabeth Anne,
     1
Wales, Alexandra, 1
Walker, Jane, 1
Walkinshaw, Clementina, 1
Wall, Mildred Ivy, 1
Wallace, Nellie, 1,2
Walpurga, Saint, 1,2
Walter, Lucy (Mrs. Barlow), 1,2
Warburton, A. M., 2
Ward, Barbara Mary, 1,2
Ward, Dorothy, 1
Ward, Genevieve, Dame, 1,2

Ward, Henrietta Mary Ada, 1
Ward, Irene, 2
Ward, Mrs. Dudley, 2
Warde, Beatrice Lamberton, 1
Wardle, Elizabeth Wardle, 2
Warren, Elizabeth Hooton, 1
Warren, Judy, 2
Warringer, June, 2
Warwick, Anne, Countess of, 1
Warwick, Frances Evelyn Maynard, 1
Waste, Joan, 2
Waterford, Louisa, Lady, 2
Watson, Caroline, 2
Watson, Maud, 2
Watt, Linnie, 2
Watts, Helen, 1,2
Watts, Mary, 2
Weamys, Anne, 1
Weaver, Elizabeth, 1
Weaver, Harriet Shaw, 2
Webb, Beatrice Potter, 1,2
Webb, Mary Gladys Meredith, 1,2
Webling, Peggy, 1
Webster, Augusta Davies, 1
Webster, Harriet, 1
Wedgwood, Veronica, 1
Weeton, Ellen, 1
Weldon, Fay, 2
Wellesley, Dorothy, 2
Wells, Becky Davies, 1
Welsh, Kit, 2
Wentworth, Bessie, 1
Wesley, Susanna Annesley, 1,2
West, Mrs. Cornwallis, 1
Westmeath, Lady, 1
Weston, Agnes E., 1
Weston, Elizabeth, 2
Wethered, Joyce, 1,2
Whale, Winifred Stephens, 1
Whall, Veronica, 2
Whateley, Anne, Sister, 1,2
Wheeler, Anna Doyle, 1
Wheelhouse, M. V., 1
Whichelo, Nellie, 2
Whigham, Margaret, 2
White, Antonia, 2
White, Diana, 2
White, Eirene Lloyd, 1
White, Florence, 1
White, Miss, 1
Whitehouse, Mary, 2
Whiteman, Elizabeth A. O., 1
Whitmore, Frances Brooke, 1
Wiedemann, Sarah Anna, 1

England/US

Mentuab, 2
Mentuvat, 1
Nicaula, 1
Sebel-Wongel, 1
Selassie, Tsahai Haile, 1
Tsahai, 1
Fiji
Dovi, Adi Losalini, 2
Finland
Aalberg, Ida Emelia, 1
Ackte-Jalander, Aino, 1
Antila, Eva, 2
Brummer, Eva, 2
Canth, Minna Ilrika Wilhelmina Johansson, 1
Elenius, Elsa, 2
Eskelin, Karolina, 1
Forsman, Eeva-Kristina, 2
Grasten, Viola, 2
Gripenberg, Alexandra, 1
Heikel, Rosina, 1
Heini, Maija Liisa, 2
Hultin, Tekla, 2
Ilvessalo, Kirsti, 2
Johansson-Pape, Lisa, 2
Jung, Dora, 2
Kaaresalo-Kasari, Ella, 2
Kallio, Elin Waenerberg, 1
Karttunen, Laila, 2
Kuusinen, Hertta (Elina), 1,2
Mannerheim, Sophie, 1
Muona, Toini, 2
Nyman, Gunnel, 2
Paasikivi, Alli, 1
Paasnuori, Tynne, 2
Rancken, Saima Tawast, 2
Ratia, Armi, 2
Runeberg, Fredrika, 1
Saarinen, Loja, 2
Salmela-Jarvinen, Martta, 2
Salmenhaara, Kyllikki, 2
Salminen, Leena, 2
Schjerfbeck, Helene, 2
Sibelius, Helena, 2
Siimes, Aune, 2
Sillanpaa, Mina, 2
Simberg-Ehrstrom, Uhra Beata, 2
Sipila, Helvi L., 2
Soldan-Brofeldt, Venny, 2
Still, Nancy, 2
Thesleff, Ellen, 2
Turpeinen, Kaisa, 2
Tuumi, Raija, 2
Tynell, Helin Helena, 2

Tyolajarvi, Pirkko Annikki, 2
Voipio, Anni, 2
Wiik, Maria, 2
Wrede, Mathilda, 1
Finland/US
Grotel, Maija, 2
Knoll-Bassett, Florence Schust, 2
Nurmi, Maila, 2
Payne, Majatta Strandell, 2
Flanders
Bijna (or Byns), Anna, 1
Bourignon, Antoinette, 1
Eyck, Margaretha von, 1,2
Lutgard, 1
Rictrude, 1
Teerlinc, Levina, 2
Van Hemessen, Caterina, 2
France
Abbema, Louise, 1
Acarie, Madame Barbe, 1
Achille-Fould, Georges, 1
Ackermann, Louise Victorine Choquet, 1
Acquillon, Duchess of, 1
Adam, Juliette Lamber, 1,2
Adam, Madame Nanny, 1
Adela of Blois, 1
Adelaide, La Petite, 1
Adelaide, Madame, 1
Adiny, Ada, 2
Adoree, Renee, 1,2
Agnes of Meran, 1
Agnes of Poiters, 1
Agoult, Marie Catherine Sophie Flavigny de, 1,2
Ahrweiller, Helene, 2
Aiguillon, Marie Madeleine de Wignerod du Pont de Corlay, Duchess of, 1
Aimee, Anouk, 2
Aisse, Mademoiselle, 1
Alacoque, Marguerite Maria, 1
Alais, 2
Alamanda, 2
Alardine Gasquiere, Sister, 2
Albret, Jeanne d', 1,2
Alencon, Emilienne, 1
Alice, 1
Allan-Despreaux, Louise, 1
Allard, Marie, 1,2
Allix, Martine, 2
Almucs de Castelnau, 2
Alphand, Nicole (Brunau-Varilla), 1
Andre, Valerie Edmee, 1

Senlis, Seraphine de, 2
Sequi, Madame, 2
Sette, Alice, 2
Severine, 2
Sevigne, Marie de Rabutinchantal,
   Marquise de, 1,2
Seyrig, Delphine, 2
Signoret, Simone, 1,2
Simon, Simone, 2
Simone, Benda, Madame, 2
Sister of the Beguines of Fl., 1
Skorik, Irene, 1
Soissons, Olympe Mancini, 1
Solange, 1
Sonrel, Elizabeth, 1
Sorel, Agnes, 1,2
Soulage, Marcelle, 1
Souza-Botelho, Adele Marie Emilie
   Fillieul, 1
Spinelly, Andree "Spi", 2
St. Laurent, Alphonsine Therese
   Bernardine, 1
St. Pol, Marie de, Countess of Pem-
   broke, 1
Staal (Stahl, Stael), Marguerite Jeanne
   Cordier D., 1,2
Stael (Stael-Holstein), Anne Louise
   Germaine Necker, 1,2
Stainville, Therese de, 1
Stella family, 2
Stephane, Nicole, 2
Stoltz, Rosine, 1
Straus, Genevieve, 1
Subligny, Marie-Therese Perdou de,
   1,2
Syamour, Marguerite, 1
Sylvia, 1
Tabouis, Genevieve R. Le Quesne, 1
Tagliafero, Magda, 1
Tailleferre, Germaine, 1
Tarsilla, 1
Tastu, Amable, Madame, 2
Tencin, Claudine Alexandrine Guerin
   de, 1
Theos, Catherine, 1
Theresa of Lisieux, 1,2
Theroigne de Mericourt, pseud., 1
Thevenin, Marie Anne Rosalie, 1
Thible, Madam, 1,2
Thomas-Soyer, Mathilde, 1
Thouret, Jeanne Antide, 1
Thurwanger, Felicite Chastanier, 1
Tible, Marie, 1
Tibors, 2

Tinayre, Marcelle Chasteau, 1
Tissot, Janou, 2
Titayana, 2
Touchet, Marie, 1
Touissant, Jeanne, 1,2
Trautmann, Claudine, 2
Trebelli, Zelia, 1
Trebuchet, Sophie, 1
Trintignant, Nadine Marquand, 2
Tristan, Flora, 1,2
Troisgros, Simone, 2
Tual, Denise Piazza, 2
Ugalde, Delphine, 1
Ursins, Mary Anne de la Tremoille,
   1,2
Uzes, Duchess d', 1
Valadon, Suzanne, 2
Valerie, 1
Vallayer-Costner, Anne, 2
Valois, Mademoiselle, 1
Vanhoutte, Marie-Leonie, 1
Varda, Agnes, 2
Varnod, Widow, 2
Vasseur, Marie le, 2
Vaubrun, Marguerite Therese,
   Marquisse de, 2
Vedres, Nicole, 2
Veil, Simone Annie Jacob, 2
Venier, Marie, 2
Verone, Maria, 2
Verrue, Jeanne Baptiste (d'Albert de
   Luynes, 1
Vesley, Jane de, 2
Vestris, Francoise-Rose, Madame, 2
Viardot, Pauline Marie, 1
Viardot-Garcia, Marie Felicitas, 1
Victoire, 2
Victoire, Madame, 1
Villers, Madame, 1
Vilmorin, Louise de, 2
Vintimille, Pauline Felicite de Nesle, 1
Vionnet, Madeleine, 2
Vivien, Renee Pauline Tarn, 2
Vix, Genevieve, 1
Waltrude, 1
Warens, Louise Francoise Elenore, 1
Weil, Simone, 1,2
Well, Simone, 2
Wittig, Monique, 2
Worth, Marie, 2
France/Brazil
   Durocher, Marie Josefina, 1
France/Canada
   Latour, Frances Mary Jacqueline, 1
   Marie de L'Incarnation, 1
   Tour, Francoise-Marie Jacquelin, 1

Rehan, Ada, 1,2
Ridge, Lola, 1,2
Russell, Mary Baptist, Mother, 2
Sadlier, Mary Anne Madden, 1,2
Sheridan, Mary, 2
Snow, Carmel White, 1
Swartz, Maud(e) O'Farrell, 2

Israel
Aloni, Shulamit, 2
Aviv, Nurith, 2
Broyde, Ruth, 2
Cohen, Zivia, 2
Damari, Shoshana, 1
Dayan, Ruth, 2
Fuld, Bracha, 1
Hazleton, Lesley, 2
Ima Shalom, 1,2
Kagan, Helen(a), 1,2
Kipnis, Hanna, 1
Klausner, Margot, 2
Levi-Tanai, Sara, 1,2
Levinson, Rena, 2
Meir, Golda Mabovitch, 1,2
Muscal, Ruth, 2
Rabin, Mrs. Yitzhak, 2
Rippin, Sarah, 2
Salzman, Pnina, 1
Samish, Zdenka, 2
Shlonsky, Verdina, 1,2
Tororek, Lily, 2
Weizmann, Vera Chatzmann, 1,2
X, Myra, 1
Yonis, Bathsheba, 1
Yoresh, Abigail, 2
Zefira, Bracha, 1

Italy
Abella, 2
Accoramboni, Vittoria, 1
Adelaide, 1
Adelaide of Susa, 1
Adelberger, Bertha, 2
Adele of Assisi, 2
Adelmota, Princess of Carrara, 2
Agnes, Maria Gaetana, 1
Agnes of Assisi, 1
Agnes of Monte Puiciano, 1
Agnesi, Maria Gaetana, 1,2
Agujari, Lucrezia, 1
Albany, Louise Maximiliana Caroline
   Stuart, 1
Alberghetti, Anna Maria, 1,2
Alboni, Marietta Contessa Pepoli, 1
Albrizzi, Isabella Teotochi, 1
Alippi-Fabretti, Quirina, 1

Amalasuntha (Amalasventa), 1,2
Andreini, Isabella, 1,2
Angela Merici, Saint, 1,2
Angela of Foligno, 1
Angeli, Pier, 1,2
Angiolina of Padua, 2
Anguisciola, Lucia, 1
Anguissola, Sofonisba, 1,2
Anselmi, Tina, 2
Antonia (Gainaci), Blessed, 1
Antonia Daniello, 2
Aqua, Eva Dell', 1
Armani, Vincenza, 1
Banti, Brigitta Giorgi, 1
Baptista Varani, 1
Barbieri, Fedora, 1
Bassani, Signora, 1
Bassi, Laura Maria Caterina, 1,2
Bat Sheba (Verona), 2
Battia, Villana, 1
Beatrice Portinari, 1
Belgiojoso, Cristina, 1
Bellincioni, Gemma, 1
Bembo, Antonia, 1
Benato-Beltrami, Elizabeth, 1
Benincasa, Caterina, 2
Benvenuta Bojani, 1
Beretta, Caterina, 2
Bernardone, Sister Pica, 1
Besanzoni, Gabriella, 2
Biancolelli, Caterina, 2
Bigottini, Emilie, 2
Biondi, Nicola, 1
Bocchi, Dorothea, 2
Bompiani-Battaglia, Clelia, 1
Bonfanti, Marie, 1,2
Bonna, 1
Borboni, Paola, 2
Bordoni, Faustina, 1
Borgia, Lucrezia, Duchess of Fer-
   rara, 1,2
Borromeo, Clelia Grillo, 1
Borsarelli, Fernanda, 2
Bortolan, Rosa, 1
Borzino, Leopoldina, 1
Bosio, Anigiolana, 1
Bozzacchi, Guiseppina, 2
Bozzidini, Bettisia, 2
Bozzino, Candida Luigia, 1
Brambilla, Marietta Cassano D'Adda,
   1
Bresegna, Isabella, 2
Brianza, Carlotta, 2
Brignone, Lilla, 2

Schrieck, Louise van der, Sister, 2
Trico, Catalina, 2
Van Es, Elizabeth, 2
Van Hamel, Martine, 2
Van Vries, Margaret Hardenbroek, 2
Zilve, Alida, 1
New Zealand
Alda, Frances, 1,2
Ashton-Warner, Sylvia, 2
Askin, Rosemary, 2
Batten, Jean, 1,2
Bethell, Mary Ursula, 2
Blood, Mrs. K. E., 1
Campbell-Purdie, Wendy, 2
Cashman, Katherine, 2
Frame, Janet, 2
Hammond, Joan, 1
Hodgkins, Frances, 1
Howard, Mabel, 2
Hyde, Robin, 2
Jackson, Rowena, 1
James, Naomi Christine, Dame, 2
Kanawa, Kiri Te, 2
Keller, Florence, 2
Kempthorne, Edith M., 1
Mansfield, Katherine, pseud., 1,2
Marsh, Edith Ngaio, Dame, 1,2
Marshall, Lucy, Carlile, 2
McKinnon, Emily H. S., 1
Mossong, Verna Elaine, 2
Park, Ruth, 1
Purdue, Connie, 2
Russell, Lilla, 2
Sheppard, Katharine, 2
Stenhouse, Caroline, 2
Sutherland-Hunter, Mary Young, 1,2
Taylor, Mary, 2
Te Kanawa, Kiri, 2
Vickers, Julia, 2
Young, Pam, 2
New Zealand/US
Eddy, Lillian E., 1
Wilson, Elsie Jane, 2
Nicaragua
De Sasallow, Olga Nunez, 2
Jagger, Bianca, 2
Nigeria
Ebigwei, Patricia, 2
Emecheta, Buchi, 2
Kwali, Ladi, 2
Mum-Zi, 2
Norway
Aarestrup, Marie Helene, 1
Abrahamsen, Hanna Christie, 2

Absalon, Anna Pedersdotter, 2
Astrid, 1
Backer-Grondahl, Agatha, 1
Bang, Maia, 1,2
Berg, Eva, 2
Berg, Sigrun, 2
Brundtland, Gro Harlem, 2
Collett(e), Camilla Wergeland, 2
Delbo, Helvig, 1
Dietrichsen, Mathilde Bonneire, 1
Dybwad, Johanne, 2
Fedde, Elizabeth, 1,2
Flagstad, Kirsten Marie, 1,2
Grondahl, Agathe Backer, 1
Guldberg, Estrid, 2
Gundersen, Herdis, 2
Haldorsen, Inger Alida, 2
Halling, Else, 2
Hansteen, Kirsten, 2
Henie, Sonja, 1,2
Ibsen, Marichen Altenburg, 2
Jansson, Metta, 2
Kielland, Kitty, 1
Korsmo, Grete Prytz, 2
Krog, Gina, 1
Krog, Karin, 2
Lorentzen, Annemarie, 2
Lund, Signe, 1
Martha, 1
Mathison, Karoline, 2
Maud, Charlotte Mary Victoria, 1
Mikkelsen, Caroline, 2
Nissen, Greta, 1,2
Norena, Eide (Kaja Hansen Eide), 1,2
Oerner, Inga, 1
Platen, Countess von, 1
Ramus, Anna Kolbjors, 1
Rustad, Guro, 2
Ryssdal, Signe, 2
Ryste, Ruth, 2
Sandel, Cora, 2
Selmer, Ragnihild, 2
Sigmond, Anna, 1
Spangberg-Holth, Marie, 1
Ullman, Liv Johanne, 2
Undset, Sigrid, 1,2
Valle, Inger Louise Andvig, 2
Vinsnes, Hanna, 1
Waitz, Grete, 2
Wold, Anita, 2
Norway/Germany
Zorina, Vera, 1,2
Norway/US
Darlington, Jennie, 2
Everson, Mary Dahl, 1

Theodosia, Saint, 2
Theonilla, 1
Titiana, Flavia, 1
Tranquillina, Turia Sabina, 1
Triaria, 1
Tullia, 1,2
Tullia, 1
Turia, 1,2
Unmmidia Quadratilla, 1
Valeria, 2
Valeria Galeria, 1
Valeria Nessalina, 1
Verginia (1), 1,2
Verginia (2), 1,2
Veturia, 1
Victoria, 1
Victoria, 1
Volumnia, 1

Rome (Pompeii)
Eumachia, 2

Samoa
Mata'a fa, Masiofo Fetaui, 2

Scandinavia
Clifford, Camille, 1
Freya Frigg, 2
Margaret (2), 1,2
Thaulow, Alexandra, 1

Scotland
Aberconway, Lady Laura Pochn, 1
Adam, Jean, 1
Agnes of Dunbar (Black Agnes), 1
Alison, Isabel of Perth, 1
Anderson, Mary Reid MacArthur, 1,2
Angus, Marion, 2
Armour, Jean, 2
Arnold, Annie R. Merrylees, 1
Baillie, Grizel (Grisell) Hume, Lady, 1,2
Baillie, Isobel, 1
Baillie, Joanna, 1,2
Balfour, Frances Campbell, Lady, 1
Balfour, Margaret Isabella, 1
Bannerman, Helen, 1,2
Barnard, Anne Lindsay, Lady, 2
Barrie, Margaret Ogilvy, 1
Barry, James (Miranda), 1,2
Blamire, Susanna, 1
Bowes, Elizabeth, 2
Bowes, Marjory, 2
Bridekirk, Lady, 1
Brightwen, Eliza, 2
Brunton, Mary, 2
Brux, Lady, 1
Buccleuch and Monmouth, Anne, Duchess of, 1

Buchan, Elspeth Simpson, 1
Burke, Kathleen, 2
Burns, Agnes Broun, 2
Burns, Jean, 1
Byron, Catherine Gordon, 2
Cadell, Jean, 1
Cameron, Katharine, 1
Campbell, Jane, Lady Kenmure, 1
Campbell, Janet Montgomery, 1
Campbell, Mary, 2
Carnegie, Margaret Morrison, 1
Carstairs, Janet Mure, 1
Carswell, Catherine MacFarlane Roxburgh, 1,2
Christie, Winifred, 1
Cochrane, Grizel, 1
Cockburn, Alison (Alicia), 1,2
Coillard, Christina, 1
Colvill, Margaret Wemyss, Lady, 1
Cowan, Minna Galbraith, 1
Craig, Isa, 2
Cromartie, Ann, Countess of, 1
Cruikshank, Helen B., 2
Cunningham, Anne, 1
Cunningham, Barbara, 1
Cunnison, Margaret, 1,2
Davie, Elspeth, 2
Dervorguilla, 1
Douglas, Margaret, 1
Dunbar, Lilias, 1
Dunnett, Dorothy, 2
Durham, Margaret Mure, 1
Eadie, Noel, 1
Eglinton, Susannah Kennedy, 1
Elliot, Jean, 1
Fairley, Grace M., 1
Falconer, Pearl, 1
Fenwick, Ethel Gordon Manson, 1
Ferrier, Susan Edmonstone, 1,2
Findlater, Jane Helen, 1
Fleming, Marjory (Margaret), 1,2
Fraser, Marjorie Kennedy, 1
Garden, Mary, 1,2
Geddes, Janet, 1
Glover, Jean, 1
Gordon, Jane, 1
Gordon, Katherine, 2
Gordon, Mary Gilmour, 2
Graham, Clementina Stirling, 1
Grahme, Dorothy, 1
Grant, Anne McVickar, 1,2
Grant, Mary R., 1
Grieve, Janet, 2
Guise, Mary, 2

Walton, Cecile, 1
Wardlaw, Elizabeth, Lady, 1,2
Watt, Agnes, 1
Webb, Mary, 1
Welsh, Elizabeth Knox, 1
Wilson, Margaret, 1
Scotland/Australia
Spence, Catherine Helen, 1
Scotland/England
Carlyle, Jane Baillie Welsh, 1,2
Patey, Janet Monach, 1
Scotland/Spain
Barca, Fanny Calderon de la, 2
Scotland/US
Boucicault, Agnes Robertson, 1,2
Bowers, Eilly Orrum, 1,2
Cameron, Donaldina Mackenzie, 2
Cumming, Kate, 1,2
Cunningham, Eliza Bertrand, 2
Curry, Peggy Simson, 1
Fleming, Williamina Paton Stevens,
   1,2
Graham, Isabella Marshall, 1,2
Hopekirk, Helen, 1,2
Inescort, Frieda, 2
Inman, Elizabeth Murray Campbell
   Smith, 2
Loftus, Marie Cecilia, 1,2
MacInnes, Helen Clark, 1,2
MacLeod, Grace, 1
MacMillan, Margaret, 1,2
O'Neil, Carolyn A., 2
Stamper, Mrs., 1
Tytler, Jane, 1
Vreeland, Diana Dalziel, 1,2
Walker, Susan Hunter, 1
Washburn, Jean Linsey Bruce, 1
Wright, Frances, 1,2
Scotland/USSR
Schlesin, Sonya, 1
Scythia
Thamyris, 1
Tomyris, 1
Senegal
Basse, Marie-Therese, 2
Jai, Anna Madgigaine, 2
Serbia
Draga Maschin, 1
Petrovic, Nadezda, 2
Sicily
Agatha, Saint, 1,2
Agnes, Saint, 1,2
Constance of Sicily, 1
Harmonia, 1
Marguerite of Bourgogne, 2

Sierra Leone
Ighodaro, Irene, 2
Thompson-Clewry, Pamela, 2
Silesia
Bloch, Blanche, 1
Bloch, Madame Elisa, 1
Hedwig, 1
Schygulla, Hanna, 2
Wiegmann, Marie Elizabeth Hanche,
   1
Silesia/US
Bloomfield-Zeisler, Fanny, 1,2
Singapore
Lim, Kim, 2
South Africa
Bam, Brigalia, 2
Barlow, Mollie, 2
Beek, Anna, 2
Cannon, Poppy, 1
Drummond, June, 2
Faulkner, Mary, 2
Goquiiolay-Arellano, Remidios, 2
Gordimer, Nadine, 1,2
Jabavu, Nontanto "Noni", 2
Jason, Sybil, 2
Johns, Glynnis, 2
Jonker, Ingrid, 2
Joseph, Helen, 2
Lessing, Doris May, 1,2
Lewis, Ethelreda, 1
Makeba, Miriam, 1,2
Malahlele, Mary Susan, 1
Malherbe, Mabel, 2
Mandela, Nomzamo Winnie, 2
Mandela, Winnie, 2
Massey, Patricia, 2
Millin, Sarah Gertrude Liebson, 1,2
Modjadji, Queen, 2
Myburgh, Helmine, 2
Neethling, Leonora, 2
Nerina, Nadia, 1
Oppenheimer, Bridget, 2
Quellerie (Quellerius), Maria de la, 1
Reitz, Mrs. Deneys, 2
Robertson, Isobel Russell, 2
Rosenkowitz, Sue, 2
Schreiner, Olive, 1,2
Seedat, Zubeda Kassim, 2
Sigean, Stella, 2
Sikharane, Joyce, 2
Suzman, Helen Gavronsky, 1
Suzman, Janet, 2
Whitmore, Joan, 2
South Africa/Canada
Wilson, Ethel Davis, 2

About the Author

Katharine Joan Phenix received her B.A. in Women's Studies and Political Science from the Sir George Williams Campus of Concordia University in Montreal, Quebec. She earned a Master of Science in Library and Information Science and a Certificate of Advanced Study (C.A.S.) in Library Automation and Women's Studies from the University of Illinois. Ms. Phenix has been active in the American Library Association women's groups and chaired the Committee on the Status of Women in Librarianship in 1984. She has published numerous essays on women in librarianship, including *On Account of Sex: An Annotated Bibliography on the Status of Women in Librarianship 1977–1981* with Kathleen Heim and edited its supplement *On Account of Sex . . . 1982–1986.* Katharine Phenix is also noted for implementing the nation's first online bookmobile at the Westminster (Colorado) Public Library in 1986. She has worked in public, academic, and special libraries and taught at the Graduate School of Library and Information Science at Louisiana State University. She wrote the "Software for Libraries" column in *Wilson Library Bulletin* from 1989 to 1994.